OCEANIA, ASIA, EUROPE
(see back endpapers for Africa, North America and South America)

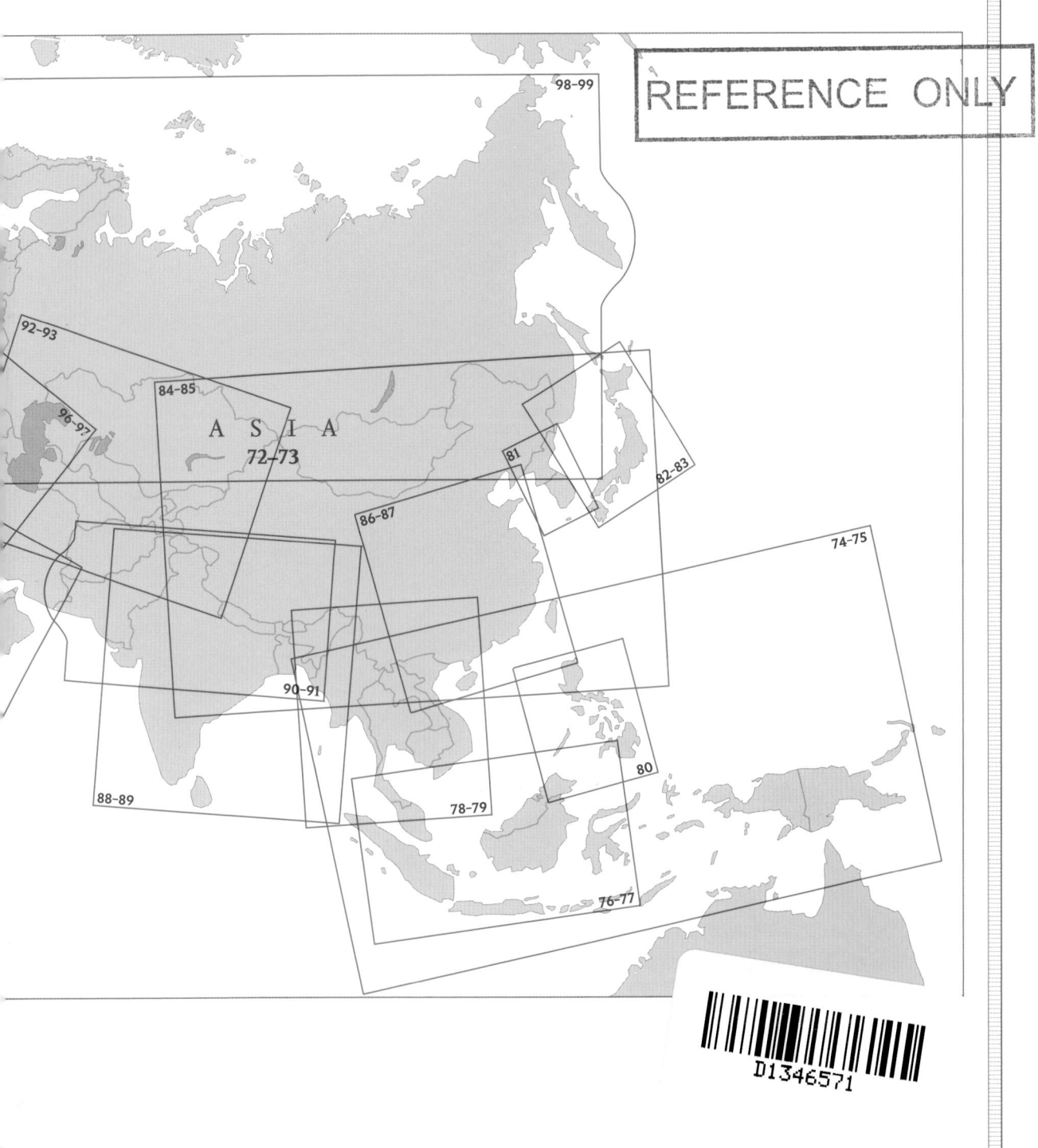

ATLAS OF THE WORLD

THE IRISH TIMES DESKTOP ATLAS OF THE WORLD

HarperCollins Publishers,
77–85 Fulham Palace Road, London, W6 8JB

First Published 2009

Printed and bound in Singapore

British Library Cataloguing in Publication Data
A catalogue record for this book is available from the British Library

ISBN 978 0 00 731816 2

Imp 001

All mapping in this atlas is generated from Collins Bartholomew digital databases.
Collins Bartholomew, the UK's leading independent geographical information supplier,
can provide a digital, custom, and premium mapping service to a variety of markets.
For further information:
Tel: +44 (0) 141 306 3752
e-mail: collinsbartholomew@harpercollins.co.uk
or visit our website at: www.collinsbartholomew.com

The representation of certain boundaries and place names in this atlas
may depart from standard Collins Bartholomew policy in order to incorporate local preferences.

THE IRISH TIMES DESKTOP
ATLAS OF THE WORLD

CONTENTS

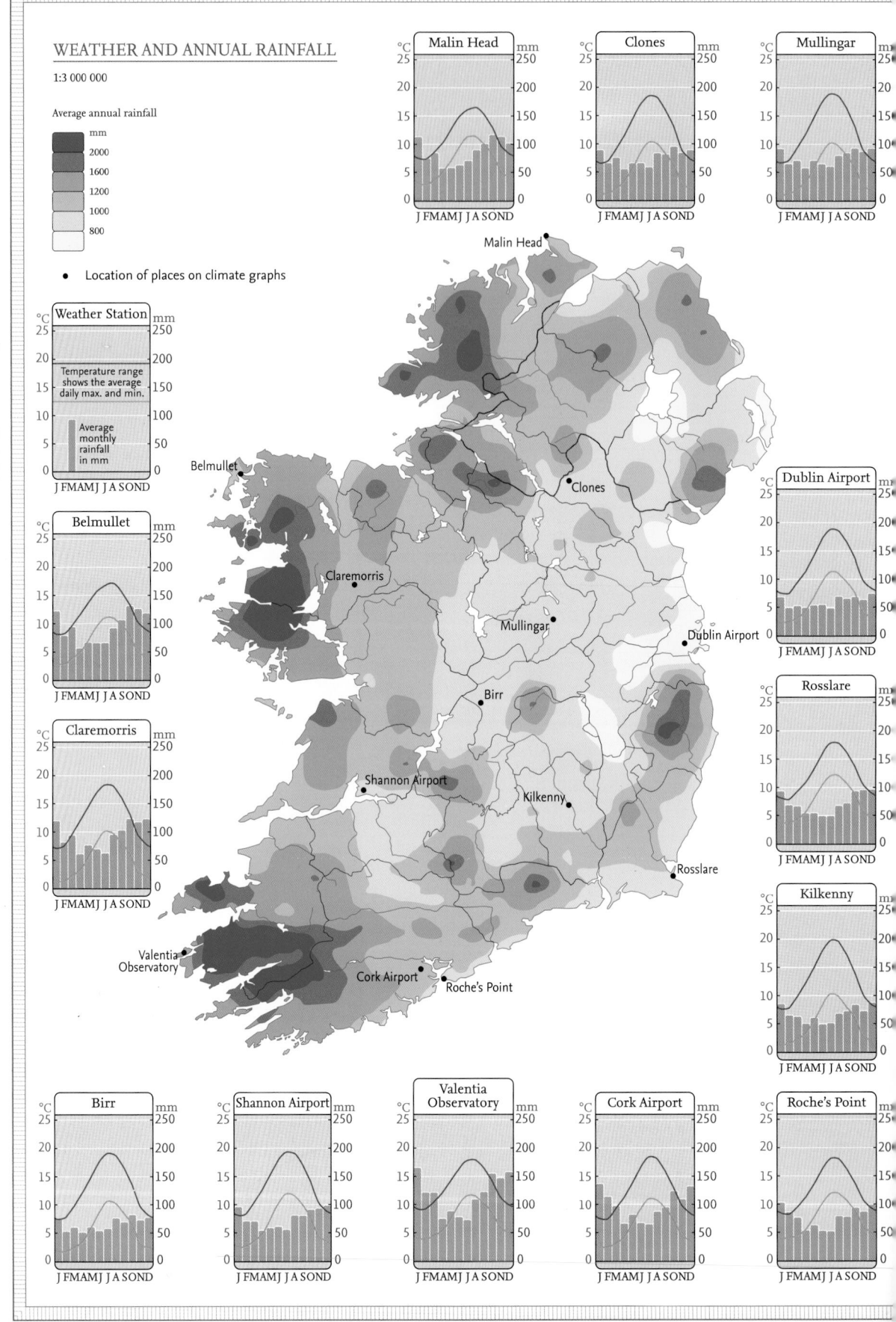

WEATHER AND ANNUAL RAINFALL

1:3 000 000

Average annual rainfall

mm
2000
1600
1200
1000
800

• Location of places on climate graphs

Weather Station

Temperature range shows the average daily max. and min.

Average monthly rainfall in mm

Malin Head

Clones

Mullingar

Belmullet

Claremorris

Dublin Airport

Rosslare

Kilkenny

Birr

Shannon Airport

Valentia Observatory

Cork Airport

Roche's Point

Malin Head

Clones

Mullingar

Belmullet

Claremorris

Birr

Shannon Airport

Kilkenny

Valentia Observatory

Cork Airport

Roche's Point

Rosslare

Dublin Airport

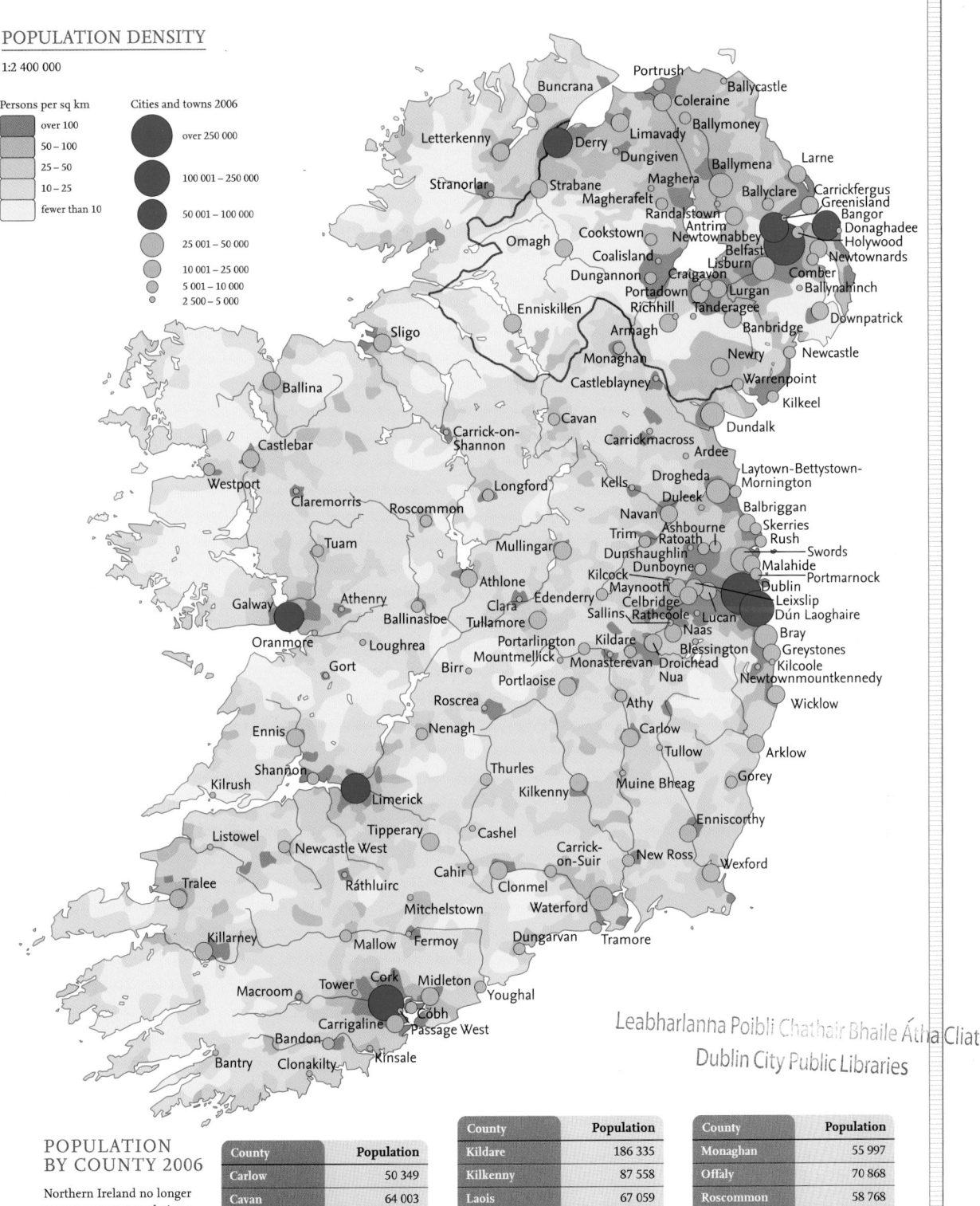

POPULATION DENSITY

1:2 400 000

Persons per sq km
- over 100
- 50 – 100
- 25 – 50
- 10 – 25
- fewer than 10

Cities and towns 2006
- over 250 000
- 100 001 – 250 000
- 50 001 – 100 000
- 25 001 – 50 000
- 10 001 – 25 000
- 5 001 – 10 000
- 2 500 – 5 000

Leabharlanna Poibli Chathair Bhaile Átha Cliath
Dublin City Public Libraries

POPULATION BY COUNTY 2006

Northern Ireland no longer reports county populations since a reorganisation of local government abolished the county as an administrative unit. However the Northern Ireland government estimates the population as 1 742 000.

County	Population	County	Population	County	Population
Carlow	50 349	Kildare	186 335	Monaghan	55 997
Cavan	64 003	Kilkenny	87 558	Offaly	70 868
Clare	110 950	Laois	67 059	Roscommon	58 768
Cork	481 295	Leitrim	28 950	Sligo	60 894
Donegal	147 264	Limerick	184 055	Tipperary	149 254
Dublin	1 187 176	Longford	34 391	Waterford	107 961
Galway	231 670	Louth	111 267	Westmeath	79 346
Kerry	139 835	Mayo	123 839	Wexford	131 749
		Meath	162 831	Wicklow	126 194

© Collins Bartholomew Ltd

7

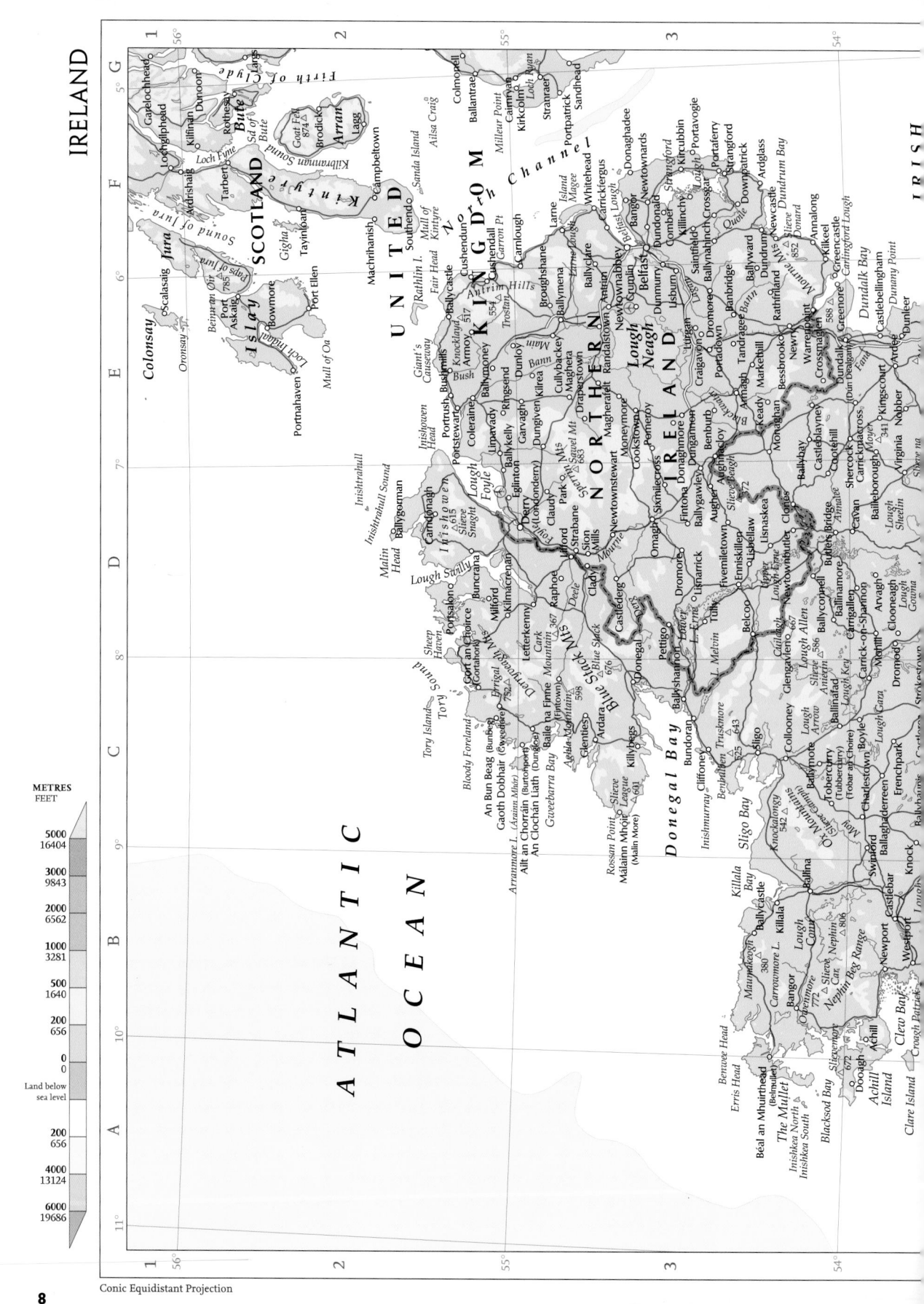

IRELAND

Conic Equidistant Projection

8

METRES
FEET

5000	16404
3000	9843
2000	6562
1000	3281
500	1640
200	656
0	0

Land below
sea level

200	656
4000	13124
6000	19686

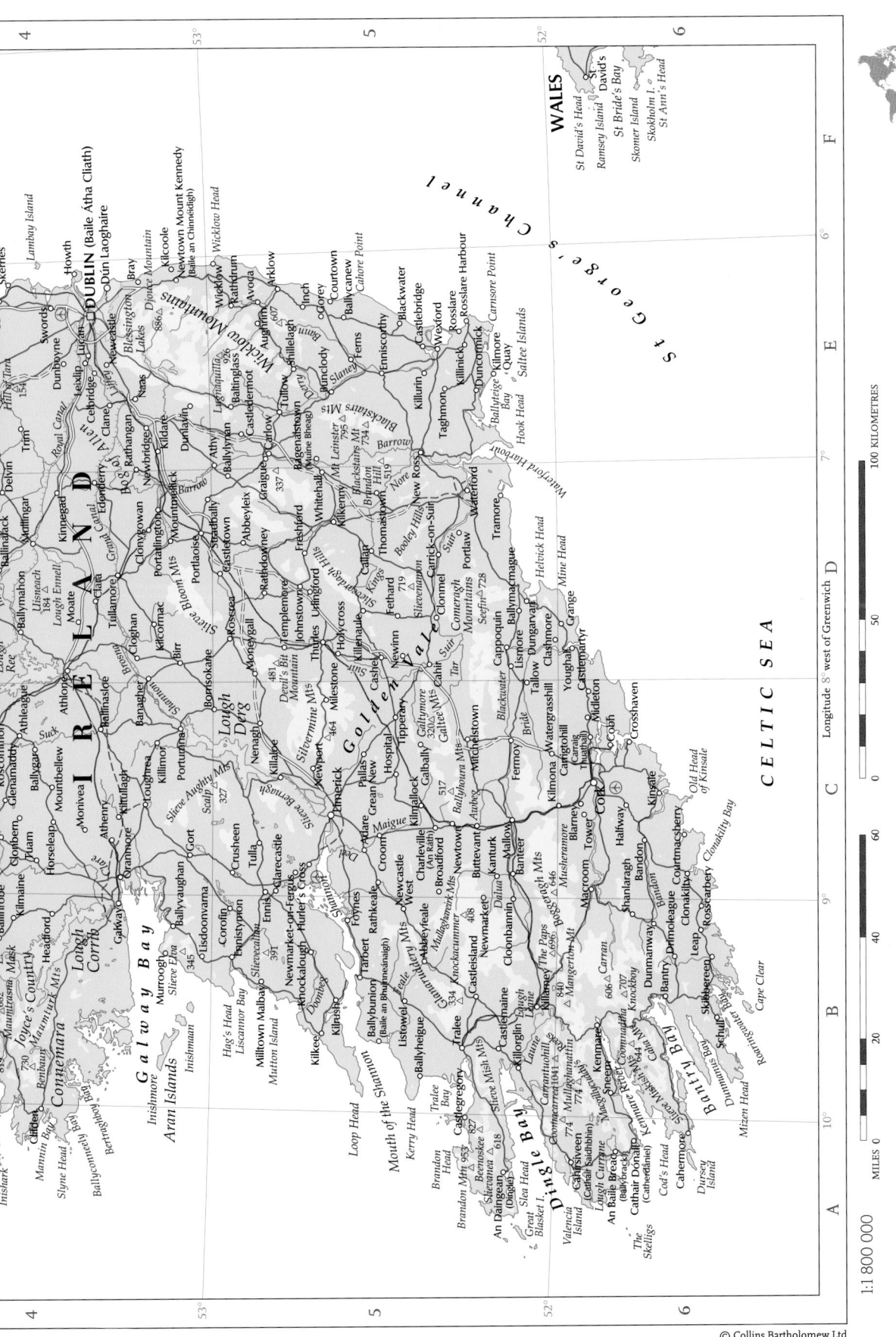

WALES

St David's Head
Ramsey Island   St David's
St Bride's Bay
Skomer Island
Skokholm I.
St Ann's Head

St George's Channel

I R E L A N D

DUBLIN (Baile Átha Cliath)
Dún Laoghaire

CELTIC SEA

Golden Vale

Wicklow Mountains

Galway Bay
Lough Corrib
Connemara
Joyce's Country
Aran Islands

Dingle Bay
Bantry Bay

Mouth of the Shannon

Longitude 8° west of Greenwich

1:1 800 000

© Collins Bartholomew Ltd

100 KILOMETRES
MILES 0

9

ATLANTIC

OCEAN

Inishtrahull
Inishtrahull

Ballygorman
Malin Head
Dunaff Head
Malin

Tory Island
Horn Head
Sheep Haven
Fanad Head
Clonmany
Camdonagh
Glentogher

Inishbofin
Tory Sound
Mulroy Bay
Rosapenna
Portsalon
Lough Swilly
Drumfree 615
Inis h

Bloody Foreland
An Fál Carrach (Falcarragh)
Ballymore
Muckish Mt. △670
Cashel
Creeslough
An Tearmann (Termon)
Rathmullan
Carrowkeel
Carrow
Scalp Mountain
Slieve Snag

Gort an Choirce (Gortahork)
Gola Island
An Bun Beag (Bunbeg)
Doirí Beaga (Derrybeg)
Gaoth Dobhair (Gweedore)
Milford
Ramelton
Inch Island
484 Muff

Owey Island
Rosses Bay
Anagaire (Annagry)
Errigal △752
Glenveagh National Park
Kilmacrenan
Newtowncunningham
Bridge End
Derryveagh Mts

Ailt an Chorráin (Burtonport)
Loch an Iúir (Loughanure)
Slieve Snaght
Gleann Doimhin
Rashedoge
Letterkenny
Carrigans
Derry (Londonderry)
New Building
Water

Aranmore Island (Árainn Mhór)
An Clochán Liath (Dungloe)
Crohy Head
Croaghleheen 383
DONEGAL
Kingarrow
Cark Mountain △367
Baile na Finne
Raphoe
Pluck
Magheramason
372
Slieveki
Donema

Mín na Croise (Meenacross)
Gweebarra Bay
Portnoo
Rossbeg
Aghla Mountain 598 △
Béal an Átha Móir
An Clochán
Drumnacross
Deele
Ballymago
Strabane

Dawros Head
Loughros More Bay
Cloghboy
Maas
Meenanarwa
Finn
An Coimín
Stranorlar
Lifford
Castlefinn
Killygordon
Sion Mills
Plumbric

An Machaire (Maghera)
Gleann Cholm Cille (Glencolumbkille)
Ardara
Kilrean
Glenties
Ballybofey
Ardstraw
Newtownstewart
N

Rossan Point
Málainn Mhóir (Malin More)
An Charraig (Carrick)
Crove
504
353
Meentullynagarn
Blue Stack Mts △676
Lough Eske
525
Castlederg
Killen
Mountjoy
T
Y
Gort
Mullagh
Soma

Rathlin O'Birne Island
Málainn Bhig (Malin Beg)
Cill Charthaigh (Kilcar)
Dunkineely
Killybegs
Croagh
Inver
Donegal
Derg
Blacktown
Drumquin
Killyclogher

Fintragh Bay
McSwynes Bay
Inver Bay
Doorin Point
Mountcharles
Tullyvoos
Laghey
Crockmore
Lough Derg
Pettigo
Ederny
Dromore
Owenragh
Fintona

Donegal Bay
Ballure
Ballyshannon
Rossnowlagh
Leggs
Kesh
Drumduff
Irvinestown
Trillick

Inishmurray
Mullaghmore
Tullaghan
Bundoran
Erne
Lower Lough Erne
Lisnarrick
Ballinamallard
Tempo

Downpatrick Head
Roskeeragh Point
Ballyconnell
Castlegal
Cliffoney
Grange
Benbulben △525
643
Truskmore
Askill
Belleek
Rosscor
Tully
Garrison
Derrygonnelly
Tullybrack
Scribbagh 376
FERMANAGH
Trory
Enniskillen
Fivemiletow

Lenadoon Point
Easky
Dromore
Rathlee West
Sligo Bay
Coney Island
Rosses Point
522
Lough Melvin
Rossinver
Dough Mountain
△461
Lough Macnean Upper
Holywell
Springfield
Lisbellaw
Brookeboro
Maguiresbridg

Rathlackan
Ballycastle
Creevagh
Maumakeogh △380
Killala Bay
Owenbeg
Beltra
Strandhill
Sligo (Sligeach)
Shanvus
Leckaun
Glenfarne
Lough Macnean Lower
Drumcard
Bellanaleck
Upper Lough Er
Lisnaskea

Killala
Belville
Castleconor
Culleens
Corbally
Knocklongy
542
Coolaney
Colooney
Dromahair
Lough Gill
Slievenakilla △667
Cuilcagh △667
Mullan
Swanlinbar
Donagh
Clor

Crossmolina
Ballina
Moylaw
Castlehill
Lahardaun
Bunnyconnellan
Ox Mountains
Slieve Gamph
Carrowneden
Largan
Cloonacool
Ballymote
Derry
Lough Arrow
Dowra
Lough Allen
Slievenakilla 547
Iron Mountains
Derrynacreeve
Teemore
Newtownbutler
Wattlebri
Scotshou

Nephin △806
Lough Conn
Knockmore
Corlee
Curry
Doocastle
Bunnanaddan
Kesh
Drumshanbo
Slieve Anierin △586
Ballyconnell
Kilconney
Belturbet
Ore

Deel
Castlehill
Cullin
Bellaghy
Roosky
Gurteen
Lough Key
Carrick-on-Shannon
Garvagh
Graadice Lough
Ballinamore
Newtown Gore
Lough Oughter
Butlers Bridge
Cavan
Strad

Derreen
Pontoon
Foxford
Cloontia
Drumsna
Garadice
LEITRIM
Killeshandra
Crossdoney
Killyconna

MAYO
Beltra Lough
Beltra
Castlebar (Caisleán an Bharraigh)
Swinford
Charlestown
Carracastle
Edmondstown
Croghan
Lough Drumharlow
Cloone
Mohill
Arvagh
Cavan
CAV
Ballinagh

Clogher
Cloonkeen
Turlough
Manulla
Bohola
Bellavary
West Airport
Knock
Ballyglass
Ballaghaderreen
Ballinameen
Croghan
Lough Bofin
Roosky
Dromod
Lough Gowna
Aghnacliff
Kilnaleck
Mount Nugen

Westport Quay
Belcarra
Ballyfarnagh
Knock
Ballyhaunis
Kiltimagh
Kilkelly
Aghamore
Lisacul
Castlerea
Bellanagare
Elphin
Roosky
Kilglass
Drumlish
Finnea
Lough Sheelin

Ballyglass
Mayo
Barneycarroll
Brickens
Ballinlough
Ballymoe
Strokestown
Kilglass Lough
Newtown Forbes
Ballinalee
Granard

IRELAND
ROSCOMMON
Tulsk
Curraghroe
Shannon
LONGFORD

Lough Carra
Partry
Nilnock
Cloonfad
Curragh West
Cashel
Glenamaddy
Creggs
Ballyleague
Lanesborough
Longford
Edgeworthstown
Castlepoll
Lough Derravar

Tuar Mhic Éadaigh (Tourmakeady)
An Trian (Trean)
Ballinrobe
Castleville
Dunmore
Gorteen
Roscommon
Ballymurry
Inny
Rathowen
Ballinalack
Ballynafid

CONNACHT
Lough Mask
Neale
Kilmaine
Milltown
Royal Canal
Danesfort
Carrickboy
Keenagh

Robe
Sinking
Glenamaddy

Conic Equidistant Projection

Longitude 8° west of Greenwich

METRES / FEET

METRES	FEET
5000	16404
3000	9843
2000	6562
1000	3281
500	1640
200	656
0	0
Land below sea level	
200	656
4000	13124
6000	19686

SCOTLAND

Saddell
Blackwaterfoot
Arran
Holy
Island
Whiting
Bay
Kilchenzie
Peninver
Lagg
Kildonan
Machrihanish
Campbeltown
*Bennan
Head*
Croc
Moy
△
446
Southend
Culzean Bay
Maidens
Turnberry

Mull of Kintyre
Sanda
Island
Ailsa Craig
Girvan
Colmonell
Ballantrae

NORTH CHANNEL

*Milleur
Point*
Kirkcolm
Cairnryan
*Loch
Ryan*
Castle
Kennedy
Stranraer
Portpatrick
Lochans
Stoneykirk
Sandhead

Port Logan
Drummore

*Mull
of Galloway*

*Inishowen
Head*
Greencastle
*Magilligan
Point*
Moville
Portstewart
Portrush
*Giant's
Causeway*
*Benbane
Head*
Causeway Head
Portballintrae
Ballintoy
*Rathlin
Island*
Carnduff
Ballyvoy
Torr
Fair Head
Ballycastle
*Runabay
Head*
Cushendun

lund
agad Head
ugh
yle
daff
Castlerock
Coleraine
Castleroe
Damhead
Bushmills
Moss-side
Armoy
Knocklayd
△
517
Stranocum
Cushendall
Glenariff
Garron Point
Glendun

Aghanloo
Crossgare
Ballybogy
Ballymoney
Dunloy
Clogh
Carnlough
Carnlough Bay

Limavady
Finvoy
Cloughmills
Carnlough
Glenarm

Derry
Burnfoot
Garvagh
Rasharkin
Clarryford
The Sheddings
Antrim Hills

**DERRY
(LONDONDERRY)**
Dungiven
Kilrea
Craigs
Glenarm

aghanloo
Feeny
Upperlands
Clady
Cullybackey
Broughshane
*Agnew's
Hill*
△
476
Larne
The Maidens
Ballygalley
Portmuck
*Island
Magee*

audy
aghy
ga
*Sawel
Mountain*
△683
Mountains
Lisnamuck
Maghera
Bellaghy
Lough Beg
Ahoghill
Ballymena
Kells
Kilwaughter
Glynn
*Larne
Lough*
Carrickfergus

Draperstown
Tobermore
Toome
Kells
Chapeltown
Ballynure
Black Head

Cranagh
Magherafelt
Castledawson
Randalstown
Ballycarry
Whitehead

THERN IRELAND
Greencastle
Moneymore
Lough
Ballyronan
Antrim
Templepatrick
Doagh
Greenisland
Belfast Lough
Groomsport
Copeland Island

NE
Creggan
Ballinderry
Cookstown
Moortown
Aldergrove
Belfast International
Newtownabbey
Nutt's
Corner
Crumlin
Hollywood
Craigavad
Bangor
Donaghadee

TE
Carrickmore
Pomeroy
Stewartstown
Tullyhogue
Glenavy
Dunmurry
Dundonald
Conlig
Millisle
Ards

UNITED KINGDOM

T
Sixmilecross
Carland
Mountjoy
R Neagh
Lower
Ballinderry
Upper Ballinderry
Belfast
Castlereagh
Comber
Greyabbey
Newtownards
Peninsula
Ballywalter

Donaghmore
Dungannon
Maghery
Lurgan
Moira
Lisburn
Carryduff
Killinchy
Ballygowan
Kircubbin
Ballyhalbert

agh
△313
Coalisland
Craigavon
Portadown
Hillsborough
Saintfield
Raffrey
*Strangford
Lough*
Ardkeen
Portavogie
Cloghy

ler
Ballygawley
Moy
Charlemont
Donaghcloney
Dromore
Ballynahinch
Crossgar
Kearney

Blackwater
gher
Aughnacloy
Benburb
Loughgall
Gilford
Lawrencetown
Dromara
Drumaness
Portaferry
Strangford
*Ballyquintin
Point*

Emyvale
Mullan
Killyleagh
Richhill
Banbridge
DOWN
Saul
Downpatrick

Glasslough
Tyholland
Milford
Tandragee
Scarva
Loughbrickland
Katesbridge
Loughinisland
Clough
Ballyhornan

Monaghan
ARMAGH
Armagh
Markethill
Poyntz Pass
Rathfriland
Castlewellan
Ardglass

ossla
Smithborough
Keady
Whitecross
Mount
Norris
*Newry
Canal*
Hilltown
*Slieve
Donard*
△852
Newcastle
St John's Point

Clontibret
Darkley
Bessbrook
Barnmeen
*Dundrum
Bay*

ewbliss
Newtownhamilton
Carnagh
Belleek
Mayobridge
*Mourne
Mountains*
Killough

MONAGHAN
Annayalla
Cullyhanna
Newry
Attical
Mullartown

Ballybay
Castleblayney
Crossmaglen
Creggan
Forkhill
Omeath
Warrenpoint
Rostrevor
Annalong
Ballymartin

Rockcorry
Cullaville
Drumbilla
Carlingford Lough
Kilkeel
Greencastle
Cranfield Point

Cootehill
Broomfield
Carlingford
Greenore
Grange

lyvin
Shercock
Innishkeen
△588
Ballagan
Point

nningstown
Carrickmacross
Dundalk
(Dún Dealgan)
Blackrock
Dundalk Bay

Drumanespick
Knockbridge
Louth
Dromiskin
Castlebellingham

ilieborough
Moyer
△341
Kingscourt
Reaghstown
Tallanstown
Dunany Point

Virginia
Lisduff
Drumcondra
Ardee
Der
Togher
Grangebellow
Clogher Head

Lough
amor
Moynalty
Woodtown
Dunleer
Clogherhead

Castletown
△246
Collon
Tullyallen
Drogheda

castle
Wilkinstown
Slane
Bettystown
Julianstown

Kilskeer
Kells
Baile Órthaí
Kilberry
*Brú na
Bóinne*
Gormanston

Clonmellon
Fordstown
Navan
Newgrange
Duleek
Balbriggan

rumcree
Maltry
(An Uaimh)

Athboy
Halltown
MEATH
Garlowcross
Balrath
Stamullen
Naul
Balrothery
Skerries

IRISH

SEA

© Collins Bartholomew Ltd

1:1 000 000

60 KILOMETRES
40
20
0

40
20
10
0
MILES

METRES
FEET

5000
16404

3000
9843

2000
6562

1000
3281

500
1640

200
656

0
0

Land below
sea level

200
656

4000
13124

6000
19686

A · 11° · B · 10° · C

1

54°

2

53°

3

Stags
of Broad Haven
Benwee Head
Port an Chlóidh (Portacloy)   Downpatrick
Head
Erris Head   Broad   Béal Deirg (Belderg)   Lenado
Haven   Point
Aghadoon   Rathlackan   Eas
Gleann na Muaidhe   380   Ballycastle   Rathl
Béal an Mhuirthead   Barr na Trá   (Glenamoy) △   Killala   Owen
(Belmullet)   (Barnatra)   Maumakeogh   Bay
An Geata Mór (Binghamstown)   Glenamoy   Creevagh   Culleens
Bun na hAbhna   Owenmore   Killala   Corbal
The   (Bunnahowen)   Belville
Mullet   Carrowmore   Attavalley   Crossmolina   Bunnyconnellan
Inishkea North   Trawmore   Lake   Bellacorick   Ballina   Castleconor
Bay   Owenmore   Crossmolina
Inishkea South   Dumha Thuama   Slieve Car   Moylaw   Castlehill   Foxford
An Fál Mór   (Doohooma)   772   Deel   Lahardaun   Swin
(Fallmore)   △   Nephin   Lough   Knockmore
Blacksod   Ballycroy   629   806   Conn
Bay   672 △   Doogort   Owenduff △   Derreen   Pontoon   Foxford
Achill Head   Bun an Churraigh   Nephin Beg Range   Beltra   Lough   Castlehill
Dooagh   (Bunacurry)   Cullin
Achill Island   Corraun   Lough   Beltra   Burren   Bohola
Dumha Éige (Dooega)   Achill Peninsula   Feeagh   Lough   Bellavary
Sound   Rosturk   Manulla
An Dumhach Bheag   Mulrany   Newport   Clogher   Belcarra
(Dooghbeg)   Kilmeena   (Caislean an Bharraigh)
Clew   Westport   Cloonkeen   Ballyfarnagh
Clare   Bay   Craagh   Mayo   Barneycarr
Island   Roonah   △765   Westport   Claremorris
Quay   Mullagh   Patrick   Quay
Inishturk   Murrisk   Liscarney   Lough Carra   Ballindin
Kinnadoohy   Cregganbaun   Partry   Ballinrobe Castle
Benwee   Bengorm   Tuar Mhic Eadaigh   Kilmaine
Inishbofin   819 △   682   (Tourmakeady)   Neale
Inishark   Killary   702 △   An Trian (Trean)   Cong
Ballynakill Bay Cashleen Harbour   Glennagevlagh   Lough Mask
Salruck   Leenane
Lough Fee   Letterfrack   Joyce's Country
Moyard   Bénbaun   Maumturk Mts
Omey   Connemara   667 △   An Mám   Corr na Móna
Island   National Park 730 △ Bencorr   (Maum)   (Cornamona)
Clifden   712 △   Sraith   An Teach Dóite   Lough
Ballinaboy   Derrylea   Salach 613   (Maam Cross)   Corrib
Doonloughan   Ballynahinch   Cashel   Derryerglinna   Oughterard Cloonb
Slyne Head   Ballyconneely   Screeb   Killarone
Roundstone   Connemara   Doire Iorrais   Ros Cathail   Baile Ch
Bertraghboy Bay   (Derryrush)   Cinn Mhara (Rosscahill)   Maigh
Ros Muc (Rosmuck)   (Kinvarra)   Cuilinn
An Aird Mhóir (Ardmore)   Lettercallow   Casla   Connemara   Baile an Dúlaigh   G
Gorumna Island   (Costelloe) (Iar Connaught) Mionlach   An C
An Cheathru Rua   Ros an Mhíl   An Spidéal   Salthill
(Carraroe)   (Rossaveel)   (Spiddal)   Galwa
North Sound   Indreabhán   Bearna   (Gaillim
(Inveran)   (Barna)
Galway Bay   Carrowmore
Eoghanacht   Inishmore   Ballinder
(Onaght)   Cill Rónáin (Kilronan)   Black Head   Burren
Inishmaan   Murroogh
Cill Éinne (Killeany)   Inisheer   Formoyle   Ballyvaughan Kinva
Aran   South Sound Burren
Islands   Lisdoonvarna   Turlough   Bost
Doolin   Kilfenora   Castletown
Cliffs   Kilnaboy
of Moher   Ennistymon   Crush
Hag's Head   Liscannor   Corofin
Lahinch   Inagh   Ruan
Liscannor Bay   Fountain
Milltown Malbay   Slievecallan   Cross
391 △

Conic Equidistant Projection

Longitude 10° west of Greenwich

A · 11° · B · C

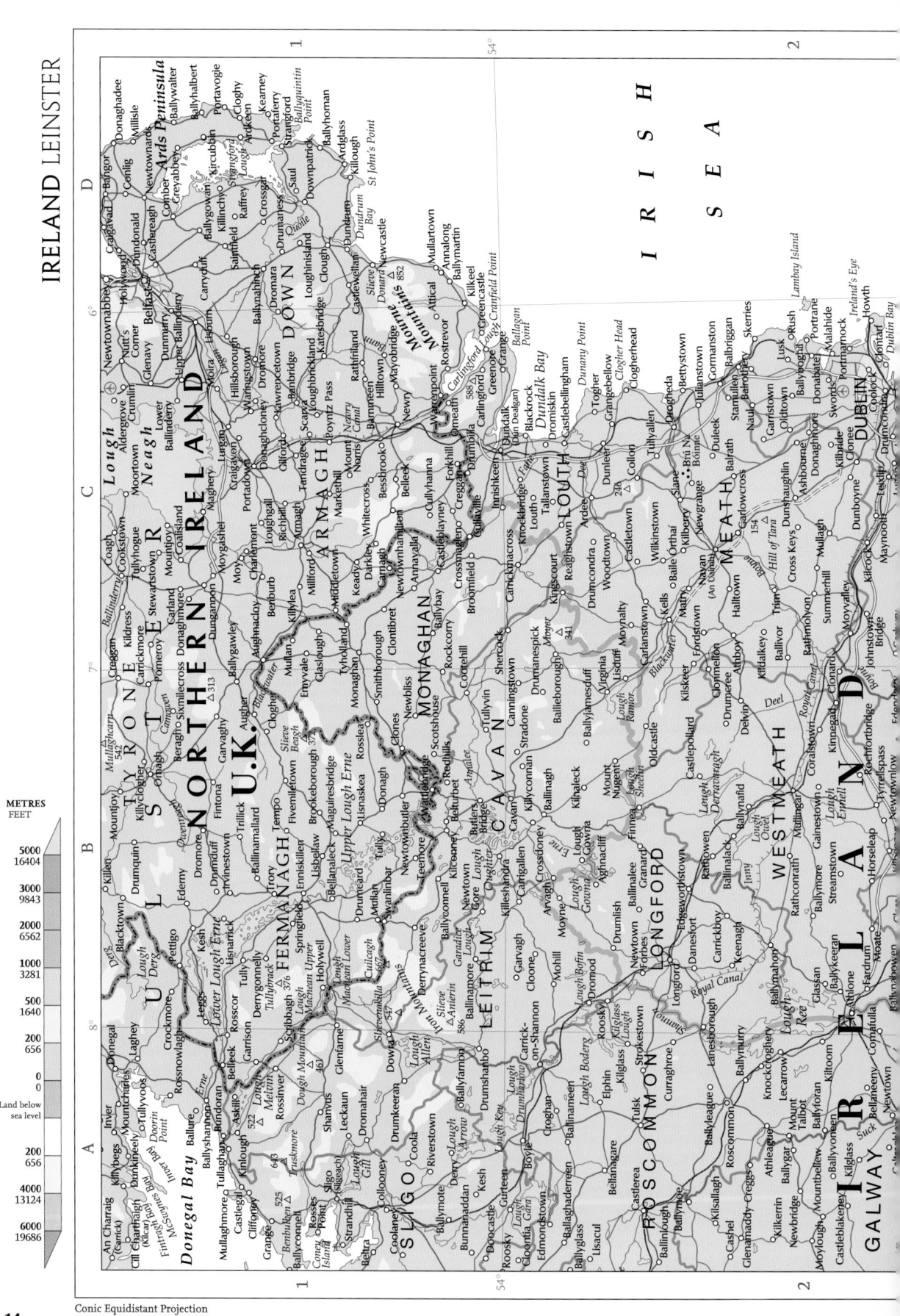

Conic Equidistant Projection

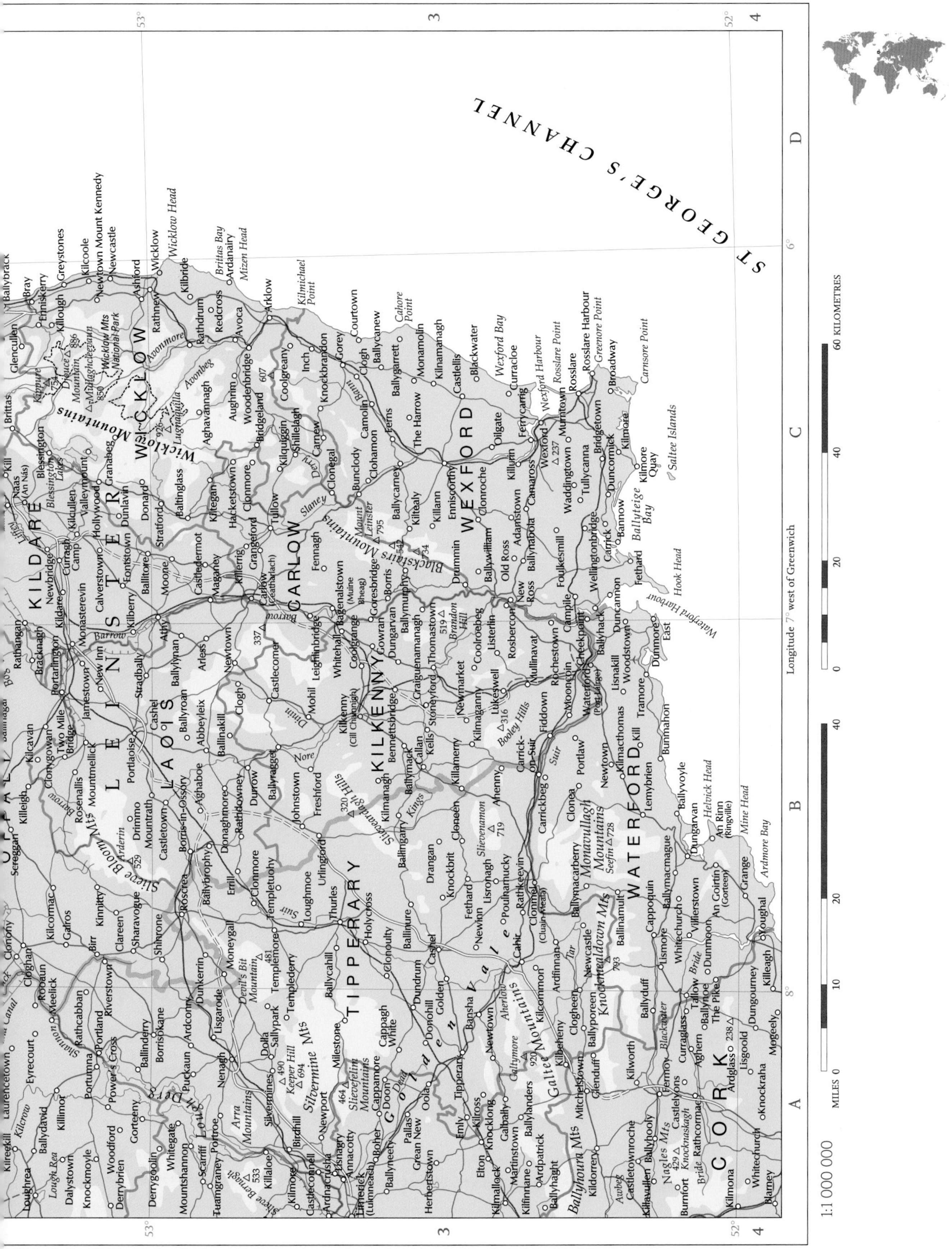

St George's Channel

1:1 000 000

MILES 0   10   20   40

KILOMETRES 0   20   40   60

Longitude 7° west of Greenwich

A 11° 10° **B** 9°

| 1 |
| 2 |
| 3 |

53°
52°

METRES
FEET

5000	16404
3000	9843
2000	6562
1000	3281
500	1640
200	656
0	0

Land below
sea level

200	656
4000	13124
6000	19686

North Sound
Galway Bay
Indreabhán (Inveran)
Bearna (Barna)
Carrowmore
Ballinder
Eoghanacht (Onaght)
Inishmore
Cill Rónáin (Kilronan)
Black Head
Murroogh
Burren
Ballyvaughan
Kinva
Cill Éinne (Killeany)
Inishmaan
Formoyle
Turlough
Aran
Islands
Inisheer
South Sound
Lisdoonvarna
Burren
Bosto
Doolin
Castletown
Cliffs of Moher
Kilfenora
Kilnaboy
Hag's Head
Liscannor
Ennistymon
Corofin
Crus
Ruan
Liscannor Bay
Lahinch
Inagh
C L
Milltown Malbay
Slievecallan 391 △
Connolly
Fountain Cross
Mutton Island
Kilmaley Clarecastle
Darragh
Newma
on-Fe
Doonbeg Bay
Mullagh
Killard
Creegh
Lissycasey
Ferigus
Killee
Doonbeg
Knockalough
Sharing
Doonbeg
Kilkee
Killadysert
Ballysteen
Doonaha
Kilrush
Foynes
Askeaton
Killimer
Knock
Kilbaha
Mouth of the Shannon
Tarbert
Glin
Capp
Loop Head
Ballylongford
Ballyhahill
Newbridge
Rathkeale
Reens
Ballybunion (Baile an Bhuinneánaigh)
Lisselton
Moyvane
Carrigkerry
Athea
Ardagh
L
Ballynaskreena
Listowel
Galey
Feale
Kilmorna
Newcastle West
Ballin
Kerry Head
Dreenagh
Causeway
Finuge
Templeglantine
Ballyheigue
Ardfert
Abbeydorney
Kilkinlea
Mountcollins
Mullagharerk Mts
Mullaghareirk 409 △
Broadfc
The Seven Hogs
Ballyheigue Bay
Ballinclogher
Glanaruddery Mts
Brosna
Feonana
All
Brandon Head
Tralee Bay
Fenit
Tralee (Trá Lí)
△ 334
Knockacummer 408 △
Cé Béhranainn (Brandon)
Brandon Bay
Castlegregory
Ballymacelligott
Castleisland
Knockanefune 439 △
Newmarket
S
Brandon Mountain
An Clochán (Cloghane)
Camp
Baurtregaum 852 △
M U N
Cordal
Blueford
Ballydavid Head
△ 953
Slievanea 618 △
Lougher
Slieve Mish Mts
Castlemaine
Farranfore
Knocknaboul
Ballydesmond
Dalu
Kantu
Sybil Point
Dingle
Lios Poll
Anascaul
Inch
Milltown
KERRY
Knocknagree
Cloonbannin
Duncannon Bridge
Ban
An Daingean (Dingle)
Gneevgullia
Great Blasket Island
Blasket Sound
Dún Chaoin (Dunquin)
Doonmanagh
Cromane
Killorglin
Rathmore
Millstreet
Slea Head
Dingle Bay
Glenbeigh
Laune
Beaufort
Killarney (Cill Airne)
Lough Leane
The Paps
Bogs
Kells
Darby's Bridge
Lough Caragh
Carrantuohill
Killarney National Park
696
Cahirsiveen (Cathair Saidhbhín)
Coomacarrea △ 774
Maghanlawaun
Macgillycuddy's Reeks
840
Poulgorm Bridge
Derrynasaggart Mts
Carriga
Doulus Head
Iveragh
1041
Mangerton Mountain
Clondro
Valencia Island
Foilclogh 500 △
Derreendarragh
Cleady
Baile Mhic Íre (Ballymakeery)
Macr
Portmagee
Inny
Letterfinish
Templenoe
Roughty
Kenmare
Carran △ 606
Béal Átha an Ghaorthaidh
Toames
Taisce Rese
Bray Head
Teeranearagh
Waterville
Lough Currane
Sneem
Tahilla
Killabunane
Lee
Inchigeelagh
Bealna
Baile an Sceilg (Ballinskelligs)
An Baile Breac (Ballybrack)
Parknasilla
Knockboy 707 △
Shehy Mts
Cappeen
Newcaste
Bolus Head
Cathair Dónall (Catherdaniel)
Coomnadiha 644 △
Togher
Castletown
Enniskear
The Skelligs (Na Scealaga)
Caha Mts
Sugarloaf Mountain
Glengarriff
Kealkill
Dunmanway
Ballineen
Scariff Island
Lamb's Head
Glenbeg Lough
Hungry Hill 575 △
Nowen Hill 537 △
Ballynacarriga
Kilco
Cod's Head
Eyeries
686 △
Adrigole
Bantry
Ilen
Ballingurteen
Ballinasc
Dursey Island
Allihies
Garinish
Slieve Miskish Mts
Whiddy Island
Drimoleague
Clonaki
Cahermore
Bere Island
Bantry Bay
Gerahies
Derreeny Bridge
Leap
Rosscarbery
Castle
Dursey Head
Ahakista
Ballydehob
Skibbereen
Unionhall
Ballyroon
Dunmanus Bay
Dumanus
Rossbrin
White Hall
Ga
He
Toormore
Schull
Three Castle Head
Baltimore
Toe Head
Mizen Head
Crookhaven
Roaringwater Bay
Sherkin Island
Cape Clear
Clear Island

Longitude 10° west of Greenwich

16 Conic Equidistant Projection

GALWAY

Craughwell   Kilregkill   Laurencetown   Clonony   Screggan   Ballinagar   Sallins
Lough Rea   Loughrea   Kilcrow   Eyrecourt   Cloghan   Killeigh   Kilcavan   Rathangan   (An Nás)

OFFALY   **KILDARE**

Ardrahan   Dalystown   Robaun   Kilcormac   Clonygowan   Bracknagh   Newbridge
Kiltartan   Knockmoyle   Meelick   Two Mile   Portarlington   Kildare   Curragh   Kilcullen
Derrybrien   Portumna   Rathcabban   Birr   Bridge   Jamestown   Monasterevin   Camp

1

Gort   Woodford   Portland   Riverstown   Kinnitty   Mountmellick   New Inn   Calverstown   Hollywood
Drumandoora   Gorteeny   Power's Cross   Clareen   Arderin   Portlaoise   Stradbally   Kilberry   Fontstown   Dunlavin

LEINSTER

ugh Graney   Derrygoolin   Ballinderry   Sharavogue   Drimmo   Cashel   Athy   Moone   Donard   **53°**
400 △   Borrisokane   Shinrone   Mountrath   Castletown   Ballylynan   Stratford
Caher   Whitegate   Puckaun   Ardcrony   529   **LAOIS**   Arless   Castledermot   Baltinglass

Mountshannon   Scarriff   Dunkerrin   Roscrea   Borris-in-Ossory   Ballyroan   Maganey   Kiltegan
Tuamgraney   Portroe   Ballybrophy   Aghaboe   Abbeyleix   Newtown   Killerrig   Grangeford
Tulla   Nenagh   Lisgarode   Moneygall   Errill   Donaghmore   Ballinakill   Clogh   337 △   Carlow   Tullow
Broadford   Arra   Devil's Bit   Rathdowney   Durrow   Ballyragget   (Ceatharlach)   **CARLOW**
Kilmurry   Killaloe   Mountains   Dolla   Mountain   Clonmore   Templetuohy   Johnstown   Castlecomer   **CARLOW**
mlebridge   Kilmore   Silvermines   Sallypark   481   Templemore   Loughmoe   Dinin   Leighlinbridge   Fennagh
533   Birdhill   Keeper Hill   Templederry   Freshford   Whitehall   Bagenalstown

Castleconnell   Newport   694 △   Thurles   Urlingford   Mohil   Coolgrange   (Muine   Clonegal
Ardnacrusha   Silvermine Mts   Milestone   Ballycahill   Kilkenny   Gowran   Bheag)   Bunclody
Limerick   Lisnagry   464 △   **TIPPERARY**   (Cill Chainnigh)   Goresbridge   Mount
(Luimneach)   Slievefelim   Holycross   320 △   Kilmanagh   **KILKENNY**   Borris   Leinster
Mungret   Boher   Mountains   Cappagh   Clonoulty   Slieveardagh Hills   Bennettsbridge   Dungarvan   795
Patrickswell   Doon   Cappamore   White   Kilmanagh   Ballymurphy
Ballyneety   Pallas   Dundrum   Ballinure   Kings   Ballysla   Callan   Graiguenamanagh   Kiltealy
Croom   Green   Donohill   Cashel   Drangan   Kells   Stoneyford   519 △   Killann

2

Herbertstown   New   Golden   Knockbrit   Cloneen   Killamery   Thomastown   Brandon   Clonroche
Emly   Tipperary   Bansha   Newmarket   367 △   Hill   Drummin
Athlacca   Kilross   Fethard   Newinn   Kilmaganny   Drummin
Rockhill   Elton   Knocklong   Newtown   Lisronagh   Slievenamon   Ahenny   Coolroebeg   Ballywilliam
Galbally   Aherlow   Lukeswell   Listerlin   Clonroche
Kilmallock   Martinstown   Galtymore   Cahir   719   Poulnamucky   **WEXFORD**
arleville   Kilfinnane   Ballylanders   920   Kilcommon   Rathkeevin   Rosbercon   Old
(An Ráth)   Ardpatrick   Galtee Mountains   Carrick-   New   Ross   Adamstown
Ballyhaght   Kilbeheny   Ardfinnan   Clonmel   on-Suir   Ross   Ballynabola   Camaross
Newtown   Clogheen   (Cluain Meala)   Carrickbeg   Fiddown   Foulkesmill
Ballyhoura Mts   Mitchelstown   Tar   Clonea   Suir   Rochestown   Waddingtown   Tullycanna
scarroll   Kildorrery   Glenduff   Ballyporeen   Newcastle   Portlaw   Mooncoin   Campile   Wellingtonbridge
Buttevant   Ballymacarbery   Waterford   Cheekpoint   Carrick   Duncormick
Castletownroche   Kilworth   **Monavullagh**   (Port Láirge)   Ballyhack   Bannow
Killavullen   Ballyhooly   Ballyduff   Cappoquin   **Mountains**   Newtown   Kilmacthomas   Lisnakill   Duncannon
Mallow   **WATERFORD**   Seefin △ 728   Kill   Tramore   Woodstown   Fethard   Ballyteige
Burnfort   Castlelyons   Lismore   Ballinamult   Lemybrien   Bay
llynamona   Nagles Mts   429 △   Ballymacmague   Bunmahon   Dunmore   Hook Head
Knocknaskagh   Curraglass   Tallow   Whitechurch   Ballyvoyle   East   Waterford Harbour
Rathcormac   Aghern   Villierstown   Dungarvan
Ardglass   238 △   Ballynoe   Dunmoon   Helvick Head
Lisgoold   The Pike   An Goirtín   An Rinn
onughmore   **CORK**   Dungourney   Grange   (Gorteen)   (Ringville)   Mine Head
Kilmona   Whitechurch   Knockraha   Killeagh   Youghal   Ardmore Bay
Tower   Blarney   Glanmire   Megeely   Castlemartyr   Youghal Bay   **52°**
Dripsey   Midleton   Ballymacoda
oachford   Clogheenmill   Carrigtohill   Garryvoe   Knockadoon Head
Ovens   **Cork**   Cloyne   Ballycotton Bay
Aherla   (Corcaigh)   Passage West   Great Island   Cobh
ookstown   Douglas   Churchtown
Ballinhassig   Ringaskiddy   Whitegate   Gyleen   Power Head
Carrigaline   Crosshaven
on   Innishannon   Ballyfeard
Bandon

3

Kilbrittain   Kinsale
Ballinspittle
oleague   Courtmacsherry   Lispatrick
Courtmacsherry   Old Head
Seven   Bay   of Kinsale
Heads

C E L T I C   S E A

60 KILOMETRES   40   20   0   40   20   10   0   MILES 0

1:1 000 000

© Collins Bartholomew Ltd

A

The index includes the names of places and physical features in Ireland. Names are indexed to the Irish province maps in the Atlas of Ireland and can be located using the grid reference letters and numbers around the edges of the map.

B

C

D

E

F

G

REFERENCES
Central Statistics Office, Ireland www.cso.ie
National Statistics Office, UK www.statistics.gov.uk
Met Éireann www.met.ie
Met Office UK www.metoffice.gov.uk

All independent countries and populated dependent and disputed territories are included in this list of the states and territories of the world; the list is arranged in alphabetical order by the conventional name form. For independent states, the full name is given below the conventional name, if this is different; for territories, the status is given. The capital city name is the same form as shown on the reference maps.

The statistics used for the area and population are the latest available and include estimates. The information on languages and religions is based on the latest information on 'de facto' speakers of the language or 'de facto' adherents to the religion. The information available on languages and religions varies greatly from country to country. Some countries include questions in censuses, others do not, in which case best estimates are used. The order of the languages and religions reflect their relative importance within the country; generally, languages or religions are included when more than one per cent of the population are estimated to be speakers or adherents.

Membership of selected international organizations is shown for each independent country. Territories are not shown as having separate memberships of these organizations.

ABBREVIATIONS

CURRENCIES

CFA	Communauté Financière Africaine
CFP	Comptoirs Français du Pacifique

ORGANIZATIONS

APEC	Asia-Pacific Economic Cooperation
ASEAN	Association of Southeast Asian Nations
CARICOM	Caribbean Community
CIS	Commonwealth of Independent States
COMM.	The Commonwealth
EU	European Union
OECD	Organization of Economic Co-operation and Development
OPEC	Organization of Petroleum Exporting Countries
SADC	Southern African Development Community
UN	United Nations

AFGHANISTAN
Islamic State of Afghanistan

Area Sq Km	652 225	Religions	Sunni Muslim, Shi'a Muslim
Area Sq Miles	251 825		
Population	27 145 000	Currency	Afghani
Capital	Kābul	Organizations	UN
Languages	Dari, Pushtu, Uzbek,Turkmen	Map page	92–93

ALBANIA
Republic of Albania

Area Sq Km	28 748	Religions	Sunni Muslim, Albanian Orthodox, Roman Catholic
Area Sq Miles	11 100		
Population	3 190 000		
Capital	Tirana (Tiranë)	Currency	Lek
Languages	Albanian, Greek	Organizations	UN
		Map page	125

ALGERIA
People's Democratic Republic of Algeria

Area Sq Km	2 381 741	Religions	Sunni Muslim
Area Sq Miles	919 595	Currency	Algerian dinar
Population	33 858 000	Organizations	OPEC, UN
Capital	Algiers (Alger)	Map page	130–131
Languages	Arabic, French, Berber		

American Samoa
United States Unincorporated Territory

Area Sq Km	197	Religions	Protestant, Roman Catholic
Area Sq Miles	76		
Population	67 000	Currency	United States dollar
Capital	Fagatogo	Map page	65
Languages	Samoan, English		

ANDORRA
Principality of Andorra

Area Sq Km	465	Religions	Roman Catholic
Area Sq Miles	180	Currency	Euro
Population	75 000	Organizations	UN
Capital	Andorra la Vella	Map page	120
Languages	Spanish, Catalan, French		

ANGOLA
Republic of Angola

Area Sq Km	1 246 700	Religions	Roman Catholic, Protestant, traditional beliefs
Area Sq Miles	481 354		
Population	17 024 000		
Capital	Luanda	Currency	Kwanza
Languages	Portuguese, Bantu, local languages	Organizations	OPEC, SADC, UN
		Map page	136

Anguilla
United Kingdom Overseas Territory

Area Sq Km	155	**Religions**	Protestant, Roman
Area Sq Miles	60		Catholic
Population	13 000	**Currency**	East Caribbean dollar
Capital	The Valley	**Map page**	163
Languages	English		

ANTIGUA AND BARBUDA

Area Sq Km	442	**Religions**	Protestant, Roman
Area Sq Miles	171		Catholic
Population	85 000	**Currency**	East Caribbean dollar
Capital	St John's	**Organizations**	CARICOM,
Languages	English, creole		Comm., UN
		Map page	163

ARGENTINA
Argentine Republic

Area Sq Km	2 766 889	**Religions**	Roman Catholic,
Area Sq Miles	1 068 302		Protestant
Population	39 531 000	**Currency**	Argentinian peso
Capital	Buenos Aires	**Organizations**	UN
Languages	Spanish, Italian,	**Map page**	168–169
	Amerindian		
	languages		

ARMENIA
Republic of Armenia

Area Sq Km	29 800	**Religions**	Armenian Orthodox
Area Sq Miles	11 506	**Currency**	Dram
Population	3 002 000	**Organizations**	CIS, UN
Capital	Yerevan (Erevan)	**Map page**	97
Languages	Armenian, Azeri		

Aruba
Self-governing Netherlands Territory

Area Sq Km	193	**Religions**	Roman Catholic,
Area Sq Miles	75		Protestant
Population	104 000	**Currency**	Aruban florin
Capital	Oranjestad	**Map page**	163
Languages	Papiamento, Dutch,		
	English		

Ascension
Dependency of St Helena

Area Sq Km	88	**Religions**	Protestant, Roman
Area Sq Miles	34		Catholic
Population	1 122	**Currency**	Pound sterling
Capital	Georgetown	**Map page**	129
Languages	English		

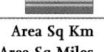

AUSTRALIA
Commonwealth of Australia

Area Sq Km	7 692 024	**Religions**	Protestant, Roman
Area Sq Miles	2 969 907		Catholic, Orthodox
Population	20 743 000	**Currency**	Australian dollar
Capital	Canberra	**Organizations**	APEC, Comm.,
Languages	English, Italian,		OECD, UN
	Greek	**Map page**	66–67

Australian Capital Territory (Federal Territory)

Area Sq Km	2 358	**Population**	329 500
Area Sq Miles	910	**Capital**	Canberra

Jervis Bay Territory (Territory)

Area Sq Km	73	**Population**	611
Area Sq Miles	28		

New South Wales (State)

Area Sq Km	800 642	**Population**	6 844 200
Area Sq Miles	309 130	**Capital**	Sydney

Northern Territory (Territory)

Area Sq Km	1 349 129	**Population**	207 700
Area Sq Miles	520 902	**Capital**	Darwin

Queensland (State)

Area Sq Km	1 730 648	**Population**	4 070 400
Area Sq Miles	668 207	**Capital**	Brisbane

South Australia (State)

Area Sq Km	983 482	**Population**	1 558 200
Area Sq Miles	379 725	**Capital**	Adelaide

Tasmania (State)

Area Sq Km	68 401	**Population**	489 600
Area Sq Miles	26 410	**Capital**	Hobart

Victoria (State)

Area Sq Km	227 416	**Population**	5 110 500
Area Sq Miles	87 806	**Capital**	Melbourne

Western Australia (State)

Area Sq Km	2 529 875	**Population**	2 061 500
Area Sq Miles	976 790	**Capital**	Perth

AUSTRIA
Republic of Austria

Area Sq Km	83 855	**Religions**	Roman Catholic,
Area Sq Miles	32 377		Protestant
Population	8 361 000	**Currency**	Euro
Capital	Vienna (Wien)	**Organizations**	EU, OECD, UN
Languages	German, Croatian,	**Map page**	118–119
	Turkish		

AZERBAIJAN
Azerbaijani Republic

Area Sq Km	86 600	**Religions**	Shi'a Muslim, Sunni
Area Sq Miles	33 436		Muslim, Russian and
Population	8 467 000		Armenian Orthodox
Capital	Baku (Bakı)	**Currency**	Azerbaijani manat
Languages	Azeri, Armenian,	**Organizations**	CIS, UN
	Russian, Lezgian	**Map page**	97

Azores (Arquipélago dos Açores)
Autonomous Region of Portugal

Area Sq Km	2 300	**Religions**	Roman Catholic,
Area Sq Miles	888		Protestant
Population	242 712	**Currency**	Euro
Capital	Ponta Delgada	**Map page**	128
Languages	Portuguese		

THE BAHAMAS
Commonwealth of The Bahamas

Area Sq Km	13 939	**Religions**	Protestant, Roman
Area Sq Miles	5 382		Catholic
Population	331 000	**Currency**	Bahamian dollar
Capital	Nassau	**Organizations**	CARICOM, Comm.,
Languages	English, creole		UN
		Map page	162–163

BAHRAIN
Kingdom of Bahrain

Area Sq Km	691	**Religions**	Shi'a Muslim, Sunni
Area Sq Miles	267		Muslim, Christian
Population	753 000	**Currency**	Bahraini dinar
Capital	Manama	**Organizations**	UN
	(Al Manāmah)	**Map page**	95
Languages	Arabic, English		

BANGLADESH
People's Republic of Bangladesh

Area Sq Km	143 998	**Religions**	Sunni Muslim, Hindu
Area Sq Miles	55 598	**Currency**	Taka
Population	158 665 000	**Organizations**	Comm., UN
Capital	Dhaka (Dacca)	**Map page**	91
Languages	Bengali, English		

BARBADOS

Area Sq Km	430	**Religions**	Protestant, Roman
Area Sq Miles	166		Catholic
Population	294 000	**Currency**	Barbados dollar
Capital	Bridgetown	**Organizations**	CARICOM,
Languages	English, creole		Comm., UN
		Map page	163

BELARUS
Republic of Belarus

Area Sq Km	207 600	**Religions**	Belorussian Orthodox,
Area Sq Miles	80 155		Roman Catholic
Population	9 689 000	**Currency**	Belarus rouble
Capital	Minsk	**Organizations**	CIS, UN
Languages	Belorussian, Russian	**Map page**	104–105

BELGIUM
Kingdom of Belgium

Area Sq Km	30 520	**Religions**	Roman Catholic,
Area Sq Miles	11 784		Protestant
Population	10 457 000	**Currency**	Euro
Capital	Brussels (Bruxelles)	**Organizations**	EU, OECD, UN
Languages	Dutch (Flemish),	**Map page**	116
	French (Walloon),		
	German		

BELIZE

Area Sq Km	22 965	**Religions**	Roman Catholic,
Area Sq Miles	8 867		Protestant
Population	288 000	**Currency**	Belize dollar
Capital	Belmopan	**Organizations**	CARICOM, Comm.,
Languages	English, Spanish,		UN
	Mayan, creole	**Map page**	163

BENIN
Republic of Benin

Area Sq Km	112 620	**Religions**	Traditional beliefs,
Area Sq Miles	43 483		Roman Catholic,
Population	9 033 000		Sunni Muslim
Capital	Porto-Novo	**Currency**	CFA franc
Languages	French, Fon,	**Organization**	UN
	Yoruba, Adja,	**Map page**	130
	local languages		

Bermuda
United Kingdom Overseas Territory

Area Sq Km	54	**Religions**	Protestant, Roman
Area Sq Miles	21		Catholic
Population	65 000	**Currency**	Bermuda dollar
Capital	Hamilton	**Map page**	141
Languages	English		

BHUTAN
Kingdom of Bhutan

Area Sq Km	46 620	**Religions**	Buddhist, Hindu
Area Sq Miles	18 000	**Currency**	Ngultrum,
Population	658 000		Indian rupee
Capital	Thimphu	**Organizations**	UN
Languages	Dzongkha,	**Map page**	91
	Nepali, Assamese		

BOLIVIA
Republic of Bolivia

Area Sq Km	1 098 581	**Religions**	Roman Catholic,
Area Sq Miles	424 164		Protestant, Baha'i
Population	9 525 000	**Currency**	Boliviano
Capital	La Paz/Sucre	**Organizations**	UN
Languages	Spanish, Quechua,	**Map page**	168
	Aymara		

Bonaire
part of Netherlands Antilles

Area Sq Km	288	**Religions**	Roman Catholic,
Area Sq Miles	111		Protestant
Population	10 638	**Currency**	Netherlands Antilles
Capital	Kralendijk		guilder
Languages	Dutch, Papiamento	**Map page**	163

Bonin Islands (Ogasawara-shotō)
part of Japan

Area Sq Km	104	**Religions**	Shintoist, Buddhist,
Area Sq Miles	40		Christian
Population	2 300	**Currency**	Yen
Capital	Ōmura	**Map page**	85
Languages	Japanese		

BOSNIA-HERZEGOVINA
Republic of Bosnia and Herzegovina

Area Sq Km	51 130	**Religions**	Sunni Muslim, Serbian
Area Sq Miles	19 741		Orthodox, Roman
Population	3 935 000		Catholic, Protestant
Capital	Sarajevo	**Currency**	Marka
Languages	Bosnian, Serbian,	**Organizations**	UN
	Croatian	**Map page**	125

BOTSWANA
Republic of Botswana

Area Sq Km	581 370	**Religions**	Traditional beliefs,
Area Sq Miles	224 468		Protestant, Roman
Population	1 882 000		Catholic
Capital	Gaborone	**Currency**	Pula
Languages	English, Setswana,	**Organizations**	Comm., SADC, UN
	Shona, local	**Map page**	136
	languages		

BRAZIL
Federative Republic of Brazil

Area Sq Km	8 514 879	**Religions**	Roman Catholic,
Area Sq Miles	3 287 613		Protestant
Population	191 791 000	**Currency**	Real
Capital	Brasília	**Organizations**	UN
Languages	Portuguese	**Map page**	166–167

BRUNEI
State of Brunei Darussalam

Area Sq Km	5 765	**Religions**	Sunni Muslim,
Area Sq Miles	2 226		Buddhist, Christian
Population	390 000	**Currency**	Brunei dollar
Capital	Bandar Seri Begawan	**Organizations**	APEC, ASEAN,
Languages	Malay, English,		Comm., UN
	Chinese	**Map page**	77

BULGARIA
Republic of Bulgaria

Area Sq Km	110 994	**Religions**	Bulgarian Orthodox,
Area Sq Miles	42 855		Sunni Muslim
Population	7 639 000	**Currency**	Lev
Capital	Sofia (Sofiya)	**Organizations**	EU, UN
Languages	Bulgarian, Turkish,	**Map page**	126
	Romany,		
	Macedonian		

BURKINA
Democratic Republic of Burkina Faso

Area Sq Km	274 200	**Religions**	Sunni Muslim,
Area Sq Miles	105 869		traditional beliefs,
Population	14 784 000		Roman Catholic
Capital	Ouagadougou	**Currency**	CFA franc
Languages	French, Moore	**Organizations**	UN
	(Mossi), Fulani, local	**Map page**	130
	languages		

BURUNDI
Republic of Burundi

Area Sq Km	27 835	**Religions**	Roman Catholic,
Area Sq Miles	10 747		traditional beliefs,
Population	8 508 000		Protestant
Capital	Bujumbura	**Currency**	Burundian franc
Languages	Kirundi (Hutu,	**Organizations**	UN
	Tutsi), French	**Map page**	135

CAMBODIA
Kingdom of Cambodia

Area Sq Km	181 000	**Religions**	Buddhist, Roman
Area Sq Miles	69 884		Catholic, Sunni
Population	14 444 000		Muslim
Capital	Phnom Penh	**Currency**	Riel
Languages	Khmer, Vietnamese	**Organizations**	ASEAN, UN
		Map page	79

CAMEROON
Republic of Cameroon

Area Sq Km	475 442	**Religions**	Roman Catholic,
Area Sq Miles	183 569		traditional beliefs,
Population	18 549 000		Sunni Muslim,
Capital	Yaoundé		Protestant
Languages	French, English,	**Currency**	CFA franc
	Fang, Bamileke,	**Organizations**	Comm., UN
	local languages	**Map page**	134

CANADA

Area Sq Km	9 984 670	**Religions**	Roman Catholic,
Area Sq Miles	3 855 103		Protestant, Eastern
Population	32 876 000		Orthodox, Jewish
Capital	Ottawa	**Currency**	Canadian dollar
Languages	English, French,	**Organizations**	APEC, Comm.,
	local languages		OECD, UN
		Map page	142–143

Alberta (Province)

Area Sq Km	661 848	**Population**	3 435 511
Area Sq Miles	255 541	**Capital**	Edmonton

British Columbia (Province)

Area Sq Km	944 735	**Population**	4 338 106
Area Sq Miles	364 764	**Capital**	Victoria

Manitoba (Province)

Area Sq Km	647 797	**Population**	1 180 004
Area Sq Miles	250 116	**Capital**	Winnipeg

New Brunswick (Province)

Area Sq Km	72 908	**Population**	748 582
Area Sq Miles	28 150	**Capital**	Fredericton

Newfoundland and Labrador (Province)

Area Sq Km	405 212	**Population**	508 548
Area Sq Miles	156 453	**Capital**	St John's

Northwest Territories (Territory)

Area Sq Km	1 346 106	**Population**	41 777
Area Sq Miles	519 734	**Capital**	Yellowknife

CANADA

Nova Scotia (Province)

Area Sq Km	55 284	Population	933 793
Area Sq Miles	21 345	Capital	Halifax

Nunavut (Territory)

Area Sq Km	2 093 190	Population	30 947
Area Sq Miles	808 185	Capital	Iqaluit (Frobisher Bay)

Ontario (Province)

Area Sq Km	1 076 395	Population	12 726 336
Area Sq Miles	415 598	Capital	Toronto

Prince Edward Island (Province)

Area Sq Km	5 660	Population	138 632
Area Sq Miles	2 185	Capital	Charlottetown

Québec (Province)

Area Sq Km	1 542 056	Population	7 676 097
Area Sq Miles	595 391	Capital	Québec

Saskatchewan (Province)

Area Sq Km	651 036	Population	987 939
Area Sq Miles	251 366	Capital	Regina

Yukon Territory (Territory)

Area Sq Km	482 443	Population	31 032
Area Sq Miles	186 272	Capital	Whitehorse

 ### Canary Islands (Islas Canarias)
Autonomous Community of Spain

Area Sq Km	7 447	Languages	Spanish
Area Sq Miles	2 875	Religions	Roman Catholic
Population	1 995 833	Currency	Euro
Capital	Santa Cruz de Tenerife/Las Palmas	Map page	130

 ### CAPE VERDE
Republic of Cape Verde

Area Sq Km	4 033	Religions	Roman Catholic, Protestant
Area Sq Miles	1 557		
Population	530 000	Currency	Cape Verde escudo
Capital	Praia	Organizations	UN
Languages	Portuguese, creole	Map page	62

 ### Cayman Islands
United Kingdom Overseas Territory

Area Sq Km	259	Religions	Protestant, Roman Catholic
Area Sq Miles	100		
Population	47 000	Currency	Cayman Islands dollar
Capital	George Town	Map page	162
Languages	English		

 ### CENTRAL AFRICAN REPUBLIC

Area Sq Km	622 436	Religions	Protestant, Roman Catholic, traditional beliefs, Sunni Muslim
Area Sq Miles	240 324		
Population	4 343 000		
Capital	Bangui	Currency	CFA franc
Languages	French, Sango, Banda, Baya, local languages	Organizations	UN
		Map page	134

 ### Ceuta
Autonomous Community of Spain

Area Sq Km	19	Religions	Roman Catholic, Muslim
Area Sq Miles	7		
Population	75 861	Currency	Euro
Capital	Ceuta	Map page	122
Languages	Spanish, Arabic		

 ### CHAD
Republic of Chad

Area Sq Km	1 284 000	Religions	Sunni Muslim, Roma Catholic, Protestant, traditional beliefs
Area Sq Miles	495 755		
Population	10 781 000		
Capital	Ndjamena	Currency	CFA franc
Languages	Arabic, French, Sara, local languages	Organizations	UN
		Map page	131

 ### Chatham Islands
part of New Zealand

Area Sq Km	963	Religions	Protestant
Area Sq Miles	372	Currency	New Zealand dollar
Population	612	Map page	65
Capital	Waitangi		
Languages	English		

 ### CHILE
Republic of Chile

Area Sq Km	756 945	Religions	Roman Catholic, Protestant
Area Sq Miles	292 258		
Population	16 635 000	Currency	Chilean peso
Capital	Santiago	Organizations	APEC, UN
Languages	Spanish, Amerindian languages	Map page	168–169

CHINA
People's Republic of China

Area Sq Km	9 584 492	Religions	Confucian, Taoist, Buddhist, Christian, Sunni Muslim
Area Sq Miles	3 700 593		
Population	1 313 437 000		
Capital	Beijing (Peking)	Currency	Yuan, Hong Kong dollar, Macao pataca
Languages	Mandarin, Wu, Cantonese, Hsiang, regional languages	Organizations	APEC, UN
		Map page	84–85

Anhui (Province)

Area Sq Km	139 000	Population	61 140 000
Area Sq Miles	53 668	Capital	Hefei

Bejing (Municipality)

Area Sq Km	16 800	Population	15 360 000
Area Sq Miles	6 487	Capital	Beijing (Peking)

Chongqing (Municipality)

Area Sq Km	23 000	Population	27 970 000
Area Sq Miles	8 880	Capital	Chongqing

Fujian (Province)

Area Sq Km	121 400	Population	35 320 000
Area Sq Miles	46 873	Capital	Fuzhou

ansu (Province)

Area Sq Km	453 700	**Population**	25 920 000
Area Sq Miles	175 175	**Capital**	Lanzhou

uangdong (Province)

Area Sq Km	178 000	**Population**	91 850 000
Area Sq Miles	68 726	**Capital**	Guangzhou (Canton)

uangxi Zhuangzu Zizhiqu (Autonomous Region)

Area Sq Km	236 000	**Population**	46 550 000
Area Sq Miles	91 120	**Capital**	Nanning

uizhou (Province)

Area Sq Km	176 000	**Population**	37 250 000
Area Sq Miles	67 954	**Capital**	Guiyang

ainan (Province)

Area Sq Km	34 000	**Population**	8 260 000
Area Sq Miles	13 127	**Capital**	Haikou

ebei (Province)

Area Sq Km	187 700	**Population**	68 440 000
Area Sq Miles	72 471	**Capital**	Shijiazhuang

eilongjiang (Province)

Area Sq Km	454 600	**Population**	38 180 000
Area Sq Miles	175 522	**Capital**	Harbin

enan (Province)

Area Sq Km	167 000	**Population**	93 710 000
Area Sq Miles	64 479	**Capital**	Zhengzhou

ong Kong (Special Administrative Region)

Area Sq Km	1 075	**Population**	6 936 000
Area Sq Miles	415	**Capital**	Hong Kong

ubei (Province)

Area Sq Km	185 900	**Population**	57 070 000
Area Sq Miles	71 776	**Capital**	Wuhan

unan (Province)

Area Sq Km	210 000	**Population**	63 200 000
Area Sq Miles	81 081	**Capital**	Changsha

iangsu (Province)

Area Sq Km	102 600	**Population**	74 680 000
Area Sq Miles	39 614	**Capital**	Nanjing

iangxi (Province)

Area Sq Km	166 900	**Population**	43 070 000
Area Sq Miles	64 440	**Capital**	Nanchang

ilin (Province)

Area Sq Km	187 000	**Population**	27 150 000
Area Sq Miles	72 201	**Capital**	Changchun

iaoning (Province)

Area Sq Km	147 400	**Population**	42 200 000
Area Sq Miles	56 911	**Capital**	Shenyang

Macao (Special Administrative Region)

Area Sq Km	17	**Population**	477 000
Area Sq Mile	7		

Nei Mongol Zizhiqu (Inner Mongolia) (Autonomous Region)

Area Sq Km	1 183 000	**Population**	23 860 000
Area Sq Miles	456 759	**Capital**	Hohhot

Ningxia Huizu Zizhiqu (Autonomous Region)

Area Sq Km	66 400	**Population**	5 950 000
Area Sq Miles	25 637	**Capital**	Yinchuan

Qinghai (Province)

Area Sq Km	721 000	**Population**	5 430 000
Area Sq Miles	278 380	**Capital**	Xining

Shaanxi (Province)

Area Sq Km	205 600	**Population**	37 180 000
Area Sq Miles	79 383	**Capital**	Xi'an

Shandong (Province)

Area Sq Km	153 300	**Population**	92 390 000
Area Sq Miles	59 189	**Capital**	Jinan

Shanghai (Municipality)

Area Sq Km	6 300	**Population**	17 780 000
Area Sq Miles	2 432	**Capital**	Shanghai

Shanxi (Province)

Area Sq Km	156 300	**Population**	33 520 000
Area Sq Miles	60 348	**Capital**	Taiyuan

Sichuan (Province)

Area Sq Km	569 000	**Population**	82 080 000
Area Sq Miles	219 692	**Capital**	Chengdu

Tianjin (Municipality)

Area Sq Km	11 300	**Population**	10 430 000
Area Sq Miles	4 363	**Capital**	Tianjin

Xinjiang Uygur Zizhiqu (Sinkiang) (Autonomous Region)

Area Sq Km	1 600 000	**Population**	20 080 000
Area Sq Miles	617 763	**Capital**	Ürümqi

Xizang Zizhiqu (Tibet) (Autonomous Region)

Area Sq Km	1 228 400	**Population**	2 760 000
Area Sq Miles	474 288	**Capital**	Lhasa

Yunnan (Province)

Area Sq Km	394 000	**Population**	44 420 000
Area Sq Miles	152 124	**Capital**	Kunming

Zhejiang (Province)

Area Sq Km	101 800	**Population**	48 940 000
Area Sq Miles	39 305	**Capital**	Hangzhou

Christmas Island
Australian External Territory

Area Sq Km	135	**Religions**	Buddhist, Sunni
Area Sq Miles	52		Muslim, Protestant,
Population	1 508		Roman Catholic
Capital	The Settlement	**Currency**	Australian dollar
Languages	English	**Map page**	74

Cocos Islands (Keeling Islands)
Australian External Territory

Area Sq Km	14	**Religions**	Sunni Muslim,
Area Sq Miles	5		Christian
Population	621	**Currency**	Australian dollar
Capital	West Island	**Map page**	74
Languages	English		

COLOMBIA
Republic of Colombia

Area Sq Km	1 141 748	**Religions**	Roman Catholic,
Area Sq Miles	440 831		Protestant
Population	46 156 000	**Currency**	Colombian peso
Capital	Bogotá	**Organizations**	UN
Languages	Spanish, Amerindian	**Map page**	166
	languages		

COMOROS
Union of the Comoros

Area Sq Km	1 862	**Religions**	Sunni Muslim, Roman
Area Sq Miles	719		Catholic
Population	839 000	**Currency**	Comoros franc
Capital	Moroni	**Organizations**	UN
Languages	Comorian, French,	**Map page**	137
	Arabic		

CONGO
Republic of the Congo

Area Sq Km	342 000	**Religions**	Roman Catholic,
Area Sq Miles	132 047		Protestant, traditional
Population	3 768 000		beliefs, Sunni Muslim
Capital	Brazzaville	**Currency**	CFA franc
Languages	French, Kongo,	**Organizations**	UN
	Monokutuba, local	**Map page**	134
	languages		

CONGO, DEMOCRATIC REPUBLIC OF THE

Area Sq Km	2 345 410	**Religions**	Christian, Sunni
Area Sq Miles	905 568		Muslim
Population	62 636 000	**Currency**	Congolese franc
Capital	Kinshasa	**Organizations**	SADC, UN
Languages	French, Lingala,	**Map page**	134–135
	Swahili, Kongo,		
	local languages		

Cook Islands
Self-governing New Zealand Overseas Territory

Area Sq Km	293	**Religions**	Protestant, Roman
Area Sq Miles	113		Catholic
Population	13 000	**Currency**	New Zealand dollar
Capital	Avarua	**Map page**	65
Languages	English, Maori		

COSTA RICA
Republic of Costa Rica

Area Sq Km	51 100	**Religions**	Roman Catholic,
Area Sq Miles	19 730		Protestant
Population	4 468 000	**Currency**	Costa Rican colón
Capital	San José	**Organizations**	UN
Languages	Spanish	**Map page**	162

CÔTE D'IVOIRE
Republic of Côte d'Ivoire

Area Sq Km	322 463	**Religions**	Sunni Muslim, Roman
Area Sq Miles	124 504		Catholic, traditonal
Population	19 262 000		beliefs, Protestant
Capital	Yamoussoukro	**Currency**	CFA franc
Languages	French, creole, Akan,	**Organizations**	UN
	local languages	**Map page**	130

CROATIA
Republic of Croatia

Area Sq Km	56 538	**Religions**	Roman Catholic,
Area Sq Miles	21 829		Serbian Orthodox,
Population	4 555 000		Sunni Muslim
Capital	Zagreb	**Currency**	Kuna
Languages	Croatian, Serbian	**Organizations**	UN
		Map page	125

CUBA
Republic of Cuba

Area Sq Km	110 860	**Religions**	Roman Catholic,
Area Sq Miles	42 803		Protestant
Population	11 268 000	**Currency**	Cuban peso
Capital	Havana (La Habana)	**Organizations**	UN
Languages	Spanish	**Map page**	162

Curaçao
part of Netherlands Antilles

Area Sq Km	444	**Religions**	Roman Catholic,
Area Sq Miles	171		Protestant
Population	135 822	**Currency**	Netherlands Antilles
Capital	Willemstad		guilder
Languages	Dutch, Papiamento	**Map page**	163

CYPRUS
Republic of Cyprus

Area Sq Km	9 251	**Religions**	Greek Orthodox,
Area Sq Miles	3 572		Sunni Muslim
Population	855 000	**Currency**	Euro
Capital	Nicosia (Lefkosia)	**Organizations**	Comm., EU, UN
Languages	Greek, Turkish,	**Map page**	96
	English		

CZECH REPUBLIC

Area Sq Km	78 864	**Religions**	Roman Catholic, Protestant
Area Sq Miles	30 450		
Population	10 186 000	**Currency**	Czech koruna
Capital	Prague (Praha)	**Organizations**	EU, OECD, UN
Languages	Czech, Moravian, Slovakian	**Map page**	118–119

DENMARK
Kingdom of Denmark

Area Sq Km	43 075	**Religions**	Protestant
Area Sq Miles	16 631	**Currency**	Danish krone
Population	5 442 000	**Organizations**	EU, OECD, UN
Capital	Copenhagen (København)	**Map page**	109
Languages	Danish		

DJIBOUTI
Republic of Djibouti

Area Sq Km	23 200	**Religions**	Sunni Muslim, Christian
Area Sq Miles	8 958		
Population	833 000	**Currency**	Djibouti franc
Capital	Djibouti	**Organizations**	UN
Languages	Somali, Afar, French, Arabic	**Map page**	133

DOMINICA
Commonwealth of Dominica

Area Sq Km	750	**Religions**	Roman Catholic, Protestant
Area Sq Miles	290		
Population	67 000	**Currency**	East Caribbean dollar
Capital	Roseau	**Organizations**	CARICOM, Comm., UN
Languages	English, creole		
		Map page	163

DOMINICAN REPUBLIC

Area Sq Km	48 442	**Religions**	Roman Catholic, Protestant
Area Sq Miles	18 704		
Population	9 760 000	**Currency**	Dominican peso
Capital	Santo Domingo	**Organizations**	UN
Languages	Spanish, creole	**Map page**	163

Easter Island (Isla de Pascua)
part of Chile

Area Sq Km	171	**Religions**	Roman Catholic
Area Sq Miles	66	**Currency**	Chilean peso
Population	3 791	**Map page**	173
Capital	Hanga Roa		
Languages	Spanish		

EAST TIMOR
Democratic Republic of Timor-Leste

Area Sq Km	14 874	**Religions**	Roman Catholic
Area Sq Miles	5 743	**Currency**	United States dollar
Population	1 155 000	**Organisations**	UN
Capital	Dili	**Map page**	75
Languages	Portuguese, Tetun, English		

ECUADOR
Republic of Ecuador

Area Sq Km	272 045	**Religions**	Roman Catholic
Area Sq Miles	105 037	**Currency**	United States dollar
Population	13 341 000	**Organizations**	APEC, OPEC, UN
Capital	Quito	**Map page**	166
Languages	Spanish, Quechua, Amerindian languages		

EGYPT
Arab Republic of Egypt

Area Sq Km	1 000 250	**Religions**	Sunni Muslim, Coptic Christian
Area Sq Miles	386 199		
Population	75 498 000	**Currency**	Egyptian pound
Capital	Cairo (Al Qāhirah)	**Organizations**	UN
Languages	Arabic	**Map page**	132

EL SALVADOR
Republic of El Salvador

Area Sq Km	21 041	**Religions**	Roman Catholic, Protestant
Area Sq Miles	8 124		
Population	6 857 000	**Currency**	El Salvador colón, United States dollar
Capital	San Salvador		
Languages	Spanish	**Organizations**	UN
		Map page	162

EQUATORIAL GUINEA
Republic of Equatorial Guinea

Area Sq Km	28 051	**Religions**	Roman Catholic, traditional beliefs
Area Sq Miles	10 831		
Population	507 000	**Currency**	CFA franc
Capital	Malabo	**Organizations**	UN
Languages	Spanish, French, Fang	**Map page**	134

ERITREA
State of Eritrea

Area Sq Km	117 400	**Religions**	Sunni Muslim, Coptic Christian
Area Sq Miles	45 328		
Population	4 851 000	**Currency**	Nakfa
Capital	Asmara	**Organizations**	UN
Languages	Tigrinya, Tigre	**Map page**	132

ESTONIA
Republic of Estonia

Area Sq Km	45 200	**Religions**	Protestant, Estonian and Russian Orthodox
Area Sq Miles	17 452		
Population	1 335 000	**Currency**	Kroon
Capital	Tallinn	**Organizations**	EU, UN
Languages	Estonian, Russian	**Map page**	104

ETHIOPIA
Federal Democratic Republic of Ethiopia

Area Sq Km	1 133 880	**Religions**	Ethiopian Orthodox, Sunni Muslim, traditional beliefs
Area Sq Miles	437 794		
Population	83 099 000		
Capital	Addis Ababa (Ādīs Ābeba)	**Currency**	Birr
		Organizations	UN
Languages	Oromo, Amharic, Tigrinya, local languages	**Map page**	133

Falkland Islands
United Kingdom Overseas Territory

Area Sq Km	12 170	**Religions**	Protestant, Roman Catholic
Area Sq Miles	4 699		
Population	3 000	**Currency**	Falkland Islands pound
Capital	Stanley		
Languages	English	**Map page**	169

Faroe Islands
Self-governing Danish Territory

Area Sq Km	1 399	**Religions**	Protestant
Area Sq Miles	540	**Currency**	Danish krone
Population	49 000	**Map page**	110
Capital	Tórshavn		
Languages	Faroese, Danish		

FIJI
Sovereign Democratic Republic of Fiji

Area Sq Km	18 330	**Religions**	Christian, Hindu, Sunni Muslim
Area Sq Miles	7 077		
Population	839 000	**Currency**	Fiji dollar
Capital	Suva	**Organizations**	UN, Comm.
Languages	English, Fijian, Hindi	**Map page**	65

FINLAND
Republic of Finland

Area Sq Km	338 145	**Languages**	Finnish, Swedish
Area Sq Miles	130 559	**Religions**	Protestant, Greek Orthodox
Population	5 277 000		
Capital	Helsinki (Helsingfors)	**Currency**	Euro
		Organizations	EU, OECD, UN
		Map page	108–109

FRANCE
French Republic

Area Sq Km	543 965	**Religions**	Roman Catholic, Protestant, Sunni Muslim
Area Sq Miles	210 026		
Population	61 647 000		
Capital	Paris	**Currency**	Euro
Languages	French, Arabic	**Organizations**	EU, OECD, UN
		Map page	120–121

French Guiana
French Overseas Department

Area Sq Km	90 000	**Religions**	Roman Catholic
Area Sq Miles	34 749	**Currency**	Euro
Population	202 000	**Map page**	167
Capital	Cayenne		
Languages	French, creole		

French Polynesia
French Overseas Territory

Area Sq Km	3 265	**Religions**	Protestant, Roman Catholic
Area Sq Miles	1 261		
Population	263 000	**Currency**	CFP franc
Capital	Papeete	**Map page**	65
Languages	French, Tahitian, Polynesian languages		

GABON
Gabonese Republic

Area Sq Km	267 667	**Religions**	Roman Catholic, Protestant, traditonal beliefs
Area Sq Miles	103 347		
Population	1 331 000		
Capital	Libreville	**Currency**	CFA franc
Languages	French, Fang, local languages	**Organizations**	UN
		Map page	134

Galapagos Islands (Islas Galápagos)
part of Ecuador

Area Sq Km	8 010	**Religions**	Roman Catholic
Area Sq Miles	3 093	**Currency**	United States dollar
Population	18 640	**Map page**	141
Capital	Puerto Baquerizo Moreno		
Languages	Spanish		

THE GAMBIA
Republic of The Gambia

Area Sq Km	11 295	**Religions**	Sunni Muslim, Protestant
Area Sq Miles	4 361		
Population	1 709 000	**Currency**	Dalasi
Capital	Banjul	**Organizations**	Comm., UN
Languages	English, Malinke, Fulani, Wolof	**Map page**	130

Gaza
Semi-autonomous region

Area Sq Km	363	**Religions**	Sunni Muslim, Shi'a Muslim
Area Sq Miles	140		
Population	1 586 008	**Currency**	Israeli shekel
Capital	Gaza	**Map page**	96
Languages	Arabic		

GEORGIA
Republic of Georgia

Area Sq Km	69 700	**Religions**	Georgian Orthodox, Russian Orthodox, Sunni Muslim
Area Sq Miles	26 911		
Population	4 395 000		
Capital	T'bilisi	**Currency**	Lari
Languages	Georgian, Russian, Armenian, Azeri, Ossetian, Abkhaz	**Organizations**	CIS, UN
		Map page	97

GERMANY
Federal Republic of Germany

Area Sq Km	357 022	**Religions**	Protestant, Roman Catholic
Area Sq Miles	137 847		
Population	82 599 000	**Currency**	Euro
Capital	Berlin	**Organizations**	EU, OECD, UN
Languages	German, Turkish	**Map page**	118

GHANA
Republic of Ghana

Area Sq Km	238 537	**Religions**	Christian, Sunni Muslim, traditional beliefs
Area Sq Miles	92 100		
Population	23 478 000		
Capital	Accra	**Currency**	Cedi
Languages	English, Hausa, Akan, local languages	**Organizations**	Comm., UN
		Map page	130

Gibraltar
United Kingdom Overseas Territory

Area Sq Km	7	Religions	Roman Catholic, Protestant, Sunni Muslim
Area Sq Miles	3		
Population	29 000		
Capital	Gibraltar	Currency	Gibraltar pound
Languages	English, Spanish	Map page	122

GREECE
Hellenic Republic

Area Sq Km	131 957	Religions	Greek Orthodox, Sunni Muslim
Area Sq Miles	50 949		
Population	11 147 000	Currency	Euro
Capital	Athens (Athina)	Organizations	EU, OECD, UN
Languages	Greek	Map page	127

Greenland
Self-governing Danish Territory

Area Sq Km	2 175 600	Religions	Protestant
Area Sq Miles	840 004	Currency	Danish krone
Population	58 000	Map page	143
Capital	Nuuk (Godthåb)		
Languages	Greenlandic, Danish		

GRENADA

Area Sq Km	378	Religions	Roman Catholic, Protestant
Area Sq Miles	146		
Population	106 000	Currency	East Caribbean dollar
Capital	St George's	Organizations	CARICOM, Comm., UN
Languages	English, creole		
		Map page	163

Guadeloupe
French Overseas Department

Area Sq Km	1 780	Religions	Roman Catholic
Area Sq Miles	687	Currency	Euro
Population	445 000	Map page	163
Capital	Basse-Terre		
Languages	French, creole		

Guam
United States Unincorporated Territory

Area Sq Km	541	Religions	Roman Catholic
Area Sq Miles	209	Currency	United States dollar
Population	173 000	Map page	75
Capital	Hagåtña		
Languages	Chamorro, English, Tagalog		

GUATEMALA
Republic of Guatemala

Area Sq Km	108 890	Religion	Roman Catholic, Protestant
Area Sq Miles	42 043		
Population	13 354 000	Currency	Quetzal, United States dollar
Capital	Guatemala City		
Languages	Spanish, Mayan languages	Organizations	UN
		Map page	162

Guernsey
United Kingdom Crown Dependency

Area Sq Km	78	Religions	Protestant, Roman Catholic
Area Sq Miles	30		
Population	63 923	Currency	Pound sterling
Capital	St Peter Port	Map page	111
Languages	English, French		

GUINEA
Republic of Guinea

Area Sq Km	245 857	Religions	Sunni Muslim, traditional beliefs, Christian
Area Sq Miles	94 926		
Population	9 370 000		
Capital	Conakry	Currency	Guinea franc
Languages	French, Fulani, Malinke, local languages	Organizations	UN
		Map page	130

GUINEA-BISSAU
Republic of Guinea-Bissau

Area Sq Km	36 125	Religions	Traditional beliefs, Sunni Muslim, Christian
Area Sq Miles	13 948		
Population	1 695 000		
Capital	Bissau	Currency	CFA franc
Languages	Portuguese, crioulo, local languages	Organizations	UN
		Map page	130

GUYANA
Co-operative Republic of Guyana

Area Sq Km	214 969	Religions	Protestant, Hindu, Roman Catholic, Sunni Muslim
Area Sq Miles	83 000		
Population	738 000		
Capital	Georgetown	Currency	Guyana dollar
Languages	English, creole, Amerindian languages	Organizations	CARICOM, Comm., UN
		Map page	166

HAITI
Republic of Haiti

Area Sq Km	27 750	Religions	Roman Catholic, Protestant, Voodoo
Area Sq Miles	10 714		
Population	9 598 000	Currency	Gourde
Capital	Port-au-Prince	Organizations	CARICOM, UN
Languages	French, creole	Map page	163

HONDURAS
Republic of Honduras

Area Sq Km	112 088	Religions	Roman Catholic, Protestant
Area Sq Miles	43 277		
Population	7 106 000	Currency	Lempira
Capital	Tegucigalpa	Organizations	UN
Languages	Spanish, Amerindian languages	Map page	163

HUNGARY
Republic of Hungary

Area Sq Km	93 030	Religions	Roman Catholic, Protestant
Area Sq Miles	35 919		
Population	10 030 000	Currency	Forint
Capital	Budapest	Organizations	EU, OECD, UN
Languages	Hungarian	Map page	119

ICELAND
Republic of Iceland

Area Sq Km	102 820	**Religions**	Protestant
Area Sq Miles	39 699	**Currency**	Icelandic króna
Population	301 000	**Organizations**	OECD, UN
Capital	Reykjavík	**Map page**	108
Languages	Icelandic		

INDIA
Republic of India

Area Sq Km	3 064 898	**Religions**	Hindu, Sunni Muslim,
Area Sq Miles	1 183 364		Shi'a Muslim, Sikh,
Population	1 169 016 000		Christian
Capital	New Delhi	**Currency**	Indian rupee
Languages	Hindi, English, many	**Organizations**	Comm., UN
	regional languages	**Map page**	88–89

INDONESIA
Republic of Indonesia

Area Sq Km	1 919 445	**Religions**	Sunni Muslim,
Area Sq Miles	741 102		Protestant, Roman
Population	231 627 000		Catholic, Hindu,
Capital	Jakarta		Buddhist
Languages	Indonesian, local	**Currency**	Rupiah
	languages	**Organizations**	APEC, ASEAN,
			OPEC, UN
		Map page	74–75

IRAN
Islamic Republic of Iran

Area Sq Km	1 648 000	**Religions**	Shi'a Muslim, Sunni
Area Sq Miles	636 296		Muslim
Population	71 208 000	**Currency**	Iranian rial
Capital	Tehrān	**Organizations**	OPEC, UN
Languages	Farsi, Azeri, Kurdish,	**Map page**	97
	regional languages		

IRAQ
Republic of Iraq

Area Sq Km	438 317	**Religions**	Shi'a Muslim, Sunni
Area Sq Miles	169 235		Muslim, Christian
Population	28 993 000	**Currency**	Iraqi dinar
Capital	Baghdād	**Organizations**	OPEC, UN
Languages	Arabic, Kurdish,	**Map page**	97
	Turkmen		

IRELAND

Area Sq Km	70 282	**Religions**	Roman Catholic,
Area Sq Miles	27 136		Protestant
Population	4 301 000	**Currency**	Euro
Capital	Dublin	**Organizations**	EU, OECD, UN
	(Baile Átha Cliath)	**Map page**	113
Languages	English, Irish		

Isle of Man
United Kingdom Crown Dependency

Area Sq Km	572	**Religions**	Protestant, Roman
Area Sq Miles	221		Catholic
Population	79 000	**Currency**	Pound sterling
Capital	Douglas	**Map page**	114
Languages	English		

ISRAEL
State of Israel

Area Sq Km	20 770	**Religions**	Jewish, Sunni Muslim,
Area Sq Miles	8 019		Christian, Druze
Population	6 928 000	**Currency**	Shekel
Capital	Jerusalem*	**Organizations**	UN
	(Yerushalayim)	**Map page**	96
	(El Quds)		
Languages	Hebrew, Arabic		

*De facto capital. Disputed.

ITALY
Italian Republic

Area Sq Km	301 245	**Religions**	Roman Catholic
Area Sq Miles	116 311	**Currency**	Euro
Population	58 877 000	**Organizations**	EU, OECD, UN
Capital	Rome (Roma)	**Map page**	124–125
Languages	Italian		

JAMAICA

Area Sq Km	10 991	**Religions**	Protestant, Roman
Area Sq Miles	4 244		Catholic
Population	2 714 000	**Currency**	Jamaican dollar
Capital	Kingston	**Organizations**	CARICOM, Comm.,
Languages	English, creole		UN
		Map page	162

Jammu and Kashmir
Disputed territory (India/Pakistan/China)

Area Sq Km	222 236	**Map page**	90–91
Area Sq Miles	85 806		
Population	13 000 000		
Capital	Srinagar		

JAPAN

Area Sq Km	377 727	**Religions**	Shintoist, Buddhist,
Area Sq Miles	145 841		Christian
Population	127 967 000	**Currency**	Yen
Capital	Tōkyō	**Organizations**	APEC, OECD, UN
Languages	Japanese	**Map page**	82–83

Jersey
United Kingdom Crown Dependency

Area Sq Km	116	**Religions**	Protestant, Roman
Area Sq Miles	45		Catholic
Population	88 200	**Currency**	Pound sterling
Capital	St Helier	**Map page**	111
Languages	English, French		

JORDAN
Hashemite Kingdom of Jordan

Area Sq Km	89 206	**Religions**	Sunni Muslim,
Area Sq Miles	34 443		Christian
Population	5 924 000	**Currency**	Jordanian dinar
Capital	'Ammān	**Organizations**	UN
Languages	Arabic	**Map page**	96

Juan Fernández Islands
part of Chile

Area Sq Km	179	**Religions**	Roman Catholic, Protestant
Area Sq Miles	69		
Population	633	**Currency**	Chilean peso
Capital	San Juan Bautista	**Map page**	173
Languages	Spanish, Amerindian languages		

KAZAKHSTAN
Republic of Kazakhstan

Area Sq Km	2 717 300	**Religions**	Sunni Muslim, Russian Orthodox, Protestant
Area Sq Miles	1 049 155		
Population	15 422 000	**Currency**	Tenge
Capital	Astana (Akmola)	**Organizations**	CIS, UN
Languages	Kazakh, Russian, Ukrainian, German, Uzbek, Tatar	**Map page**	92–93

KENYA
Republic of Kenya

Area Sq Km	582 646	**Religions**	Christian, traditional beliefs
Area Sq Miles	224 961		
Population	37 538 000	**Currency**	Kenyan shilling
Capital	Nairobi	**Organizations**	Comm., UN
Languages	Swahili, English, local languages	**Map page**	135

KIRIBATI
Republic of Kiribati

Area Sq Km	717	**Religions**	Roman Catholic, Protestant
Area Sq Miles	277		
Population	95 000	**Currency**	Australian dollar
Capital	Bairiki	**Organizations**	Comm., UN
Languages	Gilbertese, English	**Map page**	65

KOSOVO
Republic of Kosovo

Area Sq Km	10 908	**Religions**	Sunni Muslim, Serbian Orthodox
Area Sq Miles	4 212		
Population	2 070 000	**Currency**	Euro
Capital	Prishtinë (Priština)	**Map page**	125
Languages	Albanian, Serbian		

KUWAIT
State of Kuwait

Area Sq Km	17 818	**Religions**	Sunni Muslim, Shi'a Muslim, Christian, Hindu
Area Sq Miles	6 880		
Population	2 851 000	**Currency**	Kuwaiti dinar
Capital	Kuwait (Al Kuwayt)	**Organizations**	OPEC, UN
Languages	Arabic	**Map page**	94

KYRGYZSTAN
Kyrgyz Republic

Area Sq Km	198 500	**Religions**	Sunni Muslim, Russian Orthodox
Area Sq Miles	76 641		
Population	5 317 000	**Currency**	Kyrgyz som
Capital	Bishkek (Frunze)	**Organizations**	CIS, UN
Languages	Kyrgyz, Russian, Uzbek	**Map page**	93

LAOS
Lao People's Democratic Republic

Area Sq Km	236 800	**Religions**	Buddhist, traditional beliefs
Area Sq Miles	91 429		
Population	5 859 000	**Currency**	Kip
Capital	Vientiane (Viangchan)	**Organizations**	ASEAN, UN
Languages	Lao, local languages	**Map page**	78–79

LATVIA
Republic of Latvia

Area Sq Km	63 700	**Religions**	Protestant, Roman Catholic, Russian Orthodox
Area Sq Miles	24 595		
Population	2 277 000	**Currency**	Lats
Capital	Rīga	**Organizations**	EU, UN
Languages	Latvian, Russian	**Map page**	104

LEBANON
Republic of Lebanon

Area Sq Km	10 452	**Religions**	Shi'a Muslim, Sunni Muslim, Christian
Area Sq Miles	4 036		
Population	4 099 000	**Currency**	Lebanese pound
Capital	Beirut (Beyrouth)	**Organizations**	UN
Languages	Arabic, Armenian, French	**Map page**	96

LESOTHO
Kingdom of Lesotho

Area Sq Km	30 355	**Religions**	Christian, traditional beliefs
Area Sq Miles	11 720		
Population	2 008 000	**Currency**	Loti, South African rand
Capital	Maseru		
Languages	Sesotho, English, Zulu	**Organizations**	Comm., SADC, UN
		Map page	139

LIBERIA
Republic of Liberia

Area Sq Km	111 369	**Religions**	Traditional beliefs, Christian, Sunni Muslim
Area Sq Miles	43 000		
Population	3 750 000	**Currency**	Liberian dollar
Capital	Monrovia	**Organizations**	UN
Languages	English, creole, local languages	**Map page**	130

LIBYA
Socialist People's Libyan Arab Jamahiriya

Area Sq Km	1 759 540	**Religions**	Sunni Muslim
Area Sq Miles	679 362	**Currency**	Libyan dinar
Population	6 160 000	**Organizations**	OPEC, UN
Capital	Tripoli (Ṭarābulus)	**Map page**	131
Languages	Arabic, Berber		

LIECHTENSTEIN
Principality of Liechtenstein

Area Sq Km	160	**Religions**	Roman Catholic, Protestant
Area Sq Miles	62		
Population	35 000	**Currency**	Swiss franc
Capital	Vaduz	**Organizations**	UN
Languages	German	**Map page**	121

LITHUANIA
Republic of Lithuania

Area Sq Km	65 200	**Religions**	Roman Catholic, Protestant, Russian Orthodox
Area Sq Miles	25 174		
Population	3 390 000	**Currency**	Litas
Capital	Vilnius	**Organizations**	EU, UN
Languages	Lithuanian, Russian, Polish	**Map page**	104

Lord Howe Island
part of Australia

Area Sq Km	17	**Religions**	Protestant,
Area Sq Miles	6		Roman Catholic
Population	343	**Currency**	Australian dollar
Languages	English	**Map page**	67

LUXEMBOURG
Grand Duchy of Luxembourg

Area Sq Km	2 586	**Religions**	Roman Catholic
Area Sq Miles	998	**Currency**	Euro
Population	467 000	**Organizations**	EU, OECD, UN
Capital	Luxembourg	**Map page**	116
Languages	Letzeburgish,		
	German, French		

MACEDONIA (F.Y.R.O.M.)
Republic of Macedonia

Area Sq Km	25 713	**Religions**	Macedonian Orthodox,
Area Sq Miles	9 928		Sunni Muslim
Population	2 038 000	**Currency**	Macedonian denar
Capital	Skopje	**Organizations**	UN
Languages	Macedonian,	**Map page**	127
	Albanian, Turkish		

MADAGASCAR
Republic of Madagascar

Area Sq Km	587 041	**Religions**	Traditional beliefs,
Area Sq Miles	226 658		Christian, Sunni
Population	19 683 000		Muslim
Capital	Antananarivo	**Currency**	Malagasy ariary,
Languages	Malagasy, French		Malagasy franc
		Organizations	SADC, UN
		Map page	137

Madeira
Autonomous Region of Portugal

Area Sq Km	779	**Religions**	Roman Catholic,
Area Sq Miles	301		Protestant
Population	245 197	**Currency**	Euro
Capital	Funchal	**Map page**	130
Languages	Portuguese		

MALAWI
Republic of Malawi

Area Sq Km	118 484	**Religions**	Christian, traditional
Area Sq Miles	45 747		beliefs, Sunni Muslim
Population	13 925 000	**Currency**	Malawian kwacha
Capital	Lilongwe	**Organizations**	Comm., SADC, UN
Languages	Chichewa, English,	**Map page**	137
	local languages		

MALAYSIA
Federation of Malaysia

Area Sq Km	332 965	**Religions**	Sunni Muslim,
Area Sq Miles	128 559		Buddhist, Hindu,
Population	26 572 000		Christian,
Capital	Kuala Lumpur/		traditional beliefs
	Putrajaya	**Currency**	Ringgit
Languages	Malay, English,	**Organizations**	APEC, ASEAN,
	Chinese, Tamil,		Comm., UN
	local languages	**Map page**	76–77

MALDIVES
Republic of the Maldives

Area Sq Km	298	**Religions**	Sunni Muslim
Area Sq Miles	115	**Currency**	Rufiyaa
Population	306 000	**Organizations**	Comm., UN
Capital	Male	**Map page**	72
Languages	Divehi (Maldivian)		

MALI
Republic of Mali

Area Sq Km	1 240 140	**Religions**	Sunni Muslim,
Area Sq Miles	478 821		traditional beliefs,
Population	12 337 000		Christian
Capital	Bamako	**Currency**	CFA franc
Languages	French, Bambara,	**Organizations**	UN
	local languages	**Map page**	130

MALTA
Republic of Malta

Area Sq Km	316	**Religions**	Roman Catholic
Area Sq Miles	122	**Currency**	Euro
Population	407 000	**Organizations**	Comm., EU, UN
Capital	Valletta	**Map page**	100
Languages	Maltese, English		

MARSHALL ISLANDS
Republic of the Marshall Islands

Area Sq Km	181	**Religions**	Protestant, Roman
Area Sq Miles	70		Catholic
Population	59 000	**Currency**	United States dollar
Capital	Delap-Uliga-Djarrit	**Organizations**	UN
Languages	English, Marshallese	**Map page**	64

Martinique
French Overseas Department

Area Sq Km	1 079	**Religions**	Roman Catholic,
Area Sq Miles	417		traditional beliefs
Population	399 000	**Currency**	Euro
Capital	Fort-de-France	**Map page**	163
Languages	French, creole		

MAURITANIA
Islamic Arab and African Republic of Mauritania

Area Sq Km	1 030 700	**Religions**	Sunni Muslim
Area Sq Miles	397 955	**Currency**	Ouguiya
Population	3 124 000	**Organizations**	UN
Capital	Nouakchott	**Map page**	130
Languages	Arabic, French,		
	local languages		

MAURITIUS
Republic of Mauritius

Area Sq Km	2 040	**Religions**	Hindu, Roman
Area Sq Miles	788		Catholic, Sunni
Population	1 262 000		Muslim
Capital	Port Louis	**Currency**	Mauritius rupee
Languages	English, creole,	**Organizations**	Comm., SADC, UN
	Hindi, Bhojpuri,	**Map page**	129
	French		

Mayotte
French Territorial Collectivity

Area Sq Km	373	Religions	Sunni Muslim, Christian
Area Sq Miles	144		
Population	186 026	Currency	Euro
Capital	Dzaoudzi	Map page	137
Languages	French, Mahorian		

Melilla
Autonomous Community of Spain

Area Sq Km	13	Religions	Roman Catholic, Muslim
Area Sq Miles	5		
Population	66 871	Currency	Euro
Capital	Melilla	Map page	130
Languages	Spanish, Arabic		

MEXICO
United Mexican States

Area Sq Km	1 972 545	Religions	Roman Catholic, Protestant
Area Sq Miles	761 604		
Population	106 535 000	Currency	Mexican peso
Capital	Mexico City	Organizations	APEC, OECD, UN
Languages	Spanish, Amerindian languages	Map page	160–161

MICRONESIA, FEDERATED STATES OF

Area Sq Km	701	Religions	Roman Catholic, Protestant
Area Sq Miles	271		
Population	111 000	Currency	United States dollar
Capital	Palikir	Organizations	UN
Languages	English, Chuukese, Pohnpeian, local languages	Map page	64

MOLDOVA
Republic of Moldova

Area Sq Km	33 700	Religions	Romanian Orthodox, Russian Orthodox
Area Sq Miles	13 012		
Population	3 794 000	Currency	Moldovan leu
Capital	Chişinău (Kishinev)	Organizations	CIS, UN
Languages	Romanian, Ukrainian, Gagauz, Russian	Map page	106

MONACO
Principality of Monaco

Area Sq Km	2	Religions	Roman Catholic
Area Sq Miles	1	Currency	Euro
Population	33 000	Organizations	UN
Capital	Monaco-Ville	Map page	121
Languages	French, Monégasque, Italian		

MONGOLIA

Area Sq Km	1 565 000	Religions	Buddhist, Sunni Muslim
Area Sq Miles	604 250		
Population	2 629 000	Currency	Tugrik (tögrög)
Capital	Ulan Bator (Ulaanbaatar)	Organizations	UN
Languages	Khalka (Mongolian), Kazakh, local languages	Map page	84–85

MONTENEGRO

Area Sq Km	13 812	Religions	Montenegrin, Orthodox, Sunni Muslim
Area Sq Miles	5 333		
Population	598 000	Currency	Euro
Capital	Podgorica	Organizations	UN
Languages	Serbian, (Montenegrin), Albanian	Map page	125

Montserrat
United Kingdom Overseas Territory

Area Sq Km	100	Religions	Protestant, Roman Catholic
Area Sq Miles	39		
Population	6 000	Currency	East Caribbean dollar
Capital	Brades	Organizations	CARICOM
Languages	English	Map page	163

MOROCCO
Kingdom of Morocco

Area Sq Km	446 550	Religions	Sunni Muslim
Area Sq Miles	172 414	Currency	Moroccan dirham
Population	31 224 000	Organizations	UN
Capital	Rabat	Map page	130
Languages	Arabic, Berber, French		

MOZAMBIQUE
Republic of Mozambique

Area Sq Km	799 380	Religions	Traditional beliefs, Roman Catholic, Sunni Muslim
Area Sq Miles	308 642		
Population	21 397 000		
Capital	Maputo	Currency	Metical
Languages	Portuguese, Makua, Tsonga, local languages	Organizations	Comm., SADC, UN
		Map page	137

MYANMAR (Burma)
Union of Myanmar

Area Sq Km	676 577	Religions	Buddhist, Christian, Sunni Muslim
Area Sq Miles	261 228		
Population	48 798 000	Currency	Kyat
Capital	Nay Pyi Taw/ Rangoon (Yangôn)	Organizations	ASEAN, UN
Languages	Burmese, Shan, Karen, local languages	Map page	78–79

NAMIBIA
Republic of Namibia

Area Sq Km	824 292	Religions	Protestant, Roman Catholic
Area Sq Miles	318 261		
Population	2 074 000	Currency	Namibian dollar
Capital	Windhoek	Organizations	Comm., SADC, UN
Languages	English, Afrikaans, German, Ovambo, local languages	Map page	137

NAURU
Republic of Nauru

Area Sq Km	21	**Religions**	Protestant, Roman Catholic
Area Sq Miles	8		
Population	10 000	**Currency**	Australian dollar
Capital	Yaren	**Organizations**	Comm., UN
Languages	Nauruan, English	**Map page**	64

NEPAL
Federal Democratic Republic of Nepal

Area Sq Km	147 181	**Religions**	Hindu, Buddhist, Sunni Muslim
Area Sq Miles	56 827		
Population	28 196 000	**Currency**	Nepalese rupee
Capital	Kathmandu	**Organizations**	UN
Languages	Nepali, Maithili, Bhojpuri, English, local languages	**Map page**	91

NETHERLANDS
Kingdom of the Netherlands

Area Sq Km	41 526	**Religions**	Roman Catholic, Protestant, Sunni Muslim
Area Sq Miles	16 033		
Population	16 419 000		
Capital	Amsterdam/ The Hague ('s-Gravenhage)	**Currency**	Euro
		Organizations	EU, OECD, UN
		Map page	116
Languages	Dutch, Frisian		

Netherlands Antilles
Self-governing Netherlands Territory

Area Sq Km	800	**Religions**	Roman Catholic, Protestant
Area Sq Miles	309		
Population	192 000	**Currency**	Netherlands Antilles guilder
Capital	Willemstad		
Languages	Dutch, Papiamento, English	**Map page**	163

New Caledonia
French Overseas Territory

Area Sq Km	19 058	**Religions**	Roman Catholic, Protestant, Sunni Muslim
Area Sq Miles	7 358		
Population	242 000		
Capital	Nouméa	**Currency**	CFP franc
Languages	French, local languages	**Map page**	64

NEW ZEALAND

Area Sq Km	270 534	**Religions**	Protestant, Roman Catholic
Area Sq Miles	104 454		
Population	4 179 000	**Currency**	New Zealand dollar
Capital	Wellington	**Organizations**	APEC, Comm., OECD, UN
Languages	English, Maori		
		Map page	70

NICARAGUA
Republic of Nicaragua

Area Sq Km	130 000	**Religions**	Roman Catholic, Protestant
Area Sq Miles	50 193		
Population	5 603 000	**Currency**	Córdoba
Capital	Managua	**Organizations**	UN
Languages	Spanish, Amerindian languages	**Map page**	162

NIGER
Republic of Niger

Area Sq Km	1 267 000	**Religions**	Sunni Muslim, traditional beliefs
Area Sq Miles	489 191		
Population	14 226 000	**Currency**	CFA franc
Capital	Niamey	**Organizations**	UN
Languages	French, Hausa, Fulani, local languages	**Map page**	131

NIGERIA
Federal Republic of Nigeria

Area Sq Km	923 768	**Religions**	Sunni Muslim, Christian, traditional beliefs
Area Sq Miles	356 669		
Population	148 093 000		
Capital	Abuja	**Currency**	Naira
Languages	English, Hausa, Yoruba, Ibo, Fulani, local languages	**Organizations**	Comm., OPEC, UN
		Map page	131

Niue
Self-governing New Zealand Overseas Territory

Area Sq Km	258	**Religions**	Christian
Area Sq Miles	100	**Currency**	New Zealand dollar
Population	2 000	**Map page**	64
Capital	Alofi		
Languages	English, Nivean		

Norfolk Island
Australian External Territory

Area Sq Km	35	**Religions**	Protestant, Roman Catholic
Area Sq Miles	14		
Population	2 523	**Currency**	Australian dollar
Capital	Kingston	**Map page**	64
Languages	English		

Northern Mariana Islands
United States Commonwealth

Area Sq Km	477	**Religions**	Roman Catholic
Area Sq Miles	184	**Currency**	United States dollar
Population	84 000	**Map page**	75
Capital	Capitol Hill		
Languages	English, Chamorro, local languages		

NORTH KOREA
Democratic People's Republic of Korea

Area Sq Km	120 538	**Religions**	Traditional beliefs, Chondoist, Buddhist
Area Sq Miles	46 540		
Population	23 790 000	**Currency**	North Korean won
Capital	P'yŏngyang	**Organizations**	UN
Languages	Korean	**Map page**	81

NORWAY
Kingdom of Norway

Area Sq Km	323 878	Religions	Protestant, Roman
Area Sq Miles	125 050		Catholic
Population	4 698 000	Currency	Norwegian krone
Capital	Oslo	Organizations	OECD, UN
Languages	Norwegian	Map page	108–109

OMAN
Sultanate of Oman

Area Sq Km	309 500	Religions	Ibadhi Muslim, Sunni
Area Sq Miles	119 499		Muslim
Population	2 595 000	Currency	Omani riyal
Capital	Muscat (Masqaṭ)	Organizations	UN
Languages	Arabic, Baluchi,	Map page	95
	Indian languages		

PAKISTAN
Islamic Republic of Pakistan

Area Sq Km	803 940	Religions	Sunni Muslim, Shi'a
Area Sq Miles	310 403		Muslim, Christian,
Population	163 902 000		Hindu
Capital	Islamabad	Currency	Pakistani rupee
Languages	Urdu, Punjabi,	Organizations	Comm., UN
	Sindhi, Pushtu,	Map page	90
	English		

PALAU
Republic of Palau

Area Sq Km	497	Religions	Roman Catholic,
Area Sq Miles	192		Protestant, traditional
Population	20 000		beliefs
Capital	Melekeok	Currency	United States dollar
Languages	Palauan, English	Organizations	UN
		Map page	75

PANAMA
Republic of Panama

Area Sq Km	77 082	Religions	Roman Catholic,
Area Sq Miles	29 762		Protestant, Sunni
Population	3 343 000		Muslim
Capital	Panama City	Currency	Balboa
Languages	Spanish, English,	Organizations	UN
	Amerindian	Map page	162
	languages		

PAPUA NEW GUINEA
Independent State of Papua New Guinea

Area Sq Km	462 840	Religions	Protestant, Roman
Area Sq Miles	178 704		Catholic, traditional
Population	6 331 000		beliefs
Capital	Port Moresby	Currency	Kina
Languages	English, Tok Pisin	Organizations	APEC, Comm., UN
	(creole), local	Map page	75
	languages		

PERU
Republic of Peru

Area Sq Km	1 285 216	Religions	Roman Catholic,
Area Sq Miles	496 225		Protestant
Population	27 903 000	Currency	Sol
Capital	Lima	Organizations	APEC, UN
Languages	Spanish, Quechua,	Map page	166
	Aymara		

PHILIPPINES
Republic of the Philippines

Area Sq Km	300 000	Religions	Roman Catholic,
Area Sq Miles	115 831		Protestant, Sunni
Population	87 960 000		Muslim, Aglipayan
Capital	Manila	Currency	Philippine peso
Languages	English, Filipino,	Organizations	APEC, ASEAN, UN
	Tagalog, Cebuano,	Map page	80
	local languages		

Pitcairn Islands
United Kingdom Overseas Territory

Area Sq Km	45	Religions	Protestant
Area Sq Miles	17	Currency	New Zealand dollar
Population	48	Map page	65
Capital	Adamstown		
Languages	English		

POLAND
Polish Republic

Area Sq Km	312 683	Religions	Roman Catholic,
Area Sq Miles	120 728		Polish Orthodox
Population	38 082 000	Currency	Złoty
Capital	Warsaw (Warszawa)	Organizations	EU, OECD, UN
Languages	Polish, German	Map page	119

PORTUGAL
Portuguese Republic

Area Sq Km	88 940	Religions	Roman Catholic,
Area Sq Miles	34 340		Protestant
Population	10 623 000	Currency	Euro
Capital	Lisbon (Lisboa)	Organizations	EU, OECD, UN
Languages	Portuguese	Map page	122

Puerto Rico
United States Commonwealth

Area Sq Km	9 104	Religions	Roman Catholic,
Area Sq Miles	3 515		Protestant
Population	3 991 000	Currency	United States dollar
Capital	San Juan	Map page	163
Languages	Spanish, English		

QATAR
State of Qatar

Area Sq Km	11 437	Religions	Sunni Muslim
Area Sq Miles	4 416	Currency	Qatari riyal
Population	841 000	Organizations	OPEC, UN
Capital	Doha (Ad Dawḥah)	Map page	95
Languages	Arabic		

PARAGUAY
Republic of Paraguay

Area Sq Km	406 752	Religions	Roman Catholic,
Area Sq Miles	157 048		Protestant
Population	6 127 000	Currency	Guaraní
Capital	Asunción	Organizations	UN
Languages	Spanish, Guaraní	Map page	168

Réunion
French Overseas Department

Area Sq Km	2 551	Religions	Roman Catholic
Area Sq Miles	985	Currency	Euro
Population	807 000	Map page	129
Capital	St-Denis		
Languages	French, creole		

Rodrigues Island
part of Mauritius

Area Sq Km	104	Religions	Christian
Area Sq Miles	40	Currency	Rupee
Population	36 690	Map page	175
Capital	Port Mathurin		
Languages	English, creole		

ROMANIA

Area Sq Km	237 500	Religions	Romanian Orthodox,
Area Sq Miles	91 699		Protestant, Roman
Population	21 438 000		Catholic
Capital	Bucharest (Bucureşti)	Currency	Romanian leu
Languages	Romanian,	Organizations	EU, UN
	Hungarian	Map page	126

RUSSIAN FEDERATION

Area Sq Km	17 075 400	Religions	Russian Orthodox,
Area Sq Miles	6 592 849		Sunni Muslim,
Population	142 499 000		Protestant
Capital	Moscow (Moskva)	Currency	Russian rouble
Languages	Russian, Tatar,	Organizations	APEC, CIS, UN
	Ukrainian, local	Map page	98–99
	languages		

RWANDA
Republic of Rwanda

Area Sq Km	26 338	Religions	Roman Catholic,
Area Sq Miles	10 169		traditional beliefs,
Population	9 725 000		Protestant
Capital	Kigali	Currency	Rwandan franc
Languages	Kinyarwanda,	Organizations	UN
	French, English	Map page	135

Saba
part of Netherlands Antilles

Area Sq Km	13	Religions	Roman Catholic,
Area Sq Miles	5		Protestant
Population	1 434	Currency	Netherlands Antilles
Capital	Bottom		guilder
Languages	Dutch, English	Map page	163

St-Barthélémy
French Overseas Collectivity

Area Sq Km	21	Religions	Roman Catholic
Area Sq Miles	8	Currency	Euro
Population	6 852	Map page	163
Capital	Gustavia		
Languages	French		

St Helena and Dependencies
United Kingdom Overseas Territory

Area Sq Km	121	Religions	Protestant, Roman
Area Sq Miles	47		Catholic,
Population	7 000	Currency	St Helena pound
Capital	Jamestown	Map page	129
Languages	English		

ST KITTS AND NEVIS
Federation of St Kitts and Nevis

Area Sq Km	261	Religions	Protestant, Roman
Area Sq Miles	101		Catholic
Population	50 000	Currency	East Caribbean dollar
Capital	Basseterre	Organizations	CARICOM, Comm.,
Languages	English, creole		UN
		Map page	163

ST LUCIA

Area Sq Km	616	Religions	Roman Catholic,
Area Sq Miles	238		Protestant
Population	165 000	Currency	East Caribbean dollar
Capital	Castries	Organizations	CARICOM, Comm.,
Languages	English, creole		UN
		Map page	163

St-Martin
French Overseas Collectivity

Area Sq Km	54	Religions	Roman Catholic
Area Sq Miles	21	Currency	Euro
Population	33 102	Map page	163
Capital	Marigot		
Languages	French		

St Pierre and Miquelon
French Territorial Collectivity

Area Sq Km	242	Religions	Roman Catholic
Area Sq Miles	93	Currency	Euro
Population	6 000	Map page	147
Capital	St-Pierre		
Languages	French		

ST VINCENT AND THE GRENADINES

Area Sq Km	389	Religions	Protestant, Roman
Area Sq Miles	150		Catholic
Population	120 000	Currency	East Caribbean dollar
Capital	Kingstown	Organizations	CARICOM, Comm.,
Languages	English, creole		UN
		Map page	163

SAMOA
Independent State of Samoa

Area Sq Km	2 831	Religions	Protestant, Roman
Area Sq Miles	1 093		Catholic
Population	187 000	Currency	Tala
Capital	Apia	Organizations	Comm., UN
Languages	Samoan, English	Map page	65

SAN MARINO
Republic of San Marino

Area Sq Km	61	**Religions**	Roman Catholic
Area Sq Miles	24	**Currency**	Euro
Population	31 000	**Organizations**	UN
Capital	San Marino	**Map page**	124
Languages	Italian		

SÃO TOMÉ AND PRÍNCIPE
Democratic Republic of São Tomé and Príncipe

Area Sq Km	964	**Religions**	Roman Catholic,
Area Sq Miles	372		Protestant
Population	158 000	**Currency**	Dobra
Capital	São Tomé	**Organizations**	UN
Languages	Portuguese, creole	**Map page**	129

SAUDI ARABIA
Kingdom of Saudi Arabia

Area Sq Km	2 200 000	**Religions**	Sunni Muslim, Shi'a
Area Sq Miles	849 425		Muslim
Population	24 735 000	**Currency**	Saudi Arabian riyal
Capital	Riyadh (Ar Riyāḍ)	**Organizations**	OPEC, UN
Languages	Arabic	**Map page**	94–95

SENEGAL
Republic of Senegal

Area Sq Km	196 720	**Religions**	Sunni Muslim,
Area Sq Miles	75 954		Roman Catholic,
Population	12 379 000		traditional beliefs
Capital	Dakar	**Currency**	CFA franc
Languages	French, Wolof,	**Organizations**	UN
	Fulani, local	**Map page**	130
	languages		

SERBIA
Republic of Serbia

Area Sq Km	88 361	**Religions**	Roman Catholic,
Area Sq Miles	34 116		Serbian Orthodox,
Population	7 788 448		Sunni Muslim
Capital	Belgrade (Beograd)	**Currency**	Serbian dinar
Languages	Serbian, Hungarian	**Organizations**	UN
		Map page	125

SEYCHELLES
Republic of the Seychelles

Area Sq Km	455	**Religions**	Roman Catholic,
Area Sq Miles	176		Protestant
Population	87 000	**Currency**	Seychelles rupee
Capital	Victoria	**Organizations**	Comm., SADC, UN
Languages	English, French,	**Map page**	129
	creole		

SIERRA LEONE
Republic of Sierra Leone

Area Sq Km	71 740	**Religions**	Sunni Muslim,
Area Sq Miles	27 699		traditional beliefs
Population	5 866 000	**Currency**	Leone
Capital	Freetown	**Organizations**	Comm., UN
Languages	English, creole,	**Map page**	130
	Mende, Temne,		
	local languages		

SINGAPORE
Republic of Singapore

Area Sq Km	639	**Religions**	Buddhist, Taoist, Sunni
Area Sq Miles	247		Muslim, Christian,
Population	4 436 000		Hindu
Capital	Singapore	**Currency**	Singapore dollar
Languages	Chinese, English,	**Organizations**	APEC, ASEAN,
	Malay, Tamil		Comm., UN
		Map page	76

Sint Eustatius
part of Netherlands Antilles

Area Sq Km	21	**Religions**	Protestant, Roman
Area Sq Miles	8		Catholic
Population	2 584	**Currency**	Netherlands Antilles
Capital	Oranjestad		guilder
Languages	Dutch, English	**Map page**	163

Sint Maarten
part of Netherlands Antilles

Area Sq Km	34	**Religions**	Protestant, Roman
Area Sq Miles	13		Catholic
Population	35 035	**Currency**	Netherlands Antilles
Capital	Philipsburg		guilder
Languages	Dutch, English	**Map page**	163

SLOVAKIA
Slovak Republic

Area Sq Km	49 035	**Religions**	Roman Catholic,
Area Sq Miles	18 933		Protestant, Orthodox
Population	5 390 000	**Currency**	Euro
Capital	Bratislava	**Organizations**	EU, OECD, UN
Languages	Slovakian,	**Map page**	119
	Hungarian, Czech		

SLOVENIA
Republic of Slovenia

Area Sq Km	20 251	**Religions**	Roman Catholic,
Area Sq Miles	7 819		Protestant
Population	2 002 000	**Currency**	Euro
Capital	Ljubljana	**Organizations**	EU, UN
Languages	Slovenian, Croatian,	**Map page**	124–125
	Serbian		

SOLOMON ISLANDS

Area Sq Km	28 370	**Religions**	Protestant, Roman
Area Sq Miles	10 954		Catholic
Population	496 000	**Currency**	Solomon Islands dollar
Capital	Honiara	**Organizations**	Comm., UN
Languages	English, creole,	**Map page**	64
	local languages		

SOMALIA
Somali Democratic Republic

Area Sq Km	637 657	Religions	Sunni Muslim
Area Sq Miles	246 201	Currency	Somali shilling
Population	8 699 000	Organizations	UN
Capital	Mogadishu (Muqdisho)	Map page	133
Languages	Somali, Arabic		

SOUTH AFRICA, REPUBLIC OF

Area Sq Km	1 219 080	Religions	Protestant, Roman
Area Sq Miles	470 689		Catholic, Sunni
Population	48 577 000		Muslim, Hindu
Capital	Pretoria (Tshwane)/	Currency	Rand
	Cape Town	Organizations	Comm., SADC, UN
Languages	Afrikaans, English, nine official local languages	Map page	138–139

SOUTH KOREA
Republic of Korea

Area Sq Km	99 274	Religions	Buddhist, Protestant,
Area Sq Miles	38 330		Roman Catholic
Population	48 224 000	Currency	South Korean won
Capital	Seoul (Sŏul)	Organizations	APEC, OECD, UN
Languages	Korean	Map page	81

SPAIN
Kingdom of Spain

Area Sq Km	504 782	Religions	Roman Catholic
Area Sq Miles	194 897	Currency	Euro
Population	44 279 000	Organizations	EU, OECD, UN
Capital	Madrid	Map page	122–123
Languages	Spanish, Castilian, Catalan, Galician, Basque		

SRI LANKA
Democratic Socialist Republic of Sri Lanka

Area Sq Km	65 610	Religions	Buddhist, Hindu,
Area Sq Miles	25 332		Sunni Muslim,
Population	19 299 000		Roman Catholic
Capital	Sri Jayewardenepura Kotte	Currency	Sri Lankan rupee
		Organizations	Comm., UN
Languages	Sinhalese, Tamil, English	Map page	89

SUDAN
Republic of the Sudan

Area Sq Km	2 505 813	Religions	Sunni Muslim,
Area Sq Miles	967 500		traditional beliefs,
Population	38 560 000		Christian
Capital	Khartoum	Currency	Sudanese pound (Sudani)
Languages	Arabic, Dinka, Nubian, Beja, Nuer, local languages	Organizations	UN
		Map page	132–133

SURINAME
Republic of Suriname

Area Sq Km	163 820	Religions	Hindu, Roman
Area Sq Miles	63 251		Catholic, Protestant,
Population	458 000		Sunni Muslim
Capital	Paramaribo	Currency	Suriname guilder
Languages	Dutch, Surinamese, English, Hindi	Organizations	CARICOM, UN
		Map page	167

Svalbard
part of Norway

Area Sq Km	61 229	Religions	Protestant
Area Sq Miles	23 641	Currency	Norwegian krone
Population	2 400	Map page	98
Capital	Longyearbyen		
Languages	Norwegian		

SWAZILAND
Kingdom of Swaziland

Area Sq Km	17 364	Currency	Emalangeni,
Area Sq Miles	6 704		South African rand
Population	1 141 000	Organizations	Comm., SADC, UN
Capital	Mbabane	Map page	139
Languages	Swazi, English		
Religions	Christian, traditional beliefs		

SWEDEN
Kingdom of Sweden

Area Sq Km	449 964	Religions	Protestant,
Area Sq Miles	173 732		Roman Catholic
Population	9 119 000	Currency	Swedish krona
Capital	Stockholm	Organizations	EU, OECD, UN
Languages	Swedish	Map page	108–109

SWITZERLAND
Swiss Confederation

Area Sq Km	41 293	Religions	Roman Catholic,
Area Sq Miles	15 943		Protestant,
Population	7 484 000	Currency	Swiss franc
Capital	Bern	Organizations	OECD, UN
Languages	German, French, Italian, Romansch	Map page	121

SYRIA
Syrian Arab Republic

Area Sq Km	185 180	Religions	Sunni Muslim, Shi'a
Area Sq Miles	71 498		Muslim, Christian
Population	19 929 000	Currency	Syrian pound
Capital	Damascus (Dimashq)	Organizations	UN
Languages	Arabic, Kurdish, Armenian	Map page	96

TAIWAN
Republic of China

Area Sq Km	36 179	Religions	Buddhist, Taoist,
Area Sq Miles	13 969		Confucian, Christian
Population	22 880 000	Currency	Taiwan dollar
Capital	T'aipei	Organizations	APEC
Languages	Mandarin, Min, Hakka, local languages	Map page	87

The People's Republic of China claims Taiwan as its 23rd province

TAJIKISTAN
Republic of Tajikistan

Area Sq Km	143 100	**Religions**	Sunni Muslim
Area Sq Miles	55 251	**Currency**	Somoni
Population	6 736 000	**Organizations**	CIS, UN
Capital	Dushanbe	**Map page**	93
Languages	Tajik, Uzbek, Russian		

TANZANIA
United Republic of Tanzania

Area Sq Km	945 087	**Religions**	Shi'a Muslim, Sunni
Area Sq Miles	364 900		Muslim, traditional
Population	40 454 000		beliefs, Christian
Capital	Dodoma	**Currency**	Tanzanian shilling
Languages	Swahili, English,	**Organizations**	Comm., SADC, UN
	Nyamwezi, local	**Map page**	135
	languages		

THAILAND
Kingdom of Thailand

Area Sq Km	513 115	**Religions**	Buddhist, Sunni
Area Sq Miles	198 115		Muslim
Population	63 884 000	**Currency**	Baht
Capital	Bangkok	**Organizations**	APEC, ASEAN, UN
	(Krung Thep)	**Map page**	78–79
Languages	Thai, Lao, Chinese,		
	Malay, Mon-Khmer		
	languages		

TOGO
Republic of Togo

Area Sq Km	56 785	**Religions**	Traditional beliefs,
Area Sq Miles	21 925		Christian, Sunni
Population	6 585 000		Muslim
Capital	Lomé	**Currency**	CFA franc
Languages	French, Ewe, Kabre,	**Organizations**	UN
	local languages	**Map page**	130

Tokelau
New Zealand Overseas Territory

Area Sq Km	10	**Religions**	Christian
Area Sq Miles	4	**Currency**	New Zealand dollar
Population	1 000	**Map page**	65
Capital	none		
Languages	English, Tokelauan		

TONGA
Kingdom of Tonga

Area Sq Km	748	**Religions**	Protestant, Roman
Area Sq Miles	289		Catholic
Population	100 000	**Currency**	Pa'anga
Capital	Nuku'alofa	**Organizations**	Comm., UN
Languages	Tongan, English	**Map page**	65

TRINIDAD AND TOBAGO
Republic of Trinidad and Tobago

Area Sq Km	5 130	**Religions**	Roman Catholic,
Area Sq Miles	1 981		Hindu, Protestant,
Population	1 333 000		Sunni Muslim
Capital	Port of Spain	**Currency**	Trinidad and Tobago
Languages	English, creole,		dollar
	Hindi	**Organizations**	CARICOM, Comm.,
			UN
		Map page	163

Tristan da Cunha
Dependency of St Helena

Area Sq Km	98	**Religions**	Protestant, Roman
Area Sq Miles	38		Catholic
Population	284	**Currency**	Pound sterling
Capital	Settlement of	**Map page**	129
	Edinburgh		
Languages	English		

TUNISIA
Republic of Tunisia

Area Sq Km	164 150	**Religions**	Sunni Muslim
Area Sq Miles	63 379	**Currency**	Tunisian dinar
Population	10 327 000	**Organizations**	UN
Capital	Tunis	**Map page**	131
Languages	Arabic, French		

TURKEY
Republic of Turkey

Area Sq Km	779 452	**Religions**	Sunni Muslim, Shi'a
Area Sq Miles	300 948		Muslim
Population	74 877 000	**Currency**	Lira
Capital	Ankara	**Organizations**	OECD, UN
Languages	Turkish, Kurdish	**Map page**	96

TURKMENISTAN
Republic of Turkmenistan

Area Sq Km	488 100	**Religions**	Sunni Muslim, Russian
Area Sq Miles	188 456		Orthodox
Population	4 965 000	**Currency**	Turkmen manat
Capital	Aşgabat (Ashkhabad)	**Organizations**	UN
Languages	Turkmen, Uzbek,	**Map page**	92
	Russian		

Turks and Caicos Islands
United Kingdom Overseas Territory

Area Sq Km	430	**Religions**	Protestant
Area Sq Miles	166	**Currency**	United States dollar
Population	26 000	**Map page**	163
Capital	Grand Turk		
	(Cockburn Town)		
Languages	English		

TUVALU

Area Sq Km	25	**Religions**	Protestant
Area Sq Miles	10	**Currency**	Australian dollar
Population	11 000	**Organizations**	Comm., UN
Capital	Vaiaku	**Map page**	65
Languages	Tuvaluan, English		

UGANDA
Republic of Uganda

Area Sq Km	241 038	**Religions**	Roman Catholic, Protestant, Sunni Muslim, traditional beliefs
Area Sq Miles	93 065		
Population	30 884 000		
Capital	Kampala		
Languages	English, Swahili, Luganda, local languages	**Currency**	Ugandan shilling
		Organizations	Comm., UN
		Map page	135

UKRAINE
Republic of Ukraine

Area Sq Km	603 700	**Religions**	Ukrainian Orthodox, Ukrainian Catholic, Roman Catholic
Area Sq Miles	233 090		
Population	46 205 000		
Capital	Kiev (Kyiv)	**Currency**	Hryvnia
Languages	Ukrainian, Russian	**Organizations**	CIS, UN
		Map page	106–107

UNITED ARAB EMIRATES
Federation of Emirates

Area Sq Km	77 700	**Religions**	Sunni Muslim, Shi'a Muslim
Area Sq Miles	30 000		
Population	4 380 000	**Currency**	United Arab Emirates dirham
Capital	Abu Dhabi (Abū Z̧abī)		
		Organizations	OPEC, UN
Languages	Arabic, English	**Map page**	95

Abu Dhabi (Abū Z̧abī) (Emirate)

Area Sq Km	67 340	**Population**	1 292 119
Area Sq Miles	26 000	**Capital**	Abu Dhabi (Abū Z̧abī)

Ajman (Emirate)

Area Sq Km	259	**Population**	189 849
Area Sq Miles	100	**Capital**	Ajman

Dubai (Emirate)

Area Sq Km	3 885	**Population**	1 200 309
Area Sq Miles	1 500	**Capital**	Dubai

Fujairah (Emirate)

Area Sq Km	1 165	**Population**	118 617
Area Sq Miles	450	**Capital**	Fujairah

Ra's al Khaymah (Emirate)

Area Sq Km	1 684	**Population**	197 571
Area Sq Miles	650	**Capital**	Ra's al Khaymah

Sharjah (Emirate)

Area Sq Km	2 590	**Population**	724 859
Area Sq Miles	1 000	**Capital**	Sharjah

Umm al Qaywayn (Emirate)

Area Sq Km	777	**Population**	45 756
Area Sq Miles	300	**Capital**	Umm al Qaywayn

UNITED KINGDOM
of Great Britain and Northern Ireland

Area Sq Km	243 609	**Religions**	Protestant, Roman Catholic, Muslim
Area Sq Miles	94 058		
Population	60 769 000	**Currency**	Pound sterling
Capital	London	**Organizations**	Comm., EU, OECD, UN
Languages	English, Welsh, Gaelic		
		Map page	110–111

England (Constituent country)

Area Sq Km	130 433	**Population**	50 431 700
Area Sq Miles	50 360	**Capital**	London

Northern Ireland (Province)

Area Sq Km	13 576	**Population**	1 724 400
Area Sq Miles	5 242	**Capital**	Belfast

Scotland (Constituent country)

Area Sq Km	78 822	**Population**	5 094 800
Area Sq Miles	30 433	**Capital**	Edinburgh

Wales (Principality)

Area Sq Km	20 778	**Population**	2 958 600
Area Sq Miles	8 022	**Capital**	Cardiff

UNITED STATES OF AMERICA
Federal Republic

Area Sq Km	9 826 635	**Religions**	Protestant, Roman Catholic, Sunni Muslim, Jewish
Area Sq Miles	3 794 085		
Population	305 826 000		
Capital	Washington D.C.	**Currency**	United States dollar
Languages	English, Spanish	**Organizations**	APEC, OECD, UN
		Map page	148–149

Alabama (State)

Area Sq Km	135 765	**Population**	4 599 030
Area Sq Miles	52 419	**Capital**	Montgomery

Alaska (State)

Area Sq Km	1 717 854	**Population**	670 053
Area Sq Miles	663 267	**Capital**	Juneau

Arizona (State)

Area Sq Km	295 253	**Population**	6 166 318
Area Sq Miles	113 998	**Capital**	Phoenix

Arkansas (State)

Area Sq Km	137 733	**Population**	2 810 872
Area Sq Miles	53 179	**Capital**	Little Rock

California (State)

Area Sq Km	423 971	**Population**	36 457 549
Area Sq Miles	163 696	**Capital**	Sacramento

Colorado (State)

Area Sq Km	269 602	Population	4 753 377
Area Sq Miles	104 094	Capital	Denver

Connecticut (State)

Area Sq Km	14 356	Population	3 504 809
Area Sq Miles	5 543	Capital	Hartford

Delaware (State)

Area Sq Km	6 446	Population	853 476
Area Sq Miles	2 489	Capital	Dover

District of Columbia (District)

Area Sq Km	176	Population	581 530
Area Sq Miles	68	Capital	Washington

Florida (State)

Area Sq Km	170 305	Population	18 089 888
Area Sq Miles	65 755	Capital	Tallahassee

Georgia (State)

Area Sq Km	69 700	Population	9 363 941
Area Sq Miles	26 911	Capital	Atlanta

Hawaii (State)

Area Sq Km	28 311	Population	1 285 498
Area Sq Miles	10 931	Capital	Honolulu

Idaho (State)

Area Sq Km	216 445	Population	1 466 465
Area Sq Miles	83 570	Capital	Boise

Illinois (State)

Area Sq Km	149 997	Population	12 831 970
Area Sq Miles	57 914	Capital	Springfield

Indiana (State)

Area Sq Km	94 322	Population	6 313 520
Area Sq Miles	36 418	Capital	Indianapolis

Iowa (State)

Area Sq Km	145 744	Population	2 982 085
Area Sq Miles	56 272	Capital	Des Moines

Kansas (State)

Area Sq Km	213 096	Population	2 764 075
Area Sq Miles	82 277	Capital	Topeka

Kentucky (State)

Area Sq Km	104 659	Population	4 206 074
Area Sq Miles	40 409	Capital	Frankfort

Louisiana (State)

Area Sq Km	134 265	Population	4 287 768
Area Sq Miles	51 840	Capital	Baton Rouge

Maine (State)

Area Sq Km	91 647	Population	1 321 574
Area Sq Miles	35 385	Capital	Augusta

Maryland (State)

Area Sq Km	32 134	Population	5 615 727
Area Sq Miles	12 407	Capital	Annapolis

Massachusetts (State)

Area Sq Km	27 337	Population	6 437 193
Area Sq Miles	10 555	Capital	Boston

Michigan (State)

Area Sq Km	250 493	Population	10 095 643
Area Sq Miles	96 716	Capital	Lansing

Minnesota (State)

Area Sq Km	225 171	Population	5 167 101
Area Sq Miles	86 939	Capital	St Paul

Mississippi (State)

Area Sq Km	125 433	Population	2 910 540
Area Sq Miles	48 430	Capital	Jackson

Missouri (State)

Area Sq Km	180 533	Population	5 842 713
Area Sq Miles	69 704	Capital	Jefferson City

Montana (State)

Area Sq Km	380 837	Population	944 632
Area Sq Miles	147 042	Capital	Helena

Nebraska (State)

Area Sq Km	200 346	Population	1 768 331
Area Sq Miles	77 354	Capital	Lincoln

Nevada (State)

Area Sq Km	286 352	Population	2 495 529
Area Sq Miles	110 561	Capital	Carson City

New Hampshire (State)

Area Sq Km	24 216	Population	1 314 895
Area Sq Miles	9 350	Capital	Concord

New Jersey (State)

Area Sq Km	22 587	Population	8 724 560
Area Sq Miles	8 721	Capital	Trenton

UNITED STATES OF AMERICA
Federal Republic

New Mexico (State)

Area Sq Km	314 914	**Population**	1 954 599
Area Sq Miles	121 589	**Capital**	Santa Fe

New York (State)

Area Sq Km	141 299	**Population**	19 306 183
Area Sq Miles	54 556	**Capital**	Albany

North Carolina (State)

Area Sq Km	139 391	**Population**	8 856 505
Area Sq Miles	53 819	**Capital**	Raleigh

North Dakota (State)

Area Sq Km	183 112	**Population**	635 867
Area Sq Miles	70 700	**Capital**	Bismarck

Ohio (State)

Area Sq Km	116 096	**Population**	11 478 006
Area Sq Miles	44 825	**Capital**	Columbus

Oklahoma (State)

Area Sq Km	181 035	**Population**	3 579 212
Area Sq Miles	69 898	**Capital**	Oklahoma City

Oregon (State)

Area Sq Km	254 806	**Population**	3 700 758
Area Sq Miles	98 381	**Capital**	Salem

Pennsylvania (State)

Area Sq Km	119 282	**Population**	12 440 621
Area Sq Miles	46 055	**Capital**	Harrisburg

Rhode Island (State)

Area Sq Km	4 002	**Population**	1 067 610
Area Sq Miles	1 545	**Capital**	Providence

South Carolina (State)

Area Sq Km	82 931	**Population**	4 321 249
Area Sq Miles	32 020	**Capital**	Columbia

South Dakota (State)

Area Sq Km	199 730	**Population**	781 919
Area Sq Miles	77 116	**Capital**	Pierre

Tennessee (State)

Area Sq Km	109 150	**Population**	6 038 803
Area Sq Miles	42 143	**Capital**	Nashville

Texas (State)

Area Sq Km	695 622	**Population**	23 507 783
Area Sq Miles	268 581	**Capital**	Austin

Utah (State)

Area Sq Km	219 887	**Population**	2 550 063
Area Sq Miles	84 899	**Capital**	Salt Lake City

Vermont (State)

Area Sq Km	24 900	**Population**	623 908
Area Sq Miles	9 614	**Capital**	Montpelier

Virginia (State)

Area Sq Km	110 784	**Population**	7 642 884
Area Sq Miles	42 774	**Capital**	Richmond

Washington (State)

Area Sq Km	184 666	**Population**	6 395 798
Area Sq Miles	71 300	**Capital**	Olympia

West Virginia (State)

Area Sq Km	62 755	**Population**	1 818 470
Area Sq Miles	24 230	**Capital**	Charleston

Wisconsin (State)

Area Sq Km	169 639	**Population**	5 556 506
Area Sq Miles	65 498	**Capital**	Madison

Wyoming (State)

Area Sq Km	253 337	**Population**	515 004
Area Sq Miles	97 814	**Capital**	Cheyenne

URUGUAY
Oriental Republic of Uruguay

Area Sq Km	176 215	**Religions**	Roman Catholic,
Area Sq Miles	68 037		Protestant, Jewish
Population	3 340 000	**Currency**	Uruguayan peso
Capital	Montevideo	**Organizations**	UN
Languages	Spanish	**Map page**	169

UZBEKISTAN
Republic of Uzbekistan

Area Sq Km	447 400	**Religions**	Sunni Muslim, Russian
Area Sq Miles	172 742		Orthodox
Population	27 372 000	**Currency**	Uzbek som
Capital	Tashkent	**Organizations**	CIS, UN
Languages	Uzbek, Russian,	**Map page**	92–93
	Tajik, Kazakh		

VANUATU
Republic of Vanuatu

Area Sq Km	12 190	**Religions**	Protestant, Roman
Area Sq Miles	4 707		Catholic, traditional
Population	226 000		beliefs
Capital	Port Vila	**Currency**	Vatu
Languages	English, Bislama	**Organizations**	Comm., UN
	(creole), French	**Map page**	64

VATICAN CITY
Vatican City State

Area Sq Km	0.5	**Religions**	Roman Catholic
Area Sq Miles	0.2	**Currency**	Euro
Population	557	**Map page**	124
Capital	Vatican City		
Languages	Italian		

VENEZUELA
Republic of Venezuela

Area Sq Km	912 050	**Religions**	Roman Catholic,
Area Sq Miles	352 144		Protestant
Population	27 657 000	**Currency**	Bolívar fuerte
Capital	Caracas	**Organizations**	OPEC, UN
Languages	Spanish, Amerindian	**Map page**	166
	languages		

VIETNAM
Socialist Republic of Vietnam

Area Sq Km	329 565	**Religions**	Buddhist, Taoist,
Area Sq Miles	127 246		Roman Catholic,
Population	87 375 000		Cao Dai, Hoa Hoa
Capital	Ha Nôi (Hanoi)	**Currency**	Dong
Languages	Vietnamese, Thai,	**Organizations**	APEC, ASEAN, UN
	Khmer, Chinese,	**Map page**	78–79
	local languages		

Virgin Islands (U.K.)
United Kingdom Overseas Territory

Area Sq Km	153	**Religions**	Protestant, Roman
Area Sq Miles	59		Catholic
Population	23 000	**Currency**	United States dollar
Capital	Road Town	**Map page**	163
Languages	English		

Virgin Islands (U.S.)
United States Unincorporated Territory

Area Sq Km	352	**Religions**	Protestant,
Area Sq Miles	136		Roman Catholic
Population	111 000	**Currency**	United States dollar
Capital	Charlotte Amalie	**Map page**	163
Languages	English, Spanish		

Wallis and Futuna Islands
French Overseas Territory

Area Sq Km	274	**Religions**	Roman Catholic
Area Sq Miles	106	**Currency**	CFP franc
Population	15 000	**Map page**	65
Capital	Matā'utu		
Languages	French, Wallisian,		
	Futunian		

West Bank
Disputed Territory

Area Sq Km	5 860	**Religions**	Sunni Muslim, Jewish,
Area Sq Miles	2 263		Shi'a Muslim, Christian
Population	2 676 284	**Currency**	Jordanian dinar,
Capital	none		Israeli shekel
Languages	Arabic, Hebrew	**Map page**	96

Western Sahara
Disputed Territory (Morocco)

Area Sq Km	266 000	**Religions**	Sunni Muslim
Area Sq Miles	102 703	**Currency**	Moroccan dirham
Population	480 000	**Map page**	130
Capital	Laâyoune		
Languages	Arabic		

YEMEN
Republic of Yemen

Area Sq Km	527 968	**Religions**	Sunni Muslim, Shi'a
Area Sq Miles	203 850		Muslim
Population	22 389 000	**Currency**	Yemeni riyal
Capital	Şan'ā'	**Organizations**	UN
Languages	Arabic	**Map page**	94–95

ZAMBIA
Republic of Zambia

Area Sq Km	752 614	**Religions**	Christian, traditional
Area Sq Miles	290 586		beliefs
Population	11 922 000	**Currency**	Zambian kwacha
Capital	Lusaka	**Organizations**	Comm., SADC, UN
Languages	English, Bemba,	**Map page**	136–137
	Nyanja, Tonga,		
	local languages		

ZIMBABWE
Republic of Zimbabwe

Area Sq Km	390 759	**Religions**	Christian, traditional
Area Sq Miles	150 873		beliefs
Population	13 349 000	**Currency**	Zimbabwean dollar
Capital	Harare	**Organizations**	SADC, UN
Languages	English, Shona,	**Map page**	137
	Ndebele		

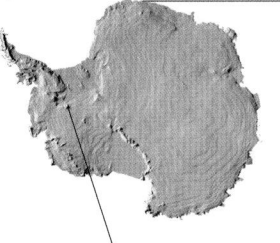

ANTARCTICA

Total Land Area
12 093 000 sq km
4 669 133 sq miles
(excluding ice shelves)

HIGHEST MOUNTAIN
Vinson Massif
4 897 m /16 066 ft

HIGHEST MOUNTAINS	metres	feet
Vinson Massif	4 897	16 066
Mt Tyree	4 852	15 918
Mt Kirkpatrick	4 528	14 855
Mt Markham	4 351	14 275
Mt Jackson	4 190	13 747
Mt Sidley	4 181	13 717

OCEANIA

Total land area
8 844 516 sq km
3 414 887 sq miles
(includes New Guinea and
Pacific Island nations)

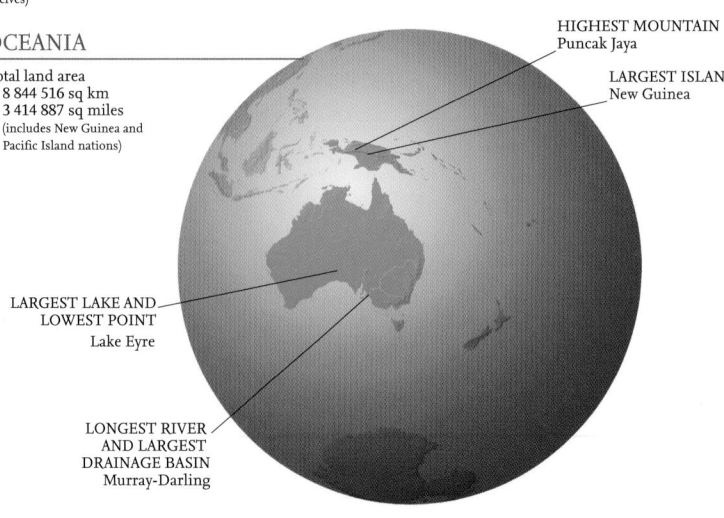

HIGHEST MOUNTAIN
Puncak Jaya

LARGEST ISLAND
New Guinea

LARGEST LAKE AND
LOWEST POINT
Lake Eyre

LONGEST RIVER
AND LARGEST
DRAINAGE BASIN
Murray-Darling

HIGHEST MOUNTAINS	metres	feet	LARGEST ISLANDS	sq km	sq miles	LARGEST LAKES	sq km	sq miles	LONGEST RIVERS	km	mile
Puncak Jaya	5 030	16 502	New Guinea	808 510	312 167	Lake Eyre	0–8 900	0–3 436	Murray-Darling	3 750	2 33
Puncak Trikora	4 730	15 518	South Island	151 215	58 384	Lake Torrens	0–5 780	0–2 232	Darling	2 739	1 70
Puncak Mandala	4 700	15 420	North Island	115 777	44 701				Murray	2 589	1 60
Puncak Yamin	4 595	15 075	Tasmania	67 800	26 178				Murrumbidgee	1 690	1 05
Mt Wilhelm	4 509	14 793							Lachlan	1 480	92
Mt Kubor	4 359	14 301							Macquarie	950	59

ASIA

Total Land Area
45 036 492 sq km
17 388 686 sq miles

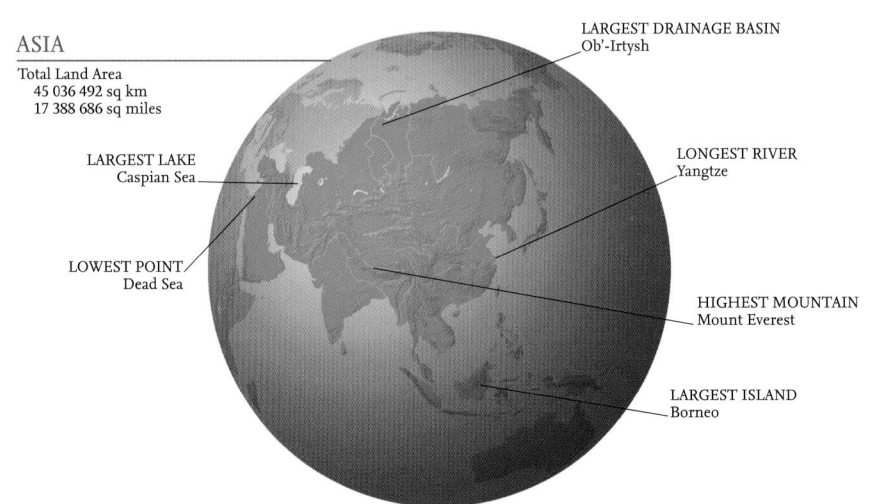

LARGEST DRAINAGE BASIN
Ob'-Irtysh

LARGEST LAKE
Caspian Sea

LONGEST RIVER
Yangtze

LOWEST POINT
Dead Sea

HIGHEST MOUNTAIN
Mount Everest

LARGEST ISLAND
Borneo

HIGHEST MOUNTAINS	metres	feet	LARGEST ISLANDS	sq km	sq miles	LARGEST LAKES	sq km	sq miles	LONGEST RIVERS	km	mile
Mt Everest	8 848	29 028	Borneo	745 561	287 861	Caspian Sea	371 000	143 243	Yangtze	6 380	3 96
K2	8 611	28 251	Sumatra	473 606	182 859	Lake Baikal	30 500	11 776	Ob'-Irtysh	5 568	3 46
Kangchenjunga	8 586	28 169	Honshū	227 414	87 805	Lake Balkhash	17 400	6 718	Yenisey-Angara-Selenga	5 550	3 44
Lhotse	8 516	27 939	Celebes	189 216	73 056	Aral Sea	17 158	6 625	Yellow	5 464	3 39
Makalu	8 463	27 765	Java	132 188	51 038	Ysyk-Köl	6 200	2 394	Irtysh	4 440	2 75
Cho Oyu	8 201	26 906	Luzon	104 690	40 421						

EUROPE

Total Land Area
9 908 599 sq km
3 825 731 sq miles

LARGEST ISLAND
Great Britain

LONGEST RIVER AND
LARGEST DRAINAGE BASIN
Volga

LARGEST LAKE AND
LOWEST POINT
Caspian Sea

HIGHEST MOUNTAIN
El'brus

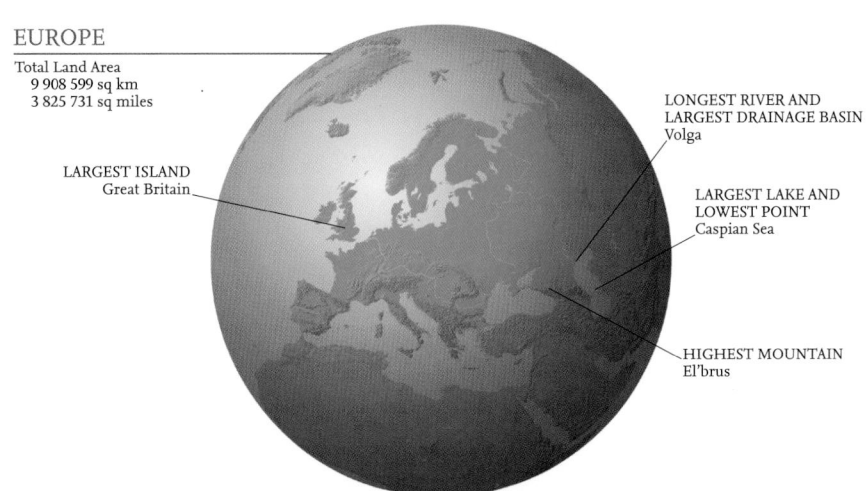

HIGHEST MOUNTAINS	metres	feet	LARGEST ISLANDS	sq km	sq miles	LARGEST LAKES	sq km	sq miles	LONGEST RIVERS	km	miles
El'brus	5 642	18 510	Great Britain	218 476	84 354	Caspian Sea	371 000	143 243	Volga	3 688	2 292
Gora Dykh-Tau	5 204	17 073	Iceland	102 820	39 699	Lake Ladoga	18 390	7 100	Danube	2 850	1 771
Shkhara	5 201	17 063	Novaya Zemlya	90 650	35 000	Lake Onega	9 600	3 707	Dnieper	2 285	1 420
Kazbek	5 047	16 558	Ireland	83 045	32 064	Vänern	5 585	2 156	Kama	2 028	1 260
Mont Blanc	4 808	15 774	Spitsbergen	37 814	14 600	Rybinskoye Vodokhranilishche	5 180	2 000	Don	1 931	1 200
Dufourspitze	4 634	15 203	Sicily (Sicilia)	25 426	9 817				Pechora	1 802	1 120

AFRICA

Total Land Area
30 343 578 sq km
11 715 721 sq miles

LONGEST RIVER
Nile

LOWEST POINT
Lake Assal

LARGEST LAKE
Lake Victoria

HIGHEST MOUNTAIN
Kilimanjaro

LARGEST ISLAND
Madagascar

LARGEST DRAINAGE BASIN
Congo

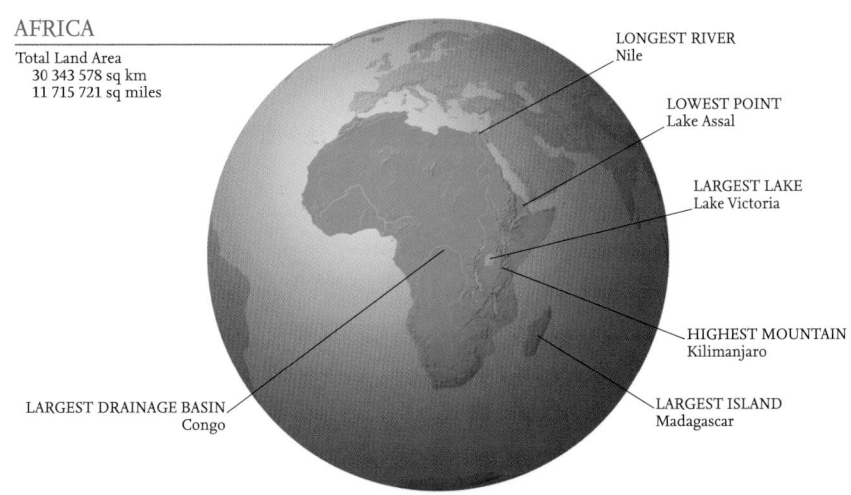

HIGHEST MOUNTAINS	metres	feet	LARGEST ISLANDS	sq km	sq miles	LARGEST LAKES	sq km	sq miles	LONGEST RIVERS	km	miles
Kilimanjaro	5 892	19 330	Madagascar	587 040	226 656	Lake Victoria	68 870	26 591	Nile	6 695	4 160
Mt Kenya	5 199	17 057				Lake Tanganyika	32 600	12 587	Congo	4 667	2 900
Margherita Peak	5 110	16 765				Lake Nyasa	29 500	11 390	Niger	4 184	2 600
Meru	4 565	14 977				Lake Volta	8 482	3 275	Zambezi	2 736	1 700
Ras Dejen	4 533	14 872				Lake Turkana	6 500	2 510	Webi Shabeelle	2 490	1 547
Mt Karisimbi	4 510	14 796				Lake Albert	5 600	2 162	Ubangi	2 250	1 398

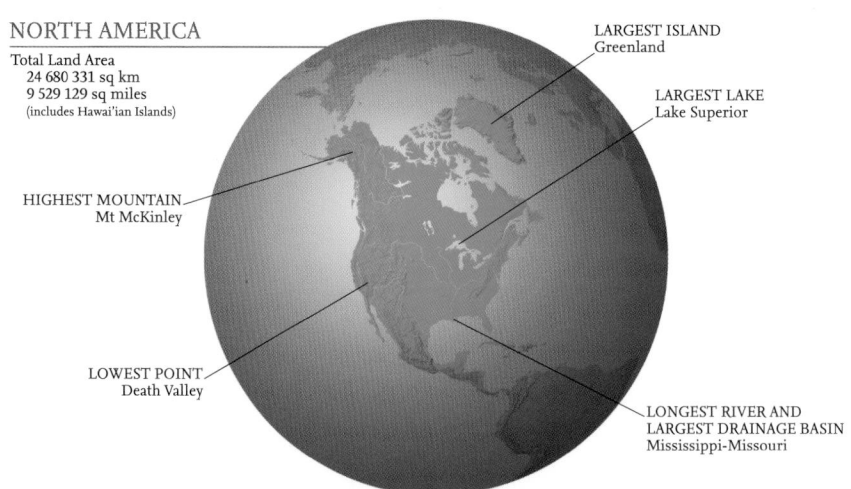

NORTH AMERICA

Total Land Area
24 680 331 sq km
9 529 129 sq miles
(includes Hawai'ian Islands)

LARGEST ISLAND
Greenland

LARGEST LAKE
Lake Superior

HIGHEST MOUNTAIN
Mt McKinley

LOWEST POINT
Death Valley

LONGEST RIVER AND
LARGEST DRAINAGE BASIN
Mississippi-Missouri

HIGHEST MOUNTAINS	metres	feet	LARGEST ISLANDS	sq km	sq miles	LARGEST LAKES	sq km	sq miles	LONGEST RIVERS	km	miles
Mt McKinley	6 194	20 321	Greenland	2 175 600	839 999	Lake Superior	82 100	31 699	Mississippi-Missouri	5 969	3 70?
Mt Logan	5 959	19 550	Baffin Island	507 451	195 927	Lake Huron	59 600	23 012	Mackenzie-Peace-Finlay	4 241	2 63?
Pico de Orizaba	5 610	18 405	Victoria Island	217 291	83 896	Lake Michigan	57 800	22 317	Missouri	4 086	2 53?
Mt St Elias	5 489	18 008	Ellesmere Island	196 236	75 767	Great Bear Lake	31 328	12 096	Mississippi	3 765	2 34?
Volcán Popocatépetl	5 452	17 887	Cuba	110 860	42 803	Great Slave Lake	28 568	11 030	Yukon	3 185	1 97?
			Newfoundland	108 860	42 031	Lake Erie	25 700	9 923			

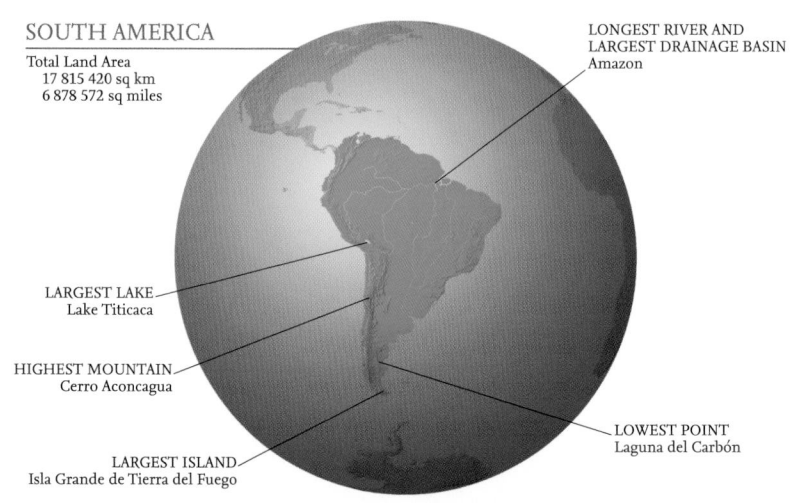

SOUTH AMERICA

Total Land Area
17 815 420 sq km
6 878 572 sq miles

LONGEST RIVER AND
LARGEST DRAINAGE BASIN
Amazon

LARGEST LAKE
Lake Titicaca

HIGHEST MOUNTAIN
Cerro Aconcagua

LOWEST POINT
Laguna del Carbón

LARGEST ISLAND
Isla Grande de Tierra del Fuego

HIGHEST MOUNTAINS	metres	feet	LARGEST ISLANDS	sq km	sq miles	LARGEST LAKES	sq km	sq miles	LONGEST RIVERS	km	mile?
Cerro Aconcagua	6 959	22 831	Isla Grande de Tierra del Fuego	47 000	18 147	Lake Titicaca	8 340	3 220	Amazon	6 516	4 04?
Nevado Ojos del Salado	6 908	22 664	Isla de Chiloé	8 394	3 241				Río de la Plata-Paraná	4 500	2 79?
Cerro Bonete	6 872	22 546	East Falkland	6 760	2 610				Purus	3 218	2 00?
Cerro Pissis	6 858	22 500	West Falkland	5 413	2 090				Madeira	3 200	1 98?
Cerro Tupungato	6 800	22 309							São Francisco	2 900	1 80?

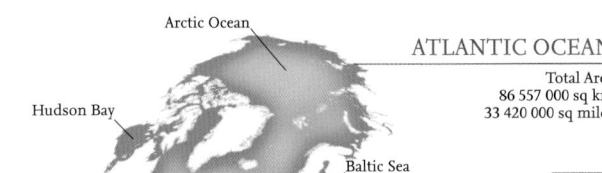

ATLANTIC OCEAN

Arctic Ocean

Hudson Bay

Baltic Sea

North Sea   Black Sea

Gulf of Mexico

Mediterranean Sea

Caribbean Sea

Deepest Point
Milwaukee Deep

Total Area
86 557 000 sq km
33 420 000 sq miles

ATLANTIC OCEAN	Area		Deepest Point	
	square km	square miles	metres	feet
Extent	86 557 000	33 420 000	8 605	28 231
Arctic Ocean	9 485 000	3 662 000	5 450	17 880
Caribbean Sea	2 512 000	970 000	7 680	25 196
Mediterranean Sea	2 510 000	969 000	5 121	16 800
Gulf of Mexico	1 544 000	596 000	3 504	11 495
Hudson Bay	1 233 000	476 000	259	849
North Sea	575 000	222 000	661	2 168
Black Sea	508 000	196 000	2 245	7 365
Baltic Sea	382 000	147 000	460	1 509

PACIFIC OCEAN

Bering Sea

Sea of Okhotsk

Sea of Japan
(East Sea)

East China Sea
and Yellow Sea

South China Sea

Deepest Point
Challenger Deep

Total Area
166 241 000 sq km
64 186 000 sq miles

PACIFIC OCEAN	Area		Deepest Point	
	square km	square miles	metres	feet
Extent	166 241 000	64 186 000	10 920	35 826
South China Sea	2 590 000	1 000 000	5 514	18 090
Bering Sea	2 261 000	873 000	4 150	13 615
Sea of Okhotsk	1 392 000	537 000	3 363	11 033
Sea of Japan (East Sea)	1 013 000	391 000	3 743	12 280
East China Sea and Yellow Sea	1 202 000	464 000	2 717	8 913

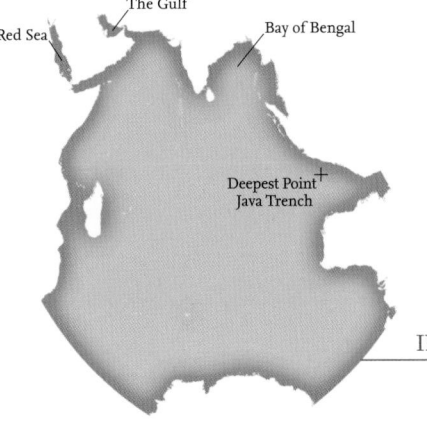

The Gulf

Red Sea

Bay of Bengal

Deepest Point
Java Trench

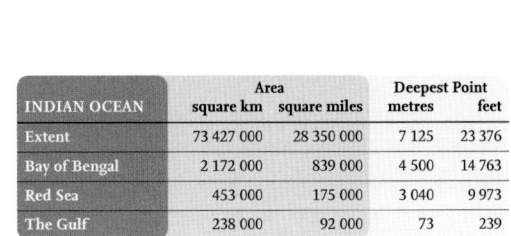

INDIAN OCEAN	Area		Deepest Point	
	square km	square miles	metres	feet
Extent	73 427 000	28 350 000	7 125	23 376
Bay of Bengal	2 172 000	839 000	4 500	14 763
Red Sea	453 000	175 000	3 040	9 973
The Gulf	238 000	92 000	73	239

INDIAN OCEAN

Total Area
73 427 000 sq km
28 350 000 sq miles

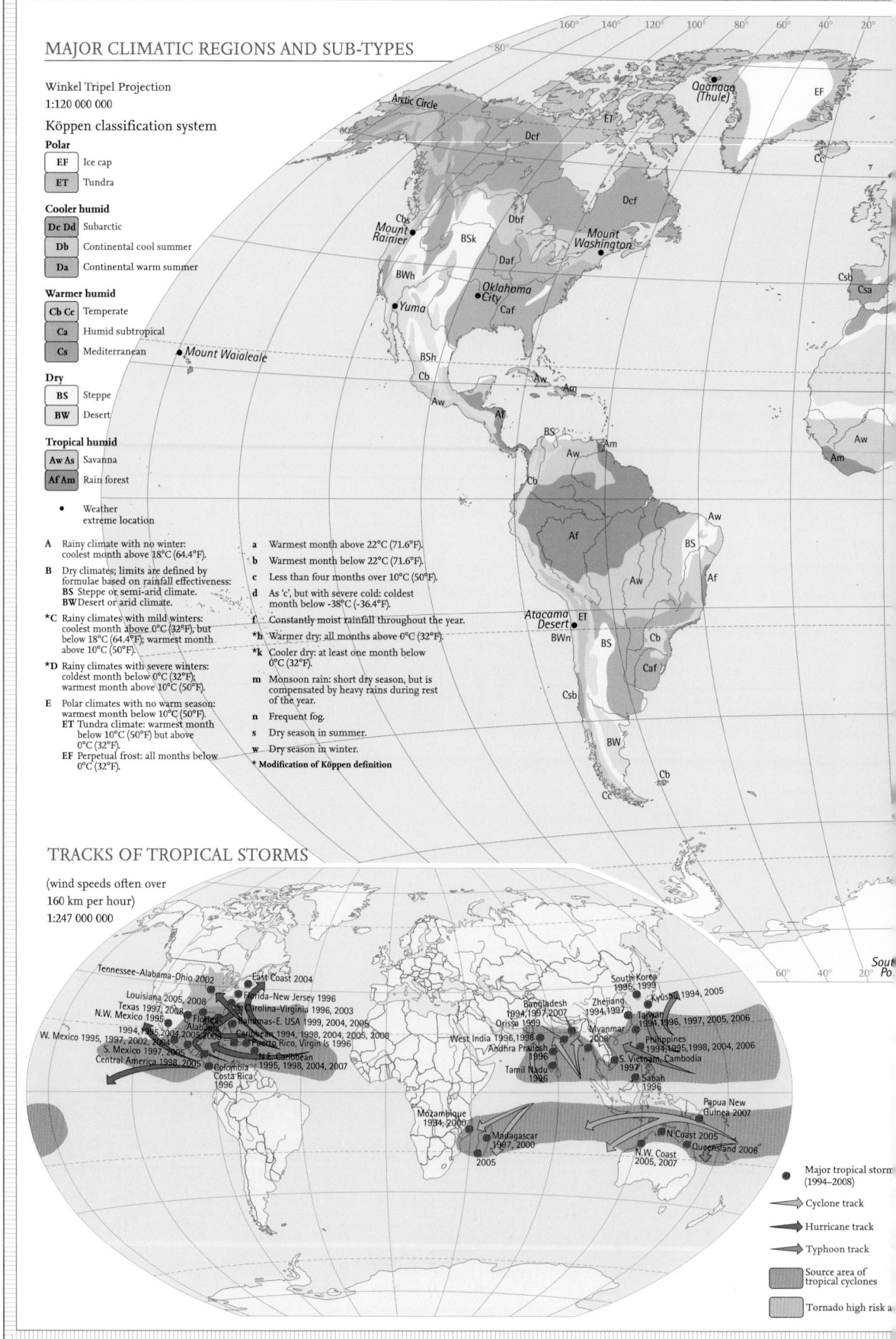

MAJOR CLIMATIC REGIONS AND SUB-TYPES

Winkel Tripel Projection
1:120 000 000

Köppen classification system

Polar

| EF | Ice cap |
| ET | Tundra |

Cooler humid

Dc Dd	Subarctic
Db	Continental cool summer
Da	Continental warm summer

Warmer humid

Cb Cc	Temperate
Ca	Humid subtropical
Cs	Mediterranean

Dry

| BS | Steppe |
| BW | Desert |

Tropical humid

| Aw As | Savanna |
| Af Am | Rain forest |

•   Weather extreme location

A   Rainy climate with no winter: coolest month above 18°C (64.4°F).

B   Dry climates; limits are defined by formulae based on rainfall effectiveness: **BS** Steppe or semi-arid climate. **BW** Desert or arid climate.

*C   Rainy climates with mild winters: coolest month above 0°C (32°F), but below 18°C (64.4°F); warmest month above 10°C (50°F).

*D   Rainy climates with severe winters: coldest month below 0°C (32°F); warmest month above 10°C (50°F).

E   Polar climates with no warm season: warmest month below 10°C (50°F). **ET** Tundra climate: warmest month below 10°C (50°F) but above 0°C (32°F). **EF** Perpetual frost: all months below 0°C (32°F).

a   Warmest month above 22°C (71.6°F).

b   Warmest month below 22°C (71.6°F).

c   Less than four months over 10°C (50°F).

d   As 'c', but with severe cold: coldest month below -38°C (-36.4°F).

f   Constantly moist rainfall throughout the year.

*h   Warmer dry: all months above 0°C (32°F).

*k   Cooler dry: at least one month below 0°C (32°F).

m   Monsoon rain: short dry season, but is compensated by heavy rains during rest of the year.

n   Frequent fog.

s   Dry season in summer.

w   Dry season in winter.

*** Modification of Köppen definition**

TRACKS OF TROPICAL STORMS

(wind speeds often over
160 km per hour)
1:247 000 000

Tennessee-Alabama-Ohio 2002
East Coast 2004
Louisiana 2005, 2008
Florida-New Jersey 1996
Texas 1997, 2008
N.W. Mexico 1995
Carolina-Virginia 1996, 2003
Bahamas-E. USA 1999, 2004, 2005
W. Mexico 1995, 1997, 2002, 2004
Florida 1994, 1995, 2004, 2005, 2006
Alabama
S. Mexico 1997, 2005
Caribbean 1994, 1998, 2004, 2005, 2008
Central America 1998, 2005
Puerto Rico, Virgin Is 1996
Colombia
Costa Rica 1996
N.E. Caribbean 1995, 1998, 2004, 2007

Bangladesh 1994, 1997, 2007
Orissa 1999
West India 1996, 1998
Andhra Pradesh
Tamil Nadu 1996
Zhejiang 1994, 1997
Kyushu 1994, 2005
South Korea 1995, 1999
Taiwan 1994, 1996, 1997, 2005, 2006
Myanmar 2008
Philippines 1994, 1995, 1998, 2004, 2006
S. Vietnam, Cambodia 1997
Sabah 1996
Papua New Guinea 2007

Mozambique 1994, 2000
Madagascar 1997, 2000
2005
N. Coast 2005, 2007
N.W. Coast 2005, 2007
Queensland 2006

•   Major tropical storm (1994–2008)

→   Cyclone track

→   Hurricane track

→   Typhoon track

  Source area of tropical cyclones

  Tornado high risk a

WORLD WEATHER EXTREMES

	Location		Location
Highest shade temperature	57.8°C/136°F Al ʿAzīzīyah, Libya (13th September 1922)	Highest surface wind speed	
		High altitude	372 km per hour/231 miles per hour Mount Washington, New Hampshire, USA (12th April 1934)
Hottest place — Annual mean	34.4°C/93.9°F Dalol, Ethiopia		
Driest place — Annual mean	0.1 mm/0.004 inches Atacama Desert, Chile	Low altitude	333 km per hour/207 miles per hour Qaanaaq (Thule), Greenland (8th March 1972)
Most sunshine — Annual mean	90% Yuma, Arizona, USA (over 4 000 hours)	Tornado	512 km per hour/318 miles per hour Oklahoma City, Oklahoma, USA (3rd May 1999)
Least sunshine	Nil for 182 days each year, South Pole		
Lowest screen temperature	-89.2°C/-128.6°F Vostok Station, Antarctica (21st July 1983)	Greatest snowfall	31 102 mm/1 224.5 inches Mount Rainier, Washington, USA (19th February 1971 — 18th February 1972)
Coldest place — Annual mean	-56.6°C/-69.9°F Plateau Station, Antarctica	Heaviest hailstones	1 kg/2.21 lb Gopalganj, Bangladesh (14th April 1986)
Wettest place — Annual mean	11 873 mm/467.4 inches Meghalaya, India	Thunder-days average	251 days per year Tororo, Uganda
Most rainy days	Up to 350 per year Mount Waialeale, Hawaii, USA	Highest barometric pressure	1 083.8 mb Agata, Siberia, Rus. Fed. (31st December 1968)
Windiest place	322 km per hour/200 miles per hour in gales, Commonwealth Bay, Antarctica	Lowest barometric pressure	870 mb 483 km/300 miles west of Guam, Pacific Ocean (12th October 1979)

WORLD LAND COVER

Winkel Tripel Projection
1:120 000 000

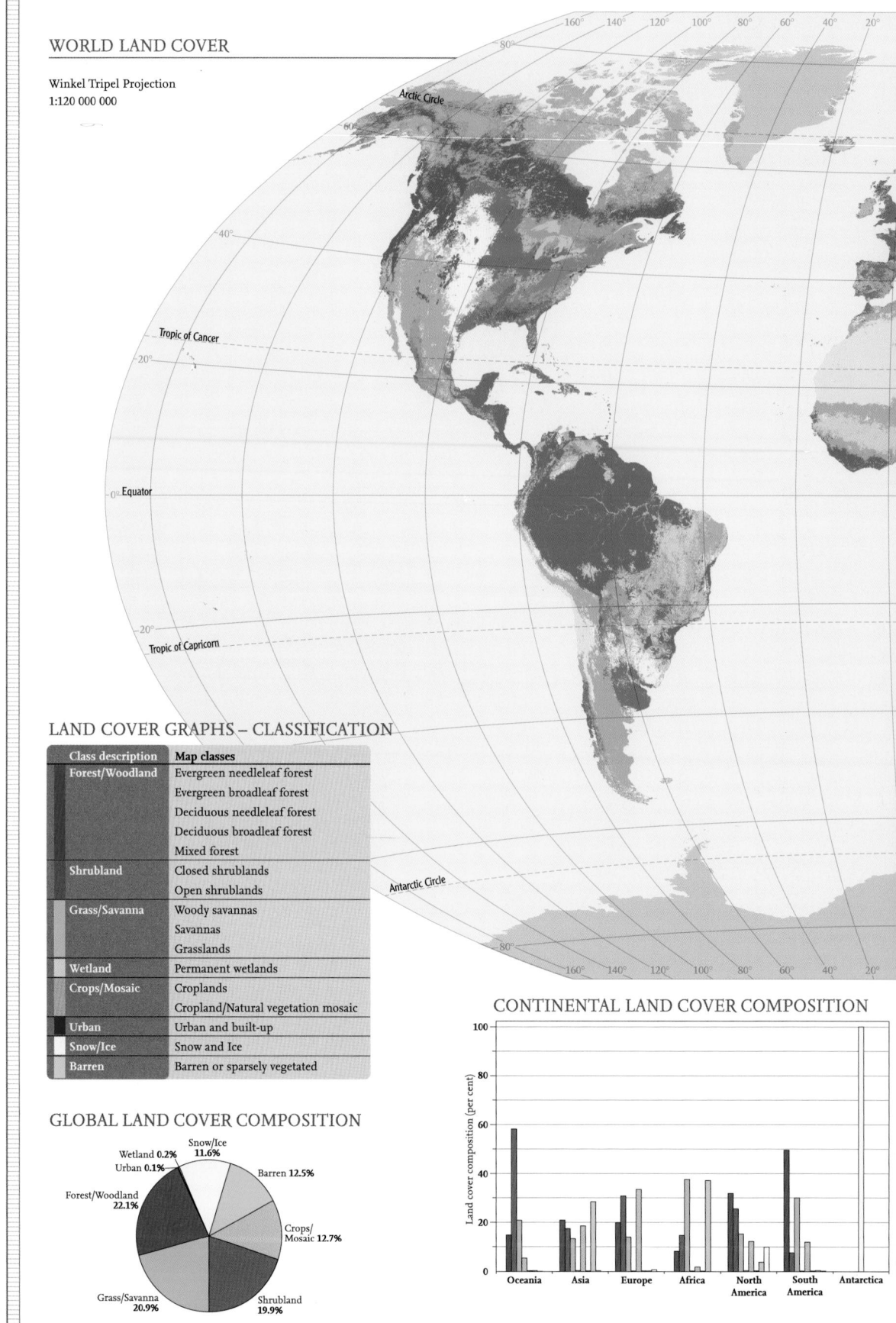

LAND COVER GRAPHS – CLASSIFICATION

Class description	Map classes
Forest/Woodland	Evergreen needleleaf forest
	Evergreen broadleaf forest
	Deciduous needleleaf forest
	Deciduous broadleaf forest
	Mixed forest
Shrubland	Closed shrublands
	Open shrublands
Grass/Savanna	Woody savannas
	Savannas
	Grasslands
Wetland	Permanent wetlands
Crops/Mosaic	Croplands
	Cropland/Natural vegetation mosaic
Urban	Urban and built-up
Snow/Ice	Snow and Ice
Barren	Barren or sparsely vegetated

GLOBAL LAND COVER COMPOSITION

Wetland **0.2%**
Snow/Ice **11.6%**
Urban **0.1%**
Barren **12.5%**
Forest/Woodland **22.1%**
Crops/Mosaic **12.7%**
Grass/Savanna **20.9%**
Shrubland **19.9%**

CONTINENTAL LAND COVER COMPOSITION

Land cover composition (per cent)

Oceania   Asia   Europe   Africa   North America   South America   Antarctica

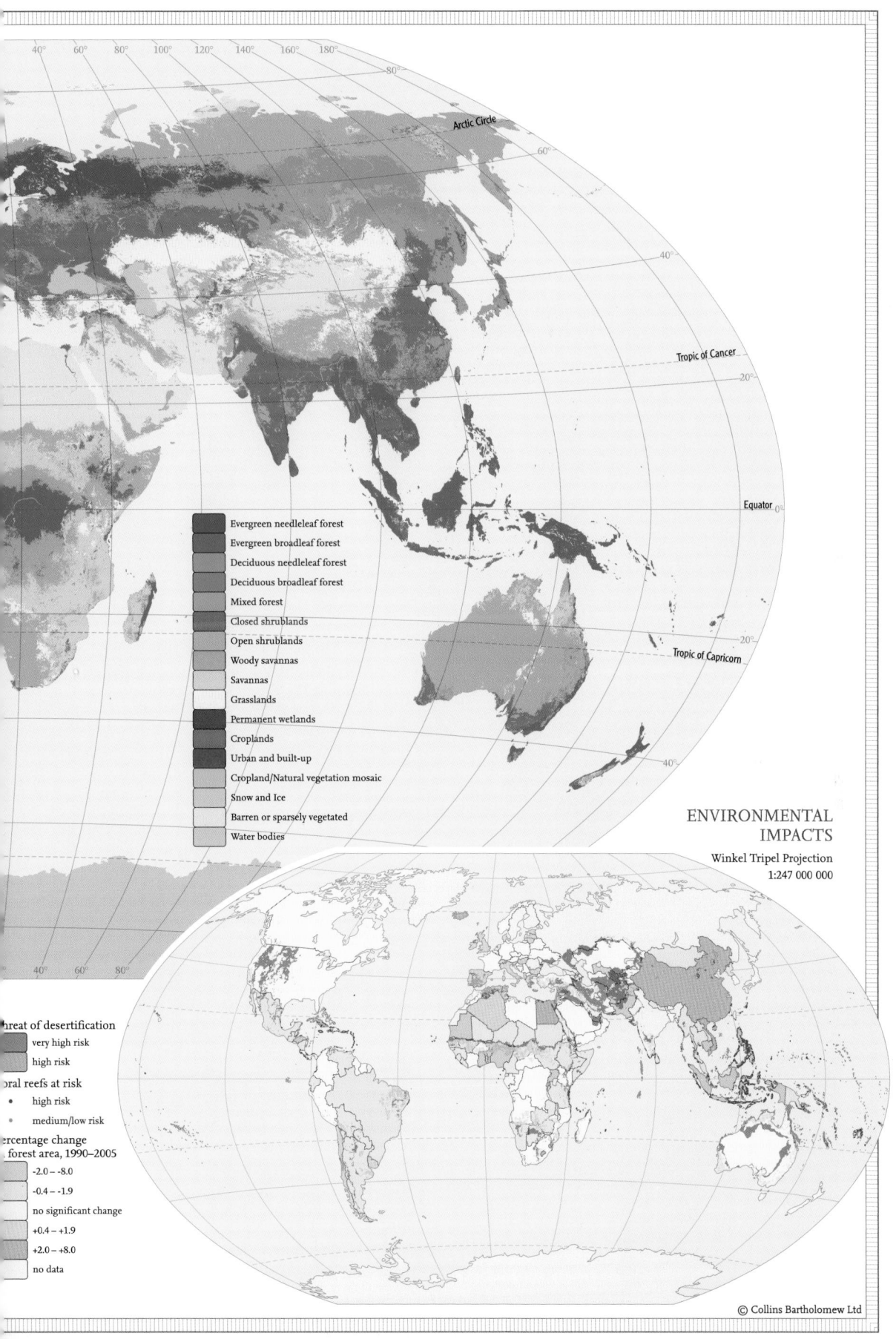

Evergreen needleleaf forest
Evergreen broadleaf forest
Deciduous needleleaf forest
Deciduous broadleaf forest
Mixed forest
Closed shrublands
Open shrublands
Woody savannas
Savannas
Grasslands
Permanent wetlands
Croplands
Urban and built-up
Cropland/Natural vegetation mosaic
Snow and Ice
Barren or sparsely vegetated
Water bodies

ENVIRONMENTAL
IMPACTS

Winkel Tripel Projection
1:247 000 000

hreat of desertification
very high risk
high risk

oral reefs at risk
• high risk
◦ medium/low risk

ercentage change
 forest area, 1990–2005
-2.0 – -8.0
-0.4 – -1.9
no significant change
+0.4 – +1.9
+2.0 – +8.0
no data

© Collins Bartholomew Ltd

53

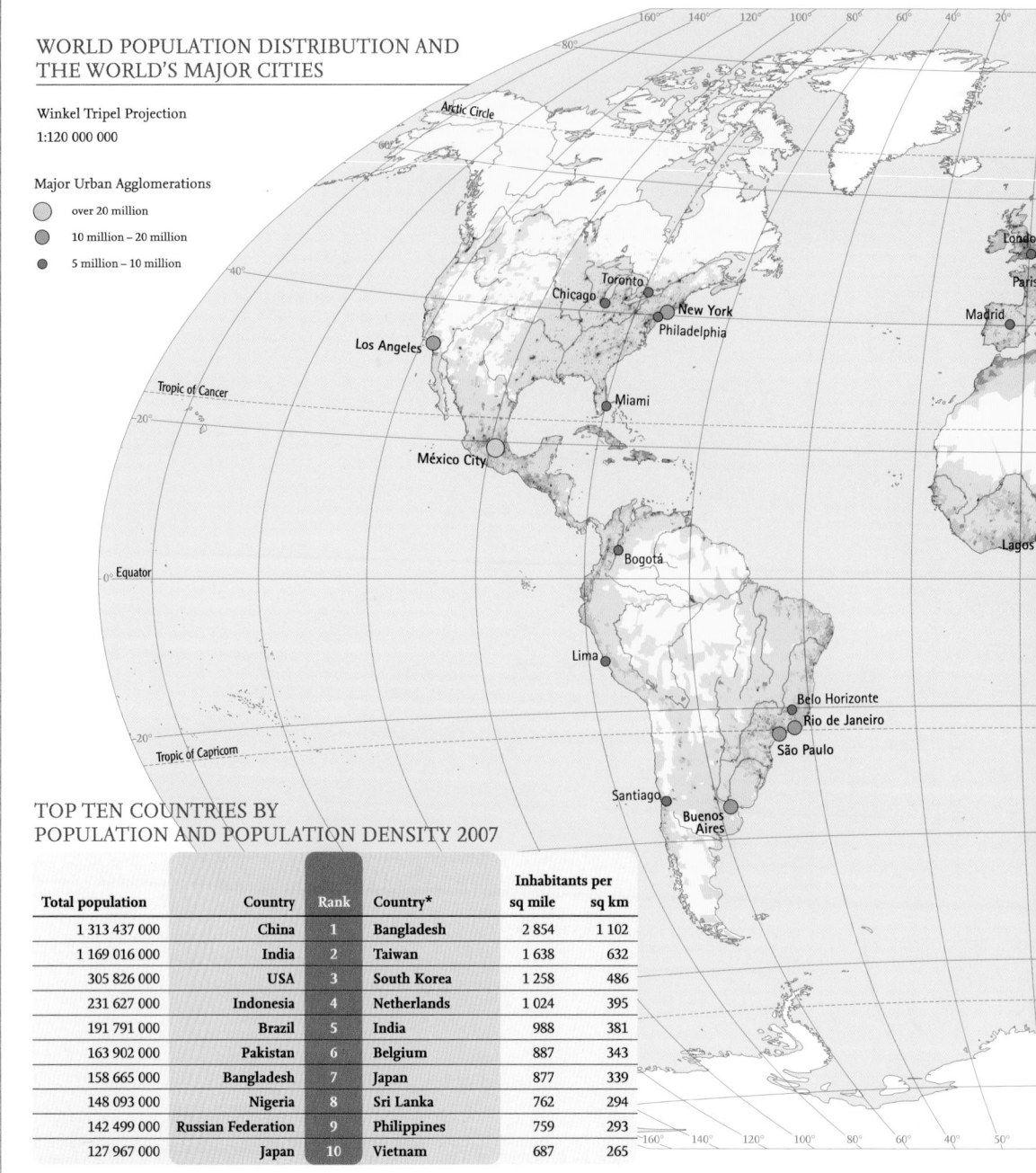

WORLD POPULATION DISTRIBUTION AND THE WORLD'S MAJOR CITIES

Winkel Tripel Projection
1:120 000 000

Major Urban Agglomerations

- over 20 million
- 10 million – 20 million
- 5 million – 10 million

TOP TEN COUNTRIES BY POPULATION AND POPULATION DENSITY 2007

Total population	Country	Rank	Country*	Inhabitants per sq mile	Inhabitants per sq km
1 313 437 000	China	1	Bangladesh	2 854	1 102
1 169 016 000	India	2	Taiwan	1 638	632
305 826 000	USA	3	South Korea	1 258	486
231 627 000	Indonesia	4	Netherlands	1 024	395
191 791 000	Brazil	5	India	988	381
163 902 000	Pakistan	6	Belgium	887	343
158 665 000	Bangladesh	7	Japan	877	339
148 093 000	Nigeria	8	Sri Lanka	762	294
142 499 000	Russian Federation	9	Philippines	759	293
127 967 000	Japan	10	Vietnam	687	265

* Only countries with a population of over 10 million are considered.

KEY POPULATION STATISTICS FOR MAJOR REGIONS

	Population 2007 (millions)	Growth (per cent)	Infant mortality rate	Total fertility rate	Life expectancy (years)	% aged 60 and over 2005	% aged 60 and over 2050
World	6 671	1.2	49	2.6	67	10	22
More developed regions	1 223	0.3	7	1.6	77	20	33
Less developed regions	5 448	1.4	54	2.8	65	8	20
Africa	965	2.3	87	4.7	53	5	10
Asia	4 030	1.1	43	2.3	69	9	24
Europe	731	0.0	8	1.5	75	21	35
Latin America and the Caribbean	572	1.2	22	2.4	73	9	24
North America	339	1.0	6	2	79	17	27
Oceania	34	1.2	26	2.3	75	14	25

Except for population and % aged 60 and over figures, the data are annual averages projected for the period 2005–2010.

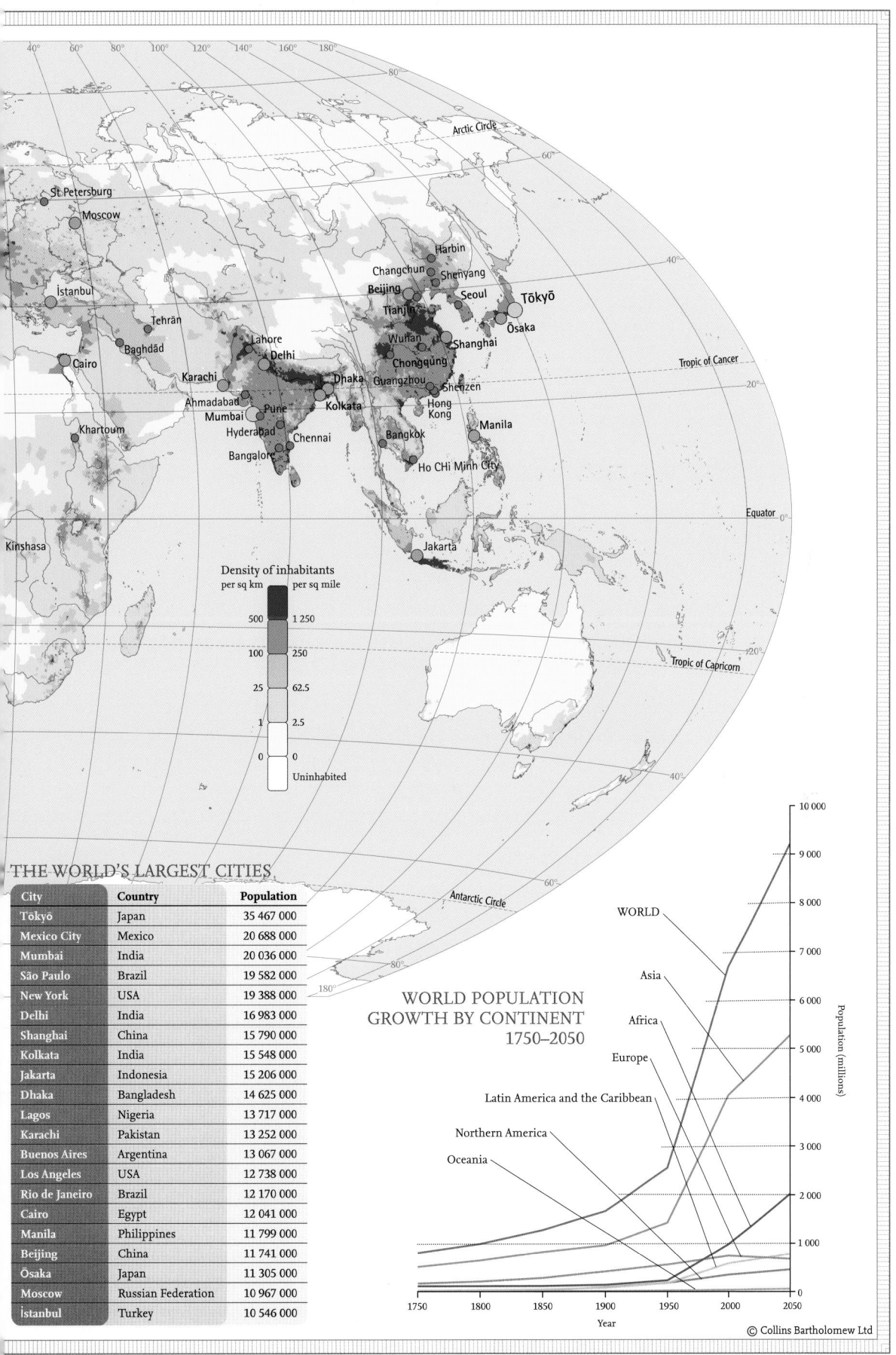

Density of inhabitants

per sq km	per sq mile
500	1 250
100	250
25	62.5
1	2.5
0	0
	Uninhabited

THE WORLD'S LARGEST CITIES

City	Country	Population
Tōkyō	Japan	35 467 000
Mexico City	Mexico	20 688 000
Mumbai	India	20 036 000
São Paulo	Brazil	19 582 000
New York	USA	19 388 000
Delhi	India	16 983 000
Shanghai	China	15 790 000
Kolkata	India	15 548 000
Jakarta	Indonesia	15 206 000
Dhaka	Bangladesh	14 625 000
Lagos	Nigeria	13 717 000
Karachi	Pakistan	13 252 000
Buenos Aires	Argentina	13 067 000
Los Angeles	USA	12 738 000
Rio de Janeiro	Brazil	12 170 000
Cairo	Egypt	12 041 000
Manila	Philippines	11 799 000
Beijing	China	11 741 000
Ōsaka	Japan	11 305 000
Moscow	Russian Federation	10 967 000
İstanbul	Turkey	10 546 000

WORLD POPULATION GROWTH BY CONTINENT 1750–2050

WORLD

Asia

Africa

Europe

Latin America and the Caribbean

Northern America

Oceania

Population (millions)

Year

© Collins Bartholomew Ltd

INTERNATIONAL TELECOMMUNICATIONS TRAFFIC

RUSSIAN FEDERATION

CANADA

UNITED STATES

CHINA

INDIA

AUSTRALIA

Telephone lines per
100 inhabitants 2006

- over 50
- 35.0–50.0
- 15.0–34.9
- 10.0–14.9
- 5.0–9.9
- 1.0–4.9
- 0–0.9
- no data

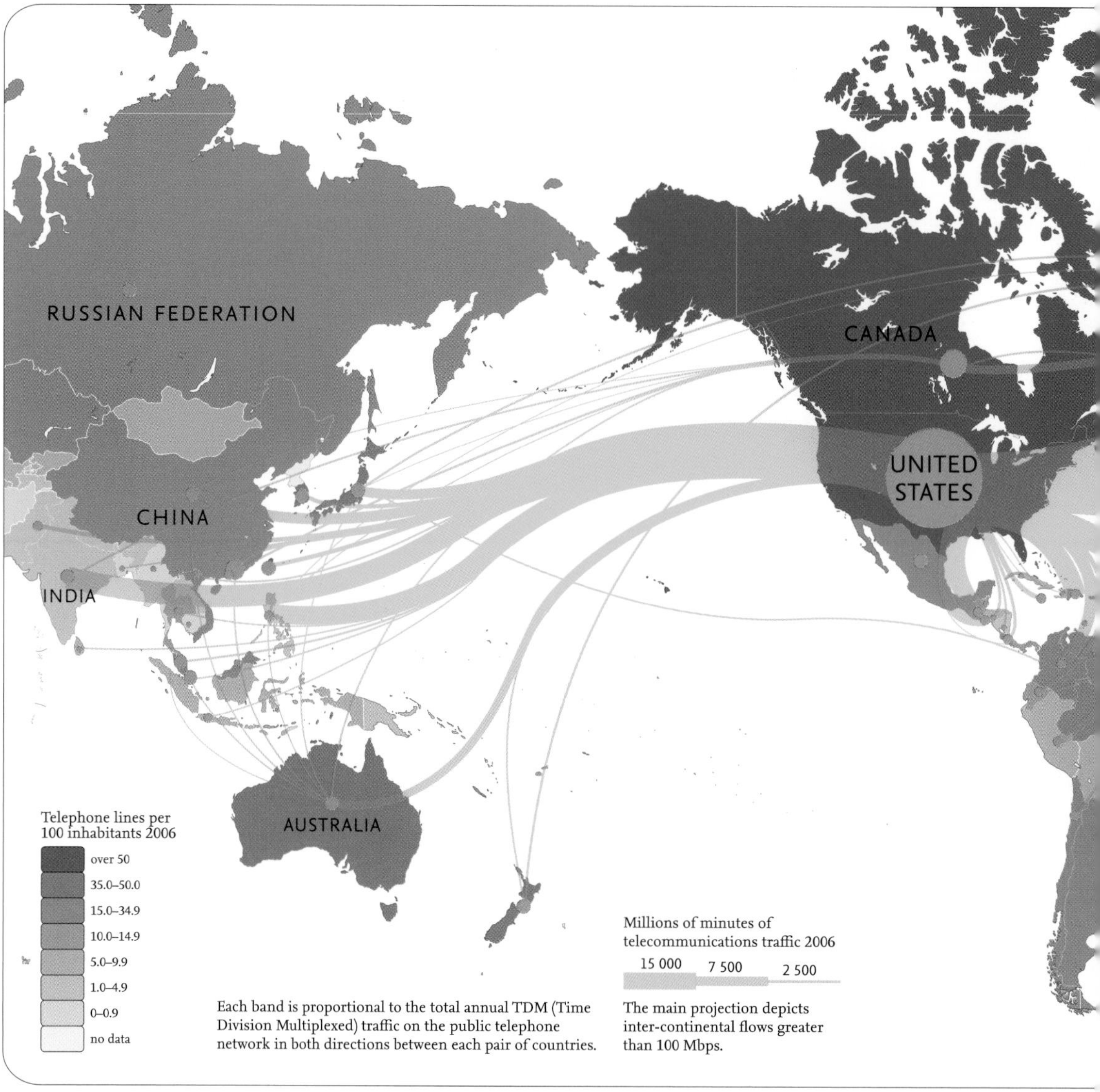

Each band is proportional to the total annual TDM (Time
Division Multiplexed) traffic on the public telephone
network in both directions between each pair of countries.

Millions of minutes of
telecommunications traffic 2006

15 000   7 500   2 500

The main projection depicts
inter-continental flows greater
than 100 Mbps.

WORLD COMMUNICATION EQUIPMENT 1993–2007

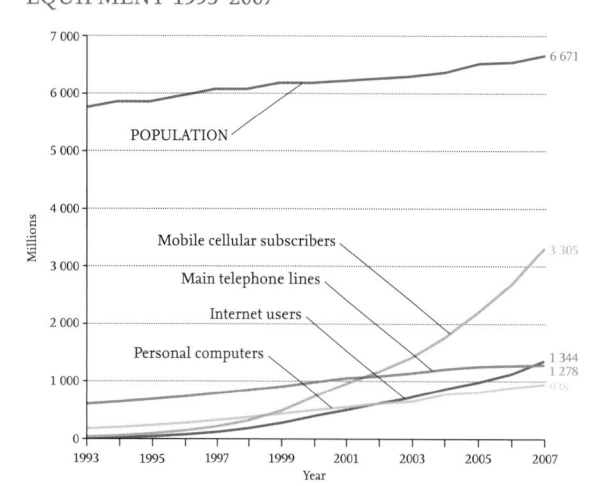

POPULATION

6 671

Mobile cellular subscribers

Main telephone lines

Internet users

Personal computers

3 305

1 344
1 278

Millions

1993 1995 1997 1999 2001 2003 2005 2007

Year

INTERNET USERS 2000 AND 2007

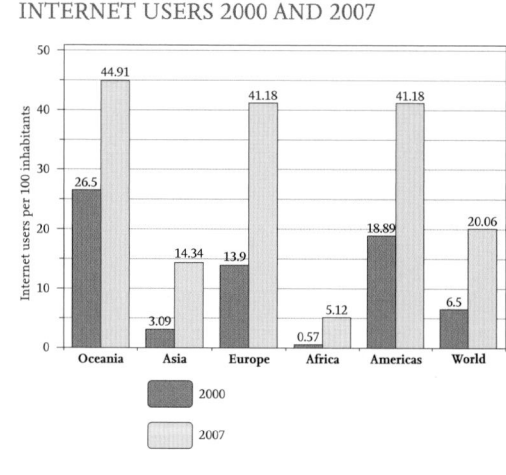

Internet users per 100 inhabitants

	Oceania	Asia	Europe	Africa	Americas	World
2000	26.5	3.09	13.9	0.57	18.89	6.5
2007	44.91	14.34	41.18	5.12	41.18	20.06

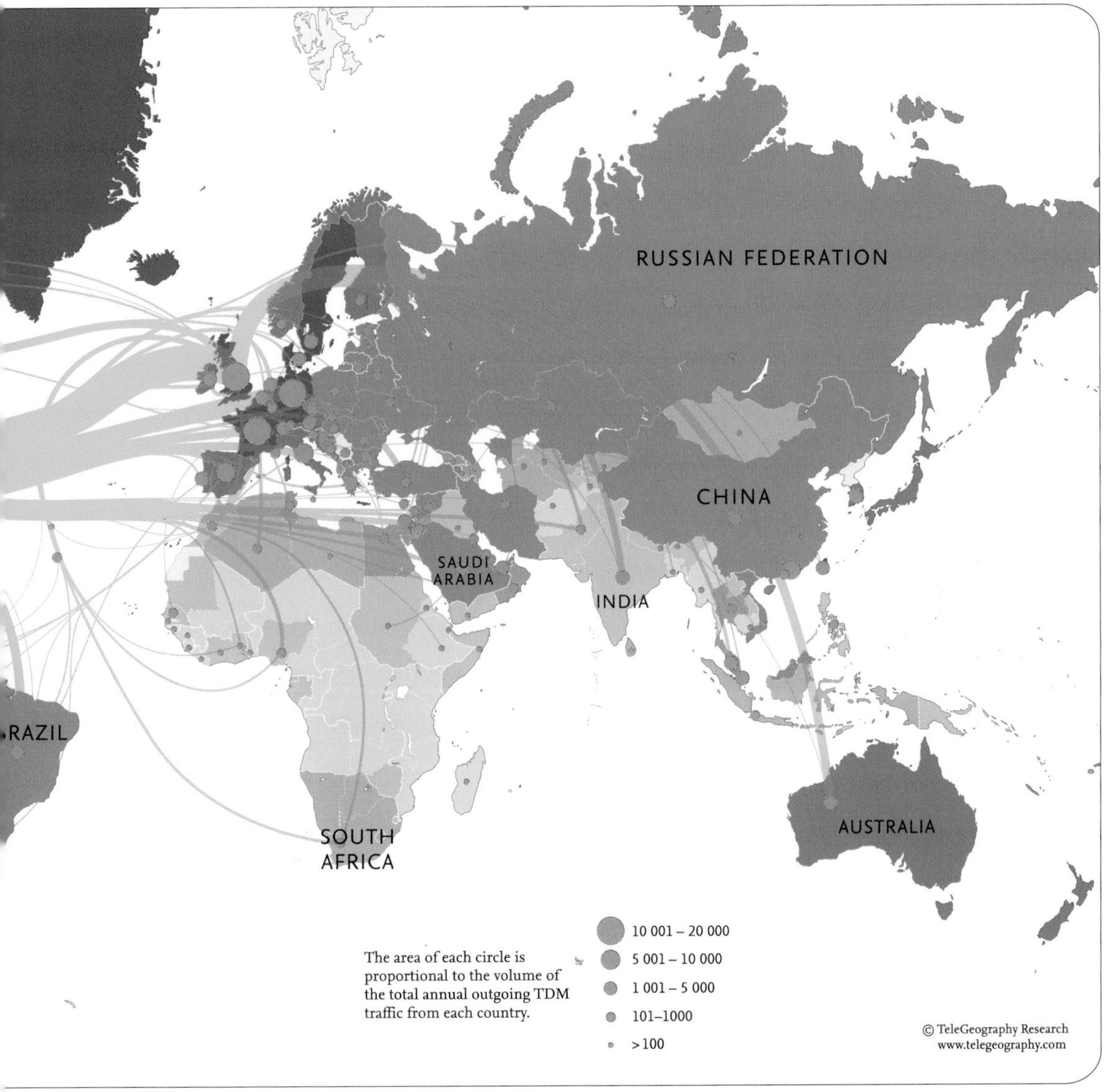

RUSSIAN FEDERATION

CHINA

SAUDI
ARABIA

INDIA

BRAZIL

SOUTH
AFRICA

AUSTRALIA

The area of each circle is
proportional to the volume of
the total annual outgoing TDM
traffic from each country.

- 10 001 – 20 000
- 5 001 – 10 000
- 1 001 – 5 000
- 101–1000
- >100

© TeleGeography Research
www.telegeography.com

TOP BROADBAND ECONOMIES 2007

Countries with highest broadband penetration rate –
subscribers per 100 inhabitants

	Top Economies	Rate
1	Denmark	36.3
2	Iceland	34.8
3	Netherlands	33.5
4	Finland	33.3
5	Switzerland	32.1
6	South Korea	30.6
7	Norway	29.0
8	Sweden	25.9
9	United Kingdom	25.6
10	France	25.2
11	Luxembourg	24.2
12	Germany	24.0
13	Canada	22.9
14	Belgium	22.6
15	Japan	22.1

INTERNET USERS

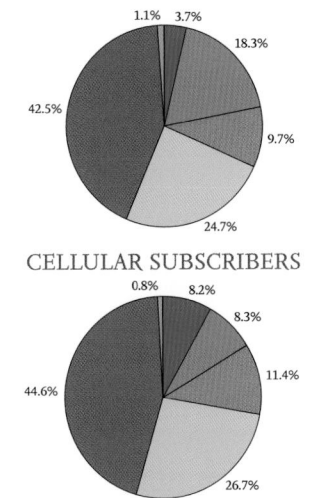

1.1% 3.7%
18.3%
42.5%
9.7%
24.7%

CELLULAR SUBSCRIBERS

0.8% 8.2%
8.3%
44.6%
11.4%
26.7%

TELEPHONE MAIN LINES

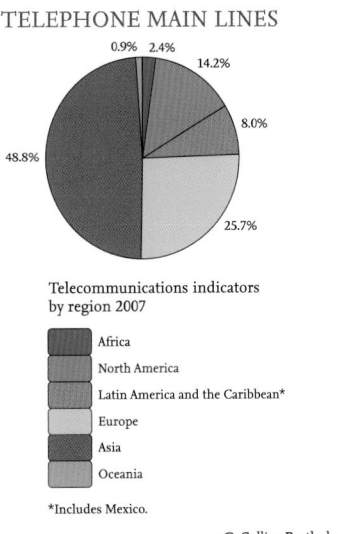

0.9% 2.4%
14.2%
8.0%
48.8%
25.7%

Telecommunications indicators
by region 2007

- Africa
- North America
- Latin America and the Caribbean*
- Europe
- Asia
- Oceania

*Includes Mexico.

© Collins Bartholomew Ltd

MAP POLICIES

PLACE NAMES

The spelling of place names on maps has always been a matter of great complexity, because of the variety of the world's languages and the systems used to write them down. There is no standard way of spelling names or of converting them from one alphabet, or symbol set, to another. Instead, conventional ways of spelling have evolved in each of the world's major languages, and the results often differ significantly from the name as it is spelled in the original language. Familiar examples of English conventional names include Munich (München), Florence (Firenze) and Moscow (from the transliterated form, Moskva).

In this atlas, local name forms are used where these are in the Roman alphabet, though for major cities, and main physical features, conventional English names are given first. The local forms are those which are officially recognized by the government of the country concerned, usually as represented by its official mapping agency. This is a basic principle laid down by the United Kingdom government's Permanent Committee on Geographical Names (PCGN) and the equivalent United States Board on Geographic Names, (BGN). Prominent English-language and historic names are not neglected, however. These, and significant superseded names and alternate spellings, are included in brackets on the maps where space permits, and are cross-referenced in the index.

Country names are shown in conventional English form and include any recent changes promulgated by national governments and adopted by the United Nations. The names of continents, oceans, seas and under-water features in international waters also appear in English throughout the atlas, as do those of other international features where such an English form exists and is in common use. International features are defined as features crossing one or more international boundary.

BOUNDARIES

The status of nations, their names and their boundaries, are shown in this atlas as they are at the time of going to press, as far as can be ascertained. Where an international boundary symbol appears in the sea or ocean it does not necessarily infer a legal maritime boundary, but shows which offshore islands belong to which country. The extent of island nations is shown by a short boundary symbol at the extreme limits of the area of sea or ocean within which all land is part of that nation.

Where international boundaries are the subject of dispute it may be that no portrayal of them will meet with the approval of any of the countries involved, but it is not seen as the function of this atlas to try to adjudicate between the rights and wrongs of political issues. Although reference mapping at atlas scales is not the ideal medium for indicating the claims of many separatist and irredentist movements, every reasonable attempt is made to show where an active territorial dispute exists, and where there is an important difference between 'de facto' (existing in fact, on the ground) and 'de jure' (according to law) boundaries. This is done by the use of a different symbol where international boundaries are disputed, or where the alignment is unconfirmed, to that used for settled international boundaries. Ceasefire lines are also shown by a separate symbol. For clarity, disputed boundaries and areas are annotated where this is considered necessary. The atlas aims to take a strictly neutral viewpoint of all such cases, based on advice from expert consultants.

MAP PROJECTIONS

Map projections have been selected specifically for the area and scale of each map, or suite of maps. As the only way to show the Earth with absolute accuracy is on a globe, all map projections are compromises. Some projections seek to maintain correct area relationships (equal area projections), true distances and bearings from a point (equidistant projections) or correct angles and shapes (conformal projections); others attempt to achieve a balance between these properties. The choice of projections used in this atlas has been made on an individual continental and regional basis. Projections used, and their individual parameters, have been defined to minimize distortion and to reduce scale errors as much as possible. The projection used is indicated at the bottom left of each map page.

SCALE

In order to directly compare like with like throughout the world it would be necessary to maintain a single scale throughout the atlas. However, the desirability of mapping the more densely populated areas of the world at larger scales, and other geographical considerations, such as the need to fit a homogeneous physical region within a uniform rectangular page format, mean that a range of scales have been used. Scales for continental maps range between 1:20 000 000 and 1:44 000 000, depending on the size of the continental land mass being covered. Scales for regional maps are typically in the range 1:12 000 000 to 1:20 000 000. Mapping for most countries is at scales between 1:4 800 000 and 1:12 000 000, although for the more densely populated areas of Europe the scale increases to 1:2 400 000.

ABBREVIATIONS

Arch.	Archipelago			L.	Lake			Ra.	Range			mountain range
B.	Bay				Loch	(Scotland)	lake	S.	South, Southern			
	Bahia, Baía	Portuguese	bay		Lough	(Ireland)	lake		Salar, Salina,			
	Bahía	Spanish	bay		Lac	French	lake		Salinas	Spanish	salt pan, salt pans
	Baie	French	bay		Lago	Portuguese, Spanish	lake	Sa	Serra	Portuguese,	mountain range
C.	Cape			M.	Mys	Russian	cape, point		Sierra	Spanish	mountain range
	Cabo	Portuguese,		Mt	Mount			Sd	Sound			
		Spanish	cape, headland		Mont	French	hill, mountain	S.E.	Southeast,			
	Cap	French	cape, headland	Mt.	Mountain				Southeastern			
Co	Cerro	Spanish	hill, peak, summit	Mte	Monte	Portuguese, Spanish	hill, mountain	St	Saint			
E.	East, Eastern			Mts	Mountains				Sankt	German	Saint
Est.	Estrecho	Spanish	strait		Monts	French	hills, mountains		Sint	Dutch	Saint
G.	Gebel	Arabic	hill, mountain	N.	North, Northern			Sta	Santa	Italian, Portuguese,	
Gt	Great			O.	Ostrov	Russian	island			Spanish	Saint
I.	Island, Isle			Pk	Puncak	Indonesian, Malay	hill, mountain	Ste	Sainte	French	Saint
	Ilha	Portuguese	island	Pt	Point			Str.	Strait			
	Islas	Spanish	island	Pta	Punta	Italian, Spanish	cape, point	Tk	Teluk	Indonesian, Malay	bay, gulf
Is	Islands, Isles			R.	River			Tg	Tanjong, Tanjung	Indonesian, Malay	cape, point
	Islas	Spanish	islands		Rio	Portuguese	river	Vdkhr.	Vodokhranilishche	Russian	reservoir
Kep.	Kepulauan	Indonesian	islands		Río	Spanish	river	W.	West, Western			strait
Khr.	Khrebet	Russian	mountain range		Rivière	French	river		Wadi, Wâdi, Wādī	Arabic	watercourse

MAP SYMBOLS

LAND AND WATER FEATURES

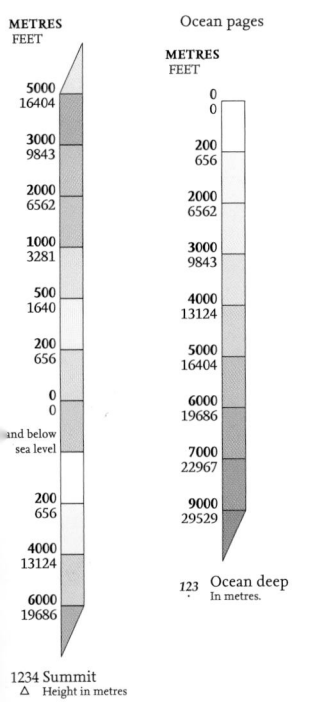

Lake		River	
Impermanent lake		Impermanent river	
Salt lake or lagoon		Ice cap / Glacier	
Impermanent salt lake		123 Pass Height in metres	
Dry salt lake or salt pan		∴ Site of special interest	
		⌄ Oasis	
		Wall	

TRANSPORT

Motorway

Main road

Track

Main railway

Canal

Main airport

BOUNDARIES

International boundary

Disputed international boundary or alignment unconfirmed

Undefined international boundary in the sea.
All land within this boundary is part of state or territory named.

Administrative boundary
Shown for selected countries only.

Ceasefire line or other boundary described on the map

RELIEF

Contour intervals used in layer-colouring, for land height and sea depth

METRES FEET		Ocean pages METRES FEET	
5000 16404		0 0	
3000 9843		200 656	
2000 6562		2000 6562	
1000 3281		3000 9843	
500 1640		4000 13124	
200 656		5000 16404	
0 0		6000 19686	
and below sea level		7000 22967	
200 656		9000 29529	
4000 13124			
6000 19686		123 Ocean deep In metres.	

1234 Summit
△ Height in metres

1234 Volcano
▲ Height in metres

STYLES OF LETTERING

Cities and towns are explained separately

		Physical features	
Country	**FRANCE**	Island	*Gran Canaria*
Overseas Territory/Dependency	**Guadeloupe**	Lake	*Lake Erie*
Disputed Territory	AKSAI CHIN	Mountain	*Mt Blanc*
Administrative name Shown for selected countries only.	**SCOTLAND**	River	*Thames*
Area name	PATAGONIA	Region	*LAPPLAND*

CITIES AND TOWNS

Population	National Capital	Administrative Capital Shown for selected countries only	Other City or Town
over 10 million	**DHAKA** ▣	**Karachi** ◉	**New York** ◉
5 million to 10 million	**MADRID** ▣	**Toronto** ◉	**Philadelphia** ◉
1 million to 5 million	**KĀBUL** ▢	**Sydney** ○	**Koahsiung** ○
500 000 to 1 million	**BANGUI** ▢	**Winnipeg** ○	**Jeddah** ○
100 000 to 500 000	WELLINGTON ▢	Edinburgh ○	Apucarana ○
50 000 to 100 000	PORT OF SPAIN ▢	Bismarck ○	Invercargill ○
under 50 000	MALABO ▢	Charlottetown ○	Ceres ○

CONTINENTAL MAPS

BOUNDARIES ——— International boundary ------ Disputed international boundary ········ Ceasefire line

CITIES AND TOWNS National Capital **Beijing** ▢ Other City or Town **New York** ○

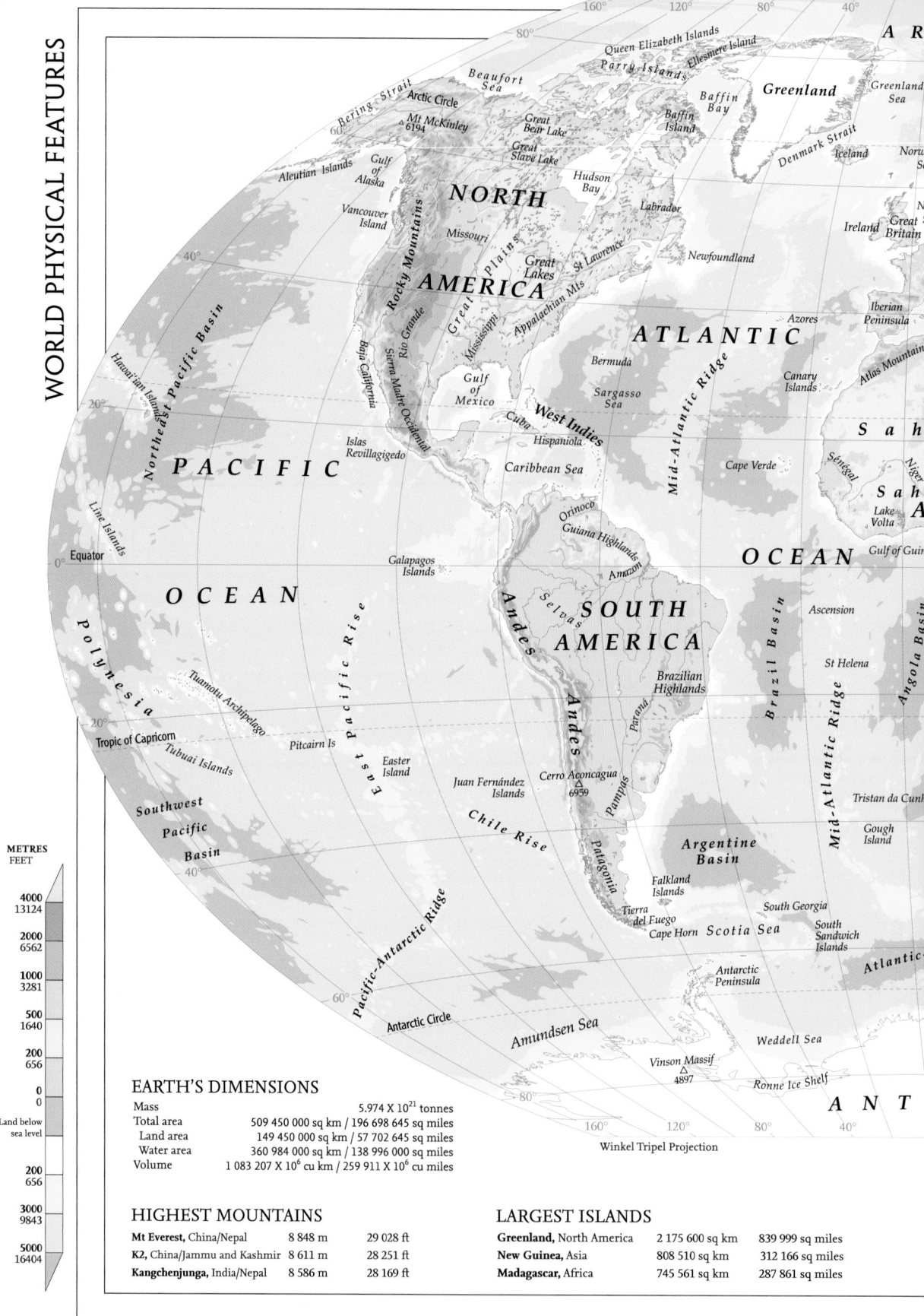

METRES
FEET

METRES	FEET
4000	13124
2000	6562
1000	3281
500	1640
200	656
0	0
Land below sea level	
200	656
3000	9843
5000	16404

Winkel Tripel Projection

EARTH'S DIMENSIONS

Mass	5.974 X 10^{21} tonnes	
Total area	509 450 000 sq km / 196 698 645 sq miles	
Land area	149 450 000 sq km / 57 702 645 sq miles	
Water area	360 984 000 sq km / 138 996 000 sq miles	
Volume	1 083 207 X 10^6 cu km / 259 911 X 10^6 cu miles	

HIGHEST MOUNTAINS

Mt Everest, China/Nepal	8 848 m	29 028 ft
K2, China/Jammu and Kashmir	8 611 m	28 251 ft
Kangchenjunga, India/Nepal	8 586 m	28 169 ft

LARGEST ISLANDS

Greenland, North America	2 175 600 sq km	839 999 sq miles
New Guinea, Asia	808 510 sq km	312 166 sq miles
Madagascar, Africa	745 561 sq km	287 861 sq miles

Lambert Azimuthal Equal Area Projection

IC **OCEAN**

albard

Novaya
Zemlya   *New Siberia*
                Islands
Barents   *Kara Sea*   *East Siberian*
Sea   *Sea*

andinavia   *Arctic Circle*   60°

                Central   *Verkhoyanskiy Khrebet*
                Siberian   *Bering*
West   *Plateau*   *Sea of*   *Sea*
Siberian   *Yenisey*   *Lena*   *Okhotsk*   *Aleutian Is*
Ob   *Siberia*   *Emperor Seamount Chain*   40°
Plain

Ural Mountains *Irtysh*   *Altai Mountains*   *Manchurian*   *Hokkaidō*
                                                     Plain
E U R O P E   *Lake*   **G o b i**
                Lake   *Baikal*   *Sea of*
Danube   *Balkhash*   *Amur*   *Japan*   *Honshū*
Dnieper   *Volga* *Aral* *Tien Shan* **A S I A**   *(East Sea)*
Black Sea   *El'brus* *Sea*   *Yellow*
                5642   *Caspian Sea* *Turan* *Qilian Shan*   **P A C I F I C**
                        Lowland   *Kunlun Shan*   *East*   *Bonin*
ranean Sea   *Euphrates* *Zagros Mts* *Plateau of Tibet*   *China*   *Islands*   *Tropic of Cancer*
                        The Gulf *Indus* *Himalaya* *Yangtze* *Sea*   20°
Libyan   *Arabian*   *Mt Everest* 8848   *Mid-Pacific Mountains*
Desert   *Red Sea* *Nile* *Ganges*   *Ryukyu Is*   **O C E A N**
a   *Peninsula* *Deccan*   *South*   *Challenger*   *Mariana Trench*
                Rub' al Khali *Arabian*   *Bay* *Mekong* *China*   *Deep*
ICA   *Gulf of Aden* *Sea*   *of*   *Sea*   *10920* •   *Marshall Islands*
                Ethiopian   *Bengal*   *Philippines*   *Micronesia*
Highlands   *Sri Lanka*   *Caroline Islands*
Congo   *White Nile*   *Maldives*   *Peninsular*
Basin   *Lake*   *Malaysia*   *Equator*   0°
                Victoria *Somali Basin*   *Borneo*   *Puncak Jaya*
Great Rift Valley *5892* △ *Kilimanjaro*   **Greater Sunda Islands** △ *New*
                Seychelles   *Laut Java* *5030* *Guinea*   *Solomon Is*   *Melanesia*
                                             I N D I A N *Java* *Laut*
                                                             Banda   *Arafura*   *Tuvalu*
Zambezi   *Timor*   *Sea*
                Madagascar *Mauritius*   *Sea*   *Great Barrier Reef* *Coral*   *Fiji*
                        Réunion   *Sea*
Kalahari   *Tonga Trench*
Desert   **O C E A N**   **AUSTRALIA**   *Tropic of Capricorn*   20°
ape of   *Crozet*   *Great*   *Norfolk I.*
od Hope   *Basin*   *Southeast Indian Ridge*   *Victoria*   *Darling* *Lord Howe I.*
                                                             Desert   *Mt Kosciuszko*
                Prince   *Îles Kerguélen*   *Great*   *Murray* *2229* △
Edward Is   *Australian*   *Tasman*   40°
                                                             Bight   *Tasmania*   *Sea*   **New Zealand** *North*
                                                                                                              Island
Antarctic Basin   *Australian-Antarctic Basin*   *Mt Cook* △ *South*
                                                                             3754 *Island*
                Davis Sea
                                Antarctic Mountains *Ross Sea* *Antarctic Circle*   60°
C T I C A

40°   80°   120°   160°   80°

1: 100 800 000

Equatorial diameter	12 756 km / 7 927 miles	
Polar diameter	12 714 km / 7 901 miles	
Equatorial circumference	40 075 km / 24 903 miles	
Meridional circumference	40 008 km / 24 861 miles	

LARGEST LAKES

Caspian Sea, Asia / Europe	371 000 sq km	143 243 sq miles
Lake Superior, North America	82 100 sq km	31 366 sq miles
Lake Victoria, Africa	68 800 sq km	6 591 sq miles

LONGEST RIVERS

Nile, Africa	6 695 km	4 160 miles
Amazon, South America	6 516 km	4 049 miles
Yangtze, Asia	6 380 km	3 965 miles

61

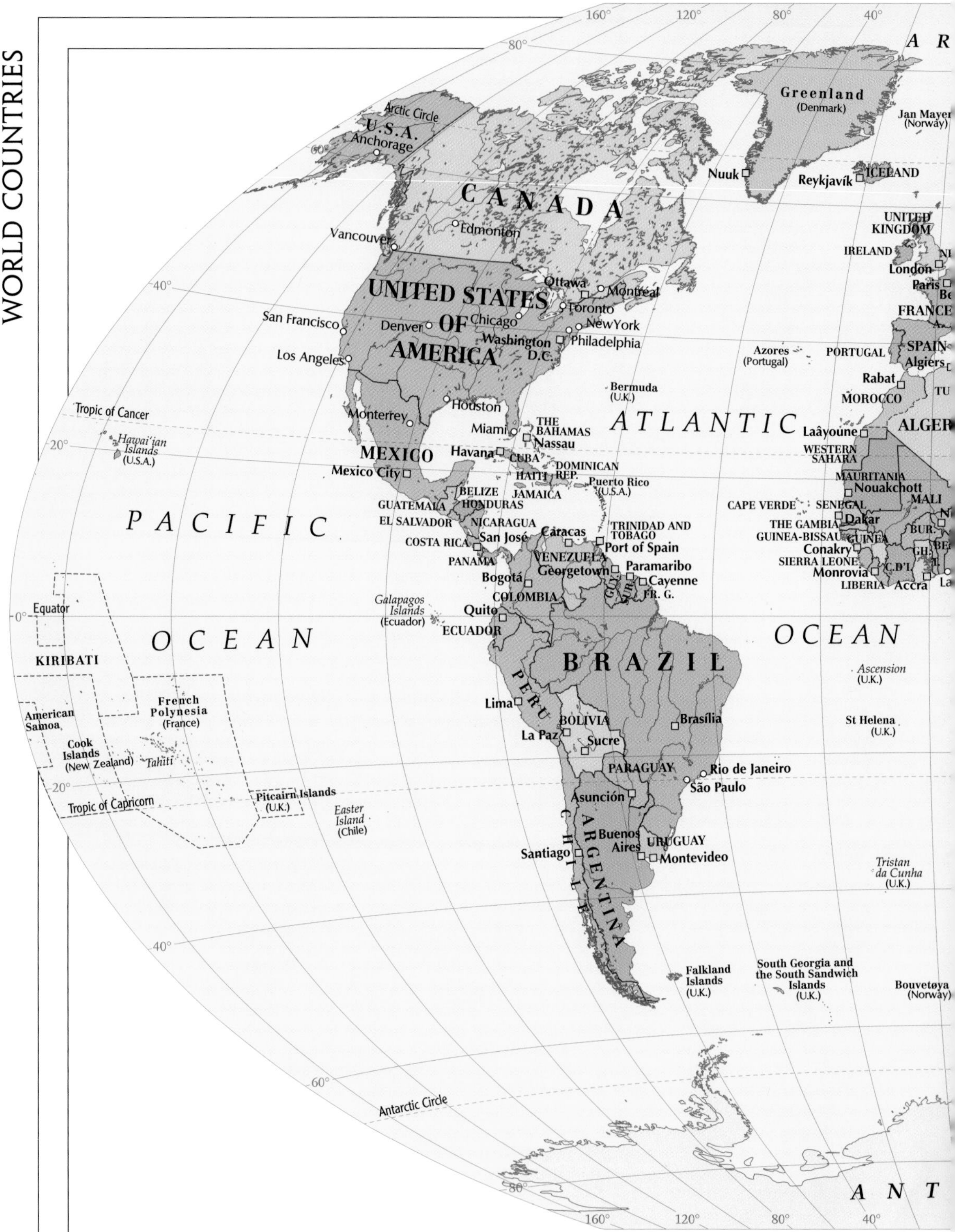

160°
120°
80°
40°
80°
A R
Arctic Circle
U.S.A.
Anchorage
60°
Greenland
(Denmark)
Jan Mayen
(Norway)
Nuuk
Reykjavík
ICELAND
CANADA
Edmonton
Vancouver
UNITED KINGDOM
IRELAND
London
Paris
FRANCE
40°
UNITED STATES OF AMERICA
Ottawa
Montreal
Toronto
Chicago
New York
San Francisco
Denver
Washington D.C.
Philadelphia
Los Angeles
Azores
(Portugal)
PORTUGAL
SPAIN
Algiers
Rabat
MOROCCO
Bermuda
(U.K.)
Houston
Tropic of Cancer
Monterrey
Miami
THE BAHAMAS
Nassau
ATLANTIC
Laâyoune
ALGER
Hawai'ian Islands
(U.S.A.)
20°
MEXICO
Havana
CUBA
DOMINICAN REP.
HAITI
Puerto Rico
(U.S.A.)
WESTERN SAHARA
Mexico City
JAMAICA
BELIZE
MAURITANIA
Nouakchott
MALI
GUATEMALA
HONDURAS
CAPE VERDE
SENEGAL
Dakar
PACIFIC
EL SALVADOR
NICARAGUA
TRINIDAD AND TOBAGO
THE GAMBIA
COSTA RICA
San José
Caracas
Port of Spain
GUINEA-BISSAU
GUINEA
BUR.
Conakry
PANAMA
VENEZUELA
Paramaribo
SIERRA LEONE
Monrovia
C.D'I.
GH.
Bogotá
Georgetown
Cayenne
LIBERIA
Accra
COLOMBIA
FR. G.
Galapagos Islands
(Ecuador)
Equator
0°
Quito
ECUADOR
OCEAN
OCEAN
KIRIBATI
BRAZIL
Ascension
(U.K.)
PERU
French Polynesia
(France)
Lima
American Samoa
BOLIVIA
Brasília
St Helena
(U.K.)
La Paz
Sucre
Cook Islands
(New Zealand)
Tahiti
PARAGUAY
Rio de Janeiro
São Paulo
20°
Pitcairn Islands
(U.K.)
Asunción
Tropic of Capricorn
Easter Island
(Chile)
CHILE
ARGENTINA
Buenos Aires
URUGUAY
Santiago
Montevideo
Tristan da Cunha
(U.K.)
40°
Falkland Islands
(U.K.)
South Georgia and the South Sandwich Islands
(U.K.)
Bouvetøya
(Norway)
60°
Antarctic Circle
80°
A N T
160°
120°
80°
40°

Winkel Tripel Projection

ABBREVIATIONS

A.	ANDORRA	BE.	BENIN	C.A.R.	CENTRAL AFRICAN REPUBLIC	DEN.	DENMARK
AL.	ALBANIA	BEL.	BELGIUM			EQ.G.	EQUATORIAL GUINEA
ARM.	ARMENIA	B.H.	BOSNIA-HERZEGOVINA	C.D'I.	CÔTE D'IVOIRE	FR.G.	FRENCH GUIANA
AUS.	AUSTRIA	BN.	BAHRAIN	CR.	CROATIA	GEOR.	GEORGIA
AZ.	AZERBAIJAN	BUR.	BURKINA	CYP.	CYPRUS	GER.	GERMANY
B.	BURUNDI	CAM.	CAMEROON	CZ.R.	CZECH REPUBLIC	GH.	GHANA

40° 80° 120° 160°

Svalbard
(Norway)

Arctic Circle

60°

RUSSIAN FEDERATION

Magadan

FINLAND

ESTONIA
LATVIA
LITH.
BELARUS
Moscow

Yekaterinburg
Omsk
Novosibirsk

40°

Kiev
SLA.
UKRAINE
MO.
ROMANIA
BULGARIA
GEOR.
Astana
KAZAKHSTAN
MONGOLIA
Ulan Bator
Harbin

Ankara
AZ.
RM.
T'bilisi
UZBEK.
Dushanbe
KYR.
Beijing
Tianjin
N.KOREA
P'yŏngyang
JAPAN

GREECE
TURKEY
SYRIA
TURKM.
TAJIK.
CHINA
Seoul
S.KOREA
Tōkyō
Osaka

ipoli
CYP.
LEB.
ISR.
Baghdad
Amman
IRAQ
KU.
Tehrān
AFGHAN.
ISTAN
Kābul
Islamabad
New
Delhi
Lanzhou
Xi'an
Chengdu
Wuhan
Shanghai

PACIFIC

Tropic of Cancer

BYA
Cairo
JOR.
BN.
NEPAL
BHUTAN
Chongqing
T'aipei
20°

EGYPT
Riyadh
U.A.E.
Muscat
PAKISTAN
Karachi
Kathmandu
BANGLA-
DESH
Dhaka
MYANMAR
(BURMA)
Ha Nôi
Hong Kong
TAIWAN

OCEAN

SAUDI
ARABIA
OMAN
INDIA
Nay Pyi Taw
Vientiane

Northern
Mariana
Islands
(U.S.A.)

Khartoum
ERITREA
YEMEN
San'a'
Mumbai
Rangoon
THAILAND
Bangkok
CAM-
BODIA
Manila
MARSHALL
ISLANDS

HAD
Ndjamena
SUDAN
Addis
Ababa
Asmara
DJIBOUTI
Chennai
PHILIPPINES

C.A.R.
ETHIOPIA
SOMALIA
SRI
LANKA
BRUNEI
FEDERATED STATES
OF MICRONESIA

Bangui
UGANDA
MALDIVES
Kuala Lumpur
Putrajaya
MALAYSIA
PALAU

DEM.
REP.
OF THE
CONGO
KENYA
Nairobi
Mogadishu
SINGAPORE

hasa
Dodoma
SEYCHELLES
British Indian
Ocean Territory
(U.K.)
INDONESIA
Equator
0°

uanda
TANZANIA
COMOROS
INDIAN
Jakarta
PAPUA
NEW
GUINEA
NAURU
KIRIBATI

GOLA
Lilongwe
ZAMBIA
Antananarivo
MADAGASCAR
MAURITIUS
Christmas
Island
(Australia)
EAST
TIMOR
Port
Moresby
SOLOMON
ISLANDS
TUVALU

Harare
ZIMBABWE
Réunion
(France)
Cocos
Islands
(Australia)
Coral Sea
Islands
Territory
(Aust.)
SAMOA

NIBIA
BOTS-
WANA
MOZAMBIQUE
OCEAN
AUSTRALIA
VANUATU
New
Caledonia
(France)
FIJI

ndhoek
Maputo
Pretoria
SWAZILAND
TONGA

Maseru
LESOTHO
Tropic of Capricorn

REP. OF
SOUTH AFRICA
Perth
Brisbane
Norfolk
Island
(Australia)

Sydney
Canberra

French Southern
and Antarctic Lands
Wellington
NEW
ZEALAND
40°

Îles Kerguélen
(France)

60°

Antarctic Circle

CTICA
80°

40° 80° 120° 160°

1: 100 800 000

GUY.	GUYANA	LEB.	LEBANON	NI.	NIGERIA	SW.	SWITZERLAND
HUN.	HUNGARY	LITH.	LITHUA	Q.	QATAR	T.	TOGO
ISR.	ISRAEL	LUX.	LUXEMBOURG	R.	RWANDA	TAJIK.	TAJIKISTAN
JOR.	JORDAN	M.	MONTENEGRO	S.	SERBIA	TURKM.	TURKMENISTAN
K.	KOSOVO	MA.	MACEDONIA	SLA.	SLOVAKIA	U.A.E.	UNITED ARAB EMIRATES
KU.	KUWAIT	MO.	MOLDOVA	SL.	SLOVENIA	UZBEK.	UZBEKISTAN
KYR.	KYRGYZSTAN	NETH.	NETHERLANDS	SUR.	SURINAME		

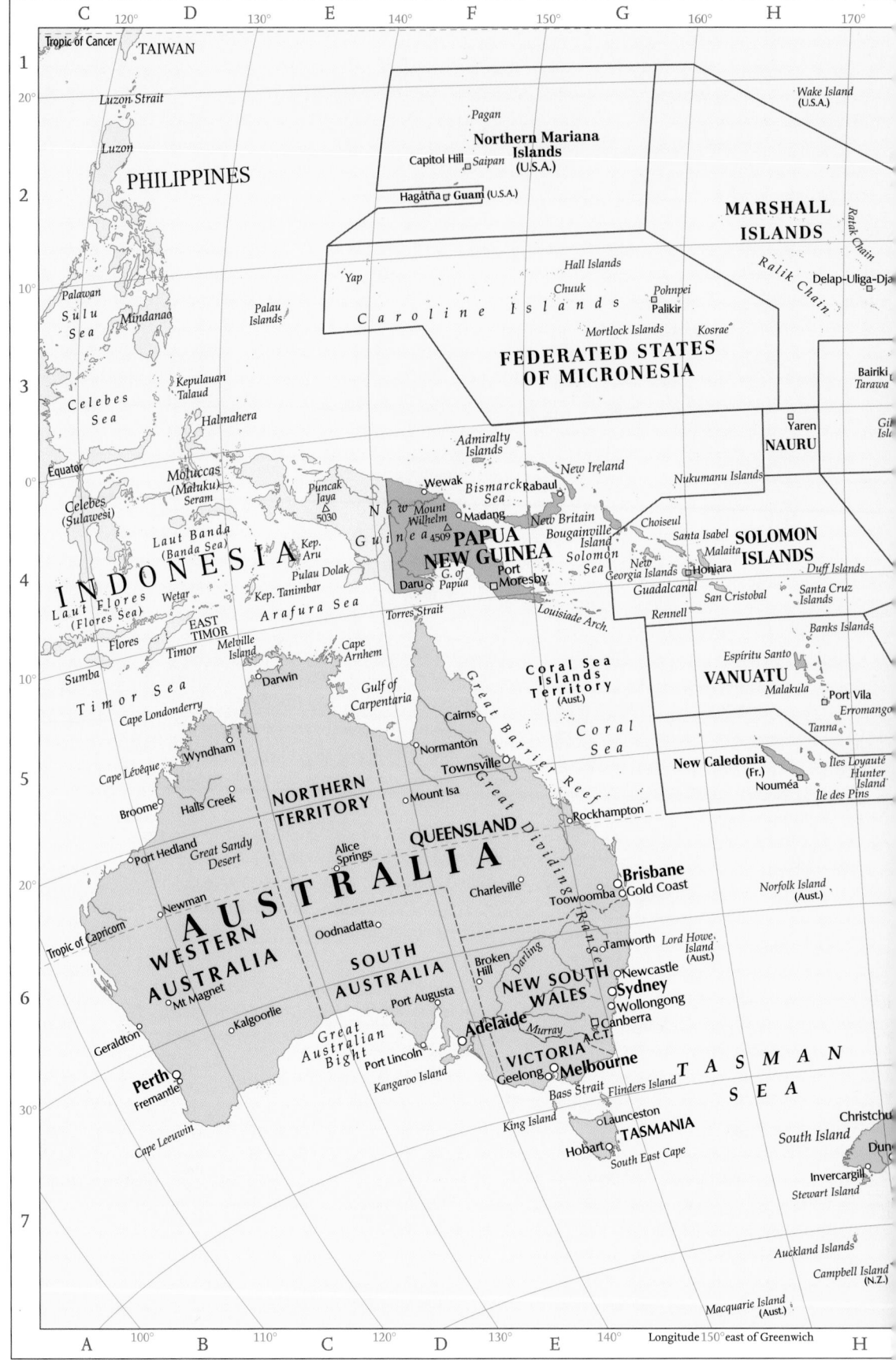

Tropic of Cancer
TAIWAN

Luzon Strait

Luzon

PHILIPPINES

Palawan

Sulu
Sea

Mindanao

Kepulauan
Talaud

Palau
Islands

Celebes
Sea

Halmahera

Pagan

Northern Mariana
Islands
(U.S.A.)

Capitol Hill ▫ Saipan

Hagåtña ▫ Guam (U.S.A.)

Yap

Hall Islands

Chuuk

Pohnpei
▫ Palikir

Caroline Islands

Mortlock Islands

Kosrae

FEDERATED STATES
OF MICRONESIA

MARSHALL
ISLANDS

Ratak Chain

Ralik Chain

Delap-Uliga-Dja

Bairiki
Tarawa

Gil
Isle

Equator

Celebes
(Sulawesi)

Moluccas
(Maluku)
Seram

Laut Banda
(Banda Sea)

Kep.
Aru

Pulau Dolak

Kep. Tanimbar

Puncak
Jaya
△
5030

Admiralty
Islands

New Ireland

Wewak
Bismarck
Sea

Rabaul

N
e
w

Mount
Wilhelm
△
4509

Madang

New Britain

Bougainville
Island

Solomon
Sea

Nukumanu Islands

Choiseul

Santa Isabel

New
Georgia Islands

Malaita
Honiara

SOLOMON
ISLANDS

Duff Islands

Yaren

NAURU

INDONESIA

Laut Flores
(Flores Sea)

Wetar

EAST
TIMOR

Timor

Flores

Sumba

Cape
Londonderry

Timor Sea

Melville
Island

Darwin

Cape
Arnhem

Gulf of
Carpentaria

G u i n e a

PAPUA
NEW GUINEA

Daru ○
G. of
Papua

Port
Moresby

Torres Strait

Louisiade Arch.

Guadalcanal

San Cristobal

Rennell

Coral Sea
Islands
Territory
(Aust.)

Santa Cruz
Islands

Banks Islands

Espíritu Santo

VANUATU

Malakula

Port Vila

Erromango

Cairns

Normanton

Townsville

Great Barrier Reef

Coral
Sea

Tanna

New Caledonia
(Fr.)

Nouméa

Îles Loyauté
Hunter
Island
Île des Pins

Cape Léveque

Broome

Wyndham

Halls Creek

NORTHERN
TERRITORY

Mount Isa

Rockhampton

Norfolk Island
(Aust.)

Port Hedland

Great Sandy
Desert

Newman

Geraldton

Mt Magnet ○

Kalgoorlie

A U S T R A L I A

Alice
Springs

WESTERN
AUSTRALIA

Oodnadatta

SOUTH
AUSTRALIA

Great
Australian
Bight

Port Lincoln

QUEENSLAND

Charleville

Toowoomba

Great Dividing

Brisbane
Gold Coast

Broken
Hill

Port Augusta

Tropic of Capricorn

Tamworth
Lord Howe
Island
(Aust.)

Darling

NEW SOUTH
WALES

Ra

Newcastle

Sydney
Wollongong

Range

Murray

Canberra
A.C.T.

VICTORIA

Geelong

Melbourne

Kangaroo Island

Adelaide

Perth

Fremantle

Cape Leeuwin

Bass Strait
Flinders Island

King Island

Hobart

TASMANIA

South East Cape

Launceston

T A S M A N

S E A

Christchu

South Island

Dune

Invercargill

Stewart Island

Auckland Islands

Campbell Island
(N.Z.)

Macquarie Island
(Aust.)

Longitude 150° east of Greenwich

Lambert Azimuthal Equal Area Projection

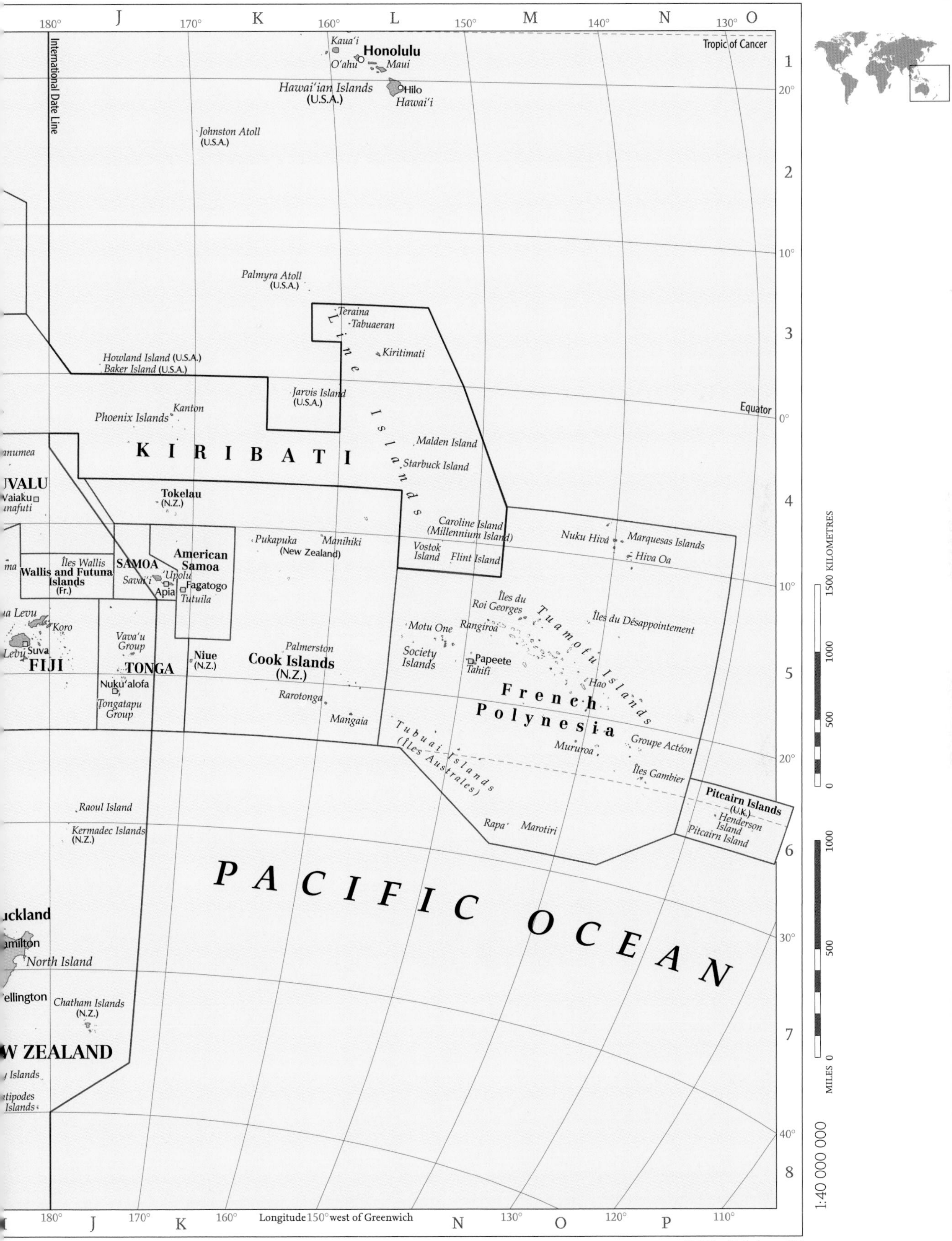

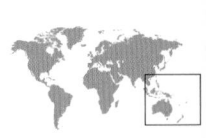

180°

International Date Line

Tropic of Cancer

Kaua'i
Honolulu
O'ahu   *Maui*

Hawai'ian Islands
(U.S.A.)
Hilo
Hawai'i

20°

Johnston Atoll
(U.S.A.)

1

2

10°

Palmyra Atoll
(U.S.A.)

3

Teraina
Tabuaeran

L
i
n
e

I
s
l
a
n
d
s

Kiritimati

Howland Island (U.S.A.)
Baker Island (U.S.A.)

Jarvis Island
(U.S.A.)

Equator

0°

nanumea

Phoenix Islands
Kanton

K I R I B A T I

Malden Island

Starbuck Island

UVALU
Vaiaku
nafuti

Tokelau
(N.Z.)

4

Caroline Island
(Millennium Island)

Nuku Hiva
Marquesas Islands

Hiva Oa

Pukapuka
Manihiki
(New Zealand)

Vostok
Island *Flint Island*

ma
Îles Wallis
Wallis and Futuna
Islands
(Fr.)

SAMOA
Savai'i
'Upolu
Apia

American
Samoa
Fagatogo
Tutuila

10°

Îles du
Roi Georges

Tuamotu Islands

Îles du Désappointement

a Levu
Koro
Levu *Suva*
FIJI

Vava'u
Group

Niue
(N.Z.)

Cook Islands
(N.Z.)

Motu One

Rangiroa

Society
Islands
Papeete
Tahiti

Hao

5

TONGA
Nuku'alofa

Tongatapu
Group

Palmerston

Rarotonga

Mangaia

F r e n c h
P o l y n e s i a

Mururoa

Groupe Actéon

20°

T u b u a i I s l a n d s
(Îles Australes)

Îles Gambier

Pitcairn Islands
(U.K.)

Raoul Island

Rapa *Marotiri*

Henderson
Island
Pitcairn Island

6

Kermadec Islands
(N.Z.)

P A C I F I C

uckland
amilton
North Island

O C E A N

30°

ellington
Chatham Islands
(N.Z.)

NW ZEALAND

7

Islands

ntipodes
Islands

40°

8

1:40 000 000

1500 KILOMETRES

1000

500

0

1000

500

0
MILES

© Collins Bartholomew Ltd

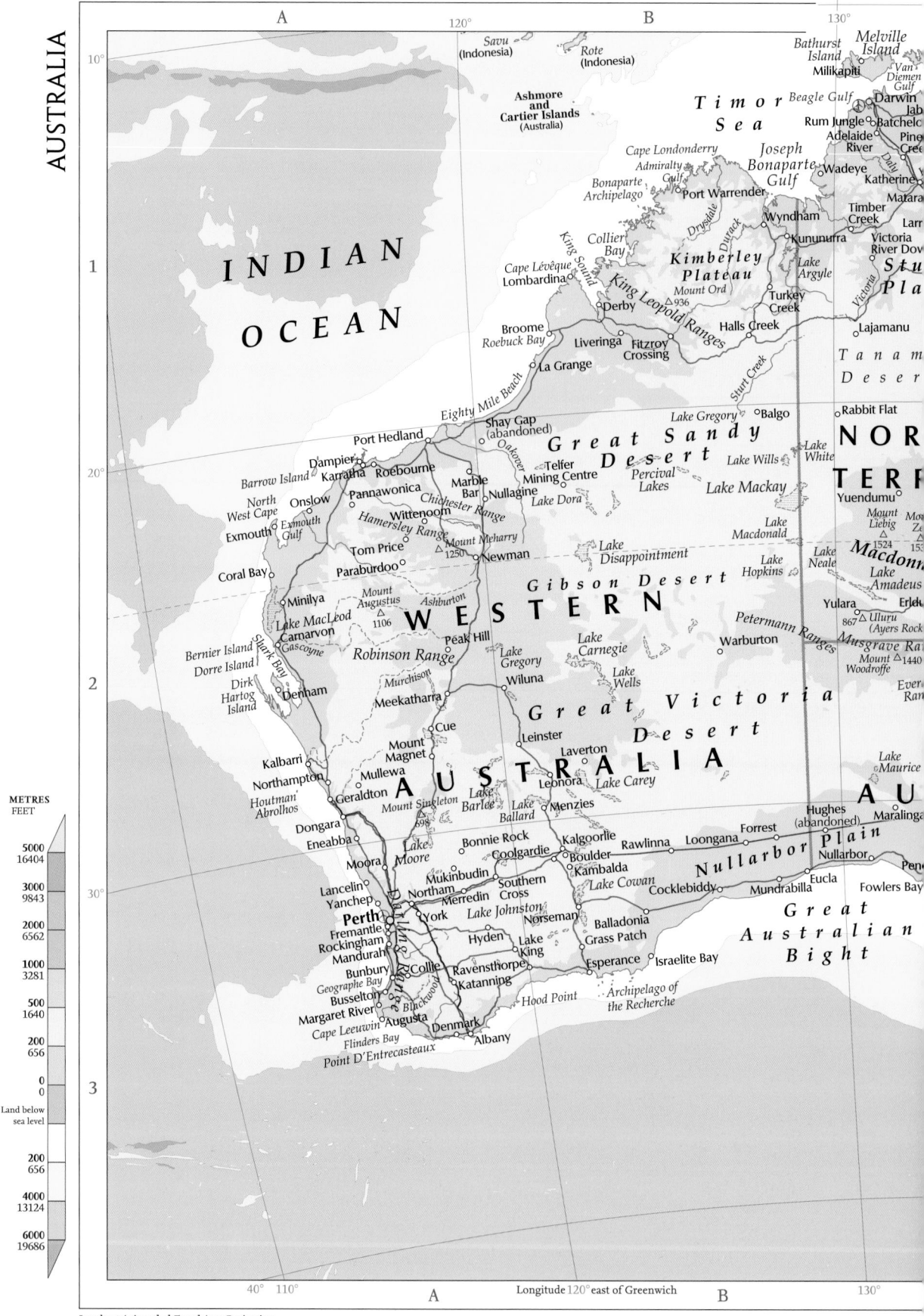

INDIAN

OCEAN

Savu
(Indonesia)
Rote
(Indonesia)

**Ashmore
and
Cartier Islands**
(Australia)

*T i m o r
S e a*

*Bathurst
Island*
Milikapiti
*Melville
Island*
*Van
Diemen
Gulf*
Beagle Gulf
Darwin
Rum Jungle
Batchelo
Adelaide
River
Pine
Cree

Cape Londonderry
*Admiralty
Gulf*
Port Warrender
*Bonaparte
Archipelago*
*Joseph
Bonaparte
Gulf*
Wadeye
Katherine
Matara

Wyndham
Kununurra
*Lake
Argyle*
Timber
Creek
Larr
Victoria
River Dov

Cape Lévêque
Lombardina
King Leopold Ranges
*Kimberley
Plateau*
Mount Ord
△936
Turkey
Creek
*Stu
Pla*

*Collier
Bay*
Derby
Halls Creek
Lajamanu

Broome
Roebuck Bay
Liveringa
Fitzroy
Crossing
Sturt Creek
*T a n a m
D e s e r*

La Grange

Eighty Mile Beach
Shay Gap
(abandoned)
Lake Gregory
Balgo
Rabbit Flat
N O R

Port Hedland
*G r e a t S a n d y
D e s e r t*
Lake Wills
*Lake
White*
T E R R

Dampier
Karratha
Roebourne
Marble
Bar
Nullagine
Telfer
Mining Centre
Percival
Lakes
Lake Mackay
Yuendumu

Barrow Island
Onslow
Pannawonica
Chichester Range
Lake Dora
*Lake
Macdonald*
*Mount
Liebig*
△1524
Mo
Ze
15

*North
West Cape*
Wittenoom
Hamersley Range
Macdonn

Exmouth
*Exmouth
Gulf*
Tom Price
Mount Meharry
△1250
Newman
*Lake
Disappointment*
*Lake
Neale*
*Lake
Amadeus*

Coral Bay
Paraburdoo
G i b s o n D e s e r t
*Lake
Hopkins*
Yulara
Erld
Uluru
△867
(Ayers Rock)

Minilya
*Mount
Augustus*
△1106
W E S T E R N
*Lake
Carnegie*
Petermann Ranges
Warburton
Musgrave Ra
Mount
△1440
Woodroffe

Lake MacLeod
Carnarvon
Gascoyne
Robinson Range
Peak Hill
*Lake
Gregory*
*Ever
Ran*

Bernier Island
Dorre Island
Shark Bay
Murchison
Meekatharra
Wiluna
*Lake
Wells*

*Dirk
Hartog
Island*
Denham
G r e a t V i c t o r i a

Cue
A U S T R A L I A
Leinster
D e s e r t
*Lake
Maurice*

Kalbarri
Mount
Magnet
Mullewa
Laverton
Leonora
Lake Carey
A U

Northampton
*Houtman
Abrolhos*
Geraldton
Mount Singleton
△698
*Lake
Barlee*
*Lake
Ballard*
Menzies
Hughes
(abandoned)
Maralinga

Dongara
Eneabba
Bonnie Rock
Coolgardie
Kalgoorlie
Boulder
Rawlinna
Loongana
Forrest
N u l l a r b o r P l a i n
Nullarbor
Pen

Moora
*Lake
Moore*
Mukinbudin
Southern
Cross
Kambalda
Lake Cowan
Cocklebiddy
Mundrabilla
Eucla
Fowlers Bay

Lancelin
Yanchep
Northam
Merredin
Lake Johnston
Norseman
*G r e a t
A u s t r a l i a n
B i g h t*

Perth
York
Hyden
*Lake
King*
Balladonia
Grass Patch

Fremantle
Rockingham
Mandurah
Collie
Ravensthorpe
Esperance
Israelite Bay

Bunbury
Geographe Bay
Busselton
Blackwood
Katanning
Hood Point
*Archipelago of
the Recherche*

Margaret River
Augusta
Denmark

Cape Leeuwin
Flinders Bay
Albany

Point D'Entrecasteaux

A 120° B 130°

10°

1

20°

2

30°

3

40° 110° A Longitude 120° east of Greenwich B 130°

Lambert Azimuthal Equal Area Projection

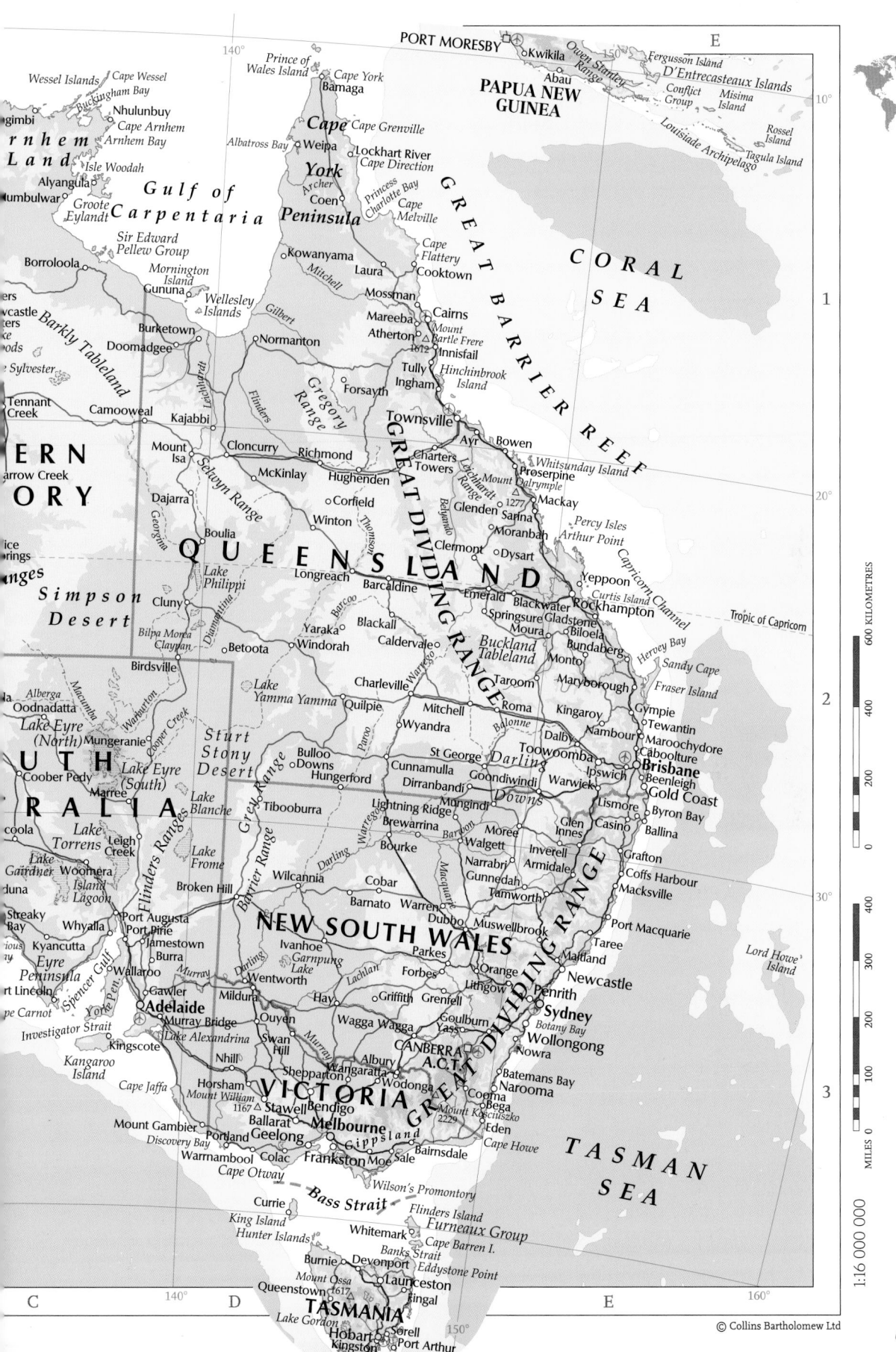

A · 140° · B

Macumba · Warburton · Cooper Creek · Noccundra · Thargomindah

Mungeranie · Innamincka · Grey Range · Bulloo

Tirari Desert · Moomba · Sturt Stony Desert · Bulloo Downs · QUE

Lake Eyre (North) · Etadunna · Caryapundy Swamp · Hungerford

Lake Blanche · Tilcha (abandoned) · Mount Sturt 427 △ · Tibooburra · Milparinka · Wanaaring · Paroo

William Creek · Lake Eyre (South) · Lake Callabonna · Hawkers Gate

Marree · Moolawatana

Millers Creek · S O U T H · 30°

Lyndhurst · Leigh Creek · Balcanoona · Packsaddle · Tongo · Darling

Parakylia · Roxby Downs · A U S T R A L I A · Lake Frome · White Cliffs · Momba · Tilpa

Beltana · Parachilna · Mootwingee

Wirraminna · Woomera · Lake Torrens · Frome Downs · Mount Robe 486 △ · Euriowie · Wilcannia

Island Lagoon · Pernatty Lagoon · Curnamona · Broken Hill · Stephens Creek · N E W

Woocalla · Hawker · Cockburn · Mingary

Lake Gairdner · Lake Macfarlane · Cradock · Olary · Menindee Lake · Menindee · Mount Man

Gawler Ranges · Quorn · Mannahill · Tandou Lake · Darnick · Ivanh

Port Augusta · Stirling North · Yunta · Coombah · 2

Nonning · Mount Remarkable △ 969 · Wilmington · Orroroo · Paratoo · Popiltah · Pooncarie · Mossgiel

Buckleboo · Iron Knob · Wirrabara · Peterborough · Terowie · Oakbank · Garnpung Lake · Boo

Kimba · Whyalla · Jamestown · Canopus · Burtundy · Hatfield

Kyancutta · Balumbah · Port Pirie · Gladstone · Darling · Lake Victoria · Oxley

Lock · Cleve · Crystal Brook · Burra · Wentworth · Murrumbidgee

Sheringa · Eyre Peninsula · Cowell · Snowtown · Clare · Morgan · Murray · Renmark · R

Ungarra · Arno Bay · Wallaroo · Blyth · Waikerie · Merbein · Mildura · Booroorba

Cockaleechie · Kadina · Port Wakefield · Balaklava · Barmera · Berri · Red Cliffs · Robinvale · Balranald · Moulam

Tumby Bay · Moonta · Maitland · Kapunda · Loxton · Werrimull · Hattah · Tooleybuc

Port Lincoln · Minlaton · Ardrossan · Nuriootpa · Alawoona · Swan Hill · Barham

Coffin Bay · Gambier Islands · Gawler · Mannum · Mindarie · Ouyen · Sea Lake · Denil

Cape Carnot · 35° · York Peninsula · Yorketown · Adelaide · Mount Barker · Murray Bridge · Pinnaroo · Murrayville · Underbool · Lake Tyrrell · Ultima · Murray · Cohu

Marion Bay · Willunga · Tailem Bend · Lameroo · Hopetoun · Kerang · Echuc

Investigator Strait · Goolwa · Lake Alexandrina · Coonalpyn · Lake Hindmarsh · Birchip · Charlton · Rochester

Cape Borda · Kingscote · Victor Harbor · Meningie · Tintinara · Warracknabeal · Wycheproof · Echuc

Penneshaw · Backstairs Passage · Younghusband Peninsula · Keith · Nhill · Donald · Dimboola · Bendigo

Cape du Couedic · Kangaroo Island · Bordertown · Kaniva · V I C T

Padthaway · Goroke · Horsham · St Arnaud · Castlemaine

Lacepede Bay · Edenhope · Stawell · Avoca · Kyneton

Kingston South East · Naracoorte · Mount William △ 1167 · Ararat · Daylesford · Ma

Cape Jaffa · Glenelg · Balmoral · The Grampians · Beaufort · Skipton · Ballarat · Sunbu

Robe · Lake George · Penola · Coleraine · Bacchus Marsh · Melton

Beachport · Millicent · Casterton · Hamilton · Wyndham · Werribe

Mount Gambier · Lake Corangamite · Geelong · Queenscliff

Port MacDonnell · Heywood · Mortlake · Camperdown · Terang · Colac · Torq · Angles

Discovery Bay · Portland · Warrnambool · Lorne

Cape Nelson · Port Fairy · Port Campbell · Apollo Bay · Cape Otway

135° · A · Longitude 140° east of Greenwich · B

METRES
FEET

5000 / 16404
3000 / 9843
2000 / 6562
1000 / 3281
500 / 1640
200 / 656
0 / 0
Land below sea level
200 / 656
4000 / 13124
6000 / 19686

3

Conic Equidistant Projection

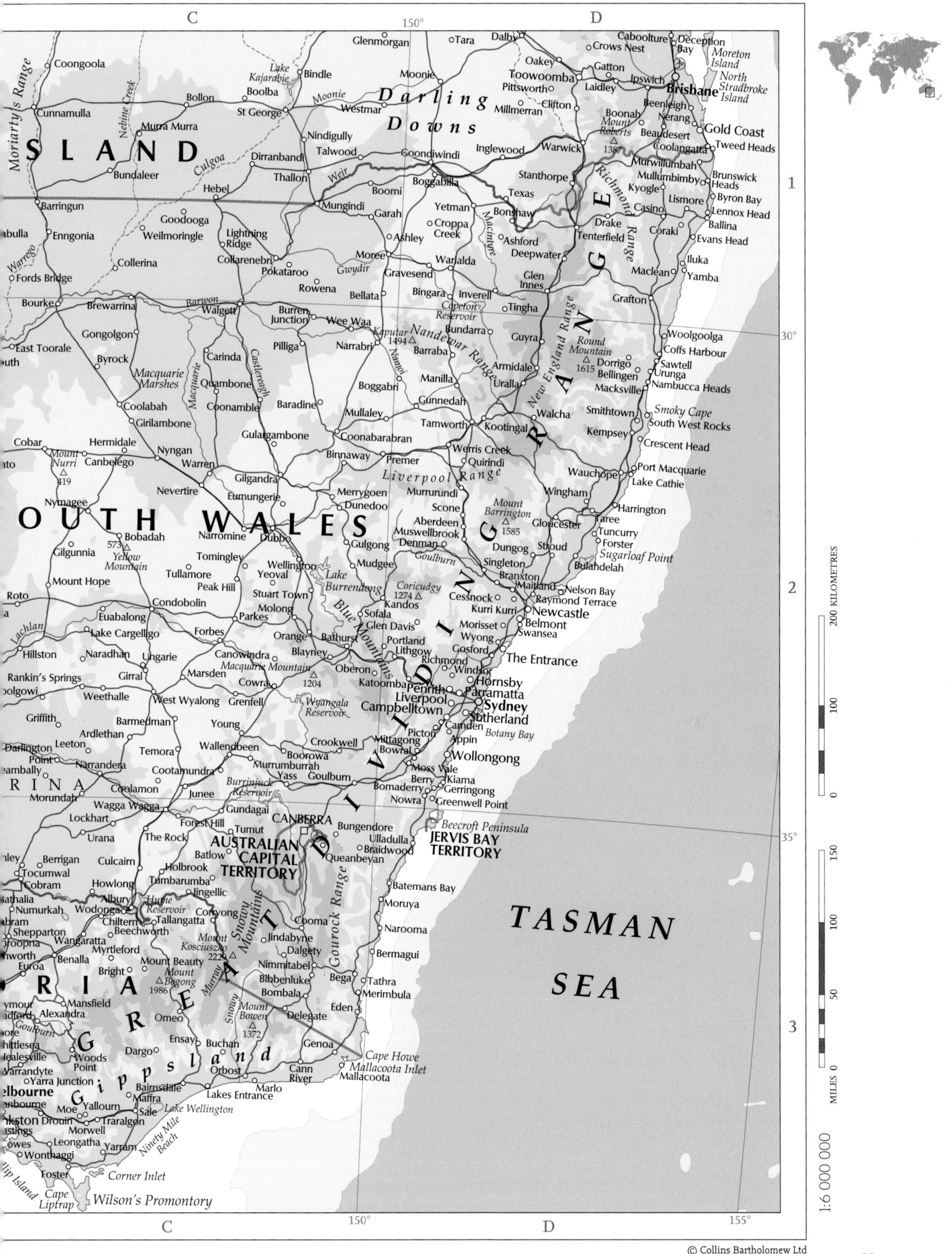

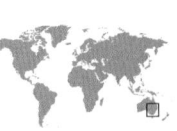

C 150° D

Coongoola · Glenmorgan · Tara · Dalby · Oakey · Crows Nest · Caboolture · Deception Bay · Moreton Island

SLAND · Cunnamulla · Bollon · Boolba · Bindle · Moonie · Toowoomba · Pittsworth · Clifton · Millmerran · Gatton · Laidley · Ipswich · Brisbane · North Stradbroke Island

Murra Murra · St George · Westmar · Darling Downs · Warwick · Boonah · Beaudesert · Beenleigh · Nerang · Gold Coast

Bundaleer · Dirranbandi · Talwood · Goondiwindi · Inglewood · Stanthorpe · Mount Roberts 1387 · Murwillumbah · Coolangatta · Tweed Heads

Barringun · Hebel · Mungindi · Boomi · Texas · Brunswick Heads · Mullumbimby · Kyogle · Byron Bay

Enngonia · Goodooga · Weilmoringle · Collarenebri · Garah · Yetman · Croppa Creek · Bonshaw · Ashford · Deepwater · Drake · Casino · Lismore · Lennox Head · Evans Head

Fords Bridge · Lightning Ridge · Pokataroo · Ashley · Warialda · Tenterfield · Coraki · Ballina · Iluka · Yamba

Bourke · Brewarrina · Collerina · Rowena · Moree · Gravesend · Bingara · Inverell · Glen Innes · Maclean · Grafton

Walgett · Bellata · Burren Junction · Wee Waa · Narrabri · Barraba · Tingha · Woolgoolga · Coffs Harbour

East Toorale · Byrock · Gongolgon · Carinda · Pilliga · Bundarra · Guyra · Round Mountain 1615 · Dorrigo · Sawtell

Macquarie Marshes · Coolabah · Quambone · Coonamble · Boggabri · Manilla · Armidale · Uralla · Bellingen · Urunga · Nambucca Heads

Cobar · Nyngan · Baradine · Mullaley · Gunnedah · Walcha · Macksville · Smithtown · Smoky Cape · South West Rocks

Hermidale · Warren · Coonabarabran · Tamworth · Kootingal · Kempsey · Crescent Head

Mount Nurri 419 · Canbelego · Gilgandra · Binnaway · Premer · Werris Creek · Quirindi · Wauchope · Port Macquarie · Lake Cathie

Nymagee · Nevertire · Eumungerie · Merrygoen · Murrurundi · Wingham · Harrington

Bobadah · Narromine · Dunedoo · Scone · Aberdeen · Mount Barrington 1585 · Gloucester · Taree · Tuncurry · Forster

Gilgunnia · Yellow Mountain 573 · Dubbo · Gulgong · Muswellbrook · Denman · Dungog · Stroud · Sugarloaf Point

Mount Hope · Tomingley · Wellington · Mudgee · Singleton · Branxton · Bulahdelah

Roto · Euabalong · Yeoval · Stuart Town · Lake Burrendong · Coricudgy 1274 · Cessnock · Maitland · Nelson Bay

Lake Cargelligo · Molong · Sofala · Glen Davis · Kandos · Kurri Kurri · Raymond Terrace · Belmont · Swansea

Hillston · Condobolin · Forbes · Parkes · Orange · Bathurst · Portland · Lithgow · Morisset · Wyong · Newcastle

Naradhan · Ungarie · Canowindra · Blayney · Oberon · Gosford · The Entrance

Rankin's Springs · Girral · Marsden · Cowra · Macquarie Mountain 1204 · Katoomba · Windsor · Richmond · Hornsby

Griffith · Weethalle · West Wyalong · Grenfell · Wyangala Reservoir · Penrith · Parramatta · Sydney

Darlington Point · Barmedman · Young · Crookwell · Liverpool · Campbelltown · Sutherland · Botany Bay

Leeton · Ardlethan · Temora · Wallendbeen · Boorowa · Mittagong · Picton · Camden · Appin · Wollongong

Narrandera · Cootamundra · Murrumburrah · Yass · Goulburn · Bowral · Kiama

Coleambally · Junee · Burrinjuck Reservoir · Moss Vale · Berry · Gerringong

Morundah · Wagga Wagga · Gundagai · Bomaderry · Nowra · Greenwell Point

RINA · Lockhart · Forest Hill · Tumut · Canberra · Bungendore · Beecroft Peninsula · Jervis Bay Territory

Urana · The Rock · Batlow · Australian Capital Territory · Ulladulla · Braidwood · Queanbeyan

Berrigan · Culcairn · Holbrook · Tumbarumba · Jingellic · Batemans Bay

Tocumwal · Cobram · Howlong · Albury · Hume Reservoir · Corryong · Tallangatta · Snowy Mountains · Gourock Range · Cooma · Moruya

Mathura · Numurkah · Wodonga · Chiltern · Beechworth · Mount Kosciuszko 2229 · Jindabyne · Dalgety · Narooma

Shepparton · Wangaratta · Myrtleford · Bright · Mount Beauty · Nimmitabel · Bermagui

Benalla · Mount Bogong 1986 · Omeo · Bibbenluke · Bega · Tathra · Merimbula

Euroa · Mansfield · Dargo · Bombala · Eden · Tasman Sea

Alexandra · Woods Point · Ensay · Buchan · Mount Bowen 1372 · Delegate · Genoa

Healesville · Dargo · Orbost · Cann River · Cape Howe · Mallacoota Inlet · Mallacoota

Warrandyte · Yarra Junction · Gippsland · Bairnsdale · Marlo

Melbourne · Drouin · Maffra · Sale · Lakes Entrance · Lake Wellington

Hastings · Morwell · Yallourn · Traralgon · Ninety Mile Beach

Cowes · Leongatha · Yarram · Corner Inlet

Foster · Cape Liptrap · Wilson's Promontory

C 150° D 155°

200 KILOMETRES
100
0

150
100
50
MILES 0

1:6 000 000

© Collins Bartholomew Ltd

69

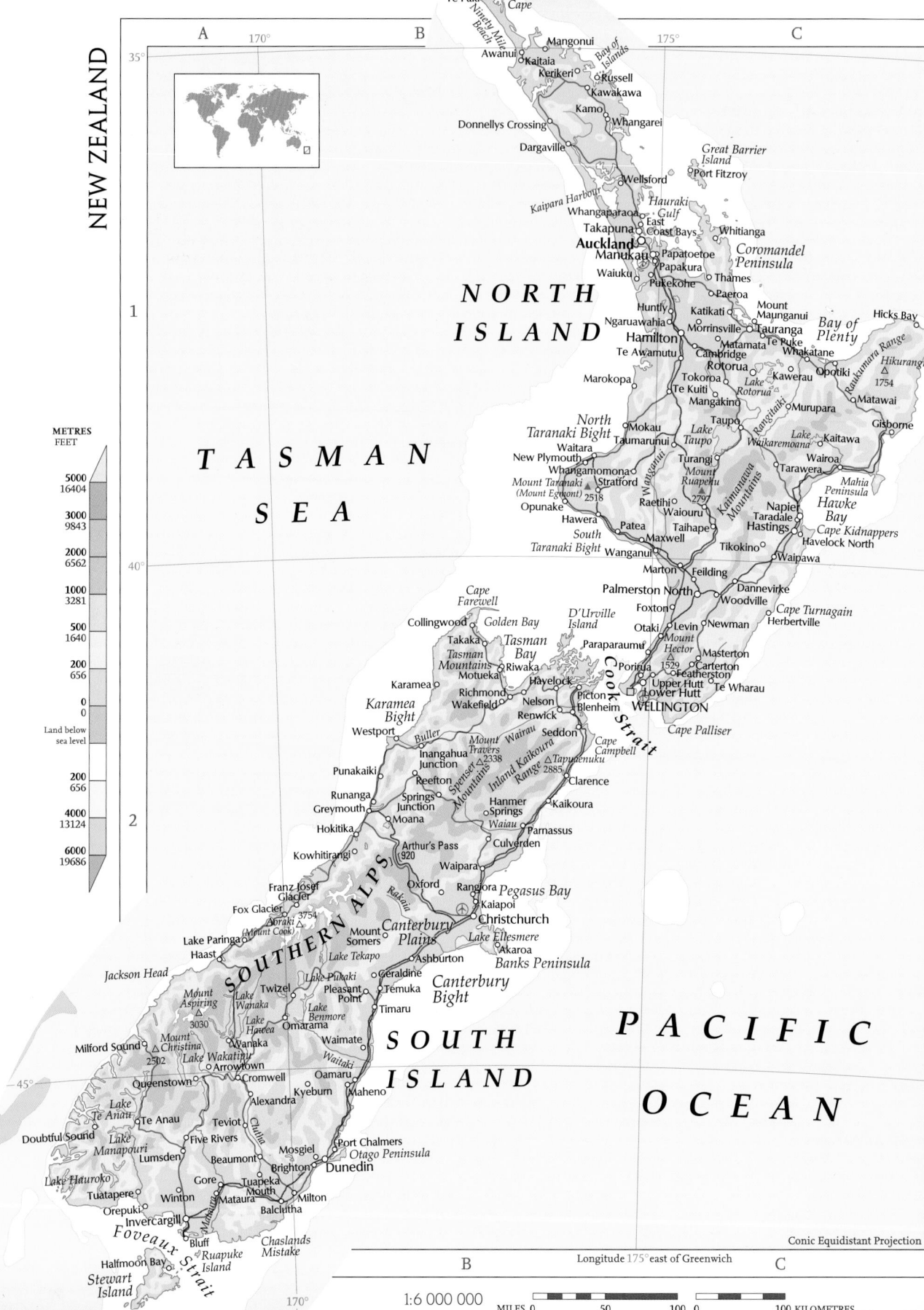

NEW ZEALAND

A 170° B 175° C

35°

Te Paki North
Cape
Ninety Mile Beach
Mangonui
Awanui Kaitaia Bay of
Kerikeri Islands
Russell
Kawakawa
Kamo
Donnellys Crossing Whangarei
Dargaville
Great Barrier
Island
Wellsford Port Fitzroy
Whangaparaoa Hauraki
Kaipara Harbour East Gulf
Takapuna Coast Bays Whitianga
Auckland Coromandel
Manukau Papatoetoe Peninsula
Waiuku Papakura Thames
Pukekohe Paeroa
Huntly Mount
Katikati Maunganui
NORTH Ngaruawahia Morrinsville Tauranga Bay of
Hamilton Te Puke Plenty Hicks Bay
Te Awamutu Cambridge Matamata Whakatane
ISLAND Marokopa Rotorua Kawerau Opotiki Rangaunu Range
Te Kuiti Tokoroa Hikurangi
Mangakino Lake Murupara 1754
North Taupo Rotorua Matawai
Taranaki Bight Mokau Taumarunui Rangitaiki Gisborne
New Plymouth Whangamomona Turangi Lake Waikaremoana Kaitawa
Waitara Stratford Mount Wairoa
Mount Taranaki Ruapehu Tarawera Mahia
(Mount Egmont) 2518 279 Waiouru Kaimanawa Peninsula
Opunake Raetihi Napier Hawke
Hawera Patea Taihape Taradale Bay
Maxwell Tikokino Hastings Cape Kidnappers
South Wanganui Havelock North
Taranaki Bight Marton Waipawa
Feilding Dannevirke
40° Palmerston North Woodville
Cape Foxton Cape Turnagain
Farewell D'Urville Herbertville
Collingwood Golden Bay Island Otaki Levin Newman
Takaka Tasman Paraparaumu Mount
Tasman Bay Porirua Hector Masterton
Mountains Motueka Riwaka Upper Hutt 1529 Carterton
Karamea Hayelock Lower Hutt Featherston
Richmond Nelson Picton WELLINGTON Te Wharau
Karamea Wakefield Renwick Blenheim
Bight Westport Seddon Cape Palliser
Buller Wairau Cape
Punakaiki Mount Campbell
Inangahua Travers Tapuaenuku
Junction Spenser 2338 Inland Kaikoura 2885
Reefton Mountains Range Clarence
Runanga Springs Kaikoura
Greymouth Junction Hanmer Parnassus
Moana Springs
Hokitika Waiau
Kowhitirangi Arthur's Pass Culverden
920 Waipara
Oxford Rangiora Pegasus Bay
Franz Josef Rakaia Kaiapoi
Glacier SOUTHERN Christchurch
Fox Glacier ALPS Mount Canterbury
Aoraki 3754 Somers Plains
Lake Paringa (Mount Cook) Ashburton Lake Ellesmere
Haast Lake Tekapo Akaroa
Geraldine Banks Peninsula
Jackson Head Twizel Pleasant Temuka
Mount Lake Pukaki Point Canterbury
Aspiring Lake Timaru Bight
3030 Wanaka Lake
Milford Sound Benmore Waimate
Mount Omarama
Christina Lake Wanaka Oamaru
2502 Hawea Arrowtown SOUTH
Lake Wakatipu Cromwell Waitaki Maheno
Queenstown Kyeburn
Alexandra ISLAND
Lake Te Anau Maheno
Te Anau Teviot Clutha PACIFIC
45° Five Rivers Port Chalmers
Doubtful Sound Lumsden Beaumont Mosgiel Otago Peninsula OCEAN
Lake Brighton Dunedin
Manapouri Gore Milton
Lake Hauroko Tuatapere Winton Mataura Tuapeka
Orepuki Mouth
Invercargill Balclutha
Bluff Chaslands
Foveaux Strait Ruapuke Mistake
Halfmoon Bay Island
Stewart
Island

TASMAN

SEA

METRES
FEET

5000
16404

3000
9843

2000
6562

1000
3281

500
1640

200
656

0
0

Land below
sea level

200
656

4000
13124

6000
19686

B Longitude 175° east of Greenwich C

Conic Equidistant Projection

1:6 000 000 MILES 0 50 100 0 100 KILOMETRES

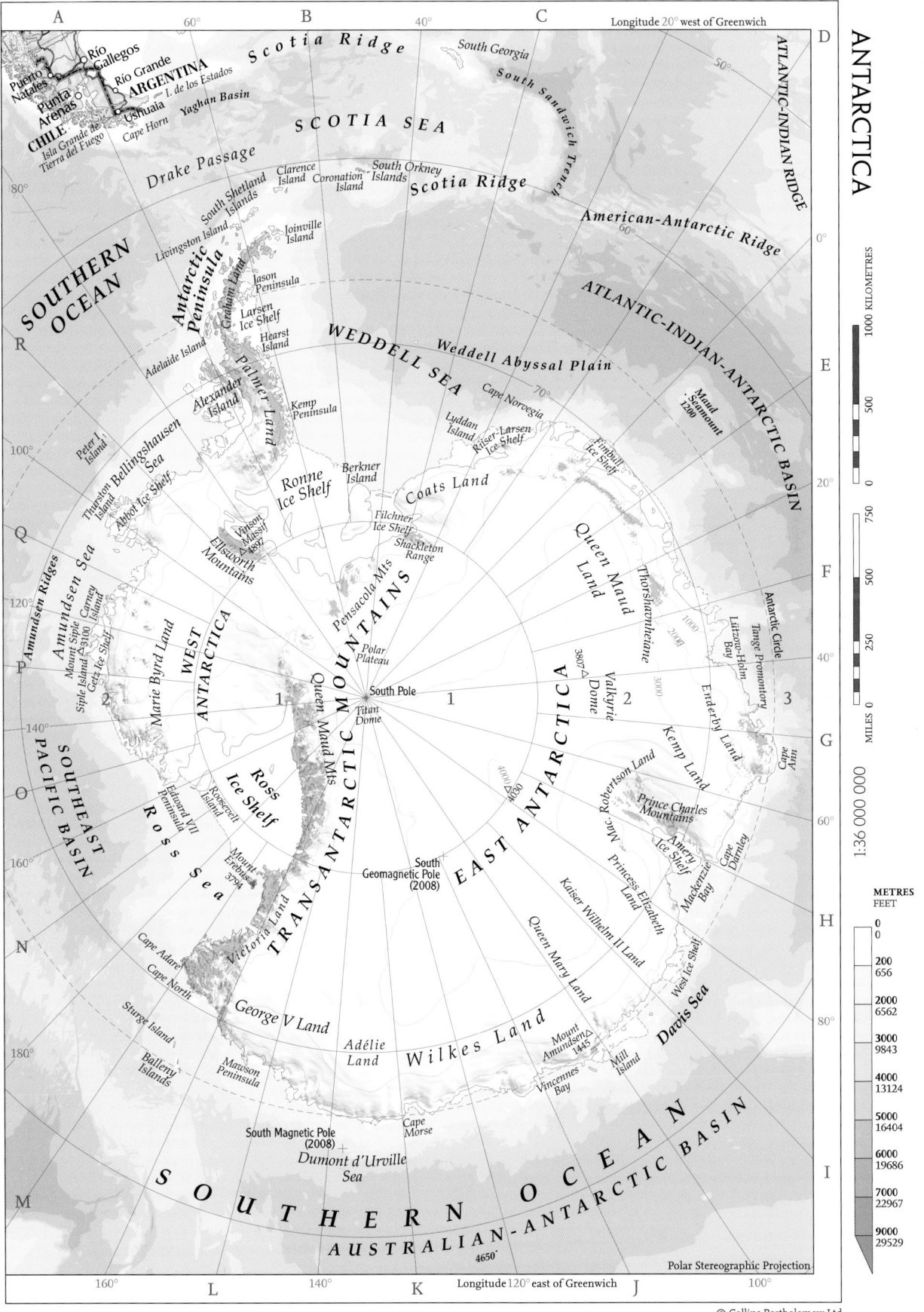

ANTARCTICA

A   60°   B   40°   C   Longitude 20° west of Greenwich   D

50°

ATLANTIC-INDIAN RIDGE

Scotia Ridge
South Georgia
South Sandwich Trench
SCOTIA SEA
60°
American-Antarctic Ridge
E
Drake Passage
Clarence Island
Coronation Island
South Orkney Islands
Scotia Ridge
ATLANTIC-INDIAN-ANTARCTIC BASIN
South Shetland Islands
Joinville Island
SOUTHERN OCEAN
Livingston Island
Antarctic Peninsula
Jason Peninsula
Graham Land
Larsen Ice Shelf
Hearst Island
WEDDELL SEA
Weddell Abyssal Plain
Cape Norvegia
70°
Maud Seamount 1200
R
Adelaide Island
Palmer Land
Kemp Peninsula
Lyddan Island
Riiser-Larsen Ice Shelf
Fimbul Ice Shelf
Alexander Island
Peter I Island
Bellingshausen Sea
Ronne Ice Shelf
Berkner Island
Coats Land
20°
Q
Thurston Island
Abbot Ice Shelf
Filchner Ice Shelf
Shackleton Range
Queen Maud Land
Thorshavnheiane
Antarctic Circle
Amundsen Ridges
Vinson Massif 4897
Ellsworth Mountains
Pensacola Mts
1000
2000
Tange Promontory
Lützow-Holm Bay
F
Amundsen Sea
Mount Siple Carney Island
WEST ANTARCTICA
TRANSANTARCTIC MOUNTAINS
Polar Plateau
3000
40°
Siple Island 3110
Getz Ice Shelf
Marie Byrd Land
Queen Maud Mts
South Pole
1
Valkyrie Dome 3807
Enderby Land
Cape Ann
P
2
1
Titan Dome
2
3807
Kemp Land
3
G
SOUTHEAST PACIFIC BASIN
Edward VII Peninsula
Ross Ice Shelf
EAST ANTARCTICA
Mac. Robertson Land
Prince Charles Mountains
Amery Ice Shelf
Cape Darnley
O
Roosevelt Island
Ross Sea
4000
Princess Elizabeth Land
Mackenzie Bay
Mount Erebus 3794
South Geomagnetic Pole (2008)
Kaiser Wilhelm II Land
West Ice Shelf
H
Victoria Land
Cape Adare
Queen Mary Land
Davis Sea
N
Cape North
George V Land
Sturge Island
Adélie Land
Wilkes Land
Mount Amundsen 1445
Mill Island
80°
Balleny Islands
Mawson Peninsula
Vincennes Bay
I
South Magnetic Pole (2008)
Cape Morse
SOUTHERN OCEAN
AUSTRALIAN-ANTARCTIC BASIN
Dumont d'Urville Sea
M
4650
Polar Stereographic Projection
160°   L   140°   K   Longitude 120° east of Greenwich   J   100°

80°
100°
140°
120°

© Collins Bartholomew Ltd

1000 KILOMETRES
500
0

750
500
250
MILES 0

1:36 000 000

METRES FEET
0 / 0
200 / 656
2000 / 6562
3000 / 9843
4000 / 13124
5000 / 16404
6000 / 19686
7000 / 22967
9000 / 29529

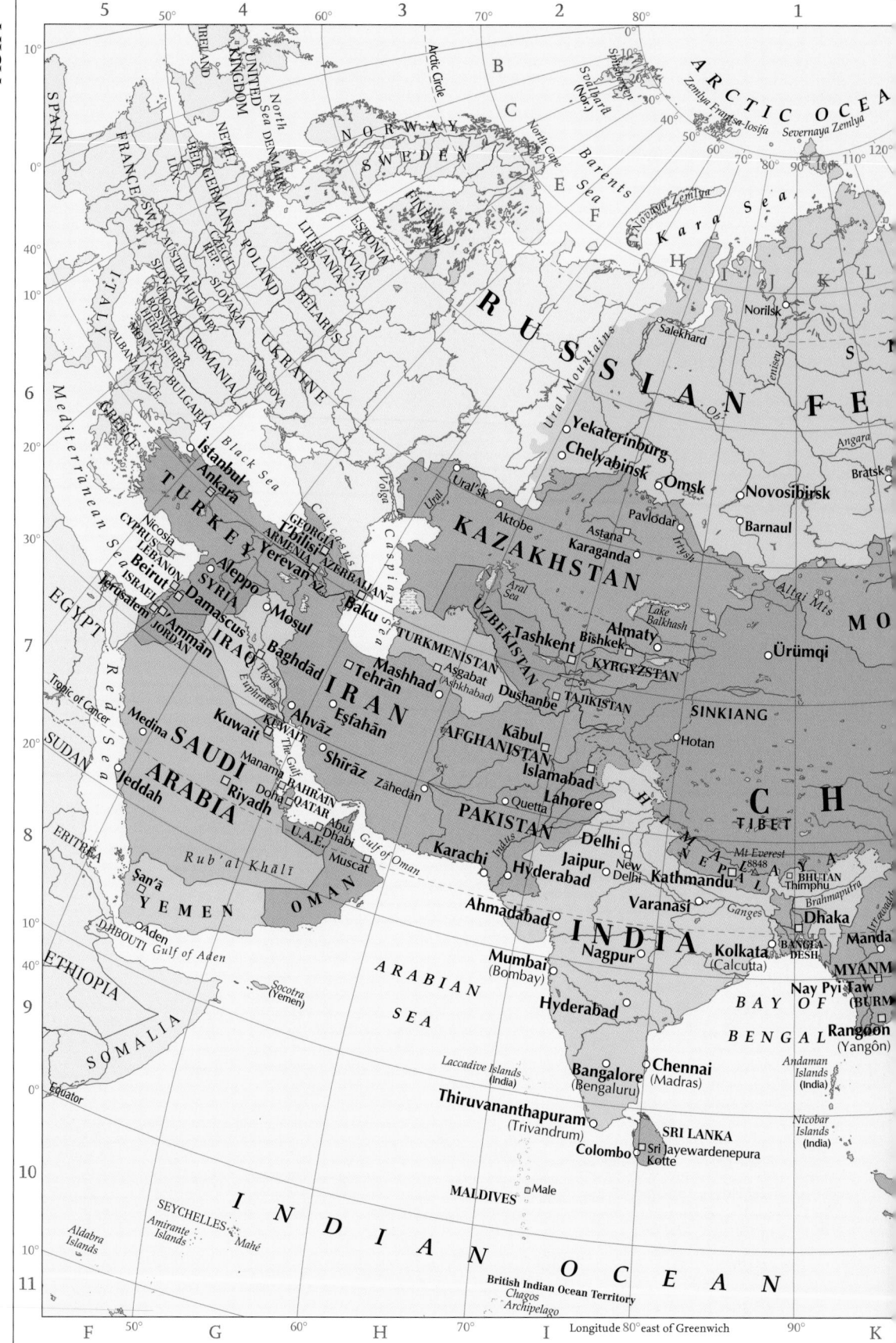

5   50°   4   60°   3   70°   2   80°   1

10°

SPAIN
FRANCE
IRELAND
UNITED KINGDOM
NETH.
DENMARK
North Sea
BELGIUM
GERMANY
SW.
LUX.
AUSTRIA
CZECH REP.
SWITZ.
SLOVAKIA
POLAND
LITHUANIA
LATVIA
ESTONIA
NORWAY
SWEDEN
FINLAND
Arctic Circle
B
C
Svalbard (Nor.)
Zemlya Frantsa-Iosifa
Severnaya Zemlya

ARCTIC OCEA

0°

ITALY
SLOVENIA
CROATIA
BOSNIA & HERZ.
MONT.
SERBIA
HUNGARY
ROMANIA
BELARUS
UKRAINE
MOLDOVA
E
North Cape
Barents Sea
Novaya Zemlya
Kara Sea
F

40°

10°

ALBANIA
MACE.
BULGARIA
GREECE
Mediterranean Sea
Black Sea
RUSSIAN FE
H
I
J
K
L
ST
Norilsk

6

20°

istanbul
Ankara
TURKEY
GEORGIA
ARMENIA
AZERBAIJAN
Tbilisi
Yerevan
Baku
Caucasus
Volga
Ural
Ural'sk
Aktobe
KAZAKHSTAN
Astana
Karaganda
Pavlodar
Irtysh
Altai Mts
Yekaterinburg
Chelyabinsk
Omsk
Novosibirsk
Barnaul
Bratsk
Angara
MO

30°

CYPRUS
Nicosia
LEBANON
Beirut
Damascus
SYRIA
Aleppo
Mosul
IRAQ
Baghdād
Tigris
Euphrates
IRAN
Tehrān
Mashhad
TURKMENISTAN
Aşgabat (Ashkhabad)
UZBEKISTAN
Tashkent
Bishkek
Almaty
KYRGYZSTAN
Dushanbe
TAJIKISTAN
Aral Sea
Caspian Sea
Lake Balkhash
Ürümqi
SINKIANG
Hotan

7

ISRAEL
Jerusalem
Amman
JORDAN
Eşfahān
Ahvāz
Shīrāz
Zāhedan
Kābul
AFGHANISTAN
Islamabad
Lāhore
Quetta
CH
TIBET
HIMALAYA
EGYPT
Red Sea
Tropic of Cancer

20°

Medina
Kuwait
KUWAIT
SAUDI
ARABIA
Riyadh
Manama
BAHRAIN
Doha
QATAR
Abu Dhabi
U.A.E.
The Gulf
Muscat
Gulf of Oman
PAKISTAN
Karachi
Hyderabad
Delhi
New Delhi
Jaipur
Kathmandu
Mt Everest 8848
BHUTAN
Thimphu
Indus
SUDAN
Jeddah

8

Rub' al Khālī
OMAN
Varanasi
Ganges
Brahmaputra
Ahmadabad
INDIA
Nagpur
Kolkata (Calcutta)
BANGLA-DESH
Dhaka
Manda

ERITREA
San'ā
YEMEN
Aden
DJIBOUTI
Gulf of Aden
ARABIAN
SEA
Socotra (Yemen)
Mumbai (Bombay)
Hyderabad
MYANM
Nay Pyi Taw
(BURM
Rangoon
(Yangôn)
BAY OF
BENGAL

9

40°

10°

ETHIOPIA
SOMALIA
Equator
Laccadive Islands (India)
Bangalore (Bengaluru)
Chennai (Madras)
Thiruvananthapuram (Trivandrum)
Andaman Islands (India)
Nicobar Islands (India)

0°

SRI LANKA
Colombo
Sri Jayewardenepura Kotte

10

Aldabra Islands
SEYCHELLES
Amirante Islands
Mahé
INDIAN OCEAN
MALDIVES
Male

10°

11

British Indian Ocean Territory
Chagos Archipelago

F   50°   G   60°   H   70°   I   Longitude 80° east of Greenwich   90°   K

Two Point Equidistant Projection

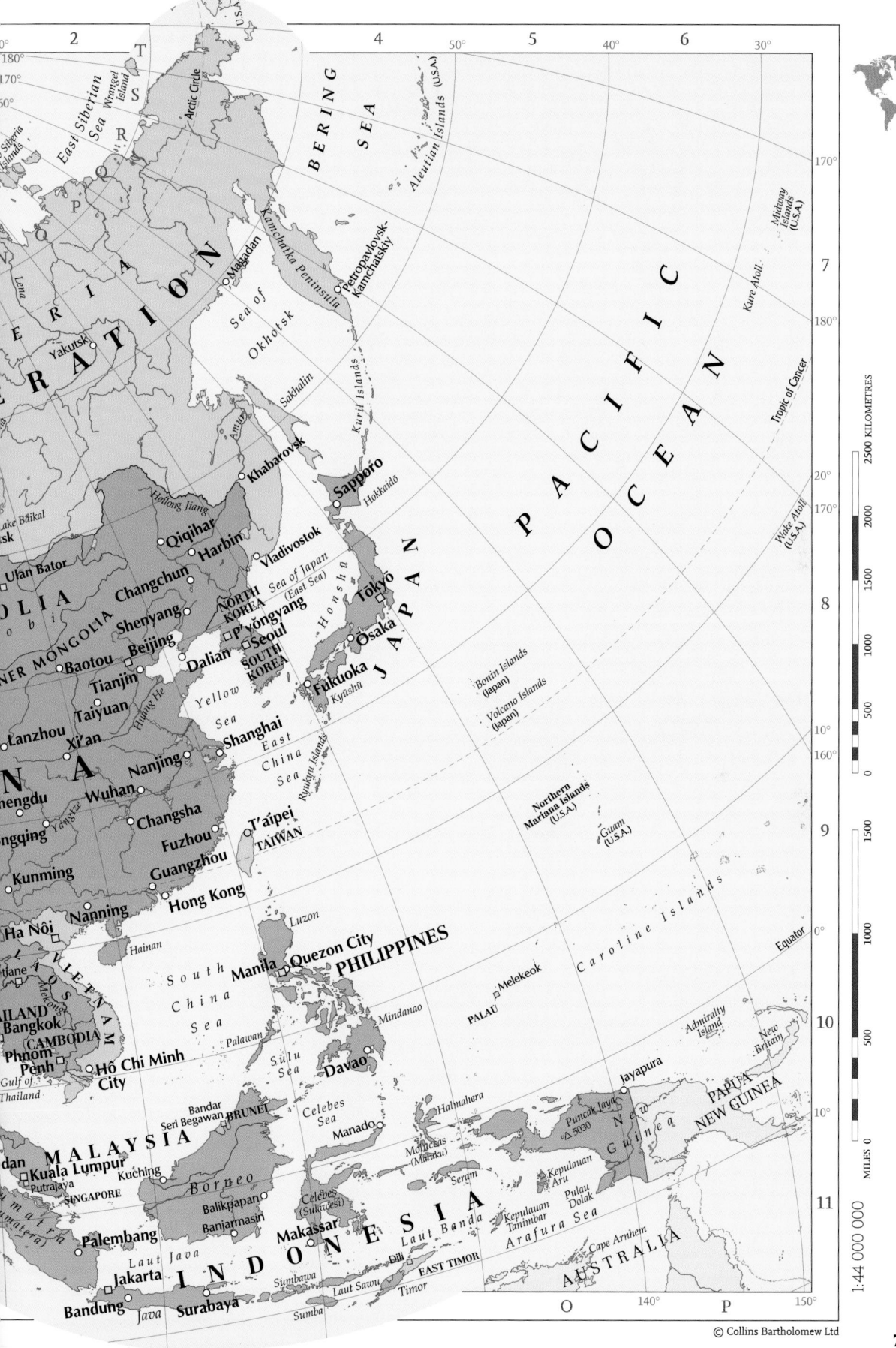

180°
170°

T
S
R
Q
P

East Siberian Sea

Wrangel Island

Arctic Circle

East Siberian Sea

Siberia

Lena

Yakutsk

ERIA
RATION

Magadan

Kamchatka Peninsula

Petropavlovsk-Kamchatskiy

BERING SEA

Aleutian Islands (U.S.A.)

170°

Kure Atoll

Midway Islands (U.S.A.)

7

180°

Sea of Okhotsk

Sakhalin

Kuril Islands

Tropic of Cancer

Wake Atoll (U.S.A.)

Khabarovsk

Sapporo

Hokkaidō

20°
170°

Heilong Jiang

Qiqihar

Harbin

Vladivostok

Lake Baikal

sk

Ulan Bator

MONGOLIA

Gobi

INNER MONGOLIA

Changchun

Shenyang

NORTH KOREA

Pyŏngyang

Sea of Japan (East Sea)

Honshū

Tōkyō

JAPAN

PACIFIC

OCEAN

8

Baotou

Beijing

Dalian

Seoul

SOUTH KOREA

Ōsaka

Tianjin

Taiyuan

Yellow Sea

Kyūshū

Fukuoka

Bonin Islands (Japan)

Lanzhou

Xi'an

Shanghai

East China Sea

Volcano Islands (Japan)

10°
160°

NA

Nanjing

Ryukyu Islands

nengdu

Wuhan

Changsha

T'aipei

ngqing

Yangtze

Fuzhou

TAIWAN

Northern Mariana Islands (U.S.A.)

9

Kunming

Guangzhou

Nanning

Hong Kong

Guam (U.S.A.)

Ha Nôi

Hainan

Luzon

Caroline Islands

0°

Equator

tiane

VIETNAM

South China Sea

Manila

Quezon City

PHILIPPINES

Melekeok

ILAND

Bangkok

CAMBODIA

Phnom Penh

Hô Chi Minh City

Palawan

Mindanao

PALAU

Admiralty Island

New Britain

10

Gulf of Thailand

Sulu Sea

Davao

Jayapura

PAPUA NEW GUINEA

Bandar Seri Begawan

BRUNEI

Celebes Sea

Manado

Halmahera

Moluccas (Maluku)

Puncak Jaya △ 5030

New Guinea

10°

dan

MALAYSIA

Kuala Lumpur

Kuching

Borneo

Seram

Kepulauan Aru

Pulau Dolak

Putrajaya

SINGAPORE

Balikpapan

Banjarmasin

Celebes (Sulawesi)

Kepulauan Tanimbar

Arafura Sea

Cape Arnhem

11

matra)

Palembang

Makassar

Laut Banda

Laut Java

INDONESIA

AUSTRALIA

Jakarta

Bandung

Java

Surabaya

Sumbawa

Dili

Sumba

Timor

EAST TIMOR

Laut Sawu

2500 KILOMETRES
2000
1500
1000
500
0

1500
1000
500
0
MILES 0

1:44 000 000

© Collins Bartholomew Ltd

METRES
FEET

5000	16404
3000	9843
2000	6562
1000	3281
500	1640
200	656
0	0
Land below sea level	
200	656
4000	13124
6000	19686

Longitude 105° east of Greenwich

Albers Equal Area Conic Projection

Tropic of Cancer

Ryukyu Islands (*Nansei-shotō*) (Japan)

IWAN
The People's Republic of China claims Taiwan as its 23rd Province.

1

Philippine

Sea

Pagan

Northern Mariana Islands (U.S.A.)

P A C I F I C

15°

O C E A N

CAPITOL HILL • Saipan
Tinian

uzon

Rota

HAGÅTÑA ⊕

Guam (U.S.A.)

PHILIPPINES

Catanduanes

Legaspi

Sorsogon Catarman

Irosin Catbalogan

Samar

Roxas Catbalogan

Tacloban

Cebu

Bohol Surigao

Bohol Sea Butuan

Cagayan de Oro

Mindanao

Iligan

Cotabato

Davao

Mati

Moro Gulf

General Santos

Ulithi

Fais

Yap ⊕
Colonia

Ngulu

Sorol

FEDERATED STATES OF MICRONESIA

Faraulep

Mariana Trench

2

Eauripik

Caroline Islands

East Caroline Basin

Kepulauan Talaud

Kepulauan Sangir

Sangir

Morotai

Daruba

Manado
Tobelo

Gorontalo
Ternate *Halmahera*

Sao-Slu

Labuha Waigeo

Selat Dampir Sorong

Bacan *Gunung Binaia*

Obi Misoöl

PALAU
MELEKEOK

Babeldaob

Equator 0°

Pelleluhu
Islands

St Matthias
Group

Mussau Island

New Hanover

Admiralty
Islands Lorengau
Hermit Islands Kavieng

Manus Island

Ysabel Channel

Umbukul

Bismarck Archipelago New
Ireland

New

S I A

Kendari

Buru Ambon

Buton

Laut Banda
(*Banda Sea*)

*Kepulauan
Alor* *Kepulauan Barat Daya*

DILI

*EAST
TIMOR*

Timor

Kupang

Timor Sea

Manokwari Biak

Numfoor *Selat Yapen*

Ransiki Serui Sarmi

Nabire *Teluk Cenderawasih*

Babo

Fakfak

Kaimana

Adi

Amamapare

Dobo Wokam

Kai Keeil *Kepulauan Kai*

Kepulauan Tanimbar

Saumlakki

Merauke

Arafura Sea

AUSTRALIA

Jayapura Vanimo

Aitape

Wewak

**PAPUA
(IRIAN JAYA)**

Pegunungan Maoke

Enarotali *Puncak Jaya*

**NEW
GUINEA**

Kiunga

Balimo Kikori

Morehead

Daru

*Gulf
of Papua*

NEW GUINEA

Mendi Mount
Hagen Goroka

Lae

Kerema

Bereina

PORT
MORESBY Abau

Thursday
Island
Prince of Wales
Island

Bamaga

Cape York

Weipa

Coen

**Cape York
Peninsula**

Bismarck Sea

Rabaul

Ulamona

Kimbe

New Britain

Gasmata

PAPUA

Mt
Wilhelm

*Huon
Peninsula*

Morobe

Mount
Victoria

*Trobriand
Islands*

D'Entrecasteaux Is

Kwikila

Alotau

Samarai

Cape Grenville

Lockhart River

Cape Melville

Cape
Flattery

Cooktown

Laura

150°

15°

© Collins Bartholomew Ltd

500 KILOMETRES
250
0

500
250
0 MILES

1:20 000 000

75

Phangnga
Ban Khok Kloi
Thalang
Krabi
Phuket
Thung Song
Nakhon Si Thammarat
Khao Chum Thong
VIETNAM
Mui Ca Mau
Nam Căn
Đao Côn Sơn

THAILAND
Trang
Phatthalung
Thale Luang
Hat Yai
Songkhla
Pattani
Satun
Sadao
Yala
Narathiwat
Kota Bharu
Pasir Putih
Kuala Kerai

SOUTH CHI

Andaman Sea
Pulau We
Sabang
Banda Aceh
Sigli
Bireun
Lhokseumawe
Calang
Takengon
Peureula
Langsa
Pangkalansusu
Gunung Abongabong △ 2985
Blangkejeren
Gunung Leuser △ 3145
Binjai
Belawan
Medan
Tebingtinggi
Pematangsiantar
Sidikalang
Kisaran
Prapat
Balige
Danau Toba
Tapaktuan

Langkawi
Kangar
Alor Star
Sungai Petani
Pinang
George Town
Butterworth
Taiping
Kuala Kangsar
Ipoh
Kampar
Teluk Intan
Bagan Datuk
Klang
KUALA LUMPUR
PUTRAJAYA
Labuhanbilik

MALAYSIA
PENINSULAR
MALAYSIA
Gunung Tahan △ 2189
Tasik Kenyir
Kuala Terengganu
Dungun
Cukai
Kuala Lipis
Temerluh
Kuantan
Pekan
Padang Endau

Kuala Lumpur

Kepulauan Anambas
Jemaja
Laut
Natuna Besar
Panarik
Kepulauan Natuna (Indonesia)
Subi Besar
Selat Serasan

Simeulue
Sinabang
Singkil
Pulau-pulau Banyak
Nias
Sirombu
Gunungsitoli
Padangsidimpuan
Sibolga
Rantauprapat
Bagansiapiapi
Dumai
Duri
Bengkalis
Daludalu
Gunungtua
Hutanopan
Minas
Natal
Airbangis
Talu
Bangkinang
Pekanbaru

Bahau
Seremban
Melaka
Segamat
Mersing
Keluang
Muar
Batu Pahat
Johor Bahru
SINGAPORE
Bintan
Tanjungpinang
Kepulauan Riau

Kepulauan Tambelan (Indonesia)
Liku
Sambas
Pemangkat
Singkawang
Mempawah
Bengkayang
Ngabang
Kuch
Siluas

Equator
Telo
Tanahmasa
Tanahbala
Pulau-pulau Batu
Payakumbuh
Padangpanjang
Bukittinggi
Padang
Solok
Kagologolo
Siberut
Painan
Muarasiberut
Sipura
Kaliet
Pagai Utara

SUMATERA

Kampar
Tembilahan
Rengat
Kualatungal
Simpang

Lingga
Daik
Singkep
Kepulauan Lingga

Pontianak
Balaiber
Kubu
Telukbatang
Pulau-pulau Karimata
Sukadana
Ketapang

Mega
Muarabungo
Sijunjung
Sungaipenuh
Gunung Kerinci △ 3805
Bangko
Sarolangun
Mukomuko
Burai
Pagai Selatan
Jambi
Muaratembesi
Batanghari
Surulangun
Sekayu
Lubuklinggau
Tebingtinggi
Curup
Bengkulu
Gunung Dempo △ 3169
Lahat
Martapura
Menggala
Muaradua
Gunung Resag △ 2232
Kotabumi
Metro
Bintuhan
Krui
Kotaagung
Bandar Lampung

Mentok
Belinyu
Sungailiat
Pangkalpinang
Bangka
Koba
Rajik
Plaju
Kayuagung
Palembang
Prabumulih
Musi
Tanjungpandan
Toboali
Manggar
Dendang
Belitung
Selat Karimata
Suk
Kendawang

INDI
LAUT
(JAV

Enggano
Sebesi
Tanjung Cina
Teluk Semangka
Krakatau
Selat Sunda
Panaitan
Deli
Teluk Palabuhanratu

JAKARTA
Serang
Rangkasbitung
Bogor
Sukabumi
Bandung
Sindangbarang
Cilacap
Karawang
Cirebon
Tanjung Indramayu
Pekalon
Tegal
Gunung Slamet △ 3428
Garut
Ciamis
Kebum
Temanggu
JAVA (JAWA)

Peg.un.ungan.Barisan

Greater Sunda Is

Kepulauan Mentawai

INDIAN OCEAN

Strait of Malacca

Strait of Malacca

0°

2

10°

A
Longitude 100° east of Greenwich
B

Albers Equal Area Conic Projection

Palawan
Rio Tuba
Bugsuk
Balabac
Balabac
SULU
SEA
Roxas
Oroquieta
Liloy
Ozamiz Iligan
Siocon
Pagadian
Zamboanga
Peninsula
Balabac Strait
Banggi
Kudat
Cagayan de
Tawi-Tawi
Kanibongan
Zamboanga
Moro
Gulf Datu Piang
SEA
Sulu
Archipelago
Isabela
Basilan Lebak
Kota Belud
Turtle Islands
(Philippines)
Cotabato
Kota
Kinabalu
Gunung
Kinabalu
△ 4095
Ranau
Sandakan
Jolo Jolo
PHILIPPINES
Gunung Trus Madi
△ 2649
Beaufort
Lamag
Tambisan
Siasi
Labuan
Tenom
Lahad
Datu
Balimbing
BANDAR SERI
BEGAWAN
Lawas
Kuamut
Tawi-Tawi
BRUNEI
Tomani
SABAH
Sibutu
Kuala Belait
Pensiangan
Semporna
Lutong
Seria
Lumbis
Tawau
CELEBES
Miri
△ *Bukit Harden*
2136
Mensalong
SEA
Labang
Long
Akah
Kubuang
Tarakan
Bintulu
Mukah
△
Igan
Tanjung
Sirik
Belaga
MALAYSIA
Tanjungselor
Sibu
SARAWAK
Sarikei
Kapit
Tanjungredeb
Saratok
Rajang
Debak
Datadian
Sri Aman
△
2988
Sepinang
Tanjung
Mangkalihat
Tolitoli
Kwandang
Lubok
Antu
Putusibau
Semenanjung Minahasa
Semitau
BORNEO
Gunung Menyapa
△ 2000
Gorontalo
Sambaliung
Sintau
Longwai
Sangkulirang
Kepulauan
Togian
Sidoan
Moutong
0°
gahpinoh
△
Longiram
Bontang
Tanjung
Pangkalsiang
Tomali
Teluk
Togian
Tomini
Tenggarong
Batudaka
Kepulauan
Muaralaung
KALIMANTAN
Donggala
Luwuk
Schwaner
Samarinda
Palu
Peleng
Tewah
Muarateweh
Samboja
Mapane
Poso
Tataba
Banggai
Seruyan
Rantaupanjang
Kahayan
Balikpapan
Uekuli
Barito
Tanahgrogot
Tenteno
Kolonedale
Kepulauan
Banggai
Palangkaraya
Tanjung
CELEBES
Babana
Teluk Towori
Sampit
Amuntai
(SULAWESI)
Bukit △ 3074
Mamuju
Masamba
Manui
Kandangan
Gandadiwata
Rantepao
Kualapembuang
Palopo
Wowoni
Kotabaru
Sambo
Makale
Malamala
Banjarmasin
Sebuku
Majene
Polewali
Kendari
Tanjung
Martapura
Parepare
Anabanua
Kolaka
Puting
Pagatan
Singkang
Laut
Raha
Muna Buton
Tanjung
Selatan
Watampone
Kepulauan
Maros
Sinjai
Baubau
Laut Kecil
Gunung Lompobattang
△ 2871
Kabaena
Makassar
Bawean
(*Ujung Pandang*)
Bulukumba
Batuata
Bontosunggu
au-pulau
imunjawa
Salayar
Tanjung
Bugel
Benteng
Masalembu
Besar
Sabalana
Tanahjampea
Kalao
Kalaotoa
Madura
Arjasa
Kepulauan
Tengah
Kepulauan Bonerate
Bangkalan
Sumenep
Kepulauan
Solor
Tuban
Genteng Raas
Situbondo
Laut Bali
(*Bali Sea*)
Kepulauan
Laut Flores
(*Flores Sea*)
Larantuka
Labala
Surabaya
Selat Madura
Banyuwangi
Sumbawa
Reo *Flores*
Pasuruan
Gunung
Raung
△ 2821
Maumere
Bajawa
Lumajang
Singaraja
Mataram
Dompu
Raba Labuhanbajo
Jember
Gianyar
Alas
Ruteng
Ende
Denpasar
Bali
Praya
Taliwang
Plampang
Selat Sumba
Sumba
Laut Sawu
(*Savu Sea*)
Waikabubak
Memboro
Waingapu
10°
120°

77

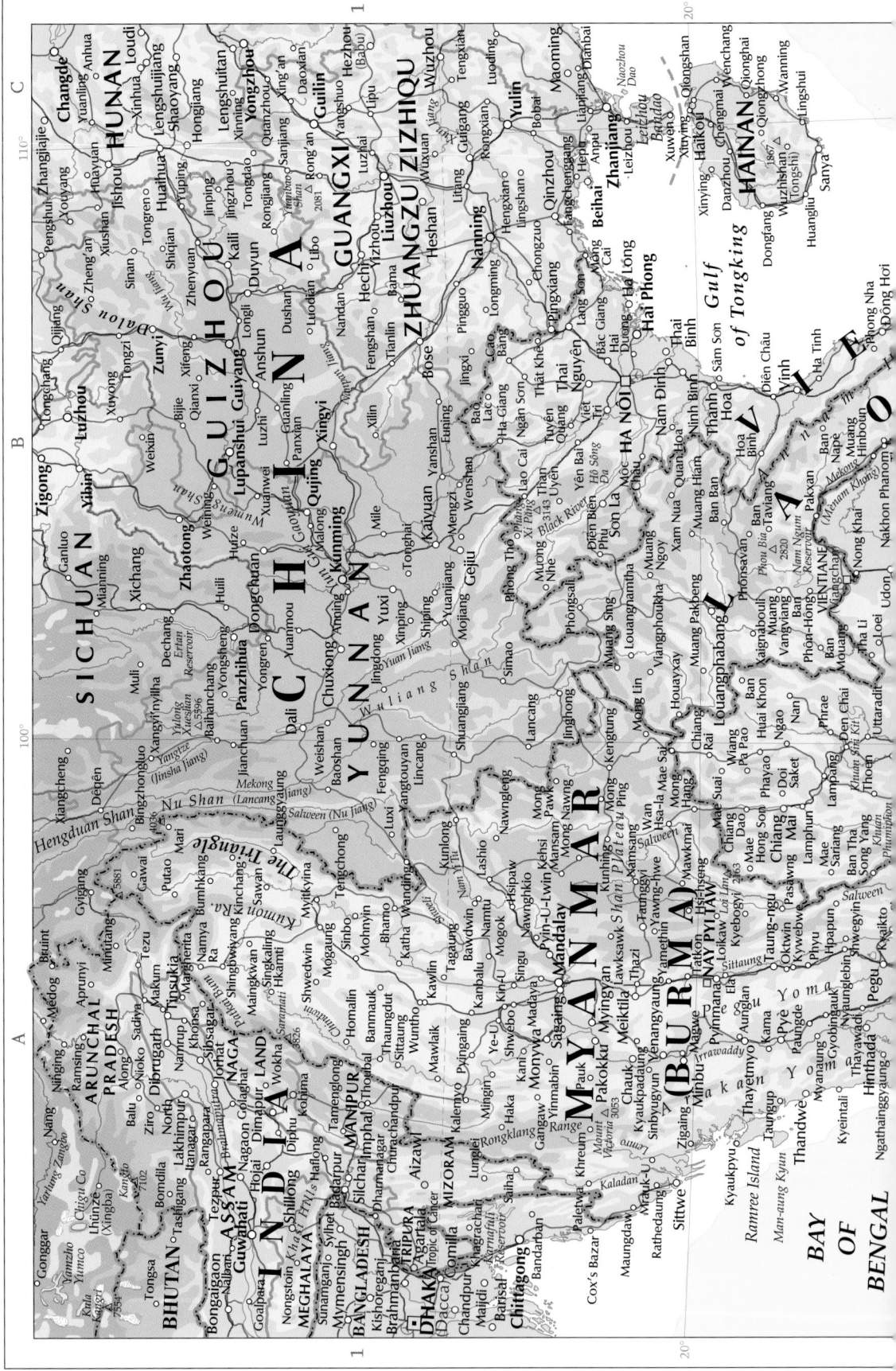

METRES
FEET

5000	16404
3000	9843
2000	6562
1000	3281
500	1640
200	656
0	0
Land below sea level	
200	656
4000	13124
6000	19686

Albers Equal Area Conic Projection

1:9 600 000

© Collins Bartholomew Ltd

200 KILOMETRES

100

0

150

100

MILES 0

1:9 600 000

METRES
FEET

5000
16404

3000
9843

2000
6562

1000
3281

500
1640

200
656

0
0

Land below
sea level

200
656

4000
13124

6000
19686

Dongsha
Qundao

1

20°

Batan
Itbayat   Islands
Luzon   Basco
Strait   Batan

Balintang Channel
Babuyan

Calayan   Babuyan
   Islands
Fuga   Camiguin
Babuyan Channel

Bangui
Laoag   San Vicente
   Aparri
Bangued   Tuguegarao
Vigan   Mount   Chico
   Sapocoy   Ilagan   Palanan
Tagudin   Bontoc
San Fernando   Mount
La Trinidad   Pulog   Santiago
Dagupan   Baguio   △ 2929   Bayombong
Lingayen   San Carlos
   Tarlac   San Jose   **LUZON**
Mount Pinatubo   Cabanatuan
Iba △ 1660   Gapan
Angeles   San Fernando
Olongapo   Valenzuela   Polillo Islands
Balanga   Quezon City
MANILA   Pasig
Tagaytay City   Santa Cruz   Labo
San Pablo   Lucena   Daet   Pandan
Lubang   Batangas   Lopez   Libmanan   Catanduanes
Islands   Calapan   Boac   Naga   Virac
Mount   Naujan   Oas   Tabaco
Halcon   **Mindoro**   Mayon
Mamburao △ 2585   Legaspi   Sorsogon
   Roxas   Burias   Irosin
San Jose   Romblon   Catarman
Busuanga   Tablas   Masbate   Calbayog
Calamian   Sibuyan   **Masbate**   **Samar**
Group   Sea
Culion   Coron   Pandan   Roxas   Catbalogan
Limpacan   Culasi   Visayan   Tacloban
El Nido   Cuyo   **Panay**   Sea
Islands   Cadiz   Ormoc   Guiuan
Taytay   Dalanganem   Pototan   Bacolod
Islands   San Jose de   Iloilo   **Cebu**   **Leyte**
Dumaran   Buenavista   △ 2450
Roxas   **Negros**   Talisay   Cebu   Maasin
   Cauayan   Dinagat
10°   Puerto Princesa   Bohol   Siargao
Apurahuan   Tanjay   Tagbilaran   Dapa
Aborlan   Bayawan   Siquijor   Surigao
Mount   Dumaguete   Mambajao   Tandag
Mantalingajan △   Camiguin   Butuan
   2054   Brooke's Point   Dipolog   Cagayan   Gingoog
Rio Tuba   Roxas   de Oro
Bugsuk   Oroquieta   Malaybalay   Bislig
Balabac   Liloy   Ozamiz   Iligan
Balabac   **MINDANAO**   Baganga
Balabac Strait   Siocon   Pagadian   Mount Ragang
Banggi   Zamboanga   △ 2815
   Peninsula   Cotabato   Tagum
Kudat   Zamboanga   Datu Piang   **Davao**
Kanibongan   Isabela   Lebak   Digos
Kota Belud   Basilan   Banga   Mati
Kota   Jolo   Kiamba   General Santos
Kinabalu   Jolo   Batulaki
Ranau   Siasi
Sandakan   Sarangani Islands
Lamag
Tambisan
MALAYSIA   Balimbing
SABAH

3

Luzon Strait

PHILIPPINE

SEA

PHILIPPINES

SOUTH

CHINA

SEA

Scarborough
Shoal

Mindoro Strait

Palawan Passage

Palawan

SULU SEA

Turtle Islands
(Philippines)

Moro
Gulf

Sulu Archipelago

Cagayan de
Tawi-Tawi

Gunung
Kinabalu
△ 4095
Gunung
Trus Madi
△ 2649

Banjaran Crocker

Lawas   Tenom
Tomani   Kuamut   Lahad
Pensiangan   Datu
Lumbis   Semporna
INDONESIA   Tawau
Mensalong
Kubuang   Tarakan

Tawi-Tawi
Sibutu

CELEBES
SEA

INDONESIA

Mount
Apo
△ 2954   Davao
Gulf

Kepulauan
Nanusa

Kepulauan
Talaud

Karakelong

Pulutan

Sangir   Tahuna

Kaburuang

Longitude 120° east of Greenwich

Albers Equal Area Conic Projection

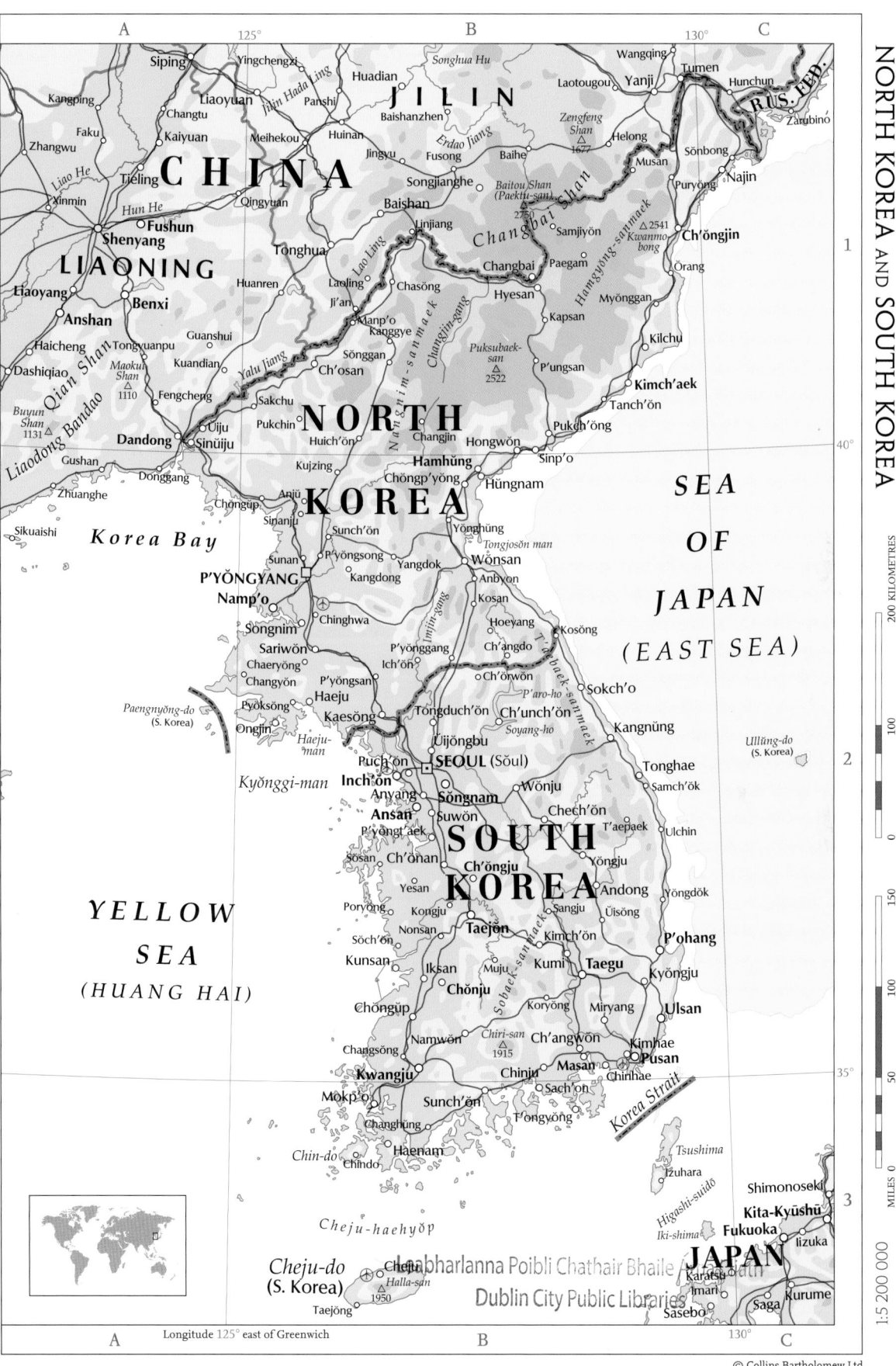

A   125°   B   130°   C

CHINA

LIAONING

JILIN

Siping
Kangping
Changtu
Faku
Zhangwu
Xinmin
Liaoyang
Anshan
Haicheng
Dashiqiao
Zhuanghe
Sikuaishi

Yingchengxi
Liaoyuan
Kaiyuan
Tieling
Fushun
Shenyang
Tongyuanpu
Guanshui
Kuandian
Fengcheng
Sakchu
Pukchin
Dandong
Sinŭiju
Gushan
Donggang
Chŏngŭp

Huadian
Baishanzhen
Meihekou
Huinan
Jingyu
Fusong
Songjianghe
Baishan
Tonghua
Huanren
Laoling
Ji'an
Manp'o
Kanggye
Sŏnggan
Ch'osan
Huich'ŏn
Kujing

Songhua Hu
Laotougou
Fusong
Baihe

Wangqing
Yanji
Tumen
Hunchun
Zarūbino
Helong
Musan
Puryŏng
Najin
Sŏnbong
Ch'ŏngjin
Ŏrang
Myŏnggan
Kilchu
Kimch'aek
Tanch'ŏn
Pukch'ŏng

RUS. FED.

N O R T H

K O R E A

Zengfeng Shan △2750
Baitou Shan (Paektu-san) △2750
Samjiyŏn
Paegam
Hyesan
Kapsan
P'ungsan
Kwanmo bong △2541

Changbai
Chasŏng

Baitou Shan

Changjin-gang
Puksubaek-san △2522

Hamhŭng
Chŏngp'yŏng
Hŭngnam
Sinp'o
Hongwŏn
Pukch'ŏng

SEA
OF
JAPAN
(EAST SEA)

P'YŎNGYANG
Namp'o
Songnim
Sariwŏn
Chaeryŏng
Changyŏn
Pyŏksŏng
Ongjin

Sunch'ŏn
Sunan
P'yŏngsong
Kangdong
Chinghwa
P'yŏnggang
Ich'ŏn
P'yŏngsan
Haeju
Kaesŏng

Yangdok
Wŏnsan
Anbyon
Kosan
Hoeyang
Ch'angdo
Ch'ŏrwŏn

Kosŏng
Sokch'o

Tongjosŏn man
Yŏnghŭng

Korea Bay

Haeju-man

Kyŏnggi-man

Paengnyŏng-do (S. Korea)

Y E L L O W
S E A
(HUANG HAI)

Tongduch'ŏn
Ch'unch'ŏn
Ŭijŏngbu
Puch'ŏn
SEOUL (Sŏul)
Inch'ŏn
Anyang
Ansan
Suwŏn
Songnam
Wŏnju
Chhech'ŏn
T'aebaek
Kangnŭng
Tonghae
Samch'ŏk
Ulchin

Soyang-ho
P'aro-ho

SOUTH
KOREA

Sŏsan
Ch'ŏnan
P'yŏngt'aek
Yesan
Kongju
Nonsan
Poryŏng
Söch'ŏn
Kunsan
Iksan
Muju
Chŏnju
Chŏngŭp

Taejŏn
Ch'ŏngju
Sangju
Ŭisŏng
Andong
Yŏngju
Yŏngdŏk
Kimch'ŏn
Kumi
Taegu
P'ohang
Kyŏngju
Ulsan

Ŭllŭng-do (S. Korea)

Koryŏng
Miryang
Ch'angwŏn
Kwangju
Namwŏn
Changsŏng
Chinju
Masan
Pusan
Kimhae
Chinhae
Sach'ŏn
Chinju

Chiri-san △1915

Mokp'o
Changhŭng
Sunch'ŏn
T'ongyŏng
Haenam
Chindo

Chin-do

Korea Strait

Tsushima
Izuhara
Higashi-suidō
Iki-shima
Shimonoseki
Kita-Kyūshū
Fukuoka
Iizuka
Karatsu
Imari
Saga
Kurume
Sasebo

JAPAN

Cheju-haehyŏp

Cheju
Cheju-do (S. Korea)
Halla-san △1950
Taejŏng

1

40°

2

35°

3

200 KILOMETRES
100
0

150
100
50
0
MILES

1:5 200 000

© Collins Bartholomew Ltd

METRES
FEET

5000
16404

3000
9843

2000
6562

1000
3281

500
1640

200
656

0
0

Land below
sea level

200
656

4000
13124

6000
19686

82

Albers Equal Area Conic Projection

Map labels

1

45°

145°

Sakhalin

Korsakov
Novikovo
Gomozavodsk
Ostrov
Moneron
Mys Aniva
Zaliv
Aniva

Mys Kril'on
La Pérouse Strait

Rebun-tō
Rishiri-tō

Teshio

Wakkanai
Sōya-misaki

Nayoro
Asahikawa

Monbetsu
Abashiri
Abashiri-
wan
Shiretoko-
misaki
Rausu
Shibetsu
Nemuro

HOKKAIDŌ

Kitami
Kushiro-ko
Menken-dake
1503
Ashoro
Bekkai
Kushiro

Obihiro

Hiroo

Erimo-
misaki

2

40°

Asahi-dake
2290
Hidaka-sammyaku

Bibai
Iwamizawa
Yūbari
Tomakomai
Samani

Takikawa
Ebetsu
Sapporo
Chitose

Otaru
Ishikari-
wan
Shikotsu-ko
Tōya-ko
Date
Muroran
Uchiura-wan
(Volcano Bay)

Rumoi

Ishikari-
hantō

Iwanai
Suttsu
Shakotan-misaki

Yakumo
Mori
Hakodate

Esashi
Matsumae
O-shima

Okushiri-tō

Ōma
Tappi-zaki
Shiriya-zaki
Mutsu
Shimokita-
hantō
Mutsu-
wan

Oshika-
hantō

Hachinohe

Aomori
Goshogawara
Hirosaki
Towada
Ninohe
Odate
Kazuno
Noshiro
Oga-hantō
Oga
Akita
Honjō

Kuji
Miyako

Morioka
Kamaishi
Kitakami-gawa
Hanamaki
Kitakami
Kesennuma
Ichinoseki
2041
Yokote
Sakata

SEA

OF

JAPAN

(EAST SEA)

C

Svetlaya

Amgu

Terney

Sikhote-Alin'

Bikin

Vostok

Kamenka

Rudnaya Pristan'

Dal'negorsk

Kavalerovo

Preobrazheniye

RUSSIAN

FEDERATION

Bikin
Luchegorsk
Dal'nerechensk
Lesozavodsk
Kirovskiy
Iman
Ussuri

Spassk-Dal'niy

Arsen'yev
Chuguyevka
Iazo
Vrangel'
Partizansk

B

Shuangyashan

Baoqing
Dongfanghong

Hulin

Mishan

Khorol
Yaroslavskiy
Mikhaylovka
Ussuriysk
Artem
Bol'shoy Kamen'
Nakhodka

CHINA

Wanda Shan

Lake
Khanka

Pogranichnyy
Poltavka
Ugloye
Ugolovoye
Slavyanka
Zaliv
Petra Velikogo
Zarubino

Qitaihe
Jixi

Boli

Linkou
Muling

Suifenhe

Vladivostok

Boli

Mudan Jiang

Muling

Tumen

Hunchun
Kraskino

A

Yilan

Fangzheng

Changting

Zhangguangcai Ling

Mudanjiang

Wangqing
Yanji

Helong

Laoye Ling

Tumen

Sŏnbong
Najin

Ch'ŏngjin

NORTH
KOREA

Kwanmo-
bong
2541

Musan

Myŏnggan

Kilchu

Kimch'aek

1

45°

130°

135°

140°

2

40°

SOUTH
KOREA

Ulchin

Ulling-do
(S. Korea)

Liancourt Rocks
Claimed and administered
by South Korea as Tok-tō;
claimed by Japan as Take-shima

Oki-shotō
Dōgo
Saigō
Dōzen

P

A

J

A

P

A

N

H

O

N

S

H

U

SHIKOKU

KYUSHU

PACIFIC

OCEAN

Tori-shima

Izu-shotō
Hachijō-jima
Aoga-shima
Sumisu-jima

Mikura-jima
Miyake-jima
Nii-jima
O-shima

Tanega-shima
Yaku-shima

SENDAI
Sendai

TOKYO
Kawasaki
Yokohama

Osaka
Kyōto
Kōbe

Nagoya

Hiroshima

Fukuoka

Kagoshima

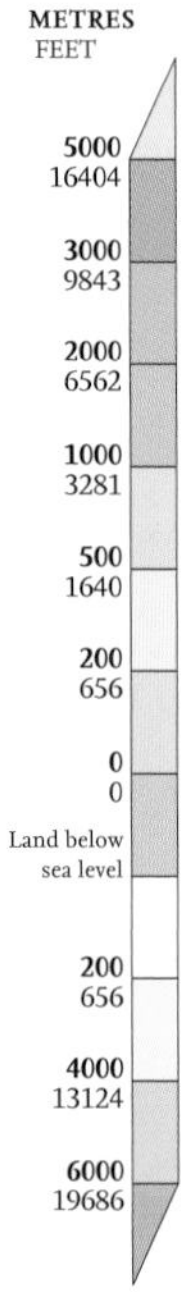

A 75° B 90° C 105°

KAZAKHSTAN

RUSSIAN FEDE

Atbasar · Akkol' · Pavlodar · Slavgorod · Barnaul · Biysk · Chernogorsk · Minusinsk · Zima · Kachug
Arkalyk · Zhaltyr · Yereymentau · Kulunda · Rubtsovsk · Mikhaylovsky · Gorno-Altaysk · Askiz · Cheremkhovo · Angarsk · Irku
Ozero Kypshak · Temirtau (Akmola) · ASTANA · Ekibastuz · Semipalatinsk · Gornyak · Zyryanovsk · Inya · Kosh-Agach · Chadan · Kyzyl · Vostochny Sayan · Slyudyanka · Kyak
Zhezkazgan · Karaganda · Karagayly · Georgiyevka · Ust'-Kamenogorsk · Teeli · Uvs Nuur · Ulaangom · Tsagaannuur · Tsetserleg · Mörön · Hatgal · Suhbaa · Darhar
Atasu · Kaynar · Zharma · Lake Zaysan (Ozero Zaysan) · Hyargas Nuur · Har Us Nuur · Hov · Hövsgöl Nuur · Hutag-Öndör · Bulgan

KYRGYZSTAN · TIEN SHAN · XINJIANG
TAJIK. · Tarim Basin (Tarim Pendi) · Taklimakan Desert (Taklimakan Shamo)
KUNLUN SHAN · Plateau of Tibet (Qingzang Gaoyuan) · TIBET
CHINA · Qaidam Pendi · Qilian Shan

INDIA · NEPAL · BHUTAN · BANGLADESH · MYANMAR (BURMA) · THAILAND · LAOS · VIETNA

MONGOLIA

BAY OF BENGAL

Longitude 90° east of Greenwich

Albers Equal Area Conic Projection

METRES / FEET
5000 / 16404
3000 / 9843
2000 / 6562
1000 / 3281
500 / 1640
200 / 656
0 / 0
Land below sea level
200 / 656
4000 / 13124
6000 / 19686

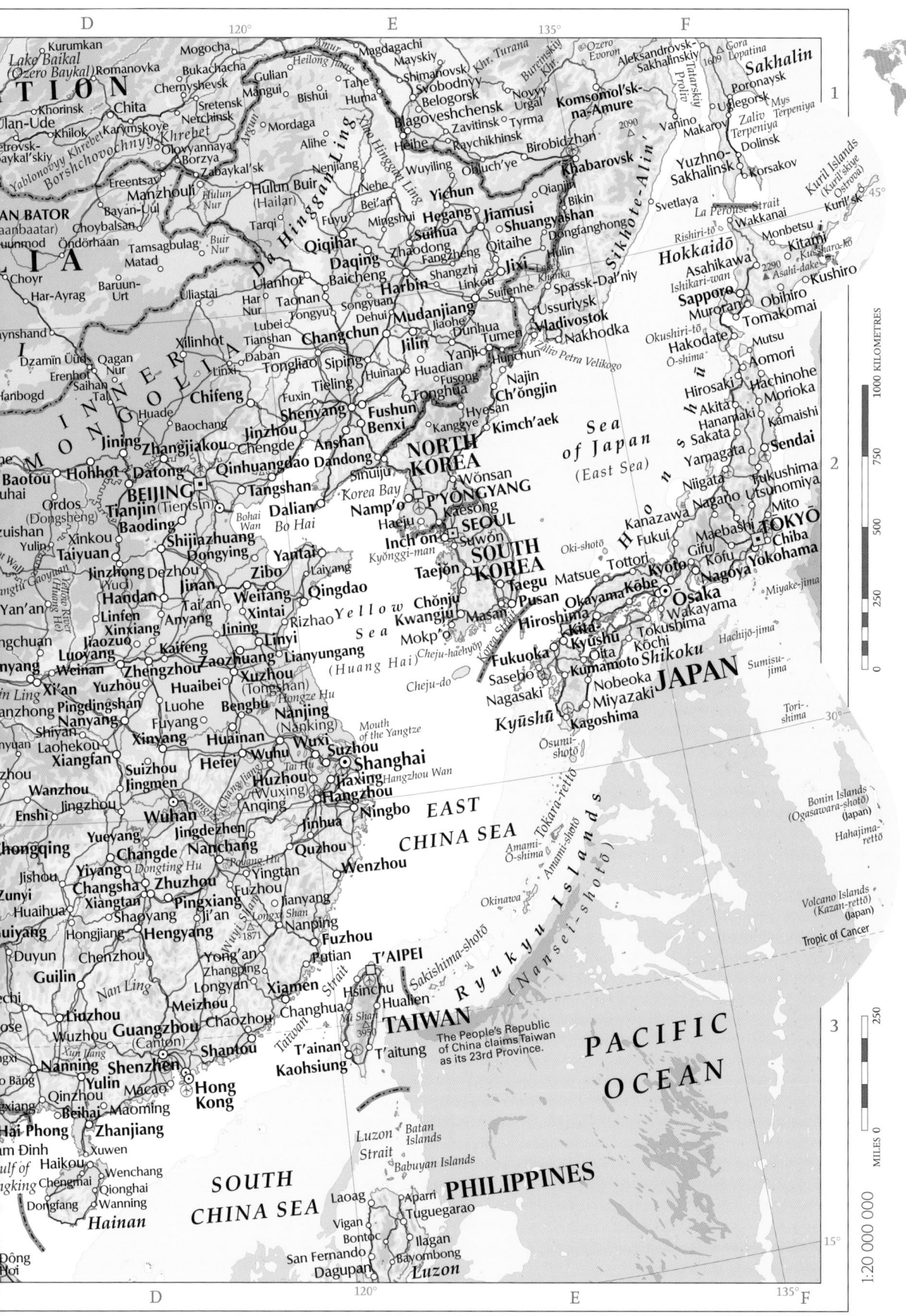

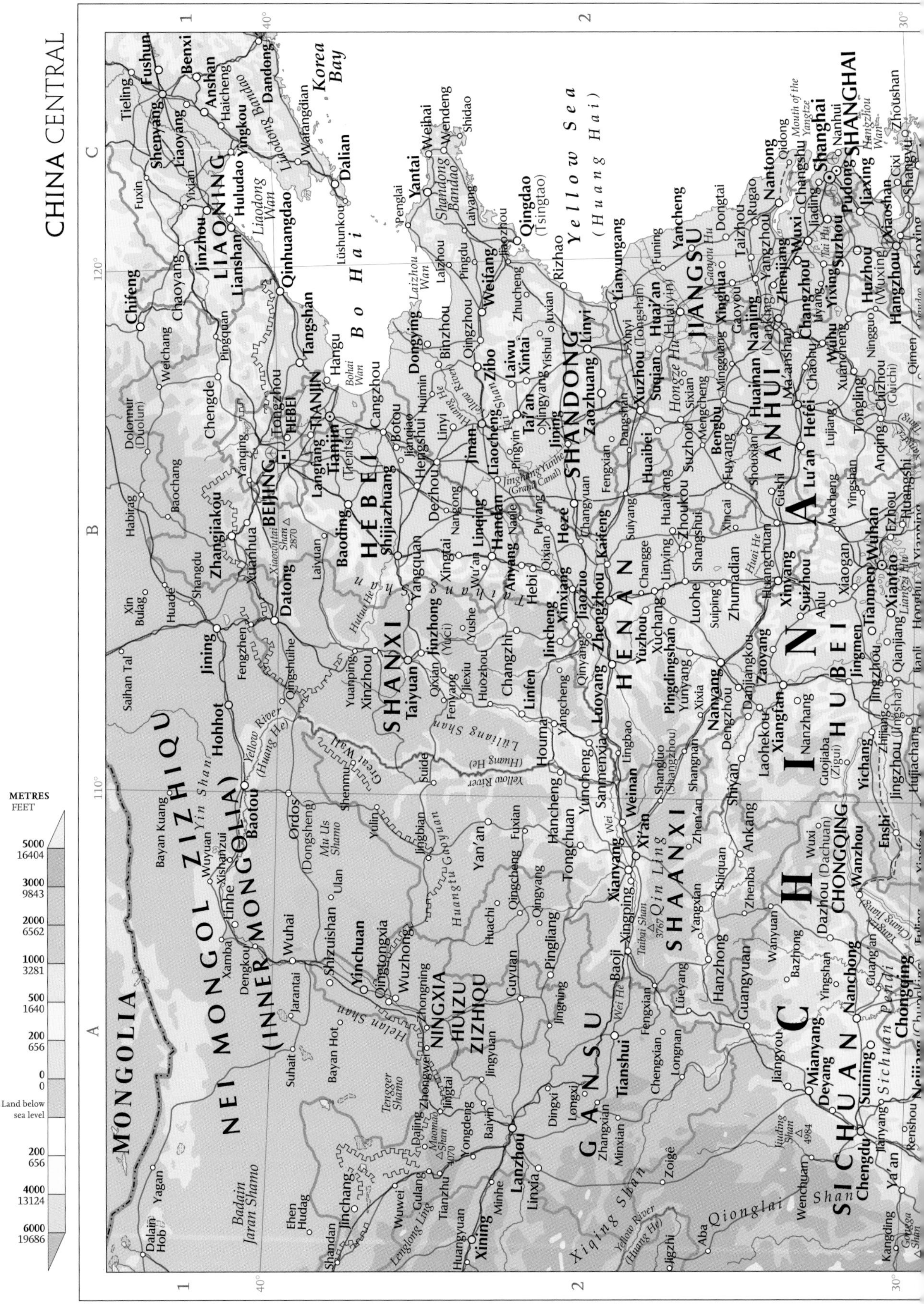

MONGOLIA

NEI MONGOL ZIZHIQU
(INNER MONGOLIA)

MONGOLIA

GANSU

NINGXIA HUIZU ZIZHIQU

SHANXI

SHAANXI

HEBEI

BEIJING

TIANJIN

LIAONING

SHANDONG

HENAN

JIANGSU

ANHUI

HUBEI

CHONGQING

SICHUAN

SHANGHAI

Seas and bays: Korea Bay, Bo Hai, Liaodong Wan, Laizhou Wan, Bohai Wan, Yellow Sea (Huang Hai)

METRES / FEET

METRES	FEET
5000	16404
3000	9843
2000	6562
1000	3281
500	1640
200	656
0	0
Land below sea level	
200	656
4000	13124
6000	19686

Selected places: Fushun, Benxi, Anshan, Shenyang, Liaoyang, Haicheng, Tieling, Fuxin, Jinzhou, Huludao, Yingkou, Dandong, Dalian, Qinhuangdao, Tangshan, Chengde, Zhangjiakou, Datong, Hohhot, Baotou, Jining, Beijing, Tianjin (Tientsin), Langfang, Cangzhou, Baoding, Shijiazhuang, Taiyuan, Jinzhong, Yangquan, Xingtai, Handan, Anyang, Hebi, Puyang, Linqing, Dezhou, Jinan, Zibo, Weifang, Qingdao (Tsingtao), Yantai, Weihai, Rizhao, Linyi, Zaozhuang, Jining, Tai'an, Heze, Kaifeng, Zhengzhou, Luoyang, Sanmenxia, Xi'an, Xianyang, Baoji, Tianshui, Lanzhou, Xining, Yinchuan, Wuzhong, Chongqing, Chengdu, Deyang, Mianyang, Nanchong, Suining, Wuhan, Hefei, Nanjing, Suzhou, Wuxi, Changzhou, Zhenjiang, Yangzhou, Nantong, Shanghai, Hangzhou, Jiaxing, Huzhou, Ningbo

Albers Equal Area Conic Projection

87

1:9 600 000

MILES 0   100   200   300

0   200   400 KILOMETRES

Longitude 110° east of Greenwich

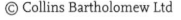

EAST CHINA SEA

SOUTH CHINA SEA

ZHEJIANG

FUJIAN

JIANGXI

HUNAN

GUIZHOU

YUNNAN

GUANGXI ZHUANGZU ZIZHIQU

GUANGDONG

HAINAN

TAIWAN

LUZON

PHILIPPINES

VIETNAM

LAOS

THAILAND

Gulf of Tongking

Taiwan Strait

Bashi Channel

Luzon Strait

Balintang Channel

Babuyan Channel

TAIPEI

Hong Kong

Macao

Shenzhen

Guangzhou

Nanning

HANOI

Hai Phong

VIENTIANE

Kunming

Guiyang

Nanchang

Changsha

Kaohsiung

T'ainan

T'aichung

Hsinchu

Hualien

T'aitung

Xiamen (Amoy)

Shantou (Swatow)

Fuzhou

Quanzhou

Wenzhou

Tropic of Cancer

The People's Republic of China claims Taiwan as its 23rd Province.

CHINA

QINGHAI

KUNLUN SHAN

Hoh Xil Shan

Ningjing Shan

Yangtze
(Tongtian He)

Guxiang Hu

Chindu

Yushu

Wuli

Ulan Ul Hu

Tanggula Shan

Migriggyangzham Co

PLATEAU OF TIBET
(QINGZANG GAOYUAN)

Tanggula Shan

Sog

Nagqu

Damxung

Lharigabbo

Lhasa

XIZANG ZIZHIQU
(TIBET)

Nyainqêntanglha Shan

Gangdisê Shan

Kangri

Gangdisê Shan

Gertse

Zanda

Co Ngoin

Ngangze

Zhari Namco

Ge'gyai

Gangrinboqê

Senge Zangbo

Saga

Zhongba

Paiku Co

Tarlung Zangbo

Lhazê

Xigazê

Thazê

Gyangzê

Gyirong

Kangmar

Nam Co

Yamzho
Yumco

Damxung

Congdü

Mount Everest
Qomolangma Feng 8848

Nyingchi

Sadiya

Tezu

Dibrugarh

Ningjing

Namrup

Jorhat

Lakhimpur North

Nagaon

Silchar

Kohima

Imphal

Aizawl

Lunglei

MYANMAR
(BURMA)

Mawlaik

Wuntho

Mingyan

Monywa

Namtü

BHUTAN

THIMPHU

Guwahati

Shillong

Bongaigaon

Rangpur

Cooch Behar

Siliguri

Darjiling

Gangtok

BANGLADESH

Rajshahi

Pabna

DHAKA
(Dacca)

Comilla

Chittagong

Cox's

Barisal

Khulna

Kolkata
(Calcutta)

Jessore

NEPAL

KATHMANDU

Patan

Bhaktapur

Pokhara

Gorakhpur

Darbhanga

Purnia

Munger

Bhagalpur

Asansol

Bardhaman

Jamshedpur

Ranchi

Raurkela

INDIA

Lucknow

Kanpur

Allahabad

Varanasi

Patna

Gaya

Jabalpur

Bhopal

Indore

Vadodara

Rajkot

Ahmadabad

Hyderabad

NEW DELHI

Delhi

Meerut

Jaipur

Agra

Gwalior

Jodhpur

Bikaner

Jaisalmer

PAKISTAN

ISLAMABAD

Rawalpindi

Lahore

Faisalabad

Multan

Bahawalpur

Peshawar

Quetta

AFGHANISTAN

KABUL

Ghazni

Jalalabad

JAMMU AND KASHMIR

Srinagar

Jammu

KARAKORAM RANGE

K2 (Qogir Feng)
(Godwin Austen)
8611

HIMALAYA

Tropic of Cancer

Rann of Kachchh

Gulf of Kachchh

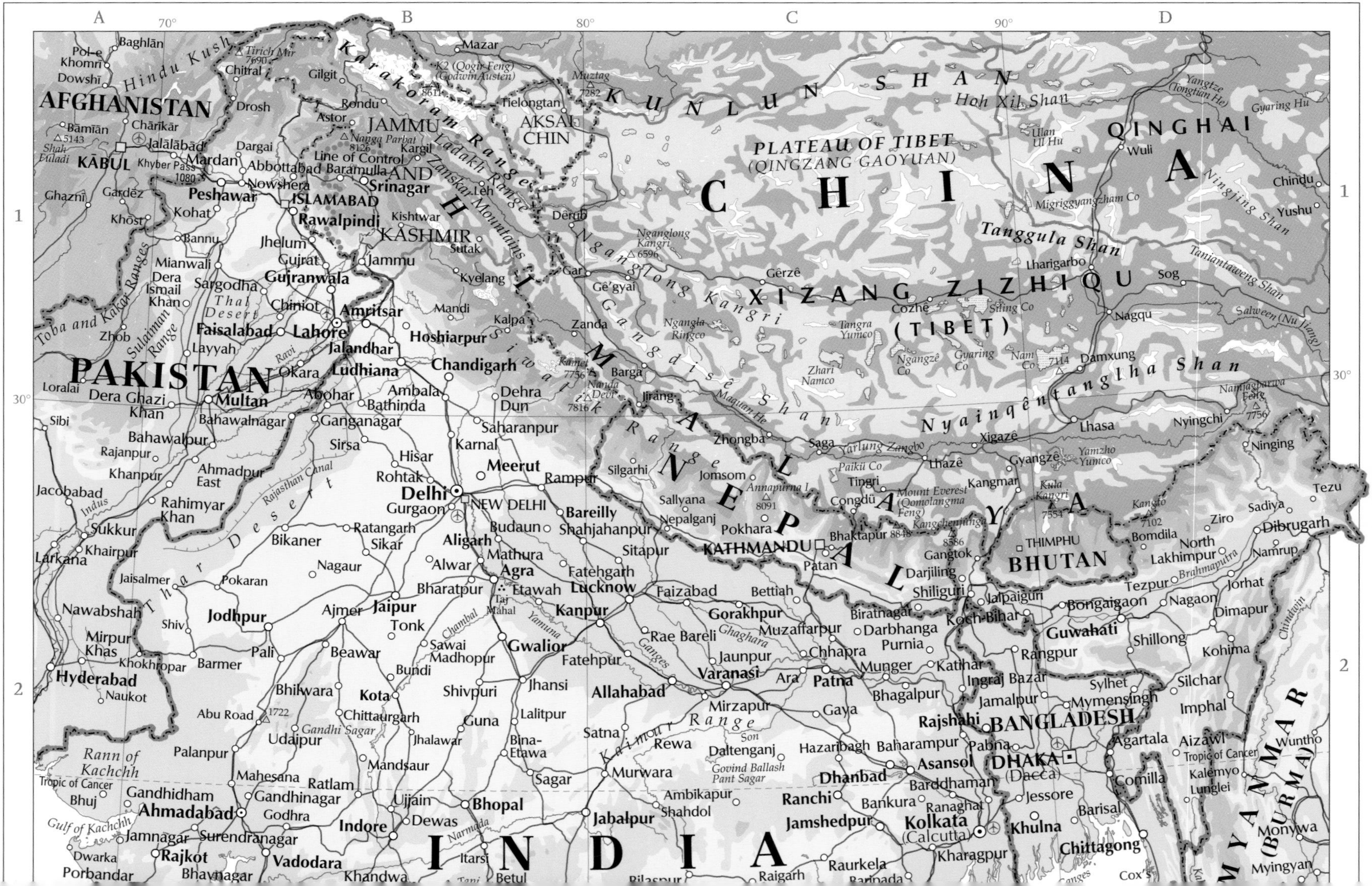

Albers Equal Area Conic Projection

METRES
FEET

5000
16404

3000
9843

2000
6562

1000
3281

500
1640

200
656

0
0

Land below
sea level

200
656

4000
13124

6000
19686

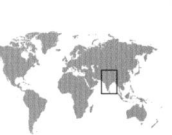

ARABIAN SEA

BAY OF BENGAL

INDIAN OCEAN

SRI LANKA

MALDIVES

1:12 000 000

MILES 0 100 200 300

0 250 500 KILOMETRES

Longitude 90° east of Greenwich

Garabil
Belentligi

TURKMENISTAN

Andkhvoy
Sheberghān
Mazar-e
Sharīf
Kholm
Khānābād
Fayzābād
Qullai Karl Marks 6626
Ishkoshim
Buzai
Gumbad
Mazar

Morghāb
Maymanah
Sar-e
Pol
Āybak
Baghlān
Talōqan
Tirich Mīr 7690
Battura Glacier
Pasu
*K2 (Qogir Feng)
(Godwin Austen)*
8611

Serhetabat
Qal'eh-ye Now
*Safīd Kūh
(Paropamisus)*
Dowshī
Pol-e Khomrī
Bāzārak
Bāmiān
Jabal as Sirāj
Chārīkār
Chitral
Drosh
Barikot
Dir
Nanga Parbat 8126
Gilgit Rakaposhi 7788
Gilgit
Chilas
Rondu
Astor
Skardu
Khaplu
Karakoram Ran

Hari Rūd
Chaghcharān
Kūh-e Bābā
Shah Fulad 5143
Mehtar
Nūrestan
Asadābād
Mahmud-e Rāqī
Dargai
Mongora
Sopur
Line of Control
Kishtwar
Chenab
JAMMU
AND
KASHMIR
Kargil
Zanskar Ran
Leh
LADAKH Ran

Delārām
Chalap Dalan
Kūh-e Qeysār
4182
Nīlī
Māidān Shahr
KABUL
Sikaram 4761
Khyber Pass 1080
Jalālābād
Mardan
Abbottabad
Nowshera
Wah
ISLAMABAD
Baramula
Srinagar
Anantnag
Udhampur
Chamba
Kyelang

AFGHANISTAN
Ghaznī
Gardēz
Khōst
Kohat
Peshawar
Rawalpindi
Jhelum
Talagang
Jammu
Kathua
Pathankot
Sujanpur
HIMACHAL
PRADESH
Mandi
Sundarnagar

HAZARAJAT
Tarīn Kowt
Sharan
Orgūn
Thal
Daud Khel
Mianwali
Bhera
Wazirabad
Sialkot
Batala
Hoshiarpur
Shimla

Dasht-e Mārgow
Gereshk
Kalāt
Bannu
Lakki
Marwat
Tank
Khushab
Sargodha
Kalur Kot
Gujranwala
Amritsar
Jalandhar
Ludhiana
Ambala
Chandigar

Lashkar Gāh
Kandahār
Arghandāb
Tarnak
Dera
Ismail Khan
Takht-i-Sulaimān 3374
Bhakkar
Chiniot
Jhang
Lahore
Faisalabad
Firozpur
Patiala
Roorkee

Helmand
Chaman
Pishin
Muslimbagh
Zhob
Thal Desert
Layyah
Shorkot
Okara
Sahiwal
Fazilka
PUNJAB
Bathinda
Saharanpur
U

Quetta
Mach
Sulaiman Range
Taunsa
Muzaffargarh
Multan
Khanewal
Burewala
Abohar
Ganganagar
Sirsa
Tohana
Karnal
Kairana

30°
Dasht-e Arbu Lut
Mastung
Central Brahui Range
Sibi
Barkhan
Dera Ghazi Khan
Lodhran
Bahawalnagar
Hanumangarh
HARYANA
Hisar
Rohtak
Sonipat
Meer

Amir
Chah
Chagai
Dalbandin
Hamun-i-Lora
Ras Koh 3007
Nushki
Kalat
Lahri
Rajanpur
Jampur
Uch
Bahawalpur
Fort Abbas
Anupgarh
Nohar
Mahajan
Rajgarh
Bhiwani
Delhi
Ghaziaba

Nok Kundi
Yakmach
Kalat
Dera Bugti
Kashmore
Ahmadpur
East
Suratgarh
Bikaner
Churu
Gurgaon
Morada
NEW DEI

Hamun-i-Mashkel
Qila Ladgasht
Washuk
Karodi
Khuzdar
Jacobabad
Shikarpur
Sadiqabad
Barsalpur
Sardarshahr
Ratangarh
Sikar
Jhunjhunun
Namaul
Faridaba

Kamarod
Nagha Kalat
Shahdad Kot
Ghotki
Ramgarh
Ghotaru
Nokha
Nagaur
Alwar
Mathura
Agra

Panjgur
Siahan Range
Srab
Larkana
Khairpur
Sukkur
Jaisalmer
Bap
Phalodi
Sujangarh
Jaipur
Bharatpur
Firozab

Diz
Central Makran Range
Wadh
Kandiaro
Pokaran
RAJASTHAN
Merta
Sambhar
Ajmer
Morena
Gwali

Tump
Turbat
Bela
Dadu
Kirthar Range
Diwana
Nawabshah
Barmer
Jodhpur
Tonk
Sawai
Madhopur
Bundi
Shivpuri
Jhans

Hoshab
Bhairi 1454
Bazdar
Goshanak
Sakrand
Tando Adam
Shiv
Balotra
Pali
Beawar
Devli
Bhilwara
Kota
Lalitpu

Dasht
Makran Coast Range
Uthal
Hyderabad
Khipro
Luni
Jalore
Deogarh
Bundi
Baran

Suntsar
Gwadar
Pasni
Ormara
Sonmiani
Sonmiani Bay
Bula Khan
Thano
Mirpur Khas
Khokhropar
Sirohi
Gitru Sikhar
Chittaurgarh
Jhalawar

Karachi
Thatta
Sujawal
Naukot
Mithi
Abu Road
1722
Udaipur
Neemuch
Guna

Mouths of the Indus
Jati
Badin
Nagar Parkar
Palanpur
Sidhpur
I Mandsaur
Biaora
Bina-Etav

Tropic of Cancer
Rann of Kachchh
Lakhpat
Radhanpur
Mahesana
Dungarpur
Banswara
Jaora
N
Bhopal
Vidish

Rapur
Bhuj
Gandhidham
Viramgam
Gandhinagar
Ratlam
Dahod
Ujjain
Dewas
Sag

Kandla
Ahmadabad
Godhra
Indore
MADHYA PR

Gulf of Kachchh
Okha
Dwarka
Surendranagar
Dhandhuka
Nadiad
Vadodara
Alirajpur
Dhar
Mhow
Harda
Itarsi
Chhindw

GUJARAT
Jamnagar
Rajkot
Gondal
Dhasa
Bhavnagar
Khambhat
Bharuch
Rajpur
Khargon
Khandwa
Betul

Porbandar
Upleta
Kathiawar
Nandurbar
Narmada
Satpura Range
Burhanpur
Achalpur

ARABIAN
Junagadh
Keshod
Amreli
Visavadar
Mahuva
Veraval
Gulf of Khambhat
Surat
Vyara
Jalgaon
Bhusawal
Amravati
Akola
Wardha

SEA
2 Diu
Gulf of Khambhat
Valsad
Dhule
Chalisgaon
Khamgaon
Hinganghat

20°
2
Daman
Silvassa
Nashik
Manmad
MAHARASHTRA
Jalna
Adila

Dahanu
Igatpuri
Aurangabad
Pusad
Penganga
Parbhani

Administrative areas not named on the map:
INDIA
Ulhasnagar
Sangamner
Kalyan
Thane
Narayangaon
Ahmadnagar
Godavari
Nanded

Mumbai (Bombay)
Navi
Mumbai

1. DADRA AND NAGAR HAVELI (B2)
2. DAMAN AND DIU (B2)

METRES
FEET
5000
16404

3000
9843

2000
6562

1000
3281

500
1640

200
656

0
0

Land below
sea level

200
656

4000
13124

6000
19686

Albers Equal Area Conic Projection

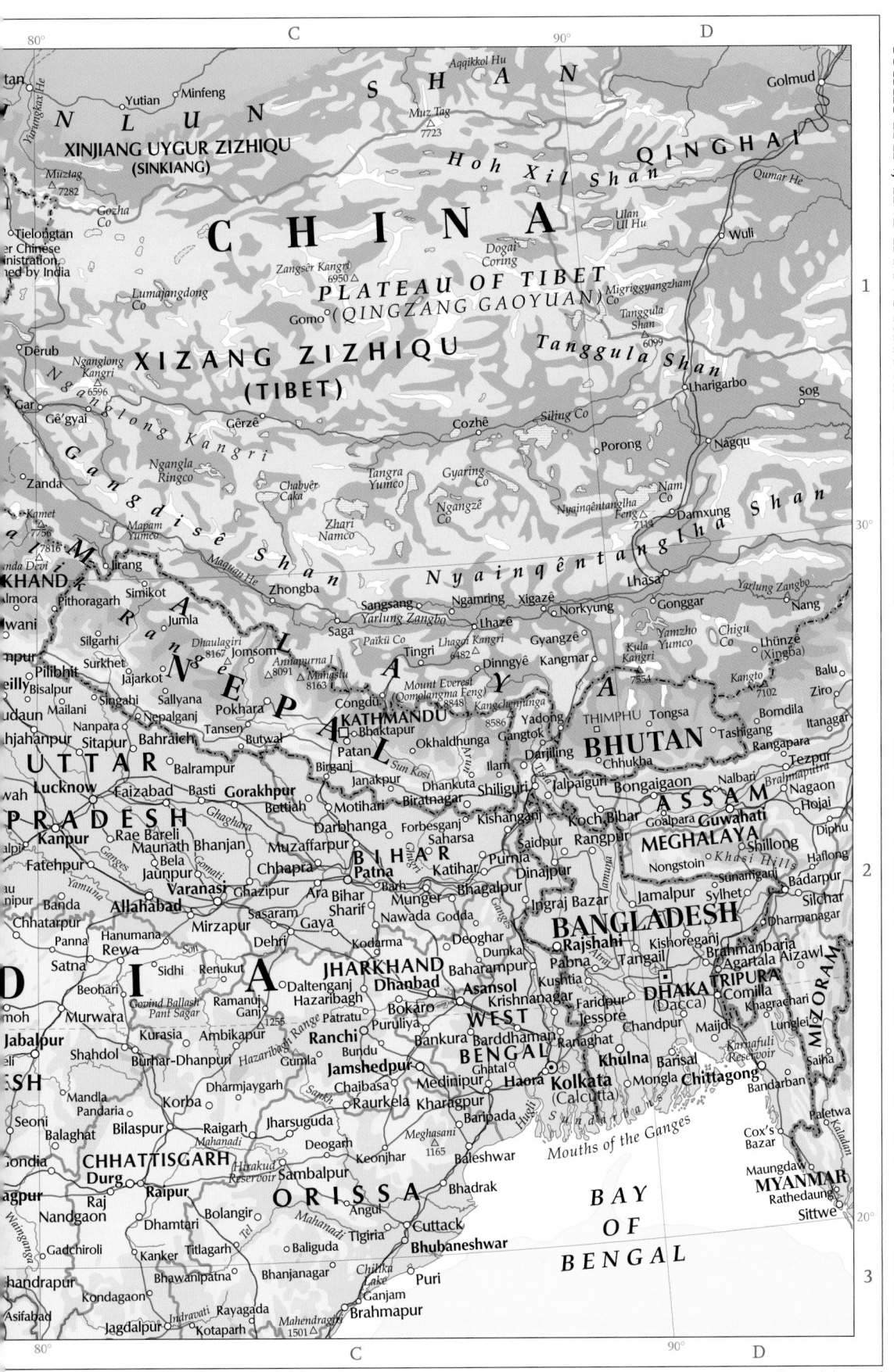

80°   C   90°   D

**XINJIANG UYGUR ZIZHIQU
(SINKIANG)**

K U N L U N   S H A N

Yutian   Minfeng

Aqqikkol Hu

Golmud

Muz Tag
7723

Hoh Xil Shan   QINGHAI

Muztag
7282

Gozha
Co

Tielongtan
Chinese
istration
ned by India

Dogai
Coring

Ulan
Ul Hu

Wuli

Qumar He

C H I N A

Zangsêr Kangri
6950

Migriggyangzham
Co

Tanggula
Shan

1

Lumajangdong
Co

Gomo

**PLATEAU OF TIBET
(QINGZANG GAOYUAN)**

Dêrub

Nganglong
Kangri
6596

**XIZANG ZIZHIQU
(TIBET)**

Lharigarbo

Sog

Gar   Gê'gyai

Gêrzê

Cozhê

Siling Co

Porong

Nagqu

6099

Tanggula Shan

Zanda

Ngangla
Ringco

Chabyêr
Caka

Tangra
Yumco

Gyaring
Co

Ngangzê
Co

Nam
Co

Nyainqêntanglha
Feng   7114

Damxung

Nyainqêntanglha   Shan

Mapam
Yumco

Zhari
Namco

30°

Kamet
7756

7816

Jirang

Maquan He

Zhongba

Sangsang   Ngamring   Xigazê   Norkyung

Lhasa

Gonggar   Nang

Yarlung Zangbo

KHAND
lmora

Simikot

G a n g d i s ê   S h a n

Saga

Yarlung Zangbo

Lhazê

Yamzho
Yumco

Chigu
Co

Lhünzê
(Xingba)

Pithoragarh   Jumla

wani

Silgarhi   Surkhet

Paiku Co

Tingri

Lhagoi Kangri
6482

Gyangzê

Kula
Kangri

Balu

pur   Pilibhit
reilly   Bisalpur   Singahi

Jajarkot

Dhaulagiri
8167   Jomsom
8091   Annapurna I
8163   Manaslu

Congdü

Mount Everest
(Qomolangma Feng)
8848

Dinngyê   Kangmar

Kangto
7554

Bomdila

7102   Ziro

udaun   Mailani   Nepalganj

Pokhara   Tansen

Butwal

KATHMANDU
Bhaktapur

Yadong

Kangchenjunga
8586

THIMPHU   Tongsa

Tashigang   Itanagar

jhanpur   Sitapur   Nanpara

Bahraich

Patan
Sun Kosi

Okhaldhunga

Darjiling

Gangtok

BHUTAN
Chhukha

Rangapara

U T T A R   Balrampur

Lucknow   Faizabad   Basti   **Gorakhpur**

Birganj   Janakpur

Ilam   Jalpaiguri   Bongaigaon

Tezpur

wah   Bettiah   Motihari   Dhankuta   Biratnagar   Shiliguri

A S S A M   Nalbari   Nagaon

PRADESH   Rae Bareli   Maunath Bhanjan

Ghaghara   Darbhanga   Forbesganj   Kishanganj

Koch Bihar   Goalpara   **Guwahati**   Hojai

Kanpur   Bela   Jaunpur

Muzaffarpur   **BIHAR**   Saharsa

Saidpur   Rangpur   **MEGHALAYA**   Shillong   Diphu

Fatehpur   Chhapra   **Patna**

Katihar   Purnia   Dinajpur   Jamalpur   Nongstoin   Khasi Hills   Sunamganj   Bádarpur

nipur   **Varanasi**   Ghazipur   Ara   Bihar
Sharif   Barh   Munger   Bhagalpur

Ingraj Bazar   Sylhet   Silchar

Brahmaputra

Yamuna   Banda

Allahabad   Mirzapur   Sasaram   Nawada   Godda

Rajshahi   Pabna   Tangail   **DHAKA**   Brahmanbaria   Aizawl   Dharmanagar

Chhatarpur   Panna   Rewa   Sidhi   Dehri   Gaya   Kodarma   Deoghar   Dumka   Baharampur   Kushtia   Jamuna   Agartala   **MIZORAM**

Satna   **JHARKHAND**   Dumri   **Pabna**   Faridpur   Khagrachari

Beohari   Renukut   Hazaribagh   **Dhanbad**   Asansol   **WEST**   Krishnanagar   Jessore   Chandpur   Comilla   Lunglei

Jabalpur   Govind Ballash
Pant Sagar   Ramanuj
Ganj   1255   Patratu   Bokaro   Puruliya   Kushtia   Maijdi

Murwara   Kurasia   Ambikapur   **Ranchi**   Bankura   **Barddhaman**   Ranaghat   **Khulna**   Barisal   **Chittagong**

eli   Shahdol   Burhar-Dhanpuri   Gumla   **Jamshedpur**   **BENGAL**   Ghatal   **Haora**   **Kolkata**   Mongla   Bandarban

oh   Hazaribagh Range   Chaibasa   Medinipur   (Calcutta)

Mandla   Pandaria   Dharmjaygarh   Korba   Raurkela   Kharagpur   Baripada   Sundarbans   Cox's
Bazar   Paletwa

Seoni   Balaghat   Bilaspur   Raigarh   Jharsuguda   Meghasani
1165   Baleshwar   **Mouths of the Ganges**   Maungdaw   **MYANMAR**

Gondia   **CHHATTISGARH**   Deogarh   Keonjhar   **BAY**   Rathedaung

Durg   **Raipur**   Sambalpur   Bhadrak

agpur   Raj
Nandgaon   Dhamtari   Bolangir   Angul   **O R I S S A**   Cuttack   **OF**   Sittwe

Gadchiroli   Kanker   Titlagarh   Baliguda   **Bhubaneshwar**   **BENGAL**

handrapur   Bhawanipatna   Bhanjanagar   Chilka
Lake   Puri   20°

Asifabad   Jagdalpur   Kondagaon   Rayagada   Ganjam

Kotaparh   **Brahmapur**

80°   C   90°   D

300 KILOMETRES
200   100   0
200   100   0   MILES

1:9 000 000

3

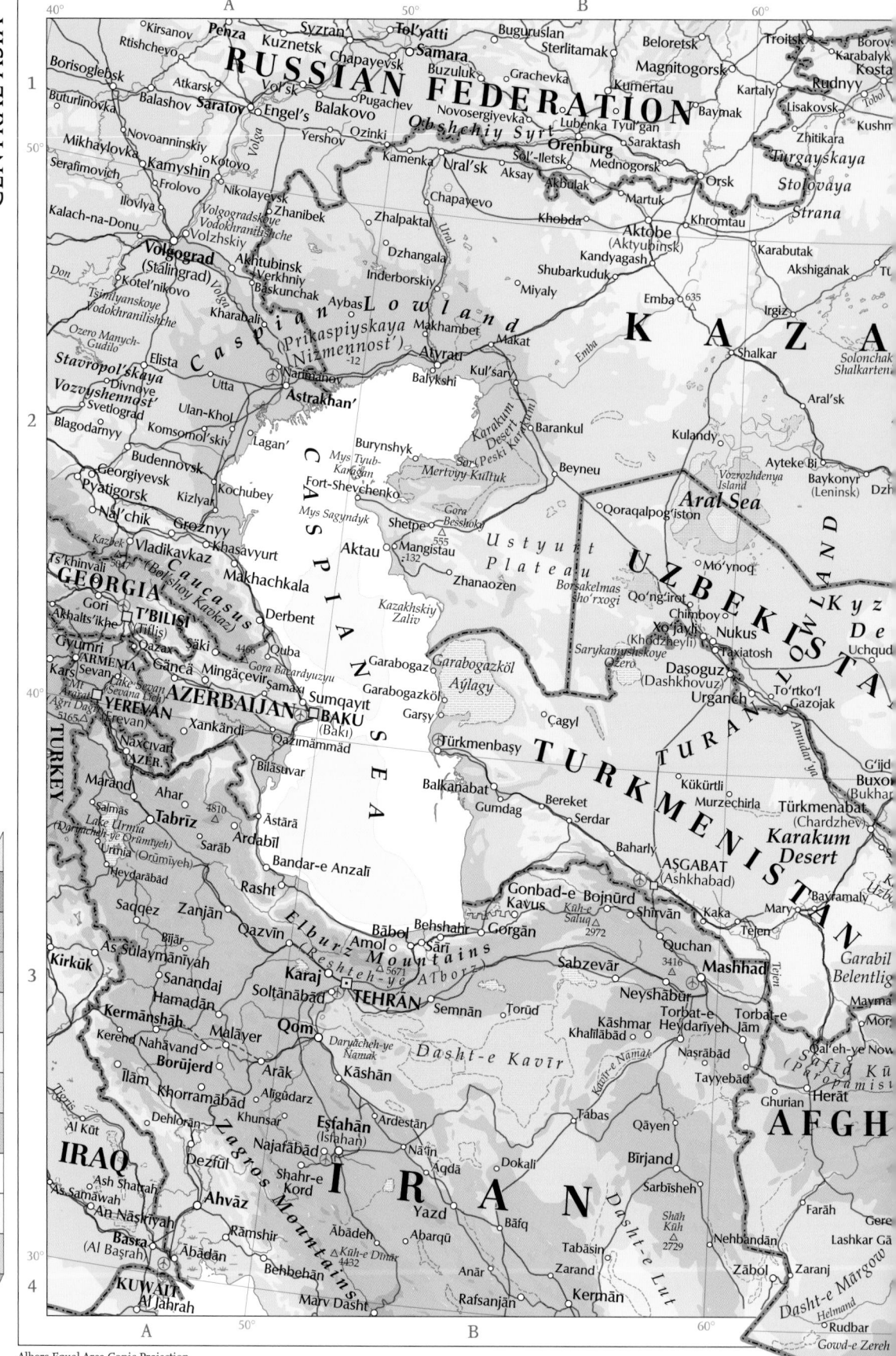

RUSSIAN FEDERATION

Penza
Kirsanov
Kuznetsk
Syzran'
Chapayevsk
Rtishchevo
Tol'yatti
Buguruslan
Sterlitamak
Beloretsk
Troitsk
Borov
Borisoglebsk
Atkarsk
Balashov
Saratov
Engel's
Balakovo
Buzuluk
Samara
Grachevka
Kumertau
Magnitogorsk
Karabalyk
Kosta
Rudnyy
Buturlinovka
Balashov
Novoanninskiy
Kamyshin
Frolovo
Pugachev
Novosergiyevka
Baymak
Kartaly
Lisakovsk
Zhitikara
Kushn
Mikhaylovka
Serafimovich
Ilovlya
Kamyshin
Nikolayevsk
Zhanibek
Yershov
Ozinki
Obshchiy Syrt
Kamenka
Ural'sk
Aksay
Akbulak
Mednogorsk
Orenburg
Saraktash
Orsk
Khromtau
Turgayskaya
Stolovaya
Kalach-na-Donu
Zhalpaktal
Chapayevo
Aktobe
(Aktyubinsk)
Karabutak
Akshiganak
Karabutak
Tu
Volgograd
(Stalingrad)
Akhtubinsk
Verkhniy
Baskunchak
Inderborskiy
Zhangala
Shubarkuduk
Kandyagash
Kaz A Z A
Don
Kotel'nikovo
Volga
Aybas
L o w l a n d
Makhambet
Miyaly
Emba 635
Shalkar
Irgiz
Tsimlyanskoye
Vodokhranilishche
Kharabali
Makat
Emba
Solonchak
Shalkarten
Ozero Manych-
Gudilo
Elista
Utta
Narimanov
Atyrau
Kul'sary
Balykshi
Vozrozhdeniya
Island
Aral'sk
Stavropol'skaya
Astrakhan'
(Prikaspiyskaya
Nizmennost')
-12
Kulandy
Aytelke Bi
Baykonyr
(Leninsk)
Dzh
Vozvyshennost'
Divnoye
Svetlograd
Ulan-Khol
Lagan'
Karakum
Desert
Barankul
Beyneu
Mo'ynoq
Uzbek I S T A
Blagodarnyy
Budennovsk
Komsomol'skiy
Burynshyk
Sor (Peski Karakum)
Mangystau
Qoraqalpog'iston
Aral Sea
Kyz
D e
Georgiyevsk
Pyatigorsk
Kizlyar
Kochubey
Mys Tyub-
Karagan
Fort-Shevchenko
Mertvyy Kultuk
Uchqud
Nal'chik
Groznyy
Khasavyurt
Mys Sagyndyk
Shetpe
Gora
Besshoky
555
Aktau
Zhanaozen
U s t y u r t
P l a t e a u
Qo'ng'irot
Chimboy
Nukus
To'rtko'l
Vladikavkaz
Makhachkala
Mangistau
-132
Zhanaozen
Borsakelmas
sho'rxogi
Xo'jayli
(Khodzheyli)
Taxiatosh
Gazojak
Kazbek
Caucasus
Bol'shoy Kavkaz
Derbent
Kazakhskiy
Zaliv
Garabogaz
Dasoguz
(Dashkhovuz)
GEORGIA
Gori
T'BILISI
(Tflis)
Quba
Garabogaz
Garabogazköl
Garabogazköl
Sarykamyshskoye
Ozero
Urganch
Gyumri
Akhalts'ikhe
Qazax
Gora Bazardyuzyu
4466
Sumqayit
Aylagy
Garşy
ARMENIA
Kars
Sevan
** Gäncä**
Mingäçevir
Şamaxı
BAKU
(Bakı)
Çagyl
Mt.
Aragats
Lake Sevan
Sevana Lich
AZERBAIJAN
Xankändi
Türkmenbaşy
TURAN L O W L A N D
G'ijd
Naxçıvan
Qazımämmäd
Amu Darya
Buxo
(Bukhar
Agri Daği
5165
(Ararat)
YEREVAN
(Erevan)
Biläsuvar
Balkanabat
Kükürtli
Murzechirla
Türkmenabat
(Chardzhev)
Kuz
Uzb
TURKEY
AZER.
Astara
Bereket
Serdar
Karakum
Desert
TURKMENISTAN
Bayramaly
Mary
4810
Marand
Ahar
Tabriz
Gumdag
AŞGABAT
(Ashkhabad)
Mary
Salmas
Lake Urmia
(Daryacheh-ye Orümiyeh)
Sarab
Ardabil
Baharly
Kül-e
Saluq
2972
Kaka
Tejen
Garabil
Belentligi
Urmia (Orümiyeh)
Heydarabad
Bandar-e Anzali
Gonbad-e
Kavus
Bojnürd
Shirvan
Quchan
Mayma
Kirkük
Saqqez
Zanjän
Rasht
Elburz Mountains
Bābol
Behshahr
Gorgan
Sabzevär
3416
Mashhad
Mor
Qazvin
Amol
Sari
Reshteh-ye Alborz
5671
Torud
Neyshäbür
As Sulaymäniyah
Sanandaj
Karaj
Soltanabad
TEHRĀN
Semnan
Torbat-e
Heydariyeh
Torbat-e
Jām
Safid Ku
(Paropamisus)
Hamadan
Kermanshah
Kerend Nahavand
Malayer
Qom
Daryacheh-ye
Namak
Käshmar
Khalilabad
Nasrabad
Koyir-e Namak
Ghurian
Herat
Borüjerd
Aräk
Käshän
Dasht-e Kavir
Tayyebad
A F G H
Ilam
Khorramabad
Aligüdarz
Ardestan
Qāyen
Khunsar
Esfahan
(Isfahan)
Näin
Aqda
Dokali
Bīrjand
Ghurian
Al Küt
Dehloran
Najafabad
Shahr-e
Kord
I R A N
Yazd
Sarbisheh
Farah
Ger
Dezfül
Zagros Mountains
Ābädeh
Ābarqu
Anar
Shah
Küh
2729
Nehbandan
Lashkar Ga
Basra
(Al Basrah)
Ahväz
Rämshir
Behbahän
Küh-e Dinar
4432
Marv Dasht
Anär
Zarand
Bäfq
Tabäsin
Dasht-e Lut
Zäbol
Zaranj
IRAQ
Ash Shatrah
An Näsiriyah
As Samäwah
Äbädän
Rafsanjän
Kermän
Dasht-e Margow
Rudbar
Helmand
KUWAIT
Al Jahrah

METRES
FEET

5000	16404
3000	9843
2000	6562
1000	3281
500	1640
200	656
0	0
Land below sea level	
200	656
4000	13124
6000	19686

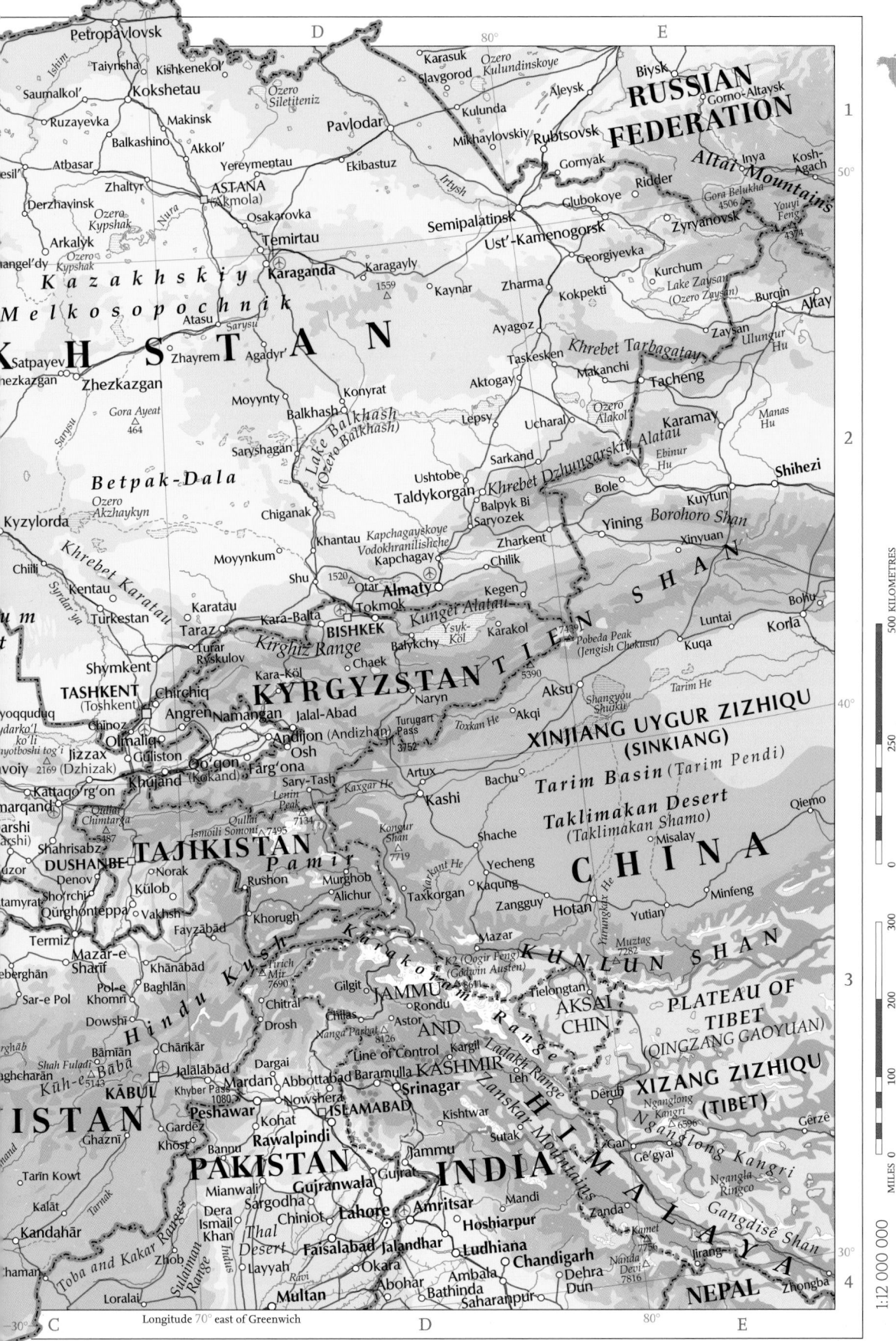

Petropavlovsk

Ishim

Taiynsha

Kishkenekol'

Kokshetau

Saumalkol'

Ruzaevka

Makinsk

Akkol'

Balkashino

Atbasar

Zhaltyr

ASTANA
(Akmola)

Derzhavinsk

Ozero
Kypshak

Osakarovka

Temirtau

Arkalyk

Ozero
Kypshak

Karaganda

esil'

angel'dy

Satpayev

nezkazgan

Zhezkazgan

Kazakhskiy

Atasu

Sarysu

Zhayrem

Agadyr'

Melkosopochnik

Gora Ayeat
464

Konyrat

Moyynty

Balkhash

Karagayly

1559

KHSTAN

STAN

Saryshagan

Sarysu

Kyzylorda

Ozero
Akzhaykyn

Betpak-Dala

Lake Balkhash
(Ozero Balkhash)

Chiganak

Ushtobe

Moyynkum

Khantau

Shu

Karasuk

Slavgorod

Ozero
Kulundinskoye

Pavlodar

Ekibastuz

Irtysh

Yereymentau

Kulunda

Mikhaylovskiy

Rubtsovsk

Semipalatinsk

Ust'-Kamenogorsk

Aleysk

Gornyak

Ridder

Glubokoye

Zyryanovsk

Kaynar

Zharma

Georgiyevka

Kurchum

Ayagoz

Taskesken

Aktogay

Makanchi

Kokpekti

Lake Zaysan
(Ozero Zaysan)

Biysk

RUSSIAN
FEDERATION

Gorno-Altaysk

Inya

Kosh-
Agach

Altai

Gora Belukha
4506

Youyi
Feng
4374

Burgin

Zaysan

Ullungur
Hu

Altay

Mountains

Lepsy

Ucharal

Sarkand

Balpyk Bi

Saryozek

Zharkent

Chilik

Ozero
Alakol

Bole

Khrebet Dzhungarskiy Alatau

Karamay

Ebinur
Hu

Manas
Hu

Shihezi

Taldykorgan

Kapchagayskoye
Vodokhranilishche

Kapchagay

Yining

Kuytun

Xinyuan

Borohoro Shan

Zhezkazgan

1520

Otar

Almaty

Kegen

S H A N

Bohu

Chilli

Khrebet Karatau

Kentau

Karatau

Syrdar'ya

Taraz

Turar
Ryskulov

Kara-Balta

Tokmok

BISHKEK

Balykchy

Kunger Alatau

Ysyk-
Köl

Karakol

Kara-Köl

Chaek

7439

Pobeda Peak
(Jengish Chokusu)

Luntai

Kuqa

Korla

Turkestan

Shymkent

Kirghiz Range

Shangyou
Shuiku

TASHKENT
(Toshkent)

Chirchiq

Angren

Namangan

KYRGYZSTAN

Naryn

5390

Aksu

Akqi

T I E N

Tarim He

yoqquduq

Chinoz

Jalal-Abad

Turugart
Pass
3752

Toxkan He

XINJIANG UYGUR ZIZHIQU

idarko'l
ko'li

Olmaliq

Andijon (Andizhan)

Osh

Artux

(SINKIANG)

nyotboshi tog'i

Jizzax
2169 (Dzhizak)

Guliston

Qo'qon
(Kokand)

Farg'ona

Kaxgar He

Bachu

Kashi

Tarim Basin (Tarim Pendi)

Qiemo

voiy

Khujand

Sary-Tash

Lenin
Peak

Taklimakan Desert
(Taklimakan Shamo)

narqand

Qullai
i Chimtarga
5487

Qullai
Somoni 7495

7134

Kongur
Shan
7719

Shache

Yecheng

Misalay

arshi

Shahrisabz

TAJIKISTAN

Pamir

Yarkant He

C H I N A

izor

DUSHANBE

Norak

Rushon

Murghob

Alichur

Taxkorgan

Kaqung

Zangguy

Hotan

Yutian

Minfeng

tamyrat

Sho'rchi

Denov

Kúlob

Khorugh

K2 (Qogir Feng)
(Godwin Austen)
8611

Karangax He

Muztag
7282

Qúrghonteppa

Vakhsh

Fayzābād

Termiz

Mazar-e
Sharif

Khānābād

Hindu Kush

Mazar

K U N L U N   S H A N

eberghān

Pol-e
Khomri

Baghlan

Tirich
Mir
7690

Gilgit

Rondu

Tielongtan

AKSAI
CHIN

*PLATEAU OF
TIBET*

Sar-e Pol

Dowshi

Chitrāl

Chilas

Astor

JAMMU

Ladakh Range

(QINGZANG GAOYUAN)

rghāb

Bāmiān

Chārikār

Drosh

Nanga Parbat
8126

AND

Kargil

Leh

Dêrub

XIZANG ZIZHIQU

Shah Fuladi

Kūh-e

agheharān
5143

Bābā

Jalālābād

Dargai

KASHMIR

Line of Control

Baramulla

Srinagar

Zanskar Mountains

Gar

Nganglong
Kangri
6596

(TIBET)

Gê'gyai

KĀBUL

Gardēz

Khyber Pass
1080

Peshawar

Mardan

Abbottabad

Nowshera

Kohat

ISLAMABAD

Jammu

Kishtwar

Sutak

Gê'gyai

Ngangse Kangri

Gêrzê

ISTAN

Ghaznī

Khost

Banpu

Rawalpindi

Gujrat

H I M A L A Y A

Zanda

Gangdisê Shan

Tarin Kowt

Toba and Kakar Ranges

Mianwali

Gujranwala

Kamet
7756

Jirang

Zhongba

Kalāt

Dera
Ismail
Khan

Sargodha

Chiniot

PAKISTAN

Lahore

Amritsar

INDIA

Mandi

Hoshiarpur

Nanda
Devi
7816

Kandahār

Sulaiman Range

Zhob

*Thal
Desert*

Faisalabad

Jalandhar

Ludhiana

Chandigarh

Dehra
Dun

NEPAL

haman

Loralai

Indus

Layyah

Ravi

Okara

Abohar

Bathinda

Ambala

Saharanpur

Multan

Tarnak

30°

C

Longitude 70° east of Greenwich

D

80°

E

1:12 000 000

© Collins Bartholomew Ltd

500 KILOMETRES

250

0

300

200

100

0

MILES 0

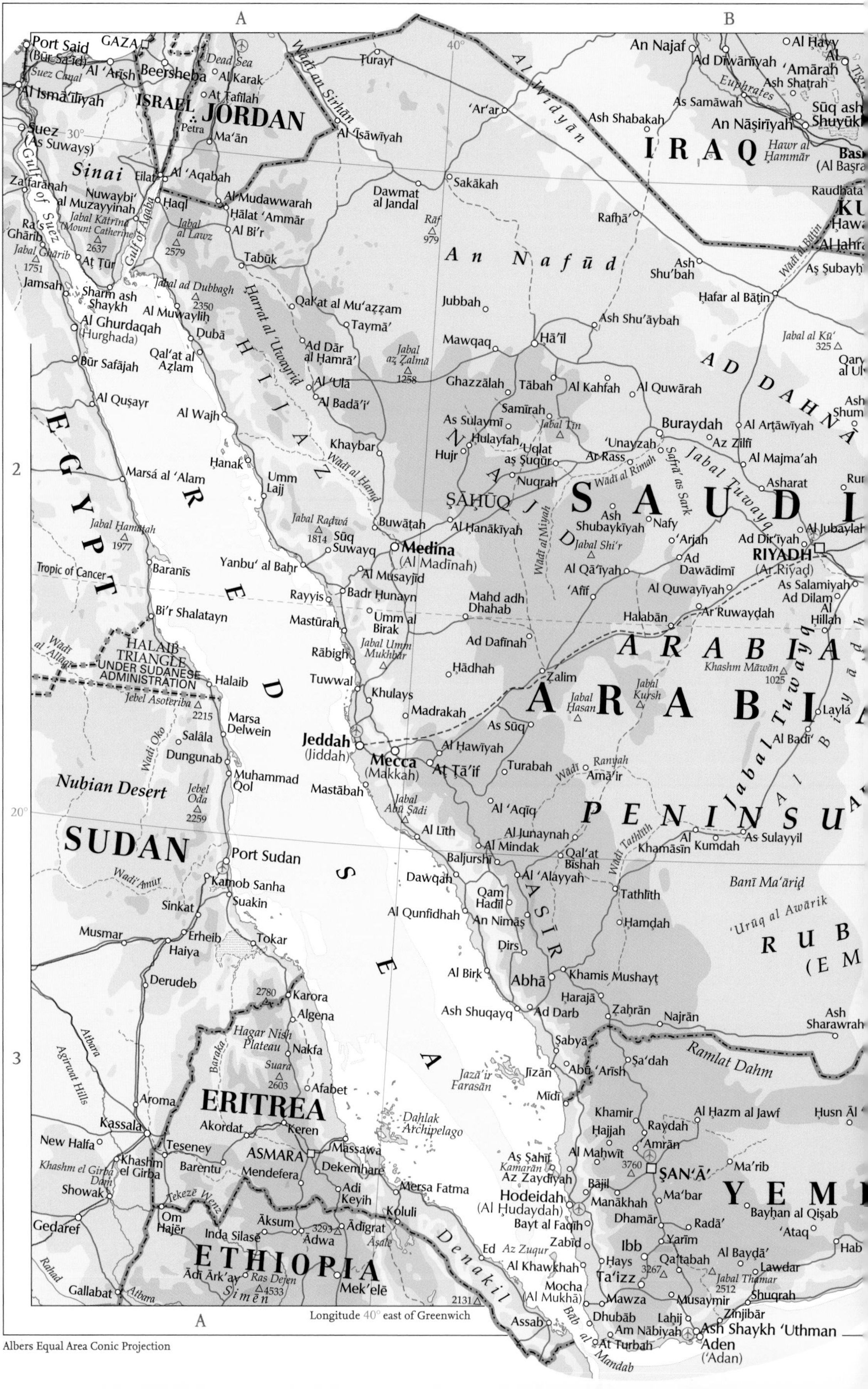

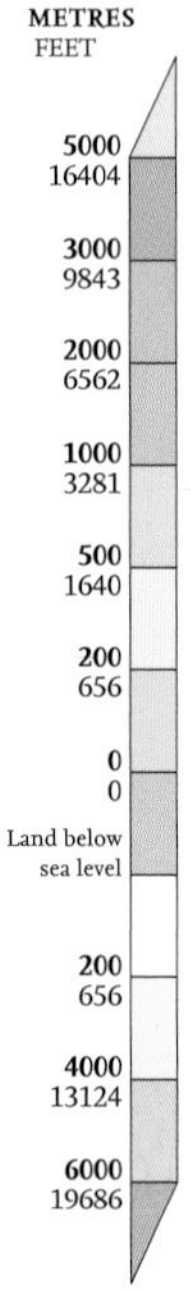

A   B

Port Said
(Būr Sa'īd) GAZA
Al 'Arīsh Beersheba Al Karak
Suez Canal Al Ismā'īlīyah At Tafīlah
Suez
(As Suways) **ISRAEL** **JORDAN**
Zaffaranah Petra Ma'ān

An Najaf Ad Dīwānīyah 'Amārah Al Hayy Al
Euphrates Ash Shatrah
'Ar'ar As Samāwah An Nāsirīyah Sūq ash
Ash Shabakah Shuyūkh
I R A Q Hawr al
Hammār Bas
(Al Basra)

Sinai Eilat Al 'Aqabah Al Mudawwarah Hālat 'Ammār
Nuwaybi' al Muzayyinah Haql Al Bi'r
Jabal Kātrīna Jabal al Lawz Tabūk
Mount Catherine 2637 2579
Ra's Ghārib Jabal Ghārib 1751 At Tūr
Jamsah Sharm ash Shaykh Al Ghurdaqah (Hurghada)
Jabal ad Dubbagh 2350 Al Muwaylih Dubā
Qal'at al Azlam Al 'Ula Al Badā'i'

Dawmat al Jandal Sakākah
Raf Rafha' Ash Shu'bah
979 An Nafūd Ash Shum
Hafar al Bātin Ash Shu'aybah Jabal al Ka' 325 Qary al Ul
Jubbah Hā'il
Mawqaq Ghazzālah Tābah Al Kahfah Al Quwārah Buraydah Al Artāwīyah
QaRat al Mu'azzam Taymā' Jabal az Zalma 1258 Samīrah Jabal Tin Az Zilfī Al Majma'ah
Ad Dār al Hamrā' As Sulaymī Hulayfah 'Unayzah Asharat
Khaybar Uqlat aş Şuqūr Ar Rass Nafy 'Arjah
Hanak Umm Lajj Nuqrah ŞĀHŪQ Ash Shubaykīyah Ad Dawādimī Ad Dir'īyah Al Jubaylah
Jabal Radwā 1814 Al Hanākīyah Jabal Shi'r Ad **RIYADH**
Sūq Suwayq Buwātah Al Qā'īyah (Ar Riyad) As Salamīyah
Yanbu' al Bahr **Medina** (Al Madīnah) 'Afīf Al Quwayīyah Ad Dilam Al Hillah
Rayyis Al Musayjīd Mahd adh Dhahab Halabān Ar Ruwaydah
Baranīs Badr Hunayn Ad Dafīnah **A R A B I A**
Bi'r Shalatayn Mastūrah Umm al Birak Khashm Māwān 1025
Rābigh Jabal Umm Mukhbar Zalim Jabal Kursh Jabal Tuwayq
HALAIB TRIANGLE Halaib Tuwwal Khulays Hādhah Jabal Hasan Laylā Al Badī'
UNDER SUDANESE ADMINISTRATION Jebel Asoteriba 2215 Madrakah As Sūq
Marsa Delwein Wadi al Allāqi **Jeddah** (Jiddah) As Sūq **P E N I N S U**
Salāla Dungunab Muhammad Qol **Mecca** (Makkah) Al Hawīyah At Tā'if Turabah 'Amā'ir
Nubian Desert Jebel Oda 2259 Mastābah Jabal Abū Sadi Al 'Aqīq Al Badī As Sulayyil
Al Līth Al Junaynah Qal'at Bīshah Banī Ma'ārid
SUDAN Port Sudan Baljurshi Al 'Alāyyah Khamāsīn Kumdah 'Urūq al Awārik
Wadi 'Amur Kamob Sanha Dawqah Qam Hadīl Tathlīth **R U B**
Sinkat Suakin Al Qunfidhah An Nimās Hamdah (E M
Musmar Erheib Haiya Tokar Dirs
Derudeb Al Birk Abhā Khamis Mushayt
2780 Karora Ash Shuqayq Ad Darb Harajā
Algena Hagar Nish Plateau Zahrān Najrān Ash Sharawrah
Hagar Nish Plateau Nakfa Suara 2603 Jīzān Sabyā
Aroma Afabet **ERITREA** Jaza'ir Farasān Abū 'Arīsh Şa'dah Ramlat Dahm
Kassala Akordat Keren Mīdī Khamir Al Hazm al Jawf Husn Āl
New Halfa Teseney Dahlak Archipelago Hajjah Raydah Amrān
Khashm el Girba Dam Barentu **ASMARA** Massawa Al Mahwīt 3760 **SAN'Ā'** Ma'rib
Showak Mendefera Dekemhare Kamarān Aş Şahīl Manākhah Ma'bar Bayhān al Qişab
Gedaref Adi Keyih Mersa Fatma Az Zaydīyah Bājil Dhamār Radā' 'Ataq Hab
Āksum Koluli **Hodeidah** (Al Hudaydah) Bayt al Faqīh Yarīm Al Baydā'
Inda Silase Ādigrat Ed Az Zuqur Zabīd **Ibb** Qatabah Lawdar
3293 Ādwa Āşale Hays Jabal Thamar 2512
ETHIOPIA 3267 **Ta'izz** Shuqrah
Ādi Ārk'ay Ras Dejen 4533 Mek'ele Al Khawkhah Mawza Musaymir Zinjibār
Gallabat Rahad Atbara Sīmēn 2131 Mocha (Al Mukhā) Dhubāb Lahij Ash Shaykh 'Uthman
Longitude 40° east of Greenwich Assab Am Nābiyah Aden ('Adan) At Turbah Bāb al Mandab

METRES FEET
5000 / 16404
3000 / 9843
2000 / 6562
1000 / 3281
500 / 1640
200 / 656
0 / 0
Land below sea level
200 / 656
4000 / 13124
6000 / 19686

Albers Equal Area Conic Projection

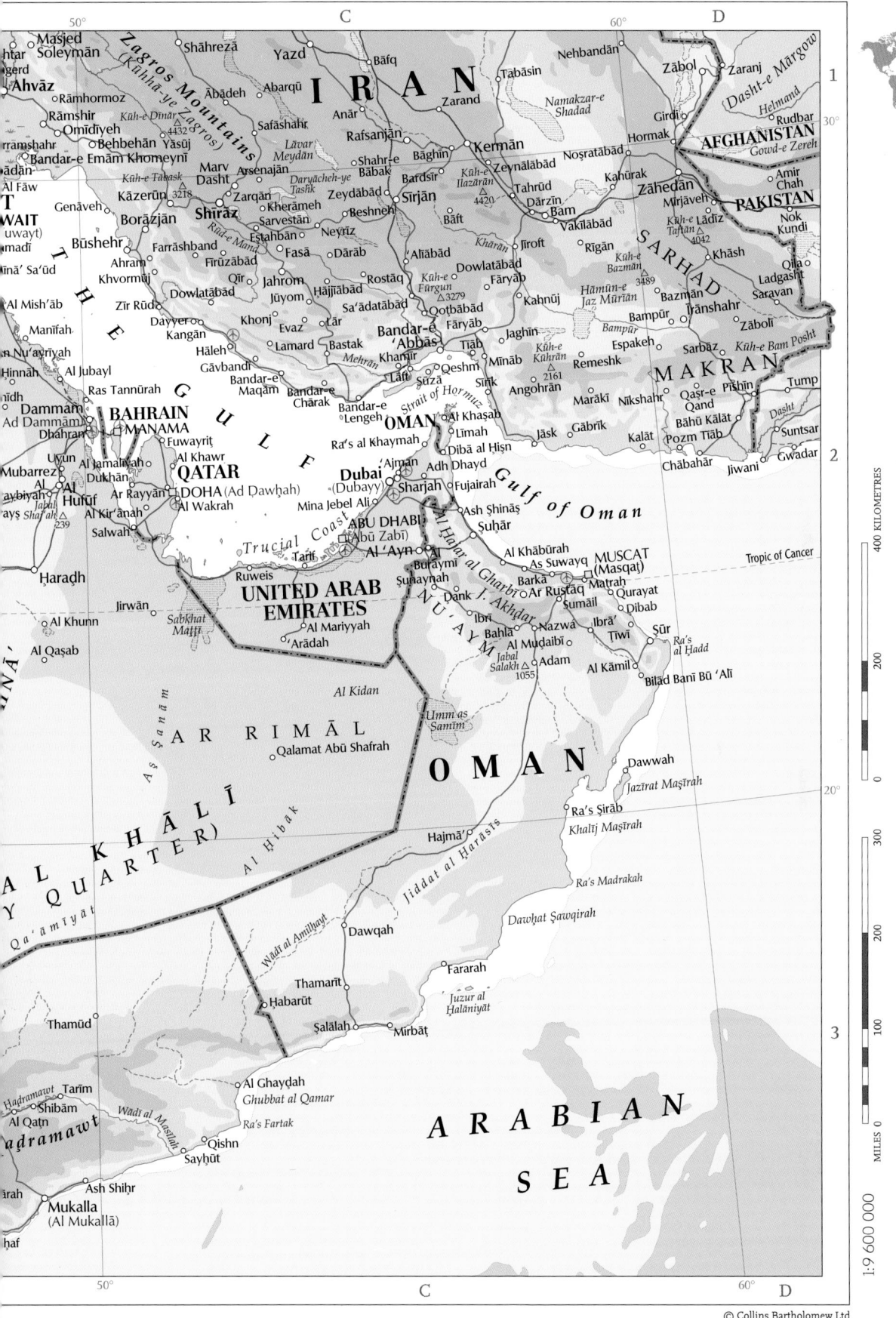

50°

Masjed
Soleymān
htar
Ahvāz
gerd
Rāmhormoz
Omīdīyeh
rramshahr
Bandar-e Emām Khomeynī
ādan
Al Fāw
T
WAIT
uwayt)
amadī
īnā' Sa'ūd
Al Mish'āb
Manīfah
n Nu'ayrīyah
Hinnah
Al Jubayl
nīdh
Dammām
Ad Dammām
Dhahrān
Mubarrez
Al Jamalīyah
Al
aybiyah
Al
Hufūf
'Ali
ays
Jabal
Shat'ah
239
Al Kir'ānah
Salwah
Haradh
Jirwān
Al Khunn
Al Qasab
īnā'
ĪNA'
AL KHĀLĪ
Y QUARTER)
Qa'āmīyāt
Thamūd
Hadramawt
Tarīm
Al Qatn
Shibām
adramawt
Wādī al Masīlah
Qishn
Sayhūt
īrah
Ash Shihr
Mukalla
(Al Mukallā)
haf

Shāhrezā
Yazd
Bāfq
Tabāsin
Nehbandān
Zābol
Zaranj
Dasht-e Mārgow
I R A N
Ābādeh
Abarqū
Zarand
Anār
Namakzar-e
Shadad
Girdī
Helmand
AFGHANISTAN
Safāshahr
Rafsanjān
Bāghīn
Kermān
Nosratābād
Hormak
Gowd-e Zereh
Kūh-e Dīnār
Kūhhā-ye Zagros
4432 △
Lāvar
Meydān
Shahr-e
Bābak
Kūh-e
Ilazaran
△
4420
Zeynālābād
Tahrūd
Kahūrak
Zāhedān
Amir
Chah
PAKISTAN
Marv
Dasht
Arsenajān
Zeydābād
Dārzīn
Mirjāveh
Kūh-e
Taftān
△4042
Nok
Kundi
Zarqān
Daryācheh-ye
Tashk
Sīrjān
Bardsīr
Bam
Vakīlābād
Khāsh
Qila
Kāzerūn
3218 △
Kherāmeh
Beshneh
Sarhad
Ladgasht
Shīrāz
Sarvestān
Khārān
Jīroft
Rīgān
Saravan
Borāzjān
Estahbān
Neyrīz
Bāft
Kūh-e
Bazmān
Bazmān
Zābolī
Būshehr
Farrāshband
Fasā
Dārāb
Aliābād
Dowlatābād
Fāryāb
Hāmūn-e
Jaz Mūrīān
△3489
Ahram
Firūzābād
Qīr
Rostāq
Kūh-e
Fārgun
△3279
Fāryāb
Kahnūj
Bampūr
Īranshahr
Khvormūj
Zīr Rūd
Jahrom
Hājjiābād
Sa'ādatābād
Qotbābād
Bampūr
Espakeh
MAKRAN
Dayyer
Dowlatābād
Jūyom
Khonj
Evaz
Lār
Bandar-e
'Abbās
Tīāb
Jaghīn
Remeshk
Sarbāz
Kūh-e Bam Posht
Kangān
Hāleh
Lamard
Bastak
Khamīr
Mīnāb
Kūh-e
Kūhran
2161 △
Marākī
Nīkshahr
Tump
Gāvbandī
Mehrān
Laft
Sūza
Qeshm
Sīrīk
Angohrān
Jāsk
Gābrīk
Kalāt
Bāhū Kālāt
Dasht
Suntsar
Bandar-e
Maqām
Bandar-e
Charak
Bandar-e
Lengeh
Strait of Hormuz
OMAN
Al Khasab
Pozm Tīāb
Gwadar
B
A
H
R
A
I
N
T H E
G U L F
Ra's al Khaymah
Līmah
Pīshīn
Qasr-e
Qand
Chābahār
Jiwani
MANAMA
Fuwayrit
Ajman
Dibā al Hisn
Dibā al Hisn
QATAR
Dubai
(Dubayy)
Sharjah
Adh Dhayd
Al Khawr
DOHA (Ad Dawhah)
Mina Jebel Ali
Fujairah
Gulf of Oman
Ar Rayyān
Al Wakrah
ABU DHABI
(Abū Zabī)
Ash Shinās
Suhār
Al Halar al Gharbī
Al 'Ayn
Barkā
As Suwayq
MUSCAT
(Masqat)
Tropic of Cancer
Ruweis
Tarīf
Buray
Ar Rustāq
Matrah
UNITED ARAB
EMIRATES
Sunaynah
Danik
J. Akhdar
Sumāil
Quryat
Al Khābūrah
Jirwān
Ibrī
Bahlā
Nazwā
Ibrā'
Dibab
Sabkhat
Matti
Al Mariyyah
N U 'A Y M
Tīwī
Arādah
Jabal
Salakh
Adam
Al Mudaibī
1055
Sūr
Ra's
al Hadd
Al Kidan
Al Kāmil
Bilād Banī Bū 'Alī
Umm as
Samīm
O M A N
Dawwah
Jazīrat Masīrah
Qalamat Abū Shafrah
Ra's Sirāb
20°
As Sanām
AR RIMĀL
Hajmā'
Khalīj Masīrah
Al Hibak
Jiddat al Harāsīs
Ra's Madrakah
Wādī al Amilhayt
Dawqah
Dawhat Sawqirah
Thamarīt
Fararah
Juzur al
Halānīyāt
Habarūt
Salālah
Mirbāt
A R A B I A N
Al Ghaydah
Ghubbat al Qamar
Ra's Fartak
S E A

400 KILOMETRES
200
0

300
200
100
0
MILES

1:9 600 000

METRES
FEET

5000
16404

3000
9843

2000
6562

1000
3281

500
1640

200
656

0
0

Land below
sea level

200
656

4000
13124

6000
19686

Longitude 30° east of Greenwich

Albers Equal Area Conic Projection

METRES
FEET

5000
16404

3000
9843

2000
6562

1000
3281

500
1640

200
656

0
0

Land below
sea level

200
656

4000
13124

6000
19686

NORWAY

SWEDEN

FINLAND

Torshavn
Faroe
Islands
(Denmark)
Shetland
Islands

Arctic Circle

Jan Mayen
(Norway)

Norwegian
Sea

Bergen
Drammen
OSLO
Kristiansand

Gulf of Bothnia
STOCKHOLM
Baltic Sea

Gulf of Finland
HELSINKI
Turku
Tampere

ESTONIA
LATVIA
RIGA
LITHUANIA
VILNIUS
KALININGRAD
BELARUS
MINSK

UKRAINE

Kirovohrad
Kryvyy Rih
Kherson
Mykolayiv
Sevastopol'
Simferopol'

Bat'umi
Trabzon
TURKEY
Kars
GEORGIA
Sochi
Novorossiysk
Krasnodar
Stavropol'

ARM.
YEREVAN
AZER.
Naxçivan
Tabriz
Ardabil
Rasht
IRAN
Qazvin

Greenland
Sea

Svalbard
(Norway)
Spitsbergen
Longyearbyen

Bjørnøya
(Norway)

A R C T I

Zemlya
Aleksandry
Nagurskoye

Ostrov
Rudol'fa
Green-Bell
Zemlya Frantsa-Iosifa

Zemlya
Vil'cheka

Mys
Zhelaniya

B A R E N T S

S E A

Stolbovoy

Novaya Zemlya

Kara Sea
(Karskoye More)

Ostrov
Belyy

Dikso

Yamal Peninsula
(Poluostrov Yamal)

Gydan
Peninsula
(Gydanskiy
Poluostrov)

Salekhard

Novyy Urengoy
Nadym

Urengoy
Turukha

Novosibirsk

Tomsk

Barnaul

KAZAKHSTAN

ASTANA
(Akmola)

Karaganda
Temirtau

Balkhash
Lake Balkhash
(Ozero Balkhash)

UZBEKISTAN
Nukus

TURKMEN.
Balkanabat

Conic Equidistant Projection

Longitude 75° east of Greenwich

1:24 000 000

© Collins Bartholomew Ltd

K. KOSOVO
LIE. LIECHTENSTEIN
MACE. MACEDONIA
MONT. MONTENEGRO

Chamberlin Trimetric Projection

© Collins Bartholomew Ltd

1:20 000 000

1000 KILOMETRES

750

500

250

0

MILES 0

250

500

BARENTS SEA

Novaya Zemlya

Vorkuta

Ostrov Kolguyev

Ob'

RUSSIAN FEDERATION

Ural Mountains

White Sea

Murmansk

Archangel

Syktyvkar

Perm

FINLAND

NLAND

Lake Onega

Lake Ladoga

Helsinki

St Petersburg

Tallinn

ESTONIA

TONIA

Nizhniy Novgorod

Kazan'

Yaroslavl

Volga

Riga

VIA

Samara

Orenburg

Moscow

NIA

ius

Ryazan'

Minsk

BELARUS

Homyel'

Voronezh

Saratov

Volgograd

Don

Kiev

Kharkiv

UKRAINE

Dnipropetrovs'k

Donets'k

Astrakhan

Volga

KAZAKHSTAN

Aral Sea

UZBEKISTAN

MOLDOVA

Chişinău

Dniepe

Rostov na-Donu

ROMANIA

MANIA

Bucharest

Odessa

Sea of Azov

Krasnodar

Groznyy

Caspian Sea

Caucasus

TURKMENISTAN

Sofia

BULGARIA

ULGARIA

Black Sea

GEORGIA

AZERBAIJAN

ARMENIA

AZER.

İstanbul

Thessaloniki

hessaloniki

TURKEY

Aegean Sea

ECE

GREECE

Athens

Crete

CYPRUS

LEBANON

SYRIA

Euphrates

IRAQ

Tigris

IRAN

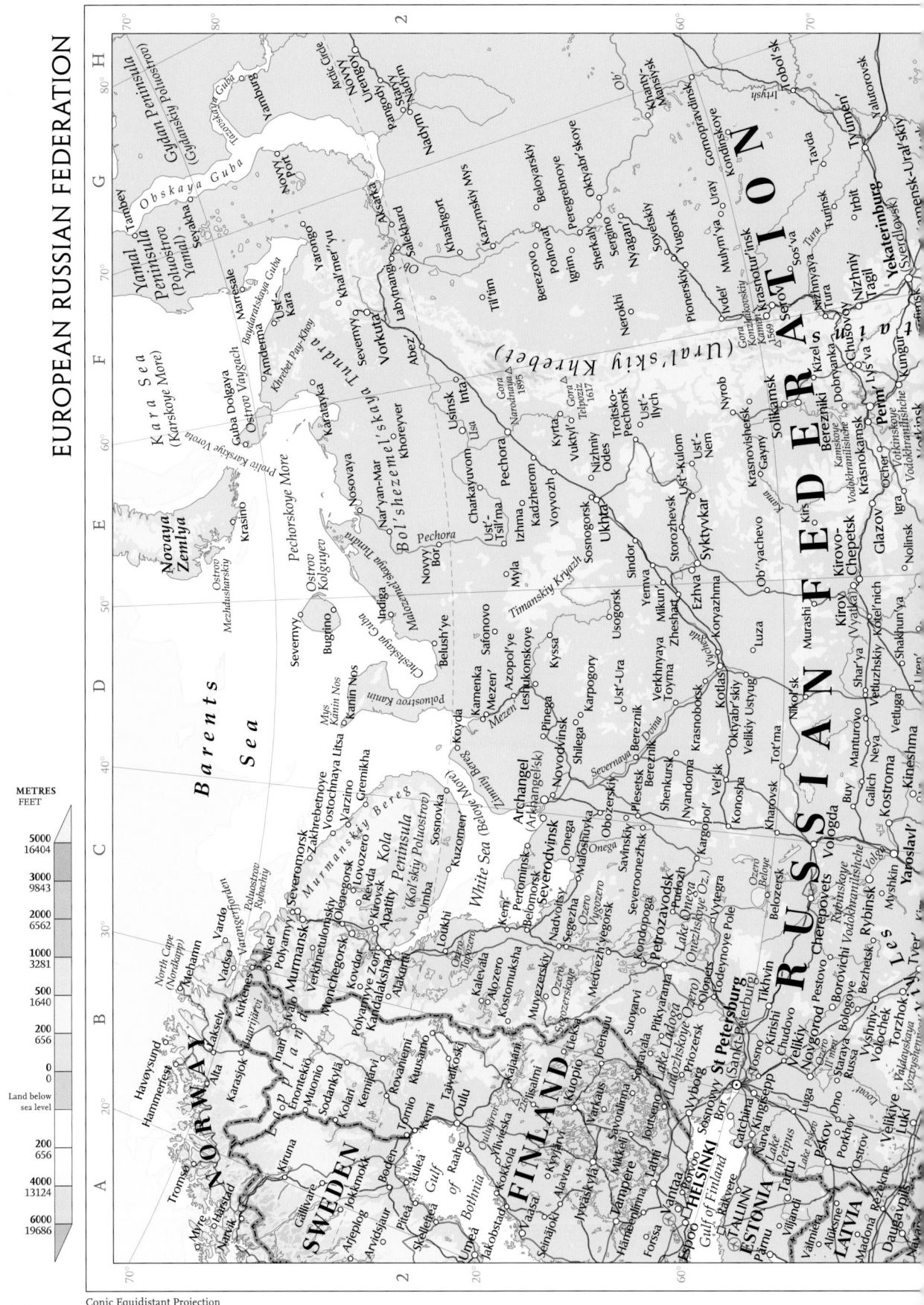

Conic Equidistant Projection

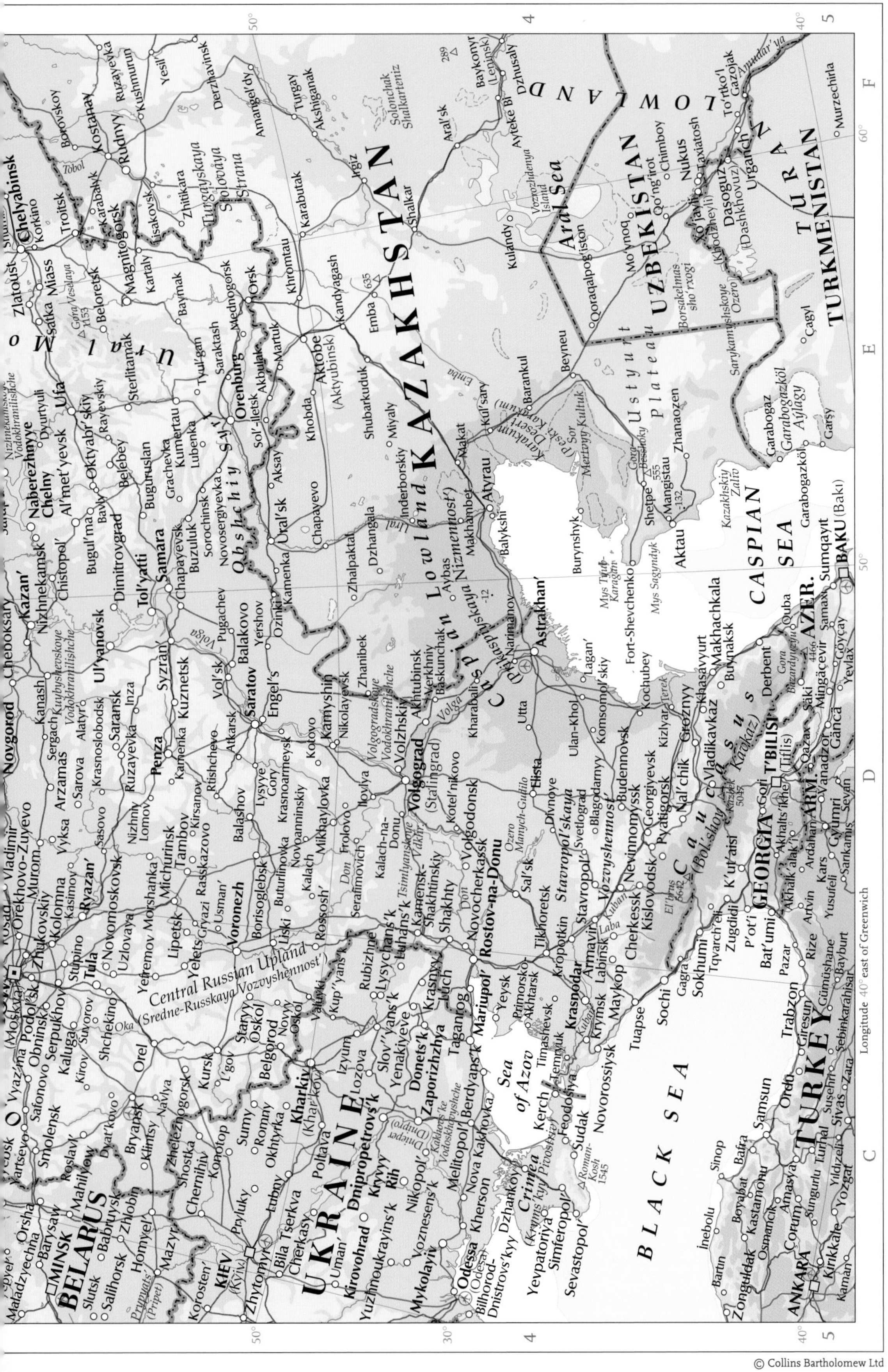

1:12 000 000

MILES 0   100   200   300

0   250   500 KILOMETRES

Longitude 40° east of Greenwich

BELARUS
UKRAINE
KAZAKHSTAN
UZBEKISTAN
TURKMENISTAN
TURAN LOWLAND
GEORGIA
ARM.
AZER.
TURKEY
CASPIAN SEA
BLACK SEA
Sea of Azov
Aral Sea
Caucasus (Bol'shoy Kavkaz)
Ustyurt Plateau
Central Russian Upland (Sredne-Russkaya Vozvyshennost')

MINSK
KIEV (Kyïv)
MOSCOW (Moskva)
ANKARA
T'BILISI (Tiflis)
BAKU (Bakı)
Astrakhan'
Volgograd (Stalingrad)
Rostov-na-Donu
Samara
Kazan'
Chelyabinsk
Orenburg
Ufa
Saratov
Voronezh
Penza
Ryazan'
Tula
Tol'yatti
Ul'yanovsk
Nizhnekamsk
Naberezhnyye Chelny
Novgorod
Cheboksary

FINLAND

Kouvola
Anjalankoski
Mäntsälä
Järvenpää
Hamina
Espoo
Tuusula
Porvoo
Loviisa
Vyborg
Kirkkonummio
Vantaa
Kotka
Vyborgskiy Zaliv
Zelenogorsk
HELSINKI
(Helsingfors)
Hanko
Ekenäs

SWEDEN
Uppsala
Norrtälje
Mariehamn
Korpo
Ostrov Gogland
Ostrov Moshchnyy
Lomonosov
Märsta
Aland Islands
Kökar
Sosnovyy Bor
Petrodvore
Sollentuna
Åkersberga
Täby
Ust'-Luga
STOCKHOLM
Tumba
Gulf of Finland
Maardu
Loksa
Narva Bay
Kingisepp
Gatch
Västerhaninge
TALLINN
Kohtla-Järve
Volosc
Paldiski
Keila
Kehra
Rakvere
Sillamäe
Narva
Nynäshamn
Kärdla
Vormsi
Turba
Vaida
Tapa
Kiviõli
Jõhvi
Narvskoye Vodokhranilishche
Sivers
Kalana
Hari Kurk
Haapsalu
Rapla
Paide
Rakke
Emumägi 166
Raja
Vasknarva
Os'mino
Mshinsk
Hiiumaa
Kaina
Muhu
Virtsu
Vändra
Põltsamaa
Jõgeva
Gdov
Luga
Emmaste
Mustjala
Orissaare
ESTONIA
Viljandi
Võrtsjärv
Lake Peipus
Plyussa
Kuressaare
Saaremaa
Kihnu
Pärnu
Mõisaküla
Tartu
Ülenurme
Elva
Yamm
Strugi-Krasnyye
Säre
Irbe Strait
Mazirbe
Kolkasrags
Ruhnu
Limbaži
Valmiera
Valka
Valga
Võru
Pskov
Lake Pskov
Porkhov
Slavkovic
Oviśrags
Roja
Gulf of Riga
Saulkrasti
Cēsis
Rauna
Smiltene
Alūksne
Ostrov
Pechory
Palkino
Dedovic
Ventspils
Dundaga
Sigulda
Gulbene
Balvi
Pytalovo
Pushkinskiye Gory
Chikhache
Pāvilosta
Akmeņrags
Kuldīga
Talsi
Tukums
Jūrmala
Garkalne
Elkas kalns 265
Madona
Kārsava
Bezhanits
Novorzhe
BALTIC SEA
Gotska Sandön
Visby
Slite
Klintehamn
Gotland (Sweden)
Fårö
LATVIA
RĪGA
Olaine
Ogre
Kārsava
Barkava
Mežvidi
Ludza
Opochka
Liepāja
Aizpute
Saldus
Dobele
Jelgava
Iecava
Aizkraukle
Koknese
Jēkabpils
Viļāni
Rēzekne
Sebezh
Puśtoshka
Nīca
Skrunda
Mažeikiai
Venta
Naujoji Akmenė
Bauska
Pasvalys
Biržai
Līvāni
Preiļi
Malta
Dagda
Nev
Skuodas
Vinta
Kuršėnai
Rokiškis
Daugava
Kretinga
Plungė
Telšiai
Šiauliai
Pakruojis
Radviliškis
Kupiškis
Daugavpils
Krāslava
Rasony
Yezyaryshc
Verkhnyadzvinsk
Klaipėda
Courland Lagoon
Gargždai
Medvėgalio kalnas 235
Zarasai
Druya
Navapolatsk
Harad Obal'
Kintai
Šilalė
Kelmė
Panevėžys
Visaginas
Braslaw
Myory
Polatsk
Ushachy
Shumilina
Nida
LITHUANIA
Raseiniai
Kėdainiai
Ukmergė
Utena
Dūkštas
Navišiu kalnas 289
Sharkawshchyna
Varapayeva
Byeshankovic
Šilutė
Pagėgiai
Tauragė
Jurbarkas
Jonava
Molėtai
Švenčionys
Ignalina
Pastavy
Hlybokaye
Mys Taran
Svetlogorsk
Zelenogradsk
Sovetsk
Neman
Šakiai
 Širvintos
Pabradė
Narach
Myadzyel
Lyepyel'
Chashniki
Syan
Baltiysk
RUS. FED.
Kaliningrad
Chernyakhovsk
Vilkaviškis
Noreikiškės
Kaunas
Grigiškės
Astravyets
Dokshytsy
Byahoml'
Gulf of Gdańsk
Svetlyy
Gvardeysk
Gusev
Kybartai
Prienai
Trakai
VILNIUS
Ashmyany
Smarhon
Vilyeyka
Plyeshchanitsy
Kokhana Talachyn
Mamonovo
Bagrationovsk
Ozersk
Marijampolė
Alytus
Salčininkai
Varena
Maladzyechna
Barysaw
Krupki
Zhlobin
Frombork
Braniewo
Korsze
Goldap
Lazdijai
Sejny
Merkinė
Voranava
Valozhyn
Zaslawye
Smalyavichy
Zhodzina
Byerazino
Elbląg
Bartoszyce
Węgorzewo
Giżycko
Suwałki
Augustów
Druskininkai
Lida
Ivye
Shchuchyn
Navahrudak
Ilwye
Byarozawka
Uskhodni
MINSK 345
Smilavichy
Chervyen'
Malbork
Pasłęk
Dobre Miasto
Olecko
Ełk
Grajewo
Masty
Nyoman
Karelichy
Stowbtsy
Mar''ina Horka
Klichaw
Kwidzyn
Ostróda
Olsztyn
Dzyarzhynsk
Kwidzyn
Iława
Dylewska Góra 312
Pojezierze Mazurskie
Jezioro Śniardwy
Mońki
Hrodna
Vawkavysk
Zel'va
Baranavichy
Asipovichy
Babruysk
Nidzica
Szczytno
Łomża
Svislach
Slonim
Nyasvizh
Kapyl'
Staraya Darohi
Rahach
Brodnica
Działdowo
Mława
Ostrołęka
Narew
Zambrów
Białystok
Hajnówka
Pruzhany
Ivatsevichy
Klyetsk
Slutsk
Salihorsk
Hlusk
Lyuban'
Svyetlaho
Dzhaldowo
Ciechanów
POLAND
Płock
Ostrów Mazowiecka
Wyszków
Węgrów
BELARUS
Byaroza
Kamyanyets
Tsyelyakhany
Dzyatlavichy
Mal'kavichy
Aktsyabrsk
Kutno
Legionowo
WARSAW (Warszawa)
Pruszków
Siedlce
Zhabinka
Drahichyn
Ivanava
Luninyets
Zhytkavichy
Kapatkyevichy
Vasilyevichy
Kalinkavichy
Łowicz
Zgierz
Łódź
Nizina Mazowiecka
Mińsk Mazowiecki
Łuków
Biała Podlaska
Brest
Kobryn
Pina
Pinsk
Pyetrykaw
Mazyr
Khoyni
Skierniewice
Vistula (Wisła)
Deblin
Łukow
Parczew
Malaryta
Ratne
Lyubeshiv
Zarichne
Pripet Marshes
Prypyats (Pripet)
Stolin
Lyel'chytsy
Yel'sk
Narowly
Tomaszów Mazowiecki
Pionki
Puławy
Lubartów
Kamin'-Kashyrs'kyy
Volodymyrets'
Dubrovytsya
Piotrków Trybunalski
Koniskie
Radom
Chełm
Lyuboml
Kuznetsov'sk
Manevychy 220
Klesiv
Sarny
Ovruch
Skarżysko-Kamienna
Starachowice
Lublin
Kovel'
Turiys'k
Rokytne
Luhyny
Narodychi
Kielce
Łysica 611
Ostrowiec Świętokrzyski
Krasnystaw
UKRAINE
Olevs'k
Uzh
Polis'k

Conic Equidistant Projection

Longitude 25° east of Greenwich

METRES / FEET
5000 / 16404
3000 / 9843
2000 / 6562
1000 / 3281
500 / 1640
200 / 656
0 / 0
Land below sea level
200 / 656
4000 / 13124
6000 / 19686

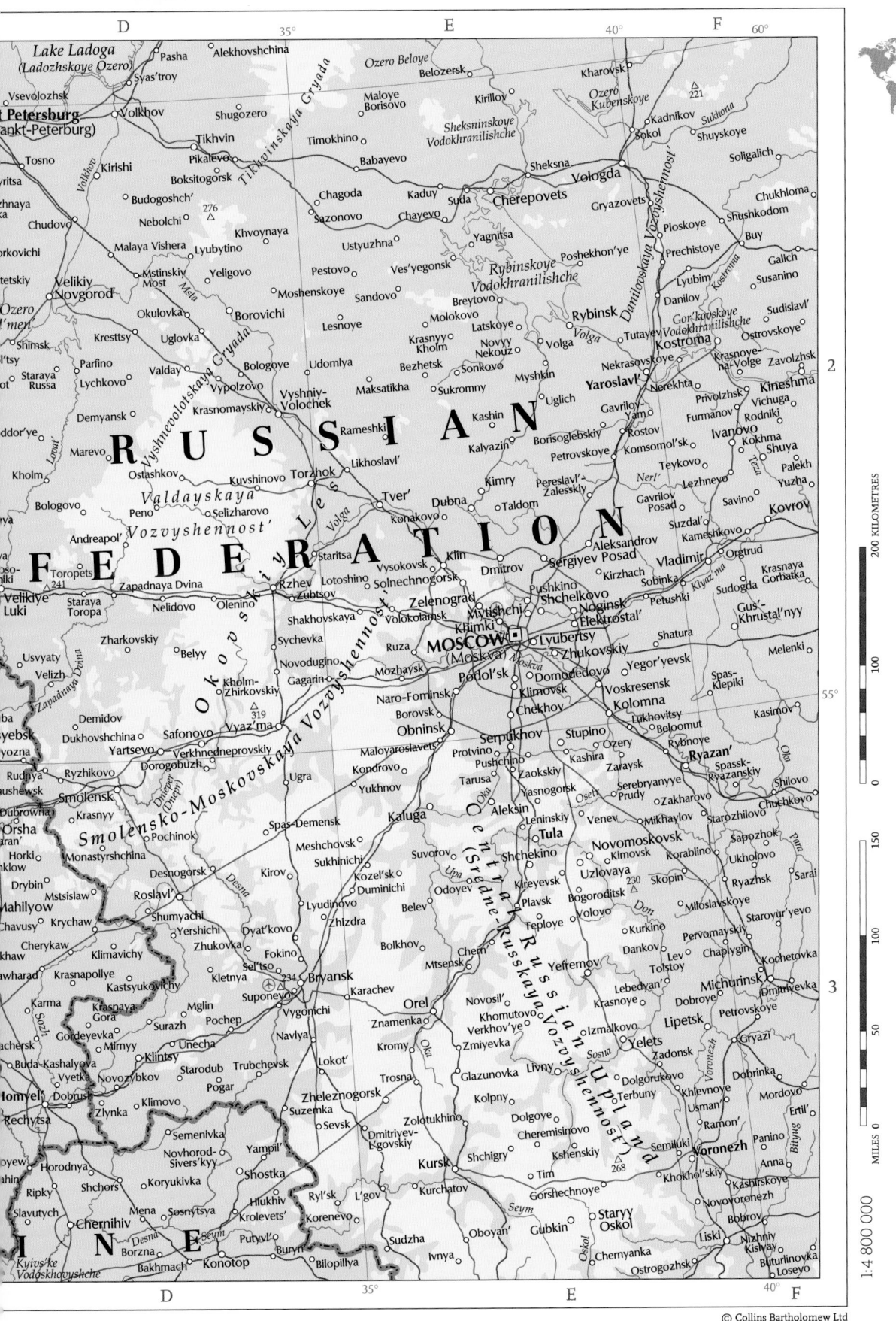

Lake Ladoga
(Ladozhskoye Ozero)
Pasha
Alekhovshchina
Ozero Beloye
Belozersk
Kharovsk
△ 221
Vsevolozhsk
Volkhov
Shugozero
Kirillov
Maloye
Borisovo
Ozero
Kubenskoye
Kadnikov
Sukhona
Soligalich
Petersburg
(ankt-Peterburg)
Tikhvin
Timokhino
Babayevo
Sheksna
Vologda
Shuyskoye
arita
Kirishi
Pikalevo
Sheksninskoye
Vodokhranilishche
Sokol
Chukhloma
Chnaya
Boksitogorsk
Chagoda
Kaduy
Suda
Cherepovets
Gryazovets
Ploskoye
Shushkodom
Buy
ka
Chudovo
Budogoshch'
Nebolchi
276
△
Sazonovo
Chayevo
Prechistoye
Galich
Susanino
orkovichi
Malaya Vishera
Khvoynaya
Ustyuzhna
Yagnitsa
Poshekhon'ye
Lyubim
Danilov
Sudislavl'
tetskiy
Lyubytino
Yeligovo
Pestovo
Ves'yegonsk
Rybinskoye
Vodokhranilishche
Krasnoye-
na-Volge
Ostrovskoye
Velikiy
Novgorod
Mstinskiy
Most
Moshenskoye
Sandovo
Breytovo
Kostroma
Zavolzhsk
Ozero
l'men'
Okulovka
Borovichi
Lesnoye
Molokovo
Latskoye
Novyy
Nekouz
Volga
Nekrasovskoye
Privolzhsk
Kineshma
Vichuga
Shimsk
Kresttsy
Uglovka
Udomlya
Bezhetsk
Sonkovo
Myshkin
Yaroslavl'
Nerekhta
Rodniki
l'tsy
Parfino
Valday
Bologoye
Maksatikha
Sukromny
Uglich
Gavrilov-
Yam
Furmanov
Ivanovo
Shuya
ot
Staraya
Russa
Vyshniy-
Volochek
Kashin
Borisoglebskiy
Rostov
Komsomol'sk
Kokhma
Palekh
dor'ye
Demyansk
Marevo
Rameshki
Likhoslavl'
Kalyazin
Petrovskoye
Teykovo
Lezhnevo
Yuzha
Kholm
Ostashkov
Kuvshinovo
Torzhok
Tver'
Dubna
Pereslavl'-
Zalesskiy
Gavrilov
Posad
Savino
Kovrov
Bologovo
Peno
Selizharovo
Konakovo
Taldom
Nerl'
Suzdal'
Kameshkovo
Ostrovskoye
Andreapol'
Staritsa
Klin
Dmitrov
Sergiyev Posad
Aleksandrov
Vladimir
Orgtrud
Krasnaya
Gorbatka
Toropets
△ 241
Zapadnaya Dvina
Rzhev
Zubtsov
Vysokovsk
Solnechnogorsk
Zelenograd
Pushkino
Shchelkovo
Noginsk
Kirzhach
Sobinka
Petushki
Sudogda
Gus'-
Khrustal'nyy
Velikiye
Luki
Staraya
Toropa
Nelidovo
Olenino
Shakhovskaya
Volokolamsk
Mytishchi
Khimki
Elektrostal'
Shatura
Melenki
Usvyaty
Velizh
Zharkovskiy
Belyy
Sychevka
Ruza
MOSCOW
(Moskva)
Lyubertsy
Zhukovskiy
Yegor'yevsk
Spas-
Klepiki
Demidov
Dukhovshchina
Novodugino
Gagarin
Mozhaysk
Podol'sk
Domodedovo
Klimovsk
Voskresensk
Kolomna
Kasimov
yebsk
yozna
Safonovo
Kholm-
Zhirkovskiy
△ 319
Naro-Fominsk
Borovsk
Obninsk
Chekhov
Lukhovitsy
Beloomut
Rybnoye
Rudnya
Demidov
Vyaz'ma
Verkhnedneprovskiy
Maloyaroslavets
Protvino
Serpukhov
Stupino
Ozery
Zaraysk
Ryazan'
Spassk-
Ryazanskiy
Shilovo
Smolensk
Krasnyy
Dorogobuzh
Ugra
Yukhnov
Pushchino
Tarusa
Kashira
Yasnogorsk
Serebryanyye
Prudy
Zakharovo
Starozhilovo
Chuchkovo
Orsha
Horki
Pochinok
Spas-Demensk
Kaluga
Aleksin
Venev
Mikhaylov
Sapozhok
Sarai
Monastyrshchina
Desnogorsk
Kirov
Meshchovsk
Sukhinichi
Leninskiy
Tula
Novomoskovsk
Korablino
Ryazhsk
Mahilyow
Krychaw
Roslavl'
Kozel'sk
Duminichi
Odoyev
Shchekino
Kireyevsk
Uzlovaya
230
△
Skopin
Pervomayskiy
Staroyur'yevo
Chavusy
Cherykaw
Shumyachi
Yershichi
Lyudinovo
Zhizdra
Belev
Plavsk
Teploye
Bogoroditsk
Volovo
Kurkino
Dankov
Lev
Tolstoy
Chaplygin
Kochetkova
khaw
Krasnapollye
Kastsyukovichy
Zhukovka
Fokino
Kletnya
Bolkhov
Chern'
Mtsensk
Yefremov
Krasnoye
Yelets
Michurinsk
Dmitriyevka
awharad
Krasnaya
Gora
Mglin
Pochep
Bryansk
Karachev
Novosil'
Dobroye
Lipetsk
Petrovskoye
Karma
Surazh
Unecha
Vygonichi
Orel
Khomutovo
Verkho-
v'ye
Izmalkovo
Yelets
Gryazi
Gordeyevka
Mirnyy
Navlya
Znamenka
Kromy
Zmiyevka
Livny
Dolgorukovo
Terbuny
Usman'
Dobrinka
Mordovo
Ertil'
omyel'
Dobrush
Klintsy
Starodub
Trubchevsk
Pogar
Zheleznogorsk
Suzemka
Glazunovka
Kolpny
Dolgoye
Ramon'
Vyetka
Novozybkov
Klimovo
Zlynka
Sevsk
Dmitriyev-
L'govskiy
Zolotukhino
Cheremisinovo
Semiluki
Voronezh
Panino
Anna
lomyel'
Rechytsa
Semenivka
Yampil'
Shostka
Kursk
Shchigry
Tim
Gorshechnoye
Khokhol'skiy
268
△
Kashirskoye
oyew
Horodnya
Novhorod-
Sivers'kyy
Koryukivka
Kurchatov
Kshenskiy
Novovoronezh
ahin
Ripky
Shchors
Hlukhiv
Ryl'sk
L'gov
Sudzha
Oboyan'
Gubkin
Staryy
Oskol
Liski
Nizhniy
Kislyay
Bobrov
Slavutych
Mena
Sosnytsya
Krolevets'
Korenevo
Ivnya
Chernyanka
Buturlinovka
Loseyo
Chernihiv
Desna
Putyvl'
Buryn
Bilopillya
Konotop
Bakhmach
Ostrogozhsk

200 KILOMETRES
100
0
150
100
50
MILES 0

1:4 800 000

© Collins Bartholomew Ltd

105

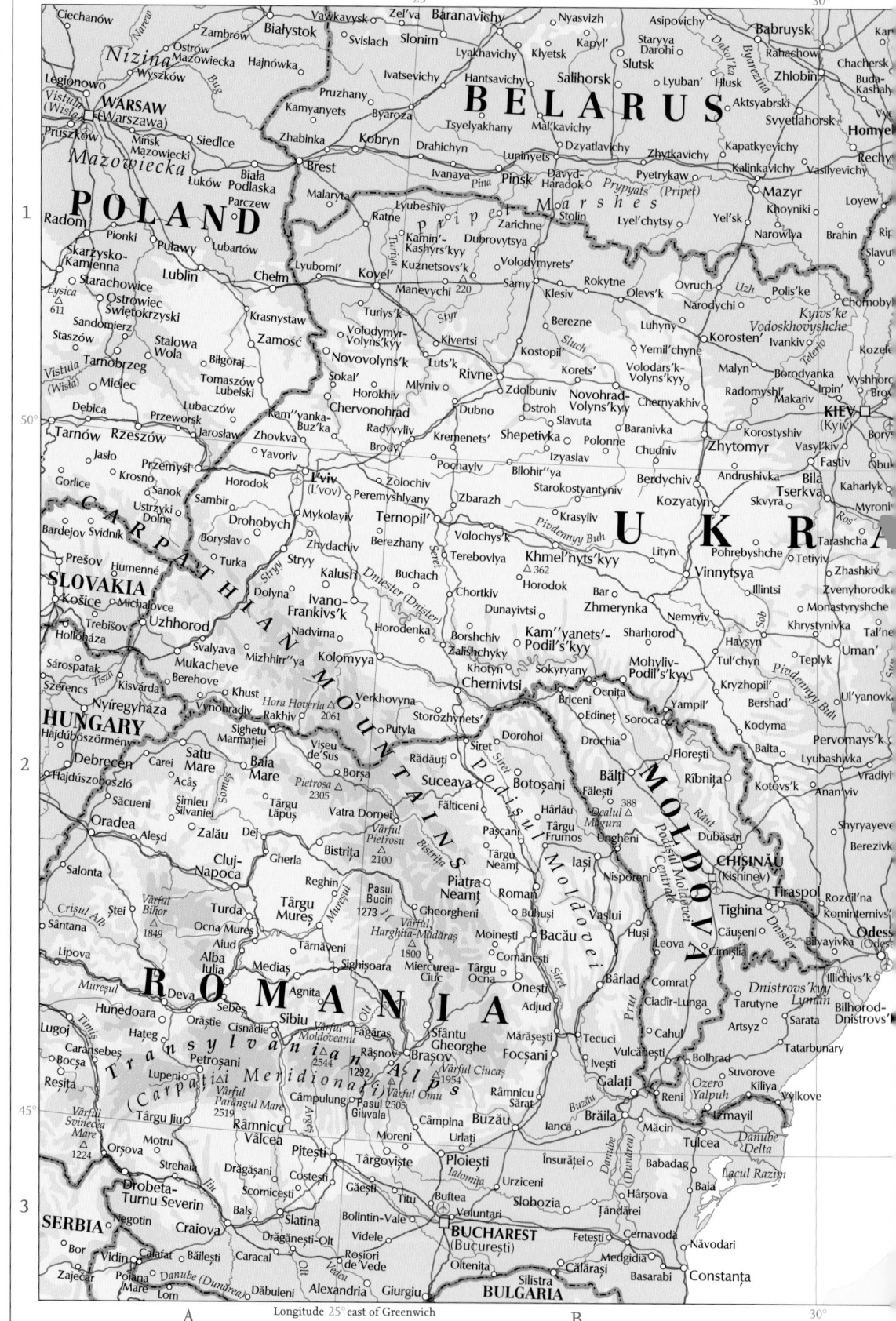

METRES
FEET

5000
16404

3000
9843

2000
6562

1000
3281

500
1640

200
656

0
0

Land below
sea level

200
656

4000
13124

6000
19686

106

Conic Equidistant Projection

Longitude 25° east of Greenwich

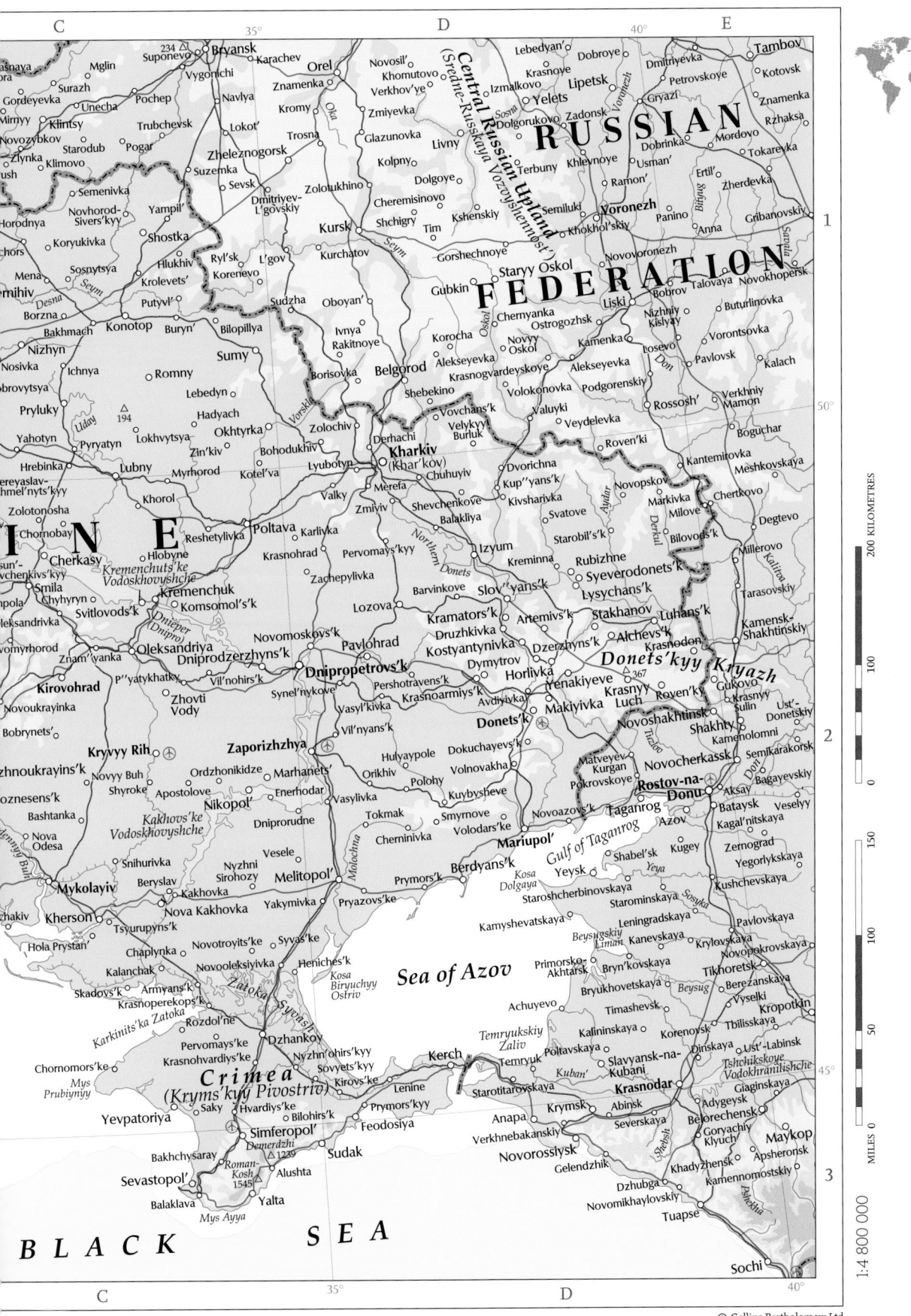

© Collins Bartholomew Ltd

1:4 800 000

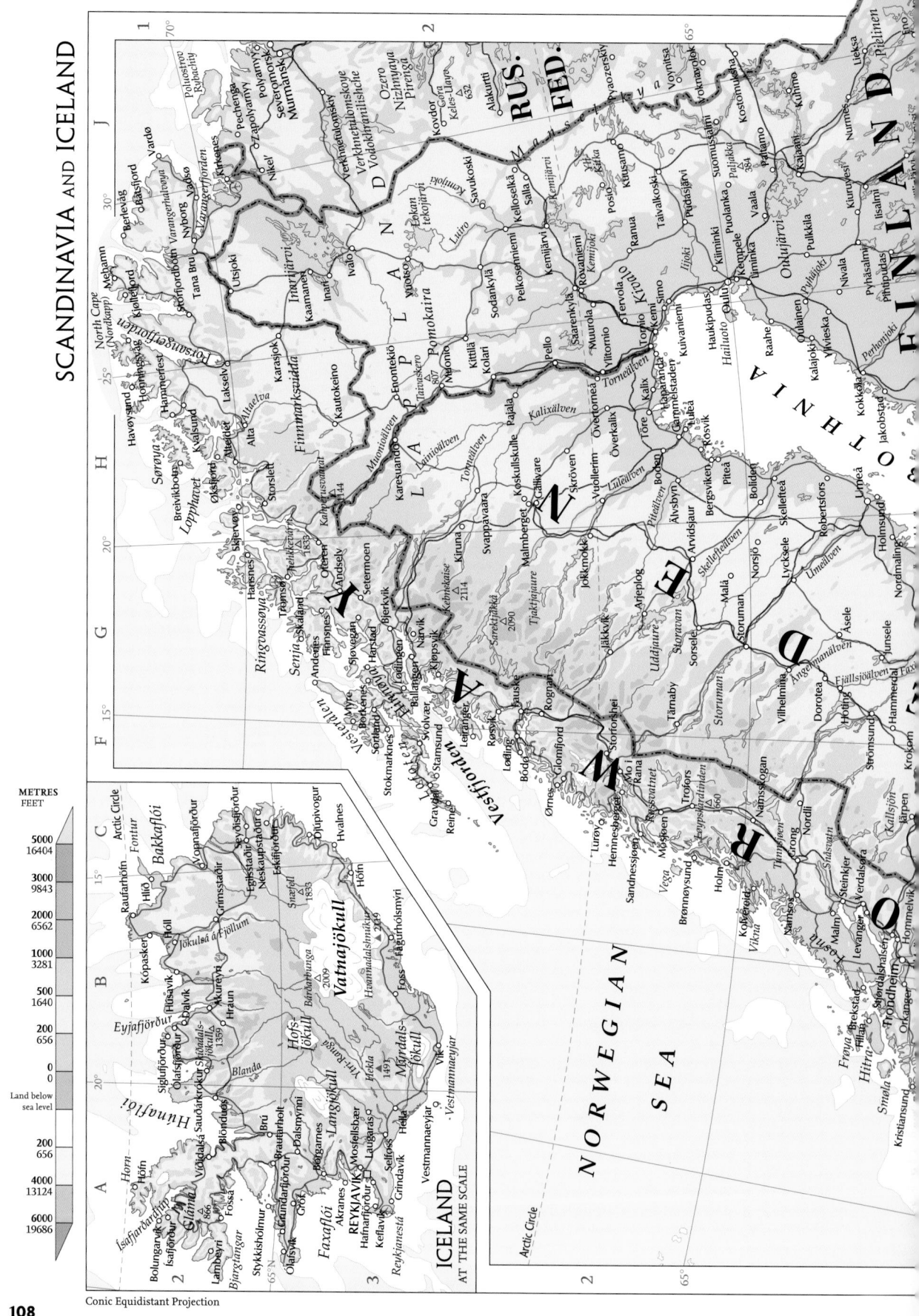

Conic Equidistant Projection

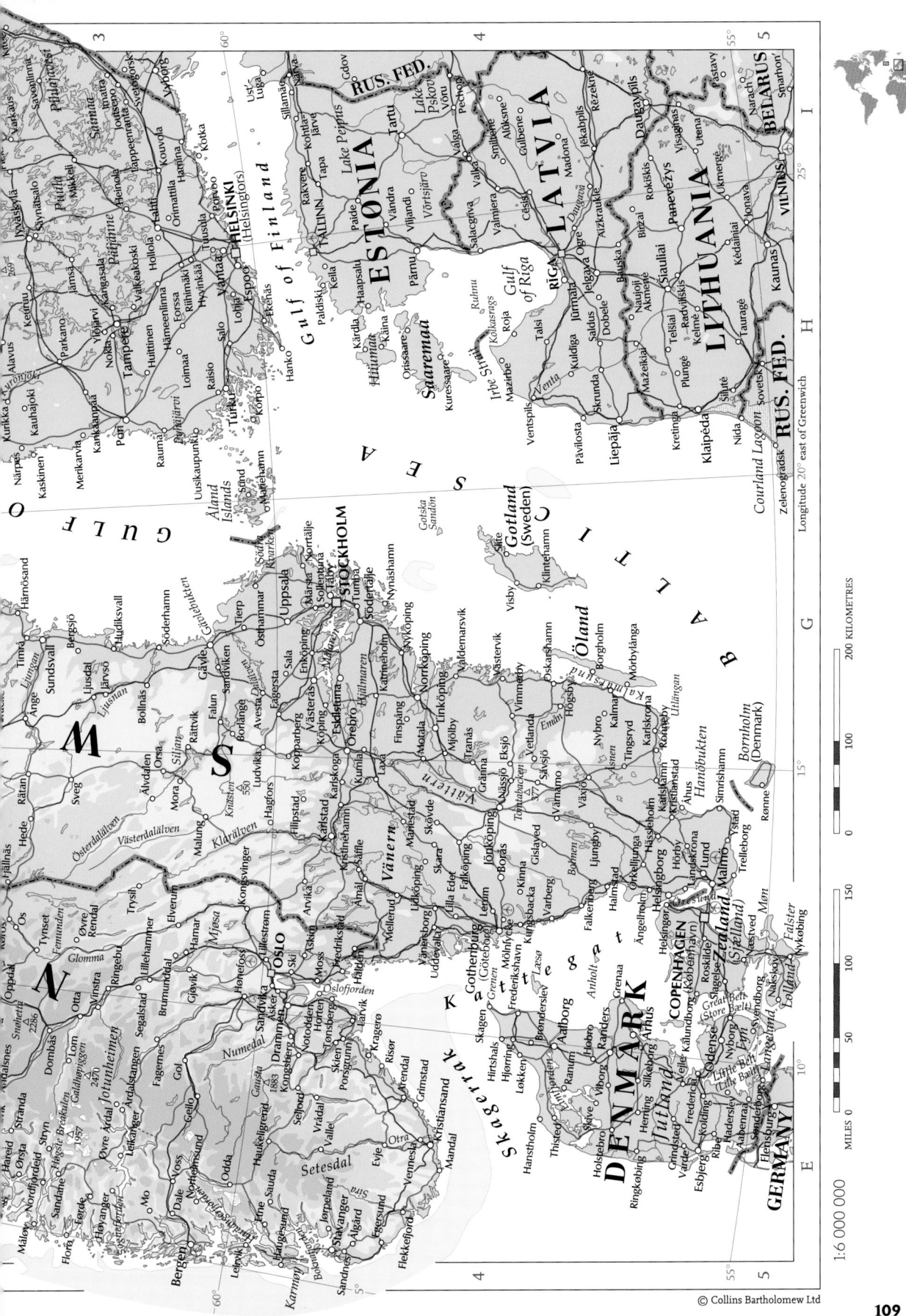

© Collins Bartholomew Ltd

1:6 000 000

MILES 0

KILOMETRES

200

Longitude 20° east of Greenwich

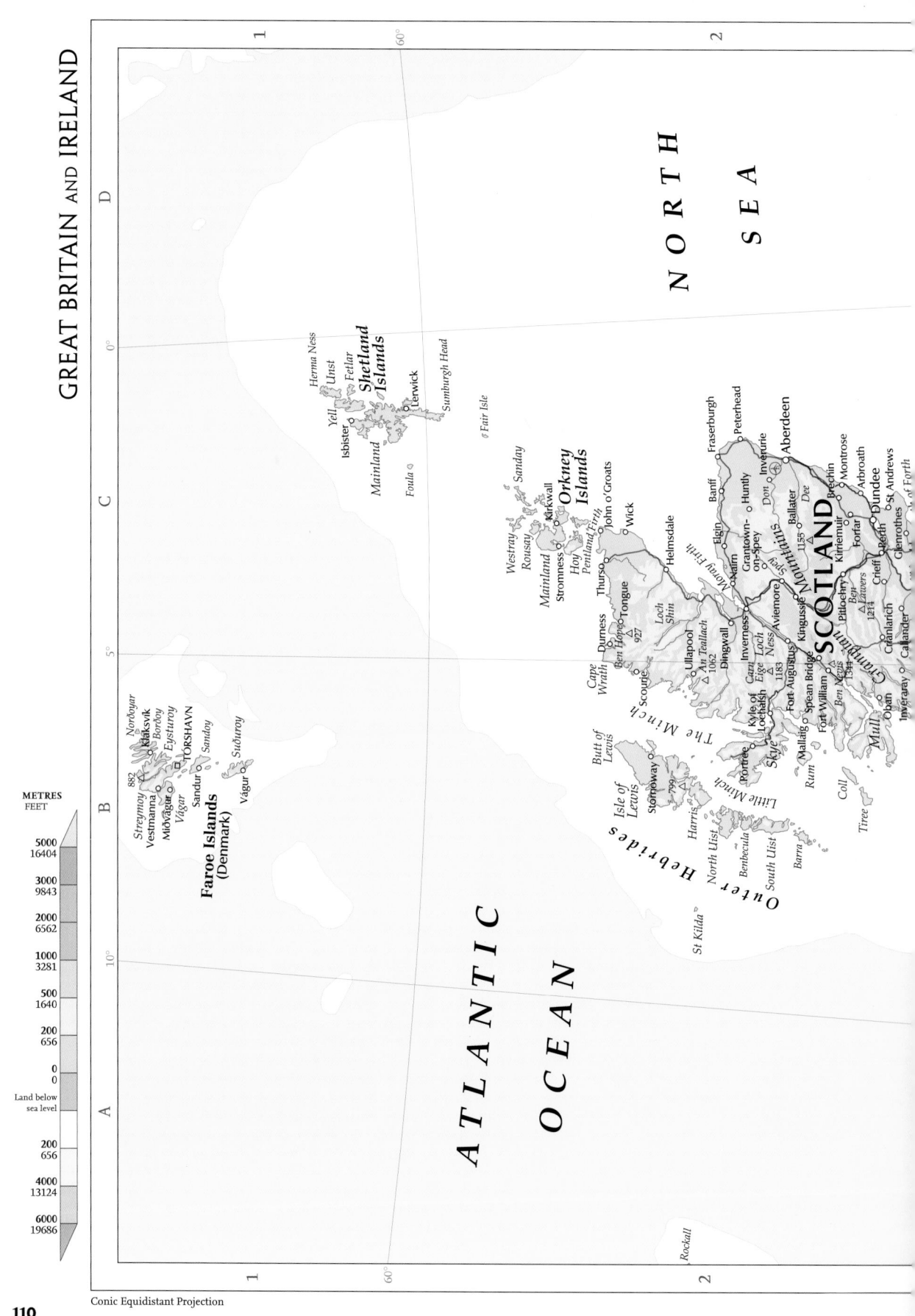

METRES
FEET

5000
16404

3000
9843

2000
6562

1000
3281

500
1640

200
656

0
0

Land below
sea level

200
656

4000
13124

6000
19686

ATLANTIC OCEAN

NORTH SEA

**Faroe Islands
(Denmark)**

Streymoy
Vestmanna
Norðoyar
Klaksvík
Borðoy
Eysturoy
882
Miðvágur
TÓRSHAVN
Vágur
Vágar
Sandur
Sandoy
Suðuroy

Herma Ness
Unst
Yell
Fetlar
Isbister
Mainland
*Shetland
Islands*
Lerwick
Sumburgh Head

Foula

Fair Isle

Sanday
Westray
Rousay
Sanday
*Orkney
Islands*
Kirkwall
Stromness
Mainland
Hoy
Pentland Firth
John o'Groats
Wick

Cape
Wrath
Dumess
Ben Hope
Tongue
Loch
Shin
Scourie
Helmsdale

Butt of
Lewis
Stornoway
799
Harris
Isle of
Lewis

Outer Hebrides

North Uist
Benbecula
South Uist
Barra

St Kilda

Ullapool
An Teallach
1062

Dingwall
Inverness
Nairn
Elgin
Fraserburgh
Peterhead
Banff
Huntly
Grantown-
on-Spey
Don
Inverurie
Aberdeen

The Minch

Little Minch
Portree
Skye
Kyle of
Lochalsh
Mallaig
Rum
Coll
Tiree

Spean Bridge
Fort Augustus
Loch
Ness
Eige
Loch
Cairn
1183
Aviemore
Kingussie
Ben Nevis
1344
Fort William

Grampian Mountains
1155
Ballater
Dee
SCOTLAND
Ben
Lawers
1214
Kirriemuir
Pitlochry
Forfar
Brechin
Montrose
Arbroath
Crieff
Perth
Dundee
St Andrews
Glenrothes
Mull
Oban
Crianlarich
Callander
Inveraray
of Forth

Moray Firth

*ATLANTIC
OCEAN*

Rockall

Conic Equidistant Projection

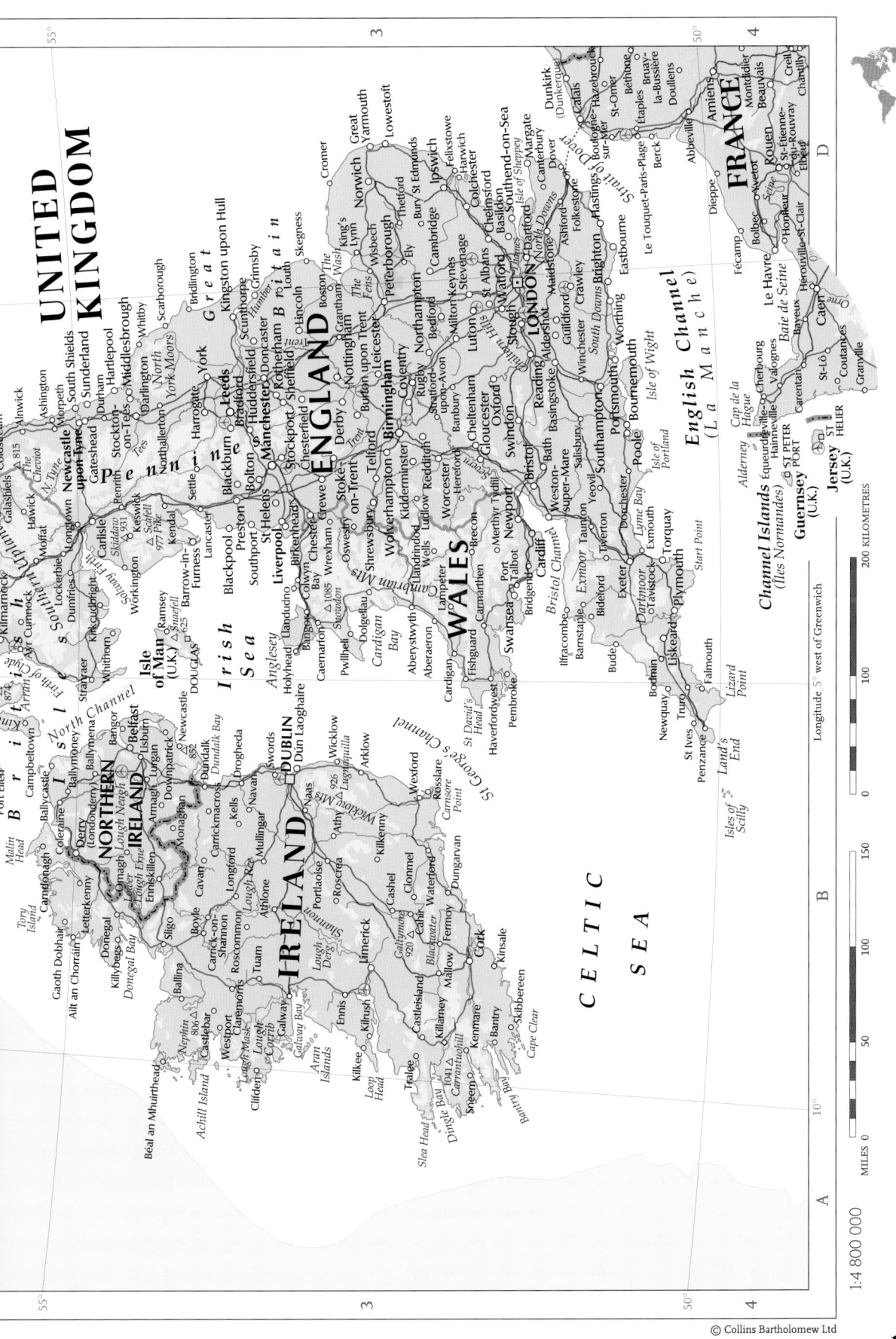

© Collins Bartholomew Ltd

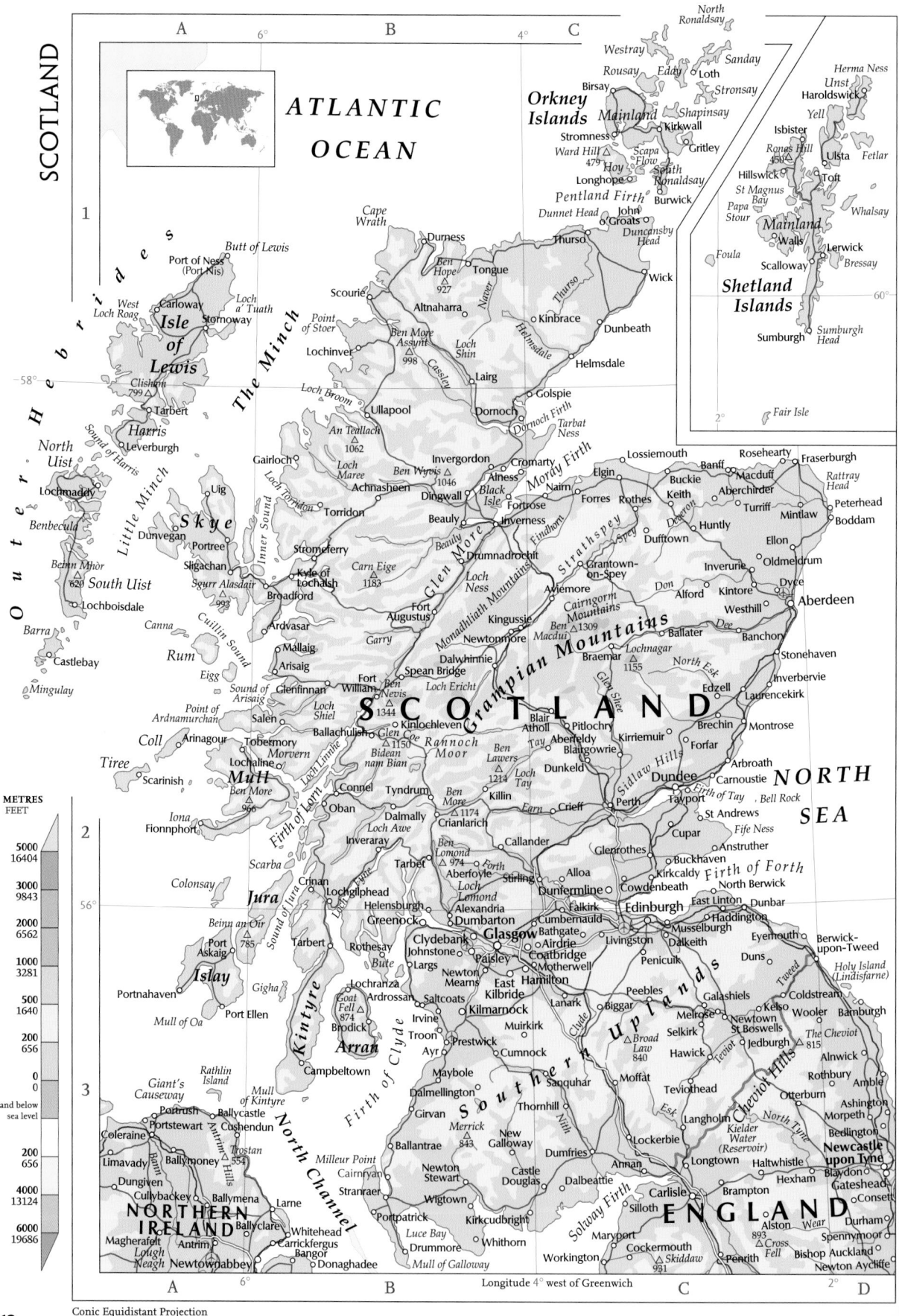

ATLANTIC

OCEAN

North
Ronaldsay

Westray
Rousay *Eday* *Sanday*
Birsay *Loth* *Stronsay*
Orkney *Mainland* *Shapinsay*
Islands Kirkwall
Stromness *Scapa* Gritley
Ward Hill △ *Flow*
479 *Hoy* *South*
Longhope *Ronaldsay*
Burwick
Pentland Firth John
Dunnet Head o'Groats *Duncansby*
Head

Herma Ness
Unst
Haroldswick
Yell
Isbister
Ronas Hill △ Ulsta *Fetlar*
450
Hillswick *Toft*
St Magnus *Whalsay*
Papa *Bay*
Stour **Mainland**
Foula *Walls*
Scalloway Lerwick
Shetland *Bressay*
Islands
Sumburgh *Sumburgh*
Head

Cape
Wrath Durness Thurso
Ben Tongue
Hope Wick
927 Altnaharra *Naver* Kinbrace
Scourie *Thurso*
Loch Dunbeath
Ben More *Shin* Helmsdale
Assynt *Loch*
△ *Shin* Lairg *Helmsdale*
998 Golspie
Lochinver *Cassley* Dornoch
Ullapool *Dornoch Firth*
Tarbat
Loch Broom *Ness*
Lossiemouth Rosehearty
An Teallach Invergordon Cromarty Elgin Banff Fraserburgh
△ Gairloch Alness Macduff
1062 *Loch* *Moray Firth* Nairn Buckie Aberchirder *Rattray*
Maree *Ben Wyvis* Dingwall Forres Keith *Head*
Achnasheen △ *Black* Fortrose Rothes Turriff Peterhead
1046 *Isle* Huntly Mintlaw Boddam
Torridon Beauly Inverness Dufftown Ellon
Inner Drumnadrochit *Findhorn* *Spey* Oldmeldrum
Stromeferry *Sound* *Beauly* *Strathspey* *Don* Inverurie Dyce
Carn Eige *Glen More* Grantown- Alford Kintore
Kyle of △ *Loch* on-Spey Westhill Aberdeen
Lochalsh 1183 *Ness* Aviemore *Cairngorm* Banchory
Broadford Fort *Mountains* Ballater Stonehaven
Ardvarsar Augustus *Monadhliath Mountains* *Ben* △ *Dee* Inverbervie
Kingussie *Macdui* 1309 Laurencekirk
Garry Newtonmore *Lochnagar* *North Esk*
Dalwhinnie △ Braemar Edzell
Mallaig 1155
Arisaig Spean Bridge *Loch Ericht* Blair *Glen Shee* Brechin
Sound of *Ben* Atholl Pitlochry Kirriemuir Montrose
Glenfinnan Fort △ *Nevis* Aberfeldy Blairgowrie Forfar Arbroath
Arisaig William 1344 *Sidlaw Hills*
Salen *Loch Shiel* *Glen* *Rannoch* *Ben* *Tay* Dunkeld Carnoustie
Point of Kinlochleven *Coe* *Moor* *Lawers* Dundee
Ardnamurchan Ballachulish △ △ Crieff Perth Tayport
Tobermory 1150 *Bidean* 1214 *Loch* St Andrews *Bell Rock*
Morvern *nam Bian* *Ben* *Tay* Killin *Firth of Tay*
Lochaline Connel *More* Callander *Earn* *Fife Ness*
Ben More Tyndrum △ Crianlarich Cupar
966 Oban *Loch Awe* 1174 Killin Glenrothes
Iona *Firth of Lorn* Dalmally *Ben* Callander Buckhaven
Fionnphort Inveraray *Lomond* *Forth* Stirling Kirkcaldy
△ 974 Aberfoyle Alloa North Berwick
Loch Dunfermline Cowdenbeath Dunbar
Lomond Falkirk Edinburgh East Linton
Crinan Helensburgh Cumbernauld Musselburgh Haddington
Lochgilphead Greenock Dumbarton Bathgate Livingston Dalkeith Eyemouth
Alexandria Airdrie Berwick-
Clydebank **Glasgow** Coatbridge Penicuik Duns upon-Tweed
Johnstone Paisley Motherwell *Holy Island*
Largs Newton Hamilton Peebles Galashiels *(Lindisfarne)*
Rothesay Mearns East Lanark Melrose Coldstream
Bute Kilbride Biggar Selkirk Newtown Kelso Wooler
Ardrossan Kilmarnock Moffat Hawick St Boswells
Saltcoats Muirkirk *Teviot* Jedburgh *The Cheviot*
Troon Prestwick Cumnock Teviothead Langholm △ 815 Alnwick
Ayr Maybole Sanquhar Rothbury
Dalmellington Thornhill *Esk* Amble
Girvan Merrick *Nith* Lockerbie Longtown Otterburn Ashington
△ New Dumfries Langholm *North Tyne* Morpeth
843 Galloway *Kielder* Bedlington
Ballantrae Newton Castle Annan *Water* Haltwhistle **Newcastle**
Stewart Douglas Dalbeattie *(Reservoir)* Hexham **upon Tyne**
Wigtown Carlisle Brampton Gateshead
Cairnryan Kirkcudbright *Solway Firth* Silloth Alston *Wear* Consett
Stranraer Maryport Cross Spennymoor
Portpatrick *Luce* Whithorn Workington 893 *Fell* Durham Bishop Auckland
Bay *Mull of Galloway* Cockermouth △ Penrith Newton Aycliffe
Skiddaw
931

Isle
of
Lewis
Port of Ness
(Port Nis)
Carloway *Butt of Lewis*
Stornoway *Loch*
West *a' Tuath*
Loch Roag
Harris
Tarbert
Leverburgh
North *Sound of Harris*
Uist
Lochmaddy Uig
Benbecula Dunvegan *Skye*
Beinn Mhòr Portree
△ 620 Sligachan
South Uist Kyle of
Lochboisdale *Sgurr Alasdair* Lochalsh
△ 993 Broadford
Barra *Canna* *Cuillin Sound*
Castlebay *Rum* *Sound of*
Mingulay *Eigg* *Arisaig*

Coll Arinagour
Tiree Scarinish
Iona
Fionnphort

Scarba
Colonsay
Jura
Beinn an Òir
△ 785
Port
Askaig *Sound of Jura*
Islay *Gigha*
Portnahaven
Mull of Oa Port Ellen

Rathlin
Island *Mull*
Giant's *of Kintyre*
Causeway Portrush Ballycastle *Milleur Point*
Portstewart Cushendun *Cairnryan*
Coleraine *Antrim Hills*
Limavady Ballymoney *Trostan*
Dungiven Cullybackey △ 554
Ballymena
NORTHERN
IRELAND Larne
Magherafelt Ballyclare Whitehead
Lough Antrim Carrickfergus
Neagh Newtownabbey Bangor
Donaghadee

Crinan
Kintyre *Firth of Clyde*
Tarbert
Campbeltown
Goat Lochranza
Fell Brodick
874 **Arran**
North Channel

SCOTLAND

Grampian Mountains

NORTH
SEA

Firth of Forth
Southern Uplands
Broad
Law
840
Cheviot Hills
Tweed

ENGLAND

s *e* *d* *i* *r* *b* *e* *H* *r* *e* *t* *u* *O*

The Minch
Point of Stoer
Little Minch
Glen More

Loch Torridon
Loch Ness
Loch Linnhe
Loch Leven
Bidean

A 6° B 4° C 2° D

1

2

3

Longitude 4° west of Greenwich

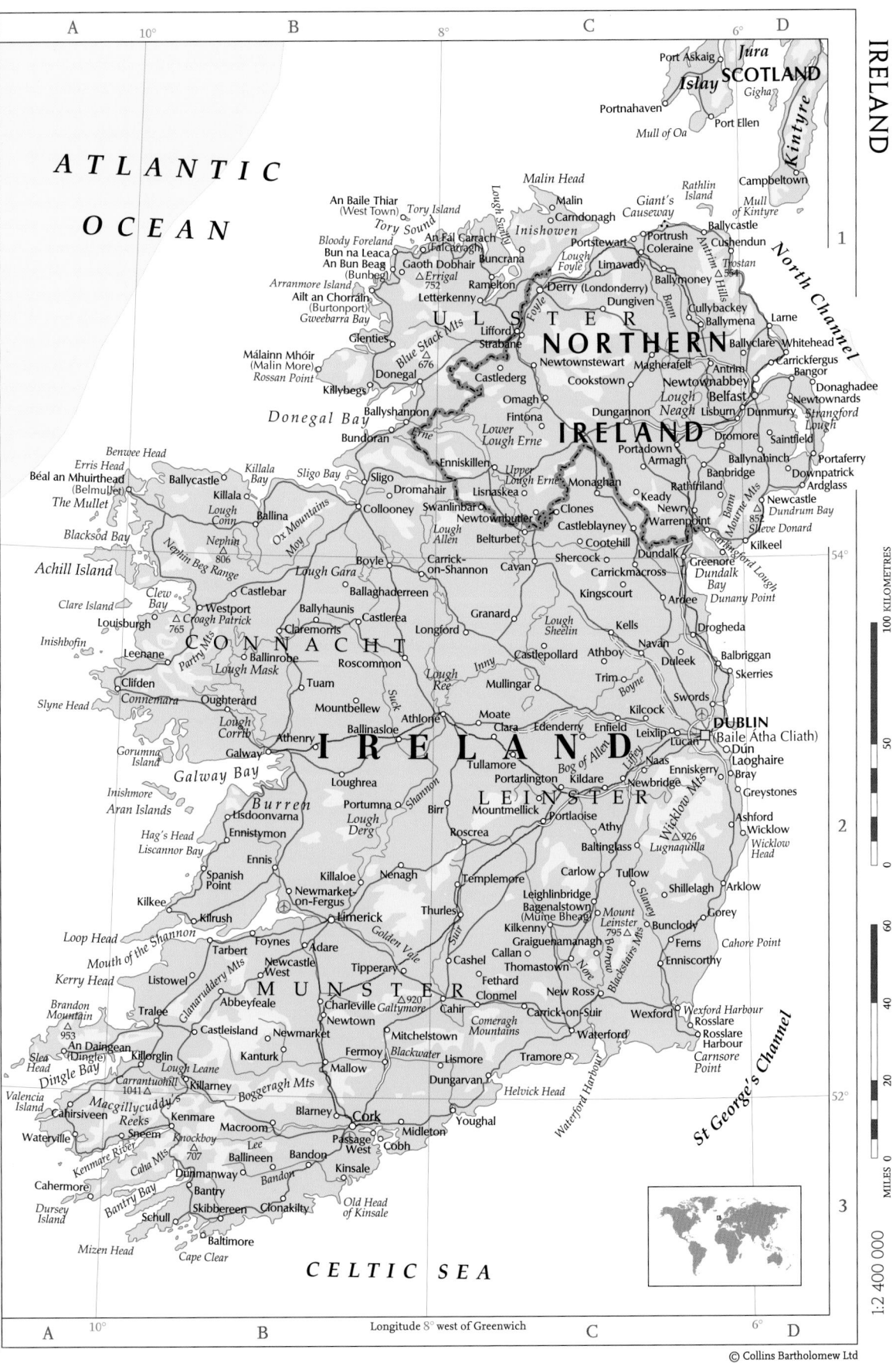

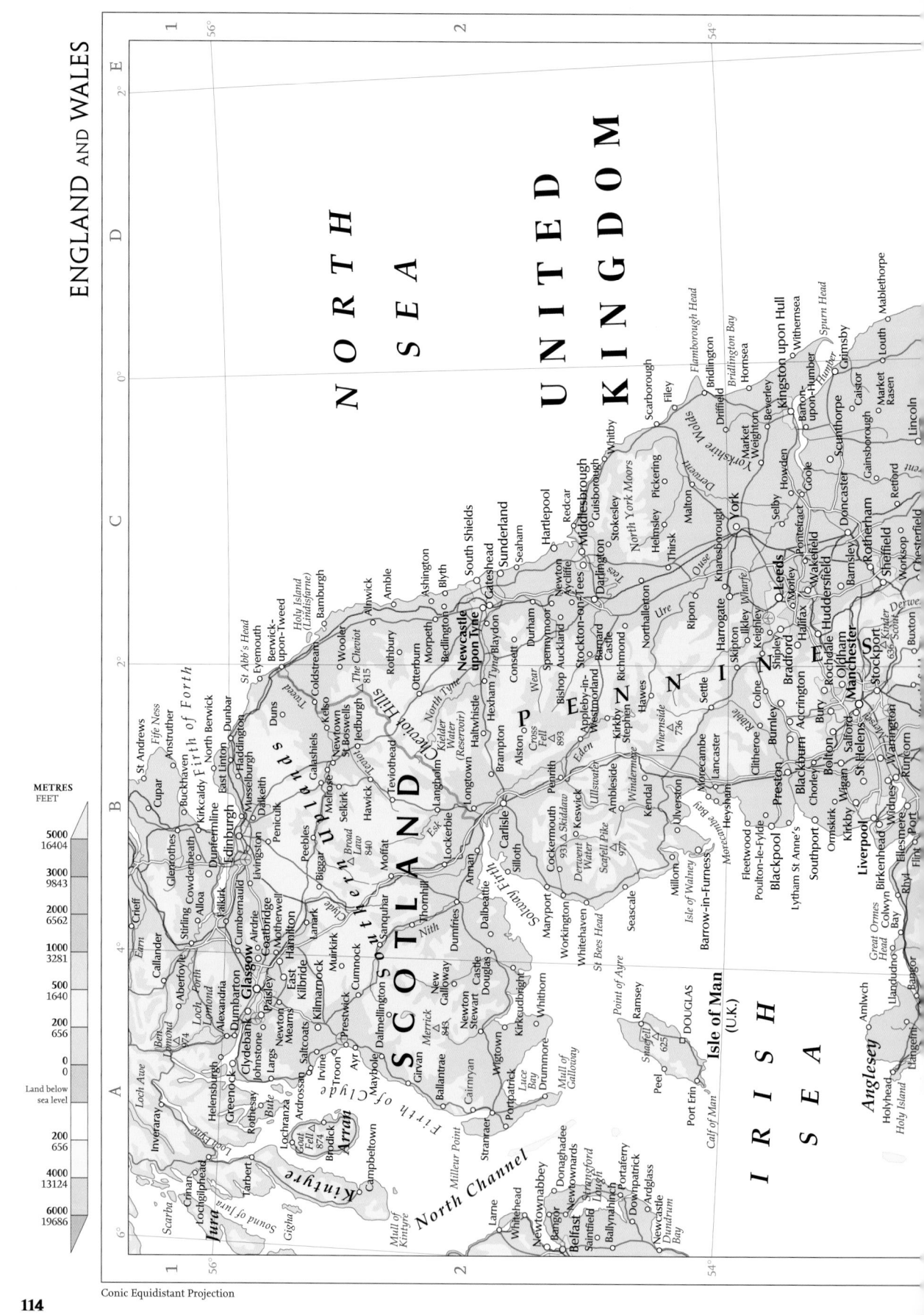

METRES
FEET

5000	16404
3000	9843
2000	6562
1000	3281
500	1640
200	656
0	0
Land below sea level	
200	656
4000	13124
6000	19686

N O R T H   S E A

U N I T E D   K I N G D O M

Flamborough Head
Bridlington
Bridlington Bay
Hornsea
Spurn Head
Withernsea
Kingston upon Hull
Beverley
Barton-upon-Humber
Grimsby
Scarborough
Filey
Market Weighton
Howden
Goole
Scunthorpe
Caistor
Market Rasen
Louth
Mablethorpe
Lincoln

Whitby
Yorkshire Wolds
Driffield
North York Moors
Pickering
Malton
Knaresborough
York
Selby
Pontefract
Doncaster
Retford
Worksop
Chesterfield

Redcar
Middlesbrough
Guisborough
Stokesley
Helmsley
Thirsk
Ripon
Harrogate
Wetherby
Leeds
Wakefield
Barnsley
Rotherham
Sheffield

Hartlepool
Sunderland
Seaham
Durham
Bishop Auckland
Darlington
Stockton-on-Tees
Northallerton
Bedale
Skipton
Keighley
Shipley
Bradford
Halifax
Morley
Huddersfield
Holmfirth
Buxton

South Shields
Gateshead
Newcastle upon Tyne
Blaydon
Consett
Newton Aycliffe
Barnard Castle
Richmond
Hawes
Settle
Colne
Burnley
Accrington
Bolton
Rochdale
Oldham
Manchester
Stockport

Ashington
Blyth
Morpeth
Bedlington
Hexham
Haltwhistle
Alston
Cross Fell
893
Appleby-in-Westmorland
Kirkby Stephen
Kirkby Lonsdale
Whernside
736
Lancaster
Morecambe
Heysham
Preston
Blackburn
Chorley
Wigan
St Helens
Warrington
Runcorn

Alnwick
Amble
Rothbury
Otterburn
The Cheviot
815
Wooler
Kidder Water (Reservoir)
North Tyne
Brampton
Penrith
Skiddaw
931
Keswick
Derwent Water
Scafell Pike
977
Ambleside
Windermere
Kendal
Ulverston
Morecambe Bay
Fleetwood
Poulton-le-Fylde
Blackpool
Lytham St Anne's
Southport
Ormskirk
Kirkby
Liverpool
Birkenhead
Bebington
Ellesmere Port
Neston
Flint

Berwick-upon-Tweed
Holy Island (Lindisfarne)
Bamburgh
Coldstream
Kelso
Jedburgh
Cheviot Hills
Longtown
Carlisle
Wigton
Silloth
Maryport
Cockermouth
Workington
Whitehaven
St Bees Head
Seascale
Millom
Isle of Walney
Barrow-in-Furness

St Abb's Head
Eyemouth
Duns
Newtown St Boswells
Melrose
Galashiels
Hawick
Selkirk
Langholm
Lockerbie
Esk
Annan
Dumfries
Dalbeattie
Castle Douglas
Kirkcudbright
Solway Firth
Whithorn
Point of Ayre
Ramsey
DOUGLAS
Snaefell
625
Isle of Man (U.K.)
Peel
Port Erin
Calf of Man

St Andrews
Anstruther
Buckhaven
Kirkcaldy
Firth of Forth
North Berwick
Dunbar
Haddington
Musselburgh
Dalkeith
Penicuik
Peebles
Biggar
Moffat
Broad Law
840
Lauder
Thornhill
Sanquhar
New Galloway
Newton Stewart
Wigtown

Cupar
Fife Ness
Glenrothes
Cowdenbeath
Dunfermline
Edinburgh
Livingston
Motherwell
Lanark
Cumbernauld
Airdrie
Coatbridge
Hamilton
East Kilbride
Muirkirk
Cumnock
Dalmellington
Girvan
Ballantrae
Cairnryan
Luce Bay
Stranraer
Portpatrick
Mull of Galloway

Crieff
Callander
Aberfoyle
Stirling
Falkirk
Alloa
Glasgow
Paisley
Clydebank
Newton Mearns
Prestwick
Kilmarnock
Saltcoats
Irvine
Troon
Ayr
Maybole
Drummore

Earn
Ben Lomond
974
Loch Lomond
Helensburgh
Dumbarton
Johnstone
Largs
Rothesay
Bute
Ardrossan
Kilbride

SOUTHERN UPLANDS

SCOTLAND

P E N N I N E S

Tees
Wear
Ure
Swale
Ouse
Nidd
Wharfe
Aire
Calder
Don
Derwent
Trent
Ribble
Eden
Lune
Clyde
Nith

N O R T H   S E A

I R I S H   S E A

North Channel
Milleur Point
Firth of Clyde
Mull of Kintyre
Kintyre
Campbeltown
Brodick
Arran
Goat Fell
874
Lochranza
Sound of Jura
Gigha
Jura
Scarba
Lochgilphead
Crinan
Tarbert
Inveraray
Loch Awe
Loch Fyne

Larne
Whitehead
Newtownabbey
Bangor
Donaghadee
Newtownards
Belfast
Saintfield
Strangford Lough
Portaferry
Ballynahinch
Downpatrick
Ardglass
Newcastle
Dundrum Bay

Anglesey
Amlwch
Holyhead
Holy Island
Great Ormes Head
Llandudno
Colwyn Bay
Rhyl
Prestatyn
Llangefni
Bangor

Conic Equidistant Projection

© Collins Bartholomew Ltd

1:2 400 000

MILES 0   20   40   60

0   50   100 KILOMETRES

FRANCE

ENGLAND

WALES

LONDON

Birmingham

Norwich

Cardiff

Swansea

Plymouth

Exeter

Bristol

Southampton

Portsmouth

Brighton

Dover

Cambridge

Ipswich

Oxford

Reading

Nottingham

Leicester

Coventry

Northampton

Gloucester

Cheltenham

Isle of Wight

ENGLISH CHANNEL
(LA MANCHE)

Bristol Channel

Cardigan Bay

Cambrian Mountains

Strait of Dover

Greenwich 0° meridian

The Wash

The Fens

Land's End

Lizard Point

Start Point

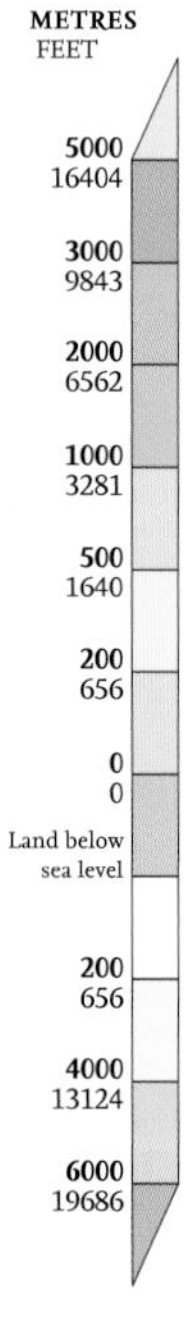

Grid reference: A 4° B 6° C

NORTH SEA

NETHERLANDS

BELGIUM

FRANCE

LUXEMBOURG

MÜNSTERLAND

East Frisian Islands
Spiekeroog
Langeoog
Norderney
Juist
Borkum
Norden
Westerholt
OSTFRIESLA...
Emden
Aurich
Wies...
Hinte (Ostfriesland)
Leer
Wester...

West Frisian Islands
Schiermonnikoog
Ameland
Hollum
Terschelling
West-Terschelling
Oost-Vlieland
Vlieland
Texel
Den Burg
Marsdiep
Den Helder

Waddenzee
Lauwersmeer
Eenrum
Uithuizen
Delfzijl
Appingedam
Groningen (Ostfriesland)
Winschoten
Strücklingen (Saterland)
Papenburg
Friesoy...
Walchum

Burdaard
Oenkerk
Dokkum
Bedum
Ferwert
Kollum
Leeuwarden
Franeker
Reduzum
Drachten
Veendam
Stadskanaal
Assen
Beilen
Emmen
Haren (Ems)
Löningen
Meppen
Lingen (Ems)
Fürster...

Witmarsum
Bolsward
Sneek
Sloten
Harlingen
Hoogezand-Sappemeer
Heerenveen
Wolvega

Schagen
Nieuwe-Niedorp
Heerhugowaard
Bergen
Alkmaar
Castricum
Wieringerwerf
IJsselmeer
Creil
Steenwijk
Hoogeveen
Coevorden
Meppen
Gross-Hesepe

Hoorn
Enkhuizen
Urk
Markermeer
Emmeloord
Meppel
Hardenberg
Kloosterhaar
Gronau (Westfalen)
Ibbenb...

Purmerend
Lelystad
Dronten
Kampen
Zwolle
Ommen
Vriezenveen
Nordhorn

Berkhout
Beverwijk
IJmuiden
Zaandam
AMSTERDAM
Driemond
Heerde
Raalte
Almelo
Oldenzaal
Rheine

Zandvoort
Haarlem
Amstelveen
Naarden
Nijkerk
Torenberg 107△
Harderwijk
Deventer
Nijverdal
Borne
Hengelo
Enschede
Emsdetten
Steinfurt

Noordwijk-Binnen
Katwijk aan Zee
Hillegom
Leiden
Alphen aan den Rijn
Hilversum
Amersfoort
Apeldoorn
Gronau (Westfalen)
Ahaus
Greven

THE HAGUE (s-Gravenhage) (Den Haag)
Waddinxveen
Utrecht
Veenendaal
Barneveld
Ede
Zutphen
Winterswijk
Havixbeck
Mür...

Hook of Holland (Hoek van Holland)
Delft
Gouda
Nieuwegein
Wageningen
Doesburg
Hoog-Keppel
Coesfeld

Vlaardingen
Rotterdam
Schoonhoven
Culemborg
Neder Rijn
Arnhem
Doetinchem
Velen
Borken
Dülmen
Dortmund-Ems-Kanal

Hellevoetsluis
Capelle aan de IJssel
Waal
Tiel
Nijmegen
Zevenaar
Kleve
Bocholt
Ascheberg
Ah...

Scharendijke
Burgh-Haamstede
Zierikzee
Spijkenisse
Middelharnis
Oosterhout
Waalwijk
Maas
Oss
Wijchen
(Rhein)
Goch
Wesel
Dorsten
Marl
Recklinghausen
Lünen

Oosterschelde
Westkapelle
Middelburg
Goes
Roosendaal
s-Hertogenbosch
Uden
Wanroij
Kevelaer
Dinslaken
Gelsenkirchen
Herne
Hamm

Koudekerke
Halsteren
Bergen op Zoom
Etten-Leur
Boxtel
Erp
St Anthonis
Venray
Bottrop
Bochum
Frondenberg

Vlissingen
Hoogerheide
Breda
Tilburg
Best
Helmond
Asten
Venlo
Duisburg
Essen
Hagen
Iserlo...

Zeebrugge
Knokke-Heist
Blankenberge
Westerschelde
Breskens
Zandvliet
Brecht
Eindhoven
Veldhoven
Deurne
Kessel
Mülheim an der Ruhr
Krefeld
Ratingen
Hattingen
Wuppertal
Lüdenscheid

Ostend (Oostende)
Nieuwpoort
Meetkerke
Sluis
St-Laureins
Philippine
Terneuzen
Kapellen
Schilde
Westmalle
Lille
Arendonk
Luyksgestel
Mönchengladbach
Viersen
Düsseldorf
Hilden
Remscheid
Pletten...

Veurne
Zedelgem
Torhout
Brugge (Bruges)
Eeklo
Evergem
Maldegem
St-Niklaas
Antwerp (Antwerpen) (Anvers)
Lier
Geel
Bocholt
Lommel
Weert
Roermond
Herkenbosch
Neuss
Solingen
Dormagen
Leverkusen
Attendor...
Gummersba...

Diksmuide
Wingene
Tielt
Deinze
Ghent (Gent)
Lokeren
Willebroek
Mechelen
Aarschot
Beringen
Hechtel
Maaseik
Albert Kanaal
Wegberg
Grevenbroich
Bergisch Gladbach

Roeselare
Zulte
Leie
Wichelen
Aalst
Vilvoorde
Diest
Hasselt
Sittard
Hückelhoven
Steie...
Geilenkirchen
Bergheim (Erft)
Köln

Ieper
Menen
Kortrijk
Oudenaarde
Schaerbeek
Anderlecht
Uccle
BRUSSELS (Bruxelles)
Leuven
Tienen
Genk
Heerlen
Kerkrade
Bürth
Cologne (Köln)
Wiehl

Roubaix
Mouscron
Ronse
Ath
Nivelles
Ottignies
Borgloon
Tongeren
Maastricht
Mechelen
Eschweiler
Düren
Kerpen
Troisdorf

Lille
Villeneuve-d'Ascq
Tournai
Péruwelz
Lens
Soignies
Fleurus
Eghezée
Oupeye
Liège
Aachen
Stolberg (Rheinland)
Kreuzau
Bonn
St Augustin
Bett...

Lens
Douai
Boussu
Mons
Frameries
Thuin
Charleroi
Châtelet
Andenne
Huy
Seraing
Verviers
Mechernich
Kallo
Bad Neuenahr-Ahrweiler
Königswinter
Altenkir...
Meckenheim (Wester...)

Valenciennes
Maubeuge
Aulnoye-Aymeries
Beaumont
Namur
Assesse
Ciney
Durbuy
Spa
Malmédy
Blankenheim
Adenau
Neuwied
Koblenz
Lahnstein

Cambrai
Caudry
Avesnes-sur-Helpe
Philippeville
Rochefort
Marche-en-Famenne
Vielsalm
St-Vith
Dahlem
Hillesheim
Mayen
Cochem
Emmelsha...
Monta...

Bohain-en-Vermandois
La Capelle
Couvin
Beauraing
La Roche-en-Ardenne
Houffalize
Prüm
Gerolstein
Daun
Manderscheid
Blankenrath
Simmer... (Hunsrü...)

Péronne
Guise
Hirson
Momignies
Monthermé
Fumay
Libin
Bastogne
Clervaux
Arzfeld
Neuerburg
Wittlich
Bad...

St-Quentin
Vervins
Rocroi
Bièvre
St-Hubert
Wiltz
Bitburg
Salmtal
Bernkastel-Kues
Bing am Rhei...

Chauny
Marle
Rozoy-sur-Serre
Bogny-sur-Meuse
Vresse
Paliseul
Libramont 567△
Neufchâteau
Ettelbruck
Mersch
Trier
Konz
Morbach
Bad Kreuznac...

Tergnier
Montcornet
Signy-l'Abbaye 316△
Charleville-Mézières
Bouillon
Redange
Echternach
Nohfelden
Idar-Oberstein
Donners...

Noyon
Laon
Omont
Sedan
Carignan
Arlon
LUXEMBOURG
Pétange
Reinsfeld
St Wendel
Erbeskopf 818△
Wolfstein

Courmelles
Rethel
Mouzon
Virton
Esch-sur-Alzette
Mettlach
Merzig
Neunkirchen
Kaisersla...

Attichy
Soissons
Vouziers
Stenay
Longuyon
Hayange
Florange
Thionville
Saarlouis
Homburg

Villers-Cotterêts
Fismes
Béthény
Guignicourt
Dun-sur-Meuse
Spincourt
Consenvoye
Rombas

Tinqueux
Reims
Aisne

Oostende
Erbeskopf

Marne/river labels:
Neder Rijn
Waal
Maas
Meuse
Rhein
Rhine
Ruhr
Mosel
Saar
Kyll
Sûre
Our
Dender
Schelde
Leie
Sambre
Ourthe
Semois
Serre
Oise
Aisne
Eemskanaal
IJssel
Berkel
Lippe

Conic Equidistant Projection

METRES / FEET
5000 16404
3000 9843
2000 6562
1000 3281
500 1640
200 656
0 0
Land below sea level
200 656
4000 13124
6000 19686

Longitude 6° east of Greenwich

A · 5° · B · 10° · C

DENMARK

NORTH SEA

METRES
FEET

5000	16404
3000	9843
2000	6562
1000	3281
500	1640
200	656
0	0

Land below
sea level

200	656
4000	13124
6000	19686

NETHERLANDS

AMSTERDAM

BELGIUM

BRUSSELS
(Bruxelles)

LUXEMBOURG

GERMANY

Hamburg

Bremen

Hannover

BERLIN

Cologne
(Köln)

Frankfurt
am Main

Nuremberg
(Nürnberg)

FRANCE

LORRAINE

Stuttgart

BAYERN

Munich
(München)

CZECH

PRAG

SWITZERLAND

LIECHTEN-
STEIN
VADUZ

BERN

Zürich

ITALY

Dolomites

Longitude 10° east of Greenwich

B · C

Conic Equidistant Projection

Map: France and Switzerland

Scale legend

METRES
FEET

5000	16404
3000	9843
2000	6562
1000	3281
500	1640
200	656
0	0
Land below sea level	
200	656
4000	13124
6000	19686

Grid references

A   5°   B   0°

1   50°

2   45°

3

A   5°   B   Greenwich 0° meridian

Major water bodies and regions

English Channel (La Manche)

Bristol Channel

Strait of Dover

Baie de Seine

Golfe de St-Malo

BAY OF BISCAY

Gulf of Gascony

Mar Cantábrico

Cordillera Cantábrica

Countries and regions

UNITED KINGDOM

FRANCE

SPAIN

ANDORRA

NORMANDY

BRITTANY

PICARDY

ARTOIS

ANJOU

AQUITAINE

GASCONY (GASCOGNE)

PYRENEES

ASTURIAS

NAVARRA

Selected place names

LONDON, Reading, Basingstoke, Guildford, Maidstone, Canterbury, Margate, Dover, Dunkirk (Dunkerque), Folkestone, Calais, Boulogne-sur-Mer, Hastings, Eastbourne, Brighton, Worthing, Portsmouth, Southampton, Bournemouth, Poole, Weymouth, Exeter, Plymouth, Torquay, Penzance, St Ives, Land's End, Falmouth, Newquay, Truro, Bodmin, Liskeard, Tavistock, Barnstaple, Bideford, Ilfracombe, Taunton, Bridgwater, Weston-super-Mare, Bath, Salisbury, Winchester, Aldershot, Crawley

Cherbourg, Le Havre, Caen, Bayeux, St-Lô, Coutances, Granville, Avranches, Rouen, Dieppe, Fécamp, Amiens, Abbeville, Beauvais, Versailles, Boulogne-Billancourt, Paris, Dreux, Chartres, Évreux, Lisieux, Alençon, Le Mans, Laval, Rennes, St-Malo, St-Brieuc, Guingamp, Morlaix, Brest, Quimper, Lorient, Vannes, Redon, Nantes, St-Nazaire, Angers, Tours, Orléans, Blois, Châteauroux, Poitiers, Niort, La Rochelle, Rochefort, Saintes, Cognac, Angoulême, Limoges, Bordeaux, Bergerac, Périgueux, Brive-la-Gaillarde, Mont-de-Marsan, Dax, Bayonne, Biarritz, St-Jean-de-Luz, Pau, Lourdes, Tarbes, Auch, Toulouse, Colomiers, Muret, Carcassonne, Foix, Andorra la Vella

Santander, Bilbao, Donostia-San Sebastián, Vitoria-Gasteiz, Pamplona, Logroño, Burgos, León, Oviedo, Gijón-Xixón, Avilés, Palencia, Huesca, Jaca, Tudela

A 10° B 5°

ATLANTIC
OCEAN

Mar Cantábrico

Cabo
Ortegal
Punta de
Estaca de Bares
Cervo
Ortigueira
Viveiro
Ferrol
Luarca
Avilés
Cabo de Peñas
Gijón-Xixón
Santander
Laredo
Algor
(Guec
A Coruña
A Gándara
de Altea
Vilalba
Ribadeo
Salas
Pola de
Siero
Ribadesella
Llanes
Santillana
Torrelavega
Barakaldo
Bilbao
Llodio
Betanzos
Cangas
del Narcea
Oviedo
Mieres
ASTURIAS
Reinosa
Arra
Vitoria-Gaster
Santiago
de Compostela
Ordes
Melide
Lugo
Villablino
Peña Ubiña
2417
Langreo
Torrecerredo
2648
Cabañaquinta
Guardo
Aguilar
de Campóo
Miranda de Ebro
Briviesca
Nájera
Logr
GALICIA
Cape Finisterre
(Cabo Fisterra)
Vilagarcía de Arousa
Santa Uxía de Ribeira
Pontevedra
Marín
Cangas
Vigo
Muros
de Arousa
A Estrada
Lalín
Chantada
Sarria
Monforte
de Lemos
Ponferrada
San Andrés
del Rabanedo
León
Astorga
Saldaña
Osorno
Cordillerá Cantábrica
Sierra de la Dem
Burgos
Redondela
Tui
Cañiza
Ourense
Xinzo
de Limia
Barco
Truchas
El Teleno
2188
Benavente
Valencia
de Don Juan
Sahagún
Palencia
Lerma
Miño
Fondevila
Verín
Sierra de la Cabrera
Medina
de Rioseco
Aranda
de Duero
Ayllón
Viana do Castelo
Bragança
Zamora
CASTILLA Y LEÓN
Valladolid
Toro
Tordesillas
Cuéllar
Braga
Chaves
Macedo
de Cavaleiros
Duero
Cerezo
de Abajo
Medin
Sigüenz
Póvoa de Varzim
Guimarães
Vila Real
Mirandela
Fermoselle
*Embalse
de Almendra*
Medina
del Campo
Olmedo
Matosinhos
Maia
Oporto
(Porto)
Torre de
Moncorvo
Sierra de Mogadouro
Ledesma
Tormes
Arévalo
Segovia
Sierra de Guadarrama
Peñalara
2430
Medin
Vila Nova de Gaia
Pedroso
São João
da Madeira
Lamego
Meda
Salamanca
Lumbrales
Guadalajara
Alcalá de
Henares
Emb
Buer
Ovar
Aveiro
Ílhavo
Águeda
Viseu
Vilari
Formoso
Ciudad
Rodrigo
Peñaranda
de Bracamonte
Ávila
Móstoles
Mealhada
Mangualde
Guarda
Nuñomoral
MADRID
Getafe
Taran
Figueira
da Foz
Coimbra
Mondego
Torre
1993
Covilhã
Sabugal
Béjar
Sierra de Gredos
Fuenlabrada
Parla
Aranjuez
Lousã
Fundão
Sierra da Estrela
Plasencia
Valle de Tiétar
Torrijos
Ocaña
Marinha
Grande
Pombal
Castelo
Branco
Coria
Navalmoral
de la Mata
Talavera
de la Reina
Toledo
Batalha
Leiria
Tomar
Alcántara
Tagus (Tejo)
Trujillo
*Embalse
de Valdecañas*
Montes de Toledo
CASTILLA-LA MANCH
Caldas da Rainha
Torres
Novas
Abrantes
Cáceres
Sierra de San Pedro
*Sierra
de Guadalupe*
Herrera
del Duque
Madridejos
Peniche
Entroncamento
Santarém
Ponte
de Sor
Portalegre
EXTREMADURA
Miajadas
Navalvillar
de Pela
*Embalse
de Cijara*
Alcázar
San Juan
Torres Vedras
Coruche
Campo Maior
Mérida
Guadiana
Ciudad
Real
Socuéllamos
Villarrobledo
Tome
Vila Franca de Xira
Amadora
LISBON
(Lisboa)
Cacém
Cascais
Almada
Montijo
Elvas
Estremoz
Redondo
Badajoz
Don
Benito
Villanueva
de la Serena
Almadén
Daimiel
Manzanares
Valdepeñas
Setúbal
Alcácer do Sal
Évora
*Barragem
de Alqueva*
Olivenza
Cabeza del Buey
Jabalón
Villanueva
de los Infantes
Cabo Espichel
Baía de Setúbal
Torrão
Amareleja
Zafra
Almendralejo
Hinojosa
del Duque
Puertollano
Grândola
Beja
Moura
Fregenal
de la Sierra
Peñarroya-Pueblonuevo
Los Pedroches
Pozoblanco
Linares
Sines
*Cabo de
Sines*
Aljustrel
Castro
Verde
Serpa
Rosal de la
Frontera
Azuaga
Sierra
Morena
Andújar
Odemira
Cortegana
Constantina
Córdoba
Baeza
Úbeda
Mértola
Valverde
del Camino
Palma del Río
Écija
Guadalquivir
Martos
Jaén
Alcaudete
Baza
Aljezur
Almodôvar
Guadiana
Huelva
Almonte
Coria
del Río
Lora
del Río
Carmona
Lucena
Montilla
Cabra
Alcalá la Real
Priego
de Córdoba
Guadix
ALGARVE
Lagos
Portimão
Loulé
Tavira
Ayamonte
*Playa de
Castilla*
Utrera
Seville
(Sevilla)
Marchena
Osuna
Puente-
Genil
Loja
Sierra de
Sierra Nevada
Mulhacén
3482
Alme
São Vicente
Sagres
Albufeira
Olhão
Cabo de Faro
Santa Maria
Las Marismas
Lebrija
Morón de
la Frontera
Antequera
Granada
Vélez-
Málaga
Motril
Adra
Alm
Sanlúcar
de Barrameda
El Puerto de
Santa María
Arcos
de la Frontera
ANDALUCÍA
Ronda
Málaga
Torremolinos
Almuñécar
*Golfo
de Cádiz*
Costa de la Luz
Jerez de la
Frontera
Cádiz
San
Fernando
Chiclana de
la Frontera
Marbella
Estepona
Costa del Sol
*Golfo
Alme*
Vejer de la Frontera
Barbate de Franco
Algeciras
La Línea de
la Concepción
Alborán
Cabo Trafalgar
Strait of Gibraltar
Gibraltar (U.K.)
Pta Almina
Ceuta
(Spain)
Cabo Negro
Sea
I. de Alborán
Tangier
(Tánger)
Asilah
Tétouan
MOROCCO
*Cap des
Trois Fourches*

PORTUGAL

SPAIN

Miño
Tuela
Sabor
Douro
Tua
Serra do Faro

1

40°

2

35°

METRES
FEET

5000
16404

3000
9843

2000
6562

1000
3281

500
1640

200
656

0
0

Land below
sea level

200
656

4000
13124

6000
19686

A 10° B 5°

122

Conic Equidistant Projection

FRANCE

Gulf of Gascony

Arcachon
la Teste-de-Buch
Gradignan
Gujan-Mestras
Langon
Marmande
Casteljaloux
Nérac
Lectoure
Castelsarrasin
Auch
Colomiers
Toulouse
Cugnaux
Muret

AQUITAINE

Figeac
Cahors
Villefranche-de-Rouergue
Rodez
Espalion
Marvejols
Mende
Les Vans
Pierrelatte
Valréas
Nyons
Sisteron
Digne-les-Bains

Villeneuve-sur-Lot
Agen
Moissac
Montauban
Gaillac
Albi
Castres

Cévennes

Aveyron
Séverac-le-Château
Millau
Florac
Ganges
Uzès
Bagnols-sur-Cèze
Orange
Bollène
Carpentras
Avignon
Cavaillon
Manosque

Mimizan
Labouheyre
Morcenx
Soustons
Mont-de-Marsan
Dax
Tartas
Aire-sur-l'Adour
Pau
Orthez
Maubourguet
Tarbes

GASCONY
(GASCOGNE)

Carmaux
Lodève
Montpellier

LANGUEDOC

Vauvert
Arles
Nîmes
Salon-de-Provence
Pertuis
Aix-en-Provence
Marignane
Aubagne
Toulon
St-Tropez
Brignoles
Draguignan
Fréjus

Biarritz
Bayonne
Irun
St-Jean-de-Luz
Ostia-an-bastián
Etxarri-Aranatz
Pamplona

NAVARRA

Oloron-Ste-Marie
Lourdes
Bagnères-de-Luchon
St-Gaudens
Foix
Vielha

PYRENEES

ANDORRA
ANDORRA LA VELLA
Les Escaldes

Châteauneuf-les-Martigues
Marseille
La Ciotat
Six-Fours-les-Plages
Cap Sicié
Hyères

Golfe du Lion

Béziers
Agde
Sète
Narbonne
Carcassonne
Pamiers
Limoux
Quillan
Durban-Corbières
Rivesaltes
Étang de Leucate
Perpignan
Port-Vendres
Céret
Prades
Cap de Creus

Pau
Billère
Gave de Pau
Aragón
Jaca
Monte Perdido 3348
Aneto 3404
Le Seu d'Urgell
Figueres
Banyoles
Cap de Begur

Tafalla
Borja
Sádaba
Ejea de los Caballeros
Arguís
Huesca
Arguís
Tremp
Berga
Ripoll
Olot
Torelló
Vic
Salt
Girona
Torroella de Montgrí
Palamós
Costa Brava

Alfaro
Tudela
Graus
Barbastro
Monzón
Tárrega
Igualada
Manresa
Sabadell
Blanes
Costa Brava

CATALUÑA

Alto del nervo
2316
Alagón
Zaragoza
Quinto
Binefar
Fraga
Lleida
Martorell
Santa Coloma de Gramanet
Mataró

ARAGÓN

Calatayud
Cariñena
Escatrón
Caspe
Valls
Reus
Tarragona
Barcelona
El Prat de Llobregat
Vilanova i la Geltrú

Daroca
Calamocha
Molina de Aragón
Monreal del Campo
Perales del Alfambra
Morella
Gandesa
Tortosa
Amposta
Sant Carles de la Ràpita
Vinarós

Costa Dorada
Golf de Sant Jordi

Tordesilos
Medinaceli
Teruel
Peñarroya 2019
Sarrión

VALENCIA

Torreblanca
Castellón de la Plana

Costa del Azahar

Minorca
(Menorca)

Punta Nati
Ciutadella
Es Mercadal
Mahón
Cap de Formentor

Serranía de Javalambre
Santa Cruz de Moya
Utiel
La Vall d'Uixó
Sagunto
Burriana
Turia

Majorca
(Mallorca)
Pollença
Alcúdia
Sóller
Sa Pobla
Cap des Freu
La Cabaneta
Manacor
Felanitx

Embalse de Alarcón
Cabriel
Manises
Requena
Torrent
Valencia
Catarroja
Burjassot
Algemesí
Sueca
Cullera

Golfo de Valencia

Sa Dragonera
Calvià
Palma de Mallorca
Cap de ses Salines

Minglanilla

La Roda
Albacete
Almansa
Xàtiva
Ontinyent
Oliva
Gandia
Dénia
Cabo de la Nao

Ibiza
(Eivissa)

Sant Joan de Labritja
Santa Eulalia del Río
Ibiza (Eivissa)
Sant Antoni de Portmany
San Francisco Javier
Formentera

Illa de Cabrera

BALEARIC ISLANDS
(ISLAS BALEARES)
(Spain)

Alcaraz
Yecla
Villena
Ibi
Alcoy-Alcoi
Elda
Novelda
Villajoyosa
La Vila Joiosa
Alicante
Benidorm
Altea

Segura
Hellín
Jumilla
Crevillent
Elche
Elx
Oriheula

Costa Blanca

Caravaca la Cruz
Cieza
Molina de Segura
Alcantarilla
Murcia
Torrevieja

MURCIA

Lorca
Alhama de Murcia
Mazarrón
Cabo de Palos

MEDITERRANEAN SEA

Huércal-Overa
Vera
Aguilas
Golfo de Mazarrón

Cabo de Gata

ALGIERS
(Alger)
Aïn Taya
Dellys
Boumerdes
Tizi Ouzou
Bejaïa
Bougaa
Jijel
Sétif

Djebel Bissa 1157
Ténès
Tipasa
Koléa
Blida
Larba
Bouira
Bordj Bou Arréridj
Aïn Azel

Sidi Ali
Ouled Farès
Aïn Defla
Miliana
Médéa
Berrouaghia
Sour el Ghozlane
Sidi Aissa
M'Sila

Mostaganem
Cap Carbon
Arzew
Aïn Tédélès
Relizane
Oued Chlef
Chlef
Khemis Miliana
Ksar el Boukhari
Barika

Oran
Oued Tlélat
Mohammadia
Mascara
Zemmora
Bordj Bounaama
Tissemsilt
Mahdia
Tiaret
Zenzach
Bou Saâda
M'Doukal

Beni Saf
Aïn Temouchent
Sig

ALGERIA

1

2

40°

35°

200 KILOMETRES
100
0

150
100
50
MILES 0

1:4 800 000

A

P

S

3738

Ortles
3905

Bolzano
Merano
Adige
Laives

Cortina
d'Ampezzo

Tarvisio
Gemona
del Friuli
Tolmezzo
Cividale
del Friuli
2864
Maniago
Tolmin

SLO

LJUBLJANA

Logatec

Bonneville
Martigny
Matterhorn
Mont-Blanc 4478
Chiavenna
Tirano
Sondrio
Bellinzona
Dolomites
Trento
Belluno
Feltre
Conegliano
Vittorio
Veneto
Udine
Pordenone
Gorizia
Monfalcone

Rumilly
Cluses
Chamonix
Mont-Blanc 4808
Verbania
Lugano
Lake Como
Riva del
Garda
Rovereto
Valdagno
Schio
Treviso
Portogruaro

Trieste

Koper

Aix-les-
Bains
Annecy
Albertville
Aosta
Arona
Como
Lecco
Lake
Garda
Bergamo
Brescia
Vicenza
Verona
Treviglio
Padua
(Padova)
Venice
(Venezia)
Gulf of
Venice

Rijek

Chambéry
St-Egrève
Isère
Borgosesia
Biella
Busto
Arsizio
Monza
Rho
Milan
(Milano)
Manerbio
Cremona
Lonigo
Rovigo
Laguna
Veneta
Chioggia
Porto Tolle
Poreč
Rovinj
Pazin
Criky

1

Voiron
Grenoble
Modane
Ivrea
Novara
Vercelli
Vigevano
Pavia
Lodi
Crema
Mantua
(Mantova)
Legnago
Codigoro
Porto
maggiore
Comacchio
Pula
Rt Kamenjak
Cre

45°

Barre des
Ecrins
4102
La Mure
Cuorgnè
Rivoli
Turin
(Torino)
Po
Casale
Monferrato
Piacenza
Parma
Reggio
nell'Emilia
Modena
Ferrara
Argenta
Po
Veli Losi
Loši

St-Bonnet-
en-Champsaur
Briançon
Giaveno
Moncalieri
Asti
Alessandria
Novi Ligure
Tortona
Reno
Bologna
Ravenna

Gap
Pinerolo
Saluzzo
Alba
Acqui
Terme
Tanaro
Carpi
Imola
Faenza
Forlì
Cesenatico

Barcelonnette
Fossano
Mondovì
Savona
Sestri
Levante
Fivizzano
Monte
Cimone
2165
Cesena
Rimini

Digne-les-
Bains
Durance
Cuneo
1871
Col de Tende
Savona
Rapallo
Carrara
Barga
Pistoia
Prato
SAN
MARINO
Pesaro
Fano
Senigallia

Sisteron
Castellane
Maritime
Alps
Tende
Albenga
La Spezia
Massa
Lucca
Florence
(Firenze)
SAN
MARINO
Ancona

Manosque
San
Remo
Ventimiglia
Imperia
Capo Mele
Gulf of
Genoa
Genoa
(Genova)
Viareggio
Pisa
Arno
Empoli
Scandicci
Sansepolcro
Arezzo
Cagli
Osimo

Draguignan
Grasse
MONTE-
CARLO
Nice
MONACO
Antibes
Livorno
Cecina
Siena
Cortona
Gubbio
Fabriano
Macerata
Civitanova
Marche

Brignoles
Fréjus
St-Raphaël
Côte d'Azur
Cannes
Cap de St-Tropez
L i g u r i a n
S e a
Isola
di Capraia
San Vincenzo
Montepulciano
Perugia
Foligno
Ascoli
Piceno
Fermo
San Bene
del Tront

Toulon
Hyères
St-Tropez
Cap
Sicié
Îles d'Hyères

Cap Corse
Monte
Stello
Isola
d'Elba
Piombino
Follonica
Marsciano
Todi
Terni
Narni
Monte
Corno
2912
L'Aquila
Giuliano
Teramo
Penne
Pes

2

L'Île-Rousse
St-Florent
1507
Bastia
Isola
Pianosa
Castiglione
della Pescaia
Grosseto
Orvieto
Lago di
Bolsena
Viterbo
Tiber (Tevere)
Rieti
Nera
Monte
Amaro
2793
Chi
Triver

Corsica
(Corse)
(France)
Calvi
Vescovato
Cervione
Arcipelago
Toscano
Isola
di Montecristo
Tarquinia
Civitavecchia
Guidonia-
Montecelio
Tivoli
Aterno
Avezzano
Sora
Pescara

Monte
Rotondo
2622
Capo Rosso
Corte
Ghisonaccia
VATICAN CITY
ROME
(Roma)
Liri
Campob

Capo di Feno
Ajaccio
Prunelli-di-Fiumorbo
Pomezia
Velletri
Sezze
Frosinone
Cassino
Venafr

Olmeto
Zonza
Sartène
Punta d'Ovace
1340
Porto-Vecchio
Aprilia
Anzio
Latina
Fondi
Sessa
Aurunc

Capo Pertusato
Bonifacio
Sabaudia
Gaeta
Golfo
di Gaeta
Naples
(Napoli)
Case

Punta Caprara
Isola Asinara
Golfo dell'
Asinara
Arzachena
La Maddalena
Capo Ferro
Strait of Bonifacio
Isole Ponziane
Pozzuoli
Ves
Pompe

Porto Torres
Punta
Balestrieri
1359
Olbia
Sorrento
Isola d'Ischia
Isola di Capri
Goi
Sal

Capo Caccia
Sassari
Oschiri
Budoni
Isole Ponziane

Alghero
Ploaghe
Buddusò
Capo Comino
Siniscola

Bonorva
Nuoro
Orosei

Sardinia
(Sardegna)
(Italy)
Macomer
Golfo di Orosei

Abbasanta
Punta La
Marmora
Capo di Monte Santu

40°
Oristano
Laconi
1834
Tortolì

Capo della Frasca
Mandas
Tertenia
T Y R R H E N I A N
S E A

3

Guspini
San Gavino Monreale
Serramanna
Villaputzu

Iglesias
Monte Linas
1236
Assemini

Portoscuso
Punta
Maxia
Quartu Sant'Elena
Isola di Ustica

Isola di San Pietro
Sant'Antioco
Cagliari
Capo Carbonara
Isol
Lipa

Isola di Sant'Antioco
1017
Pula
Golfo di
Cagliari
Isola Filic

M E D I T E R R A N E A N   S E A
Sicily
(Sicilia)

Capo San Vito
Monte Sparagio
Partinico
Palermo
Cefalù

Isola Marettimo
Trapani
1110
Alcamo
Rocca
Busambra
1613
Termini
Imerese
Mo

La Galite
Marsala
Partanna
Leonforte
Dit

Mazara del Vallo
Castelvetrano
Caltanissetta

Menzel
Bourguiba
Bizerte
Rass Jebel
Capo Granitola
Sciacca
Canicatti

Collo
Cap
de Fer
Chetaïbi
Cap
de Garde
Nefza
Mateur
Golfe de
Tunis
Cap
Bon
Agrigento
Caltagir
Niscemi
Gela

Skikda
Annaba
El Kala
Tabarka
Licata
Golfo di Gela

ALGERIA
Azzaba
El Hadjar
El Tarf
TUNISIA
Jedeida

Conic Equidistant Projection

Longitude 10° east of Greenwich

A
B

METRES
FEET

5000
16404

3000
9843

2000
6562

1000
3281

500
1640

200
656

0
0

Land below
sea level

200
656

4000
13124

6000
19686

© Collins Bartholomew Ltd

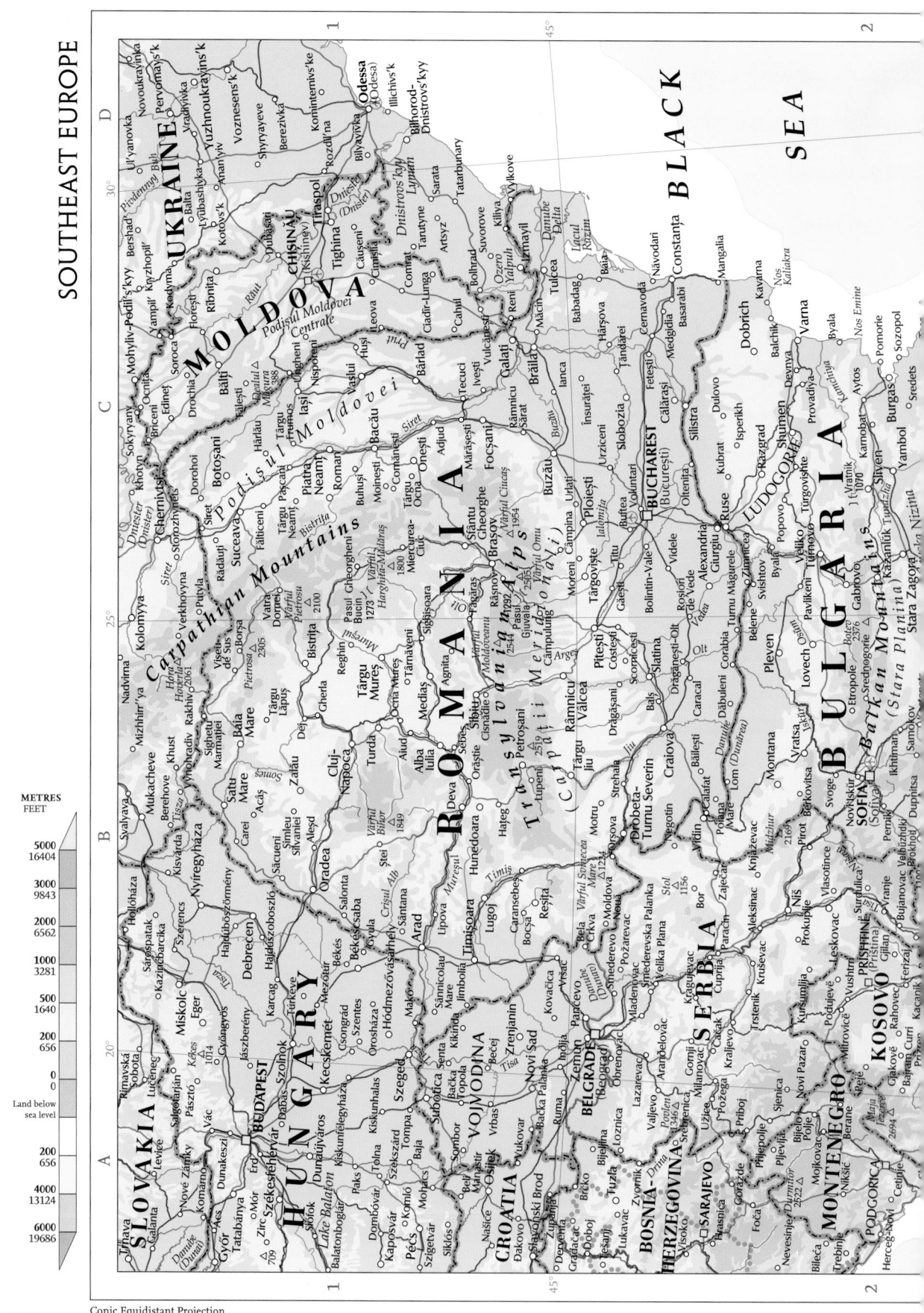

Conic Equidistant Projection

METRES
FEET

5000
16404

3000
9843

2000
6562

1000
3281

500
1640

200
656

0
0

Land below
sea level

200
656

4000
13124

6000
19686

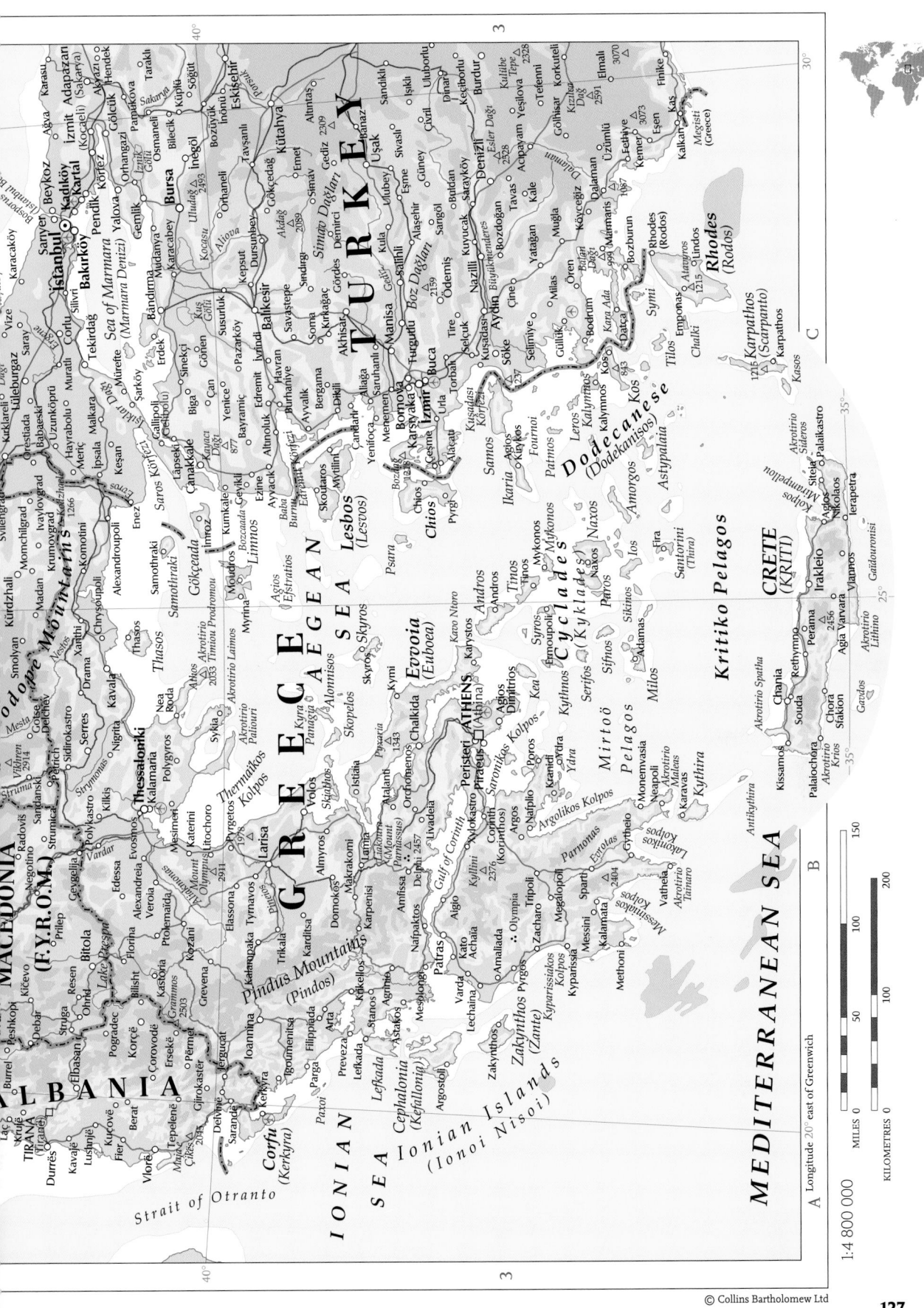

© Collins Bartholomew Ltd

1:4 800 000

A   Longitude 20° east of Greenwich

MILES   0   50   100   150

KILOMETRES   0   100   200

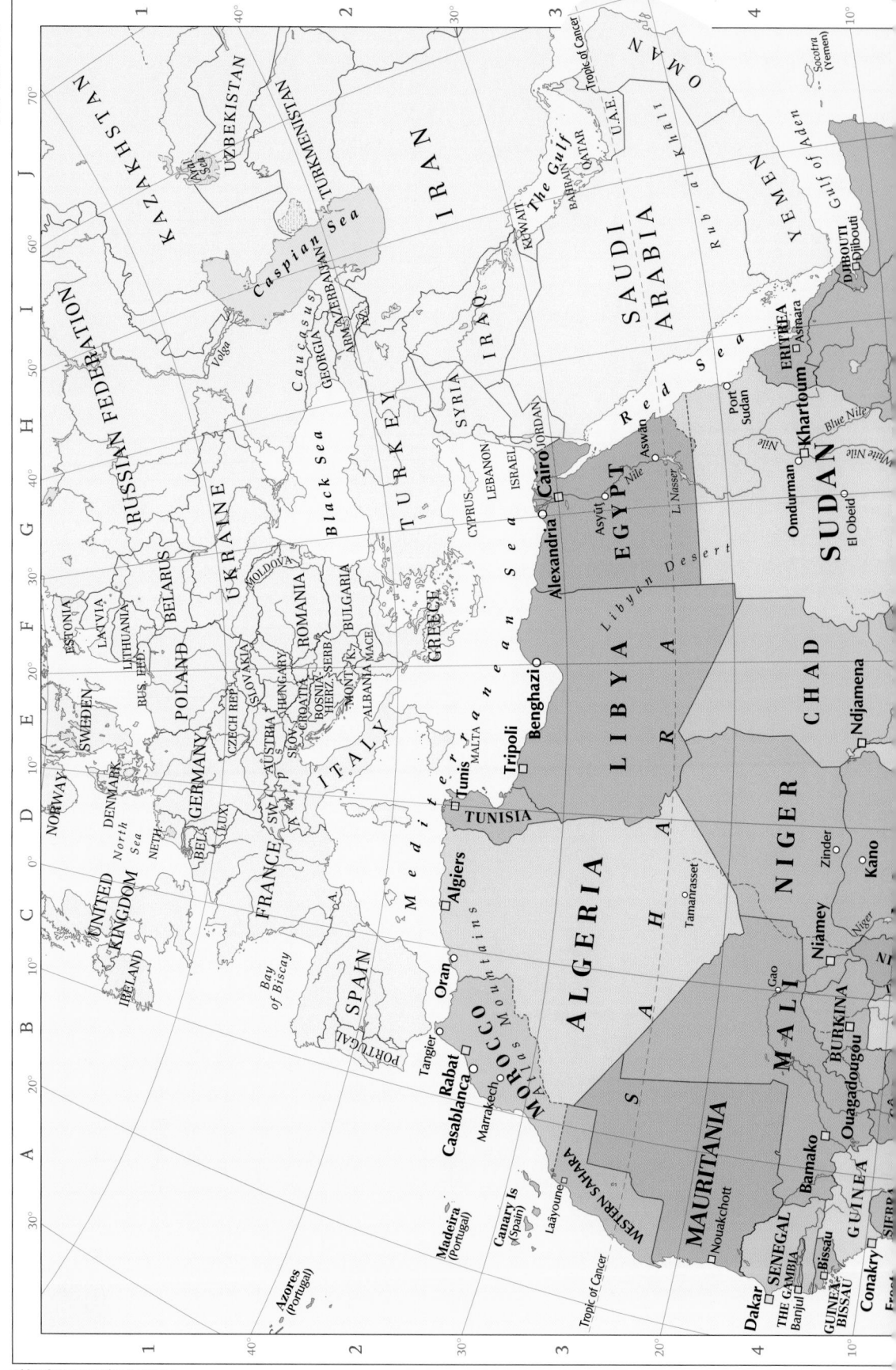

Oblated Stereographic Projection

Equator 0°

I N D I A N

O C E A N

SEYCHELLES

Victoria Mahé

Coëtivy

Farquhar Group (Seychelles)

Agalega Islands (Mauritius)

Tropic of Capricorn

MAURITIUS

Port Louis

St-Denis Réunion (France)

Tanjona Bobaomby

MADAGASCAR

Mayotte (France)

Antananarivo

Aldabra Islands (Seychelles)

Fianarantsoa

COMOROS

Moroni

Tanjona Volimena

Mozambique Channel

Tanjona Vohimena

S O M A L I A

Mogadishu

Mombasa

Dar es Salaam

Zanzibar

Mahajanga

Nampula

KENYA

Nairobi

TANZANIA

Dodoma

Lake Turkana

Kilimanjaro 5892

Tabora

UGANDA

Kampala

Kigali

RWANDA

BURUNDI

Bujumbura

Lake Victoria

Lake Tanganyika

Lake Nyasa

MALAWI

Lilongwe

Blantyre

MOZAMBIQUE

Beira

Kisangani

DEMOCRATIC

REPUBLIC

OF THE CONGO

Lubumbashi

Ndola

ZAMBIA

Lusaka

Livingstone

Kalemie

Zambezi

ZIMBABWE

Harare

Bulawayo

Limpopo

Maputo

Mbabane

SWAZILAND

Durban

Pretoria (Tshwane)

Johannesburg

LESOTHO

Maseru

REPUBLIC

OF

SOUTH AFRICA

Port Elizabeth

BOTSWANA

Francistown

Gaborone

Kalahari Desert

Mbandaka

Kananga

Kinshasa

Brazzaville

CONGO

Congo

Congo

ANGOLA

Huambo

Luanda

CABINDA (Angola)

Namibe

NAMIBIA

Windhoek

Namib Desert

Orange

Cape Town

Cape of Good Hope

Cape Agulhas

CAMEROON

Douala

Yaoundé

Bangui

CENTRAL AFRICAN REPUBLIC

GABON

Libreville

Port Gentil

EQUAT. GUINEA

Malabo

Bioko

SÃO TOMÉ AND PRÍNCIPE

São Tomé

São Tomé

Gulf of Guinea

Accra

Abidjan

LIBERIA

Equator 0°

Accra Novo

A T L A N T I C

O C E A N

St Helena (U.K.)

Ascension Island (U.K.)

Tristan da Cunha (U.K.)

Tropic of Capricorn

Greenwich 0° meridian

1:36 000 000

MILES 0   250   500   750   1000

0   500   1000   1500 KILOMETRES

© Collins Bartholomew Ltd

129

A T L A N T I C
O C E A N

Madeira
(Portugal)
FUNCHAL

SANTA
CRUZ DE
TENERIFE
La Palma
Pico del
Teide
3718
La Gomera
El Hierro
Canary Islands
(Islas Canarias)
(Spain)
Tenerife
Gran
Canaria
LAS PALMAS
DE GRAN
CANARIA
Lanzarote
Fuerteventura
Jandía

SPAIN
Gibraltar
(UK)
Málaga Almería Cartag
Strait of Gibraltar
Tangier Ceuta (Spain) Mostaganem Ch
(Tanger) **Oran** Sidi Be
Tétouan Melilla (Spain) **Abbès**
Ksar el Kebir Larache Tlemcen
Kenitra Sidi Taounate Oujda
Ben Slimane Kacem Taza Taourirt S Bay
RABAT Meknès **Fès** Atta
El Jadida (Fez)
Casablanca Hauts Platea
Settat **MOROCCO**
El Kelaâ des srarhna Oued Zem
Safi Khouribga Beni Mellal Bouârfa Figuig (Saha
Essaouira Marrakech Haut Atlas (High Atlas) Aïn Sefra
ATLAS MOUNTAINS
Jbel Toubkal 4167 Grand Erg
Taroudannt Er Rachidia Occiden
Agadir Ouarzazate Béchar El Hom
Tiznit Zagora Abadla
Sidi Ifni Anti-Atlas Beni Timimo
Abbès
Guelmine Hamada du Drâa Tabelbala Plate
Tan- Ksabi
Tan Adrar Sbaa Seb
Erg Meker
Iabès
Al Mahbas Tindouf Chenachane Reggane Aoulef In
Es Semara El Eglab Sebkha Azzel
Matti
Bordj Flye
Ste-Marie Poste
Chegga Weygand
Boujdour Aïn
Galtat Ben Tili Taoudenni Bordj
Zemmour Bir Mokhtar
Mogreïn Erg Iguidi Oued Ilalen
Skaymat Tiguesmat Erg Chech Adrar e
WESTERN El Hammâmi El Hank Taoudenni Aguelhok
Ad Dakhla **SAHARA** S Tanezrouft Ifôgha
Maqteïr OURÂNE Aoukâr
Zouérat Tichla Guelb er Richât 485 A L G E R I A

Tropic of Cancer

Nouâdhibou
Atâr
Akchâr
Nouâmghâr
Akjoujt
MAURITANIA
Sebkhet Araouane Kidal
Te-n-Dghâmcha Azaouâd Anéfis
NOUAKCHOTT Tidjikja Dhar Tîchît Dhar Oualâta
Moudjéria Tichît Oualâta Araouane
Boutilimit Magta Lahjar HÔD IRÎGUI **MALI**
Tiguent Aleg Ayoûn el Néma Gourma-
Rosso Bogué Atroûs Rharous
St-Louis Sénégal Kaédi Kiffa Lac Timbuktu Bourem
Dagana Mbout Timbedgha Faguibine (Tombouctou) Gao
Louga Linguère Bassikounou Goundam Ménaka
Matam Sélibabi Néma Niger
Thiès Dara Yélimané Nioro Youvarou Doro Ansongo
DAKAR Diourbel Bakel Timbedgha Lac Débo Hombori
Mbour Fatick Kidira Kayes Diéma Kogoni Mopti Gorom
Kaffrine Goudiri Sandaré Nampala Douentza Gorom
Kaolack **SENEGAL** Bafoulabé Boron Niono Ténenkou Djibo
BANJUL Gambia Tambacounda Kolokani Macina San Koro Bandiagara Dori
THE GAMBIA Brikama Kolda Kédougou Kita Ségou Djenné Tougan Ouahigouya Tillabé
Sedhiou Gabú Satadougou Kati Dioïla Bla Nouna Gourcy Kaya Bogandé NIAM
Ziguinchor Buba Mali Koundara Bamako Bougouni Sikasso San Gayéri
GUINEA Bafata Gaoual Siguiri Kangaba Mahou **BURKINA** Fada-N'Gourma
BISSAU Koubia Lac de Kolondiéba Manga Léo Pô Tenkodogo
BISSAU Boké Pita Labé Dinguiraye Sélingué Orodara **OUAGADOUGOU** Bawku BEN
Bolama Cacine Fria Dabola Kouroussa Mandiana Banfora Bolgatanga Dapaong Natiting
Arquipélago Fouta Djallon Kankan Kadiolo Lawra Wa Porga Djoug
dos Bijagós Dubréka Mamou Faranah Minniéni Gaoua Tehini Yendi Paral
GUINEA Kindia Odienné Ferkéssédougou Boundiali Tamale KA
CONAKRY Falaba Kissidougou Bouna Damongo Bimbila Bassila
Lungi Makeni Kérouané Korhogo Salaga Sokodé
Port Loko Magburaka Beyla Séguéla **CÔTE** Bondoukou **GHANA** Kete Krachi
FREETOWN Tunsar Sefadu Nzérékoré Katiola Kintampo Salavou
SIERRA Bo Kailahun Touba Man Béoumi Bouaké Wenchi Techiman Atakpame Abomey Abed
LEONE Kenema Lola 752 **D'IVOIRE** Daoukro Mampong Lac de **PORTO-N**
Bonthe Zimmi Sanniquellie Danané Daloa Bouaflé Bongouanou Kossou Bekwai Kumasi Lake Volta **LOMÉ**
Robertsport Zorzor Bamga Gagnoa Divo Adzopé Obuasi **ACCRA**
MONROVIA Kakata Tapeta Zwedru Lakota Tiassalé Aboisso Tarkwa Winneba Tema
Harbel **LIBERIA** Sassandra **YAMOUSSOUKRO** Koforidua Aného Slave Co
Buchanan Grand- Bingerville Axim Cape Coast
River Cess Greenville **Abidjan** Lahou Sekondi Gold Coast Big
Barclayville San-Pédro of Ben
Harper Tabou Cape Three Points
Cape Palmas

G U L F   O F   G U I N E A

METRES
FEET

5000	16404
3000	9843
2000	6562
1000	3281
500	1640
200	656
0	0
Land below sea level	
200	656
4000	13124
6000	19686

Lambert Azimuthal Equal Area Projection

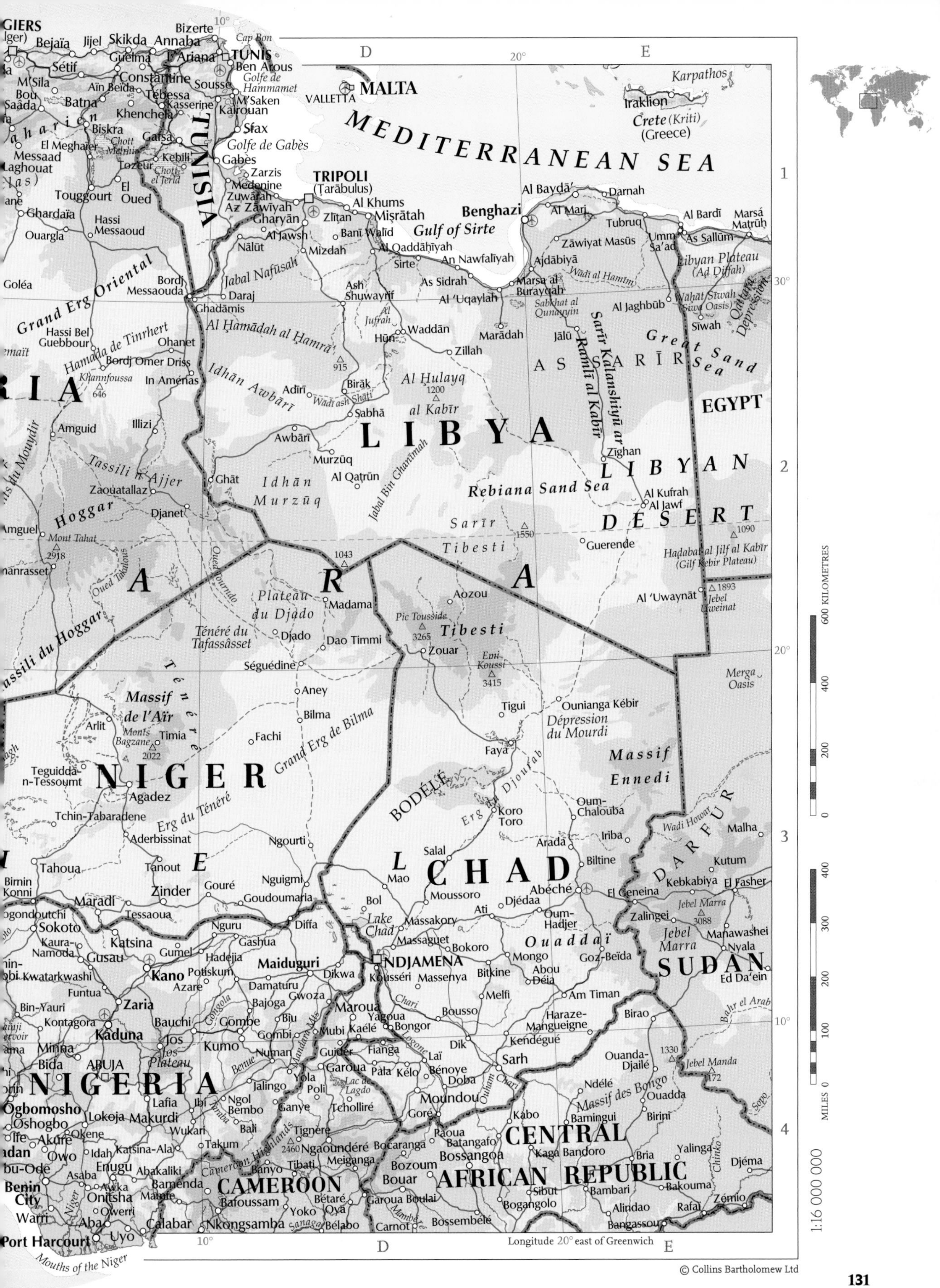

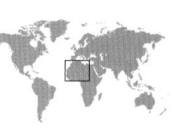

D

C

B

A

IRAN

Yazd
Anār
Abarqū
Khunsar
Na'īn
Eşfahān
(Isfahān)
Shīrāz
Neyrīz
Dārāb
Jahrom
Bastak
Ābādeh
Shahr-e kord
Borūjān
Fīrūzābād
Dezfūl
Khorramābād
Ahvāz
Ābādān
Īlām
Ālī al-Gharbī

The Gulf

BAHRAIN
MANAMA
QATAR
DOHA
ABU DHABI (Abū Zabī)
U.A.E.
Harād
Al Dawḥah
Ad Dawādimī

OMAN

AR RIMĀL

KUWAIT
Al Kuwayt
Al Jahrāh
Al Aḥmadī

Basra
(Al Başrah)
An Naşīrīyah
As Samāwah
An Najaf

BAGHDAD
Fallūjah
Ar Ramādī
Ba'qūbah
Ar Rutbah

SYRIA
DAMASCUS

IRAQ

ARABIAN
DESERT

AD DAHNĀ'

SAUDI
ARABIA

PENINSULA

AR RUB' AL KHĀLĪ
(EMPTY QUARTER)

RIYADH
(Ar Riyāḍ)

YEMEN
SAN'A'
Ta'izz
Ibb
Dhamār
Mocha
Al Bayḍā'

ERITREA
ASMARA

SUDAN
KHARTOUM
Omdurman

EGYPT
CAIRO
(Al Qāhirah)
Giza (Al Jīzah)
Alexandria
(Al Iskandarīyah)

LIBYA
Benghazi

CHAD

Western Desert

LIBYAN DESERT

Nubian Desert

MEDITERRANEAN SEA

ISRAEL
JERUSALEM
Tel Aviv-Yafo
GAZA

LEBANON
BEIRUT

JORDAN
AMMAN

HIJAZ

Medina
(Al Madīnah)

Mecca
(Makkah)
At Tā'if

Jeddah
(Jiddah)

METRES / FEET

METRES	FEET
5000	16404
3000	9843
2000	6562
1000	3281
500	1640
200	656
0	0
Land below sea level	
200	656
4000	13124
6000	19686

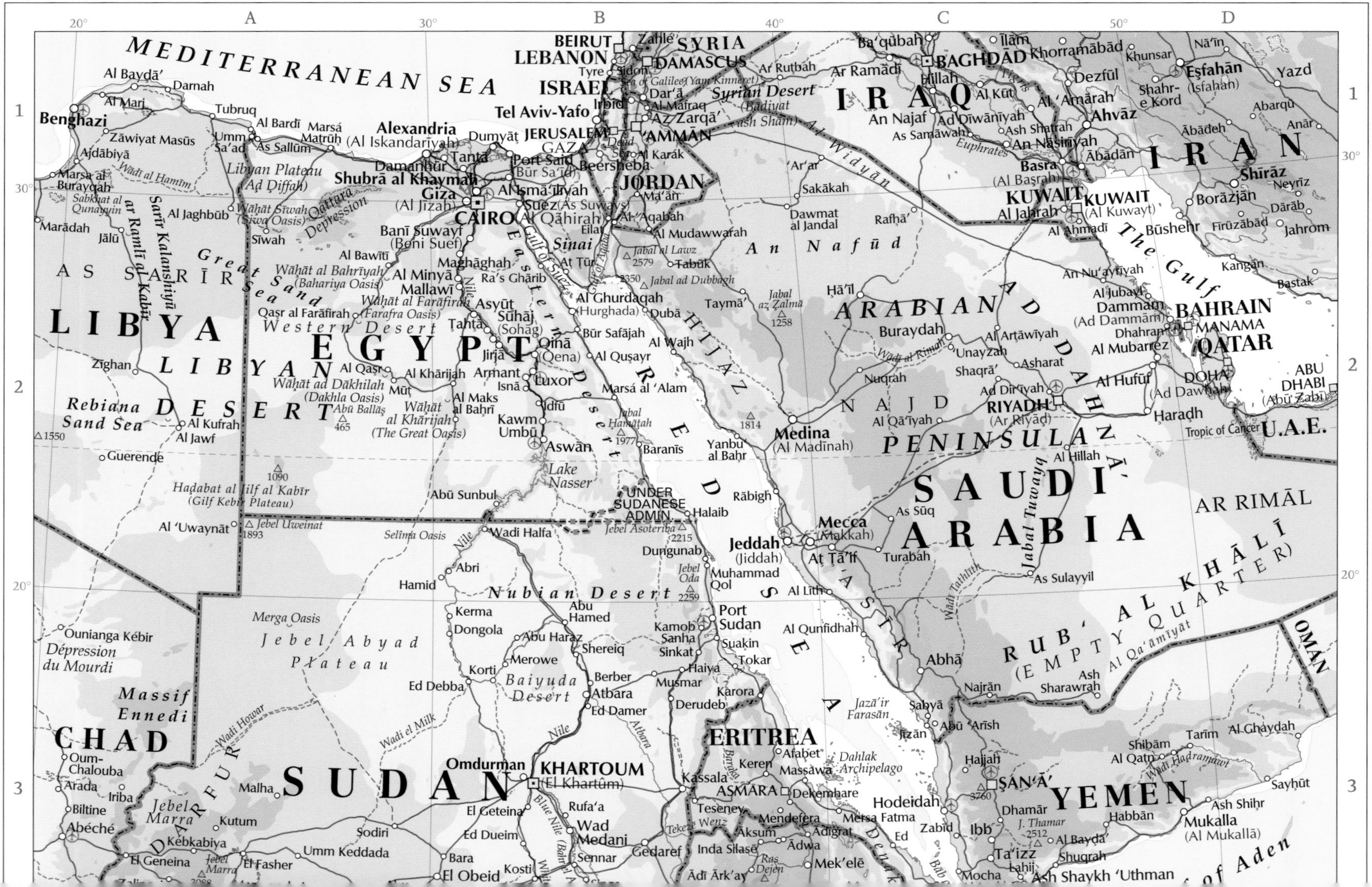

Lambert Azimuthal Equal Area Projection

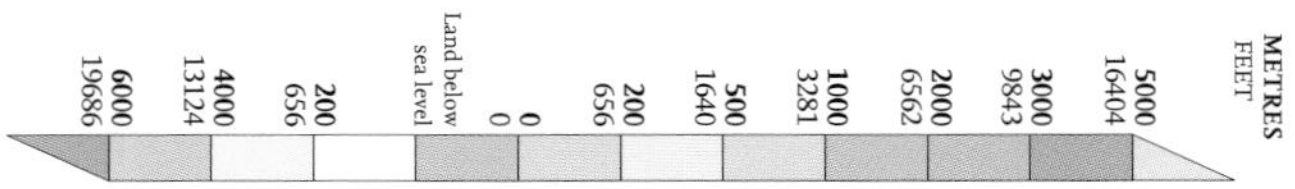

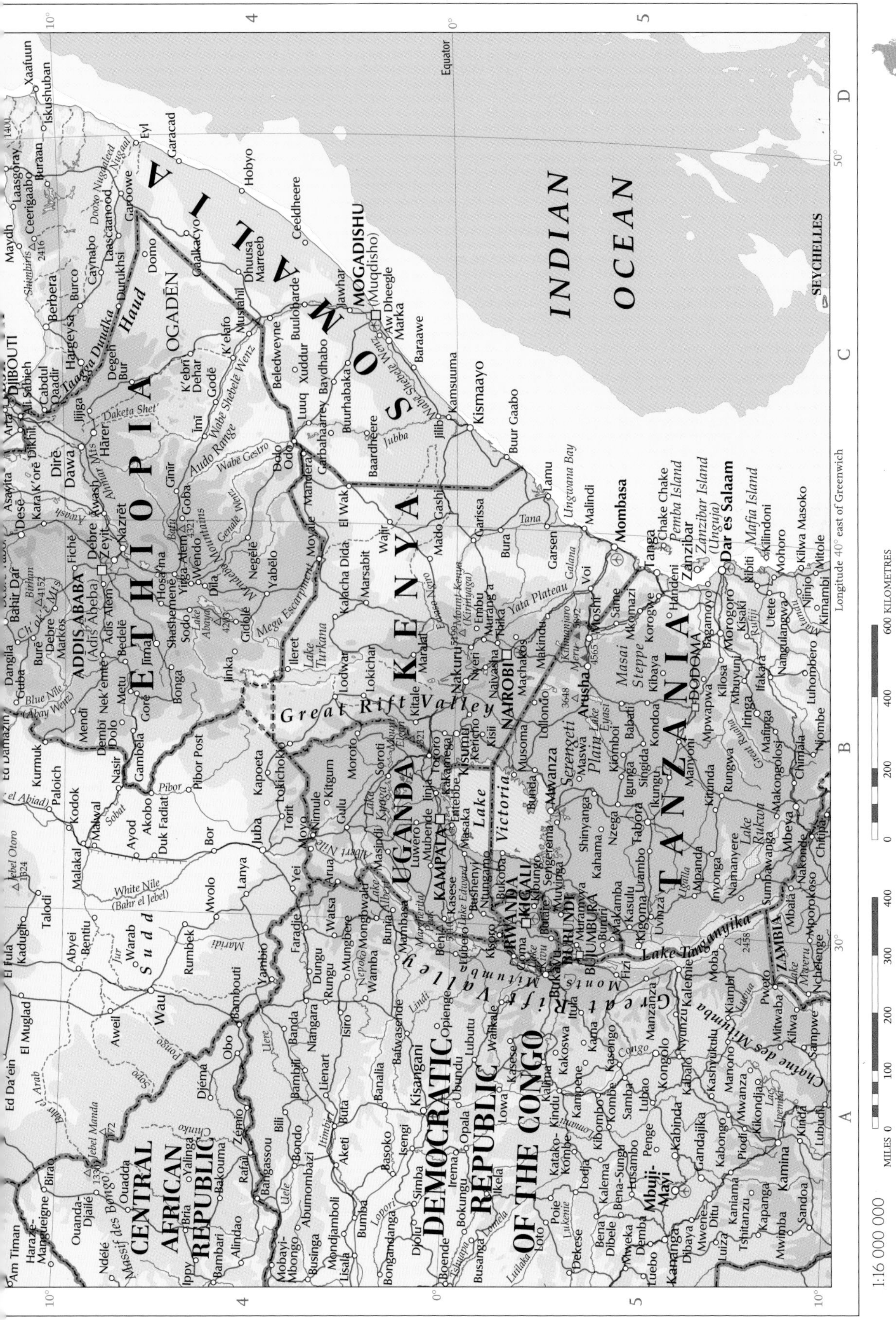

1:16 000 000

© Collins Bartholomew Ltd

A 10° B 20°

1

Tudun-Wada • Kari • Damboa • Mora • Massenya • Melfi • Abou Déia • Bourtoutou • Plaine de Garar

Bauchi • Gombe • Bajoga • Biu • Gwoza • Mokolo • Maroua • Yagoua • Bousso • Am Timan • Birao

10° Jos • Dindima • Kumo • Combi • Mubi • Kaélé • Bongor • Dik • Kendégué • Haraze-Mangueigne • Délémbé • 1330

Jos Plateau • Pankshin • Kaltungo • Guider • Fianga • Laï • Koumra • Sarh • Tiroungoulou • Ouanda-Djailé

NIGERIA • Numan • Garoua • Pala • Kélo • Bénoye • Kabo • Markounda • Bamingui • Ouadda • Birini

Shendam • Jalingo • Yola • Poli • Tchollire • Koum • Béinamar • Doba • Maro • Gore • Ndélé • Massif des Bongo • Ouadda • Bani

Lafia • Ibi • Ganye • Ngol Bembo • Mbé • Touboro • Moundou • Gribingui • Kaga • Bandoro • Ippy • Bria • Yalinga

Wukari • Donga • Bali • Gashaka • Tignère • Ngaoundéré • Baibokoum • Paoua • Batangafo • Dékoa • Bambari • Bakouma

Makurdi • Gboko • Takum • 2460 • Banyo • Bélèl • **CENTRAL** • Bossangoa • Grimari • Alindao • Rafaï

Katsina-Ala • Nkambe • Meiganga • Bocaranga • Bozoum • Sibut • Bangassou

Ikom • Wum • Bamenda • Tibati • Ngaoundal • Garoua Boulai • Bouar • Baoro • Bogangolo • Damara • **AFRICAN REPUBLIC**

Mamfe • Mbouda • Foumban • Yoko • Bétaré Oya • Carnot • Gadzi • **BANGUI** • Zongo • Mobayi-Mbongo

2 Calabar • Kumba • Nkongsamba • Kétté • Bélabo • Nanga • Bertoua • Berbérati • Boda • Bimbo • Bosobolo • Uele • Abumombazi

Mont Cameroun 4100 • Loum • Mbanga • Baffa • Eboko • Mbandjok • Batouri • Bambio • Mbaïki • Libenge • Bondo • Bûsinga

Limbe • Buea • Monatélé • **YAOUNDÉ** • Abong Mbang • Nola • Salo • Libenge • Gemena • Aketi

MALABO • Douala • Obala • Akonolinga • Yokadouma • Dongou • Kungu • Mondjamboli

Edéa • Mbalmayo • Bioko • Kribi • Ebolowa • Sangmélima • Djoum • Moloundou • Impfondo • Makanza • Lisala • Bumba • Lolo

EQUATORIAL Bata • Niefang • Ebebiyin • Souanké • Quesso • Epéna • Bolomba • Basankusu • Bongandanga

GUINEA Cogo • Oyem • Sembé • Mékambo • Makoua • Mbandaka • Embondo • Boende • Watsi Kengo • Busanga • Ikela

Ntoum • Mitzic • Mbomo • **CONGO** • Owando • Bikoro • Bokatola • Bolobo

0° **LIBREVILLE** • Alembé • Booué • Owando • Lac Tumba • Congo Basin • Bokele • Bolobo

Bifoun • **GABON** • Okondja • Obouya • Loukoléla • Bolia • Boleko • Ifumo

Port-Gentil • Lambaréné • Koulamoutou • Akiéni • Okoyo • Gamboma • Inongo • Lac Mai-Ndombe

Fougamou • Mimongo • Moanda • Franceville • Ntandembele • Buna • Oshwe • Dekese • Lodja

Iguéla • Mouila • Mayoko • Boumango • Lékana • Ngo • Bolobo • Mushie • Kutu • Loto • Poie

Tchibanga • Ndendé • Nyanga • Mossendjo • Komono • Djambala • Ngabé • Bandundu • Bagata • Bunianga

Mayumba • Nzambi • Sibiti • Makabana • Loudima • Madingou • Mindouli • Kasangulu • Kenge • Ilebo • Domiongo • Bena Dibele

3 Loubomo • **BRAZZAVILLE** • **KINSHASA** • Masi-Manimba • Idiofa • Mweka • Lusam

Pointe-Noire • Belize • Luozi • Kisantu • Kikwit • Kingandu • Luebo • Demba

CABINDA • Tshela • Kimpese • Mbanza-Ngungu • Popokabaka • Gungu • Kilembe • Kananga

(Angola) Cabinda • Boma • Matadi • Maquela do Zombo • Mawanga • Feshi • Tshikapa • Kazumba • Dibaya • Gandajika

Muanda • Kitona • M'banza Congo • Damba • Quimbele • Kasongo-Lunda • Bumba • Kamonia • Mwene-Ditu

Tomboco • Lucunga • Songo • Uíge • Negage • Massango • Cuango • Tembo Aluma • Kahemba • Luiza • Kimpa

N'zeto • Ambriz • Muxaluando • Camabatela • Bindu • Caungula • Cambulo • Lucapa • Plateau du Kasaï • Tshita

ATLANTIC Caxito • Quimbundo • Chitato • Kapanga

10° **LUANDA** • Catete • N'dalatando • Lucala • Calandula • Capenda-Camulemba • Mona Quimbundo • Chiluage • Mwimba

OCEAN Dondo • Malanje • Xá-Muteba • Quitapa • Cacolo • Saurimo • Sandoa • Kafakumba

Calulo • Cuanza • 1613 • Muriege • Muconda • Malonga • Kasaji

Gabela • Quibala • **ANGOLA** • Dala • Luau • Dilolo • Caianda

4 Waku-Kungo • Andulo • Quirima • Luacano • Mwhilung

Sumbe • N'harea • Camanóngue • Cazombo • Calunda

Planalto do Bié • Camacupa • Luena • Sachanga

A 10° B Longitude 20° east of Greenwich

METRES / FEET

METRES	FEET
5000	16404
3000	9843
2000	6562
1000	3281
500	1640
200	656
0	0

Land below sea level

200	656
4000	13124
6000	19686

Lambert Azimuthal Equal Area Projection

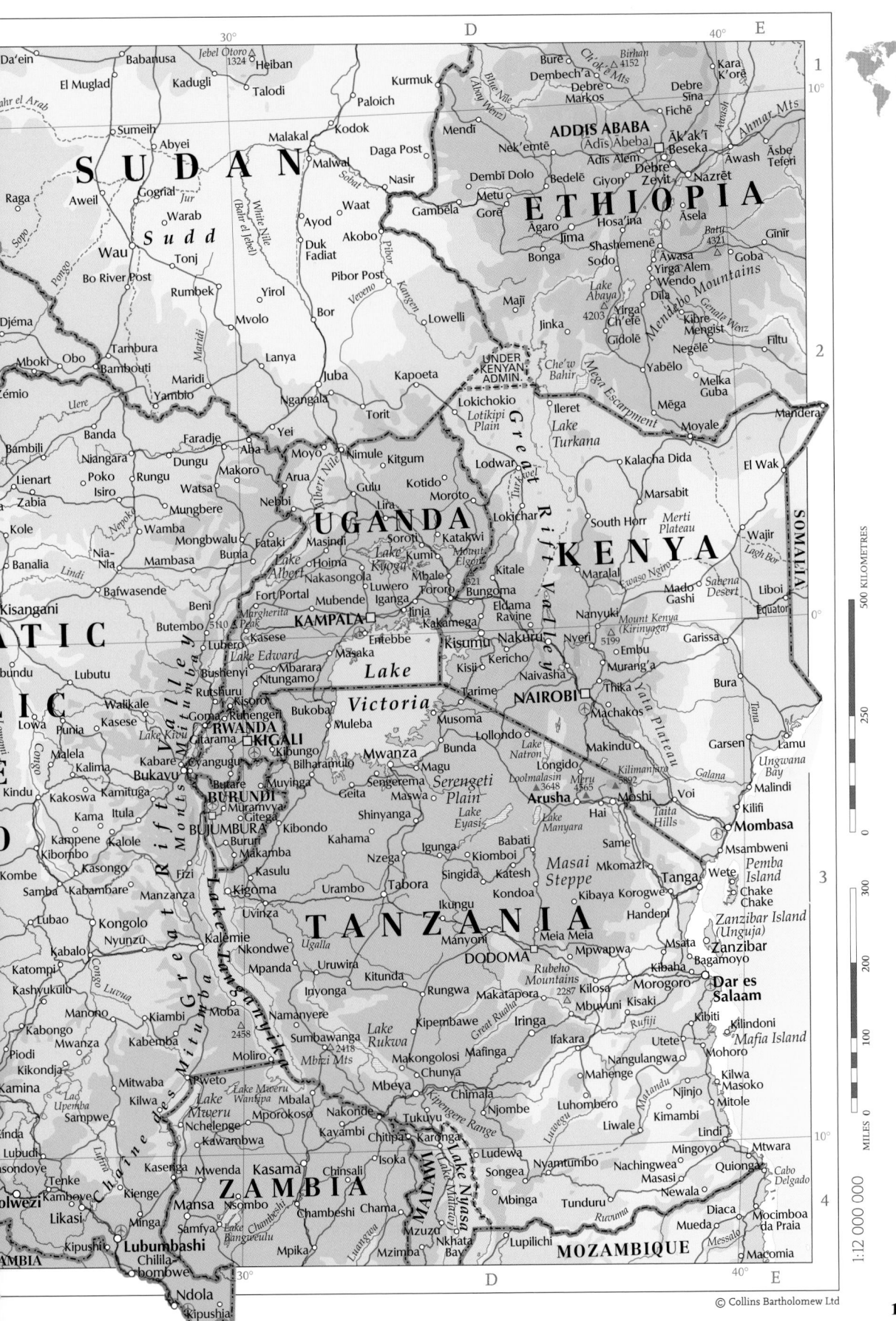

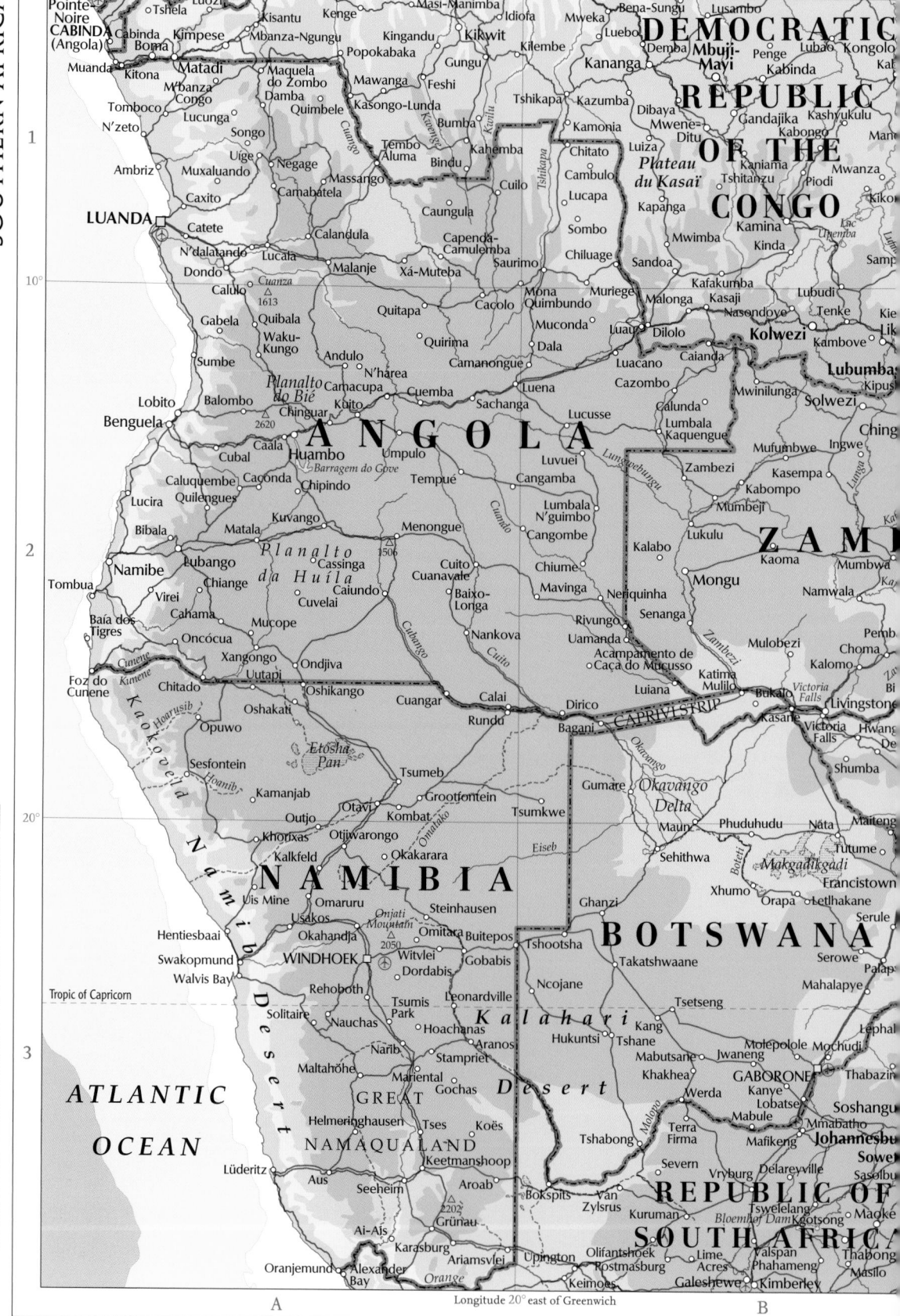

METRES
FEET

5000
16404

3000
9843

2000
6562

1000
3281

500
1640

200
656

0
0

Land below
sea level

200
656

4000
13124

6000
19686

ATLANTIC

OCEAN

Pointe-
Noire
CABINDA
(Angola)
Cabinda
Boma
Muanda
Kitona
M'banza
Congo
Tomboco
N'zeto
Ambriz
Caxito
LUANDA
Catete
N'dalatando
Dondo
Calulu
Gabela
Sumbe
Lobito
Benguela

Luozi
Tshela
Kisantu
Kimpese
Mbanza-Ngungu
Matadi
Maquela
do Zombo
Damba
Quimbele
Lucunga
Songo
Uíge
Negage
Muxaluando
Camabatela
Calandula
Lucala
Malanje
Quibala
Waku-
Kungo
Andulo
Balombo
Chinguar
Caala
Huambo

Kenge
Kingandu
Gungu
Popokabaka
Mawanga
Feshi
Tembo
Aluma
Massango
N'harea
Camacupa
Cuemba

Masi-Manimba
Idiofa
Kikwit
Kilembe
Kahemba
Bindu
Caungula
Capenda-
Camulemba

Mweka
Luebo
Demba
Tshikapa
Kazumba
Bumba
Chitato
Cacolo
Mona
Quimbundo
Muconda
Quitapa
Quirima
Camanongue
Luena
Sachanga
Lucusse

Bena-Sungu
**Mbuji-
Mayi**
Dibaya
Mwene-
Ditu
Luiza
Cambulo
Lucapa
Saurimo
Sombo
Chiluage
Sandoa
Malonga
Dala
Luacano
Cazombo
Calunda
Lumbala
Kaquengue

Lusambo
Penge
Kananga
Gandajika
Kaniama
Kapanga
Kafakumba
Luau
Dilolo
Caianda
Mwinilunga

DEMOCRATIC
REPUBLIC
OF THE
CONGO
Lubao Kongolo
Kabinda
Mwanza
Kamina
Kinda
Nasondoye
Tenke
Lubudi
Kolwezi
Kambove
Lubumbashi
Solwezi
Mufumbwe
Ingwe
Kasempa
Kabompo
Mumbeji

ANGOLA
Umpulo
Tempué
Luvuei
Cangamba
Cangombe
Lumbala
N'guimbo
Kalabo
Mongu
Lukulu
Zambezi

ZAMBIA
Kaoma
Namwala

LONGITUDE continue...

Cubal
Caluquembe
Lucira
Bibala
Namibe
Tombua
Virei
Baía dos
Tigres
Foz do
Cunene

Caconda
Chipindo
Quilengues
Matala
Lubango
Chiange
Cahama
Oncócua
Xangongo
Mucope
Cuvelai
Chitado
Uutapi
Oshikango
Oshakati
Opuwo
Sesfontein
Kamanjab

Caála
Cassinga
Cuvango
Menongue
Cuito
Cuanavale
Baixo-
Longa
Nankova
Ondjiva
Cuangar
Rundu
Calai
Bagani
Dirico

Chiume
Mavinga
Neriquinha
Rivungo
Uamanda
Luiana
Acampamento de
Caça do Mucusso
Katima
Mulilo
CAPRIVI STRIP

Senanga
Mulobezi
Choma
Kalomo
**Victoria
Falls**
Livingstone
Victoria
Falls
Shumba

Bukalo
Kasane

Namibe
Etosha
Pan
Tsumeb
Otavi
Kombat
Grootfontein
Tsumkwe

Gumare
Maun
Okavango
Delta
Phuduhudu
Nata
Tutume
Francistown
Letlhakane

NAMIBIA
Outjo
khorixas
Otjiwarongo
Kalkfeld
Okakarara
Uis Mine
Omaruru
Usakos
Okahandja
WINDHOEK
Witvlei
Dordabis
Hentiesbaai
Swakopmund
Walvis Bay
Rehoboth

Steinhausen
Omitara
Buitepos
Gobabis
Leonardville
Ghanzi
Tshootsha
Sehithwa
Xhumo
Orapa

BOTSWANA
Takatshwaane
Serowe
Mahalapye

Solitaire
Nauchas
Tsumis
Park
Hoachanas
Maltahöhe
Mariental
Gochas
Helmeringhausen
Tses
Koës
NAMAQUALAND
Lüderitz
Aus
Seeheim
Aroab
Ai-Ais
Karasburg
Ariamsvlei
Oranjemund
Alexander
Bay

Kalahari
Kang
Hukuntsi
Tshane
Ncojane
Tsetseng
Werda
Tshabong
Bokspits
Van
Zylsrus
Upington

Desert
Mabutsane
Jwaneng
Khakhea
Kanye
Mabule
Severn
Vryburg
Kuruman
Olifantshoek
Keimoes
Postmasburg

Molepolole Mochudi
GABORONE
Lobatse
Johannesburg
Mafikeng
Delareyville
REPUBLIC OF
SOUTH AFRICA

Longitude 20° east of Greenwich

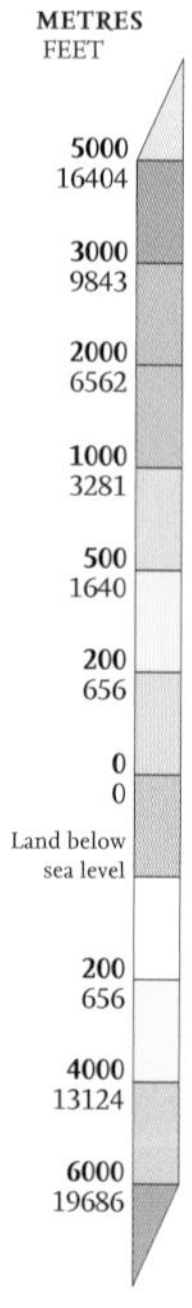

Lambert Azimuthal Equal Area Projection

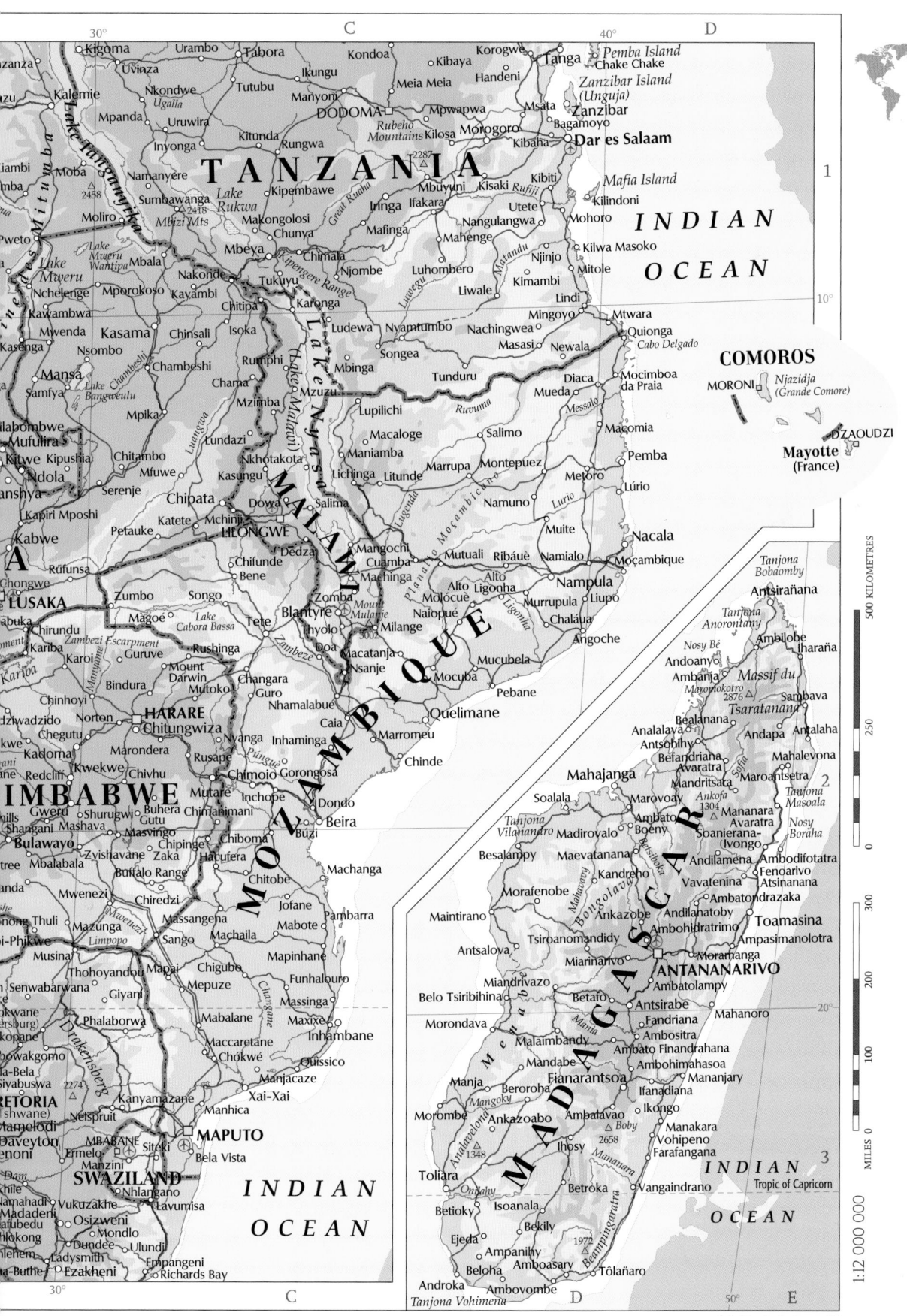

30°

Kigoma
Uvinza
Urambo
Tabora
Kondoa
Kibaya
Korogwe
Tanga
Pemba Island
Chake Chake

Nkondwe
Ugalla
Tutubu
Manyoni
Meia Meia
Handeni
Zanzibar Island
(Unguja)

Mpanda
Uruwira
DODOMA
Mpwapwa
Msata
Bagamoyo
Zanzibar

Kitunda
Rungwa
Rubeho
Mountains
Kilosa
Morogoro
Kibaha
Dar es Salaam

TANZANIA
2287

Namanyere
Sumbawanga
Kipembawe
Great Ruaha
Mbuyuni
Kisaki
Rufiji
Mafia Island

2458
Mbizi Mts
Lake
Rukwa
Makongolosi
Chunya
Iringa
Ifakara
Nangulangwa
Utete
Kilindoni

INDIAN

Moba
Molero
Nchelenge
Lake
Mwero
Wantipa
Mbeya
Chimala
Njombe
Mahenge
Mohoro

Nakonde
Kayambi
Tukuyu
Karonga
Luhombero
Liwale
Kimambi
Kilwa Masoko
Mitole

OCEAN

Chitipa
Kapengere Range
Lindi

Kawambwa
Isoka
Ludewa
Nyamtumbo
Nachingwea
Mtwara

Kasama
Chinsali
Rumphi
Songea
Masasi
Newala
Quionga
Cabo Delgado

Nsombo
Chambeshi
Mbinga
Tunduru
Diaca
Mocimboa
da Praia

COMOROS

Mansa
Lake
Bangweulu
Mzuzu
Lupilichi
Salimo
Mueda
Messalo
Macomia

MORONI
Njazidja
(Grande Comore)

Samfya
Mpika
Mzimba
Macaloge
Maniamba
Marrupa
Montepuez
Metoro
Pemba

Mufulira
Chitambo
Nkhotakota
Lichinga
Litunde
Namuno
Lurio
Lúrio

Kitwe Kipushia
Mfuwe
Kasungu
Salima
Lugenda
Muite
Nacala

Ndola
Serenje
Dowa
Mangochi
Cuamba
Ribáuè
Namialo
Moçambique

Kapiri Mposhi
Chipata
Katete
Mchinji
LILONGWE
Machinga
Alto
Ligonha
Nampula
Liupo

Kabwe
Petauke
Chifunde
Dedza
Alto Molócuè
Murrupula
Chaláua

Rufunsa
Bene
Zomba
Naiopuè
Angoche

LUSAKA
Zumbo
Songo
Blantyre
Mount
Mulanje
3002
Milange
Mucubela

Chirundu
Magoé
Tete
Thyolo
Doa
Mocuba

Kariba
Zambezi Escarpment
Rushinga
Macatanja
Nsanje
Pebane

Karoi
Guruve
Changara
Guro
Nhamalabue
Quelimane

Chinhoyi
Mount
Darwin
Mutoko
Caia
Inhaminga
Chinde

HARARE
Chitungwiza
Nyanga
Púngoè
Gorongosa

Chegutu
Rusape
Chimoio
Dondo

MADAGASCAR

ZIMBABWE

Gweru
Shurugwi
Mutare
Buhera
Chimanimani
Beira

Bulawayo
Gutu
Chiboma

Mbalabala
Buffalo Range
Chiredzi
Machanga

Mwenezi
Jofane
Pambarra

Thuli
Mazunga
Massangena
Mabote

Phikwe
Sango
Machaila
Mapinhane

Musina
Mapai
Chigubo
Funhalouro

Thohoyandou
Mabalane
Massinga

Giyani
Maxixe
Inhambane

Phalaborwa
Maccaretane
Chókwè

Kanyamazane
Xai-Xai
Manjacaze
Quissico

PRETORIA
Nelspruit
Manhica

MBABANE
Siteki
Bela Vista

MAPUTO

SWAZILAND
Manzini

Nhlangano
Lavumisa

INDIAN

OCEAN

30°

© Collins Bartholomew Ltd

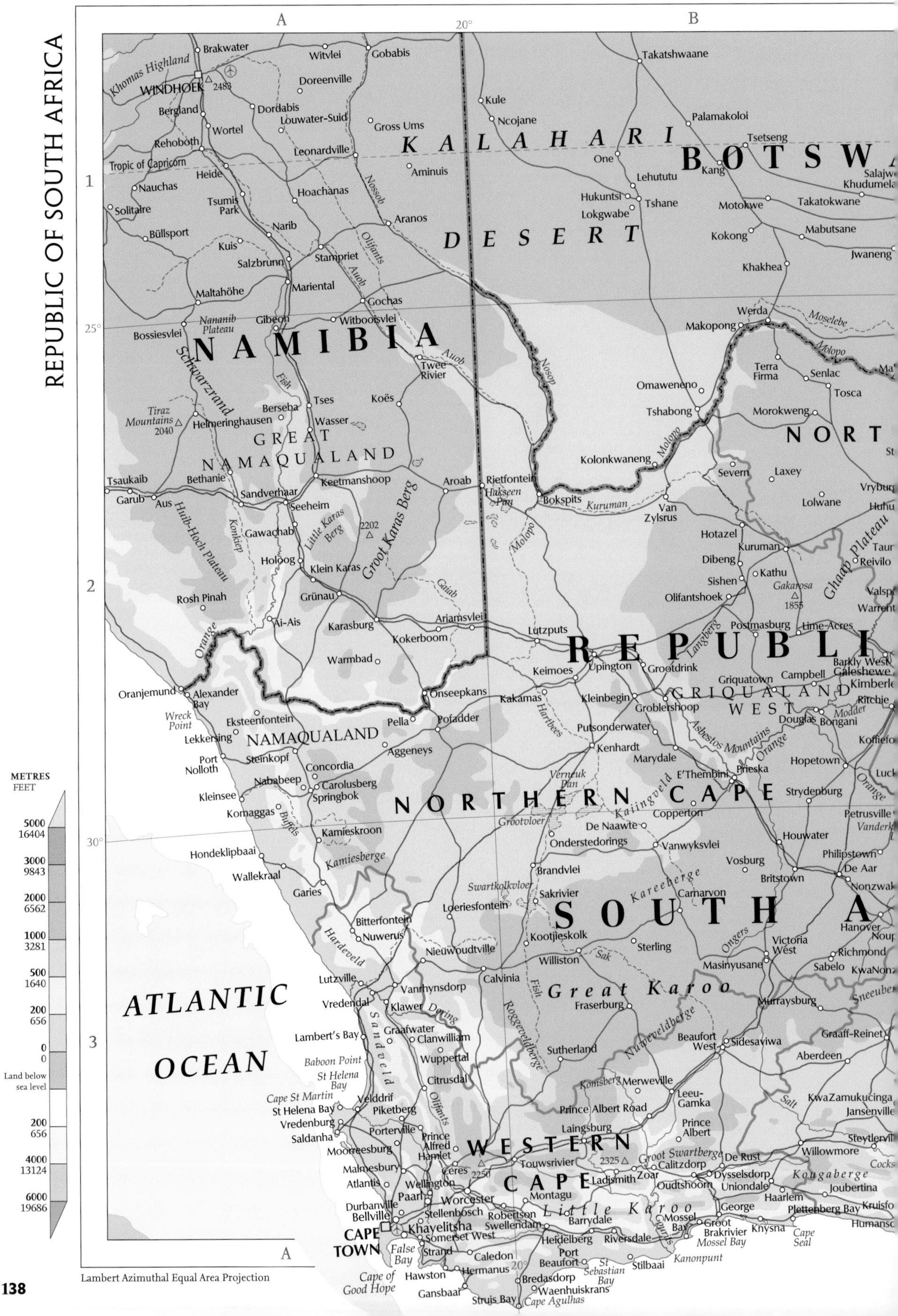

Brakwater
Witvlei
Gobabis
Takatshwaane
Khomas Highland
WINDHOEK
△ 2489
Doreenville
Kule
Palamakoloi
Tsetseng

K A L A H A R I

B O T S W A

Bergland
Dordabis
Louwater-Suid
Gross Ums
One
Lehututu
Kang
Khudumela
Salajwe
Rehoboth
Wortel
Tropic of Capricorn
Heide
Leonardville
Aminuis
Hukuntsi
Tshane
Motokwe
Takatokwane
Nauchas
Hoachanas
Lokgwabe
Kokong
Mabutsane
Solitaire
Tsumis Park
Narib
Aranos
Khakhea
Jwaneng
Büllsport
Kuis

D E S E R T

Salzbrunn
Stampriet
Werda
Maltahöhe
Mariental
Gochas
Makopong
Moselebe
Nananib Plateau
Gibeon
Witbootsvlei
Terra Firma
Senlac
Tosca
Bossiesvlei
Omaweneno
Morokweng

N A M I B I A

Twee Rivier
Tshabong

N O R T

Schwarzrand
Berseba
Tses
Koës
Severn
Laxey
Vrybur
Tiraz Mountains 2040
Helmeringhausen
Wasser
Kolonkwaneng
Hotazel
Huhu

G R E A T
N A M A Q U A L A N D
Aroab
Rietfontein
Bokspits
Van Zylsrus
Dibeng
Sishen
Kathu
Reivilo
Tsaukaib
Bethanie
Sandverhaar
Keetmanshoop
Hakseen Pan
Kuruman
Kuruman
Gakarosa 1855
Valspr
Garub
Aus
Seeheim
Olifantshoek
Warrent

R E P U B L I

Oranjemund
Alexander Bay
Eksteenfontein
Pella
Pofadder
Putsonderwater
GRIQUALAND WEST
Ritchie
Koffiefon
Bongani

N O R T H E R N   C A P E
Copperton

S O U T H   A

Lambert Azimuthal Equal Area Projection

A T L A N T I C

O C E A N

METRES
FEET

5000 16404
3000 9843
2000 6562
1000 3281
500 1640
200 656
0 0
Land below sea level
200 656
4000 13124
6000 19686

CAPE TOWN

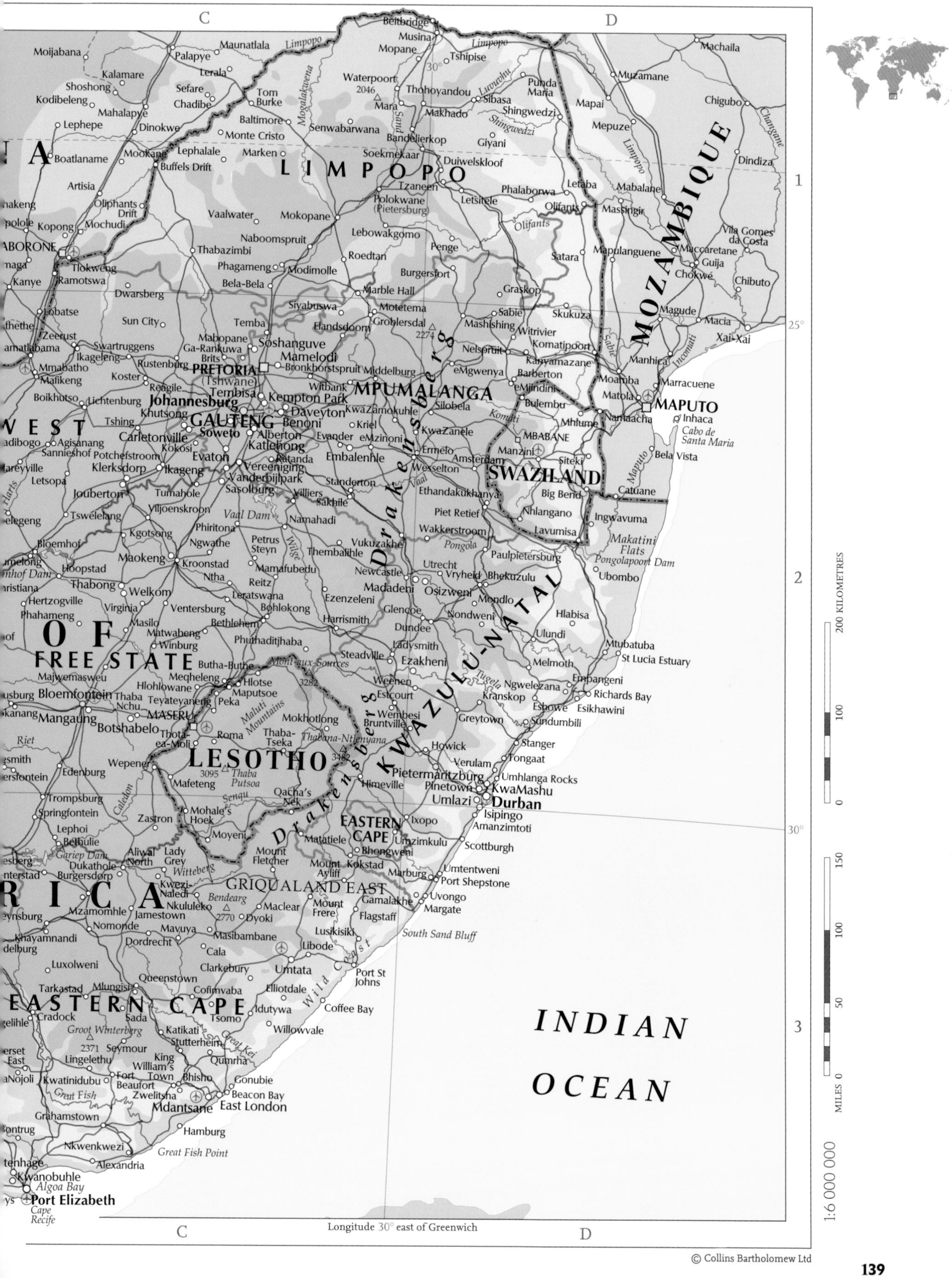

C   D

LIMPOPO

MOZAMBIQUE

MPUMALANGA

GAUTENG

PRETORIA (Tshwane)

Johannesburg

Soweto

NORTH WEST

FREE STATE

OF

LESOTHO

MASERU

SWAZILAND

MBABANE

MAPUTO

KWAZULU-NATAL

Durban

Pietermaritzburg

EASTERN CAPE

GRIQUALAND EAST

RICA

Port Elizabeth

East London

Umtata

Bloemfontein

Drakensberg

Maluti Mountains

INDIAN

OCEAN

1 : 6 000 000

200 KILOMETRES

100

0

150

100

50

MILES 0

Longitude 30° east of Greenwich

© Collins Bartholomew Ltd

139

ICELAND

Arctic Circle

Jan Mayen (Nor.)

Denmark Strait

Ammassalik

Kong Frederik VI Kyst

Kong Christian IX Land

R

Q

P

O

N

Kong Christian X Land

Greenland
(Denmark)

Kong Frederik VIII Land

Kong ... Land

Illulissat

Nuuk

Baffin
Bay

Davis Strait

Labrador
Sea

NEWFOUNDLAND AND LABRADOR

St John's
C. Race

St Pierre
St Pierre and Miquelon (Fr.)

Newfoundland

Cabot Strait

Gulf of St Lawrence

Île d'Anticosti

NEW BRUNSWICK

PRINCE EDWARD ISLAND

NOVA SCOTIA

Fredericton

St Lawrence

Labrador

Smallwood Res.

Kuujjuaq

Kuujjuak

Iqaluit

Hudson Strait

QUÉBEC

Québec

Montréal

Baffin Island

Foxe Basin

Southampton I.

Repulse Bay

Coats I.

Mansel I.

Belcher Is

Chisasibi

ONTARIO

MICH

WISCONS

Queen Elizabeth Islands

Ellesmere Island

Parry Islands

Melville Island

Devon Island

Dundas

Atanarjuat

Somerset Island

Prince of Wales I.

Boothia Pen.

Bathurst Inlet

NUNAVUT

Hudson
Bay

Churchill

Thunder Bay

Lake Superior

MINNESOTA

St Paul

Victoria Island

Banks Island

Amundsen Gulf

Sachs Harbour

Great Bear Lake

Great Slave Lake

Yellowknife

NORTHWEST TERRITORIES

CANADA

Lake Athabasca

SASKATCHEWAN

Lake Winnipeg

MANITOBA

Winnipeg

Regina

NORTH DAKOTA

Bismarck

SOUTH DAKOTA

Pierre

Rapid City

ARCTIC OCEAN

Beaufort
Sea

Inuvik

Mackenzie

Peace

ALBERTA

Edmonton

Saskatoon

Calgary

ROCKY

MOUNTAIN

MONTANA

Billings

Helena

WYOMING

YUKON TERRITORY

Whitehorse

BRITISH COLUMBIA

Prince George

Kamloops

IDAHO

Boise

Salt Lake City

U.S.A.

ALASKA

Fairbanks

Mt McKinley
△ 6194

Anchorage

Juneau

Alexander Archipelago

Queen Charlotte Islands

Vancouver Island

Victoria

Vancouver

Seattle

Olympia

WASHINGTON

Columbia

Portland

Salem

OREGON

Reno

Carson City

NEV

CALI

Sacramento

San Francisco

Yukon

Barrow

Arctic Circle

RUS. FED.

Bering Str.

Nome

St Lawrence I.

St Matthew Island

Nunivak I.

Pribilof Islands

Kodiak I.

Alaska Pen.

Gulf of
Alaska

Bering
Sea

Aleutian Islands

3

70°

2

80°

10°

20°

30°

40°

50°

60°

1

110°

120°

130°

140°

150°

160°

170°

80°

70°

60°

A

B

C

D

E

F

G

H

I

J

K

L

M

2

3

4

50°

60°

40°

4

5

6

50°

60°

Bi-Polar Oblique Projection

ATLANTIC OCEAN

PACIFIC OCEAN

CARIBBEAN SEA

GULF OF MEXICO

UNITED STATES OF AMERICA

MEXICO

BRAZIL

VENEZUELA

COLOMBIA

GUYANA

CUBA

THE BAHAMAS

HAITI

DOMINICAN REP.

JAMAICA

GUATEMALA

HONDURAS

NICARAGUA

COSTA RICA

PANAMA

BELIZE

EL SALVADOR

Washington D.C.
New York
Philadelphia
Boston
Detroit
Chicago
Columbus
Indianapolis
Nashville
Atlanta
Memphis
Jacksonville
Tampa
Miami
New Orleans
Houston
Dallas
Austin
Denver
Las Vegas
Phoenix
Los Angeles
San Diego
Kansas City
Monterrey
Ciudad Juárez
Guadalajara
León
Mexico City
Puebla
Acapulco
Mérida
Havana
Santiago de Cuba
Port-au-Prince
Santo Domingo
Kingston
Nassau
Guatemala City
San Salvador
Tegucigalpa
Managua
San José
Panama City
Belmopan

Raleigh
Columbia
Richmond
Charleston
Frankfort
Montgomery
Tallahassee
Baton Rouge
Little Rock
Oklahoma City
Tulsa
Jefferson City
Topeka
Springfield
Des Moines
Lincoln
Santa Fe
Albuquerque
Harrisburg
Chihuahua

PENNSYLVANIA
OHIO
INDIANA
ILLINOIS
TENNESSEE
GEORGIA
ALABAMA
MISS.
LOUISIANA
ARKANSAS
MISSOURI
KANSAS
OKLAHOMA
TEXAS
NEW MEXICO
ARIZONA
VIRGINIA
NORTH CAROLINA
SOUTH CAROLINA
FLORIDA
KEN.
IOWA

GULF OF CALIFORNIA
Gulf of California
Rio Grande
Colorado
Mississippi
Red
Arkansas

Bahia de Campeche
Yucatán
Bahia

Tropic of Cancer
Equator
Longitude 90° west of Greenwich
Tropic of Cancer
Equator

Bermuda (U.K.)
Turks and Caicos Is (U.K.)
Cayman Is (U.K.)
Virgin Is (U.K.)
Virgin Is (U.S.A.)
Puerto Rico (U.S.A.)
Anguilla (U.K.)
ANTIGUA AND BARBUDA
Guadeloupe (Fr.)
DOMINICA
Martinique (Fr.)
ST LUCIA
BARBADOS
ST VINCENT AND THE GRENADINES
GRENADA
TRINIDAD AND TOBAGO
ST KITTS AND NEVIS
Netherlands Antilles (Neth.)
Aruba (Neth.)
Lesser Antilles
Greater Antilles
Hispaniola
Orinoco
ECUADOR

Galapagos Islands (Ecu.)
Isla de Malpelo (Col.)
Isla de Coco (Costa Rica)
Clipperton Island (Fr.)
Islas Revillagigedo (Mex.)
Guadalupe (Mex.)

C. Hatteras
Lake Erie

CONNECTICUT
DELAWARE
KENTUCKY
MASSACHUSETTS
MARYLAND
MISSISSIPPI
NEW HAMPSHIRE
NEW JERSEY
RHODE ISLAND
VERMONT
WEST VIRGINIA

C.
DEL.
KEN.
MASS.
MD.
MISS.
N.H.
N.J.
R.I.
VT.
W.V.

1:32 000 000

MILES 0   200   400   600   800
KILOMETRES 0   400   800   1200

© Collins Bartholomew Ltd

141

Lambert Azimuthal Equal Area Projection

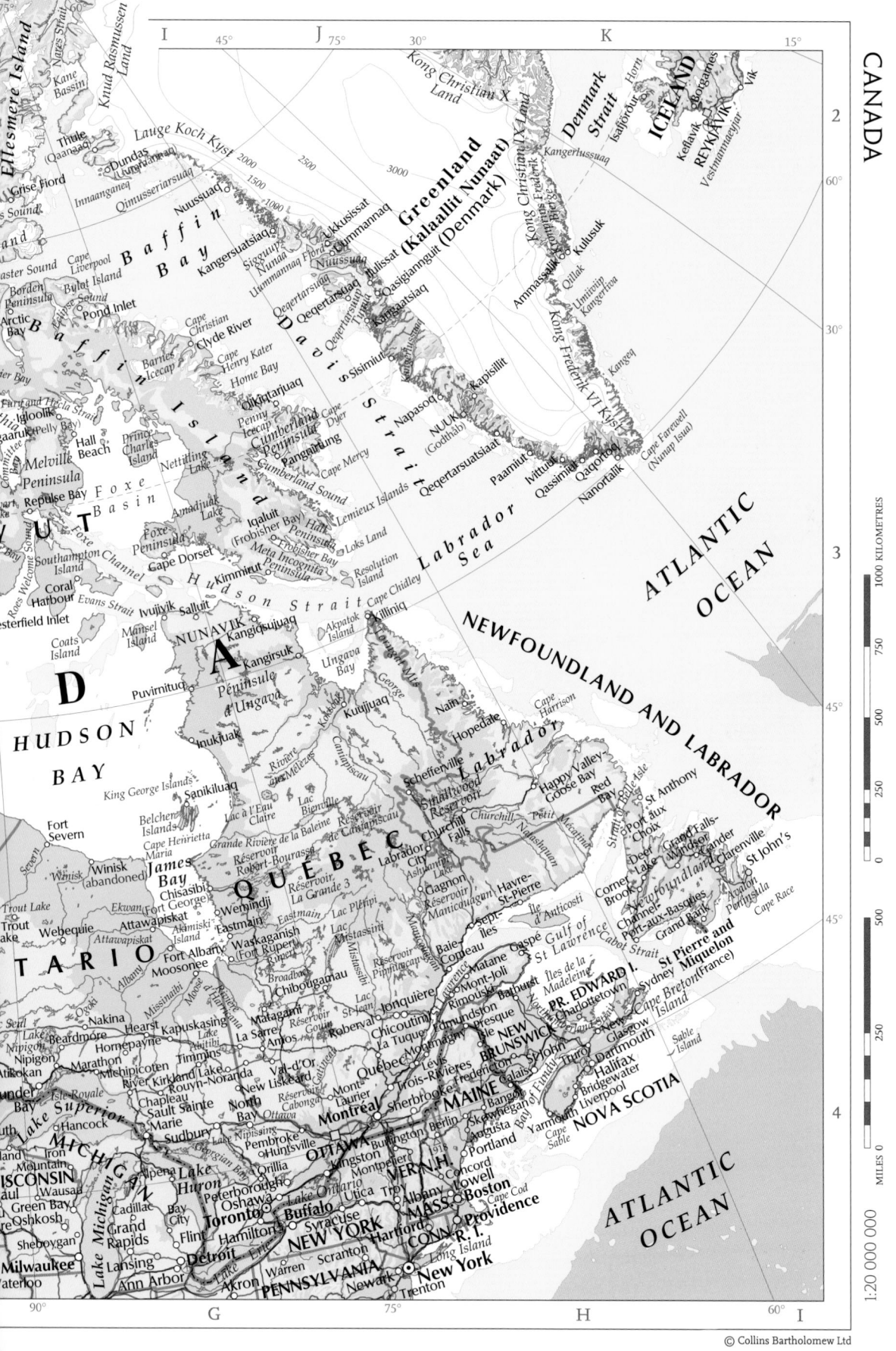

Ellesmere Island

Nares Strait
Kane Bassin
Knud Rasmussen Land

I 45° **J** 75° 30° **K** 15°

Kong Christian X Land

Lauge Koch Kyst 2000
1500 2500
3000

Thule (Qaanaaq)
Dundas
Innaanganeq
Qimusseriarsuaq

Greenland (Kalaallit Nunaat) (Denmark)

Kong Christian IX Land

Denmark Strait
Horn
Isafjördur
Kangerlussuaq

ICELAND
Keflavík REYKJAVÍK
Vestmannaeyjar
Vík
Esjubjörur

2
60°

Grise Fiord
s Sound
land

Baffin Bay

Cape Liverpool
Bylot Island
Arctic Bay
Pond Inlet

Nuussuaq
Kangersuatsiaq
Siggup
Nunaa
Upernavik
Uummannaq Fjord
Nuussuaq
Uummannaaq
Qegertarsuaq
Ikerasak
Ilulissat

Ammassalik (Tasiilaq)
Sermilik
Qillak
Umiivip Kangertiva
Kulusuk

30°

Kong Frederik VI Kyst

3

Baffin Island

Cape Christian
Clyde River
Barnes Icecap
Cape Henry Kater
Home Bay

Qegertarsuaq
Qegertat
Tutut
Ilulissat
Qasigiannguit
Kangaatsiaq
Napasoq
Kapisillit

Kangeq

Sisimiut

Davis Strait

Qikiqtarjuaq
Penny Icecap
Cumberland Peninsula
Pangnirtung
Cumberland Sound

Cape Christian
Cape Dyer
Cape Mercy

NUUK (Godthåb)

Qegertarsuatsiaat

Paamiut
Ivittuut
Qassimiut

Cape Farewell (Nunap Isua)

Borden Peninsula
Kater Sound

Foxe Basin

Farquhar and Hecla Strait
Igloolik
aaruk (Pelly Bay)
Committee

Melville Peninsula
Hall Beach

Prince Charles Island
Nettling Lake

Iqaluit (Frobisher Bay)
Hall Peninsula
Frobisher Bay
Meta Incognita Peninsula

Lemieux Islands
Loks Land

Labrador Sea

Qaqortoq
Nanortalik

45°

Repulse Bay
NUT

Amadjuak Lake
Foxe Peninsula
Cape Dorset

Kimmirut
Resolution Island

Cape Chidley

NEWFOUNDLAND AND LABRADOR

ATLANTIC OCEAN

Southampton Island
Roes Welcome Sound
Coral Harbour

Foxe Channel

Evans Strait

Hudson Strait

Akpatok Island

Killiniq

A

sterfield Inlet
Coats Island
Mansel Island

Salluit
Ivujivik

NUNAVIK
Kangiqsujuaq
Kangirsuk

Ungava Bay

Koksoak
George

Nain
Cape Harrison

D

HUDSON BAY

King George Islands
Sanikiluaq

Puvirnituq
Inukjuak

Péninsule d'Ungava

Kuujjuaq

Rivière aux Mélèzes

Caniapiscau

Hopedale

Labrador

Happy Valley-Goose Bay
Red Bay

St Anthony
Port au Choix

45°

Fort Severn

Belcher Islands
Cape Henrietta Maria

Lac à l'Eau Claire

Lac Bignelle

Schefferville
Smallwood Reservoir

Churchill Falls
Churchill
Petit Mécatina

Deer Lake
Grand Falls-Windsor
Gander
St John's

HUDSON BAY

Winisk (abandoned)
James Bay
Chisasibi
Fort George
Wemindji

Grande Rivière de la Baleine
Réservoir Robert-Bourassa

QUÉBEC
Réservoir La Grande 3

Labrador City
Ashuanipi
Gagnon
Réservoir Manicouagan

Strait of Belle Isle
Corner Brook
Newfoundland
Port-aux-Basques
Channel-Port aux Basques
Grand Bank
Avalon Peninsula
Cape Race

Winisk
Ekwan
Attawapiskat
Akimiski Island
Fort Albany
Moosonee

Eastmain
Waskaganish (Fort Rupert)
Broadback

Lac Mistassini

Réservoir Pipmuacan

Baie-Comeau
Sept-Îles
Île d'Anticosti
Havre-St-Pierre

Gaspé
Gulf of St Lawrence

St Pierre and Miquelon (France)

Sydney
Cape Breton Island
Sable Island

Trout Lake
Trout Lake

Webequie
Ogoki
Attawapiskat
Ogoki

Matagami
Chibougamau

Lac St-Jean
Roberval
Chicoutimi
Jonquière

Rimouski
Mont-Joli
Matane

Îles de la Madeleine

PR. EDWARD I.
Charlottetown

New Glasgow
NOVA SCOTIA

TARIO

Nakina
Beardmore

Hearst
Kapuskasing
Hornepayne

La Sarre
Amos

Val-d'Or
New Liskeard

Réservoir Gouin
La Tuque

Edmundston
Presque Isle
Matapédia

Truro
Dartmouth
Halifax

Marathon
Michipicoten
Atikokan

Timmins
Kirkland Lake
Rouyn-Noranda

North Bay

Trois-Rivières
Québec
Lévis
Sherbrooke

NEW BRUNSWICK
Fredericton
Saint John
St Stephen

Bridgewater
Liverpool
Yarmouth
Bay of Fundy

ATLANTIC OCEAN

under
Isle Royale
Bay
Lake Superior

Chapleau
Sault Sainte Marie

Sudbury
Lake Nipissing
Pembroke

Huntsville

Montréal
Ottawa
OTTAWA

Montpelier
Burlington
VERM.
N.H.
Augusta

Calais
MAINE
Bangor
Skowhegan

Portland
Concord
Lowell
MASS.
Boston
Cape Cod

Hancock
Iron Mountain

MICHIGAN

Marquette
Alpena

Georgian Bay

Orillia
Peterborough
Oshawa

Kingston

Lake Ontario

Cobourg

Hamilton

St Catharines

Syracuse
Utica
Albany
Hartford
CONN.
Providence
R.I.

Long Island

'ISCONSIN
aul
Green Bay
Oshkosh
Milwaukee
aterloo
Sheboygan

Lake Michigan

Cadillac
Bay City
Grand Rapids
Flint
Lansing

Toronto
Buffalo

NEW YORK
Scranton
Warren
Akron
PENNSYLVANIA

Newark
Trenton

New York

Iron Mountain
Green Bay

Detroit
Ann Arbor

90° **G** 75° **H** 60° **I**

1:20 000 000

1000 KILOMETRES
750
500
250
0

500
250
0
MILES

© Collins Bartholomew Ltd

143

Lambert Azimuthal Equal Area Projection

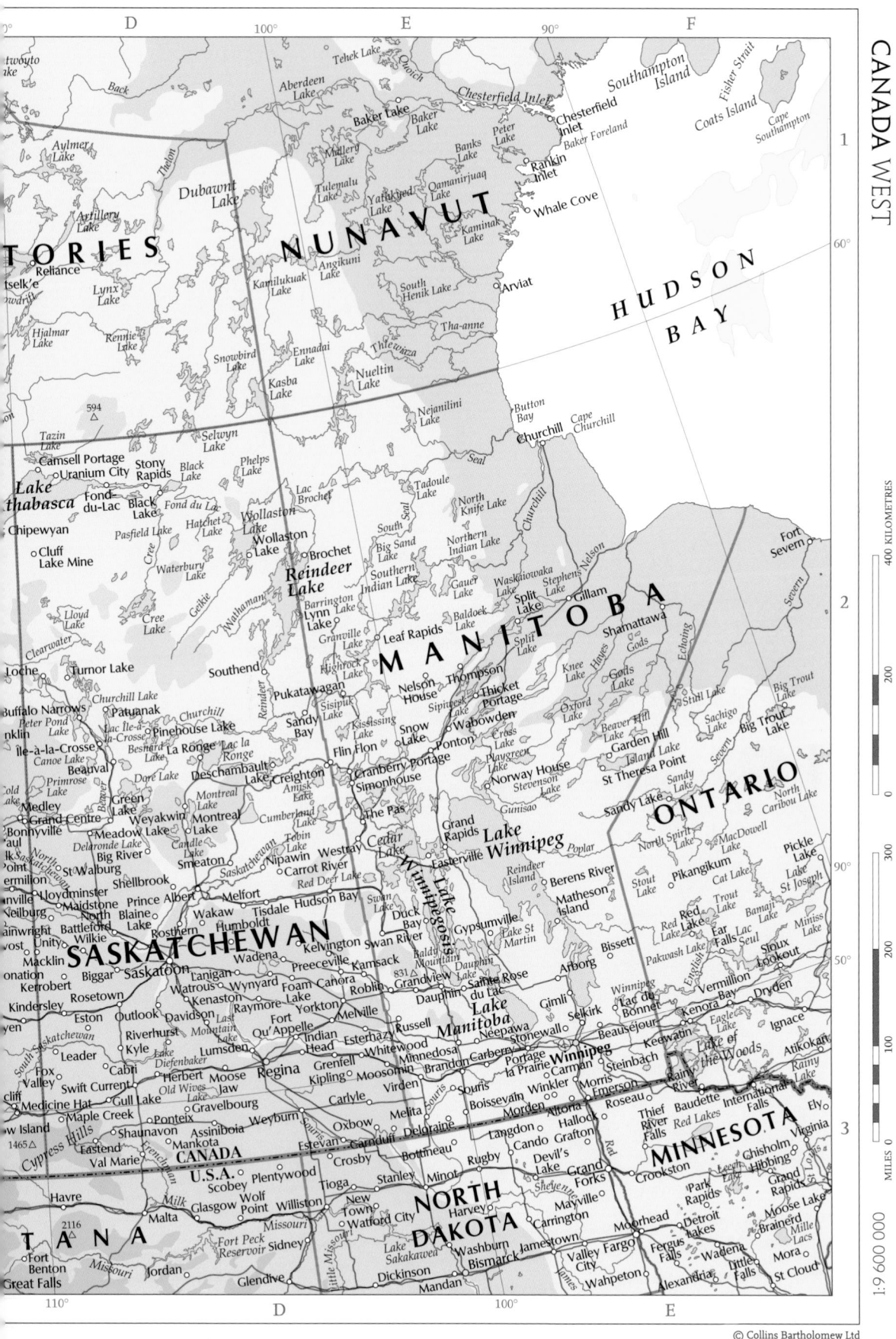

D 100° E 90° F

CANADA WEST

1

60°

HUDSON

BAY

NUNAVUT

MANITOBA

2

ONTARIO

SASKATCHEWAN

90°

50°

Lake
Winnipeg

Lake
Manitoba

3

MINNESOTA

CANADA
U.S.A.

NORTH
DAKOTA

110° D 100° E

1:9 000 000

KILOMETRES
400 200 0

MILES
300 200 100 0

© Collins Bartholomew Ltd

A · 90° · 60° · B · 80° · C

HUDSON BAY

Cape Churchill
North Knife Lake
Churchill
Churchill

Puvirnituq
Gilmour Island
Ottawa Islands
Hopewell Islands

Lac Payne
Tasialuf
Lac Tasiat
Arnaud
Fariba

MANITOBA
Stephens Lake
Nelson
Gillam

Inukjuak
Lac Le Roy
Lac Ned

NUNAVUT

Lac Chavigny
Lac Bacqueville
Rivière aux Fer

Fort Severn

Sleeper Islands
North Belcher Islands
King George Islands
Sanikiluaq

Nastapoka Islands
Naskapoca
Lac Minto

Knee Lake
Hayes
Gods
Gods Lake
Echoing
Shamattawa

Belcher Islands
Flaherty Island

Lacs des Loups Marins

Winisk (abandoned)

Kuujjuarapik (Poste-de-la-Baleine)

Lac à l'Eau Claire

Stull Lake
Sachigo Lake
Severn
Winisk

Cape Henrietta Maria
Long Island

Lac Guillaume-Delisle

James Bay

Grande Rivière de la Baleine

Lac Bienville

Sandy Lake
Big Trout Lake
Big Trout Lake
Kasabonika Lake
Ekwan

Chisasibi (Fort George)
North Twin Island

Lac Burton
Réservoir Robert-Bourassa

Réservoir La Grande 4
Lac

Stout Lake
North Spirit Lake
Webequie
Wunnummin Lake
Winisk Lake
Attawapiskat
Radisson
Wemindji

Réservoir La Grande 3
Lac St-Jean

QUÉ

Pikangikum
MacDowell
Cat Lake
North Caribou Lake
Attawapiskat Lake
Missisa Lake
Kapiskau
Fort Albany
Akimiski Island
South Twin Island

Réservoir Opinaca
Eastmain

Red Lake
Red Lake
Trout Lake
Bamaji Lake
Lake St Joseph
Pickle Lake
Ogoki Reservoir
Albany
Charlton Island
Rupert Bay
Eastmain
Waskaganish (Fort Rupert)

ONTARIO

Pakwash Lake
English
Ear Falls
Miniss Lake
Savant Lake
Whitewater Lake
Ogoki
Pledger Lake
Moosonee
Rupert

Lac Evans
Mistassini

Vermilion Bay
Red Lake
Lac Seul
Sturgeon Lake
Caribou Lake
Albany
Moose Factory
Rivière d'Harricana

Lac Comencho
Lac Opataca
Mistassini

Kenora
Eagle Lake
Dryden
Sioux Lookout
Armstrong
Lake Nipigon
Nakina
Missinaibi
Moose
Nottaway

Lac Matagami
Lac au Goéland
Chibougamau

Lake of the Woods
Ignace
Lac des Mille Lacs
Longlac
Beardmore
Hearst
Kesagami Lake
Fraserdale

Lac Matagami
Matagami
Lac Wasuanipi

Fort Frances
Atikokan
Nipigon
Terrace Bay
Manitouwadge
Hornepayne
Kapuskasing
Smooth Rock Falls
Cochrane
Lebel-sur-Quévillon
La Sarre

Réservoir Gouin
Dolbea
Mistass

CANADA
U.S.A.
Thunder Bay
Nipigon Bay
Marathon
Missinaibi Lake
Iroquois Falls
Timmins
Lake Abitibi
Rouyn-Noranda
Amos
Senneterre
Lac Parent

Lac St-Jea
Métabetcho

Grand Marais
Pigeon River
Thunder Cape
St Ignace Island
Michipicoten Island
Wawa
Michipicoten River
Foleyet
Chapleau
Kirkland Lake
Malartic
Val-d'Or

Réservoir Parent
La Tuque

Ashland
Copper Harbor
Keweenaw Peninsula
Batchawana Mountain
Ramsey Lake
New Liskeard
Englehart
Lac Simard
Réservoir Dozois
Lac Kempt

St-Michel-des-Saints
Shawinigan
Trois-Rivières

Lake Superior

Hancock
Houghton
Ishpeming
Marquette
Newberry
Sault Sainte Marie
Sudbury
Sturgeon Falls
North Bay
Mattawa
Lac Kipawa
Réservoir Baskatong

Mont-Laurier
Maniwaki
Mont Tremblant
Joliette
Sté-Adèle

Park Falls
Gogebic Range
Bruce Crossing
Crystal Falls
Iron Mountain
Escanaba
St Ignace
Thessalon
Blind River
Espanola
Nipissing
Deep River
Petawawa
Pembroke
Arnprior

Sorel
Ashes

MICHIGAN

Rhinelander
Merrill Menominee
Marinette
St Joseph Islands
North Channel
Manitoulin Island
Wikwemikong
South River
Huntsville
Barrys
Bracebridge
Carleton Place
Smiths Falls
Cornwall
Massena

Montréal
Salaberry-de-Valleyfield
Hull
OTTAWA

St-Jean-Richelie
Sherbro

Wausau
Shawano
Green Bay
Cheboygan
Petoskey
Alpena
Tobermory
Bruce Peninsula
Owen Sound
Parry Sound
Gravenhurst
Bancroft
Rideau Lakes
Brockville

Champlain
Plattsburgh
St Johns

WISCONSIN
Appleton
Oshkosh
Sheboygan
Manitou Islands
Traverse City
Gaylord
South Baymouth
Georgian Bay
Midland
Orillia
Kawartha Lakes
Peterborough
Belleville
Kingston
Watertown
Lowville

VERMO

Wisconsin Rapids
Fond du Lac
West Bend
Manistee
Cadillac
Grayling
Tawas City
Port Elgin
Kincardine
Barrie
Oshawa
Cobourg
Oswego
Rome

Mount Marcy
Rutland
Lebanon

Portage
Madison
Milwaukee
Grand Rapids
Muskegon
Saginaw Bay
Bay City
Harbor Beach
Goderich
Hanover
Lindsay
Lake Ontario
Rochester
Oneida
Syracuse
Auburn
Utica
Glens Falls

Waukesha
Racine
Kenosha
Grand Rapids
Lansing
Flint
Port Huron
Stratford
Kitchener
Guelph
Toronto
Scarborough
Hamilton
St Catharines
Buffalo
Batavia
Geneva
Finger Lakes
Schenectady
Troy
Albany
Pittsfield

Rockford
Elgin
Waukegan
Battle Creek
Pontiac
Livonia
London
Brantford
Niagara
Rochester
Dunkirk
Hornell
Cortland
Ithaca
Norwich
Oneonta
MA
Worces

Aurora
Ottawa
Chicago
Kalamazoo
Jackson
Ann Arbor
Detroit
Windsor
St Thomas
Lake Erie
Erie
Jamestown
Olean
Elmira
Corning
Binghamton

Joliet
Gary
Michigan City
South Bend
Elkhart
Adrian
Sylvania
Pelee Island
Cleveland
Ashtabula
Warren
Bradford
Sayre
NEW YORK
Springfield

ILLINOIS
Pontiac
Watseka
Plymouth
Fort Wayne
Toledo
Lorain
Maumee
OHIO

INDIANA

METRES FEET

5000	16404
3000	9843
2000	6562
1000	3281
500	1640
200	656
0	0

Land below sea level

200	656
4000	13124
6000	19686

Longitude 80° west of Greenwich

B · C

Lambert Azimuthal Equal Area Projection

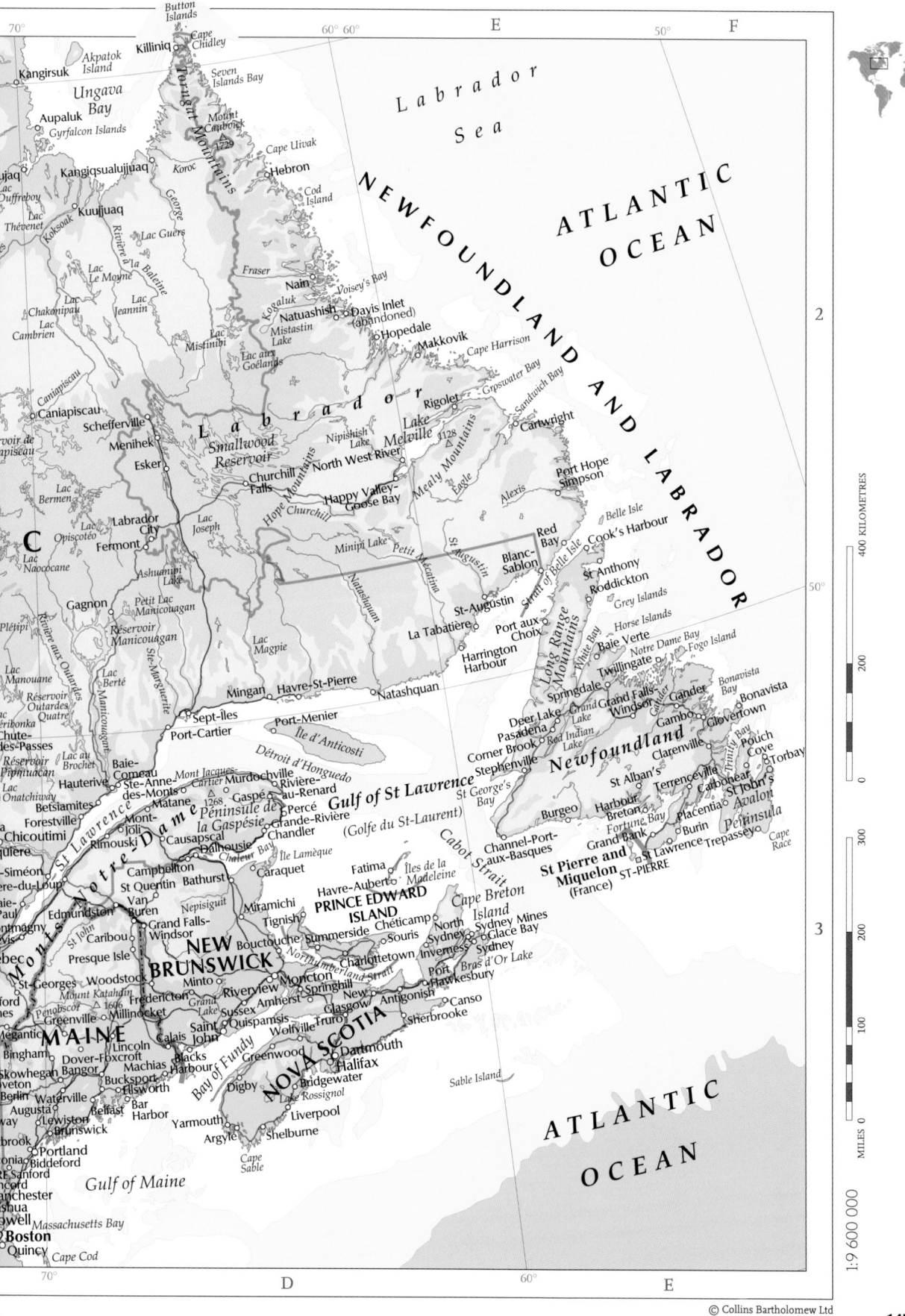

Button
Islands
70°   60° 60°   E   50°   F

Cape
Killiniq C'hidley
Akpatok
Island
Kangirsuk   Seven   L a b r a d o r
Ungava   Toungat Mountains   Islands Bay
Aupaluk   Bay   S e a
Gyrfalcon Islands   Mount
Cairboick
1329   Cape Uivak
iujaq   Kangiqsualujjuaq   Hebron
Lac   Koroc   Cod
Duffreboy   Island
Lac
Thévenet   Kuujjuaq   George   Fraser   N E W F O U N D L A N D
Koksoak   Lac Guers   Nain
Riviere à la Baleine   Logaluk   Voisey's Bay   ATLANTIC
Chakonipau   Jeannin   Natuashish   Davis Inlet
Lac   Lac   Mistastin   (abandoned)   OCEAN
Cambrien   Misfinibi   Lake   Hopedale
Lac aux   Makkovik
Goélands   Cape Harrison
Caniapiscau   Rigolet Groswater Bay
rvoir de   Scheffervillle   L a b r a d o r   Lake   Sandwich Bay
apiseau   Caniapiscau   Nipishish   Melville   Cartwright   A N D
Menihek   Smallwood   Lake   △1128
Esker   Reservoir   North West River   Mealy Mountains   Port Hope
Lac   Churchill   Happy Valley-   Eagle   Simpson   L A B R A D O R
Bermen   Falls   Goose Bay   Alexis
Hope Mountains   Churchill   Belle Isle
Lac   Labrador   Lac   Red   Cook's Harbour
Opiscotéo   City   Joseph   Minim Lake Petit Mécatina   Bay   2
C   Fermont   Ashuanipi   St Augustin   Blanc-   St Anthony
Lac   Lake   Sablon   Roddickton   50°
Navocane   Gagnon   Petit Lac   Lac   La Tabatière   Port aux   Grey Islands
Manicouagan   Magpie   St-Augustin   Choix   Horse Islands
Plétipi   Réservoir   Natashkuan   Harrington   Baie Verte   Fogo Island
Manicouagan   Harbour   White Bay   Notre Dame Bay
Lac   Mingan Havre-St-Pierre   Natashquan   Long Range Mountains   Twillingate
Manouane   Ste-Marguerite   Springdale   Grand   Gander   Bonavista
Réservoir   Sept-îles   Deer Lake   Grand Falls-   Bay
ac   Outardes   Port-Menier   Île d'Anticosti   Pasadena   Lake   Windsor   Gander   Glovertown Bonavista
Onatchiway   Quatre   Port-Cartier   Corner Brook Red Indian   Gambo   Trinity Pouch
Chute-   Détroit d'Honguedo   Lake   Clarenville   Bay Cove
des-Passes   Baie-   Mont Jacques-   Stephenville   Newfoundland   Torbay
Réservoir   Comeau   Cartier Murdochville Rivière-   St Alban's   Terrenceville Carbonear St John's
Pipmuacan   Hauterive   Ste-Anne-   au-Renard   St George's   Harbour   Placentia Avalon
Lac   des-Monts Mont Jacques   Gulf of St Lawrence   Bay   Breton   Peninsula
quière   Betsiamites   Matane 1268 Gaspé   Burgeo   Fortune   Burin Cape
a   Forestville   Mont-   Grande-Rivière   Channel-Port-   Bay   St Lawrence Race
Chicoutimi   joli   Péninsule de   Percé   (Golfe du Saint-Laurent)   aux-Basques   Grand Bank Trepassey
Rimouski   la Gaspésie Chandler   St Pierre and   St Lawrence
Île Lamèque   Miquelon   ST-PIERRE
-Siméon   Campbellton   Fatima   Îles de la   (France)   3
ère-du-Loup   St Quentin Bathurst   Havre-Aubert Madeleine
aie-   Van-   Nepisiguit   PRINCE EDWARD   Cape Breton
Paul   Edmundston Buren   Miramichi   Island
ontmagny   Grand Falls-   Tignish   Chéticamp   North Sydney Mines
evis   St John Windsor   Bouctouche Summerside   Souris   Sydney Glace Bay
ébec   Caribou   NEW   Charlottetown Inverness   Sydney
St-Georges Woodstock   BRUNSWICK   Northumberland Strait   Port Bras d'Or Lake
tford   Presque Isle   Grand Moncton   Hawkesbury
nes   Fredericton Lake Riverview Springhill   New
Penobscot Minto   Amherst Glasgow   Antigonish
Megantic   MAINE Mount Katahdin   Sussex   Truro   Canso
Bingham   △1606   Quispamsis Wolfville   Sherbrooke
Skowhegan Greenville   Saint NOVA SCOTIA
oveton   Millinocket   Lincoln   John   New   Dartmouth
Berlin   Dover-Foxcroft   Calais   Glasgow Halifax
Bangor   Machias Blacks   Greenwood   Sable Island
way   Waterville   Bucksport   Harbour Bridgewater
Augusta   Ellsworth   Digby   Bar   Bay of Fundy   Lake Rossignol
Lewiston   Belfast   Harbor   NOVA SCOTIA
way   Brunswick   Yarmouth   Liverpool   ATLANTIC
Portland   Argyle Shelburne
conia Biddeford   Cape
RE Sanford   Sable   OCEAN
ncord
anchester   Gulf of Maine
shua
owell Massachusetts Bay
Boston
Quincy Cape Cod
70°   D   60°   E

1:9 600 000   400 KILOMETRES

200

0

300

200

100

MILES 0

147

© Collins Bartholomew Ltd

50° 130° A 120° B 110° C 100°

CANADA

BRITISH COLUMBIA
ALBERTA
SASKATCHEWAN
MANITOBA

Port Hardy • Gold River • Campbell River • Powell River • Nanaimo • Victoria • Vancouver Island • Cape Flattery

Mount Waddington 4042 • 100 Mile House • Kamloops • Kelowna • Vernon • Penticton • Nelson • Cranbrook

Jasper • Edmonton • Wetaskiwin • Leduc • Camrose • Vegreville • Lloydminster • Meadow Lake • The Pas • Cedar Lake

Banff • Airdrie • Calgary • Okotoks • Brooks • Medicine Hat • Lethbridge

Prince Albert • Saskatoon • Rosthern • Biggar • Unity • Kindersley • Moose Jaw • Swift Current • Regina • Weyburn

Nipawin • Humboldt • Canora • Wynyard • Yorkton • Melville • Virden • Estevan • Brandon

WASHINGTON • Seattle • Tacoma • Olympia • Spokane • Yakima • Bellingham • Everett
Mount Baker 3285 • Mount Olympus 2428 • Mount Rainier 4392 • Mount St Helens 2550

OREGON • Portland • Salem • Eugene • Albany • Bend • Astoria • Coos Bay • Grants Pass • Klamath Falls
Oregon City • Pendleton • La Grande

Coast Range • Blue Mountains • Columbia • Snake

MONTANA • Helena • Butte • Bozeman • Billings • Great Falls • Missoula • Dillon • Glendive • Miles City • Shelby • Havre • Glasgow
Fort Peck Reservoir • Lewis Range • Bitterroot Range • Absaroka Ra. • Bighorn Mts • Yellowstone • Missouri

N. DAKOTA • Bismarck • Dickinson • Bowman • Minot • Williston • Jamestown • Bottineau • Devils Lake • Mobridge

S. DAKOTA • Pierre • Rapid City • Aberdeen • Black Hills • Lake Oahe

IDAHO • Boise • Idaho Falls • Twin Falls • Nampa • Jerome • Caldwell • Burns • Pocatello • Grangeville
Grand Teton 4190 • Gannett Peak 4202

WYOMING • Casper • Cheyenne • Laramie • Cody • Lander • Green River • Evanston • Pinedale
Kings Peak 4123 • Uinta Mts • North Platte • Sweetwater

NEBRASKA • Chadron • Scottsbluff • Ogallala • Sidney • North Platte • McCook • Kearney
Niobrara • South Platte • Republican

NEVADA • Reno • Sparks • Carson City • Elko • Winnemucca • Lovelock • Tonopah • Ely • Caliente • Wendover
Pyramid Lake • Humboldt • Great Basin • Wheeler Peak 3982 • Sevier Lake • Great Salt Lake

CALIFORNIA • Sacramento • San Francisco • Oakland • San Jose • Stockton • Modesto • Fresno • Visalia • Bakersfield
Santa Rosa • Salinas • Santa Maria • Santa Barbara • Oxnard • Los Angeles • Long Beach • Pasadena • Riverside • Santa Ana
Oceanside • San Diego • Redding • Red Bluff • Ukiah • Eureka • Crescent City • Point Arena • Point Conception
Mount Shasta 4317 • Mount Whitney 4418 • Death Valley • Monterey Bay • Channel Islands • Salton Sea
Coast Range • Sierra Nevada

UTAH • Salt Lake City • Provo • Ogden • Logan • Cedar City • Richfield • St George • Moab • Kanab • Page
Lake Powell • Colorado

COLORADO • Denver • Aurora • Colorado Springs • Pueblo • Boulder • Greeley • Grand Junction • Craig • Durango • Trinidad • Alamosa
Mount Elbert 4398 • Sangre de Cristo Range

KANSAS • Dodge City • Liberal • Ulysses • Great Bend • Garden City • Stratford • Dumas

ARIZONA • Phoenix • Mesa • Glendale • Tucson • Flagstaff • Yuma • Prescott • Kingman • Winslow • Casa Grande
Lake Havasu City • Grand Canyon • Tuba City • Kayenta • Colorado Plateau • Gila • Baldy Peak 3476

NEW MEXICO • Albuquerque • Santa Fe • Las Cruces • Roswell • Farmington • Gallup • Clovis • Hobbs • Lovington • Artesia
Los Alamos • Taos • Socorro • St Johns • Clayton • Tucumcari • Portales • Alamogordo • Deming • Silver City • Las Vegas
Llano Estacado • Sacramento Mountains • Pecos • Canadian

TEXAS • El Paso • Amarillo • Lubbock • Midland • Odessa • Pecos • Van Horn • Fort Stockton • Alpine • Del Rio • San Angelo
Abilene • Brady • Snyder • Post • Vernon • Wichita Falls • Edwards Plateau • Emory Peak 2388

MEXICO • Ciudad Juárez • Chihuahua • Hermosillo • Culiacán • Durango • Torreón • Monterrey • Saltillo • Mazatlán
Ciudad Obregón • Los Mochis • Guaymas • Navojoa • Ciudad Delicias • Hidalgo del Parral • Gómez Palacio
Monclova • Nuevo Laredo • Matamoros • Piedras Negras • Ciudad Acuña • Sabinas • Camargo • Jiménez
Cuauhtémoc • Guamúchil • Guasave • Madera • Yécora • Moctezuma • Agua Prieta • Nogales • Douglas • Nogales
Magdalena • Caborca • Puerto Peñasco • Benjamin Hill • Nuevo Casas Grandes • Bolsón de Mapimí • Sierra Madre Occidental
Río Bravo del Norte / Río Grande • Conchos • Yaqui • Mayo • Nazas • Sonora

BAJA CALIFORNIA • Tijuana • Mexicali • Ensenada • San Luis Río Colorado • Lázaro Cárdenas • San Felipe • Rosarito
Villa Insurgentes • La Paz • San José del Cabo • Ciudad Constitución • Santa Rosalía • Bahía Tortugas
Isla Cedros • Isla Ángel de la Guarda • Isla Tiburón • Isla San José • Isla Carmen • Isla Cerralvo • Isla Margarita
Picacho del Diablo 3096 • Bahía Sebastián Vizcaíno • Punta Eugenia • Guadalupe (Mexico)
Gulf of California • Costa Rica • Cerro Peña Nevada 3664

PACIFIC OCEAN
Tropic of Cancer

Longitude 110° west of Greenwich

A 120° B 110° C 100° 20°

METRES / FEET

METRES	FEET
5000	16404
3000	9843
2000	6562
1000	3281
500	1640
200	656
0	0
Land below sea level	
200	656
4000	13124
6000	19686

Lambert Azimuthal Equal Area Projection

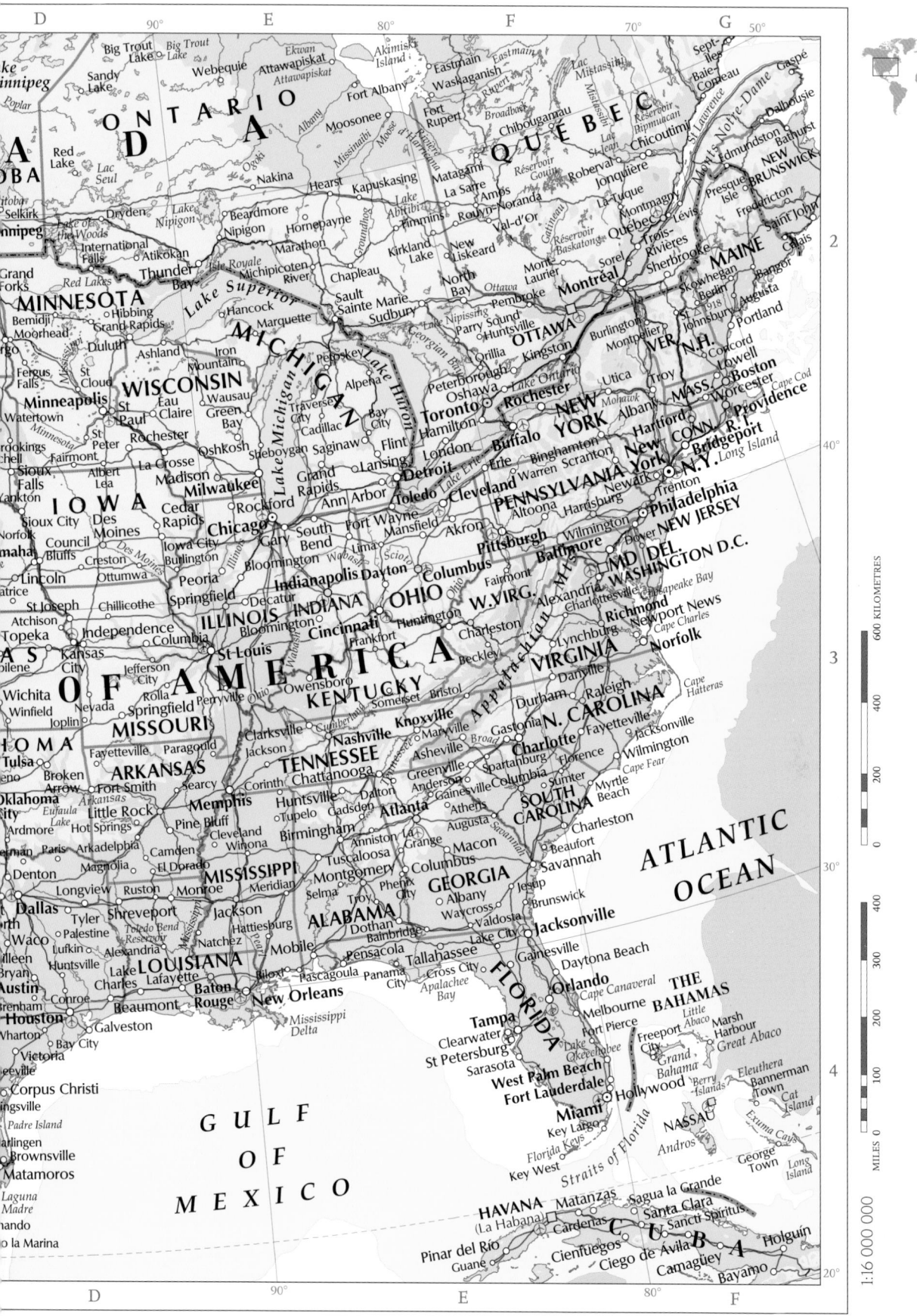

© Collins Bartholomew Ltd

1:16 000 000

ROCKY MOUNTAINS

MONTANA

IDAHO

WYOMING

WASHINGTON

OREGON

BRITISH COLUMBIA

ALBERTA

SASKATCHEWAN

CANADA
U.S.A.

Vancouver Island

Lewis Range

Selkirk Mountains

Kettle River Range

Bitterroot Range

Salmon River Mountains

Sawtooth Range

Big Belt Mountains

Crazy Mountains

Absaroka Range

Wind River Range

Wasatch Range

Blue Mountains

Columbia Plateau

High Desert

Harney Basin

Warner Mountains

Klamath Mountains

Santa Rosa Range

Independence Mountains

Great Salt Lake Desert

Cities and towns:

Frenchman, Val Marie, Milk River, Nelson Reservoir, Malta, Milk, Jordan, Fort Peck Reservoir, Hardin, Crow Agency, Lowell, Greybull, Worland, Thermopolis, Fort Washakie, Lander, Riverton, Rock Springs, Flaming Gorge Reservoir

Chinook, Havre, Gildford, Lothair, Shelby, Cut Bank, Browning, Cardston, Keremeos, Osoyoos, Okanagan Falls

Roundup, Bighorn, Billings, Laurel, Columbus, Red Lodge, Powell, Cody, Granite Peak 3901, Lovell

Lewistown, Harlowton, Big Timber, Livingston, Bozeman, White Sulphur Springs, Armington, Great Falls, Fort Benton, Choteau, Kalispell, Columbia Falls, Whitefish, Libby, Eureka, Yahk

Belgrade, Three Forks, Townsend, Boulder, Helena, Canyon Ferry Lake, Deer Lodge, Anaconda, Butte, Dillon, Salmon, Challis, Mount Haggin 3230, Hamilton, Stevensville, Missoula, Ravalli, Ronan, Polson, Flathead Lake, Thompson Falls, Snowshoe Peak 2663, Sandpoint, Bonners Ferry, Creston, Castlegar, Nelson, Trail, Rossland

Electric Peak 3490, West Yellowstone, West Thumb, Yellowstone Lake, Grand Teton 4190, Jackson, Moran, Pinedale, Gros Ventre Range, Gannett Peak 4202, Afton, Soda Springs, Montpelier, Preston, Logan, Smithfield, Tremonton, Brigham City, Ogden, Roy, Evanston, Lyman, Kemmerer, Green River

St Anthony, Rexburg, Rigby, Idaho Falls, Blackfoot, Pocatello, American Falls, American Falls Reservoir, Rupert, Burley, Twin Falls, Malad City, Spencer, Arco, Ketchum, Bellevue, Shoshone, Gooding, Jerome, Mountain Home, Glenns Ferry, Boise, Meridian, Nampa, Caldwell, Parma, Ontario, Nyssa, Cinnabar Mountain 2562, Matterhorn 3304, Wells, Contact, McDermitt, Granite Peak 2946, Denio

McCall, Cascade, Payette, Mount McGuire 3073, Grangeville, Kooskia, Kamiah, Lewiston, Clarkston, Moscow, Pullman, Colfax, Orofino, Dworshak Reservoir, Wallace, Kellogg, Coeur d'Alene, Hayden, Newport, Opportunity, Spokane, Cheney, Ritzville, Franklin D. Roosevelt Lake, Pend Oreille Lake, Colville, Grand Forks

Enterprise, Union, Eagle Cap 2925, La Grande, Baker, Jordan Valley, Juntura, Burns Junction, Burns, Hines, Riley, John Day, Strawberry Mountain 2755, Malheur Lake, Steens Mountain, Lake Malheur, Owyhee, Owyhee

Moses Lake, Ephrata, Othello, Connell, Pasco, Richland, Kennewick, Finley, Walla Walla, Hermiston, Boardman, Pendleton, Condon, John Day, Shaniko, Madras, Prineville, Redmond, Bend, Brothers, Lakeview, Warner Lakes, Lake Abert, Alturas, Goose Lake, Upper Klamath Lake, Klamath Falls

Grand Coulee, Lake Chelan, Wenatchee, Ellensburg, Roslyn, Yakima, Selah, Toppenish, Sunnyside, Grandview, Goldendale, The Dalles, Hood River, Mount Hood 3427, Woodburn, Oregon City, Sisters, Cottage Grove, Chemult, Klamath Lake, Medford, Ashland, Yreka, Central Point

Okanogan, Brewster, Glacier Peak 3213, Mount Baker 3285, Bellingham, Ferndale, Anacortes, Oak Harbor, Port Townsend, Everett, Lynnwood, Bellevue, Seattle, Bremerton, Tacoma, Parkland, Mount Rainier 4392, Lacey, Olympia, Centralia, Chehalis, Kelso, Longview, Astoria, Tillamook, McMinnville, Salem, Keizer, Albany, Lebanon, Corvallis, Harrisburg, Springfield, Eugene, Oakridge, Sutherlin, Roseburg, Canyonville, Grants Pass, Brookings, O'Brien, Crescent City

Mount Olympus 2428, Port Angeles, Port Renfrew, Victoria, Saanich, Sidney, Duncan, Ladysmith, Nanaimo, Ucluelet, Vancouver, Richmond, Mission, Chilliwack, Cowichan, Sooke

Shelton, Hoquiam, Aberdeen, Raymond, Willapa Bay, Cape Disappointment, Cape Flattery, Forks, Willamette, Keizer, Florence, Reedsport, Coos Bay, Myrtle Point, Port Orford, Cape Blanco, McKinleyville, Eureka

Mount Cleveland 3184, Mount Bonaparte 2212

Rivers/Lakes:

Missouri, Bighorn, Sweetwater, Green, Bear, Snake, Snake River Plain, Columbia, Okanogan, Yakima, Deschutes, John Day, Limpqua, Rogue, Klamath, Sprague, Madison, Clark Fork, Bitterroot, Flathead, St Joe, Clearwater, Salmon, Payette, Owyhee, Cowlitz, Milk

Reservoir:

Carson, Big Hole, Deer Lodge

45°, 110°, 115°, 120°, 125°

1, 2

A, B, C, D, E

Lambert Azimuthal Equal Area Projection

COLORADO

NEW MEXICO

UTAH

Colorado Plateau

Grand Canyon

ARIZONA

NEVADA

Great Basin

Confusion Range

Death Valley

Panamint Range

Mojave Desert

SIERRA NEVADA

CALIFORNIA

Sacramento Valley

San Francisco

Sacramento

Las Vegas

Black Mountains

Phoenix

Tucson

MEXICO

Los Angeles

San Diego

Tijuana

Channel Islands

PACIFIC

OCEAN

Longitude 120° west of Greenwich

1:6 400 000

MILES 0   50   100   150

KILOMETRES 0   100   200

A 110° B 105° C

SASKATCHEWAN

Val Marie · Estevan · Carnduff · Deloraine

Cut Bank · Gildford · Havre · Chinook · Scobey · Plentywood · Crosby · Kenmare · Minot · Bottineau

Browning · Shelby · Lothair · Nelson Reservoir · Tioga · Stanley · New

Conrad · Lairmore · Malta · Glasgow · Wolf Point · Williston · Watford City · New Town · Underwood · Washburn

Choteau · Fort Benton · Bear Paw Mountain 2116 · Milk · Fort Peck Reservoir · Fort Peck · Sidney · Beulah

Great Falls · Missouri · Jordan · Circle · Beach · Belfield · Dickinson · Mandan · Bismarck

Armington · MONTANA · Lewistown · Rock Springs · Glendive · Little Missouri · Badlands · Lemmon

Helena · Canyon Ferry Lake · White Sulphur Springs · Harlowton · Roundup · Forsyth · Miles City · Baker · Bowman · Hettinger · Lint

Townsend · Boulder · Three Forks · Belgrade · Big Timber · Billings · Hardin · Colstrip · Broadus · Buffalo · Mobridge · Selb

Bozeman · Livingston · Columbus · Laurel · Red Lodge · Crow Agency · Alzada · Belle Fourche · Faith · Dupree · Lake Oahe

45° · Electric Peak 3490 · Granite Peak 3901 · Absaroka Range · Lovell · Powell · Sheridan · Sundance · Spearfish · Sturgis · SOUTH

West Yellowstone · Cody · Greybull · Cloud Peak 4016 · Buffalo · Gillette · Newcastle · Lead · Rapid City · Pierre

St Anthony · Yellowstone Lake · Worland · Bighorn Mountains · Kaycee · Wright · Black Hills · Custer · Philip · Murdo · Viv

Rexburg · Rigby · Grand Teton 4190 · Moran · Thermopolis · Boysen Reservoir · Cheyenne · Hot Springs · Pine Ridge · Martin · Winner

Jackson · Gros Ventre Range · Gannett Peak 4202 · Fort Washakie · Riverton · Oelrichs · Chadron · Merriman · Valentine · Ainswo

2 · Afton · Wind River Range · Lander · Mills · Casper · Douglas · Lusk · Gordon · Rushville

Soda Springs · Pinedale · Glenrock · Crawford · Valentine

Montpelier · WYOMING · Muddy Gap · Pathfinder Reservoir · Torrington · Alliance · Mullen · Thedford

Kemmerer · Green · Rawlins · Seminoe Reservoir · Hanna · Wheatland · Scottsbluff · Wild Horse Hill 1281 · Hyannis · NEBR

Evanston · Lyman · Green River · Rock Springs · Saratoga · Medicine Bow Mountains · Laramie · Mitchell · Bayard · Bridgeport · Lake McConaughy

Wasatch Range · Flaming Gorge Reservoir · Medicine Bow Peak 3661 · Laramie · Cheyenne · Kimball · Sidney · Ogallala · North Platte

Kings Peak 4123 · Vernal · Craig · Steamboat Springs · North Platte · Fort Collins · Wellington · Pine Bluffs · Sutherland

Uinta Mountains · Roosevelt · Meeker · Kremmling · Boulder · Loveland · Greeley · Sterling · Julesburg · Gothenburg · Lexing

40° · Duchesne · Green · Sheep Mountain 3732 · Estes Park · Longmont · Brush · Holyoke · Imperial

Price · Wellington · Roan Plateau · Glenwood Springs · Vail · Thornton · Arvada · Fort Morgan · Akron · Wray · Benkelman · McCoo

UTAH · Rifle · Frisco · Denver · Aurora · Yuma

Green River · Grand Junction · Carbondale · Gypsum · Leadville · Lakewood · Limon · Burlington · Goodland · Oakley · WaKeen

Crescent Junction · Whitewater · Aspen · Mount Elbert 4399 · Woodland Park · Castle Rock · Kansas · St Francis · Colby · Oberl

Moab · Delta · Sawatch Ra. · Manitou Springs · Colorado Springs · Cheyenne Wells · Scott City · Ne

Hanksville · Mount Peale 3877 · Gunnison · Garfield · Salida · Canon City · Pikes Peak 4301 · Pueblo · Rocky Ford · Las Animas · Garden City

3 · COLORADO · Montrose · Olathe · Uncompahgre Peak 4363 · Sangre de Cristo Range · Fowler · Lamar · Syracuse · Dodge City

Lake Powell · Colorado · Abajo Peak 3462 · Monticello · Silverton · Rio Grande · Monte Vista · Walsenburg · La Junta · Ulysses · Satanta · Meade

Blanding · San Juan · Del Norte · Alamosa · Springfield · Liberal · Ash

Bluff · Cortez · Durango · San Juan Mountains · Trinidad

ARIZONA · Shiprock · Bayfield · Pagosa Springs · Dulce · Chama · Raton

Kayenta · Farmington · Bloomfield · NEW MEXICO

A 110° B Longitude 105° west of Greenwich C

Lambert Azimuthal Equal Area Projection

METRES / FEET

5000 / 16404
3000 / 9843
2000 / 6562
1000 / 3281
500 / 1640
200 / 656
0 / 0
Land below sea level
200 / 656
4000 / 13124
6000 / 19686

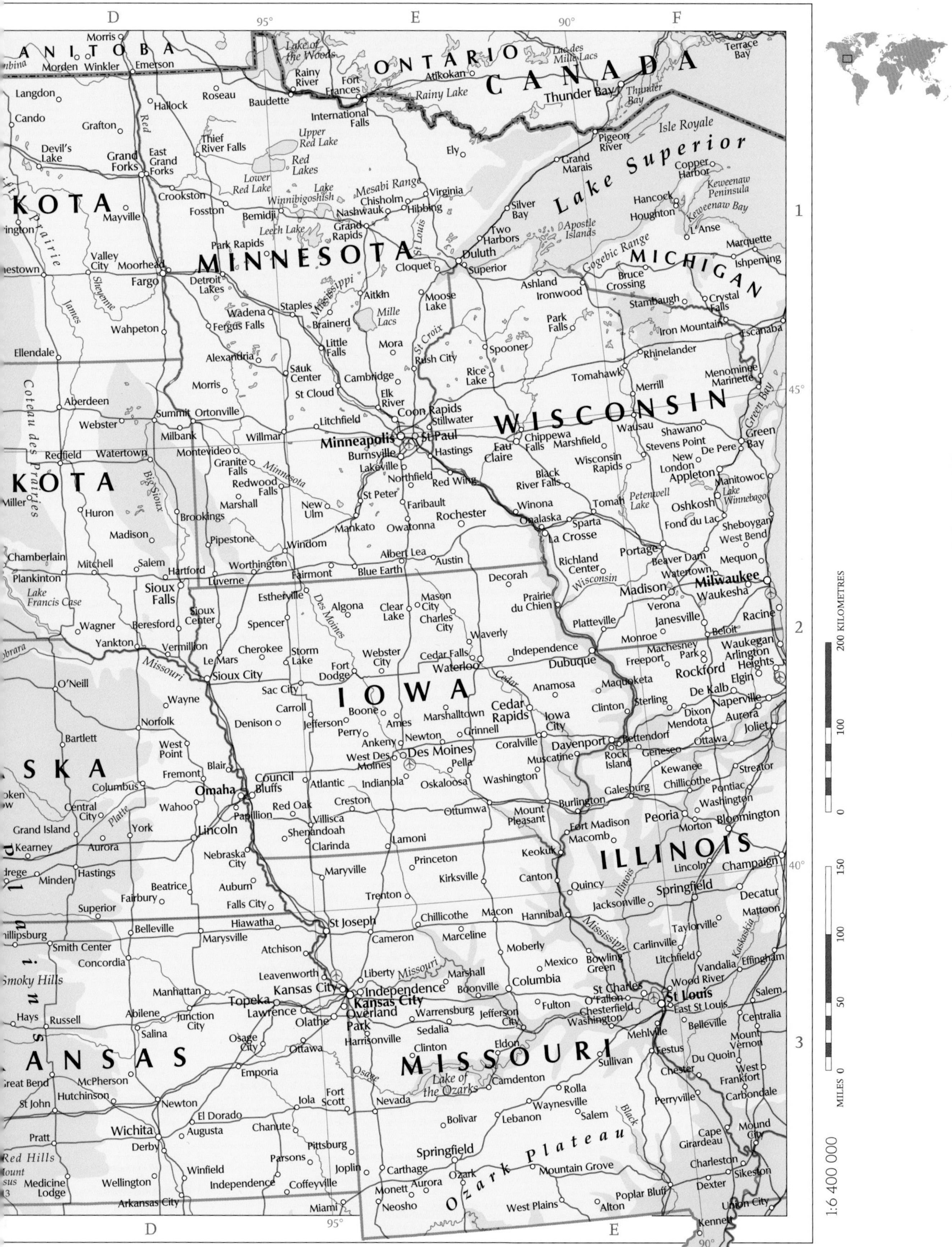

1:6 400 000

200 KILOMETRES

MILES

© Collins Bartholomew Ltd

ONTARIO

MINNESOTA

Lake Superior

MICHIGAN

WISCONSIN

IOWA

ILLINOIS

MISSOURI

INDIANA

OHIO

KENTUCKY

TENNESSEE

WEST VIRGINIA

Lake Michigan

Lake Huron

Lake Erie

Lake St Clair

Georgian Bay

Nipigon · Thunder Bay · St Ignace Island · Terrace Bay · Marathon · Kabinakagami Lake · Iroquois Fall · Nighthawk Lake · Abi

Ely · Virginia · Chisholm · Wawa · Missinaibi Lake · Timmins · Kirkla · L · Foleyet

Duluth · Two Harbors · Silver Bay · Apostle Islands · Copper Harbor · Keweenaw Peninsula · Michipicoten Bay · Michipicoten Island · Michipicoten River · Chapleau · Sultan · Temaga · L

Superior · Cloquet · Ashland · Houghton · Keweenaw Bay · Batchawana Mountain 653 · Ramsey Lake · Onaping Lake · Wanapitei Lake · Green

Grand Marais · Pigeon River · Isle Royale · Hancock · L'Anse

Ironwood · Bruce Crossing · Stambaugh · Marquette · Ishpeming · Newberry · Sault Sainte Marie · Elliot Lake · Thessalon · Blind River · Sudbury · Espanola · Sturg

Park Falls · Spooner · Crystal Falls · Iron Mountain · Ste Marie · St Joseph Island · North Channel · Little Current · Wikwemikong

Rice Lake · Rhinelander · Escanaba · Drummond Island · Manitoulin Island · South Baymouth · Tobermory · Bruce Peninsula

Hastings · Tomahawk · Merrill · Menominee · Manistique · St Ignace · Cheboygan · Rogers City · Owen Sound · Collingwo

Eau Claire · Chippewa Falls · Marshfield · Wausau · Shawano · Marinette · Beaver Island · Petoskey · Charlevoix · Alpena · Port Elgin · Kincardine · Hanover · Orangevil

Black River Falls · Wisconsin Rapids · Stevens Point · New London · Green Bay · Door Peninsula · Sturgeon Bay · Manitou Islands · Traverse City · Gaylord · Au Sable · Oscoda · Harbor Beach · Goderich · Guel

Winona · Sparta · Tomah · Appleton · De Pere · Manitowoc · Frankfort · Grayling · Tawas City · Bay City · Saginaw Bay · Stratford · Cambridg · Woodstock

Onalaska · La Crosse · Oshkosh · Fond du Lac · Sheboygan · Manistee · Cadillac · Standish · Midland · Saginaw · Lapeer · Port Huron · Sarnia · London · Brantfo

Decorah · Richland Center · Portage · Beaver Dam · West Bend · Ludington · Big Rapids · Mount Pleasant · Bay City · East Lansing · Pontiac · Sterling Heights · Simco · St Thomas

Prairie du Chien · Madison · Watertown · Mequon · Glendale · Shelby · Muskegon · Owosso · Flint · Detroit · Chatham

Platteville · Verona · Waukesha · Milwaukee · Grand Haven · Wyoming · Lansing · Brighton · Livonia · Windsor · Pelee Island

Independence · Dubuque · Monroe · Janesville · Racine · Holland · South Haven · Kalamazoo · Jackson · Ann Arbor · Taylor · Edinb

Anamosa · Freeport · Beloit · Kenosha · Grand Rapids · Benton Harbor · Battle Creek · Adrian · Monroe · Sylvania · Toledo · Ashtabula · Painesville · Meadvi

Cedar Rapids · Maquoketa · Rockford · Belvidere · Waukegan · Three Rivers · Sturgis · Angola · Perrysburg · Sandusky · Lorain · Cleveland · Euclid · Warren · Shar

Clinton · Sterling · Dixon · Arlington Heights · Elgin · Evanston · Michigan City · Niles · Elkhart · Auburn · Bowling Green · Fremont · Norwalk · Akron · Youngstown

Iowa City · Davenport · Bettendorf · Rock Island · Geneseo · De Kalb · Wheaton · Chicago · Gary · South Bend · Warsaw · Defiance · Findlay · Tiffin · Ashland · Mansfield · Wooster · Alliance · Canton · New · Cas

Muscatine · Mendota · Aurora · Joliet · Oak Lawn · Merrillville · Plymouth · Fort Wayne · Van Wert · Lima · Marion · Massillon · New · Philadelphia · East Liverpool

Washington · Ottawa · Kankakee · Rensselaer · Huntington · Bellefontaine · Mount Vernon · Delaware · Steubenville · Washington

Mount Pleasant · Burlington · Kewanee · Streator · Pontiac · Watseka · Logansport · Peru · Marion · Sidney · Springfield · Newark · Cambridge · Moundsville · Whee

Fort Madison · Galesburg · Chillicothe · Washington · Bloomington · Lafayette · Kokomo · Anderson · Muncie · Dayton · Lancaster · Zanesville

Keokuk · Macomb · Peoria · Morton · Crawfordsville · Noblesville · Kettering · Columbus · Washington Court House · Athens · Vienna · Marietta · Clarksb

Canton · Lincoln · Bloomington · Danville · Indianapolis · Lawrence · Richmond · Vandalia · Hamilton · Wilmington · Hillsboro · Chillicothe · Parkersburg · WEST

Springfield · Champaign · Decatur · Greencastle · Terre Haute · Shelbyville · Middletown · Fairfield · Cincinnati · Reading · Point Pleasant · Weston · VIRGIN

Jacksonville · Carlinville · Taylorville · Charleston · Mattoon · Greensburg · Greensburg · Portsmouth · Ironton · St Albans · Sutton · E

Bowling Green · St Charles · Wood River · Litchfield · Effingham · Bloomington · Sullivan · Columbus · Seymour · Covington · Maysville · Ashland · Huntington · Charleston · Summersville · A

O'Fallon · St Louis · Vandalia · Olney · Washington · Bedford · Madison · Frankfort · Georgetown · Morehead · Madison · Oak Hill · Beckley · Lewisburg · Covin

Chesterfield · East St Louis · Salem · Centralia · Vincennes · New Albany · Louisville · Lexington · Winchester · Richmond · Salyersville · Williamson · Welch · Blacksburg · Blue Ridge

Washington · Belleville · Mount Vernon · Princeton · Jasper · Pleasure Ridge Park · Elizabethtown · Danville · Richmond · Pikeville · Bluefield · Wytheville

Festus · Du Quoin · West Frankfort · Evansville · Henderson · Radcliff · Munfordville · Campbellsville · London · Hazard · Norton · Marion

Perryville · Chester · Harrisburg · Owensboro · Madisonville · Columbia · Somerset · Williamsburg · Middlesboro · Abingdon · Mount Rogers 1746 · Bristol · Martins

Cape Girardeau · Mound City · Charleston · Paducah · Hopkinsville · Bowling Green · Glasgow · Kingsport

Poplar Bluff · Dexter · Sikeston · Mayfield · Kentucky Lake · Oak Grove · Russellville · Springfield · Gallatin · Dale Hollow Lake · Cumberland

Kennett · Murray · Union City · Clarksville · Paris

Paragould

KENTUCKY · TENNESSEE

Lambert Azimuthal Equal Area Projection

Longitude 85° west of Greenwich

METRES / FEET

METRES	FEET
5000	16404
3000	9843
2000	6562
1000	3281
500	1640
200	656
0	0

Land below sea level

200	656
4000	13124
6000	19686

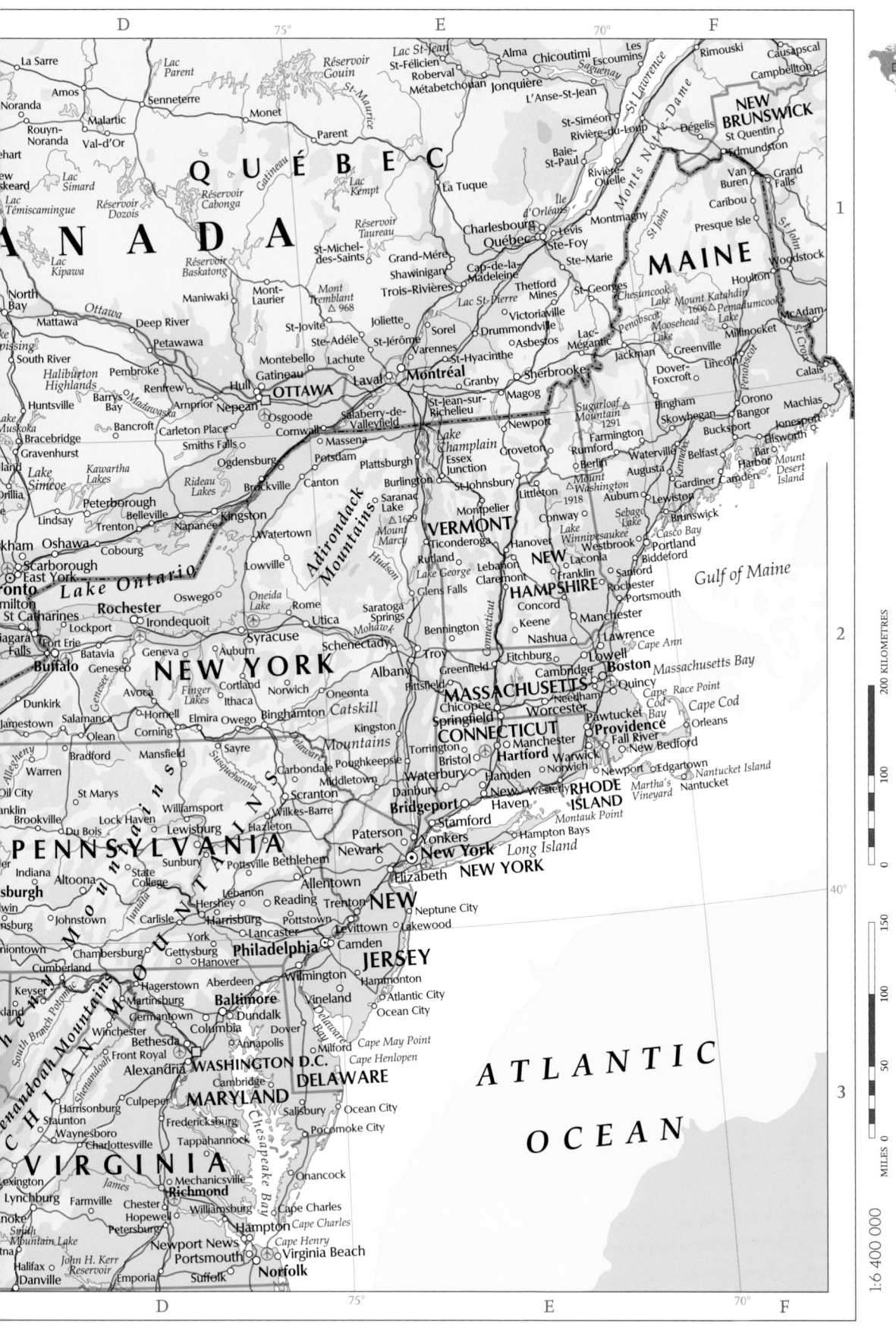

La Sarre
Lac Parent
Amos
Senneterre
Monet
Rimouski
Causapscal
Campbellton
Noranda
Malartic
Parent
NEW BRUNSWICK
Rouyn-Noranda
Val-d'Or
St Quentin
Edmundston
Van Buren
Grand Falls
QUÉBEC
Réservoir Cabonga
Réservoir Dozois
St-Maurice
Lac Kempt
Woodstock
Lac Simard
Réservoir Taureau
Caribou
Presque Isle
St-Michel-des-Saints
MAINE
Lac Kipawa
Réservoir Baskatong
Houlton
McAdam
Mont Tremblant
Mont-Laurier
Mount Katahdin
Pemadumcook Lake
Maniwaki
Moosehead Lake
Lincoln
Millinocket
Penobscot
St Croix
ATLANTIC

OCEAN

1:6 400 000

MISSOURI

TENNESSEE

ARKANSAS

OKLAHOMA

MISSISSIPPI

TEXAS

LOUISIANA

ALABAMA

KENTU

Vinita · Owasso · Tulsa · Pryor · Bentonville · Rogers · West Plains · Poplar Bluff · Charleston · Paducah · Hopkinsville · Glasgow
Broken Arrow · Siloam Springs · Springdale · Harrison · Mountain Home · Alton · Dexter · Sikeston · Mayfield · Oak Grove · Russellville · Clarksville
Sapulpa · Muskogee · Fayetteville · Pocahontas · Kennett · Murray · Kentucky Lake · Springfield · Gallatin
Okmulgee · Tahlequah · Boston Mountains · Hoxie · Paragould · Union City · Paris · Dyersburg · McKenzie · Nashville · Cumberland
Henryetta · Van Buren · Clarksville · Batesville · White · Jonesboro · Blytheville · Humboldt · Dickson · Franklin · Murfreesboro
Chicotah · Sallisaw · Fort Smith · Heber Springs · Newport · Trumann · Jackson · Brownsville · Linden · Columbia · Shelbyville · Manchester
Eufaula Lake · Mansfield · Magazine Mountain · Russellville · Searcy · Wynne · West Memphis · Millington · Bartlett · Savannah · Lewisburg · Tullahoma
McAlester · Poteau · Morrilton · Conway · Jacksonville · Forrest City · Memphis · Bolivar · Lawrenceburg · Fayetteville
Atoka · Mena · Lake Ouachita · Little Rock · Marianna · Southaven · Corinth · Florence · Athens · Huntsville
Ouachita Mountains · Hot Springs · Stuttgart · Helena · Holly Springs · Booneville · Russellville · Decatur · Scottsboro
Hugo · Idabel · Arkadelphia · Malvern · Pine Bluff · Oxford · Batesville · Tupelo · Hamilton · Cullman · Gadsden
Paris · De Queen · Hope · Fordyce · Dumas · Clarksdale · Grenada · Amory · Jasper · Center Point · Annis
New Boston · Ashdown · Camden · Warren · Monticello · Cleveland · Birmingham · Vestavia Hills · Cheaha Mountain
Commerce · Texarkana · Magnolia · El Dorado · Hamburg · Crossett · Greenville · Indianola · Columbus · Bessemer · Sylacauga
Sulphur Springs · Mount Pleasant · Homer · Minden · Bastrop · Lake Providence · Leland · Greenwood · Winona · Starkville · Tuscaloosa · Alabaster
Gladewater · Longview · Shreveport · Ruston · Monroe · Tallulah · Yazoo City · Louisville · Macon · Eutaw · Clanton · Alexander City
Tyler · Kilgore · Henderson · Carthage · Bossier City · Gibsland · Driskill Mountain · Winnsboro · Vicksburg · Canton · Meridian · Demopolis · Prattville · Auburn
Athens · Jacksonville · Marshall · Jonesboro · Mansfield · Winnfield · Olla · Jackson · Ridgeland · Forest · York · Selma · Montgomery · Tuskegee
Palestine · Nacogdoches · Tenaha · Natchitoches · Many · Pineville · Natchez · Brookhaven · Crystal Springs · Brandon · Thomasville · Greenville · Troy
Crockett · Lufkin · Toledo Bend Reservoir · Alexandria · Marksville · Lecompte · Hattiesburg · Petal · Jackson · Monroeville · Evergreen
Sam Rayburn Reservoir · Jasper · Leesville · De Ridder · Oakdale · Ville Platte · McComb · Laurel · Andalusia · Enterprise
Huntsville · Corrigan · Livingston · Opelousas · Kentwood · Bogalusa · Lumberton · Atmore · Century · Crestview
Lake Livingston · Conroe · The Woodlands · Beaumont · Sulphur · Jennings · New Roads · Baker · Hammond · Picayune · Mobile · Prichard · Pensacola · Fort Walton Beach
Humble · Orange · Lake Charles · Crowley · Lafayette · Port Allen · Baton Rouge · Gulfport · Biloxi · Pascagoula · Mississippi Sound · De Funiak Springs
Houston · Nederland · Vidor · Abbeville · New Iberia · Plaquemine · Kenner · New Orleans · Metairie · Gretna · Mobile Bay · Santa Rosa Island · Panama City
Baytown · Groves · Port Arthur · White Lake · Morgan City · Thibodaux · Houma · Raceland · Port Sulphur · Breton Sound · Mobile Point · Chandeleur Islands
Pasadena · Galveston Bay · Sugar Land · Texas City · Lake Jackson · Galveston · Galveston Island · Marsh Island · Atchafalaya Bay · Terrebonne Bay · Grand Isle · Mississippi Delta
Freeport

GULF OF MEXICO

Red · Sabine · Arkansas · Mississippi · Ouachita · White · Tennessee · Pearl · Yazoo · Tombigbee · Trinity · Neches

Mount Magazine 839
762
163

METRES / FEET

METRES	FEET
5000	16404
3000	9843
2000	6562
1000	3281
500	1640
200	656
0	0
Land below sea level	
200	656
4000	13124
6000	19686

95° 90°
35° 30° 25°

Longitude 90° west of Greenwich

Lambert Azimuthal Equal Area Projection

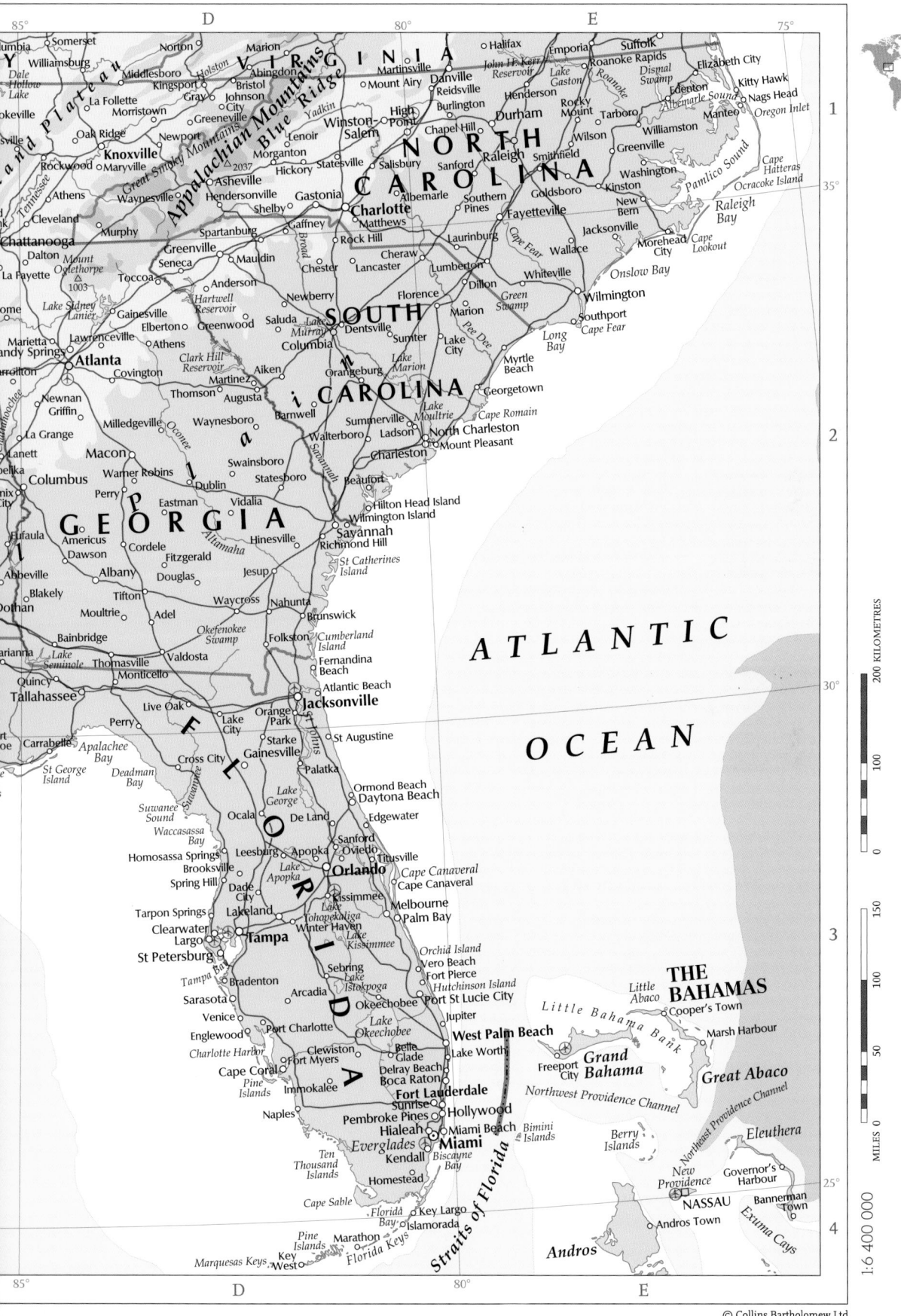

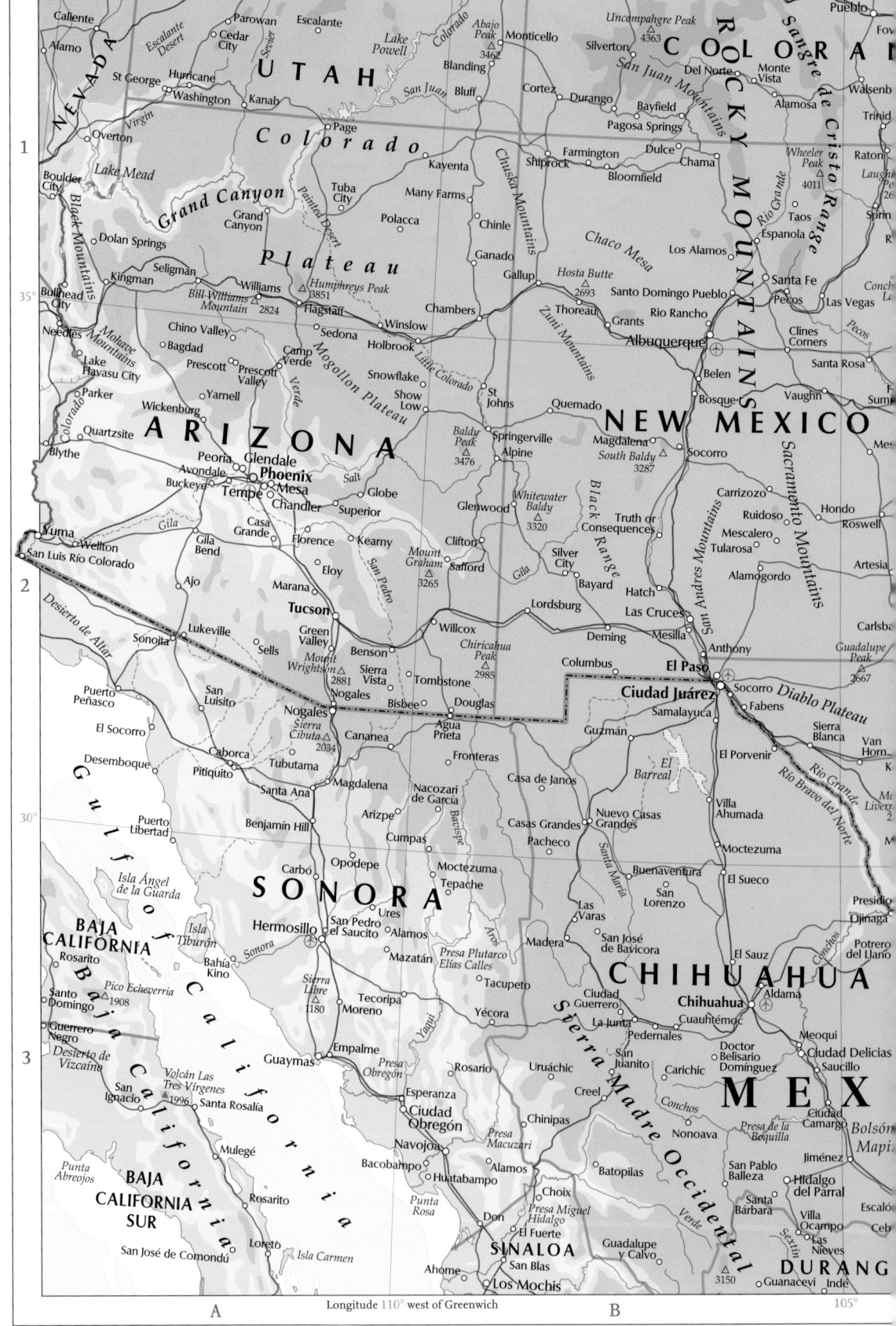

METRES
FEET

5000
16404

3000
9843

2000
6562

1000
3281

500
1640

200
656

0
0

Land below
sea level

200
656

4000
13124

6000
19686

Longitude 110° west of Greenwich

Lambert Azimuthal Equal Area Projection

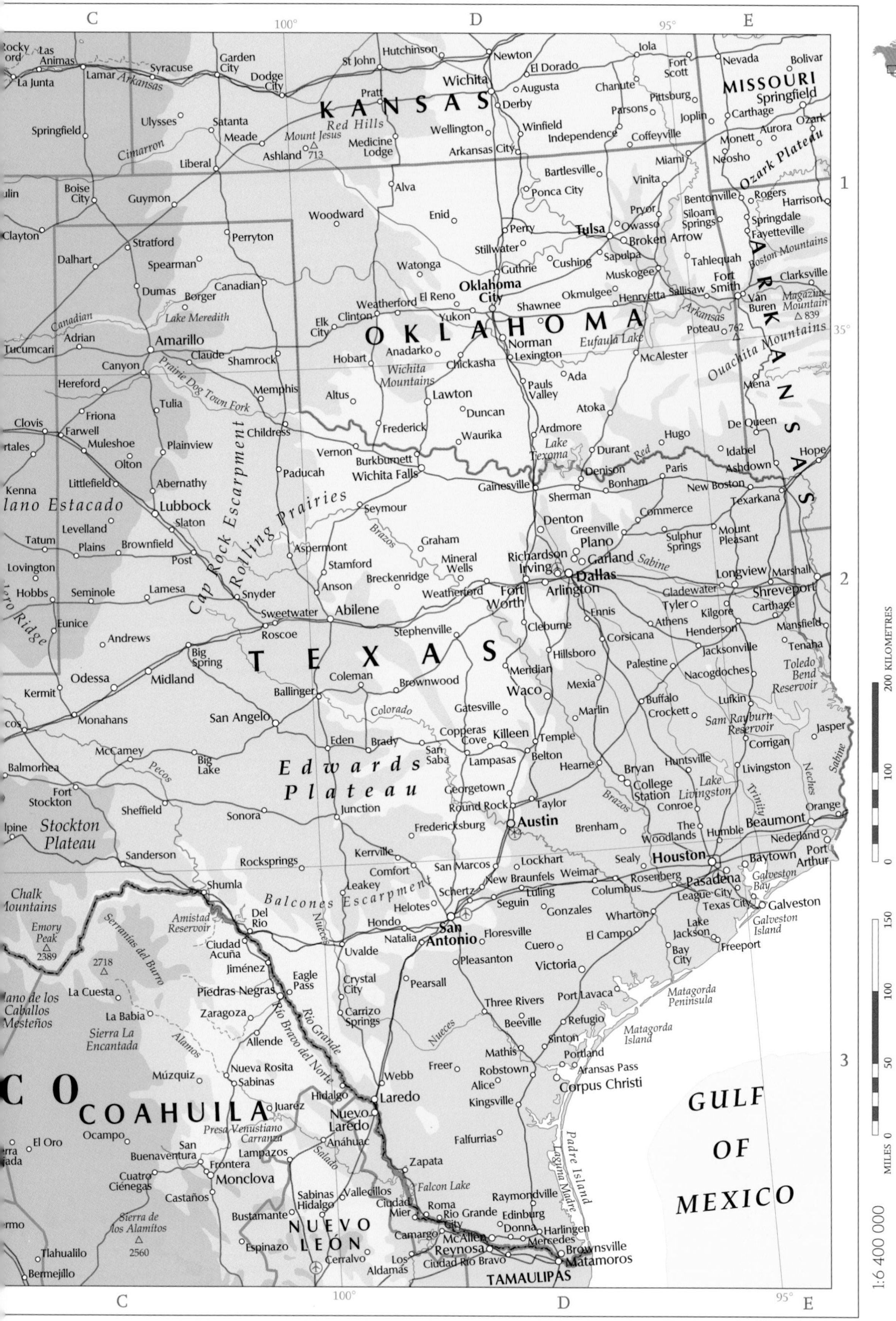

1:6 400 000

© Collins Bartholomew Ltd

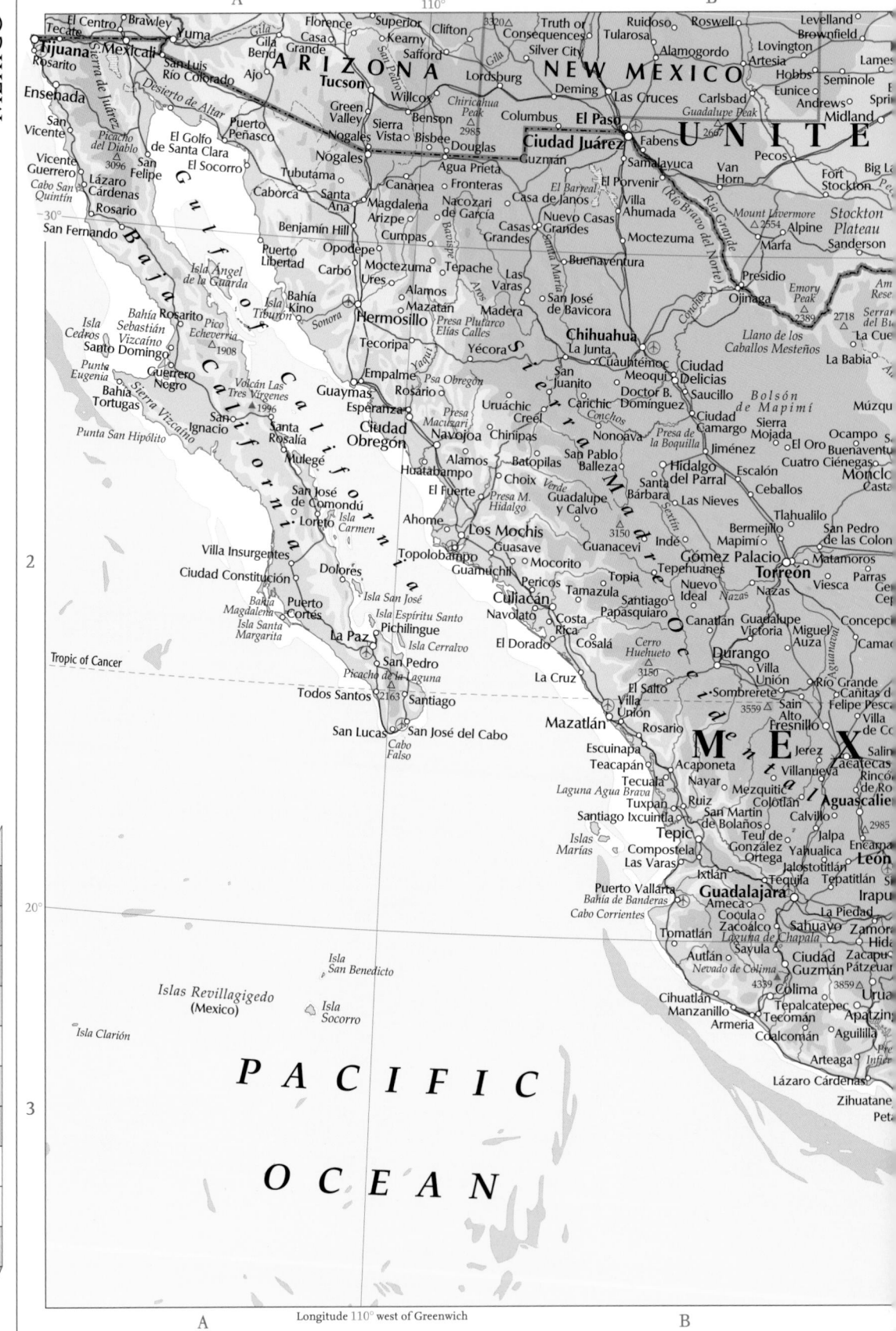

A · 110° · B

El Centro Brawley
Tecate Yuma
Tijuana Mexicali
San Luis Gila Florence Superior Clifton 3320△ Truth or Ruidoso Roswell Levelland
Rosarito Río Colorado Casa Bend Kearny Safford Consequences Tularosa Alamogordo Lovington Brownfield
Grande Silver City Hobbs Seminole
Ensenada Desierto de Altar ARIZONA Lordsburg NEW MEXICO Artesia Eunice Andrews
San Puerto Tucson Willcox Deming Las Cruces Carlsbad Midland
Vicente Peñasco Green Benson Columbus El Paso Guadalupe Peak Spri
San El Golfo Valley Sierra Bisbee Ciudad Juárez Fabens UNITE
Vicente de Santa Clara Nogales Vista Douglas Guzmán Samalayuca Van Pecos
Guerrero El Socorro Nogales Agua Prieta El Porvenir Horn Fort Big
Lázaro Tubutama Cananea Fronteras El Barreal Villa Stockton
Cárdenas San Felipe Caborca Santa Nacozari Casa de Janos Ahumada Mount Livermore Stockton
Rosario Picacho Benjamín Hill Ana de García Nuevo Casas Moctezuma △2554 Alpine Plateau
del Diablo Magdalena Arizpe Casas Grandes Marfa Sanderson
San Fernando 3096 Opodepe Cumpas Grandes Buenaventura Presidio Am
Carbó Moctezuma Tepache Ojinaga Emory △ Rese
Isla Ángel Ures Peak 2389 2718 Serr
Puerto de la Guarda Alamos San José Conchos 2667 del C
Libertad Bahía Mazatán de Bavicora La Cue
Isla Kino Madera Chihuahua Llano de los
Cedros Santo Bahía Hermosillo Cuauhtémoc La Junta Caballos Mesteños La Babia
Domingo Tiburón Tecoripa Meoqui Ciudad
Bahía Rosarito Pico Sonora San Juanito Delicias Bolsón
Isla Sebastián Echeverria Empalme Psa Obregón Juanito Doctor B. de Mapimí Múzqu
Punta Vizcaíno 1908 Guaymas Rosario Uruáchic Carichic Domínguez Sierra Ocampo
Eugenia Guerrero Volcán Las Esperanza Creel Nonoava Ciudad Mojada El Oro Buenaventu
Bahía Negro Tres Vírgenes Ciudad Presa Chínipas Camargo El Oro Cuatro Ciénegas Monclo
Tortugas Santa 1996 Obregón Macuzari Batopilas San Pablo Jiménez Escalón Ceballos Casta
Ignacio Rosalía Navojoa Chinipas Balleza Hidalgo Tlahualilo
Punta San Hipólito Mulegé Álamos Choix Verde del Parral San Pedro
Isla Santa El Fuerte Guadalupe Bermejillo de las Colon
San José Carmen Ahome y Calvo Santa 3150 Mapimí Matamoros
de Comondú Loreto Los Mochis Bárbara Indé Gómez Palacio Parras
Villa Insurgentes Topolobampo Guasave Las Nieves Tepehuanes Torreón Viesca Cep
Ciudad Constitución Dolores Guamúchil Mocorito Guanacevi Nuevo Nazas Concepci
Isla San José Culiacán Topia Ideal Nazas
Bahía Isla Espíritu Santo Navolato Tamazula Santiago Canatlán Guadalupe Miguel Camac
Magdalena Puerto Pichilingue Costa Papasquiaro Victoria Auza
Isla Santa Cortés La Paz El Dorado Rica Cerro Durango Concepci
Margarita San Pedro Cosalá Huehueto Villa
Tropic of Cancer Picacho de la Laguna La Cruz 3180 El Salto Unión Río Grande
Todos Santos △2163 Santiago Villa Sombrerete 3559△ Sain Cañitas de
San Lucas San José del Cabo Mazatlán Unión Alto Felipe Pesca
Cabo Rosario Fresnillo Villa
Falso Escuinapa MEX Jerez Vi de
Teacapán Acaponeta Zacatecas Salin
Tecuala Nayar Villanueva Rincón
Tuxpan Mezquitic de Ro
Laguna Agua Brava Ruiz Colotlán Aguascalie
Santiago Ixcuintla San Martin Calvillo
Isla Tepic de Bolaños Teul de △2985 Encarna
San Benedicto Compostela Yahualica Jalpa León
Islas Las Varas González Jalostotitlán Irapu
Marías Ixtlán Ortega Tepatitlán
Isla Puerto Vallarta Ameca Tequila La Piedad
San Benedicto Bahía de Banderas Guadalajara Cocula Zamor
Cabo Corrientes Zacoalco Sahuayo Hida
Islas Revillagigedo Isla Tomatlán Sayula Laguna de Chapala Ciudad Zacapu
(Mexico) Socorro Autlán Colima Ciudad Guzmán Pátzcuar
Nevado de Colima 4339△ Colima 3859△ Uru
Isla Clarión Cihuatlán Tepalcatepec Tecomán Apatzin
Manzanillo Coalcomán Aguilla
Armería Arteaga Infier
Lázaro Cárdenas
Zihuatane
PACIFIC Pet

OCEAN

A · Longitude 110° west of Greenwich · B

2

3

20°

30°

METRES
FEET

5000
16404

3000
9843

2000
6562

1000
3281

500
1640

200
656

0
0

Land below
sea level

200
656

4000
13124

6000
19686

Lambert Azimuthal Equal Area Projection

GULF

OF

MEXICO

Tropic of Cancer

UNITED STATES OF AMERICA

TEXAS

LOUISIANA

MISSISSIPPI

ALABAMA

FLORIDA

MEXICO

YUCATÁN

Bahía
de Campeche

GUATEMALA

BELIZE

HONDURAS

Gulf of
Tehuantepec

Yucatan Channel

200 KILOMETRES

100

0

150

100

0

MILES

1:9 600 000

A · 90° · B · 80°

30°

UNITED STATES OF AMERICA

LOUISIANA

Lake Charles · Jennings · Mobile · Bainbridge · Waycross · Valdosta · Brunswick
Orange · Lafayette · **Baton Rouge** · Pascagoula · Pensacola · Tallahassee · Lake City · **Jacksonville**
Beaumont · Morgan City · Biloxi · Panama City · *Cape San Blas* · *Apalachee Bay* · Cross City · Gainesville · Ocala · Daytona Beach
New Orleans · Houma · *Mississippi Delta* · **Orlando** · Titusville · *Cape Canaveral*
Waccasassa Bay · **Tampa** · Lakeland · Melbourne
Clearwater · St Petersburg · Fort Pierce
Sarasota · Port Charlotte · **West Palm Beach** · Fort Myers · *Lake Okeechobee* · **Fort Lauderdale**
Everglades · Hollywood
FLORIDA · **Miami**

Grand Bahama · *Little Abaco* · Marsh Harbo
Freeport City · *Great Abaco* · Eleuthe
Berry Islands · **NASSAU** · Banner Tow
Andros · George T

GULF OF MEXICO

Tropic of Cancer

Arrecife Alacrán

HAVANA (La Habana) · Matanzas · *Archipiélago de Sabana*
Pinar del Río · Cárdenas · Sagua la Grande · Santa Clara · *Archipiélago de Camagüey*
Guane · *Golfo de Batábano* · Cienfuegos · Placetas · Esmeralda
Sancti Spíritus · Ciego de Ávila · Camagüey
Isla de la Juventud · **CUBA** · Las Tunas · Hol
Golfo de Guacanayabo · Manzanillo · Bayar
Cabo Cruz · Santi de C

Yucatan Channel

Bahía de Campeche

Progreso · *Cabo Catoche*
Mérida · Tizimín · Cancún
Muna · Valladolid · *Golfo de Batábano*
Campeche · Tekax · Cozumel
Champotón · **YUCATÁN** · *Isla de Cozumel*
Ciudad del Carmen
Frontera · **MEXICO** · Chetumal
Laguna de Términos
Villahermosa · Escárcega
Palenque · *Banco Chinchorro*
Teapa · Tenosique · BELMOPAN · Belize · *Ambergris Cay*
Flores · *Turneffe Islands*
San Cristóbal de las Casas · La Libertad! · Dangriga
BELIZE · *Gulf of Honduras*
GUATEMALA · Punta Gorda · Puerto Barrios · *Islas de la Bahía* · Roatán · Trujillo
Tapachula · Cobán · *Lago de Izabal* · La Ceiba
Huehuetenango · San Pedro Sula
Quetzaltenango · El Progreso · *Patuca* · *Laguna de Caratasca*
Mazatenango · Santa Rosa de Copán · Puerto Lempira
GUATEMALA CITY · **HONDURAS** · *Coco*
Santa Ana · **TEGUCIGALPA** · Danlí · *Cayos Miskitos*
Puerto San José · San Vicente · San Miguel · Somoto · Puerto Cabezas
Sonsonate · **SAN SALVADOR** · Usulután · Jinotega · *Cordillera Isabelia* · *Isla de Providencia (Colombia)*
EL SALVADOR · Matagalpa · *Río Grande* · *Costa de Mosquitos*
Golfo de Fonseca · León · Boaco · *Isla de San Andrés (Colombia)*
NICARAGUA · Juigalpa · *Islas del Maíz (Nicaragua)*
MANAGUA · Granada · Bluefields
Jinotepe · Rivas · *Lake Nicaragua*
San Juan
Liberia · **COSTA RICA** · Puerto Limón
Puntarenas · **SAN JOSÉ** · *Canal de Panamá* · Colón · *Punta San Blas* · *Golfo del Darién*
Cartago · Changuinola
Chirripó △3819 · *Golfo de los Mosquitos* · Bocas del Toro · Aguadulce · **PANAMA CITY** · Monte
Península de Osa · La Concepción · *P A N A M A* · La Chorrera · La Palma · Turbo
Cordillera de Talamanca · David · Santiago · Chitré · *Gulf of Panama*
Puerto Armuelles · *Golfo de Chiriquí* · *Península de Azuero* · *Punta Mala*
Isla de Coiba

PACIFIC OCEAN

Grand Cayman · *Little Cayman* · **Cayman Islands (U.K.)**
Montego Bay · Spanish Town · Jam
JAMAICA · **KINGSTON**

C A R I B B E A N

Great Bahama Bank
Straits of Florida
Florida Keys · Key Largo · Key West

20°

10°

METRES / FEET
5000 / 16404
3000 / 9843
2000 / 6562
1000 / 3281
500 / 1640
200 / 656
0 / 0
Land below sea level
200 / 656
4000 / 13124
6000 / 19686

Lambert Azimuthal Equal Area Projection

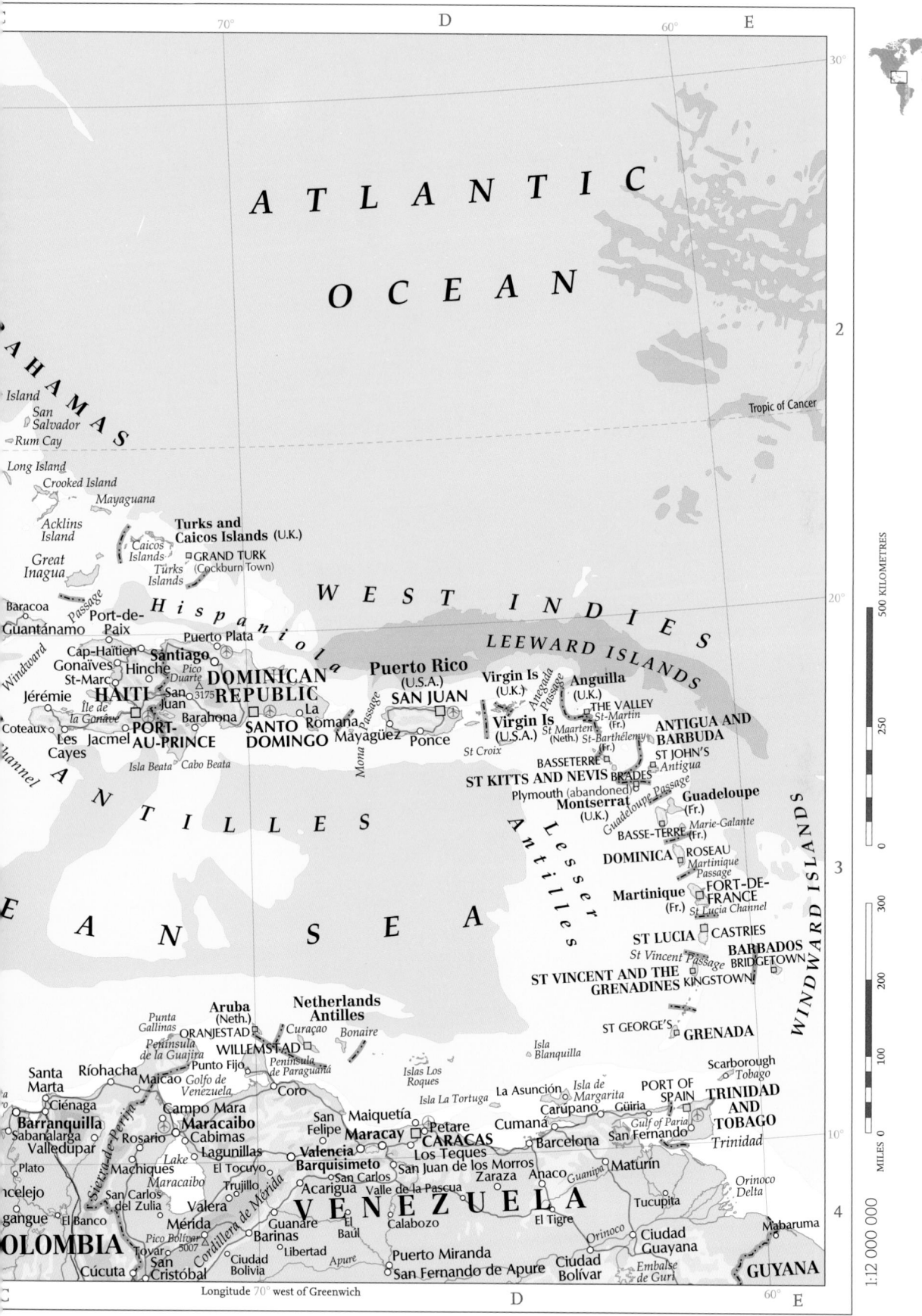

A T L A N T I C

O C E A N

Tropic of Cancer

BAHAMAS

Island
San
Salvador
Rum Cay

Long Island
Crooked Island
Mayaguana

Acklins
Island

Great
Inagua

**Turks and
Caicos Islands** (U.K.)

Caicos
Islands

□ GRAND TURK
(Cockburn Town)

Turks
Islands

W E S T   I N D I E S

L E E W A R D   I S L A N D S

Baracoa
Guantánamo
Port-de-
Paix

Hispaniola

Cap-Haïtien
Gonaïves
Santiago
St-Marc
HAITI Hinche
Jérémie
Île de
la Gonâve
Coteaux
Les
Cayes Jacmel
**PORT-
AU-PRINCE**

Pico
Duarte
△ 3175
San
Juan

**DOMINICAN
REPUBLIC**

Barahona

La
SANTO Romana
DOMINGO

Isla Beata Cabo Beata

Mayagüez

Puerto Rico
(U.S.A.)

SAN JUAN

Ponce

St Croix

Virgin Is
(U.K.)

Anegada
Passage

Virgin Is
(U.S.A.)

St-Martin
St Maarten (Fr.)
(Neth.) St-Barthélemy
(Fr.)

Anguilla
(U.K.)

THE VALLEY

□ ST JOHN'S
Antigua

**ANTIGUA AND
BARBUDA**

BASSETERRE
ST KITTS AND NEVIS BRADES

Plymouth (abandoned)
Montserrat
(U.K.)

Guadeloupe
Passage

Guadeloupe
(Fr.)

BASSE-TERRE
(Fr.)

Marie-Galante

DOMINICA
□ ROSEAU

Martinique
Passage

Martinique
(Fr.)

**FORT-DE-
FRANCE**

St Lucia Channel

ST LUCIA □ CASTRIES

St Vincent Passage

BARBADOS
BRIDGETOWN

**ST VINCENT AND THE
GRENADINES** KINGSTOWN

*Windward
Passage*

*Mona
Passage*

A N T I L L E S

*Lesser
Antilles*

C A R I B B E A N   S E A

WINDWARD ISLANDS

Baracoa

ST GEORGE'S
GRENADA

Aruba
(Neth.)
ORANJESTAD

**Netherlands
Antilles**

Curaçao
WILLEMSTAD Bonaire

Punta
Gallinas
Península
de la Guajira

Santa
Marta Ríohacha
Maicao

Ciénaga
BARRANQUILLA
Sabanalarga
Valledupar
Plato

Punto Fijo

Golfo de
Venezuela

Coro

Península
de Paraguaná

Islas Los
Roques

Isla
Blanquilla

La Tortuga

La Asunción

Isla de
Margarita

Carúpano

Güiria

Scarborough
Tobago

**PORT OF
SPAIN**

**TRINIDAD
AND
TOBAGO**

Rosario
MARACAIBO
Campo Mara
Cabimas
Lagunillas

Machiques
Lake
Maracaibo
San Carlos
del Zulia

El Banco
El Tocuyo
Trujillo
Valera

San
Felipe
Maracay
Valencia
Barquisimeto
San Carlos

Los Teques
Petare
CARACAS

Maiquetía

San Juan de los Morros

Barcelona

Cumaná

Gulf of Paria

San Fernando

Trinidad

Acarigua
Valle de la Pascua
Zaraza
Anaco
Maturín

Mérida
△ Pico Bolívar
5007

Guanare
Barinas

Apure

Calabozo

El Tigre

Tucupita

Orinoco
Delta

Mabaruma

Tovar
San
Cristóbal
Cúcuta

Ciudad
Bolivia

El
Baúl

Libertad

VENEZUELA

Puerto Miranda
San Fernando de Apure

Orinoco

Ciudad
Bolívar

Ciudad
Guayana

Embalse
de Guri

GUYANA

COLOMBIA

500 KILOMETRES

250

0

300

200

100

MILES 0

1:12 000 000

SOUTH AMERICA

Map grid references (top): 1 · 2 · 3 · 4
Map grid references (side): G · F · E · D · C · B

Equator

A T L A N T I C

O C E A N

Mouths of the Amazon

Ilha de Marajó

Belém
São Luís
Fortaleza
Natal
João Pessoa
Recife
Maceió
Aracaju
Salvador

Teresina
Parnaíba

Barragem de Sobradinho

São Francisco

Vitória
Rio de Janeiro

Brasília
Goiânia
Belo Horizonte
Campinas
São Paulo

B R A Z I L

Cayenne
Georgetown
Paramaribo
SURINAME French Guiana
GUYANA

Macapá
Santarém
Marabá

Tocantins
Araguaia
Xingu
Tapajós
Amazon
Iriri

Cuiabá

Campo Grande

Paraguay

PARAGU

Boa Vista
Branco
Negro

Manaus

Madeira
Purus
Juruá
Japurá

Porto Velho

Santa Cruz
BOLIVIA
Sucre

La Paz
Lake Titicaca

S E L V A S

Rio Branco

Amazon
Iquitos
Marañón

Pucallpa
A N D E S

P E R U
Ayacucho
Arequipa
Arica

Callao Lima
Trujillo

a Desert

ECUADOR
□Quito
Guayaquil

Medellín
Bogotá
Cali
COLOMBIA

VENEZUELA
Caracas
Ciudad Bolívar
Orinoco

Maracaibo
Barquisimeto

Barranquilla

C A R I B B E A N   S E A

ST LUCIA
ST VINCENT AND THE GRENADINES
BARBADOS
GRENADA
TRINIDAD AND TOBAGO
Netherlands Antilles
Aruba (Neth.)

NICARAGUA
Lake Nicaragua
COSTA RICA
PANAMA

Isla de Malpelo (Colombia)

Equator

Ilha da Trindade (Brazil)

10°
0°
10°
20°
80°
70°
60°
50°
40°
20°

Bi-Polar Oblique Projection

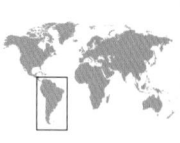

ATLANTIC OCEAN

PACIFIC OCEAN

ARGENTINA

Florianópolis

Porto Alegre

Rio Grande

Lagoa dos Patos

URUGUAY

Montevideo

Rio de la Plata

Mar del Plata

La Plata

Buenos Aires

Rosario

Bahía Blanca

Corrientes

Paraná

Salado

Córdoba

San Miguel de Tucumán

Mendoza

Cerro Aconcagua 6959

Valparaíso

Santiago

Concepción

Puerto Montt

Isla de Chiloé

Archipiélago de los Chonos

Islas Desventuradas (Chile)

Archipiélago Juan Fernández (Chile)

C H I L E

A N D E S

Neuquén

Colorado

Negro

P A T A G O N I A

Golfo de San Jorge

Comodoro Rivadavia

Río Gallegos

Tierra del Fuego

Punta Arenas

Isla de los Estados

Cape Horn

Drake Passage

South Shetland Islands (U.K.)

Antarctic Peninsula

South Orkney Islands (U.K.)

Scotia Sea

Stanley

Falkland Islands (U.K.)

South Georgia

South Georgia and the South Sandwich Islands (U.K.)

South Sandwich Islands

Longitude 20° west of Greenwich

Tropic of...

1:28 000 000

MILES 0 | 200 | 400 | 600

0 | 500 | 1000 KILOMETRES

5 30° 6 40° 7 50° 8

A 100° B 90° C 80° D 70° E 60° F 50° G 40° H 30°

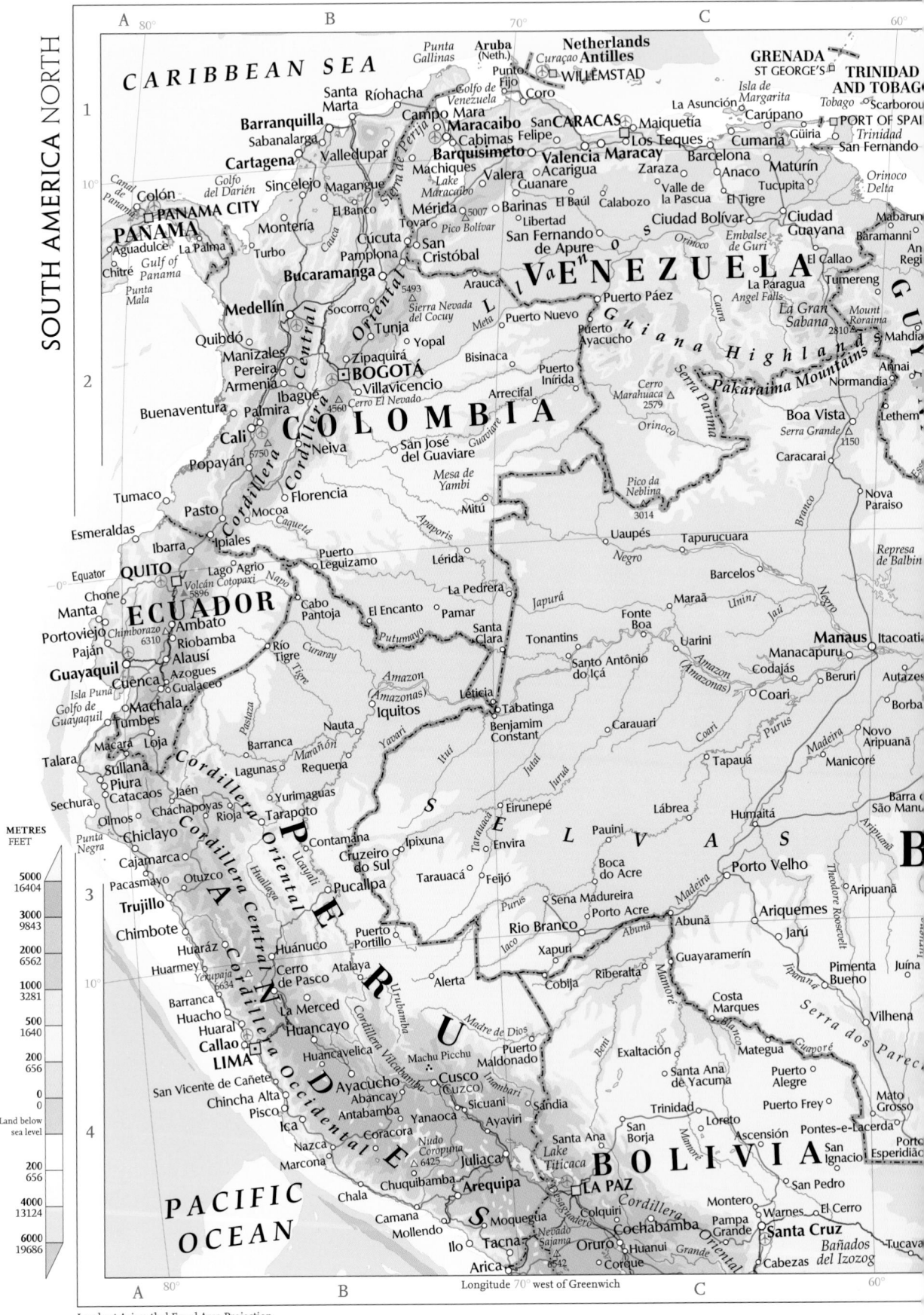

Lambert Azimuthal Equal Area Projection

ATLANTIC

OCEAN

GEORGETOWN
Paradise
New Amsterdam
den Totness PARAMARIBO
ieuw Albina St-Laurent-du-Maroni
kerie Brokopondo Sinnamary
Professor van Kourou
Blommestein Meer CAYENNE
SURINAME Guisanbourg
French Oiapoque
Juliana Top Guiana
1230 Inini
Pontoetoe
Lourenço Calçoene
Amapá Ilha de
Maracá
Serra Tumucumaque Mouths of the
Amazon
Trombetas Macapá Equator
Arere Paru Porto Santana Ilha
Serra Mazagão Chaves Caviana
Parauaquara Almeirim Cabo
Oriximiná 359 Breves Ilha de Maguarinho
Óbidos Portel Marajó Salinópolis
Juruti Monte Cametá Muaná Bragança
rucara Alegre Baía de Marajó Viseu
rucurituba Parintins Santarém Belém Cururupu
Castanhal São Luís
Altamira Acará Pinheiro Baía de São Marcos
Itaituba Tucuruí Viana Parnaíba Camocim
Represa Itapicuru Luzilândia
Tucuruí Santa Mirim Fortaleza
Jacunda Luzia Bacabal Tianguá Caucaia
Maraba Pedreiras Codó Piripiri Sobral Cascavel
Imperatriz Pres. Dutra Caxias Campo Maior Canindé Aracati
Araras Grajaú Timon Teresina Crateús Boa Quixadá Macau
acareacanga Tocantinópolis Barra do Buriti Viagem Mossoró Touros
São Corda Bravo Taua Icó Ponta
Xinguara Félix Porto Franco Açude Boa Floriano Iguatu do Calcanhar
Manuelzinho Fresco Carolina Esperança Palmeiras Sousa Natal
Jerumenha Picos Juazeiro Campina
R A Z I L Araguaína Balsas Uruçu Oeiras Crato do Norte Grande João
Conceição do Araguaia Canto do Buriti Paulistana Jaboatão dos Pessoa
São Raimundo Floresta Salgueiro Guararapes Olinda
Serra Santa Maria Nonato Caruaru Recife
do Cachimbo das Barreiras Nova Petrolina Cabo de Santo
Pedro Remanso Juazeiro Paulo Agostinho
Peixoto de Afonso Senhor do Bonfim Afonso Rio Largo
Azevedo Palmas Barragem de Xique Monte Santo Maceió
rto dos Sobradinho Xique Lagarto Arapiraca
uchos Porto Nacional Corrente Irecê Jacobina Aracaju
idos Ilha do Dianópolis Feira Serrinha
Porto Artur Bananal Natividade Barreiras Ibotirama de Santana Estância
São Gurupi Santana Alagoinhas
Diamantino Félix Cavalcante Bom Jesus Itaberaba Camaçari
Rosário Oeste Porangatu Correntina da Lapa Santo Antônio de Jesus Salvador
Barra do Bugres Uruaçu Posse Jequié Ipiaú
Cuiabá Represa Brumado Itabuna Ubaitaba
ceres Rondonópolis Niquelândia Serra da Mesa Guanambi Ilhéus
Iporá Formosa Januária Vitória da Una
Alto BRASÍLIA Arinos Espinosa Conquista Itapetinga
Garças Anápolis Janaúba Salinas
Itiquira Goiás Trindade Luziânia Unaí Montes Almenara Porto Seguro
Coxim Vianópolis Claros
uerto Paraúna Goiânia Teófilo Alcobaça
sabel Rio Verde Jataí Racatu Jequitaí Otôni
Corumbá Itumbiara Araguari Patos
Rio Verde de Mato Grosso Uberlândia de Minas

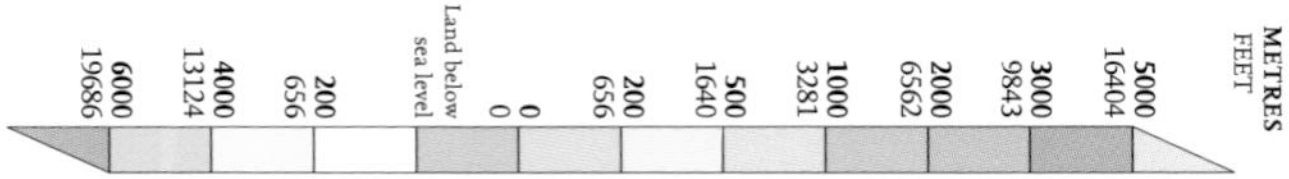

BRAZIL

BOLIVIA

PARAGUAY

PERU

ARGENTINA

CHILE

Major cities and features:

Salvador, Vitória, Rio de Janeiro, Belo Horizonte, São Paulo, Santos, Curitiba, Florianópolis, Porto Alegre, BRASÍLIA, Goiânia, Campo Grande, Cuiabá, Corumbá

LA PAZ, Santa Cruz, SUCRE, Potosí, Cochabamba, Oruro

ASUNCIÓN, Concepción, Filadelfia

Arequipa, Tacna, Arica

Córdoba, Santa Fé, Salta, Catamarca, La Rioja, Tucumán, Jujuy

Antofagasta, Iquique, Copiapó, La Serena, Coquimbo

Physical features:

Serra Geral de Goiás, Chapada Diamantina, Serra do Espinhaço, Mato Grosso, Serra dos Parecis, Serra dos Caiabis, Serra do Roncador, Altiplano, Cordillera Oriental, Atacama Desert, Chaco Boreal, São Francisco, Paraná, Paraguay, Lake Titicaca, Salar de Uyuni, Tropic of Capricorn

Scale legend:

METRES / FEET

5000	16404
3000	9843
2000	6562
1000	3281
500	1640
200	656
0	0
Land below sea level	
200	656
4000	13124
6000	19686

Lambert Azimuthal Equal Area Projection

ATLANTIC

OCEAN

URUGUAY
MONTEVIDEO
La Plata
Mar del Plata

BUENOS AIRES

A R G E N T I N A

SANTIAGO

C H I L E

P A T A G O N I A

Falkland Islands
(U.K.)

West
Falkland

STANLEY

East
Falkland

Port
Stephens

South Georgia
(U.K.)

Cape
Alexandra
Mount Paget
2934
Grytviken
Cape
Disappointment

1:16 000 000

Longitude 50° west of Greenwich

600 KILOMETRES

400

200

0

300

200

100

0

MILES

B — C

Map labels (Brazil Southeast):

Planalto do Mato Grosso

Rio das Mortes · Serra do Taquaral

Coronel Ponce · Presidente Murtinho · Araguaiana · Barra do Garças · Itapuranga · Ceres · Goianésia · Rialma · Rianópolis · Brasilândia

Cabeceira Rio Manso · Poxoréu · Torixoréu · Aragarças · Bom Jardim de Goiás · Jussara · Goiás · Jaraguá · Pirenópolis · Corumbá de Goiás · DISTRITO FEDERAL · BRASÍLIA · Planaltina · Form

Jaciara · Tesouro · Diamantino · Iporá · Itaberaí · Gama · Luziânia · Ur

MATO Rondonópolis · Guiratinga · Anicuns · Nerópolis · Anápolis · Silvânia · Vianópolis · Cabec

São Lourenço · Anhumas · Ponte de Pedra · Alto Garças · Caiapônia · Aurilândia · Trindade · **Goiânia** · Hidrolândia · Orizona · Cristalina

GROSSO Itiquira · Alto Araguaia · Santa Rita do Araguaia · Serra do Caiapó · Paraúna · Edéia · Piracanjuba · Pirés do Rio · Ipameri · Catalão · Para · Guarda Mor · Vazan

Correntes · Mineiros · Jataí · **Rio Verde** · Montividiu · Santa Helena de Goiás · Goiatuba · Caldas Novas · Goiandira · Morrinhos

Pedro Gomes · Alto Taquarí · Serranópolis · Claro · Verde · Buriti Alegre · Barragem Itumbiara · Corumb

GOIAS

Coxim · Jauru · Baús · Caçu · São Simão · Quirinópolis · Itumbiara · Tupaciguara · Araguari · Côromandel · Represa de Emborcação · Patrocíni

Rio Verde de Mato Grosso · Costa Rica · Aporé · Itarumã · Barragem de São Simão · Santa Vitória · Monte Alegre de Minas · Uberlândia · Monte Carmel

Rochedo · Corguinho · Paraíso · Cassilândia · Aporé · Gurinhatã · Prata · Nova Ponte · Patrocíni

Camapuã · Alto Sucuriú · Paranaíba · Iturama · **B R A Z** · Campina Verde · Campo Florido · Arax

MATO GROSSO Ponte do Rio Verde · Inocência · Itapajipe · Uberaba · Sacram

Jaraguari · Aparecida do Tabuado · Santa Fé do Sul · Jales · Cardoso · Frutal · Planura · Igarapava · Pedrégulho

Terenos · **DO SUL** · Represa Ilha Solteíra · Fernandópolis · Votuporanga · Colômbia · São Joaquim da Barra · Represa Peixoto

Campo Grande · Ribas do Rio Pardo · Agua Clara · Garças · Pereira Barreto · General Salgado · Nova Granada · Olímpia · **Barretos** · Orlândia · Franca · Cas

Jango · Sidrolândia · Ferreiros · Três Lagoas · Andradina · Araçatuba · São José do Rio Preto · Bebedouro · Morro Agudo · São Sebast do Para

Aroeira · Porto Alegre · Represa Jupiá · Mirandópolis · Birigüi · **São Paulo** · Catanduva · Jaboticabal · Sertãozinho · Batatais

Maracaju · Rio Brilhante · Bataguassu · Panorama · Dracena · Valparaíso · Lucélia · Penápolis · Promissão · Lins · Novo Horizonte · Tabatinga · Cravinhos · Ribeirão Preto · Mococ

Dourados · Ivinheima · Presidente Epitácio · Santo Anastácio · Tupã · Pirajuí · Cafelândia · Araraquara · São Carlos · Piraçununga · Casa Bra

Ponta Porã · Teodoro Sampaio · Represa Porto Primavera · Presidente Prudente · Peixe · Rancharia · Marília · Vera Cruz · Garça · Jaú · **PAULO** · Rio Claro · Lem

Bocajá · Caarapó · Porto São José · Nova Londrina · Porecatu · Represa Capivara · Assis · Palmital · Bauru · Agudos · São Manuel · Piracicaba · Limeira · Americ

Amambaí · Juti · Loanda · Paranavaí · Rolândia · Cornélio Procópio · Ourinhos · Botucatu · Conchas · Piraju · Avaré · Boituva · Salto · Itu · Campinas

Capitán Bado · Represa Ilha Grande · Nova Esperança · Rondon · Maringá · Arapongas · Apucarana · Santo Antônio da Platina · Itaí · Represa de Jurumirim · Tatuí · Itapetininga · Sorocaba · Pa

Coronel Sapucaia · Querência do Norte · Porto Camargo · Cianorte · Tomazina · Ibaití · Venceslau Bráz · Jaguariaíva · Itararé · Capão Bonito · Piedade · Itanh · Peruíb

Ypé-Jhú · Iguatemi · Umuarama · Campo Mourão · Telêmaco Borba · Piraí do Sul · Itapeva · Buri · Juquiá · 1350 · Dedo de Deus

Ygatimí · Salto del Guairá · Guaíra · Goio-Erê · Cândido de Abreu · Tibagi · Castro · Apiaí · Eldorado · Jacupiranga · Iguape

Porto Mendes · Campos Eré · **PARANÁ** · Reserva · Pitanga · Serra Paranapiacaba · Cerro Azul · Registro · Cananéia

Montes de Araçanguy · Toledo · Ipiranga · Rio Branco do Sul · Antonina · Guaraqueçaba

PARAGUAY · Represa de Itaipu · Cascavel · Catanduvas · Serra das Araras · Serra do Cavernoso · Prudentópolis · Guarapuava · Ponta Grossa · Campo Largo · **Curitiba** · Ilha das Peças

Hernandarias · Laranjeiras do Sul · Irati · Palmeira · São José dos Pinhais · Paranaguá

Ciudad del Este · Foz do Iguaçu · Iguaçu · Represa Salto Osório · Rio Azul · Lapa · Guaratuba

Iguaçu Falls · Chópimzinho · Represa de Foz de Areia · São Mateus do Sul · Rio Negro · Ilha de São Francisco

Dionísio Cerqueira · Mangueirinha · União da Vitória · Canoinhas · Mafra · **Joinville** · São Francisco do Sul

Wanda · Rato Branco · Clevelândia · Porto União · Itaiópolis · Araquari

Eldorado · Palmas · Campos de Palmas · Caçador · Jaraguá do Sul

Puerto Rico · Montecarlo · Xanxerê · **SANTA CATARINA** · Blumenau · Itajaí

ARGENTINA

Lambert Azimuthal Equal Area Projection

Longitude 50° west of Greenwich

METRES / FEET

METRES	FEET
5000	16404
3000	9843
2000	6562
1000	3281
500	1640
200	656
0	0
Land below sea level	
200	656
4000	13124
6000	19686

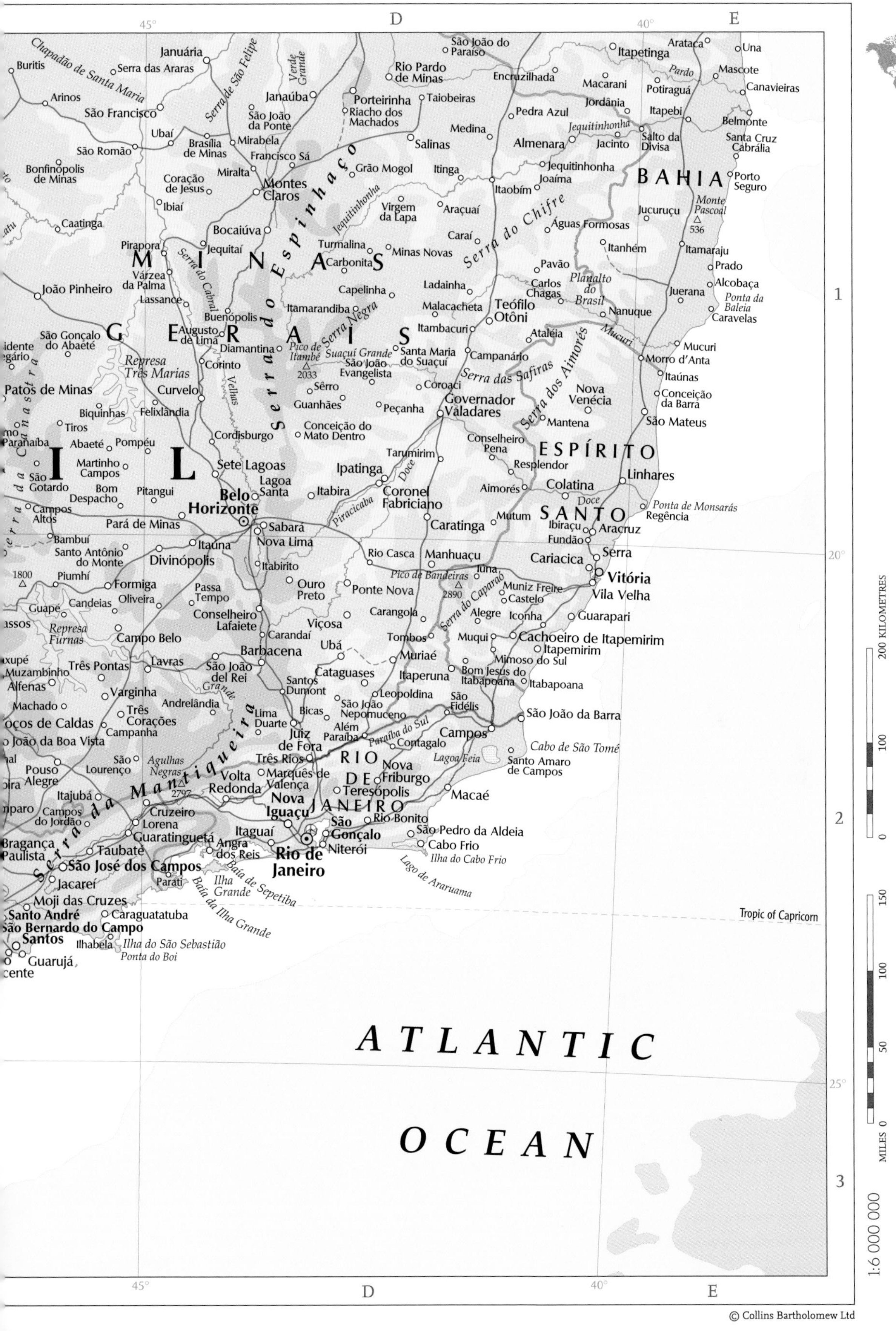

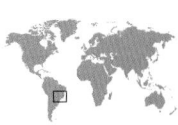

D
E
45°
40°
Chapadão de Santa Maria
Januária
Buritis
Serra das Araras
Arinos
São Francisco
Serra de São Felipe
Verde Grande
Janaúba
São João da Ponte
Ubaí
Brasília de Minas
Mirabela
São Romão
Francisco Sá
Bonfinópolis de Minas
Miralta
Coração de Jesus
Montes Claros
Ibiaí
Caatinga
Bocaiúva
Pirapora
Jequitaí
Várzea da Palma
Serra do Cabral
João Pinheiro
Lassance
Buenópolis
Augusto de Lima
São Gonçalo do Abaeté
Represa Três Marias
Corinto
Patos de Minas
Curvelo
Biquinhas
Felixlândia
Tiros
Paranaíba
Abaeté
Pompéu
Martinho Campos
São Gotardo
Bom Despacho
Campos Altos
Pitangui
Cordisburgo
Sete Lagoas
Lagoa Santa
Belo Horizonte
Pará de Minas
Bambuí
Santo Antônio do Monte
Divinópolis
Itaúna
1800
Piumhí
Formiga
Candeias
Oliveira
Passa Tempo
Guapé
Represa Furnas
Campo Belo
Conselheiro Lafaiete
Lavras
Três Pontas
Muzambinho
Alfenas
Varginha
Machado
Três Corações
Campanha
Andrelândia
Poços de Caldas
São João da Boa Vista
São Lourenço
Agulhas Negras
2797
Pouso Alegre
Itajubá
Campos do Jordão
Bragança Paulista
Taubaté
São José dos Campos
Jacareí
Moji das Cruzes
Santo André
São Bernardo do Campo
Santos
Guarujá
Caraguatatuba
Ilhabela
Ilha do São Sebastião
Ponta do Boi
Serra da Mantiqueira
Serra da Canastra
MINAS GERAIS
Serra do Espinhaço
Grão Mogol
Porteirinha
Riacho dos Machados
Taiobeiras
Rio Pardo de Minas
São João do Paraíso
Salinas
Medina
Itinga
Jequitinhonha
Virgem da Lapa
Araçuaí
Turmalina
Minas Novas
Carbonita
Capelinha
Itamarandiba
Serra Negra
Diamantina
Pico de Itambé
2033
Suaçuí Grande
São João Evangelista
Santa Maria do Suaçuí
Sêrro
Guanhães
Peçanha
Conceição do Mato Dentro
Itabira
Ipatinga
Coronel Fabriciano
Piracicaba
Doce
Tarumirim
Caratinga
Sabará
Nova Lima
Itabirito
Ouro Preto
Ponte Nova
Viçosa
Carandaí
Barbacena
Ubá
São João del Rei
Grande
Santos Dumont
Cataguases
Lima Duarte
Juiz de Fora
Bicas
São João Nepomuceno
Além Paraíba
Três Rios
Volta Redonda
Marquês de Valença
Cruzeiro
Lorena
Guaratinguetá
Angra dos Reis
Parati
Ilha Grande
Baía de Sepetiba
Baía da Ilha Grande
Itaguaí
Nova Iguaçu
Rio de Janeiro
São Gonçalo
Niterói
Teresópolis
Nova Friburgo
RIO DE JANEIRO
Rio Bonito
Macaé
São Pedro da Aldeia
Cabo Frio
Ilha do Cabo Frio
Lago de Araruama
Lagoa Feia
Campos
Contagalo
Paraíba do Sul
Leopoldina
São Fidélis
São João da Barra
Cabo de São Tomé
Santo Amaro de Campos
Itaperuna
Bom Jesus do Itabapoana
Itabapoana
Muriaé
Tombos
Carangola
Manhuaçu
Rio Casca
Pico de Bandeiras
2890
Serra do Caparaó
Iúna
Muniz Freire
Castelo
Alegre
Iconha
Muqui
Cachoeiro de Itapemirim
Itapemirim
Mimoso do Sul
Guarapari
Vila Velha
Vitória
Serra
Cariacica
Fundão
Ibiraçu
Aracruz
ESPÍRITO SANTO
Colatina
Doce
Linhares
Regência
Ponta de Monsarás
Mutum
Aimorés
Resplendor
Conselheiro Pena
Mantena
Nova Venécia
São Mateus
Conceição da Barra
Itaúnas
Morro d'Anta
Mucuri
Governador Valadares
Coroaci
Campanário
Serra das Safiras
Serra dos Aimorés
Itambacuri
Malacacheta
Teófilo Otôni
Ataléia
Ladainha
Caraí
Serra do Chifre
Itaobím
Pavão
Carlos Chagas
Planalto do Brasil
Nanuque
Águas Formosas
Itanhém
Joaíma
Jequitinhonha
Almenara
Pedra Azul
Encruzilhada
Macarani
Jordânia
Jequitinhonha
Jacinto
Salto da Divisa
Itapetinga
Pardo
Potiraguá
Itapebi
Arataca
Una
Mascote
Canavieiras
Belmonte
Santa Cruz Cabrália
Porto Seguro
BAHIA
Monte Pascoal
536
Jucuruçu
Itamaraju
Prado
Alcobaça
Juerana
Ponta da Baleia
Caravelas
Mucuri
20°
25°
1
2
3
Tropic of Capricorn
ATLANTIC OCEAN
200 KILOMETRES
100
0
MILES 0
50
100
150
1:6 000 000

A 90° **B** 120° **C** 150° **D** 180°

3 45° 2 Arctic Circle

Chukchi Sea

60°

Heilong Jiang

Sea of Okhotsk

Bering Sea

Ostrov Beringa · Aleutian Basin · Nuni Islar

Attu Island · 7822 · Aleutian Island

30°

A S I A

Sakhalin

Aleutian Chain

Aleutian Trenc

Vladivostok

Kuril Basin · Kuril Islands · (Kuril'skiye Ostrova)

4 Tropic of Cancer

Yellow River

·3510

Hokkaido 9550 Kuril Trench

6671 · Emperor Seamount Chain · 1240 · Emperor Trough

·7900

Ganges

Yangtze

Sea of Japan

Yellow Sea

Kolkata

Shanghai

East China Sea

Honshū

·8412

Tōkyō

Northwest Pacific Basin

15°

Bay of Bengal

Shikoku Kyūshū

7187 Ryukyu Islands (Nansei-shotō)

·6345

18.

Kure Atoll

Hawa

Rangoon

Hainan

7460 Ryukyu Trench

Izu-Ogasawara Trench 9780

Volcano Islands (Kazan-retto)

Mapmakers Seamounts

Midway Islands

Necker Island

Hawaii

Taiwan

Luzon Strait

Kyushu–Palau Ridge

South Honshu Ridge

Mid-Pacific Mountains

Andaman Islands

South China Sea

Philippine Basin

West Mariana Basin

Saipan

6530

Central Pacific Basin

Andaman Basin

5560

Luzon

Mariana Trench

Mariana Trench

·1564

M I C R O N E S I A

Sri Lanka

Philippines

10057 Challenger Deep

Guam·

Marshall Islands

Nicobar Islands

Palawan

Sulu Sea

Palau Islands

8967

10920

Kwajalein

Gilbert Islands

P O L Y N E

Mindanao

8054

Caroline Islands

Chuuk

Kosrae

Gilbert Ridge

Celebes Sea

·5484

West Caroline Basin

East Caroline Basin

7208

Melanesian Basin

Phoenix Islan

Equator 0°

S u m a t r a

Singapore

Halmahera

Admiralty Islands

M E L A N E S I A

2302·

Kepulauan Mentawai

Borneo

Celebes

Seram

New Guinea

New Britain

Solomon Islands

Funafuti

Fakaofo

Cocos Basin

Bangka

Laut Banda

8940

Solomon Sea

·13

Savai'i

Samoa Basin

Jakarta

Laut Jawa

7288

Laut Flores

Sumba

Timor

Arafura Sea

Torres Strait Cape York

8322

Vanua Levu

Tonga Trench

Niue

J a v a

7125

Java Trench (Sunda Trench)

Coral Sea Basin

Espíritu Santo

Viti Levu

6

Timor Sea

North Australian Basin

·6360

Great Barrier Reef

Coral Sea

7633

New Hebrides Trench

Horizon Deep 10800

I N D I A N

O C E A N

West Australian Basin

Exmouth Plateau

North West Cape

New Caledonia

South Fiji Basin

Kermadec Trench

Sou

Pacif

15°

1924·

Lord Howe Rise

Norfolk Island

New Caledonia Trough

Kermadec Islands

10047

A U S T R A L I A

Sydney

New Caledonia

North Island

Perth Basin

Perth

Great Australian Bight

Melbourne

Tasman Sea

Auckland

New Zealand

Wellington

Chatham Rise

Chatham Islands

7 Tropic of Capricorn

·549

Cape Leeuwin

South Australian Basin

·5670

Tasmania

5176.

Tasman Basin

South Island

60.

Broken Plateau

7102.

Diamantina Deep 6602

South Tasman Rise

Auckland Islands

Campbell Plateau

Antipodes Islands

Southeast Indian Ridge

Indian–Antarctic Ridge

S O U T H

8

Île Amsterdam Île St-Paul

1840

Macquarie Ridge

1646

·956

Balleny Islands

R

S

4181

Australian–Antarctic Basin

4650

Antarctic Circle

Cape Adare

9 60°

45° 90° 120° 150° 180

Lambert Azimuthal Equal Area Projection

A N T A

METRES / FEET scale:

METRES	FEET
0	0
200	656
2000	6562
3000	9843
4000	13124
5000	16404
6000	19686
7000	22967
9000	29529

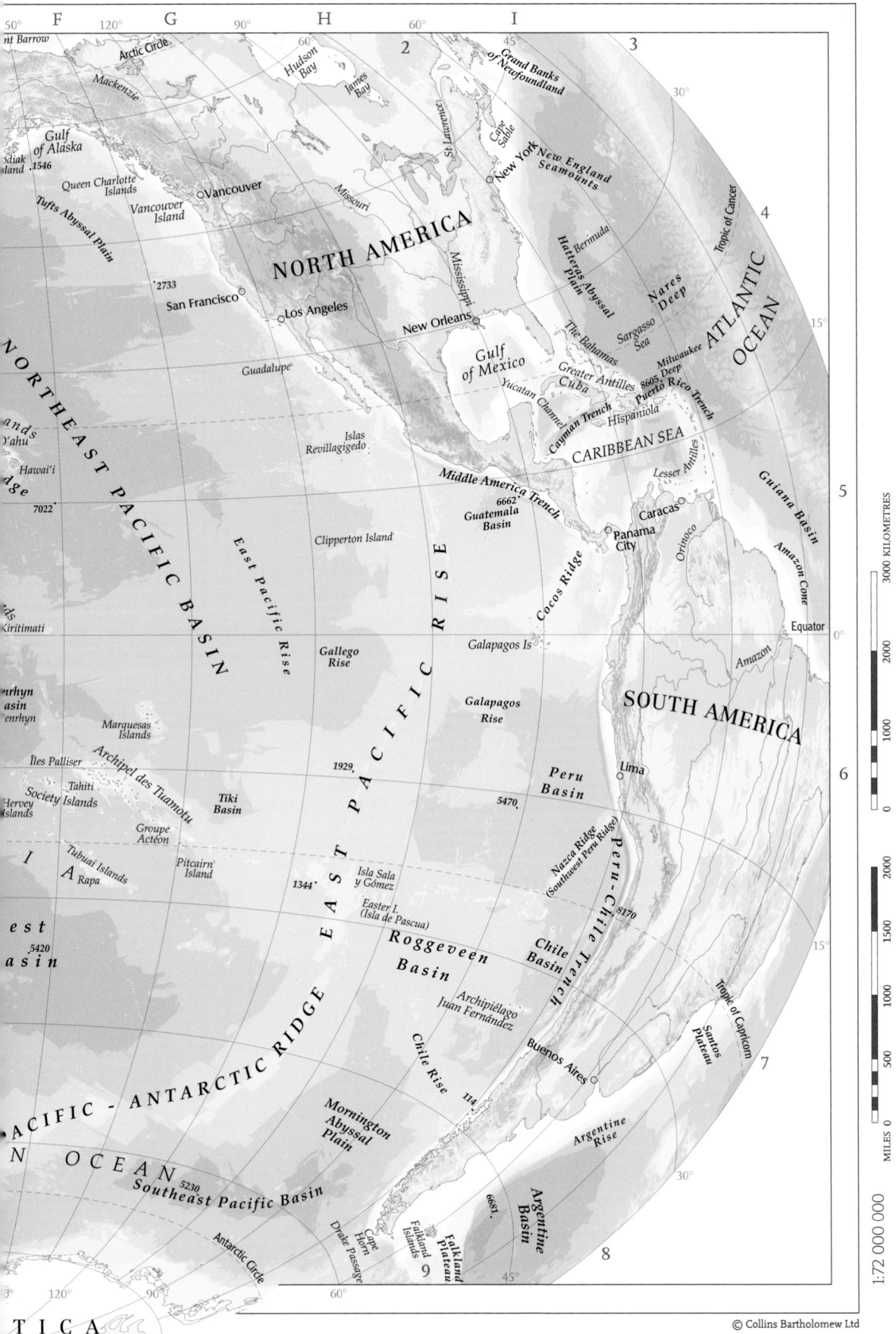

F   G   H   I

120°   90°   60°

50°

nt Barrow

Arctic Circle

Mackenzie

Hudson
Bay

James
Bay

60°

2

Grand Banks
of Newfoundland

3

Gulf
of Alaska

odiak
land ·1546

Queen Charlotte
Islands

Vancouver

Vancouver
Island

Missouri

St. Lawrence

Cape
Sable

New York

New England
Seamounts

30°

Tufts Abyssal Plain

·2733

San Francisco

Los Angeles

NORTH AMERICA

Mississippi

Bermuda

Hatteras Abyssal
Plain

Sargasso
Sea

Nares
Deep

ATLANTIC

OCEAN

4

15°

Guadalupe

New Orleans

Gulf
of Mexico

The Bahamas

Milwaukee
8605 Deep

ands
Yahu

Hawai'i

Islas
Revillagigedo

Yucatan Channel

Greater Antilles
Cuba

Hispaniola

Puerto Rico Trench

NORTHEAST

7022·

Middle America Trench

Cayman Trench

CARIBBEAN SEA

Lesser Antilles

Guiana Basin

5

PACIFIC

East Pacific Rise

Clipperton Island

6662
Guatemala
Basin

Cocos Ridge

Caracas

Panama
City

Orinoco

Amazon Cone

BASIN

EAST

Kiritimati

Galapagos Is

Galapagos
Rise

SOUTH AMERICA

Amazon

Equator   0°

rhyn
asin
enrhyn

Marquesas
Islands

PACIFIC

1929.

Peru
Basin

Lima

6

Îles Palliser

Archipel des Tuamotu

Tahiti

Tiki
Basin

5470.

Nazca Ridge
(Southwest Peru Ridge)

Society
Islands
Hervey
slands

RISE

Groupe
Actéon

8170

Peru-Chile Trench

15°

I
A
Rapa

Tubuai Islands

Pitcairn
Island

1344·

Isla Sala
y Gómez

Chile
Basin

Easter I.
(Isla de Pascua)

Roggeveen
Basin

Archipiélago
Juan Fernández

Buenos Aires

est
asin

·5420

EAST

Chile Rise

114

Tropic of Capricorn

Santos
Plateau

7

PACIFIC – ANTARCTIC RIDGE

Mornington
Abyssal
Plain

Argentine
Rise

30°

N   OCEAN

5230
Southeast Pacific Basin

Cape
Horn

6681

Drake Passage

Falkland
Islands

Argentine
Basin

Falkland
Plateau

8

Antarctic Circle

9

120°   90°

60°

45°

TICA

1:72 000 000

3000 KILOMETRES

2000

1000

0

2000

1500

1000

500

MILES 0

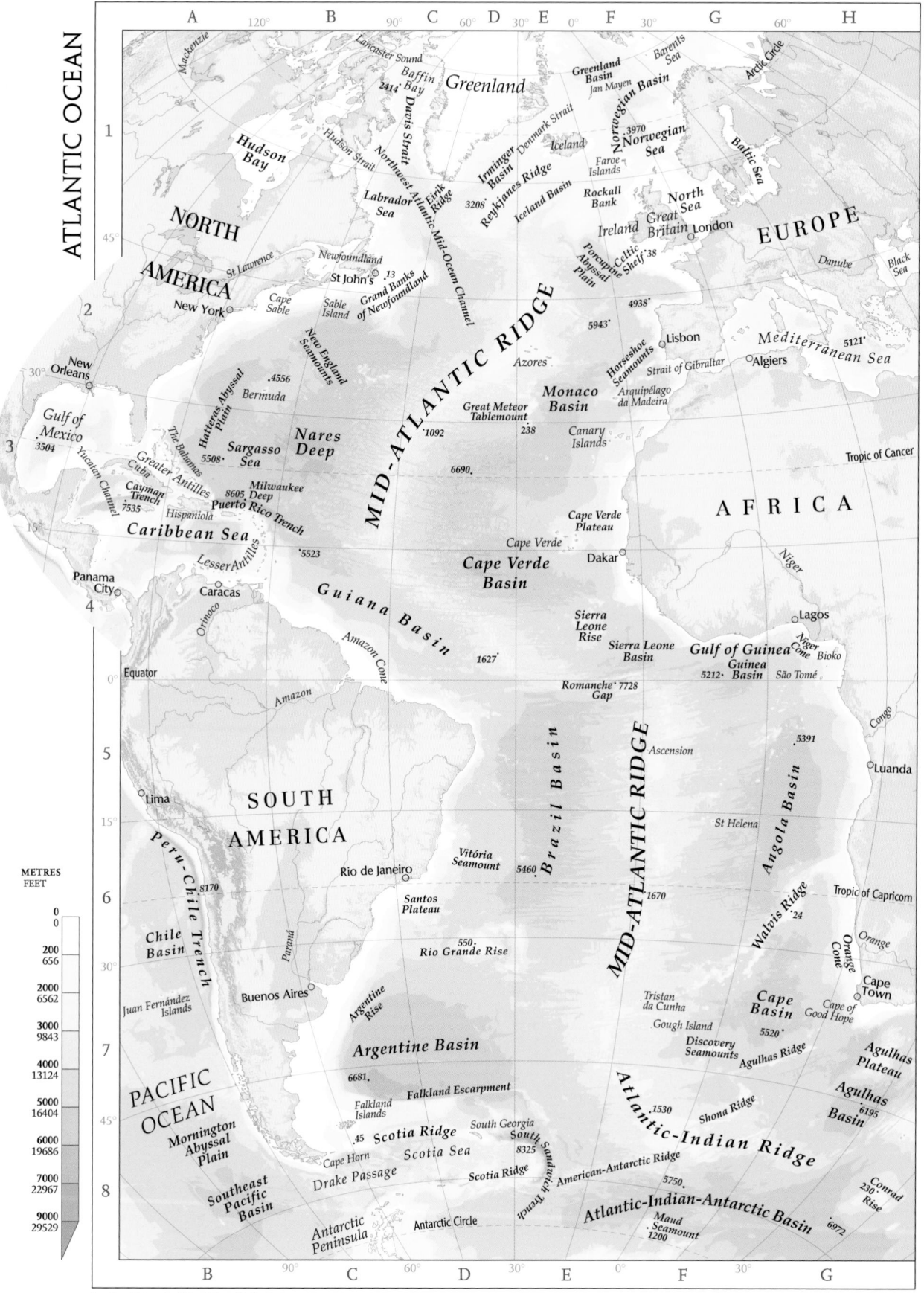

Mackenzie

Lancaster Sound

Greenland Basin
Jan Mayen

Barents Sea

Arctic Circle

120°

90°

60°

30°

0°

30°

60°

A B C D E F G H

Baffin Bay
2414

Greenland

Hudson Bay

Davis Strait

Northwest Atlantic Mid-Ocean Channel

Irminger Basin

Denmark Strait

Iceland

Norwegian Basin

Norwegian Sea
3970

Faroe Islands

Baltic Sea

1

Hudson Strait

Eirik Ridge

Reykjanes Ridge

3208

Iceland Basin

Rockall Bank

North Sea

NORTH

Labrador Sea

Ireland

Great Britain
London

EUROPE

45°

St Lawrence

Newfoundland

Porcupine Abyssal Plain

Celtic Shelf
38

Danube

Black Sea

AMERICA

St John's
13

Grand Banks of Newfoundland

2

New York

Cape Sable

Sable Island

4938

Mediterranean Sea

5121

30°

New Orleans

New England Seamounts

MID-ATLANTIC RIDGE

5943

Horseshoe Seamounts

Lisbon

Strait of Gibraltar

Algiers

Gulf of Mexico
3504

.4556

Bermuda

Great Meteor Tablemount

Azores

Monaco Basin

Arquipélago da Madeira

Hatteras Abyssal Plain

Nares Deep

238

Tropic of Cancer

3

Greater Antilles
Cuba

The Bahamas

5508

Sargasso Sea

1092

6690

Canary Islands

AFRICA

Cayman Trench
7535

8605 Milwaukee Deep
Puerto Rico Trench

Hispaniola

Cape Verde Plateau

Niger

15°

Caribbean Sea

Lesser Antilles

5523

Cape Verde

Dakar

Cape Verde Basin

Panama City

Caracas

Orinoco

Guiana Basin

Sierra Leone Rise

Lagos

4

Amazon Cone

1627

Sierra Leone Basin

Gulf of Guinea

Niger Cone
Bioko

Equator

Amazon

Romanche 7728 Gap

5212

Guinea Basin

São Tomé

0°

SOUTH

Brazil Basin

Ascension

5391

Congo

Luanda

5

AMERICA

Angola Basin

15°

Peru-Chile Trench

8170

Vitória Seamount

St Helena

Lima

Rio de Janeiro

5460

MID-ATLANTIC RIDGE

METRES
FEET

Santos Plateau

1670

Walvis Ridge
24

Tropic of Capricorn

6

0 / 0

Chile Basin

Paraná

550
Rio Grande Rise

Orange Cone

Orange

200 / 656

Juan Fernández Islands

Argentine Rise

Tristan da Cunha

Cape Basin

Cape of Good Hope

Cape Town

2000 / 6562

Buenos Aires

Gough Island

5520

3000 / 9843

7

4000 / 13124

Argentine Basin

Discovery Seamounts

Agulhas Ridge

Agulhas Plateau

5000 / 16404

6681

Falkland Islands

Falkland Escarpment

1530

Shona Ridge

Agulhas Basin
6195

6000 / 19686

PACIFIC OCEAN

45°

Mornington Abyssal Plain

45 Scotia Ridge

South Georgia

Atlantic-Indian Ridge

7000 / 22967

Cape Horn

Drake Passage

Scotia Sea

8325
South Sandwich Trench

Conrad 230 Rise

9000 / 29529

Southeast Pacific Basin

Scotia Ridge

American-Antarctic Ridge

5750

6972

8

Antarctic Peninsula

Antarctic Circle

Atlantic-Indian-Antarctic Basin

Maud Seamount
1200

90° 60° 30° 0° 30°

B C D E F G

Lambert Azimuthal Equal Area Projection

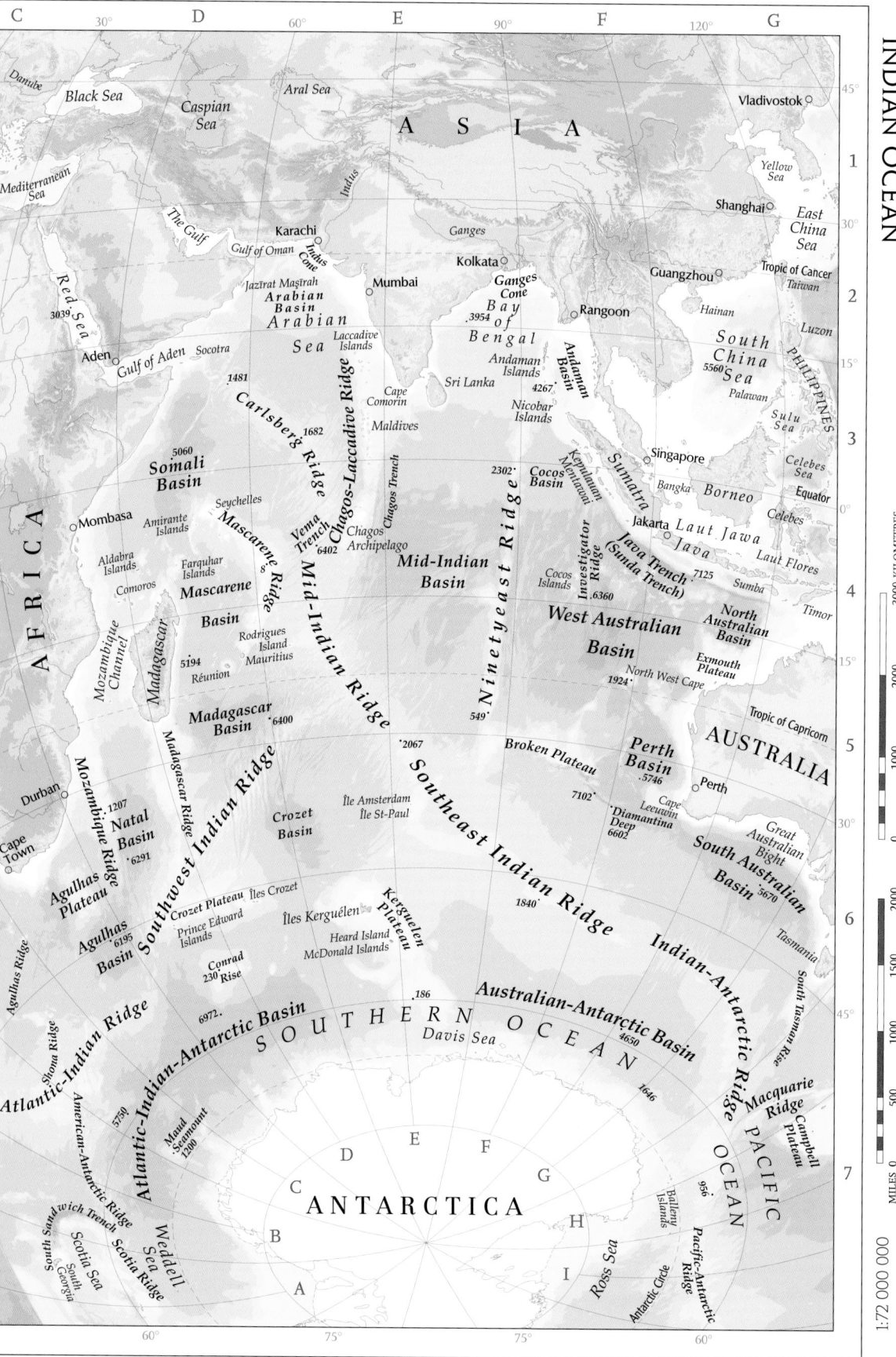

C · 30° · D · 60° · E · 90° · F · 120° · G

ASIA

Danube
Black Sea
Caspian Sea
Aral Sea
Vladivostok
1

Mediterranean Sea
The Gulf
Karachi
Indus
Indus Cone
Ganges
Kolkata
Guangzhou
Shanghai
Yellow Sea
East China Sea
Tropic of Cancer
Taiwan

Red Sea
3039
Gulf of Oman
Jazīrat Maşīrah
Arabian Basin
Mumbai
Ganges Cone
Rangoon
Hainan
South China Sea
Luzon
2

Aden
Gulf of Aden · Socotra
Arabian Sea
Laccadive Islands
.3954
Bay of Bengal
Andaman Basin
5560
PHILIPPINES

1481
Cape Comorin
Sri Lanka
Andaman Islands
4267
Palawan
Sulu Sea
15°

Carlsberg Ridge
1682
Maldives
Nicobar Islands
Singapore
Celebes Sea
3

Somali Basin
5060
Chagos-Laccadive Ridge
Chagos Trench
2302.
Cocos Basin
Kepulauan Mentawai
Sumatra
Bangka
Borneo
Jakarta
Laut Jawa
Celebes
Equator
0°

Mombasa
Seychelles
Amirante Islands
Mascarene Ridge
Vema Trench
6402
Chagos Archipelago
Ninetyeast Ridge
Investigator Ridge
.6360
Java Trench (Sunda Trench)
Java
7125
Laut Flores
Sumba
Timor
4

Aldabra Islands
Comoros
Farquhar Islands
Mascarene Basin
8.
Mid-Indian Ridge
Mid-Indian Basin
Cocos Islands
West Australian Basin
North Australian Basin

AFRICA
Mozambique Channel
Madagascar
5194
Rodrigues Island
Mauritius
Réunion
549.
Exmouth Plateau
North West Cape
15°

Madagascar Basin
.6400
2067
Broken Plateau
1924.
Tropic of Capricorn
AUSTRALIA

Durban
1207
Madagascar Ridge
.2067
Perth Basin
.5746
Perth
5

Cape Town
Natal Basin
.6291
Southwest Indian Ridge
Crozet Basin
Île Amsterdam Île St-Paul
Southeast Indian Ridge
7102.
Cape Leeuwin
Diamantina Deep
6602
Great Australian Bight
30°

Agulhas Plateau
Agulhas Basin
6195
Crozet Plateau
Prince Edward Islands
Îles Crozet
Îles Kerguélen
Kerguelen Plateau
1840.
South Australian Basin
.5670

Agulhas Ridge
Agulhas
Conrad Rise 230
Heard Island
McDonald Islands
Indian-Antarctic Ridge
Tasmania
6

Shona Ridge
5759.
Atlantic-Indian Ridge
6972.
186.
Australian-Antarctic Basin
4650.
Macquarie Ridge
South Tasman Rise
45°

American-Antarctic Ridge
Maud Seamount
1200
Atlantic-Indian-Antarctic Basin
SOUTHERN OCEAN
Davis Sea
1646.
Campbell Plateau
PACIFIC

South Sandwich Trench
Scotia Sea
South Georgia
Scotia Ridge
Weddell Sea
D
E
F
G
956.
Balleny Islands
Pacific-Antarctic Ridge
OCEAN
7

C
B
A
ANTARCTICA
H
I
Ross Sea
Antarctic Circle

60° · 75° · 75° · 60°

3000 KILOMETRES
2000
1000
0

2000
1500
1000
500
0
MILES

1:72 000 000

© Collins Bartholomew Ltd

175

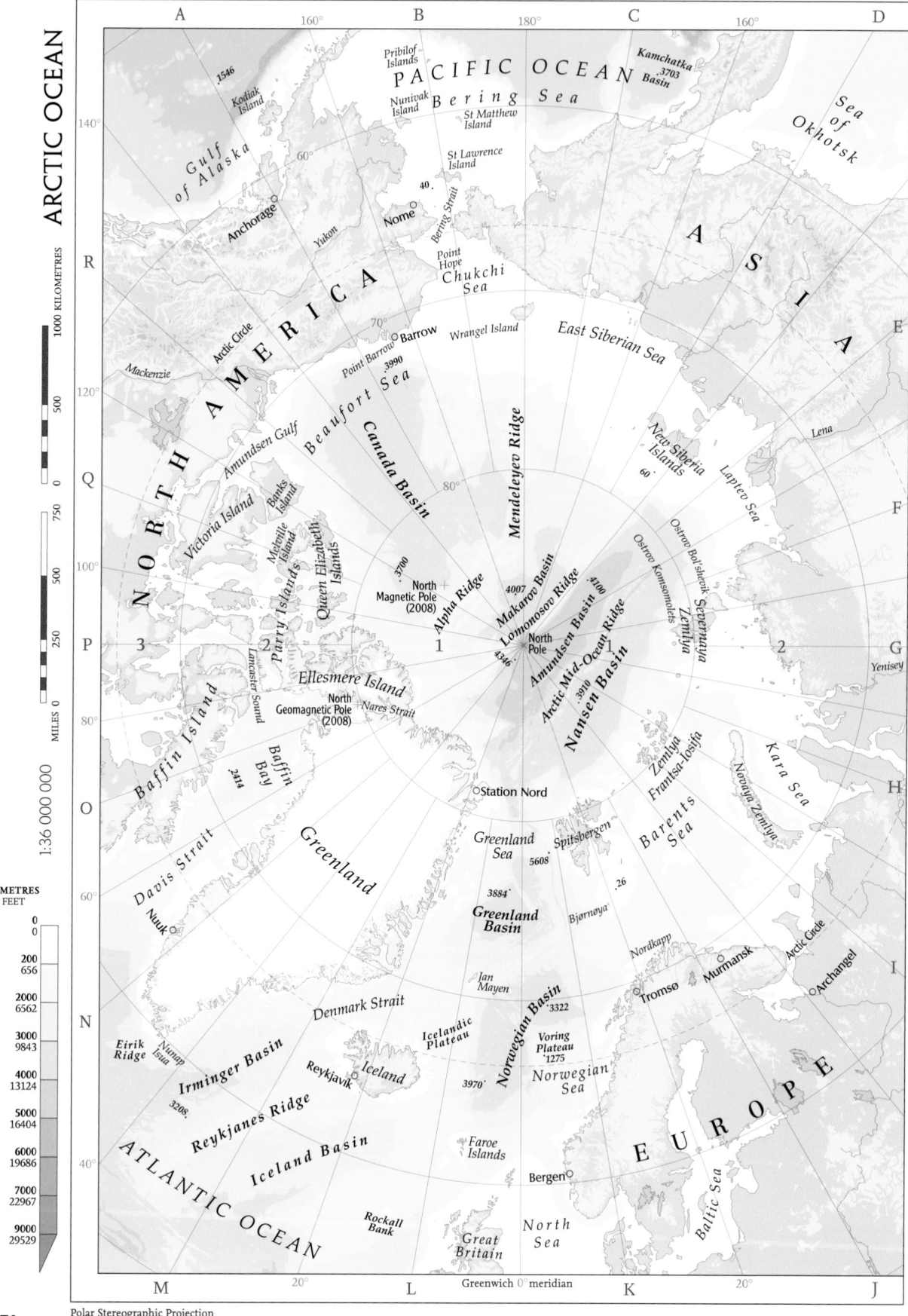

1000 KILOMETRES

500

0

750

500

250

MILES 0

1:36 000 000

METRES
FEET

0	0
200	656
2000	6562
3000	9843
4000	13124
5000	16404
6000	19686
7000	22967
9000	29529

Polar Stereographic Projection

PACIFIC OCEAN

Pribilof
Islands

Bering Sea

Kamchatka
.3703
Basin

.1546

Kodiak
Island

Nunivak
Island

St Matthew
Island

Sea
of
Okhotsk

Gulf
of Alaska

60°

St Lawrence
Island

40.

Nome

Bering Strait

A S I A

Anchorage

Yukon

Point
Hope

Chukchi
Sea

R

Arctic Circle

70°

Point Barrow

Barrow

Wrangel Island

East Siberian Sea

E

Mackenzie

120°

3990

Beaufort Sea

New Siberia
Islands

Lena

N O R T H   A M E R I C A

Amundsen Gulf

Canada Basin

Mendeleyev Ridge

60

Laptev Sea

Q

80°

Ostrov Bol'shevik

F

Victoria Island

Banks
Island

Ostrov Komsomolets

Severnaya
Zemlya

5700

Makarov Basin

4007

Lomonosov Ridge

North
Magnetic Pole
(2008)

Alpha Ridge

1

1

100°

Melville
Island

Queen Elizabeth
Islands

Parry Islands

4100

2

G

P

3

North
Pole

4546

Amundsen Basin

Arctic Mid-Ocean Ridge

Yenisey

Lancaster Sound

1

3910

Nansen Basin

Ellesmere Island

North
Geomagnetic Pole
(2008)

Nares Strait

Zemlya
Frantsa-Iosifa

Kara
Sea

80°

Baffin Island

Baffin
Bay

2414

Station Nord

Barents
Sea

Novaya Zemlya

H

O

Davis Strait

Greenland

Greenland
Sea

Spitsbergen

5608

.26

60°

3884

Bjørnøya

Nuuk

Greenland
Basin

Nordkapp

Arctic Circle

Murmansk

Archangel

I

N

Jan
Mayen

Tromsø

Denmark Strait

Icelandic
Plateau

Norwegian Basin

3322

Voring
Plateau
1275

Eirik
Ridge

Nunap
Isua

Irminger Basin

Reykjavik

Iceland

3970

Norwegian
Sea

E U R O P E

3208.

Reykjanes Ridge

Faroe
Islands

Bergen

Baltic Sea

40°

Iceland Basin

A T L A N T I C   O C E A N

Rockall
Bank

Great
Britain

North
Sea

A 160° B 180° C 160° D

M 20° L Greenwich 0° meridian K 20° J

WORLD FACTS AND FIGURES

	Total Population	2050 Projected Population	Gross National Income (GNI) Per Capita (US$)	Literacy Rate (%)	International Dialling Code	Time Zone	Official Website *Tourism Website*
WORLD	6 651 873 557	9 075 903 000	1 700	80.1	...	...	
AFGHANISTAN	27 145 000	97 324 000	...	28.0	93	+4.5	... ...
ALBANIA	3 190 000	3 458 000	2 930	99.0	355	+1	www.km.gov.al *www.albaniantourism.com*
ALGERIA	33 858 000	49 500 000	3 030	75.4	213	+1	www.el-mouradia.dz *www.matet.dz*
ANDORRA	75 000	58 000	...	...	376	+1	www.andorra.ad *www.andorra.ad*
ANGOLA	17 024 000	43 501 000	1 970	67.4	244	+1	www.angola.org *www.angola.org.uk/prov_tourism.htm*
ANTIGUA AND BARBUDA	85 000	112 000	11 050	...	1 268	-4	www.ab.gov.ag *www.antigua-barbuda.org*
ARGENTINA	39 531 000	51 382 000	5 150	97.6	54	-3	www.info.gov.ar *www.turismo.gov.ar*
ARMENIA	3 002 000	2 506 000	1 920	99.5	374	+4	www.gov.am *www.turismo.gov.ar*
AUSTRALIA	20 743 000	27 940 000	35 860	...	61	+8 to +10.5	www.gov.au *www.australia.com*
AUSTRIA	8 361 000	8 073 000	39 750	...	43	+1	www.oesterreich.at *www.austria.info*
AZERBAIJAN	8 467 000	9 631 000	1 840	99.4	994	+4	www.president.az ...
THE BAHAMAS	331 000	466 000	...	...	1 242	-5	www.bahamas.gov.bs *www.bahamas.com*
BAHRAIN	753 000	1 155 000	19 350	88.8	973	+3	www.bahrain.gov.bh *www.bahraintourism.com*
BANGLADESH	158 665 000	242 937 000	450	53.5	880	+6	www.bangladesh.gov.bd *www.parjatan.org*
BARBADOS	294 000	255 000	...	...	1 246	-4	www.barbados.gov.bb *www.barbados.org/bta.htm*
BELARUS	9 689 000	7 017 000	3 470	99.7	375	+2	www.government.by *www.mst.by*
BELGIUM	10 457 000	10 302 000	38 460	...	32	+1	www.belgium.be *www.visitflanders.com Wallonia: www.opt.b*
BELIZE	288 000	442 000	3 740	...	501	-6	www.belize.gov.bz *www.travelbelize.org*
BENIN	9 033 000	22 123 000	530	40.5	229	+1	www.gouv.bj *www.benintourisme.com*
BHUTAN	658 000	4 393 000	1 430	55.6	975	+6	www.bhutan.gov.bt *www.tourism.gov.bt*
BOLIVIA	9 525 000	14 908 000	1 100	90.3	591	-4	www.bolivia.gov.bo ...
BOSNIA-HERZEGOVINA	3 935 000	3 170 000	3 230	96.7	387	+1	www.fbihvlada.gov.ba *www.bhtourism.ba*
BOTSWANA	1 882 000	1 658 000	5 570	82.9	267	+2	www.gov.bw ...
BRAZIL	191 791 000	253 105 000	4 710	90.5	55	-2 to -5	www.brazil.gov.br *www.braziltour.com*
BRUNEI	390 000	681 000	26 930	94.9	673	+8	www.brunei.gov.bn *www.tourismbrunei.com*
BULGARIA	7 639 000	5 065 000	3 990	98.3	359	+2	www.government.bg *www.bulgariatravel.org*
BURKINA	14 784 000	39 093 000	440	28.7	226	GMT	www.primature.gov.bf *www.culture.gov.bf*
BURUNDI	8 508 000	25 812 000	100	59.3	257	+2	www.burundi.gov.bi ...
CAMBODIA	14 444 000	25 972 000	490	76.3	855	+7	www.cambodia.gov.kh *www.visit-mekong.com/cambodia/mot/*
CAMEROON	18 549 000	26 891 000	990	67.9	237	+1	... ...
CANADA	32 876 000	42 844 000	36 650	...	1	-3.5 to -8	canada.gc.ca *www.canada.travel*
CAPE VERDE	530 000	1 002 000	2 130	83.8	238	-1	www.governo.cv ...
CENTRAL AFRICAN REPUBLIC	4 343 000	6 747 000	350	48.6	236	+1	www.spm.gov.cm ...
CHAD	10 781 000	31 497 000	450	25.7	235	+1	www.primature-tchad.org ...
CHILE	16 635 000	20 657 000	6 810	96.5	56	-4	www.gobiernodechile.cl *www.visit-chile.org*

	Total Population	2050 Projected Population	Gross National Income (GNI) Per Capita (US$)	Literacy Rate (%)	International Dialling Code	Time Zone	Official Website / *Tourism Website*
CHINA	1 313 437 000	1 402 062 000	2 000	93.3	86	+8	www.china.org.cn ...
COLOMBIA	46 156 000	65 679 000	3 120	93.6	57	-5	www.gobiernoenlinea.gov.co *www.idct.gov.co*
COMOROS	839 000	1 781 000	660	75.1	269	+3	www.beit-salam.km ...
CONGO	3 768 000	13 721 000	1 050	86.8	242	+1	www.congo-site.com ...
CONGO, DEMOCRATIC REPUBLIC OF THE	62 636 000	177 271 000	130	67.2	243	+1 to +2	www.un.int/drcongo ...
COSTA RICA	4 468 000	6 426 000	4 980	95.9	506	-6	www.casapres.go.cr *www.visitcostarica.com*
CÔTE D'IVOIRE	19 262 000	33 959 000	880	48.7	225	GMT	www.cotedivoire-pr.ci *www.tourismeci.org*
CROATIA	4 555 000	3 686 000	9 310	98.7	385	+1	www.vlada.hr *www.croatia.hr*
CUBA	11 268 000	9 749 000	...	99.8	53	-5	www.cubagob.gov.cu *www.cubatravel.cu*
CYPRUS	855 000	1 174 000	23 270	97.7	357	+2	www.cyprus.gov.cy *www.visitcyprus.com*
CZECH REPUBLIC	10 186 000	8 452 000	12 790	...	420	+1	www.czech.cz *www.czechtourism.com*
DENMARK	5 442 000	5 851 000	52 110	...	45	+1	www.denmark.dk *www.visitdenmark.com*
DJIBOUTI	833 000	1 547 000	1 060	...	253	+3	www.presidence.dj *www.office-tourisme.dj*
DOMINICA	67 000	98 000	4 160	...	1 767	-4	www.ndcdominica.dm *www.ndcdominica.dm*
DOMINICAN REPUBLIC	9 760 000	12 668 000	2 910	89.1	1 809	-4	www.cig.gov.do ...
EAST TIMOR	1 155 000	3 265 000	840	...	670	+9	www.timor-leste.gov.tl ...
ECUADOR	13 341 000	19 214 000	2 910	92.6	593	-5	... *www.vivecuador.com*
EGYPT	75 498 000	125 916 000	1 360	72.0	20	+2	www.sis.gov.eg ...
EL SALVADOR	6 857 000	10 823 000	2 680	85.5	503	-6	www.casapres.gob.sv *www.elsalvador.travel*
EQUATORIAL GUINEA	507 000	1 146 000	8 510	...	240	+1	www.ceiba-equatorial-guinea.org ...
ERITREA	4 851 000	11 229 000	190	...	291	+3	shabait.com ...
ESTONIA	1 335 000	1 119 000	11 400	99.8	372	+2	www.valitsus.ee *visitestonia.com*
ETHIOPIA	83 099 000	170 190 000	170	35.9	251	+3	www.ethiopar.net *www.tourismethiopia.org*
FIJI	839 000	934 000	3 720	...	679	+12	www.fiji.gov.fj *www.bulafiji.com*
FINLAND	5 277 000	5 329 000	41 360	...	358	+2	www.valtioneuvosto.fi *www.visitfinland.com*
FRANCE	61 647 000	63 116 000	36 560	...	33	+1	www.premier-ministre.gouv.fr *www.franceguide.com*
GABON	1 331 000	2 279 000	5 360	86.2	241	+1	www.legabon.org *www.tourisme-gabon.com*
THE GAMBIA	1 709 000	3 106 000	290	...	220	GMT	www.statehouse.gm ...
GEORGIA	4 395 000	2 985 000	1 580	...	995	+4	www.parliament.ge ...
GERMANY	82 599 000	78 765 000	36 810	...	49	+1	www.bundesregierung.de *www.germany-tourism.de*
GHANA	23 478 000	40 573 000	510	65.0	233	GMT	www.ghana.gov.gh *www.touringghana.com*
GREECE	11 147 000	10 742 000	27 390	97.1	30	+2	www.greece.gov.gr *www.gnto.gr*
GRENADA	106 000	157 000	4 650	...	1 473	-4	www.gov.gd *grenadagrenadines.com*
GUATEMALA	13 354 000	25 612 000	2 590	73.2	502	-6	www.congreso.gob.gt ...
GUINEA	9 370 000	22 987 000	400	29.5	224	GMT	... *www.mirinet.net.gn/ont/*
GUINEA-BISSAU	1 695 000	5 312 000	190	64.6	245	GMT	www.republica-da-guine-bissau.org ...

	Total Population	2050 Projected Population	Gross National Income (GNI) Per Capita (US$)	Literacy Rate (%)	International Dialling Code	Time Zone	Official Website Tourism Website
GUYANA	738 000	488 000	1 150	...	592	-4	www.gina.gov.gy www.guyana-tourism.com
HAITI	9 598 000	12 996 000	430	62.1	509	-5	www.haiti.org www.haititourisme.org
HONDURAS	7 106 000	12 776 000	1 270	83.1	504	-6	www.congreso.gob.hn www.letsgohonduras.com
HUNGARY	10 030 000	8 262 000	10 870	98.9	36	+1	www.magyarorszag.hu www.hungarytourism.hu
ICELAND	301 000	370 000	49 960	...	354	GMT	www.iceland.is www.visiticeland.com
INDIA	1 169 016 000	1 592 704 000	820	66.0	91	+5.5	www.india.gov.in www.tourismofindia.com
INDONESIA	231 627 000	284 640 000	1 420	91.4	62	+7 to +9	... www.budpar.go.id
IRAN	71 208 000	101 944 000	2 930	84.7	98	+3.5	www.president.ir www.itto.org
IRAQ	28 993 000	63 693 000	...	74.1	964	+3	www.cabinet.iq ...
IRELAND	4 301 000	5 762 000	44 830	...	353	GMT	www.irlgov.ie www.discoverireland.ie
ISRAEL	6 928 000	10 403 000	20 170	...	972	+2	www.gov.il www.tourism.gov.il
ITALY	58 877 000	50 912 000	31 990	98.9	39	+1	www.governo.it www.enit.it
JAMAICA	2 714 000	2 586 000	3 560	86.0	1 876	-5	www.jis.gov.jm www.visitjamaica.com
JAPAN	127 967 000	112 198 000	38 630	...	81	+9	web-japan.org www.jnto.go.jp
JORDAN	5 924 000	10 225 000	2 650	93.1	962	+2	www.jordan.gov.jo www.see-jordan.com
KAZAKHSTAN	15 422 000	13 086 000	3 870	99.6	7	+5 to +6	www.government.kz ...
KENYA	37 538 000	83 073 000	580	73.6	254	+3	www.kenya.go.ke www.magicalkenya.com
KIRIBATI	95 000	177 000	1 240	...	686	+12 to +14	... ...
KOSOVO	2 070 000	...	...	...			... ...
KUWAIT	2 851 000	5 279 000	30 630	93.9	965	+3	www.kuwaitmission.com ...
KYRGYZSTAN	5 317 000	6 664 000	500	99.3	996	+6	www.gov.kg ...
LAOS	5 859 000	11 586 000	500	73.2	856	+7	www.un.int/lao ...
LATVIA	2 277 000	1 678 000	8 100	99.8	371	+2	www.saeima.lv www.latviatourism.lv
LEBANON	4 099 000	4 702 000	5 580	...	961	+2	www.presidency.gov.lb www.destinationlebanon.com
LESOTHO	2 008 000	1 601 000	980	82.2	266	+2	www.lesotho.gov.ls ...
LIBERIA	3 750 000	10 653 000	130	55.5	231	GMT	www.embassyofliberia.org ...
LIBYA	6 160 000	9 553 000	7 290	86.8	218	+2	www.micat.gov.lr ...
LIECHTENSTEIN	35 000	44 000	...	...	423	+1	www.liechtenstein.li www.tourismus.li
LITHUANIA	3 390 000	2 565 000	7 930	99.7	370	+2	www.lrv.lt www.tourism.lt
LUXEMBOURG	467 000	721 000	71 240	...	352	+1	www.gouvernement.lu www.ont.lu
MACEDONIA (F.Y.R.O.M.)	2 038 000	1 884 000	3 070	97.0	389	+1	www.vlada.mk www.exploringmacedonia.com
MADAGASCAR	19 683 000	43 508 000	280	70.7	261	+3	www.madagascar.gov.mg ...
MALAWI	13 925 000	29 452 000	230	71.8	265	+2	www.malawi.gov.mw ...
MALAYSIA	26 572 000	38 924 000	5 620	91.9	60	+8	www.gov.my www.tourism.gov.my
MALDIVES	306 000	682 000	3 010	97.0	960	+5	www.maldivesinfo.gov.mv www.visitmaldives.com
MALI	12 337 000	41 976 000	460	23.3	223	GMT	www.maliensdelexterieur.gov.ml www.malitourisme.com

	Total Population	2050 Projected Population	Gross National Income (GNI) Per Capita (US$)	Literacy Rate (%)	International Dialling Code	Time Zone	Official Website _Tourism Website_
MALTA	407 000	428 000	15 310	91.6	356	+1	www.gov.mt _www.visitmalta.com_
MARSHALL ISLANDS	59 000	150 000	2 980	…	692	+12	www.rmiembassyus.org _www.visitmarshallislands.com_
MAURITANIA	3 124 000	7 497 000	760	55.8	222	GMT	www.mauritania.mr _…_
MAURITIUS	1 262 000	1 465 000	5 430	87.4	230	+4	www.gov.mu _www.mauritius.net_
MEXICO	106 535 000	139 015 000	7 830	92.4	52	-6 to -8	www.gob.mx _www.visitmexico.com_
MICRONESIA, FEDERATED STATES OF	111 000	99 000	2 390	…	691	+10 to +11	www.fsmgov.org _visit-fsm.org_
MOLDOVA	3 794 000	3 312 000	1 080	99.2	373	+2	www.moldova.md _www.turism.md_
MONACO	33 000	55 000	…	…	377	+1	www.visitmonaco.com _www.monaco-congres.com_
MONGOLIA	2 629 000	3 625 000	1 000	97.3	976	+8	www.pmis.gov.mn _www.mongoliatourism.gov.mn_
MONTENEGRO	598 000	650 000	4 130	…	382	+1	www.montenegro.yu _www.visit-montenegro.com_
MOROCCO	31 224 000	46 397 000	2 160	55.6	212	GMT	www.maroc.ma _www.tourism-in-morocco.com_
MOZAMBIQUE	21 397 000	37 604 000	310	44.4	258	+2	www.mozambique.mz _…_
MYANMAR	48 798 000	63 657 000	…	89.9	95	+6.5	www.myanmar.com _www.myanmar-tourism.com_
NAMIBIA	2 074 000	3 060 000	3 210	88.0	264	+1	www.grnnet.gov.na _www.namibiatourism.com.na_
NAURU	10 000	18 000	…	…	674	+12	www.un.int/nauru _…_
NEPAL	28 196 000	51 172 000	320	56.5	977	+5.75	www.nepalhmg.gov.np _www.welcomenepal.com_
NETHERLANDS	16 419 000	17 139 000	43 050	…	31	+1	www.overheid.nl _www.us.holland.com_
NEW ZEALAND	4 179 000	4 790 000	26 750	…	64	+12 to +12.75	www.newzealand.govt.nz _www.newzealand.com_
NICARAGUA	5 603 000	9 371 000	930	80.5	505	-6	www.asamblea.gob.ni _www.visit-nicaragua.com_
NIGER	14 226 000	50 156 000	270	30.4	227	+1	_…_ _…_
NIGERIA	148 093 000	258 108 000	620	72.0	234	+1	www.nigeria.gov.ng _www.nigeriatourism.net_
NORTH KOREA	23 790 000	24 192 000	…	…	850	+9	www.korea-dpr.com _…_
NORWAY	4 698 000	5 435 000	68 440	…	47	+1	www.norway.no _www.visitnorway.com_
OMAN	2 595 000	4 958 000	11 120	84.4	968	+4	www.omanet.om _www.omantourism.gov.om_
PAKISTAN	163 902 000	304 700 000	800	54.9	92	+5	www.infopak.gov.pk _www.tourism.gov.pk_
PALAU	20 000	21 000	7 990	…	680	+9	www.palauembassy.com _visit-palau.com_
PANAMA	3 343 000	5 093 000	5 000	93.4	507	-5	www.pa _www.visitpanama.com_
PAPUA NEW GUINEA	6 331 000	10 619 000	740	57.8	675	+10	www.pngonline.gov.pg _www.pngtourism.org.pg/_
PARAGUAY	6 127 000	12 095 000	1 410	93.7	595	-4	www.presidencia.gov.py _www.senatur.gov.py_
PERU	27 903 000	42 552 000	2 980	90.5	51	-5	www.peru.gob.pe _www.peru.info_
PHILIPPINES	87 960 000	127 068 000	1 390	93.4	63	+8	www.gov.ph _www.tourism.gov.ph_
POLAND	38 082 000	31 916 000	8 210	99.3	48	+1	www.poland.gov.pl _www.poland.travel/en/_
PORTUGAL	10 623 000	10 723 000	17 850	94.9	351	GMT	www.portugal.gov.pt _www.visitportugal.com_
QATAR	841 000	1 330 000	…	90.2	974	+3	www.mofa.gov.qa _www.experienceqatar.com_
ROMANIA	21 438 000	16 757 000	4 830	97.6	40	+2	www.guv.ro _www.romaniatravel.com_
RUSSIAN FEDERATION	142 499 000	111 752 000	5 770	99.5	7	+2 to +12	www.gov.ru _www.russiatourism.ru_

	Total Population	2050 Projected Population	Gross National Income (GNI) Per Capita (US$)	Literacy Rate (%)	International Dialling Code	Time Zone	Official Website Tourism Website
RWANDA	9 725 000	18 153 000	250	64.9	250	+2	www.gov.rw www.rwandatourism.com
ST KITTS AND NEVIS	50 000	59 000	8 460	...	1 869	-4	www.gov.kn www.stkittstourism.kn
ST LUCIA	165 000	188 000	5 060	...	1 758	-4	www.stlucia.gov.lc www.stlucia.org
ST VINCENT AND THE GRENADINES	120 000	105 000	3 320	...	1 784	-4	... www.svgtourism.com
SAMOA	187 000	157 000	2 270	98.7	685	-11	www.govt.ws www.visitsamoa.ws
SAN MARINO	31 000	30 000	45 130	...	378	+1	www.consigliograndeegenerale.sm www.visitsanmarino.com
SÃO TOMÉ AND PRÍNCIPE	158 000	295 000	800	87.9	239	GMT	www.parlamento.st www.saotome.st
SAUDI ARABIA	24 735 000	49 464 000	13 980	85.0	966	+3	www.saudinf.com ...
SENEGAL	12 379 000	23 108 000	760	42.6	221	GMT	www.gouv.sn www.senegal-tourism.com
SERBIA	7 788 000	...	4 030	...	381	+1	www.srbija.gov.rs www.serbia-tourism.org
SEYCHELLES	87 000	99 000	8 870	91.8	248	+4	www.virtualseychelles.sc www.virtualseychelles.sc
SIERRA LEONE	5 866 000	13 786 000	240	38.1	232	GMT	www.statehouse-sl.org ...
SINGAPORE	4 436 000	5 213 000	28 730	94.4	65	+8	www.gov.sg www.visitsingapore.com
SLOVAKIA	5 390 000	4 612 000	9 610	...	421	+1	www.government.gov.sk www.slovakia.travel
SLOVENIA	2 002 000	1 630 000	18 660	99.7	386	+1	www.gov.si www.slovenia.info
SOLOMON ISLANDS	496 000	921 000	690	...	677	+11	www.commerce.gov.sb www.commerce.gov.sb
SOMALIA	8 699 000	21 329 000	...	...	252	+3	www.somali-gov.info ...
SOUTH AFRICA, REPUBLIC OF	48 577 000	48 660 000	5 390	88.0	27	+2	www.gov.za www.southafrica.net
SOUTH KOREA	48 224 000	44 629 000	17 690	...	82	+9	www.korea.net english.visitkorea.or.kr
SPAIN	44 279 000	42 541 000	27 340	97.4	34	+1	www.la-moncloa.es www.spain.info
SRI LANKA	19 299 000	23 554 000	1 310	91.5	94	+5.5	www.priu.gov.lk www.srilankatourism.org
SUDAN	38 560 000	66 705 000	800	60.9	249	+3	www.sudan.gov.sd ...
SURINAME	458 000	429 000	4 210	90.4	597	-3	www.kabinet.sr.org www.mintct.sr
SWAZILAND	1 141 000	1 026 000	2 400	79.6	268	+2	www.gov.sz ...
SWEDEN	9 119 000	10 054 000	43 530	...	46	+1	www.sweden.se www.visitsweden.com
SWITZERLAND	7 484 000	7 252 000	58 050	...	41	+1	www.admin.ch www.myswitzerland.com
SYRIA	19 929 000	35 935 000	1 560	83.1	963	+2	www.moi-syria.com www.syriatourism.org
TAIWAN	22 880 000	...	...	...	886	+8	www.gov.tw www.tbroc.gov.tw
TAJIKISTAN	6 736 000	10 423 000	390	99.6	992	+5	www.tjus.org ...
TANZANIA	40 454 000	66 845 000	350	72.3	255	+3	www.tanzania.go.tz www.tanzaniatouristboard.com
THAILAND	63 884 000	74 594 000	3 050	94.1	66	+7	www.thaigov.go.th www.tourismthailand.org
TOGO	6 585 000	13 544 000	350	53.2	228	GMT	www.republicoftogo.com ...
TONGO	100 000	75 000	2 250	99.2	676	+13	www.pmo.gov.to www.tongaholiday.com
TRINIDAD AND TOBAGO	1 333 000	1 230 000	12 500	98.7	1 868	-4	www.gov.tt www.gotrinidadandtobago.com
TUNISIA	10 327 000	12 927 000	2 970	77.7	216	+1	www.tunisiaonline.com www.tourismtunisia.coom
TURKEY	74 877 000	101 208 000	5 400	88.7	90	+2	www.mfa.gov.tr www.kultur.gov.tr

	Total Population	2050 Projected Population	Gross National Income (GNI) Per Capita (US$)	Literacy Rate (%)	International Dialling Code	Time Zone	Official Website *Tourism Website*
TURKMENISTAN	4 965 000	6 780 000	...	99.5	993	+5	www.turkmenistanembassy.org *www.turkmenistanembassy.org*
TUVALU	11 000	12 000	...	...	688	+12	... *www.timelesstuvalu.com*
UGANDA	30 884 000	126 950 000	300	73.6	256	+3	www.mofa.go.ug *www.visituganda.com*
UKRAINE	46 205 000	26 393 000	1 940	99.7	380	+2	www.kmu.gov.ua *www.tourism.gov.ua*
UNITED ARAB EMIRATES	4 380 000	9 056 000	...	90.4	971	+4	www.government.ae *...*
UNITED KINGDOM	60 769 000	67 143 000	40 560	...	44	GMT	www.direct.gov.uk *www.visitbritain.com*
UNITED STATES OF AMERICA	305 826 000	394 976 000	44 710	...	1	-5 to -10	www.usa.gov *www.seeamerica.org*
URUGUAY	3 340 000	4 043 000	5 310	98.0	598	-3	www.presidencia.gub.uy *www.turismo.gub.uy*
UZBEKISTAN	27 372 000	38 665 000	610	96.9	998	+5	www.gov.uz *www.uzbektourism.uz*
VANUATU	226 000	375 000	1 690	78.1	678	+11	www.vanuatugovernment.gov.vu *www.vanuatutourism.com*
VATICAN CITY	557	1 000	...	...	39	+1	www.vatican.va *www.vaticanstate.va*
VENEZUELA	27 657 000	41 991 000	6 070	93.0	58	-4.5	www.gobiernoenlinea.ve *...*
VIETNAM	87 375 000	116 654 000	700	...	84	+7	www.na.gov.vn *www.vietnamtourism.com*
YEMEN	22 389 000	59 454 000	760	58.9	967	+3	www.nic.gov.ye *www.yementourism.com*
ZAMBIA	11 922 000	22 781 000	630	...	260	+2	www.statehouse.gov.zm *www.zambiatourism.com*
ZIMBABWE	13 349 000	15 805 000	340	91.2	263	+2	www.zim.gov.zw *www.zimbabwetourism.co.zw*

INDICATOR	DEFINITION
Total population	Interpolated mid-year population, 2007.
2050 projected population	Projected total population for the year 2050.
GNI per capita	Gross National Income per person in U.S. dollars using the World Bank Atlas method, from latest available data.
Literacy rate	Percentage of population aged 15–24 with at least a basic ability to read and write, 2007.
International dialling code	The country code prefix to be used when dialling from another country.
Time zone	Time difference in hours between local standard time and Greenwich Mean Time (GMT).
Official website	The official country website where available.
Tourism website	The country website for tourists where available.

MAIN STATISTICAL SOURCES

United Nations Department of Economic and Social Affairs (UDESA)
World Population Prospects: The 2006 Revision
World Urbanization Prospects: The 2005 Revision

World Bank World Development Indicators online

UNESCO Education Data Centre

International Telecommunications Union (ITU)

WEB LINKS

www.un.org/esa/population/unpop

www.worldbank.org/data

stats.uis.unesco.org

www.itu.int

The system of timekeeping throughout the world is based on twenty-four time zones, each stretching over fifteen degrees of longitude – the distance equivalent to a time difference of one hour. The Prime, or Greenwich Meridian (0 degrees west), is the basis for Greenwich Mean Time (GMT) or Universal Coordinated Time (UTC), by which other times are measured. This universal reference point was agreed at an international conference in 1884.

Times are the local Standard Times observed compared with 12:00 (noon) Greenwich Mean Time (GMT). Daylight Saving Time, normally one hour ahead of local Standard Time, which is observed by certain countries for part of the year, is not shown on the map.

Organization	Web Address	Theme
Greenwich Royal Observatory	www.rog.nmm.ac.uk	The home of time
Greenwich Mean Time	wwp.greenwichmeantime.com	World time since 1884
World time zones	www.worldtimezones.com	Detailed time zones information
The Official US time	www.time.gov/	The home of US time
International Date Line	aa.usno.navy.mil/faq/docs/international_date.php	Understanding the international date line

| 14 +2 | 15 +3 | 16 +4 | 17 +5 | 18 +6 | 19 +7 | 20 +8 | 21 +9 | 22 +10 | 23 +11 | MIDNIGHT PM\AM | 1 -11 | 2 -10 | 3 -9 | 4 -8 |

19.00

21.00

23.00

24.00

Yekaterinburg

15.00

Yakutsk

Magadan

22.00

Anchorage

Moscow

16.00

Novosibirsk

Astana

17.00

18.00

Ulan Bator

Beijing

Monday
Sunday

INTERNATIONAL DATE LINE

60°

charest

16.00

Dushanbe

Ankara

Tehrān

15.30

16.30

Delhi

17.45

Chengdu

Shanghai

Tōkyō

20.00

30°

Cairo

Riyadh

17.00

17.30

18.30

Hong Kong

18.00

Mumbai

Manila

Bangkok

amena

Addis Ababa

17.30

Singapore

Equator

0°

Nairobi

shasa

Dar es Salaam

Jakarta

Port Moresby

Harare

Antananarivo

18.30

CENTRAL
STANDARD
TIME

retoria

WESTERN
STANDARD
TIME

21.30

EASTERN
STANDARD
TIME

23.30

01.00
Monday

pe Town

Perth

Sydney

22.30

Auckland

30°

17.00

0.45

| 30° | 45° | 60° | 75° | 90° | 105° | 120° | 135° | 150° | 165° | 180° | 165° | 150° |

Time zone boundaries can be altered to suit international or internal boundaries. China uses only one time zone although it should theoretically have five, while the Russian Federation stretches over eleven zones. The four mainland USA time zones do not always follow state boundaries.

The International Date Line is an imaginary line at approximately 180° west (or east) of Greenwich, across which the date changes by one day. The line has no international legal status and countries near to the line can choose which date they will observe. The line was amended recently so that Caroline Island, in Kiribati in the Pacific Ocean, would be the first land area to greet the year 2000. The island was renamed Millennium Island in recognition of this.

Daylight Saving Time allows nations to adjust their clocks to extend daylight during the working day. It was first introduced to the UK during the First World War to reduce the demand for artificial heating and lighting.

TIME DIFFERENCES FOR
MAJOR CITIES FROM GMT

	hours
Los Angeles	-8
New York	-5
Buenos Aires	-3
Berlin	+1
Cape Town	+2
Mumbai	+5.5
Singapore	+8
Beijing	+8
Tōkyō	+9
Sydney	+10

© Collins Bartholomew Ltd

HIGHEST MOUNTAINS	Height metres	feet	Location
Mt Everest	8 848	29 028	China/Nepal
K2	8 611	28 251	Pakistan
Kangchenjunga	8 586	28 169	India/Nepal
Lhotse	8 516	27 939	China/Nepal
Makalu	8 463	27 765	China/Nepal
Cho Oyu	8 201	26 906	China/Nepal
Dhaulagiri	8 167	26 794	Nepal
Manaslu	8 163	26 781	Nepal
Nanga Parbat	8 126	26 660	Pakistan
Annapurna I	8 091	26 545	Nepal
Gasherbrum I	8 068	26 469	China/Pakistan
Broad Peak	8 047	26 401	China/Pakistan
Gasherbrum II	8 035	26 361	China/Pakistan
Xixabangma Feng	8 012	26 286	China
Annapurna II	7 937	26 040	Nepal

LONGEST RIVERS	Length km	miles	Continent
Nile	6 695	4 160	Africa
Amazon	6 516	4 049	South America
Yangtze	6 380	3 965	Asia
Mississippi-Missouri	5 969	3 709	North America
Ob'-Irtysh	5 568	3 460	Asia
Yenisey-Angara-Selenga	5 550	3 449	Asia
Yellow River	5 464	3 395	Asia
Congo	4 667	2 900	Africa
Río de la Plata-Paraná	4 500	2 796	South America
Irtysh	4 440	2 759	Asia
Mekong	4 425	2 750	Asia
Heilong Jiang-Argun'	4 416	2 744	Asia
Lena-Kirenga	4 400	2 734	Asia
MacKenzie-Peace-Finlay	4 241	2 635	North America
Niger	4 184	2 600	Africa

LARGEST LAKES	Area sq km	sq miles	Continent
Caspian Sea	371 000	143 243	Asia/Europe
Lake Superior	82 100	31 699	North America
Lake Victoria	68 870	26 591	Africa
Lake Huron	59 600	23 012	North America
Lake Michigan	57 800	22 317	North America
Lake Tanganyika	32 600	12 587	Africa
Great Bear Lake	31 328	12 096	North America
Lake Baikal	30 500	11 776	Asia
Lake Nyasa	29 500	11 390	Africa
Great Slave Lake	28 568	11 030	North America
Lake Erie	25 700	9 923	North America
Lake Winnipeg	24 387	9 416	North America
Lake Ontario	18 960	7 320	North America
Lake Ladoga	18 390	7 100	Europe
Lake Balkhash	17 400	6 718	Asia

LARGEST DRAINAGE BASINS	Area sq km	sq miles	Continent
Amazon	7 050 000	2 722 000	South America
Congo	3 700 000	1 429 000	Africa
Nile	3 349 000	1 293 000	Africa
Mississippi-Missouri	3 250 000	1 255 000	North America
Río de la Plata-Paraná	3 100 000	1 197 000	South America
Ob'-Irtysh	2 990 000	1 154 000	Asia
Yenisey-Angara-Selenga	2 580 000	996 000	Asia
Lena-Kirenga	2 490 000	961 000	Asia
Yangtze	1 959 000	756 000	Asia
Niger	1 890 000	730 000	Africa
Heilong Jiang-Argun'	1 855 000	716 000	Asia
Mackenzie-Peace-Finlay	1 805 000	697 000	North America
Ganges-Brahmaputra	1 621 000	626 000	Asia
St Lawrence-St Louis	1 463 000	565 000	North America
Volga	1 380 000	533 000	Europe

ATLANTIC OCEAN	Area sq km	sq miles	Deepest Point metres	feet
Total extent	86 557 000	33 420 000	8 605 Milwaukee Deep 28 231	
Arctic Ocean	9 485 000	3 662 000	5 450	17 880
Caribbean Sea	2 512 000	970 000	7 680	25 196
Mediterranean Sea	2 510 000	969 000	5 121	16 800
Gulf of Mexico	1 544 000	596 000	3 504	11 495
Hudson Bay	1 233 000	476 000	259	849
North Sea	575 000	222 000	661	2 168
Black Sea	508 000	196 000	2 245	7 365
Baltic Sea	382 000	147 000	460	1 509

INDIAN OCEAN	Area sq km	sq miles	Deepest Point metres	feet
Total extent	73 427 000	28 350 000	7 125 Java Trench 23 376	
Bay of Bengal	2 172 000	839 000	4 500	14 763
Red Sea	453 000	175 000	3 040	9 973
The Gulf	238 000	92 000	73	239

PACIFIC OCEAN	Area sq km	sq miles	Deepest Point metres	feet
Total extent	166 241 000	64 186 000	10 920 Challenger Deep 35 826	
South China Sea	2 590 000	1 000 000	5 514	18 090
Bering Sea	2 261 000	873 000	4 150	13 615
Sea of Okhotsk	1 392 000	537 000	3 363	11 033
Sea of Japan (East Sea)	1 013 000	391 000	3 743	12 280
East China Sea and Yellow Sea	1 202 000	464 000	2 717	8 913

LARGEST ISLANDS	Area sq km	sq miles	Continent
Greenland	2 175 600	839 999	North America
New Guinea	808 510	312 166	Oceania
Borneo	745 561	287 861	Asia
Madagascar	587 040	266 656	Africa
Baffin Island	507 451	195 927	North America
Sumatra	473 606	182 859	Asia
Honshū	227 414	87 805	Asia
Great Britain	218 476	84 354	Europe
Victoria Island	217 291	83 896	North America
Ellesmere Island	196 236	75 767	North America
Celebes	189 216	73 056	Asia
South Island, New Zealand	151 215	58 384	Oceania
Java	132 188	51 038	Asia
North Island, New Zealand	115 777	44 701	Oceania
Cuba	110 860	42 803	North America

DEEPEST LAKES	Depth metres	feet	Continent
Lake Baïkal	1 741	5 712	Asia
Lake Tanganyika	1 471	4 826	Africa
Caspian Sea	1 025	3 363	Asia/Europe
Lake Nyasa	706	2 316	Africa
Ysyk-Köl	702	2 303	Asia

LOWEST POINTS ON LAND	Depth below sea level metres	feet	Location
Dead Sea	-421	-1 381	Asia
Lake Assal	-156	-512	Djibouti
Turpan Pendi	-154	-505	China
Qattara Depression	-133	-436	Egypt
Poluostrov Mangyshlak	-132	-433	Kazakhstan

HIGHEST WATERFALLS	Height metres	feet	Location
Angel Falls	979	3 212	Venezuela
Tugela	948	3 110	South Africa
Utigård	800	2 625	Norway
Mongfossen	774	2 539	Norway
Mtarazi	762	2 500	Zimbabwe

EARTH'S DIMENSIONS	
Mass	5.974×10^{21} tonnes
Total area	509 450 000 sq km /196 698 645 sq miles
Land area	149 450 000 sq km / 57 702 645 sq miles
Water area	360 000 000 sq km /138 996 000 sq miles
Volume	$1\ 083\ 207 \times 10^{6}$ cubic km /
	$259\ 911 \times 10^{6}$ cubic miles
Equatorial diameter	12 756 km / 7 927 miles
Polar diameter	12 714 km / 7 901 miles
Equatorial circumference	40 075 km / 24 903 miles
Meridional circumference	40 008 km / 24 861 miles

LARGEST COUNTRIES BY POPULATION	Population
China	1 313 437 000
India	1 169 016 000
United States of America	305 826 000
Indonesia	231 627 000
Brazil	191 791 000
Pakistan	163 902 000
Bangladesh	158 665 000
Nigeria	148 093 000
Russian Federation	142 499 000
Japan	127 967 000

LARGEST COUNTRIES BY AREA	Area sq km	sq miles
Russian Federation	17 075 400	6 592 849
Canada	9 984 670	3 855 103
United States of America	9 826 635	3 794 085
China	9 584 492	3 700 593
Brazil	8 514 879	3 287 613
Australia	7 692 024	2 969 907
India	3 064 898	1 183 364
Argentina	2 766 889	1 068 302
Kazakhstan	2 717 300	1 049 155
Sudan	2 505 813	967 500

LARGEST CITIES	Population	Location
Tōkyō	35 467 000	Japan
Mexico City	20 688 000	Mexico
Mumbai	20 036 000	India
São Paulo	19 582 000	Brazil
New York	19 388 000	United States of America
Delhi	16 983 000	India
Shanghai	15 790 000	China
Kolkata	15 548 000	India
Jakarta	15 206 000	Indonesia
Dhaka	14 625 000	Bangladesh
Lagos	13 717 000	Nigeria
Karachi	13 252 000	Pakistan
Buenos Aires	13 067 000	Argentina
Los Angeles	12 738 000	United States of America
Rio de Janeiro	12 170 000	Brazil

BUSIEST AIRPORTS (2007)	Location	Passengers
Atlanta (ATL)	USA	89 379 287
Chicago (ORD)	USA	76 177 855
London (LHR)	UK	68 068 304
Tōkyō (HND)	Japan	66 823 414
Los Angeles (LAX)	USA	61 896 075
Paris (CDG)	France	59 922 177
Dallas/Fort Worth Airport (DFW)	USA	59 786 476
Frankfurt am Main (FRA)	Germany	54 161 856
Beijing (PEK)	China	53 583 664
Madrid (MAD)	Spain	52 122 702
Denver (DEN)	USA	49 863 352
Amsterdam (AMS)	Netherlands	47 794 994
New York (JFK)	USA	47 716 941
Hong Kong (HKG)	China	47 042 419
Las Vegas (LAS)	USA	46 961 011

Climate is defined by the long-term weather conditions prevalent in any part of the world. The classification of climate types is based on the relationship between temperature and humidity and also on how these are affected by latitude, altitude, ocean currents and wind. Weather is how climatic conditions affect local areas. Weather stations collect data on temperature and rainfall, which can be plotted on graphs as shown here. These are based on average monthly figures over a minimum period of thirty years and can help to monitor climate change.

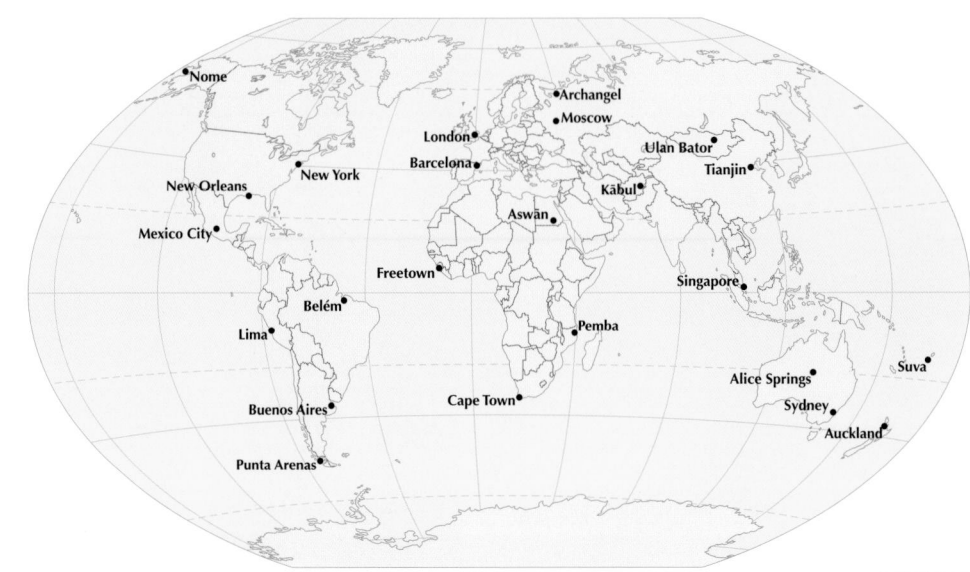

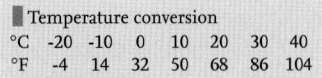

Temperature conversion							
°C	-20	-10	0	10	20	30	40
°F	-4	14	32	50	68	86	104

Rainfall conversion							
mm	25.4	127	254	381	508	635	762
ins	1	5	10	15	20	25	30

FREETOWN

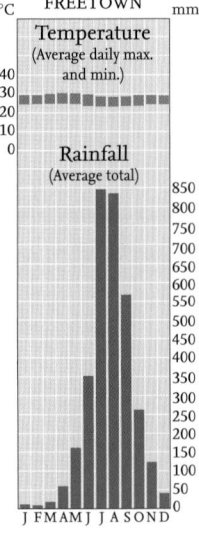

AFRICA

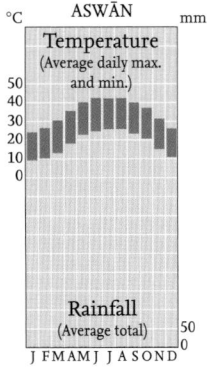

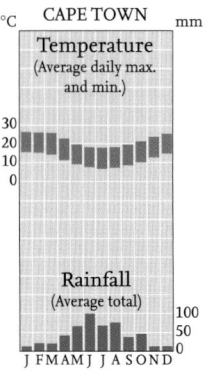

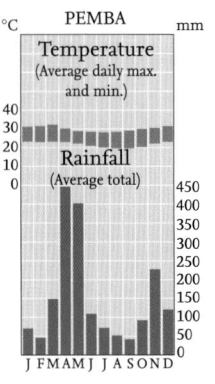

ASIA

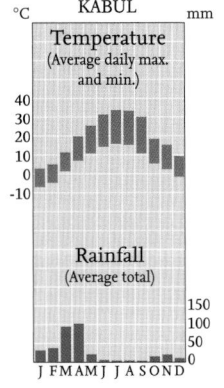

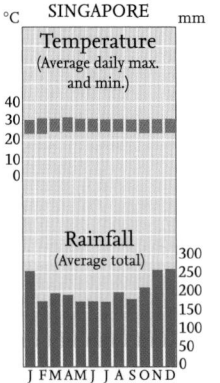

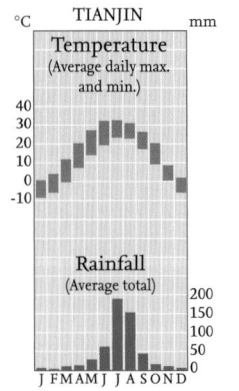

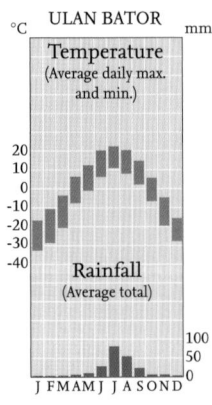

EUROPE

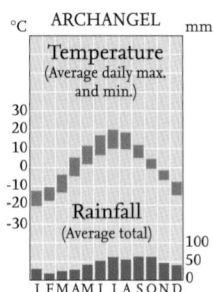

ARCHANGEL

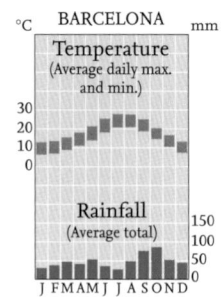

BARCELONA

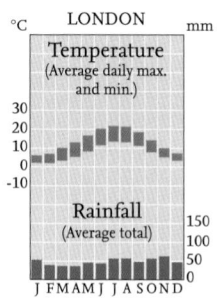

LONDON

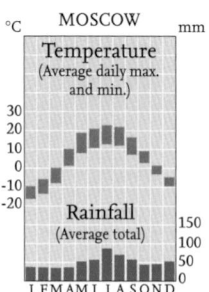

MOSCOW

NORTH AMERICA

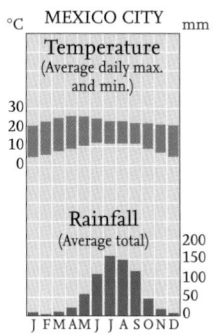

MEXICO CITY

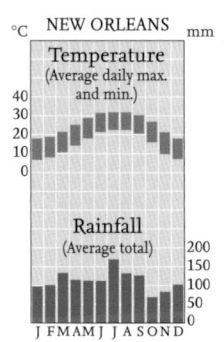

NEW ORLEANS

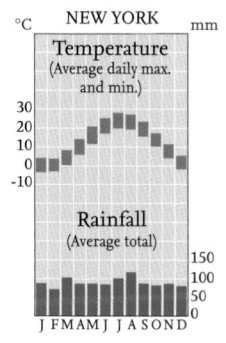

NEW YORK

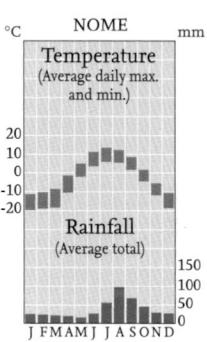

NOME

SOUTH AMERICA

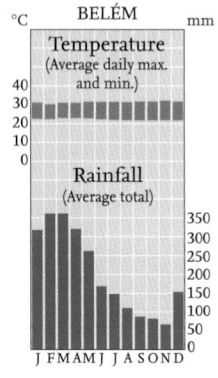

BELÉM

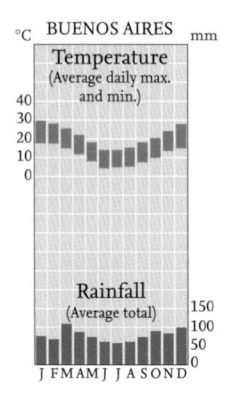

BUENOS AIRES

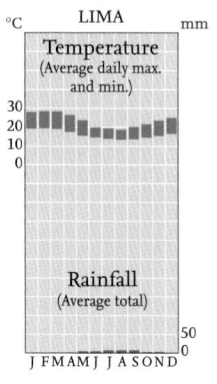

LIMA

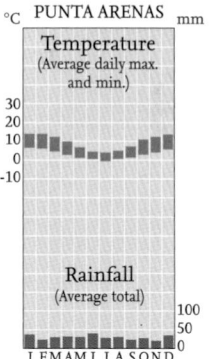

PUNTA ARENAS

OCEANIA

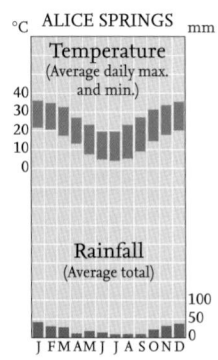

ALICE SPRINGS

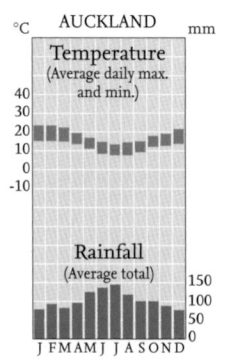

AUCKLAND

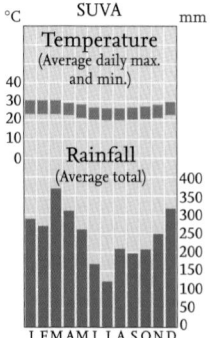

SUVA

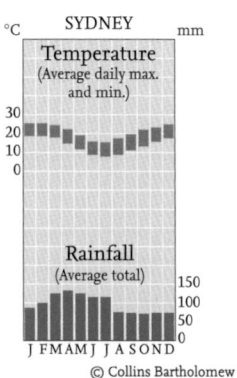

SYDNEY

© Collins Bartholomew Ltd

ENVIRONMENT

The earth has a rich environment with a wide range of habitats. Forest and woodland form the predominant natural land cover and tropical rain forests are believed to be home to the majority of the world's bird, animal and plant species. These forests are part of a delicate land-atmosphere relationship disturbed by changes in land use. Grassland, shrubland and deserts cover most of the unwooded areas of the earth with low-growing tundra in the far northern latitudes. Grassland and shrubland regions in particular have been altered greatly by man through agriculture, livestock grazing and settlements.

Organization	Web address	Theme
Earth Observatory	earthobservatory.nasa.gov	Observing the earth
USGS National Earthquake Information Center	neic.usgs.gov	Monitoring earthquakes
Scripps Institution of Oceanography	sio.ucsd.edu	Exploration of the oceans
Visible Earth	visibleearth.nasa.gov	Satellite images of the earth
USGS Volcano Hazards Program	volcanoes.usgs.gov	Volcanic activity
UNESCO World Heritage Centre	whc.unesco.org	World Heritage Sites
British Geological Survey	www.bgs.ac.uk	Geology
International Union for the Conservation of Nature	www.iucn.org	World and ocean conservation
World Rainforest Information Portal	www.rainforestweb.org	Rainforest information and resources
United Nations Environment Programme	www.unep.org	Environmental protection by the UN
World Conservation Monitoring Centre	www.unep-wcmc.org	Conservation and the environment
World Resources Institute	www.wri.org	Monitoring the environment and resources
IUCN Red List	www.iucnredlist.org	Threatened species

OCEANS

Between them, the world's oceans cover approximately 70 per cent of the earth's surface. They contain 96 per cent of the earth's water and a vast range of flora and fauna. They are a major influence on the world's climate, particularly through ocean currents – the circulation of water within and between the oceans. Our understanding of the oceans has increased enormously over the last twenty years through the development of new technologies, including that of satellite images, which can generate vast amounts of data relating to the sea floor, ocean currents and sea surface temperatures.

Organization	Web address	Theme
International Maritime Organization	www.imo.org	Shipping and the environment
General Bathymetric Chart of the Oceans	www.gebco.net	Mapping the oceans
National Oceanography Centre	www.soc.soton.ac.uk	Researching the oceans
Scott Polar Research Institute	www.spri.cam.ac.uk	Polar research

CLIMATE

The Earth's climate system is highly complex. It is recognized and accepted that man's activities are affecting this system, and monitoring climate change, including human influences upon it, is now a major issue. Future climate change depends critically on how quickly and to what extent the concentration of greenhouse gases in the atmosphere increase. Change will not be uniform across the globe and the information from sophisticated mathematical climate models is invaluable in helping governments and industry to assess the impacts climate change will have.

Organization	Web address	Theme
BBC Weather	www.bbc.co.uk/weather	Worldwide weather forecasts
Climatic Research Unit	www.cru.uea.ac.uk	Climatic research
Meteorological Office	www.met-office.gov.uk	Weather information and climatic research
National Climatic Data Center	www.ncdc.noaa.gov	Global climate data
US National Hurricane Center	www.nhc.noaa.gov	Tracking hurricanes
National Oceanic and Atmospheric Administration	www.noaa.gov	Monitoring climate and the oceans
World Meteorological Organization	www.wmo.ch	The world's climate
El Niño	www.elnino.noaa.gov	El Niño research and observations

POPULATION

The world's population reached 6 billion in 1999. Rates of population growth vary between continents, but overall, the rate of growth has been increasing and it is predicted that by 2050 another 3 billion people will inhabit the planet. The process of urbanization, in particular migration from countryside to city, has led to the rapid growth of many cities. It is estimated that by the end of 2008, more people will be living in urban areas than in rural areas, and that by 2010 there will be 473 cities with over 1 million inhabitants and twenty-one with over 10 million.

Organization	Web address	Theme
Office for National Statistics	www.statistics.gov.uk/census	UK census information
City Population	www.citypopulation.de	Statistics and maps about population
US Census Bureau	www.census.gov	US and world population
UN World Urbanization Prospects	www.un.org/esa/population/publications/2007_PopDevt	Population estimates and projections
UN Population Information Network	www.un.org/popin	World population statistics
UN Population Division	www.un.org/esa/population/unpop	Monitoring world population

COUNTRIES

The present picture of the political world is the result of a long history of exploration, colonialism, conflict and negotiation. In 1950 there were eighty-two independent countries. Since then there has been a significant trend away from colonial influences and although many dependent territories still exist, there are now 195 independent countries. The newest country is Kosovo which declared independence from Serbia in February 2008. The shapes of countries reflect a combination of natural features, such as mountain ranges, and political agreements. There are still areas of the world where boundaries are disputed or only temporarily settled as ceasefire lines.

Organization	Web address	Theme
European Union	europa.eu	Gateway to the European Union
Permanent Committee on Geographical Names	www.pcgn.org.uk	Place names research in the UK
The World Factbook	www.odci.gov/cia/publications/factbook	Country profiles
US Board on Geographic Names	geonames.usgs.gov	Place names research in the USA
United Nations	www.un.org	The United Nations
International Boundaries Research Unit	www.dur.ac.uk/ibru	International boundaries resources and research
Organisation for Economic Cooperation and Development	www.oecd.org	Economic statistics
The World Bank	www.worldbank.org/data	World development data and statistics

TRAVEL

Travelling as a tourist or on business to some countries, or travelling within certain areas can be dangerous because of wars and political unrest. The UK Foreign Office provides the latest travel advice and security warnings. Some areas of the world, particularly tropical regions in the developing world, also carry many risks of disease. Advice should be sought on precautions to take and medications required.

Organization	Web address	Theme
UK Foreign and Commonwealth Office	www.fco.gov.uk	Travel, trade and country information
US Department of State	www.state.gov	Travel, trade and country information
World Health Organization	www.who.int	Health advice and world health issues
Centers for Disease Control and Prevention	www.cdc.gov/travel	Advice for travellers
Airports Council International	www.airports.org	The voice of the world's airports
Travel Daily News	www.traveldailynews.com	Travel and tourism newsletter

ORGANIZATIONS

Throughout the world there are many international, national and local organizations representing the interests of individual countries, groups of countries, regions and specialist groups. These can provide enormous amounts of information on economic, social, cultural, environmental and general geographical issues facing the world. The following is a selection of such sites.

Organization	Web address	Theme
United Nations	www.un.org	The United Nations
United Nations Educational, Scientific and Cultural Organization	www.unesco.org	International collaboration
United Nations Children's Fund	www.unicef.org	Children's health, education, equality and protection
United Nations High Commissioner for Refugees	www.unhcr.org	The UN refugee agency
Food and Agriculture Organization of the United Nations	www.fao.org	Agriculture and defeating hunger
United Nations Development Programme	www.undp.org	The UN global development network
North Atlantic Treaty Organization	www.nato.int	North Atlantic freedom and security
European Environment Agency	www.eea.europa.eu/	Europe's environment
European Centre for Nature Conservation	www.ecnc.nl/	Nature conservation in Europe
Europa - The European Union On-line	europa.eu/index.en.htm	European Union facts and statistics
World Health Organisation	www.who.int	Health issues and advice
Association of Southeast Asian Nations	www.aseansec.org	Economic, social and cultural development
Africawater	www.africawater.org	Water resources in Africa
Joint United Nations Programme on HIV/AIDS	www.unaids.org	The AIDS crisis
African Union	www.africa-union.org	African international relations
World Lakes Network	www.worldlakes.org/	Lakes around the world
Secretariat of the Pacific Commmunity	www.spc.int	The Pacific community
The Maori world	www.maori.org.nz	Maori culture
US National Park Service	www.nps.gov	National Parks of the USA
Parks Canada	www.pc.gc.ca	Natural heritage of Canada
Panama Canal Authority	www.pancanal.com	Explore the Panama Canal
Caribbean Community Secretariat	www.caricom.org	Caribbean Community
Organization of American States	www.oas.org	Inter-American cooperation
The Latin American Network Information Center	lanic.utexas.edu	Latin America
World Wildlife Fund	www.worldwildlife.org	Global environmental conservation
Amazon Conservation Team	www.amazonteam.org	Conservation in tropical America

DISTANCES

This table shows air distances in both kilometres and *miles* for 27 cities around the world. These are the shortest distances between cities and are known as Great Circle routes.

Abu Dhabi
8075 9793 5905 6918 4303 11764 5247 11040 3422 3735 10647 14374 11689 5632 13481 5478 2043 2987 2317 7498 2367 13534 4637 5972 4795 14244
5018 6085 3669 4299 2674 7310 3260 6860 2126 2321 6616 8932 7263 3500 8377 3404 1270 1856 1440 4659 1471 8410 2881 3711 3091 8851

Auckland
8811 2161 8411 9596 18400 12288 18540 14187 13966 16194 14379 10947 2629 19592 10479 18330 16287 17042 12482 11796 16573 10372 17743 10388 9566
5475 1343 5227 5963 11433 7636 11521 8816 8678 10063 8935 6802 1634 12174 6512 11390 10121 10590 7756 7330 10298 6445 11025 6455 5944

Bangkok
4610 7523 1427 3720 8842 16081 9457 13949 7218 7070 13417 15760 7359 10196 13319 9544 6895 7477 2917 10144 7279 16885 8613 3291
2865 4675 887 2312 5494 9993 5877 8668 4393 4337 9739 4573 6336 8276 5931 4285 4646 1813 6303 4523 10492 5352 2045

Beijing
2104 8923 4465 958 8144 17325 8236 11012 9216 5809 10490 12478 9093 9243 10082 8160 7135 7072 3788 12947 7557 19265 7375
1307 5545 2775 595 5061 10766 5118 6843 5727 3610 6518 7754 5650 5744 6265 5071 4434 4354 8045 4696 11971 4583

Berlin
8942 16090 9927 8150 1182 9989 880 6403 6353 1612 6018 9746 15970 1871 9332 934 2903 1739 5791 9588 2891 11890
5556 9998 6169 5064 735 6207 547 3979 3948 1002 3740 6056 9924 1163 5799 580 1804 1081 3599 5958 1796 7388

Buenos Aires
18365 11821 15889 19429 11135 1968 11029 8490 10416 13461 9001 7366 11629 10024 9828 11105 12236 12235 15800 6891 11811
11412 7345 9873 12073 6919 1223 6853 5276 6472 8365 5593 4577 7226 6229 6107 6901 7603 7603 9818 4282 7339

Cairo
9587 14415 8270 8504 2135 9882 3215 9042 3518 2899 8733 12392 13966 3355 12223 3513 426 1234 4436 7208
5957 8957 5139 5284 1327 6141 1998 5618 2186 1801 5427 7700 8678 2085 7595 2183 265 767 2757 4479

Cape Town
14737 11034 9671 13710 8417 6075 9307 12551 4090 10101 10338 8536 16054 9635 7481 8367 9284
9157 6856 6009 8519 5230 3775 5783 7799 2542 6277 7919 8515 6424 5304 9976 5987 4649 5199 5769

Delhi
5857 10415 4142 4699 5929 14080 6601 11779 5428 4349 11286 14679 10192 7288 12882 6724 4032 4560
3640 6472 2574 2920 3684 8749 4102 7319 3373 2702 7014 9121 6333 4529 8005 4178 2505 2834

İstanbul
8970 14944 8652 7975 1379 10268 2261 8089 4751 1755 7730 11448 14628 2744 11043 2504 1170
5574 9286 5376 4956 857 6380 1405 5026 2952 1091 4803 7114 9090 1705 6862 1556 727

Jerusalem
9171 14126 7924 8083 2310 10308 3339 9190 3662 2671 8854 12552 13713 3602 12210 3615
5699 8778 4924 5023 1435 6405 2075 5711 2276 1660 5502 7800 8521 2238 7587 2246

London
9585 16990 10860 8882 9254 341 5586 6805 5206 4947 16902 1264 8778
5956 10557 6748 5519 891 5750 212 3471 4229 1557 3256 5560 10503 785 5455

Los Angeles
8828 12065 14136 9605 10212 10129 9106 3945 15553 9793 3973 2492 12762 9387
5486 7497 8784 5968 6346 6294 5658 2451 9664 6085 2469 1549 7930 5833

Madrid
10789 17687 10021 11396 1365 8118 1054 5785 6177 3446 5551 9083 17315
6704 10990 7081 6227 848 5044 655 3595 3838 2141 3449 5644 10759

Melbourne
8159 711 6050 8551 15987 13227 16793 16671 11513 14418 16730 13557
5070 442 3759 5314 9934 8219 10435 10359 7154 8959 10396 8424

Mexico City
11319 12972 16623 12071 10260 7669 9213 3362 14834 10740 3728
7034 8061 10329 7501 6375 4765 5725 2089 9218 6674 2317

Montréal
10409 16026 14816 10577 6601 8175 5522 533 11692 7077
6468 9958 9207 6572 4102 5080 3431 331 7265 4398

Moscow
7502 14487 8426 6626 2378 11529 2492 7530 6323
4662 9002 5236 4117 1478 7164 1549 4679 3929

Nairobi
11266 12162 7467 10115 5374 8941 6471 11849
7001 7557 4640 6285 3339 5556 4021 7363

New York
10870 16959 15349 11078 6907 7729 5851
6755 9936 9538 6884 4292 4803 3636

Paris
9738 16959 10743 8990 1108 9146
6051 10538 6676 5586 689 5683

Rio de Janeiro
18557 13539 15740 18135 9181
10288 8413 9781 11269 5705

Rome
9881 16322 10030 8991
6140 10142 6232 5587

Seoul
1160 8298 4666
721 5156 2899

Singapore
5317 6293
3304 3910

Sydney
7794
4843

Tōkyō

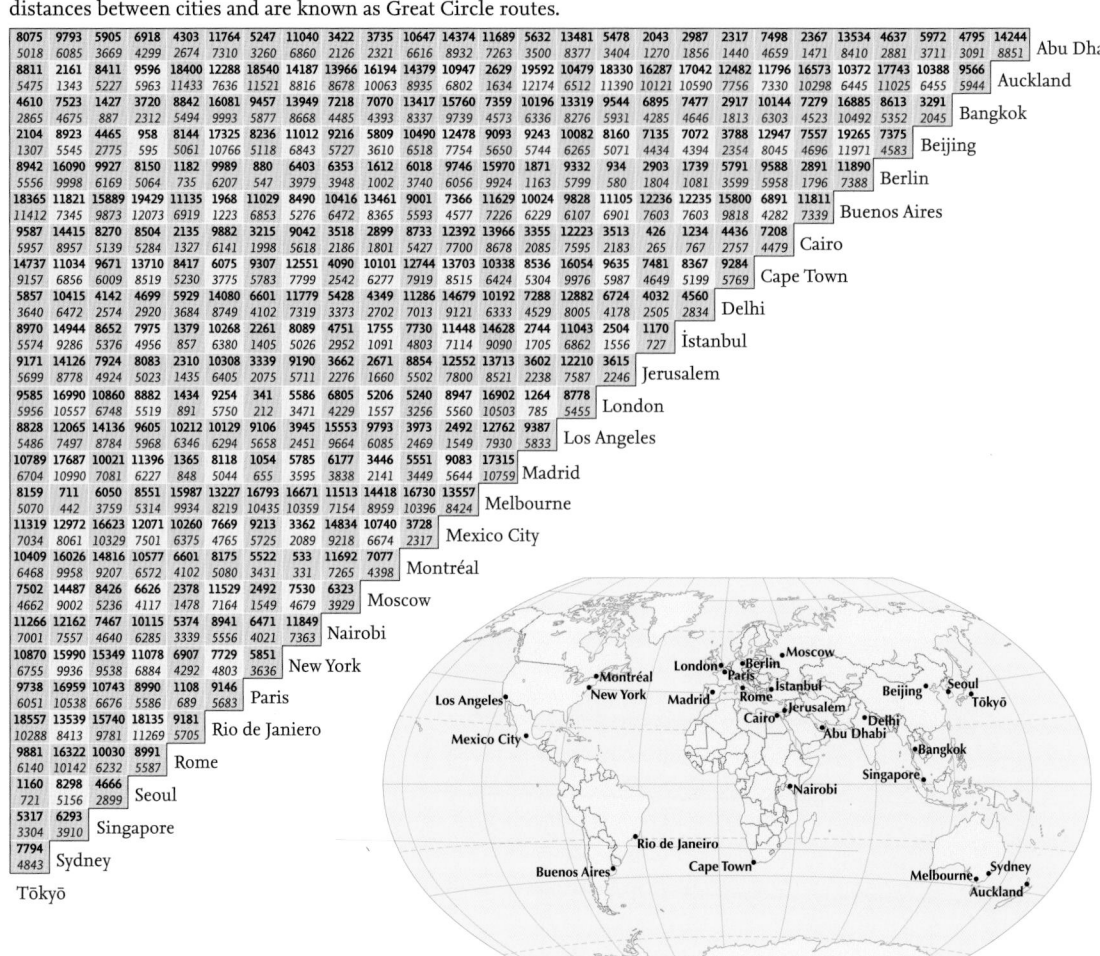

CONVERSION CHARTS

To convert	into	multiply by
LENGTH AND AREA		
millimetres	inches	0.0394
centimetres	inches	0.3937
metres	feet	3.2808
metres	yards	1.0936
kilometres	miles	0.6214
inches	millimetres	25.4
inches	centimetres	2.54
feet	metres	0.3048
yards	metres	0.9144
miles	kilometres	1.6093
acres	hectares	0.4047
hectares	acres	2.4711
square miles	square kilometres	2.5900
square kilometres	square miles	0.3861

To convert	into	multiply by
WEIGHT		
grams	ounces	0.0353
kilograms	pounds	2.2046
metric tonnes (1000 kg)	tons (2 240lbs)	0.9842
ounces	grams	28.3495
pounds	kilograms	0.4536
tons (2 240lbs)	metric tonnes (1000 kg)	1.0161
VOLUME		
pints (20fl oz)	litres	0.5683
imperial gallons	litres	4.5461
litres	pints (20fl oz)	1.7598
litres	imperial gallons	0.2200

To convert	into	multiply by
TEMPERATURE		
°C	°F	multiply by 1.8 and add 32
°F	°C	subtract 32 and divide by 1.8

To convert	into	multiply by
SPEED		
km/h	mph	0.6214
mph	km/h	1.6093

INTRODUCTION TO THE INDEX

The index includes all names shown on the maps in the Atlas of the World. Names are referenced by page number and by a grid reference. The grid reference correlates to the alphanumeric values which appear within each map frame. Each entry also includes the country or geographical area in which the feature is located. Entries relating to names appearing on insets are indicated by a small box symbol: □, followed by a grid reference if the inset has its own alphanumeric values.

Name forms are as they appear on the maps, with additional alternative names or name forms included as cross-references which refer the user to the entry for the map form of the name. Names beginning with Mc or Mac are alphabetized exactly as they appear. The terms Saint, Sainte, Sankt, etc, are abbreviated to St, Ste, St, etc, but alphabetized as if in the full form.

Names of physical features beginning with generic geographical terms are permuted – the descriptive term is placed after the main part of the name. For example, Lake Superior is indexed as Superior, Lake; Mount Everest as Everest, Mount. This policy is applied to all languages.

Entries, other than those for towns and cities, include a descriptor indicating the type of geographical feature. Descriptors are not included where the type of feature is implicit in the name itself.

Administrative divisions are included to differentiate entries of the same name and feature type within the one country. In such cases, duplicate names are alphabetized in order of administrative division. Additional qualifiers are also included for names within selected geographical areas.

INDEX ABBREVIATIONS

admin. div.	administrative division	g.	gulf	Port.	Portugal
Afgh.	Afghanistan	Ger.	Germany	prov.	province
Alg.	Algeria	Guat.	Guatemala	pt	point
Arg.	Argentina	hd	headland	r.	river
Austr.	Australia	Hond.	Honduras	r. mouth	river mouth
aut. comm.	autonomous community	i.	island	reg.	region
aut. reg.	autonomous region	imp. l.	impermanent lake	resr	reservoir
aut. rep.	autonomous republic	Indon.	Indonesia	rf	reef
Azer.	Azerbaijan	is.	islands	Rus. Fed.	Russian Federation
b.	bay	isth.	isthmus	S.	South
B.I.O.T.	British Indian Ocean Territory	Kazakh.	Kazakhstan	salt l.	salt lake
Bangl.	Bangladesh	Kyrg.	Kyrgyzstan	sea chan.	sea channel
Bol.	Bolivia	l.	lake	special admin. reg.	special administrative region
Bos.-Herz.	Bosnia Herzegovina	lag.	lagoon		
Bulg.	Bulgaria	Lith.	Lithuania	str.	strait
c.	cape	Lux.	Luxembourg	Switz.	Switzerland
Can.	Canada	Madag.	Madagascar	Tajik.	Tajikistan
C.A.R.	Central African Republic	Maur.	Mauritania	Tanz.	Tanzania
Col.	Colombia	Mex.	Mexico	terr.	territory
Czech Rep.	Czech Republic	Moz.	Mozambique	Thai.	Thailand
Dem. Rep. Congo	Democratic Republic of the Congo	mt.	mountain	Trin. and Tob.	Trinidad and Tobago
		mts	mountains	Turkm.	Turkmenistan
depr.	depression	mun.	municipality	U.A.E.	United Arab Emirates
des.	desert	N.	North	U.K.	United Kingdom
Dom. Rep.	Dominican Republic	Neth.	Netherlands	Ukr.	Ukraine
Equat. Guinea	Equatorial Guinea	Neth. Antilles	Netherlands Antilles	union terr.	union territory
		Nic.	Nicaragua	Uru.	Uruguay
esc.	escarpment	N.Z.	New Zealand	U.S.A.	United States of America
est.	estuary	Pak.	Pakistan	Uzbek.	Uzbekistan
Eth.	Ethiopia	Para.	Paraguay	val.	valley
Fin.	Finland	pen.	peninsula	Venez.	Venezuela
for.	forest	Phil.	Philippines	vol.	volcano
Fr. Guiana	French Guiana	plat.	plateau	vol. crater	volcanic crater
Fr. Polynesia	French Polynesia	P.N.G.	Papua New Guinea		
		Pol.	Poland		

1

144 B2 100 Mile House Can.

A

109 E4 Aabenraa Denmark
116 C2 Aachen Ger.
109 E4 Aalborg Denmark
118 C2 Aalen Ger.
116 B2 Aalst Belgium
109 I3 Äänekoski Fin.
121 D2 Aarau Switz.
116 B2 Aarschot Belgium
86 A2 Aba China
135 D2 Aba Dem. Rep. Congo
131 C4 Aba Nigeria
97 C2 Ābādān Iran
97 D2 Ābādeh Iran
97 D3 Ābādeh Ţashk Iran
130 B1 Abadla Alg.
171 C1 Abaeté Brazil
Abagnar Qi China see Xilinhot
151 E3 Abajo Peak U.S.A.
131 C4 Abakaliki Nigeria
99 H3 Abakan Rus. Fed.
166 B4 Abancay Peru
97 D2 Abarqū Iran
82 D2 Abashiri Japan
82 D2 Abashiri-wan b. Japan
75 D3 Abau P.N.G.
Abaya, Lake l. Eth. see Lake Abaya
Ābay Wenz r. Eth. see Blue Nile
99 H3 Abaza Rus. Fed.
124 A2 Abbasanta Italy
120 C1 Abbeville France
157 C2 Abbeville AL U.S.A.
156 B3 Abbeville LA U.S.A.
113 B2 Abbeyfeale Ireland
71 R2 Abbot Ice Shelf Antarctica
90 B1 Abbottabad Pak.
131 E3 Abéché Chad
130 B4 Abengourou Côte d'Ivoire
130 C4 Abeokuta Nigeria
115 A3 Aberaeron U.K.
112 C2 Aberchirder U.K.
Abercorn Zambia see Mbala
115 B4 Aberdare U.K.
115 A3 Aberdaron U.K.
69 D2 Aberdeen Austr.
138 B3 Aberdeen S. Africa
112 C2 Aberdeen U.K.
155 D3 Aberdeen MD U.S.A.
153 D1 Aberdeen SD U.S.A.
150 B1 Aberdeen WA U.S.A.
145 E1 Aberdeen Lake Can.
112 C2 Aberfeldy U.K.
112 B2 Aberfoyle U.K.
115 B4 Abergavenny U.K.
Abergwaun U.K. see Fishguard
Aberhonddu U.K. see Brecon
159 C2 Abernathy U.S.A.
150 B2 Abert, Lake l. U.S.A.
Abertawe U.K. see Swansea
Aberteifi U.K. see Cardigan
115 B4 Abertillery U.K.
115 A3 Aberystwyth U.K.
102 F2 Abez' Rus. Fed.
94 B3 Abhā Saudi Arabia
97 C2 Abhar Iran
Abiad, Bahr el r. Sudan/Uganda see White Nile
130 B4 Abidjan Côte d'Ivoire
153 D3 Abilene KS U.S.A.
159 D2 Abilene TX U.S.A.
115 C4 Abingdon U.K.
154 C3 Abingdon U.S.A.
107 D3 Abinsk Rus. Fed.
146 B3 Abitibi, Lake Can.
Åbo Fin. see Turku
90 B1 Abohar India
130 B4 Aboisso Côte d'Ivoire
130 C4 Abomey Benin
76 A1 Abongabong, Gunung mt. Indon.
134 B2 Abong Mbang Cameroon
80 A3 Aborlan Phil.
131 D3 Abou Déia Chad
122 B2 Abrantes Port.
168 B2 Abra Pampa Arg.
158 A3 Abreojos, Punta pt Mex.
132 B2 'Abri Sudan
152 A2 Absaroka Range mts U.S.A.
97 C1 Abşeron Yarımadası pen. Azer.
94 B3 Abū 'Arīsh Saudi Arabia
132 A2 Abū Ballāş h. Egypt
95 C2 Abu Dhabi U.A.E.
132 B3 Abu Hamed Sudan
132 B3 Abu Haraz Sudan
131 C4 Abuja Nigeria
97 C2 Abū Kamāl Syria
134 C2 Abumombazi Dem. Rep. Congo
168 B1 Abunã r. Bol./Brazil
166 C3 Abunã Brazil
90 B2 Abu Road India
94 B2 Abū Şādī, Jabal h. Saudi Arabia
132 B2 Abu Sunbul Egypt
132 A3 Abu Zabad Sudan
Abū Zabī U.A.E. see Abu Dhabi
133 A4 Abyei Sudan
161 B2 Acambaro Mex.

136 B2 Acampamento de Caça do Mucusso Angola
122 B1 A Cañiza Spain
160 B2 Acaponeta Mex.
161 C3 Acapulco Mex.
167 E3 Acará Brazil
170 A3 Acaray, Represa de resr Para.
166 C2 Acariguana Venez.
126 B1 Acâş Romania
161 C3 Acatlán Mex.
161 C3 Acayucán Mex.
130 B4 Accra Ghana
114 B3 Accrington U.K.
90 B2 Achalpur India
113 A2 Achill Island Ireland
117 D1 Achim Ger.
112 B2 Achnasheen U.K.
107 D2 Achuyevo Rus. Fed.
127 C2 Acıpayam Turkey
125 C3 Acireale Italy
163 C2 Acklins Island Bahamas
169 A3 Aconcagua, Cerro mt. Arg.
122 B1 A Coruña Spain
124 A2 Acqui Terme Italy
119 D2 Ács Hungary
161 C2 Actopán Mex.
159 D2 Ada U.S.A.
Adabazar Turkey see Adapazarı
95 C2 Adam Oman
127 B3 Adamas Greece
151 B3 Adams Peak U.S.A.
'Adan Yemen see Aden
96 B2 Adana Turkey
127 D2 Adapazarı Turkey
113 B2 Adare Ireland
71 M2 Adare, Cape Antarctica
124 A1 Adda r. Italy
94 B2 Ad Dafinah Saudi Arabia
94 B2 Ad Dahnā' des. Saudi Arabia
95 B2 Ad Dahnā' des. Saudi Arabia
130 A2 Ad Dakhla Western Sahara
Ad Dammām Saudi Arabia see Dammam
94 A2 Ad Dār al Ḥamrā' Saudi Arabia
94 B3 Ad Darb Saudi Arabia
94 B2 Ad Dawādimī Saudi Arabia
Ad Dawḥah Qatar see Doha
Aḑ Ḑiffah plat. Egypt/Libya see Libyan Plateau
94 B2 Ad Dilam Saudi Arabia
94 B2 Ad Dir'īyah Saudi Arabia
133 B4 Addis Ababa Eth.
97 C2 Ad Dīwānīyah Iraq
157 D2 Adel U.S.A.
68 A2 Adelaide Austr.
71 A3 Adelaide Island Antarctica
66 C1 Adelaide River Austr.
117 D2 Adelebsen Ger.
71 K2 Adélie Land reg. Antarctica
94 B3 Aden Yemen
132 C3 Aden, Gulf of Somalia/Yemen
116 C2 Adenau Ger.
131 C3 Aderbissinat Niger
95 C2 Adh Dhayd U.A.E.
75 C3 Adi i. Indon.
132 B3 Ādī Ārk'ay Eth.
124 B1 Adige r. Italy
132 B3 Ādīgrat Eth.
94 A3 Adi Keyih Eritrea
90 B3 Adilabad India
131 D2 Adirī Libya
155 E2 Adirondack Mountains U.S.A.
Ādīs Ābeba Eth. see Addis Ababa
133 B4 Ādīs Alem Eth.
96 B2 Adıyaman Turkey
126 C1 Adjud Romania
66 B1 Admiralty Gulf Austr.
144 A2 Admiralty Island U.S.A.
75 D3 Admiralty Islands P.N.G.
89 B3 Adoni India
120 B3 Adour r. France
122 C2 Adra Spain
130 B2 Adrar Alg.
154 C2 Adrian MI U.S.A.
159 C1 Adrian TX U.S.A.
124 B2 Adriatic Sea Europe
132 B3 Ādwa Eth.
99 K2 Adycha r. Rus. Fed.
107 D2 Adygeysk Rus. Fed.
130 B4 Adzopé Côte d'Ivoire
127 B3 Aegean Sea Greece/Turkey
117 D1 Aerzen Ger.
122 B1 A Estrada Spain
132 B3 Afabet Eritrea
Affreville Alg. see Khemis Miliana
92 C3 Afghanistan country Asia
94 B2 'Afīf Saudi Arabia
152 A2 Afton U.S.A.
96 B2 Afyon Turkey
131 C3 Agadez Niger
130 B1 Agadir Morocco
93 D2 Agadyr' Kazakh.
129 I7 Agalega Islands Mauritius
Agana Guam see Hagåtña
122 B1 A Gándara de Altea Spain
90 B2 Agar India
135 D2 Agaro Eth.
91 D2 Agartala India
97 C2 Ağdam Azer.
121 C3 Agde France
120 C3 Agen France
Agedabia Libya see Ajdābiyā

138 A2 Aggeneys S. Africa
127 C3 Agia Varvara Greece
127 B3 Agios Dimitrios Greece
127 C3 Agios Efstratios i. Greece
127 C3 Agios Kirykos Greece
127 C3 Agios Nikolaos Greece
94 A3 Agirwat Hills Sudan
139 C2 Agisanang S. Africa
126 B1 Agnita Romania
90 B2 Agra India
97 C2 Ağrı Turkey
Ağrı Dağı mt. Turkey see Ararat, Mount
124 B2 Agrigento Italy
127 B3 Agrinio Greece
125 B2 Agropoli Italy
103 E3 Agryz Rus. Fed.
160 B2 Agua Brava, Laguna lag. Mex.
170 B2 Agua Clara Brazil
161 C3 Aguada Mex.
162 B4 Aguadulce Panama
160 B2 Aguanaval r. Mex.
160 B1 Agua Prieta Mex.
160 B2 Aguascalientes Mex.
171 D1 Águas Formosas Brazil
170 C2 Agudos Brazil
122 B1 Águeda Port.
130 C3 Aguelhok Mali
122 C1 Aguilar de Campóo Spain
123 C2 Águilas Spain
160 B3 Aguililla Mex.
138 B3 Agulhas, Cape S. Africa
171 D2 Agulhas Negras mt. Brazil
174 F7 Agulhas Basin Southern Ocean
174 F7 Agulhas Plateau Southern Ocean
174 F7 Agulhas Ridge S. Atlantic Ocean
127 C2 Ağva Turkey
97 C2 Ahar Iran
116 C1 Ahaus Ger.
97 C2 Ahlat Turkey
116 C2 Ahlen Ger.
90 B2 Ahmadabad India
90 B3 Ahmadnagar India
90 B2 Ahmadpur East Pak.
90 B1 Ahmadpur Sial Pak.
133 C4 Ahmar Eth.
Ahmedabad India see Ahmadabad
Ahmednagar India see Ahmadnagar
160 B2 Ahome Mex.
97 D3 Ahram Iran
117 E1 Ahrensburg Ger.
120 C2 Ahun France
109 F4 Åhus Sweden
97 C2 Ahvāz Iran
Ahvenanmaa is Fin. see Åland Islands
138 A2 Ai-Ais Namibia
96 B2 Aigialousa Cyprus
127 B3 Aigio Greece
Aihui China see Heihe
Aijal India see Aizawl
157 D2 Aiken U.S.A.
113 B1 Ailt an Chorráin Ireland
171 D1 Aimorés Brazil
171 D1 Aimorés, Serra dos hills Brazil
121 D2 Ain r. France
123 C2 Aïn Beïda Alg.
131 C1 Aïn Beïda Alg.
130 B2 'Aïn Ben Tili Maur.
123 D2 Aïn Defla Alg.
130 B1 Aïn Sefra Alg.
152 D2 Ainsworth U.S.A.
Aintab Turkey see Gaziantep
123 D2 Aïn Taya Alg.
123 C2 Aïn Tédélès Alg.
123 C2 Aïn Temouchent Alg.
131 C3 Aïr, Massif de l' mts Niger
76 A1 Airbangis Indon.
144 A2 Airdrie Can.
112 C3 Airdrie U.K.
120 B3 Aire-sur-l'Adour France
117 E3 Aisch r. Ger.
144 A1 Aishihik Lake Can.
116 A3 Aisne r. France
75 D3 Aitape P.N.G.
153 E1 Aitkin U.S.A.
126 B1 Aiud Romania
121 D3 Aix-en-Provence France
Aix-la-Chapelle Ger. see Aachen
121 D2 Aix-les-Bains France
91 D2 Aizawl India
104 C2 Aizkraukle Latvia
104 B2 Aizpute Latvia
83 C3 Aizu-Wakamatsu Japan
121 D3 Ajaccio France
131 E1 Ajdābiyā Libya
95 C1 'Ajman U.A.E.
90 B2 Ajmer India
Ajmer-Merwara India see Ajmer
158 A2 Ajo U.S.A.
135 D2 Ak'ak'ī Beseka Eth.
Akamagaseki Japan see Shimonoseki
70 B2 Akaroa N.Z.
103 E3 Akbulak Rus. Fed.
96 B2 Akçakale Turkey
130 A3 Akchâr reg. Maur.
127 C3 Akdağ mt. Turkey
96 B2 Akdağmadeni Turkey
104 A2 Åkersberga Sweden
134 C2 Aketi Dem. Rep. Congo
97 C1 Akhalk'alak'i Georgia
97 C1 Akhalts'ikhe Georgia
95 C2 Akhḍar, Jabal mts Oman

127 C3 Akhisar Turkey
103 D4 Akhtubinsk Rus. Fed.
134 B3 Akiéni Gabon
146 B3 Akimiski Island Can.
82 D3 Akita Japan
130 A3 Akjoujt Maur.
Akkerman Ukr. see Bilhorod-Dnistrovs'kyy
93 D1 Akkol' Kazakh.
Ak-Mechet Kazakh. see Kyzylorda
104 B2 Akmenrags pt Latvia
Akmola Kazakh. see Astana
Akmolinsk Kazakh. see Astana
83 B4 Akō Japan
133 B4 Akobo Sudan
90 B2 Akola India
134 B2 Akonolinga Cameroon
94 A3 Akordat Eritrea
147 D1 Akpatok Island Can.
93 D2 Akqi China
108 □A3 Akranes Iceland
152 C2 Akron CO U.S.A.
154 C2 Akron OH U.S.A.
91 B1 Aksai Chin terr. Asia
96 B2 Aksaray Turkey
102 F2 Aksarka Rus. Fed.
92 B1 Aksay Kazakh.
107 D2 Aksay Rus. Fed.
96 B2 Akşehir Turkey
92 C2 Akshiganak Kazakh.
93 E2 Aksu China
132 B3 Āksum Eth.
92 B2 Aktau Kazakh.
92 B1 Aktobe Kazakh.
93 D2 Aktogay Kazakh.
104 C3 Aktsyabrski Belarus
Aktyubinsk Kazakh. see Aktobe
83 B4 Akune Japan
131 C4 Akure Nigeria
108 □B2 Akureyri Iceland
Akyab Myanmar see Sittwe
127 D2 Akyazı Turkey
156 C2 Alabama r. U.S.A.
156 C2 Alabama state U.S.A.
156 C2 Alabaster U.S.A.
127 C2 Alaçatı Turkey
161 D2 Alacrán, Arrecife rf Mex.
97 C1 Alagir Rus. Fed.
167 F4 Alagoinhas Brazil
123 C1 Alagón Spain
94 B3 Al Aḥmadī Kuwait
93 E2 Alakol', Ozero salt l. Kazakh.
108 J2 Alakurtti Rus. Fed.
94 B3 Al 'Alayyah Saudi Arabia
97 C2 Al 'Amādīyah Iraq
97 C2 Al 'Amārah Iraq
96 A2 Al 'Āmirīyah Egypt
159 C2 Alamítos, Sierra de los mt. Mex.
151 C3 Alamo U.S.A.
158 B2 Alamogordo U.S.A.
160 A2 Alamos Mex.
160 B2 Alamos Mex.
160 B2 Alamos r. Mex.
152 B3 Alamosa U.S.A.
Åland is Fin. see Åland Islands
109 G3 Åland Islands is Fin.
127 C2 Alanya Turkey
89 B4 Alappuzha India
96 B3 Al 'Aqabah Jordan
94 B2 Al 'Aqīq Saudi Arabia
123 C2 Alarcón, Embalse de resr Spain
96 A2 Al 'Arīsh Egypt
94 B2 Al Arṭāwīyah Saudi Arabia
77 C2 Alas Indon.
127 C2 Alaşehir Turkey
144 A2 Alaska state U.S.A.
140 D4 Alaska, Gulf of U.S.A.
142 B3 Alaska Peninsula U.S.A.
142 C2 Alaska Range mts U.S.A.
97 C2 Ālāt Azer.
103 D3 Alatyr' Rus. Fed.
166 B3 Alausí Ecuador
109 H3 Alavus Fin.
68 A2 Alawoona Austr.
95 C2 Al 'Ayn U.A.E.
124 A2 Alba Italy
123 C2 Albacete Spain
94 A2 Al Bada'i' Saudi Arabia
94 B2 Al Badī' Saudi Arabia
126 B1 Alba Iulia Romania
125 C2 Albania country Europe
66 A3 Albany Austr.
83 C3 Albany r. Can.
157 D2 Albany GA U.S.A.
155 F2 Albany NY U.S.A.
150 B2 Albany OR U.S.A.
131 E1 Al Bardī Libya
Al Başrah Iraq see Basra
67 D1 Albatross Bay Austr.
132 A2 Al Bawītī Egypt
131 E1 Al Bayḍā' Libya
94 B3 Al Bayḍā' Yemen
157 E1 Albemarle U.S.A.
157 E1 Albemarle Sound sea chan. U.S.A.
124 A2 Albenga Italy
67 C2 Alberga watercourse Austr.
135 D2 Albert, Lake Dem. Rep. Congo/Uganda
144 C2 Alberta prov. Can.
116 C2 Albert Kanaal canal Belgium
153 E2 Albert Lea U.S.A.
133 B4 Albert Nile r. Sudan/Uganda
139 C2 Alberton S. Africa

'Amur, Wadi

Albertville Dem. Rep. Congo *see* **Kalemie**
121 D2 **Albertville** France
120 C3 **Albi** France
167 D2 **Albina** Suriname
94 A2 **Al Bi'r** Saudi Arabia
94 B3 **Al Birk** Saudi Arabia
94 B2 **Al Biyāḍh** *reg.* Saudi Arabia
122 C2 **Alborán, Isla de** *i.* Spain
122 C2 **Alborán Sea** Europe
Alborz, Reshteh-ye *mts* Iran *see* **Elburz Mountains**
123 C2 **Albox** Spain
122 B2 **Albufeira** Port.
158 B1 **Albuquerque** U.S.A.
95 C2 **Al Buraymī** Oman
69 C3 **Albury** Austr.
122 B2 **Alcácer do Sal** Port.
122 C1 **Alcalá de Henares** Spain
122 C2 **Alcalá la Real** Spain
124 B3 **Alcamo** Italy
123 C1 **Alcañiz** Spain
122 B2 **Alcántara** Spain
123 C2 **Alcantarilla** Spain
122 C2 **Alcaraz** Spain
122 C2 **Alcaraz, Sierra de** *mts* Spain
122 C2 **Alcaudete** Spain
122 C2 **Alcázar de San Juan** Spain
Alcazarquivir Morocco *see* **Ksar el Kebir**
107 D2 **Alchevs'k** Ukr.
171 E1 **Alcobaça** Brazil
123 C2 **Alcoy-Alcoi** Spain
123 D2 **Alcúdia** Spain
129 H6 **Aldabra Islands** Seychelles
158 B3 **Aldama** Mex.
161 C2 **Aldama** Mex.
99 J3 **Aldan** Rus. Fed.
99 J2 **Aldan** *r.* Rus. Fed.
115 D3 **Aldeburgh** U.K.
111 C4 **Alderney** *i.* Channel Is
115 C4 **Aldershot** U.K.
130 A3 **Aleg** Maur.
171 D2 **Alegre** Brazil
168 C2 **Alegrete** Brazil
105 D1 **Alekhovshchina** Rus. Fed.
105 E2 **Aleksandrov** Rus. Fed.
Aleksandrovsk Ukr. *see* **Zaporizhzhya**
99 K3 **Aleksandrovsk-Sakhalinskiy** Rus. Fed.
98 E1 **Aleksandry, Zemlya** *i.* Rus. Fed.
Alekseyevka Kazakh. *see* **Akkol'**
107 D1 **Alekseyevka** Rus. Fed.
107 D1 **Alekseyevka** Rus. Fed.
105 E3 **Aleksin** Rus. Fed.
125 D2 **Aleksinac** Serbia
134 B3 **Alèmbé** Gabon
171 D2 **Além Paraíba** Brazil
109 F3 **Ålen** Norway
120 C2 **Alençon** France
96 B2 **Aleppo** Syria
166 B4 **Alerta** Peru
144 B2 **Alert Bay** Can.
121 C3 **Alès** France
126 B1 **Aleşd** Romania
Aleshki Ukr. *see* **Tsyurupyns'k**
124 A2 **Alessandria** Italy
Alessio Albania *see* **Lezhë**
109 E3 **Ålesund** Norway
172 D2 **Aleutian Basin** Bering Sea
140 A4 **Aleutian Islands** U.S.A.
99 L3 **Alevina, Mys** *c.* Rus. Fed.
144 A2 **Alexander Archipelago** *is* U.S.A.
138 A2 **Alexander Bay** S. Africa
156 C2 **Alexander City** U.S.A.
71 A2 **Alexander Island** Antarctica
69 C3 **Alexandra** Austr.
70 A3 **Alexandra** N.Z.
169 E5 **Alexandra, Cape** S. Georgia
Alexandra Land *i.* Rus. Fed. *see* **Aleksandry, Zemlya**
127 B2 **Alexandreia** Greece
132 A1 **Alexandria** Egypt
126 C2 **Alexandria** Romania
139 C3 **Alexandria** S. Africa
112 B3 **Alexandria** U.K.
156 B2 **Alexandria** *LA* U.S.A.
153 D1 **Alexandria** *MN* U.S.A.
155 D3 **Alexandria** *VA* U.S.A.
68 A3 **Alexandrina, Lake** Austr.
127 C2 **Alexandroupoli** Greece
147 E2 **Alexis** *r.* Can.
144 B2 **Alexis Creek** Can.
93 E1 **Aleysk** Rus. Fed.
123 C1 **Alfaro** Spain
97 C3 **Al Fāw** Iraq
96 B3 **Al Fayyūm** Egypt
117 D2 **Alfeld (Leine)** Ger.
171 C2 **Alfenas** Brazil
112 C2 **Alford** U.K.
Al Fujayrah U.A.E. *see* **Fujairah**
Al Furāt *r.* Iraq/Syria *see* **Euphrates**
109 E4 **Ålgård** Norway
122 B2 **Algarve** *reg.* Port.
122 B2 **Algeciras** Spain
123 C2 **Algemesí** Spain
94 A3 **Algena** Eritrea
Alger Alg. *see* **Algiers**
130 C2 **Algeria** *country* Africa
95 C3 **Al Ghayḍah** Yemen
124 A2 **Alghero** Italy
132 B2 **Al Ghurdaqah** Egypt
95 B2 **Al Ghwaybiyah** Saudi Arabia
131 C1 **Algiers** Alg.
139 C3 **Algoa Bay** S. Africa
153 E2 **Algona** U.S.A.
122 C1 **Algorta** Spain
Algueirao Moz. *see* **Hacufera**
97 C2 **Al Ḥadīthah** Iraq
95 C2 **Al Ḥajar al Gharbī** *mts* Oman
123 C2 **Alhama de Murcia** Spain
96 A2 **Al Ḥammām** Egypt
94 B2 **Al Ḥanākīyah** Saudi Arabia
97 C2 **Al Ḥasakah** Syria
94 B2 **Al Ḥawīyah** Saudi Arabia
97 C2 **Al Ḥayy** Iraq
94 B3 **Al Ḥazm al Jawf** Yemen
95 C3 **Al Ḥibāk** *des.* Saudi Arabia
Al Ḥillah Iraq *see* **Hillah**
94 B2 **Al Ḥillah** Saudi Arabia
95 B2 **Al Ḥinnāh** Saudi Arabia
Al Ḥudaydah Yemen *see* **Hodeidah**
95 B2 **Al Hufūf** Saudi Arabia
131 D2 **Al Ḥulayq al Kabīr** *hills* Libya
95 C2 **'Alīābād** Iran
127 C3 **Aliağa** Turkey
127 B2 **Aliakmonas** *r.* Greece
97 C2 **Äli Bayramlı** Azer.
123 C2 **Alicante** Spain
159 D3 **Alice** U.S.A.
125 C3 **Alice, Punta** *pt* Italy
67 C2 **Alice Springs** Austr.
93 D3 **Alichur** Tajik.
90 B2 **Aligarh** India
97 C2 **Alīgūdarz** Iran
85 E1 **Alihe** China
134 B3 **Alima** *r.* Congo
134 C2 **Alindao** C.A.R.
127 C3 **Aliova** *r.* Turkey
90 B2 **Alirajpur** India
133 C3 **Ali Sabieh** Djibouti
94 A1 **Al 'Īsāwīyah** Saudi Arabia
Al Iskandarīyah Egypt *see* **Alexandria**
132 B1 **Al Ismā'īlīyah** Egypt
139 C3 **Aliwal North** S. Africa
131 E2 **Al Jaghbūb** Libya
94 B2 **Al Jahrah** Kuwait
95 C2 **Al Jamalīyah** Qatar
131 E2 **Al Jawf** Libya
131 D1 **Al Jawsh** Libya
122 B2 **Aljezur** Port.
Al Jīzah Egypt *see* **Giza**
95 B2 **Al Jubayl** Saudi Arabia
94 B2 **Al Jubaylah** Saudi Arabia
131 D2 **Al Jufrah** Libya
94 B2 **Al Junaynah** Saudi Arabia
122 B2 **Aljustrel** Port.
94 B2 **Al Kahfah** Saudi Arabia
95 C2 **Al Kāmil** Oman
96 B2 **Al Karak** Jordan
97 C2 **Al Kāẓimīyah** Iraq
95 C2 **Al Khābūrah** Oman
94 B2 **Al Khamāsīn** Saudi Arabia
132 B2 **Al Khārijah** Egypt
95 C2 **Al Khaṣab** Oman
94 B3 **Al Khawkhah** Yemen
95 C2 **Al Khawr** Qatar
131 D1 **Al Khums** Libya
95 B2 **Al Khunn** Saudi Arabia
95 C2 **Al Kidan** *well* Saudi Arabia
95 C2 **Al Kir'ānah** Qatar
116 B1 **Alkmaar** Neth.
131 E2 **Al Kufrah** Libya
97 C2 **Al Kūt** Iraq
Al Kuwayt Kuwait *see* **Kuwait**
Al Lādhiqīyah Syria *see* **Latakia**
91 C2 **Allahabad** India
99 K2 **Allakh-Yun'** Rus. Fed.
94 A2 **'Allāqī, Wādī al** *watercourse* Egypt
155 D2 **Allegheny** *r.* U.S.A.
155 C3 **Allegheny Mountains** U.S.A.
113 B1 **Allen, Lough** *l.* Ireland
161 B2 **Allende** Mex.
161 B2 **Allende** Mex.
155 D2 **Allentown** U.S.A.
Alleppey India *see* **Alappuzha**
117 D1 **Aller** *r.* Ger.
152 C2 **Alliance** *NE* U.S.A.
154 C2 **Alliance** *OH* U.S.A.
94 B2 **Al Līth** Saudi Arabia
112 C2 **Alloa** U.K.
147 C3 **Alma** Can.
Alma-Ata Kazakh. *see* **Almaty**
122 B2 **Almada** Port.
122 C2 **Almadén** Spain
Al Madīnah Saudi Arabia *see* **Medina**
96 B2 **Al Mafraq** Jordan
130 B2 **Al Mahbas** Western Sahara
94 B3 **Al Maḥwīt** Yemen
94 B2 **Al Majma'ah** Saudi Arabia
132 B2 **Al Maks al Baḥrī** Egypt
Al Manāmah Bahrain *see* **Manama**
151 B2 **Almanor, Lake** U.S.A.
123 C2 **Almansa** Spain
96 B2 **Al Manṣūrah** Egypt
95 C2 **Al Mariyyah** U.A.E.
131 E1 **Al Marj** Libya
93 D2 **Almaty** Kazakh.
Al Mawṣil Iraq *see* **Mosul**
97 C2 **Al Mayādīn** Syria
122 C1 **Almazán** Spain
167 D3 **Almeirim** Brazil
116 C1 **Almelo** Neth.
171 D1 **Almenara** Brazil
122 B1 **Almendra, Embalse de** *resr* Spain
122 B2 **Almendralejo** Spain
122 C2 **Almería** Spain
122 C2 **Almería, Golfo de** *b.* Spain
103 E3 **Al'met'yevsk** Rus. Fed.
94 B2 **Al Mindak** Saudi Arabia
132 B2 **Al Minyā** Egypt
95 B2 **Al Mish'āb** Saudi Arabia
122 B2 **Almodôvar** Port.
122 B2 **Almonte** Spain
91 B2 **Almora** India
95 B2 **Al Mubarrez** Saudi Arabia
95 C2 **Al Muḍaibī** Oman
96 B3 **Al Mudawwarah** Jordan
Al Mukallā Yemen *see* **Mukalla**
Al Mukhā Yemen *see* **Mocha**
122 C2 **Almuñécar** Spain
97 C2 **Al Muqdādīyah** Iraq
94 A2 **Al Musayjīd** Saudi Arabia
94 A2 **Al Muwayliḥ** Saudi Arabia
127 B3 **Almyros** Greece
112 B2 **Alness** U.K.
114 C2 **Alnwick** U.K.
78 A1 **Along** India
127 B3 **Alonnisos** *i.* Greece
75 C3 **Alor** *i.* Indon.
75 C3 **Alor, Kepulauan** *is* Indon.
Alor Setar Malaysia *see* **Alor Star**
76 B1 **Alor Star** Malaysia
Alost Belgium *see* **Aalst**
75 E3 **Alotau** P.N.G.
102 C2 **Alozero** Rus. Fed.
154 C1 **Alpena** U.S.A.
176 Q1 **Alpha Ridge** Arctic Ocean
116 B1 **Alphen aan den Rijn** Neth.
158 B2 **Alpine** *AZ* U.S.A.
159 C2 **Alpine** *TX* U.S.A.
100 E4 **Alps** *mts* Europe
95 B3 **Al Qa'āmīyāt** *reg.* Saudi Arabia
131 D1 **Al Qaddāḥīyah** Libya
Al Qāhirah Egypt *see* **Cairo**
94 B2 **Al Qā'īyah** Saudi Arabia
97 C2 **Al Qāmishlī** Syria
96 B2 **Al Qaryatayn** Syria
95 B2 **Al Qaṣab** Saudi Arabia
132 A2 **Al Qaṣr** Egypt
95 B3 **Al Qaṭn** Yemen
131 D2 **Al Qaṭrūn** Libya
122 B2 **Alqueva, Barragem de** *resr* Port.
96 B2 **Al Qunayṭirah** Syria
94 B3 **Al Qunfidhah** Saudi Arabia
132 B2 **Al Quṣayr** Egypt
94 B2 **Al Quwārah** Saudi Arabia
94 B2 **Al Quwayīyah** Saudi Arabia
117 D2 **Alsfeld** Ger.
114 B2 **Alston** U.K.
108 H2 **Alta** Norway
108 H2 **Altaelva** *r.* Norway
84 B1 **Altai Mountains** Asia
157 D2 **Altamaha** *r.* U.S.A.
167 D3 **Altamira** Brazil
125 C2 **Altamura** Italy
160 A1 **Altar, Desierto de** *des.* Mex.
93 E2 **Altay** China
84 C1 **Altay** Mongolia
121 D2 **Altdorf** Switz.
123 C2 **Altea** Spain
108 H1 **Alteidet** Norway
117 F2 **Altenburg** Ger.
116 C2 **Altenkirchen (Westerwald)** Ger.
117 F1 **Altentreptow** Ger.
127 C3 **Altınoluk** Turkey
127 D3 **Altıntaş** Turkey
168 B1 **Altiplano** *plain* Bol.
112 B1 **Altnaharra** U.K.
170 B1 **Alto Araguaia** Brazil
123 C1 **Alto del Moncayo** *mt.* Spain
170 B1 **Alto Garças** Brazil
137 C2 **Alto Ligonha** Moz.
137 C2 **Alto Molócuè** Moz.
115 C4 **Alton** U.K.
153 E3 **Alton** U.S.A.
145 E3 **Altona** Can.
155 D2 **Altoona** U.S.A.
170 B1 **Alto Sucuriú** Brazil
170 B1 **Alto Taquarí** Brazil
118 C2 **Altötting** Ger.
84 C2 **Altun Shan** *mt.* China
84 B2 **Altun Shan** *mts* China
150 B2 **Alturas** U.S.A.
159 D2 **Altus** U.S.A.
104 C2 **Alūksne** Latvia
94 A2 **Al 'Ulā** Saudi Arabia
131 D1 **Al 'Uqaylah** Libya
Al Uqṣur Egypt *see* **Luxor**
107 C3 **Alushta** Ukr.
131 E2 **Al 'Uwaynāt** Libya
159 D1 **Alva** U.S.A.
161 C3 **Alvarado** Mex.
109 F3 **Älvdalen** Sweden
108 H2 **Älvsbyn** Sweden
94 A2 **Al Wajh** Saudi Arabia
95 C2 **Al Wakrah** Qatar
90 B2 **Alwar** India
97 C2 **Al Widyān** *plat.* Iraq/Saudi Arabia
Alxa Youqi China *see* **Ehen Hudag**
Alxa Zuoqi China *see* **Bayan Hot**
67 C1 **Alyangula** Austr.
104 B3 **Alytus** Lith.
152 C1 **Alzada** U.S.A.
117 D3 **Alzey** Ger.
66 C2 **Amadeus, Lake** *imp. l.* Austr.
143 H2 **Amadjuak Lake** Can.
122 B2 **Amadora** Port.
94 B2 **Amā'ir** Saudi Arabia
83 B4 **Amakusa-Shimo-shima** *i.* Japan
109 F4 **Åmål** Sweden
127 B3 **Amaliada** Greece
75 D3 **Amamapare** Indon.
170 A2 **Amambaí** Brazil
170 B2 **Amambaí** *r.* Brazil
170 A2 **Amambaí, Serra de** *hills* Brazil/Para.
85 E3 **Amami-Ō-shima** *i.* Japan
85 E3 **Amami-shotō** *is* Japan
93 C1 **Amangel'dy** Kazakh.
125 C3 **Amantea** Italy
139 D3 **Amanzimtoti** S. Africa
167 D2 **Amapá** Brazil
122 B2 **Amareleja** Port.
104 B2 **Ämari** Estonia
159 C1 **Amarillo** U.S.A.
124 B2 **Amaro, Monte** *mt.* Italy
96 B1 **Amasya** Turkey
166 D2 **Amazon** *r.* S. America
167 E2 **Amazon, Mouths of the** Brazil
Amazonas *r.* S. America *see* **Amazon**
173 I5 **Amazon Cone** S. Atlantic Ocean
90 B1 **Ambala** India
137 □D3 **Ambalavao** Madag.
137 □D2 **Ambanja** Madag.
120 B3 **Ambarès-et-Lagrave** France
166 B3 **Ambato** Ecuador
137 □D2 **Ambato Boeny** Madag.
137 □D3 **Ambato Finandrahana** Madag.
137 □D2 **Ambatolampy** Madag.
137 □D2 **Ambatondrazaka** Madag.
117 E3 **Amberg** Ger.
162 B3 **Ambergris Cay** *i.* Belize
91 C2 **Ambikapur** India
137 □D2 **Ambilobe** Madag.
114 C2 **Amble** U.K.
114 B2 **Ambleside** U.K.
137 □D3 **Amboasary** Madag.
137 □D2 **Ambodifotatra** Madag.
137 □D2 **Ambohidratrimo** Madag.
137 □D3 **Ambohimahasoa** Madag.
Amboina Indon. *see* **Ambon**
75 C3 **Ambon** Indon.
75 C3 **Ambon** *i.* Indon.
137 □D3 **Ambositra** Madag.
137 □D3 **Ambovombe** Madag.
151 C4 **Amboy** U.S.A.
Ambre, Cap d' *c.* Madag. *see* **Bobaomby, Tanjona**
136 A1 **Ambriz** Angola
Ambrizete Angola *see* **N'zeto**
102 F2 **Amderma** Rus. Fed.
Amdo China *see* **Lharigarbo**
161 B2 **Amealco** Mex.
160 B2 **Ameca** Mex.
116 B1 **Ameland** *i.* Neth.
170 C2 **Americana** Brazil
71 D4 **American-Antarctic Ridge** S. Atlantic Ocean
150 D2 **American Falls** U.S.A.
150 D2 **American Falls Reservoir** U.S.A.
151 D2 **American Fork** U.S.A.
65 J5 **American Samoa** *terr.* S. Pacific Ocean
157 D2 **Americus** U.S.A.
116 B1 **Amersfoort** Neth.
71 H2 **Amery Ice Shelf** Antarctica
153 E2 **Ames** U.S.A.
127 B3 **Amfissa** Greece
99 J2 **Amga** Rus. Fed.
82 C1 **Amgu** Rus. Fed.
131 C2 **Amguid** Alg.
99 K3 **Amgun'** *r.* Rus. Fed.
147 D3 **Amherst** Can.
120 C2 **Amiens** France
95 C3 **Amilḥayt, Wādī al** *r.* Oman
89 B3 **Amindivi Islands** India
138 A1 **Aminuis** Namibia
90 A2 **Amir Chah** Pak.
145 D2 **Amisk Lake** Can.
159 C3 **Amistad Reservoir** Mex./U.S.A.
114 A3 **Amlwch** U.K.
96 B2 **'Ammān** Jordan
143 J2 **Ammassalik** Greenland
94 B3 **Am Nābiyah** Yemen
97 D2 **Amol** Iran
127 C3 **Amorgos** *i.* Greece
156 C2 **Amory** U.S.A.
146 C3 **Amos** Can.
Amoy China *see* **Xiamen**
137 □D3 **Ampanihy** Madag.
171 C2 **Amparo** Brazil
137 □D2 **Ampasimanolotra** Madag.
123 D1 **Amposta** Spain
94 B3 **'Amrān** Yemen
Amraoti India *see* **Amravati**
90 B2 **Amravati** India
90 B2 **Amreli** India
90 B1 **Amritsar** India
116 B1 **Amstelveen** Neth.
116 B1 **Amsterdam** Neth.
139 D2 **Amsterdam** S. Africa
172 A8 **Amsterdam, Île** *i.* Indian Ocean
119 C2 **Amstetten** Austria
131 E3 **Am Timan** Chad
92 B2 **Amudar'ya** *r.* Asia
142 F1 **Amund Ringnes Island** Can.
71 J3 **Amundsen, Mount** Antarctica
176 H1 **Amundsen Basin** Arctic Ocean
142 D2 **Amundsen Gulf** Can.
71 P2 **Amundsen Ridges** Southern Ocean
71 P2 **Amundsen Sea** Antarctica
77 C2 **Amuntai** Indon.
Amur *r.* China *see* **Heilong Jiang**
94 A3 **'Amur, Wadi** *watercourse* Sudan

Anabanua

77 D2 **Anabanua** Indon.
99 I2 **Anabar** *r.* Rus. Fed.
99 I2 **Anabarskiy Zaliv** *b.* Rus. Fed.
166 C2 **Anaco** Venez.
150 D1 **Anaconda** U.S.A.
150 B1 **Anacortes** U.S.A.
159 D1 **Anadarko** U.S.A.
96 B1 **Anadolu Dağları** *mts* Turkey
99 M2 **Anadyr'** Rus. Fed.
99 M2 **Anadyr'** *r.* Rus. Fed.
97 C2 **'Ānah** Iraq
161 B2 **Anáhuac** Mex.
89 B3 **Anai Mudi** India
137 □D2 **Analalava** Madag.
137 □D3 **Analavelona** *mts* Madag.
76 B1 **Anambas, Kepulauan** *is* Indon.
153 E2 **Anamosa** U.S.A.
96 B2 **Anamur** Turkey
83 B4 **Anan** Japan
89 B3 **Anantapur** India
90 B1 **Anantnag** India
106 B2 **Anan'yiv** Ukr.
107 D3 **Anapa** Rus. Fed.
170 C1 **Anápolis** Brazil
97 D2 **Anār** Iran
168 B2 **Añatuya** Arg.
113 B1 **An Baile Thiar** Ireland
113 B1 **An Bun Beag** Ireland
81 B2 **Anbyon** N. Korea
120 B2 **Ancenis** France
142 C2 **Anchorage** U.S.A.
124 B2 **Ancona** Italy
169 A4 **Ancud** Chile
Anda China *see* **Daqing**
113 A2 **An Daingean** Ireland
109 E3 **Åndalsnes** Norway
122 C2 **Andalucía** *aut. comm.* Spain
Andalusia *aut. comm.* Spain *see* **Andalucía**
156 C2 **Andalusia** U.S.A.
175 F3 **Andaman Basin** Indian Ocean
89 D3 **Andaman Islands** India
79 A2 **Andaman Sea** Indian Ocean
137 □D2 **Andapa** Madag.
116 B2 **Andelst** Neth.
108 G2 **Andenes** Norway
116 B2 **Andenne** Belgium
116 B2 **Anderlecht** Belgium
121 D2 **Andermatt** Switz.
142 D2 **Anderson** *r.* Can.
142 C2 **Anderson** *AK* U.S.A.
154 B2 **Anderson** *IN* U.S.A.
157 D2 **Anderson** *SC* U.S.A.
164 C3 **Andes** *mts* S. America
93 D2 **Andijon** Uzbek.
137 □D2 **Andilamena** Madag.
137 □D2 **Andilanatoby** Madag.
Andizhan Uzbek. *see* **Andijon**
90 A1 **Andkhvoy** Afgh.
137 □D2 **Andoany** Madag.
Andong China *see* **Dandong**
81 B2 **Andong** S. Korea
120 C3 **Andorra** *country* Europe
120 C3 **Andorra la Vella** Andorra
115 C4 **Andover** U.K.
170 B2 **Andradina** Brazil
105 D2 **Andreapol'** Rus. Fed.
171 D2 **Andrelândia** Brazil
159 C2 **Andrews** U.S.A.
125 C2 **Andria** Italy
137 □D3 **Androka** Madag.
Andropov Rus. Fed. *see* **Rybinsk**
162 C2 **Andros** *i.* Bahamas
127 B3 **Andros** Greece
127 B3 **Andros** *i.* Greece
157 E4 **Andros Town** Bahamas
89 B3 **Andrott** *i.* India
106 B1 **Andrushivka** Ukr.
108 G2 **Andselv** Norway
122 C2 **Andújar** Spain
136 A2 **Andulo** Angola
130 C3 **Anéfis** Mali
163 D3 **Anegada Passage** Virgin Is (U.K.)
130 C4 **Aného** Togo
123 D1 **Aneto** *mt.* Spain
131 D3 **Aney** Niger
113 B1 **An Fál Carrach** Ireland
99 H3 **Angara** *r.* Rus. Fed.
84 C1 **Angarsk** Rus. Fed.
109 G3 **Ånge** Sweden
Angel, Salto del *waterfall* Venez. *see* **Angel Falls**
160 A2 **Ángel de la Guarda, Isla** *i.* Mex.
80 B2 **Angeles** Phil.
166 C2 **Angel Falls** Venez.
109 F4 **Ängelholm** Sweden
108 G3 **Ångermanälven** *r.* Sweden
120 B2 **Angers** France
145 E1 **Angikuni Lake** Can.
68 B3 **Anglesea** Austr.
114 A3 **Anglesey** *i.* U.K.
137 C2 **Angoche** Moz.
95 C2 **Angohrān** Iran
136 A2 **Angola** *country* Africa
154 C2 **Angola** U.S.A.
174 F6 **Angola Basin** S. Atlantic Ocean
144 A2 **Angoon** U.S.A.
120 C2 **Angoulême** France
171 D2 **Angra dos Reis** Brazil
93 D2 **Angren** Uzbek.
163 D3 **Anguilla** *terr.* West Indies
91 C2 **Angul** India
109 F4 **Anholt** *i.* Denmark
87 B3 **Anhua** China
86 B2 **Anhui** *prov.* China
170 B1 **Anhumas** Brazil
Anhwei *prov.* China *see* **Anhui**
170 C1 **Anicuns** Brazil
82 D1 **Aniva, Mys** *c.* Rus. Fed.
82 D1 **Aniva, Zaliv** *b.* Rus. Fed.
104 C1 **Anjalankoski** Fin.
120 B2 **Anjou** *reg.* France
81 B2 **Anjŭ** N. Korea
86 A2 **Ankang** China
96 B2 **Ankara** Turkey
137 □D3 **Ankazoabo** Madag.
137 □D2 **Ankazobe** Madag.
153 E2 **Ankeny** U.S.A.
118 C1 **Anklam** Ger.
137 □D2 **Ankofa** *mt.* Madag.
86 B2 **Anlu** China
71 G3 **Ann, Cape** Antarctica
155 E2 **Ann, Cape** U.S.A.
105 F3 **Anna** Rus. Fed.
131 C1 **Annaba** Alg.
117 F2 **Annaberg-Buchholtz** Ger.
96 B2 **An Nabk** Syria
94 B2 **An Nafūd** *des.* Saudi Arabia
166 D2 **Annai** Guyana
97 C2 **An Najaf** Iraq
79 B2 **Annam Highlands** *mts* Laos/Vietnam
112 C3 **Annan** U.K.
155 D3 **Annapolis** U.S.A.
91 C2 **Annapurna I** *mt.* Nepal
154 C2 **Ann Arbor** U.S.A.
166 D2 **Anna Regina** Guyana
An Nás Ireland *see* **Naas**
97 C2 **An Nāşirīyah** Iraq
131 D1 **An Nawfalīyah** Libya
121 D2 **Annecy** France
94 B3 **An Nimāş** Saudi Arabia
87 A3 **Anning** China
156 C2 **Anniston** U.S.A.
121 C2 **Annonay** France
95 B2 **An Nu'ayrīyah** Saudi Arabia
137 □D2 **Anorontany, Tanjona** *hd* Madag.
87 B3 **Anpu** China
86 B2 **Anqing** China
81 B2 **Ansan** S. Korea
117 E3 **Ansbach** Ger.
86 C1 **Anshan** China
87 A3 **Anshun** China
159 D2 **Anson** U.S.A.
130 C3 **Ansongo** Mali
112 C2 **Anstruther** U.K.
166 B4 **Antabamba** Peru
96 B2 **Antakya** Turkey
137 □E2 **Antalaha** Madag.
96 B2 **Antalya** Turkey
96 B2 **Antalya Körfezi** *g.* Turkey
137 □D2 **Antananarivo** Madag.
71 A2 **Antarctic Peninsula** Antarctica
112 B2 **An Teallach** *mt.* U.K.
122 C2 **Antequera** Spain
158 B2 **Anthony** U.S.A.
130 B2 **Anti-Atlas** *mts* Morocco
121 D3 **Antibes** France
147 D3 **Anticosti, Île d'** *i.* Can.
147 D3 **Antigonish** Can.
163 D3 **Antigua** *i.* Antigua
163 D3 **Antigua and Barbuda** *country* West Indies
161 C2 **Antiguo-Morelos** Mex.
127 B3 **Antikythira** *i.* Greece
Antioch Turkey *see* **Antakya**
65 I8 **Antipodes Islands** N.Z.
An t-Ob U.K. *see* **Leverburgh**
168 A2 **Antofagasta** Chile
170 C3 **Antonina** Brazil
António Enes Moz. *see* **Angoche**
113 C1 **Antrim** U.K.
113 C1 **Antrim Hills** U.K.
137 □D2 **Antsalova** Madag.
Antseranana Madag. *see* **Antsirañana**
137 □D2 **Antsirabe** Madag.
137 □D2 **Antsirañana** Madag.
137 □D2 **Antsohihy** Madag.
116 B2 **Antwerp** Belgium
Antwerpen Belgium *see* **Antwerp**
An Uaimh Ireland *see* **Navan**
90 B2 **Anupgarh** India
89 C4 **Anuradhapura** Sri Lanka
Anvers Belgium *see* **Antwerp**
67 C3 **Anxious Bay** Austr.
86 B2 **Anyang** China
81 B2 **Anyang** S. Korea
124 B2 **Anzio** Italy
83 C4 **Aoga-shima** *i.* Japan
82 D2 **Aomori** Japan
70 B2 **Aoraki** N.Z.
124 A1 **Aosta** Italy
130 B2 **Aoukâr** *reg.* Mali/Maur.
130 C2 **Aoulef** Alg.
131 D2 **Aozou** Chad
157 D3 **Apalachee Bay** U.S.A.
166 C3 **Apaporis** *r.* Col.
170 B2 **Aparecida do Tabuado** Brazil
80 B2 **Aparri** Phil.
102 C2 **Apatity** Rus. Fed.
160 B3 **Apatzingán** Mex.
116 B1 **Apeldoorn** Neth.
116 C1 **Apen** Ger.
124 A2 **Apennines** *mts* Italy
65 J5 **Apia** Samoa
170 C2 **Apiaí** Brazil
80 B3 **Apo, Mount** *vol.* Phil.
117 E2 **Apolda** Ger.
68 B3 **Apollo Bay** Austr.
157 D3 **Apopka** U.S.A.
157 D3 **Apopka, Lake** U.S.A.
170 B1 **Aporé** Brazil
170 B1 **Aporé** *r.* Brazil
154 A1 **Apostle Islands** U.S.A.
96 B2 **Apostolos Andreas, Cape** Cyprus
107 C2 **Apostolove** Ukr.
149 F3 **Appalachian Mountains** U.S.A.
Appennino *mts* Italy *see* **Apennines**
69 D2 **Appin** Austr.
116 C1 **Appingedam** Neth.
114 B2 **Appleby-in-Westmorland** U.K.
154 B2 **Appleton** U.S.A.
124 B2 **Aprilia** Italy
78 A1 **Aprunyi** India
107 D3 **Apsheronsk** Rus. Fed.
Apsheronskaya Rus. Fed. *see* **Apsheronsk**
170 B2 **Apucarana** Brazil
170 B2 **Apucarana, Serra da** *hills* Brazil
80 A3 **Apurahuan** Phil.
163 D4 **Apure** *r.* Venez.
94 A2 **Aqaba, Gulf of** Asia
97 D2 **'Aqdā** Iran
91 C1 **Aqqikkol Hu** *salt l.* China
170 A1 **Aquidauana** *r.* Brazil
120 B3 **Aquitaine** *reg.* France
91 C2 **Ara** India
133 A4 **Arab, Bahr el** *watercourse* Sudan
Arabian Gulf *g.* Asia *see* **The Gulf**
94 B2 **Arabian Peninsula** Asia
72 B4 **Arabian Sea** Indian Ocean
167 F4 **Aracaju** Brazil
170 A2 **Aracanguy, Montes de** *hills* Para.
167 F3 **Aracati** Brazil
170 B2 **Araçatuba** Brazil
171 D1 **Aracruz** Brazil
171 D1 **Araçuaí** Brazil
126 B1 **Arad** Romania
131 E3 **Arada** Chad
95 C2 **'Arādah** U.A.E.
172 C6 **Arafura Sea** Austr./Indon.
170 B1 **Aragarças** Brazil
123 C1 **Aragón** *aut. comm.* Spain
123 C1 **Aragón** *r.* Spain
167 E3 **Araguaia** *r.* Brazil
170 B1 **Araguaiana** Brazil
167 E3 **Araguaína** Brazil
170 C1 **Araguari** Brazil
83 C3 **Arai** Japan
131 C2 **Arak** Alg.
97 C2 **Arāk** Iran
78 A1 **Arakan Yoma** *mts* Myanmar
97 C1 **Arak's** *r.* Armenia
92 C2 **Aral Sea** *salt l.* Kazakh./Uzbek.
92 C2 **Aral'sk** Kazakh.
Aral'skoye More *salt l.* Kazakh./Uzbek. *see* **Aral Sea**
122 C1 **Aranda de Duero** Spain
125 D2 **Aranđelovac** Serbia
113 B2 **Aran Islands** Ireland
122 C1 **Aranjuez** Spain
138 A1 **Aranos** Namibia
159 D3 **Aransas Pass** U.S.A.
83 B4 **Arao** Japan
130 B3 **Araouane** Mali
167 F3 **Arapiraca** Brazil
170 B2 **Arapongas** Brazil
170 C3 **Araquari** Brazil
94 B1 **'Ar'ar** Saudi Arabia
170 C2 **Araraquara** Brazil
167 D3 **Araras** Brazil
170 C2 **Araras** Brazil
170 B1 **Araras, Serra das** *hills* Brazil
170 B3 **Araras, Serra das** *mts* Brazil
97 C2 **Ararat** Armenia
68 B3 **Ararat** Austr.
97 C2 **Ararat, Mount** Turkey
171 D2 **Araruama, Lago de** *lag.* Brazil
171 E1 **Arataca** Brazil
Aratürük China *see* **Yiwu**
166 B2 **Arauca** Col.
170 C1 **Araxá** Brazil
97 C2 **Arbīl** Iraq
145 E2 **Arborg** Can.
112 C2 **Arbroath** U.K.
90 A2 **Arbu Lut, Dasht-e** *des.* Afgh.
120 B3 **Arcachon** France
157 D3 **Arcadia** U.S.A.
150 B2 **Arcata** U.S.A.
161 B3 **Arcelia** Mex.
102 D2 **Archangel** Rus. Fed.
67 D1 **Archer** *r.* Austr.
65 M5 **Archipel des Tuamotu** *is* Fr. Polynesia
165 B6 **Archipiélago Juan Fernández** S. Pacific Ocean
150 D2 **Arco** U.S.A.
122 B2 **Arcos de la Frontera** Spain
143 G2 **Arctic Bay** Can.
Arctic Institute Islands *is* Rus. Fed. *see* **Arkticheskogo Instituta, Ostrova**
176 J1 **Arctic Mid-Ocean Ridge** Arctic Ocean
176 **Arctic Ocean**
142 D2 **Arctic Red** *r.* Can.
97 C2 **Ardabīl** Iran
97 C1 **Ardahan** Turkey
109 E3 **Årdalstangen** Norway
113 C2 **Ardee** Ireland
116 B3 **Ardennes** *plat.* Belgium
151 B3 **Arden Town** U.S.A.
97 D2 **Ardestān** Iran
113 D1 **Ardglass** U.K.
69 C2 **Ardlethan** Austr.
159 D2 **Ardmore** U.S.A.
112 A2 **Ardnamurchan, Point of** U.K.
68 A2 **Ardrossan** Austr.
112 B3 **Ardrossan** U.K.
112 B2 **Ardvasar** U.K.
151 B3 **Arena, Point** U.S.A.
109 E4 **Arendal** Norway
116 B2 **Arendonk** Belgium
117 E1 **Arendsee (Altmark)** Ger.
166 B4 **Arequipa** Peru
167 D3 **Arere** Brazil
122 C1 **Arévalo** Spain
124 B2 **Arezzo** Italy
124 B2 **Argenta** Italy
120 B2 **Argentan** France
169 C2 **Argentina** *country* S. America
174 D7 **Argentine Basin** S. Atlantic Ocean
173 I8 **Argentine Rise** S. Atlantic Ocean
169 A5 **Argentino, Lago** *l.* Arg.
120 C2 **Argenton-sur-Creuse** France
126 C2 **Argeş** *r.* Romania
90 A1 **Arghandab** *r.* Afgh.
127 B3 **Argolikos Kolpos** *b.* Greece
127 B3 **Argos** Greece
127 B3 **Argostoli** Greece
123 C1 **Arguís** Spain
85 E1 **Argun'** *r.* China/Rus. Fed.
147 D3 **Argyle** Can.
66 B1 **Argyle, Lake** Austr.
Argyrokastron Albania *see* **Gjirokastër**
Ar Horqin Qi China *see* **Tianshan**
109 F4 **Århus** Denmark
138 A2 **Ariamsvlei** Namibia
168 A1 **Arica** Chile
112 A2 **Arinagour** U.K.
171 C1 **Arinos** Brazil
166 D4 **Aripuanã** Brazil
166 C3 **Aripuanã** *r.* Brazil
166 C3 **Ariquemes** Brazil
170 B1 **Ariranhá** *r.* Brazil
112 B2 **Arisaig** U.K.
112 B2 **Arisaig, Sound of** *sea chan.* U.K.
120 B3 **Arizgoiti** Spain
158 A2 **Arizona** *state* U.S.A.
160 A1 **Arizpe** Mex.
94 B2 **'Arjah** Saudi Arabia
77 C2 **Arjasa** Indon.
108 G2 **Arjeplog** Sweden
156 B2 **Arkadelphia** U.S.A.
93 C1 **Arkalyk** Kazakh.
156 B2 **Arkansas** *r.* U.S.A.
156 B1 **Arkansas** *state* U.S.A.
153 D3 **Arkansas City** U.S.A.
Arkhangel'sk Rus. Fed. *see* **Archangel**
113 C2 **Arklow** Ireland
118 C1 **Arkona, Kap** *c.* Ger.
98 G1 **Arkticheskogo Instituta, Ostrova** *is* Rus. Fed.
121 C3 **Arles** France
159 D2 **Arlington** U.S.A.
154 B2 **Arlington Heights** U.S.A.
131 C3 **Arlit** Niger
116 B3 **Arlon** Belgium
113 C1 **Armagh** U.K.
132 B2 **Armant** Egypt
103 D4 **Armavir** Rus. Fed.
97 C1 **Armenia** *country* Asia
166 B2 **Armenia** Col.
Armenopolis Romania *see* **Gherla**
160 B3 **Armeria** Mex.
69 D2 **Armidale** Austr.
150 D1 **Armington** U.S.A.
146 B2 **Armstrong** Can.
107 C2 **Armyans'k** Ukr.
Armyanskaya S.S.R. *country* Asia *see* **Armenia**
Arnaouti, Cape *c.* Cyprus *see* **Arnauti, Cape**
146 D2 **Arnaud** *r.* Can.
96 B2 **Arnauti, Cape** Cyprus
116 B2 **Arnhem** Neth.
67 C1 **Arnhem, Cape** Austr.
67 C1 **Arnhem Bay** Austr.
67 C1 **Arnhem Land** *reg.* Austr.
124 B2 **Arno** *r.* Italy
68 A2 **Arno Bay** Austr.
146 C3 **Arnprior** Can.
117 D2 **Arnsberg** Ger.
117 E2 **Arnstadt** Ger.
138 A2 **Aroab** Namibia
170 B2 **Aroeira** Brazil
117 D2 **Arolsen** Ger.
94 A3 **Aroma** Sudan
124 A1 **Arona** Italy
160 B2 **Aros** *r.* Mex.
Arquipélago dos Açores *aut. reg.* Port. *see* **Azores**
Arrah India *see* **Ara**
97 C2 **Ar Ramādī** Iraq
112 B3 **Arran** *i.* U.K.
113 B1 **Arranmore Island** Ireland
96 B2 **Ar Raqqah** Syria
121 C1 **Arras** France
122 C1 **Arrasate** Spain
94 B2 **Ar Rass** Saudi Arabia
95 C2 **Ar Rayyān** Qatar
166 C2 **Arrecifal** Col.
161 C3 **Arriagá** Mex.
95 C2 **Ar Rimāl** *reg.* Saudi Arabia
Ar Riyāḑ Saudi Arabia *see* **Riyadh**
70 A2 **Arrowtown** N.Z.

Bad Lauterberg im Harz

151 B3 Arroyo Grande U.S.A.
161 C2 Arroyo Seco Mex.
95 C2 Ar Rustāq Oman
97 C2 Ar Ruṭbah Iraq
94 B2 Ar Ruwayḍah Saudi Arabia
97 D3 Arsenajān Iran
82 B2 Arsen'yev Rus. Fed.
133 C3 Arta Djibouti
127 B3 Arta Greece
160 B3 Arteaga Mex.
82 B2 Artem Rus. Fed.
107 D2 Artemivs'k Ukr.
120 C2 Artenay France
158 C2 Artesia U.S.A.
67 E2 Arthur Point Austr.
70 B2 Arthur's Pass N.Z.
168 C3 Artigas Uru.
145 D1 Artillery Lake Can.
139 C1 Artisia Botswana
120 C1 Artois reg. France
106 B2 Artsyz Ukr.
Artur de Paiva Angola see Kuvango
93 D3 Artux China
97 C1 Artvin Turkey
75 C3 Aru, Kepulauan is Indon.
135 D2 Arua Uganda
163 D3 Aruba terr. West Indies
91 C2 Arun r. Nepal
135 D3 Arusha Tanz.
152 B3 Arvada U.S.A.
84 C1 Arvayheer Mongolia
145 E1 Arviat Can.
108 G2 Arvidsjaur Sweden
109 F4 Arvika Sweden
124 A2 Arzachena Italy
103 D3 Arzamas Rus. Fed.
123 C2 Arzew Alg.
116 C2 Arzfeld Ger.
Arzila Morocco see Asilah
117 F2 Aš Czech Rep.
131 C4 Asaba Nigeria
90 B1 Asadābād Afgh.
82 D2 Asahi-dake vol. Japan
82 D2 Asahikawa Japan
94 B3 Āsalē l. Eth.
91 C2 Asansol India
133 C3 Āsayita Eth.
146 C3 Asbestos Can.
138 B2 Asbestos Mountains S. Africa
135 E2 Āsbe Teferi Eth.
125 C2 Ascea Italy
168 B1 Ascensión Bol.
129 B6 Ascension i. S. Atlantic Ocean
161 D3 Ascensión, Bahía de la b. Mex.
117 D3 Aschaffenburg Ger.
116 C2 Ascheberg Ger.
117 E2 Aschersleben Ger.
124 B2 Ascoli Piceno Italy
135 D2 Āsela Eth.
108 G3 Åsele Sweden
127 B2 Asenovgrad Bulg.
92 B3 Aşgabat Turkm.
94 B2 Asharat Saudi Arabia
66 A2 Ashburton watercourse Austr.
70 B2 Ashburton N.Z.
156 B2 Ashdown U.S.A.
157 D1 Asheville U.S.A.
69 D1 Ashford Austr.
113 C2 Ashford Ireland
115 D4 Ashford U.K.
82 D2 Ashibetsu Japan
114 C2 Ashington U.K.
83 B4 Ashizuri-misaki pt Japan
Ashkhabad Turkm. see Aşgabat
152 D3 Ashland KS U.S.A.
154 C3 Ashland KY U.S.A.
154 C2 Ashland OH U.S.A.
150 B2 Ashland OR U.S.A.
154 A1 Ashland WI U.S.A.
69 C1 Ashley Austr.
104 C3 Ashmyany Belarus
82 D2 Ashoro Japan
97 C2 Ash Shabakah Iraq
94 B3 Ash Sharawrah Saudi Arabia
Ash Shāriqah U.A.E. see Sharjah
97 C2 Ash Sharqāṭ Iraq
97 C2 Ash Shaṭrah Iraq
94 B3 Ash Shaykh 'Uthman Yemen
95 B3 Ash Shiḥr Yemen
95 C2 Ash Shināṣ Oman
94 B2 Ash Shu'āybah Saudi Arabia
94 B2 Ash Shu'bah Saudi Arabia
94 B2 Ash Shubaykīyah Saudi Arabia
94 B2 Ash Shumlūl Saudi Arabia
94 B3 Ash Shuqayq Saudi Arabia
131 D2 Ash Shuwayrif Libya
154 C2 Ashtabula U.S.A.
147 D2 Ashuanipi Lake Can.
91 B3 Asifabad India
122 B2 Asilah Morocco
124 A2 Asinara, Golfo dell' b. Italy
124 A2 Asinara, Isola i. Italy
98 G3 Asino Rus. Fed.
104 C3 Asipovichy Belarus
94 B2 'Asīr reg. Saudi Arabia
109 F4 Asker Norway
109 F4 Askim Norway
84 C1 Askiz Rus. Fed.
132 B3 Asmara Eritrea
109 F4 Åsnen l. Sweden
132 B2 Asoteriba, Jebel mt. Sudan
119 D2 Aspang-Markt Austria
152 B3 Aspen U.S.A.
159 C2 Aspermont U.S.A.
70 A2 Aspiring, Mount N.Z.
132 C3 Assab Eritrea
94 B3 Aş Şahīf Yemen
Aş Şaḥrā' al Gharbīyah des. Egypt see Western Desert
Aş Şaḥrā' ash Sharqīyah des. Egypt see Eastern Desert
94 B2 As Salamiyah Saudi Arabia
91 D2 Assam state India
97 C2 As Samāwah Iraq
95 C2 Aş Şanām reg. Saudi Arabia
131 E2 As Sarīr reg. Libya
124 A3 Assemini Italy
116 C1 Assen Neth.
116 B2 Assesse Belgium
131 D1 As Sidrah Libya
145 D3 Assiniboia Can.
144 C2 Assiniboine, Mount Can.
170 B2 Assis Brazil
94 B2 Aş Şubayḥīyah Kuwait
97 C2 As Sulaymānīyah Iraq
94 B2 As Sulaymī Saudi Arabia
94 B2 As Sulayyil Saudi Arabia
94 B2 As Sūq Saudi Arabia
96 B2 As Suwaydā' Syria
95 C2 As Suwayq Oman
As Suways Egypt see Suez
127 B3 Astakos Greece
93 D1 Astana Kazakh.
97 C2 Āstārā Iran
116 B2 Asten Neth.
Asterabad Iran see Gorgān
124 A2 Asti Italy
90 B1 Astor Pak.
122 B1 Astorga Spain
150 B1 Astoria U.S.A.
Astrabad Iran see Gorgān
103 D4 Astrakhan' Rus. Fed.
Astrakhan' Bazar Azer. see Cälilabad
104 C3 Astravyets Belarus
Astrida Rwanda see Butare
122 B1 Asturias aut. comm. Spain
127 C3 Astypalaia i. Greece
168 C2 Asunción Para.
132 B2 Aswān Egypt
132 B2 Asyūţ Egypt
Atacama, Desierto de des. Chile see Atacama Desert
168 B2 Atacama, Puna de plat. Arg.
168 B2 Atacama, Salar de salt flat Chile
168 B3 Atacama Desert des. Chile
130 C4 Atakpamé Togo
127 B3 Atalanti Greece
166 B4 Atalaya Peru
171 D1 Ataléia Brazil
93 C3 Atamyrat Turkm.
94 B3 'Ataq Yemen
130 A2 Atâr Maur.
151 B3 Atascadero U.S.A.
93 D2 Atasu Kazakh.
127 C3 Atavyros mt. Greece
132 B3 Atbara Sudan
132 B3 Atbara r. Sudan
93 C1 Atbasar Kazakh.
156 B3 Atchafalaya Bay U.S.A.
153 D3 Atchison U.S.A.
Ateransk Kazakh. see Atyrau
124 B2 Aterno r. Italy
124 B2 Atessa Italy
116 A2 Ath Belgium
144 C2 Athabasca Can.
145 C2 Athabasca r. Can.
145 D2 Athabasca, Lake Can.
113 C2 Athboy Ireland
113 B2 Athenry Ireland
127 B3 Athens Greece
156 C2 Athens AL U.S.A.
157 D2 Athens GA U.S.A.
154 C3 Athens OH U.S.A.
157 D1 Athens TN U.S.A.
159 D2 Athens TX U.S.A.
67 D1 Atherton Austr.
Athina Greece see Athens
113 C2 Athlone Ireland
127 B2 Athos mt. Greece
113 C2 Athy Ireland
131 D3 Ati Chad
146 A3 Atikokan Can.
103 D3 Atkarsk Rus. Fed.
157 D2 Atlanta U.S.A.
153 D2 Atlantic U.S.A.
157 D2 Atlantic Beach U.S.A.
155 E3 Atlantic City U.S.A.
71 D3 Atlantic-Indian-Antarctic Basin S. Atlantic Ocean
174 E8 Atlantic-Indian Ridge Southern Ocean
174 Atlantic Ocean
138 A3 Atlantis S. Africa
130 B1 Atlas Mountains Africa
130 C1 Atlas Saharien mts Alg.
144 A2 Atlin Can.
144 A2 Atlin Lake Can.
156 C2 Atmore U.S.A.
168 B2 Atocha Bol.
159 D2 Atoka U.S.A.
91 C2 Atrai r. India
96 B2 Aţ Ţafilah Jordan
94 B2 Aţ Ţā'if Saudi Arabia
79 B2 Attapu Laos
146 B2 Attawapiskat Can.
146 B2 Attawapiskat r. Can.
146 B2 Attawapiskat Lake Can.
116 C2 Attendorn Ger.
116 A3 Attichy France
132 B2 Aţ Ţūr Egypt
94 B3 At Turbah Yemen
151 B3 Atwater U.S.A.
92 B2 Atyrau Kazakh.
121 D3 Aubagne France
121 C3 Aubenas France
142 D2 Aubry Lake Can.
156 C2 Auburn AL U.S.A.
151 B3 Auburn CA U.S.A.
154 B2 Auburn IN U.S.A.
155 E2 Auburn ME U.S.A.
153 D2 Auburn NE U.S.A.
155 D2 Auburn NY U.S.A.
120 C2 Aubusson France
120 C3 Auch France
70 B1 Auckland N.Z.
64 H9 Auckland Islands N.Z.
133 C4 Audo mts Eth.
117 F2 Aue Ger.
117 F2 Auerbach Ger.
118 C2 Augsburg Ger.
66 A3 Augusta Austr.
125 C3 Augusta Italy
157 D2 Augusta GA U.S.A.
153 D3 Augusta KS U.S.A.
155 F2 Augusta ME U.S.A.
171 D1 Augusto de Lima Brazil
119 E1 Augustów Pol.
66 A2 Augustus, Mount Austr.
116 A2 Aulnoye-Aymeries France
Aumale Alg. see Sour el Ghozlane
78 A2 Aunglan Myanmar
138 B2 Auob watercourse Namibia/S. Africa
147 D2 Aupaluk Can.
90 B3 Aurangabad India
120 B2 Auray France
116 C1 Aurich Ger.
170 B1 Aurilândia Brazil
120 C3 Aurillac France
152 C3 Aurora CO U.S.A.
154 B2 Aurora IL U.S.A.
153 E3 Aurora MO U.S.A.
153 D2 Aurora NE U.S.A.
138 A2 Aus Namibia
154 C2 Au Sable r. U.S.A.
153 E2 Austin MN U.S.A.
151 C3 Austin NV U.S.A.
159 D2 Austin TX U.S.A.
Australes, Îles is Fr. Polynesia see Tubuai Islands
66 B2 Australia country Oceania
71 K4 Australian-Antarctic Basin sea feature Southern Ocean
69 C3 Australian Capital Territory admin. div. Austr.
118 C2 Austria country Europe
166 D3 Autazes Brazil
160 B3 Autlán Mex.
121 C2 Autun France
120 C3 Auvergne reg. France
121 C2 Auvergne, Monts d' mts France
121 C2 Auxerre France
121 D2 Auxonne France
121 C2 Avallon France
147 E3 Avalon Peninsula Can.
170 C2 Avaré Brazil
107 D2 Avdiyivka Ukr.
122 B1 Aveiro Port.
125 B2 Avellino Italy
124 B2 Aversa Italy
116 A2 Avesnes-sur-Helpe France
109 G3 Avesta Sweden
120 C3 Aveyron r. France
124 B2 Avezzano Italy
112 C2 Aviemore U.K.
125 C2 Avigliano Italy
121 C3 Avignon France
122 C1 Ávila Spain
122 B1 Avilés Spain
68 B3 Avoca Austr.
155 D2 Avoca U.S.A.
125 C3 Avola Italy
115 B3 Avon r. England U.K.
115 B4 Avon r. England U.K.
115 C4 Avon r. England U.K.
158 A2 Avondale U.S.A.
120 B2 Avranches France
70 B1 Awanui N.Z.
94 B3 Awārik, 'Urūq al des. Saudi Arabia
135 D2 Āwasa Eth.
133 C4 Āwash Eth.
133 C3 Āwash r. Eth.
131 D2 Awbārī Libya
131 D2 Awbārī, Idhān des. Libya
133 C4 Aw Dheegle Somalia
112 B2 Awe, Loch l. U.K.
133 A4 Aweil Sudan
131 C4 Awka Nigeria
130 A2 Awserd Western Sahara
142 F1 Axel Heiberg Island Can.
130 B4 Axim Ghana
166 B4 Ayacucho Peru
93 E2 Ayagoz Kazakh.
Ayaguz Kazakh. see Ayagoz
84 B2 Ayakkum Hu salt l. China
122 B2 Ayamonte Spain
99 K3 Ayan Rus. Fed.
166 B4 Ayaviri Peru
90 A1 Āybak Afgh.
92 A2 Aybas Kazakh.
107 D2 Aydar r. Ukr.
93 C2 Aydarko'l ko'li l. Uzbek.
127 C3 Aydın Turkey
93 C2 Ayeat, Gora h. Kazakh.
Ayers Rock h. Austr. see Uluṟu
99 I2 Aykhal Rus. Fed.
115 C4 Aylesbury U.K.
122 C1 Ayllón Spain
145 D1 Aylmer Lake Can.
133 B4 Ayod Sudan
99 M2 Ayon, Ostrov i. Rus. Fed.
130 B3 'Ayoûn el 'Atroûs Maur.
67 D1 Ayr Austr.
112 B3 Ayr U.K.
114 A2 Ayre, Point of Isle of Man
92 C2 Ayteke Bi Kazakh.
126 C2 Aytos Bulg.
161 C3 Ayutla Mex.
79 B2 Ayutthaya Thai.
127 C3 Ayvacık Turkey
127 C3 Ayvalık Turkey
107 C3 Ayya, Mys pt Ukr.
130 B3 Azaouâd reg. Mali
130 C3 Azaouagh, Vallée de watercourse Mali/Niger
131 D3 Azare Nigeria
Azbine mts Niger see Aïr, Massif de l'
97 C1 Azerbaijan country Asia
Azerbaydzhanskaya S.S.R. country Asia see Azerbaijan
166 B3 Azogues Ecuador
102 D2 Azopol'ye Rus. Fed.
128 A2 Azores aut. reg. Port.
107 D2 Azov Rus. Fed.
107 D2 Azov, Sea of Rus. Fed./Ukr.
Azraq, Bahr el r. Sudan see Blue Nile
122 B2 Azuaga Spain
162 B4 Azuero, Península de pen. Panama
169 C3 Azul Arg.
124 A3 Azzaba Alg.
Aẓ Ẓahrān Saudi Arabia see Dhahran
96 B2 Az Zaqāzīq Egypt
96 B2 Az Zarqā' Jordan
131 D1 Az Zāwīyah Libya
94 B3 Az Zaydīyah Yemen
130 C2 Azzel Matti, Sebkha salt pan Alg.
94 B2 Az Zilfī Saudi Arabia
94 B3 Az Zuqur i. Yemen

B

79 B2 Ba, Sông r. Vietnam
133 C4 Baardheere Somalia
93 C3 Bābā, Kūh-e mts Afgh.
127 C3 Baba Burnu pt Turkey
126 C2 Babadag Romania
127 C2 Babaeski Turkey
132 C3 Bāb al Mandab str. Africa/Asia
77 C2 Babana Indon.
135 C1 Babanusa Sudan
75 C3 Babar i. Indon.
135 D3 Babati Tanz.
105 E2 Babayevo Rus. Fed.
75 C2 Babeldaob i. Palau
144 B2 Babine r. Can.
144 B2 Babine Lake Can.
75 C3 Babo Indon.
97 D2 Bābol Iran
138 A3 Baboon Point S. Africa
104 C3 Babruysk Belarus
Babu China see Hezhou
80 B2 Babuyan i. Phil.
80 B2 Babuyan Channel Phil.
80 B2 Babuyan Islands Phil.
167 E3 Bacabal Brazil
161 D3 Bacalar Mex.
75 C3 Bacan i. Indon.
126 C1 Bacău Romania
68 B3 Bacchus Marsh Austr.
78 B1 Bắc Giang Vietnam
93 D3 Bachu China
145 E1 Back r. Can.
125 C1 Bačka Palanka Serbia
125 C1 Bačka Topola Serbia
68 A3 Backstairs Passage Austr.
79 B3 Bạc Liêu Vietnam
158 B3 Bacobampo Mex.
80 B2 Bacolod Phil.
146 C2 Bacqueville, Lac l. Can.
Bada China see Xilin
86 A1 Badain Jaran Shamo des. China
122 B2 Badajoz Spain
Badaojiang China see Baishan
91 D2 Badarpur India
117 E2 Bad Berka Ger.
117 D2 Bad Berleburg Ger.
117 E1 Bad Bevensen Ger.
117 D3 Bad Dürkheim Ger.
116 C2 Bad Ems Ger.
119 D2 Baden Austria
118 B2 Baden-Baden Ger.
117 E2 Bad Harzburg Ger.
117 D2 Bad Hersfeld Ger.
118 C2 Bad Hofgastein Austria
117 D2 Bad Homburg vor der Höhe Ger.
117 D1 Bad Iburg Ger.
90 A2 Badin Pak.
Bādiyat ash Shām des. Asia see Syrian Desert
117 E2 Bad Kissingen Ger.
116 C3 Bad Kreuznach Ger.
152 C1 Badlands reg. ND U.S.A.
152 C2 Badlands reg. SD U.S.A.
117 E2 Bad Lauterberg im Harz Ger.

Bensheim

117 D3 Bensheim Ger.
130 B1 Ben Slimane Morocco
158 A2 Benson U.S.A.
77 D2 Benteng Indon.
133 A4 Bentiu Sudan
154 B2 Benton Harbor U.S.A.
156 B1 Bentonville U.S.A.
79 B2 Bên Tre Vietnam
131 C4 Benue r. Nigeria
113 B1 Benwee Head hd Ireland
112 B2 Ben Wyvis mt. U.K.
86 C1 Benxi China
Beograd Serbia see Belgrade
91 C2 Beohari India
130 B4 Béoumi Côte d'Ivoire
83 B4 Beppu Japan
125 C2 Berane Montenegro
125 C2 Berat Albania
75 C3 Berau, Teluk b. Indon.
132 B3 Berber Sudan
133 C3 Berbera Somalia
134 B2 Berbérati C.A.R.
120 C1 Berck France
107 D2 Berdyans'k Ukr.
106 B2 Berdychiv Ukr.
106 A2 Berehove Ukr.
75 D3 Bereina P.N.G.
92 B3 Bereket Turkm.
145 E2 Berens River Can.
153 D2 Beresford U.S.A.
107 D2 Berezanskaya Rus. Fed.
106 A2 Berezhany Ukr.
106 C2 Berezivka Ukr.
106 B1 Berezne Ukr.
102 D2 Bereznik Rus. Fed.
102 E3 Berezniki Rus. Fed.
Berezov Rus. Fed. see Berezovo
102 F2 Berezovo Rus. Fed.
123 D1 Berga Spain
127 C3 Bergama Turkey
124 A1 Bergamo Italy
118 C1 Bergen Ger.
117 D1 Bergen Ger.
116 B1 Bergen Neth.
109 E3 Bergen Norway
116 B2 Bergen op Zoom Neth.
120 C3 Bergerac France
116 C2 Bergheim (Erft) Ger.
116 C2 Bergisch Gladbach Ger.
138 A1 Bergland Namibia
109 G3 Bergsjö Sweden
108 H2 Bergsviken Sweden
Berhampur India see Baharampur
99 M3 Beringa, Ostrov i. Rus. Fed.
116 B2 Beringen Belgium
140 A4 Bering Sea N. Pacific Ocean
140 B3 Bering Strait Rus. Fed./U.S.A.
116 C1 Berkel r. Neth.
151 B3 Berkeley U.S.A.
116 B1 Berkhout Neth.
71 B2 Berkner Island Antarctica
126 B2 Berkovitsa Bulg.
108 I1 Berlevåg Norway
117 F1 Berlin Ger.
155 E2 Berlin U.S.A.
117 E2 Berlingerode Ger.
69 D3 Bermagui Austr.
160 B2 Bermejíllo Mex.
168 B2 Bermejo Bol.
147 D2 Bermen, Lac l. Can.
141 L6 Bermuda terr. N. Atlantic Ocean
121 D2 Bern Switz.
117 E2 Bernburg (Saale) Ger.
143 G2 Bernier Bay Can.
66 A2 Bernier Island Austr.
116 C3 Bernkastel-Kues Ger.
137 □D3 Beroroha Madag.
68 B2 Berri Austr.
131 C1 Berriane Alg.
69 C3 Berrigan Austr.
123 D2 Berrouaghia Alg.
69 D2 Berry Austr.
162 C2 Berry Islands Bahamas
138 A2 Berseba Namibia
117 C1 Bersenbrück Ger.
106 B2 Bershad' Ukr.
147 D2 Berté, Lac l. Can.
134 B2 Bertoua Cameroon
166 C3 Beruri Brazil
114 B2 Berwick-upon-Tweed U.K.
107 C2 Beryslav Ukr.
137 □D2 Besalampy Madag.
121 D2 Besançon France
97 D3 Beshneh Iran
145 D2 Besnard Lake Can.
156 C2 Bessemer U.S.A.
92 B2 Besshoky, Gora h. Kazakh.
116 B2 Best Neth.
137 □D2 Betafo Madag.
122 B1 Betanzos Spain
134 B2 Bétaré Oya Cameroon
138 A2 Bethanie Namibia
116 B3 Bétheny France
155 D3 Bethesda U.S.A.
139 C2 Bethlehem S. Africa
155 D2 Bethlehem U.S.A.
139 C3 Bethulie S. Africa
121 C1 Béthune France
137 □D3 Betioky Madag.
67 D2 Betoota Austr.
93 D2 Betpak-Dala plain Kazakh.
137 □D3 Betroka Madag.
147 D3 Betsiamites Can.
137 □D2 Betsiboka r. Madag.
153 E2 Bettendorf U.S.A.
91 C2 Bettiah India
90 B2 Betul India
90 B2 Betwa r. India
115 B3 Betws-y-coed U.K.
116 C2 Betzdorf Ger.
152 C1 Beulah U.S.A.
114 C3 Beverley U.K.
117 D2 Beverungen Ger.
116 B1 Beverwijk Neth.
115 D4 Bexhill U.K.
127 C2 Beykoz Turkey
130 B4 Beyla Guinea
92 B2 Beyneu Kazakh.
96 B1 Beypazarı Turkey
Beyrouth Lebanon see Beirut
96 B2 Beyşehir Turkey
96 B2 Beyşehir Gölü l. Turkey
107 D2 Beysug r. Rus. Fed.
107 D2 Beysugskiy Liman lag. Rus. Fed.
104 C2 Bezhanitsy Rus. Fed.
105 E2 Bezhetsk Rus. Fed.
121 C3 Béziers France
Bhadgaon Nepal see Bhaktapur
91 C2 Bhadrak India
89 B3 Bhadravati India
91 C2 Bhagalpur India
90 A2 Bhairi Hol mt. Pak.
90 B1 Bhakkar Pak.
91 C2 Bhaktapur Nepal
78 A1 Bhamo Myanmar
91 C3 Bhanjanagar India
90 B2 Bharatpur India
90 B2 Bharuch India
90 B2 Bhavnagar India
91 C3 Bhawanipatna India
139 D2 Bhekuzulu S. Africa
90 B1 Bhera Pak.
90 B2 Bhilwara India
89 B3 Bhima r. India
90 B2 Bhind India
139 C3 Bhisho S. Africa
90 B2 Bhiwani India
139 C3 Bhongweni S. Africa
90 B2 Bhopal India
91 C2 Bhubaneshwar India
Bhubaneswar India see Bhubaneshwar
90 A2 Bhuj India
90 B2 Bhusawal India
91 D2 Bhutan country Asia
78 B2 Bia, Phou mt. Laos
Biafra, Bight of g. Africa see Benin, Bight of
75 D3 Biak Indon.
75 D3 Biak i. Indon.
119 E1 Biała Podlaska Pol.
119 D1 Białogard Pol.
119 E1 Białystok Pol.
125 C3 Bianco Italy
90 B2 Biaora India
120 B3 Biarritz France
121 D2 Biasca Switz.
82 D2 Bibai Japan
136 A2 Bibala Angola
69 C3 Bibbenluke Austr.
118 B2 Biberach an der Riß Ger.
171 D2 Bicas Brazil
89 B3 Bid India
131 C4 Bida Nigeria
89 B3 Bidar India
155 E2 Biddeford U.S.A.
112 B2 Bidean nam Bian mt. U.K.
115 A4 Bideford U.K.
Bié Angola see Kuito
136 A2 Bié, Planalto do Angola
117 D2 Biedenkopf Ger.
121 D2 Biel Switz.
117 D1 Bielefeld Ger.
124 A1 Biella Italy
119 D2 Bielsko-Biała Pol.
79 B2 Biên Hoa Vietnam
146 C2 Bienville, Lac l. Can.
116 B3 Bièvre Belgium
134 B3 Bifoun Gabon
127 C2 Biga Turkey
150 D1 Big Belt Mountains U.S.A.
139 D2 Big Bend Swaziland
145 D2 Biggar Can.
112 C3 Biggar U.K.
115 C3 Biggleswade U.K.
150 D1 Big Hole r. U.S.A.
150 E1 Bighorn U.S.A.
152 B1 Bighorn r. U.S.A.
152 B2 Bighorn Mountains U.S.A.
159 C2 Big Lake U.S.A.
154 B2 Big Rapids U.S.A.
145 D2 Big River Can.
145 E2 Big Sand Lake Can.
153 D2 Big Sioux r. U.S.A.
159 C2 Big Spring U.S.A.
150 E1 Big Timber U.S.A.
146 B2 Big Trout Lake Can.
146 A2 Big Trout Lake l. Can.
125 C2 Bihać Bos.-Herz.
91 C2 Bihar state India
91 C2 Bihar Sharif India
126 B1 Bihor, Vârful mt. Romania
130 A3 Bijagós, Arquipélago dos is Guinea-Bissau
89 B3 Bijapur India
97 C2 Bījār Iran
125 C2 Bijeljina Bos.-Herz.
125 C2 Bijelo Polje Montenegro
87 A3 Bijie China
90 B2 Bikaner India
82 B1 Bikin Rus. Fed.
82 B1 Bikin r. Rus. Fed.
134 B3 Bikoro Dem. Rep. Congo
95 C2 Bilād Banī Bū 'Alī Oman
91 C2 Bilaspur India
97 C2 Biläsuvar Azer.
106 C2 Bila Tserkva Ukr.
79 A2 Bilauktaung Range mts Myanmar/Thai.
122 C1 Bilbao Spain
125 C2 Bileća Bos.-Herz.
127 C2 Bilecik Turkey
119 E1 Biłgoraj Pol.
135 D3 Bilharamulo Tanz.
106 C2 Bilhorod-Dnistrovs'kyy Ukr.
135 C2 Bili Dem. Rep. Congo
99 M2 Bilibino Rus. Fed.
125 D2 Bilisht Albania
120 B3 Billère France
150 E1 Billings U.S.A.
115 B4 Bill of Portland hd U.K.
158 A1 Bill Williams Mountain U.S.A.
131 D3 Bilma Niger
131 D3 Bilma, Grand Erg de des. Niger
67 E2 Biloela Austr.
107 C2 Bilohirs'k Ukr.
106 B1 Bilohir"ya Ukr.
107 C1 Bilopillya Ukr.
107 D2 Bilovods'k Ukr.
156 C2 Biloxi U.S.A.
67 C2 Bilpa Morea Claypan salt flat Austr.
117 E2 Bilshausen Ger.
131 E3 Biltine Chad
106 C2 Bilyayivka Ukr.
130 C4 Bimbila Ghana
134 B2 Bimbo C.A.R.
157 E3 Bimini Islands Bahamas
90 B2 Bina-Etawa India
75 C3 Binaija, Gunung mt. Indon.
69 C1 Bindle Austr.
134 B3 Bindu Dem. Rep. Congo
137 C2 Bindura Zimbabwe
123 D1 Binefar Spain
136 B2 Binga Zimbabwe
69 D1 Bingara Austr.
116 C3 Bingen am Rhein Ger.
130 B4 Bingerville Côte d'Ivoire
155 F1 Bingham U.S.A.
155 D2 Binghamton U.S.A.
131 D2 Bin Ghanīmah, Jabal hills Libya
97 C2 Bingöl Turkey
78 A1 Bingzhongluo China
76 A1 Binjai Indon.
69 C2 Binnaway Austr.
76 B1 Bintan i. Indon.
76 B2 Bintuhan Indon.
77 C1 Bintulu Malaysia
131 C3 Bin-Yauri Nigeria
86 B2 Binzhou China
125 C2 Biograd na Moru Croatia
134 A2 Bioko i. Equat. Guinea
171 C1 Biquinhas Brazil
131 D2 Birāk Libya
134 C1 Birao C.A.R.
91 C2 Biratnagar Nepal
68 B3 Birchip Austr.
144 C2 Birch Mountains Can.
67 C2 Birdsville Austr.
96 B2 Birecik Turkey
Birendranagar Nepal see Surkhet
76 A1 Bireun Indon.
91 C2 Birganj Nepal
133 B3 Birhan mt. Eth.
170 B2 Birigüi Brazil
134 C2 Birini C.A.R.
92 B3 Bīrjand Iran
114 B3 Birkenhead U.K.
115 C3 Birmingham U.K.
156 C2 Birmingham U.S.A.
130 A2 Bîr Mogreïn Maur.
131 C3 Birnin-Kebbi Nigeria
131 C3 Birnin Konni Niger
85 E1 Birobidzhan Rus. Fed.
113 C2 Birr Ireland
112 C1 Birsay U.K.
94 A2 Bi'r Shalatayn Egypt
104 B2 Biržai Lith.
91 B2 Bisalpur India
158 B2 Bisbee U.S.A.
120 A2 Biscay, Bay of sea France/Spain
157 D3 Biscayne Bay U.S.A.
118 C2 Bischofshofen Austria
93 D2 Bishkek Kyrg.
151 C3 Bishop U.S.A.
114 C2 Bishop Auckland U.K.
85 E1 Bishui China
166 C2 Bisinaca Col.
131 C1 Biskra Alg.
80 B3 Bislig Phil.
152 C1 Bismarck U.S.A.
75 D3 Bismarck Archipelago is P.N.G.
75 D3 Bismarck Sea P.N.G.
123 D2 Bissa, Djebel mt. Alg.
130 A3 Bissau Guinea-Bissau
145 E2 Bissett Can.
144 C2 Bistcho Lake Can.
126 B1 Bistrița Romania
126 C1 Bistrița r. Romania
116 C3 Bitburg Ger.
121 D2 Bitche France
131 D3 Bitkine Chad
97 C2 Bitlis Turkey
127 B2 Bitola Macedonia
Bitolj Macedonia see Bitola
125 C2 Bitonto Italy
117 F2 Bitterfeld Ger.
138 A3 Bitterfontein S. Africa
150 D1 Bitterroot r. U.S.A.
150 C1 Bitterroot Range mts U.S.A.
105 E3 Bityug r. Rus. Fed.
131 D3 Biu Nigeria
83 C3 Biwa-ko l. Japan
93 E1 Biysk Rus. Fed.
Bizerta Tunisia see Bizerte
131 C1 Bizerte Tunisia
108 □A2 Bjargtangar hd Iceland
108 G3 Bjästa Sweden
125 C1 Bjelovar Croatia
108 G2 Bjerkvik Norway
Björneborg Fin. see Pori
98 C2 Bjørnøya Arctic Ocean
130 B3 Bla Mali
153 E3 Black r. U.S.A.
67 D2 Blackall Austr.
114 B3 Blackburn U.K.
150 D2 Blackfoot U.S.A.
118 B2 Black Forest mts Ger.
152 C2 Black Hills U.S.A.
112 B2 Black Isle pen. U.K.
145 D2 Black Lake Can.
145 D2 Black Lake l. Can.
115 B4 Black Mountains hills U.K.
158 A1 Black Mountains U.S.A.
114 B3 Blackpool U.K.
158 B2 Black Range mts U.S.A.
78 B1 Black River r. Vietnam
154 A2 Black River Falls U.S.A.
150 C2 Black Rock Desert U.S.A.
154 C3 Blacksburg U.S.A.
96 B1 Black Sea Asia/Europe
147 D3 Blacks Harbour Can.
113 A1 Blacksod Bay Ireland
113 C2 Blackstairs Mountains hills Ireland
130 B4 Black Volta r. Africa
67 D2 Blackwater Austr.
113 C2 Blackwater r. Ireland
144 B1 Blackwater Lake Can.
66 A3 Blackwood r. Austr.
103 D4 Blagodarnyy Rus. Fed.
127 B2 Blagoevgrad Bulg.
85 E1 Blagoveshchensk Rus. Fed.
145 D2 Blaine Lake Can.
153 D2 Blair U.S.A.
112 C2 Blair Atholl U.K.
112 C2 Blairgowrie U.K.
157 D2 Blakely U.S.A.
121 D2 Blanc, Mont mt. France/Italy
169 B3 Blanca, Bahía b. Arg.
68 A1 Blanche, Lake imp. l. Austr.
168 B1 Blanco r. Bol.
150 B2 Blanco, Cape U.S.A.
147 E2 Blanc-Sablon Can.
108 □A2 Blanda r. Iceland
115 B4 Blandford Forum U.K.
151 E3 Blanding U.S.A.
123 D1 Blanes Spain
76 A1 Blangkejeren Indon.
116 A2 Blankenberge Belgium
116 C2 Blankenheim Ger.
116 C2 Blankenrath Ger.
163 D3 Blanquilla, Isla i. Venez.
119 D2 Blansko Czech Rep.
137 C2 Blantyre Malawi
113 B3 Blarney Ireland
114 C2 Blaydon U.K.
69 C2 Blayney Austr.
70 B2 Blenheim N.Z.
131 C1 Blida Alg.
146 B3 Blind River Can.
139 C2 Bloemfontein S. Africa
139 C2 Bloemhof S. Africa
139 C2 Bloemhof Dam S. Africa
120 C2 Blois France
108 □A2 Blönduós Iceland
113 B1 Bloody Foreland pt Ireland
158 B1 Bloomfield U.S.A.
154 B2 Bloomington IL U.S.A.
154 B3 Bloomington IN U.S.A.
118 B2 Bludenz Austria
153 E2 Blue Earth U.S.A.
154 C3 Bluefield U.S.A.
162 B3 Bluefields Nic.
69 C2 Blue Mountains Austr.
150 C1 Blue Mountains U.S.A.
132 B3 Blue Nile r. Eth./Sudan
142 E2 Bluenose Lake Can.
154 C3 Blue Ridge mts U.S.A.
144 C2 Blue River Can.
113 B1 Blue Stack Mountains hills Ireland
70 A3 Bluff N.Z.
151 E3 Bluff U.S.A.
170 C3 Blumenau Brazil
68 A2 Blyth Austr.
114 C2 Blyth U.K.
151 D4 Blythe U.S.A.
156 C1 Blytheville U.S.A.
130 A4 Bo Sierra Leone
80 B2 Boac Phil.
162 B3 Boaco Nic.
167 E3 Boa Esperança, Açude resr Brazil
150 C1 Boardman U.S.A.
139 C1 Boatlaname Botswana
167 F3 Boa Viagem Brazil
166 C2 Boa Vista Brazil
69 C2 Bobadah Austr.
87 B3 Bobai China

137 □D2 Bobaomby, Tanjona c. Madag.
130 B3 Bobo-Dioulasso Burkina
137 B3 Bobonong Botswana
Bobriki Rus. Fed. see Novomoskovsk
105 F3 Bobrov Rus. Fed.
107 C2 Bobrovytsya Ukr.
107 C2 Bobrynets' Ukr.
137 □D3 Boby mt. Madag.
166 C3 Boca do Acre Brazil
171 D1 Bocaiúva Brazil
170 A2 Bocajá Brazil
134 B2 Bocaranga C.A.R.
157 D3 Boca Raton U.S.A.
162 M4 Bocas del Toro Panama
119 E2 Bochnia Pol.
116 B2 Bocholt Belgium
116 C2 Bocholt Ger.
116 C2 Bochum Ger.
117 E1 Bockenem Ger.
126 B1 Bocşa Romania
134 B2 Boda C.A.R.
99 I3 Bodaybo Rus. Fed.
112 D2 Boddam U.K.
131 D3 Bodélé reg. Chad
108 H2 Boden Sweden
Bodensee l. Ger./Switz. see Constance, Lake
115 A4 Bodmin U.K.
115 A4 Bodmin Moor moorland U.K.
108 F2 Bode Norway
127 C3 Bodrum Turkey
134 C3 Boende Dem. Rep. Congo
79 A2 Bogale Myanmar
156 C2 Bogalusa U.S.A.
130 B3 Bogandé Burkina
134 B2 Bogangolo C.A.R.
96 B2 Boğazlıyan Turkey
84 B2 Bogda Shan mts China
69 D1 Boggabilla Austr.
69 D2 Boggabri Austr.
113 B2 Boggeragh Mountains hills Ireland
Boghari Alg. see Ksar el Boukhari
75 D3 Bogia P.N.G.
116 B3 Bogny-sur-Meuse France
113 C2 Bog of Allen reg. Ireland
69 C3 Bogong, Mount Austr.
76 B2 Bogor Indon.
105 E3 Bogoroditsk Rus. Fed.
166 B2 Bogotá Col.
99 G3 Bogotol Rus. Fed.
Bogoyavlenskoye Rus. Fed. see Pervomayskiy
99 H3 Boguchany Rus. Fed.
107 E2 Boguchar Rus. Fed.
130 A3 Bogué Maur.
86 B2 Bo Hai g. China
116 A3 Bohain-en-Vermandois France
86 B2 Bohai Wan b. China
Bohemian Forest mts Ger. see Böhmer Wald
139 C2 Bohlokong S. Africa
117 F3 Böhmer Wald mts Ger.
107 D1 Bohodukhiv Ukr.
80 B3 Bohol i. Phil.
80 B3 Bohol Sea Phil.
93 E2 Bohu China
171 C2 Boi, Ponta do pt Brazil
139 C2 Boikhutso S. Africa
170 B3 Boi Preto, Serra de hills Brazil
170 B1 Bois r. Brazil
142 D2 Bois, Lac des l. Can.
150 C2 Boise U.S.A.
159 C1 Boise City U.S.A.
145 D3 Boissevain Can.
139 C2 Boitumelong S. Africa
170 C2 Boituva Brazil
117 E1 Boizenburg Ger.
92 B3 Bojnürd Iran
91 C2 Bokaro India
134 B3 Bokatola Dem. Rep. Congo
130 A3 Boké Guinea
134 C3 Bokele Dem. Rep. Congo
109 E4 Boknafjorden sea chan. Norway
131 D3 Bokoro Chad
79 A2 Bokpyin Myanmar
105 D2 Boksitogorsk Rus. Fed.
138 B2 Bokspits Botswana
134 C3 Bokungu Dem. Rep. Congo
131 D3 Bol Chad
130 A3 Bolama Guinea-Bissau
91 C2 Bolangir India
79 B2 Bolavén, Phouphiang plat. Laos
120 C2 Bolbec France
93 E2 Bole China
134 B3 Boleko Dem. Rep. Congo
130 B3 Bolgatanga Ghana
106 B2 Bolhrad Ukr.
82 B1 Boli China
134 B3 Bolia Dem. Rep. Congo
108 H3 Boliden Sweden
126 C2 Bolintin-Vale Romania
153 E1 Bolivar MO U.S.A.
156 C1 Bolivar TN U.S.A.
166 B2 Bolívar, Pico mt. Venez.
168 B1 Bolivia country S. America
105 E3 Bolkhov Rus. Fed.
121 C3 Bollène France
109 G3 Bollnäs Sweden
69 C1 Bollon Austr.
117 E2 Bollstedt Ger.
109 F4 Bolmen l. Sweden
134 B3 Bolobo Dem. Rep. Congo
124 B2 Bologna Italy
105 D2 Bologovo Rus. Fed.

105 D2 Bologoye Rus. Fed.
139 C2 Bolokanang S. Africa
134 B2 Bolomba Dem. Rep. Congo
124 B2 Bolsena, Lago di l. Italy
99 H1 Bol'shevik, Ostrov i. Rus. Fed.
102 E2 Bol'shezemel'skaya Tundra lowland Rus. Fed.
82 B2 Bol'shoy Kamen' Rus. Fed.
Bol'shoy Kavkaz mts Asia/Europe see Caucasus
99 K2 Bol'shoy Lyakhovskiy, Ostrov i. Rus. Fed.
Bol'shoy Tokmak Kyrg. see Tokmok
Bol'shoy Tokmak Ukr. see Tokmak
160 B2 Bolsón de Mapimí des. Mex.
116 B1 Bolsward Neth.
114 B3 Bolton U.K.
96 B1 Bolu Turkey
75 E3 Bolubolu P.N.G.
108 □A2 Bolungarvík Iceland
124 B1 Bolzano Italy
134 B3 Boma Dem. Rep. Congo
69 D2 Bomaderry Austr.
69 C3 Bombala Austr.
Bombay India see Mumbai
171 C1 Bom Despacho Brazil
91 D2 Bomdila India
170 B1 Bom Jardim de Goiás Brazil
167 E4 Bom Jesus da Lapa Brazil
171 D2 Bom Jesus do Itabapoana Brazil
131 D1 Bon, Cap c. Tunisia
163 D3 Bonaire i. Neth. Antilles
150 C1 Bonaparte, Mount U.S.A.
66 B1 Bonaparte Archipelago is Austr.
147 E2 Bonavista Can.
147 E3 Bonavista Bay Can.
134 C2 Bondo Dem. Rep. Congo
130 B4 Bondoukou Côte d'Ivoire
Bône Alg. see Annaba
77 D2 Bonerate, Kepulauan is Indon.
171 C1 Bonfinópolis de Minas Brazil
133 B4 Bonga Eth.
91 D2 Bongaigaon India
134 C2 Bongandanga Dem. Rep. Congo
138 B2 Bongani S. Africa
134 C2 Bongo, Massif des mts C.A.R.
137 □D2 Bongolava mts Madag.
131 D3 Bongor Chad
130 B4 Bongouanou Côte d'Ivoire
79 B2 Bông Sơn Vietnam
159 D2 Bonham U.S.A.
121 D3 Bonifacio France
124 A2 Bonifacio, Strait of France/Italy
85 F3 Bonin Islands is Japan
116 C2 Bonn Ger.
150 C1 Bonners Ferry U.S.A.
121 D2 Bonneville France
66 A3 Bonnie Rock Austr.
145 C2 Bonnyville Can.
124 A2 Bonorva Italy
69 D1 Bonshaw Austr.
77 C1 Bontang Indon.
130 A4 Bonthe Sierra Leone
80 B2 Bontoc Phil.
77 C2 Bontosunggu Indon.
77 C2 Bontrug S. Africa
69 C1 Boolba Austr.
68 B2 Booligal Austr.
69 C1 Boomi Austr.
69 D1 Boonah Austr.
153 E2 Boone U.S.A.
156 C2 Booneville U.S.A.
153 E3 Boonville U.S.A.
68 B2 Booroorban Austr.
69 C2 Boorowa Austr.
133 C3 Boosaaso Somalia
142 G2 Boothia, Gulf of Can.
142 F2 Boothia Peninsula Can.
134 B3 Booué Gabon
116 C2 Boppard Ger.
160 B2 Boquilla, Presa de la resr Mex.
109 B4 Bor Serbia
133 B4 Bor Sudan
96 B2 Bor Turkey
135 E2 Bor, Lagh watercourse Kenya/Somalia
137 □E2 Boraha, Nosy i. Madag.
109 F4 Borås Sweden
97 D3 Borāzjān Iran
166 D3 Borba Brazil
120 B3 Bordeaux France
142 F1 Borden Island Can.
143 G2 Borden Peninsula Can.
68 B3 Bordertown Austr.
123 C3 Bordj Bou Arréridj Alg.
123 C2 Bordj Bounaama Alg.
130 B2 Bordj Flye Ste-Marie Alg.
131 C1 Bordj Messaouda Alg.
130 C2 Bordj Mokhtar Alg.
Bordj Omar Driss Alg. see Bordj Omer Driss
131 C2 Bordj Omer Driss Alg.
110 B1 Borðoy i. Faroe Is
Borgå Fin. see Porvoo
108 □A3 Borgarnes Iceland
159 C1 Borger U.S.A.
109 G4 Borgholm Sweden
116 B2 Borgloon Belgium
124 A1 Borgosesia Italy
103 B3 Borisoglebsk Rus. Fed.
105 E2 Borisoglebskiy Rus. Fed.
107 D1 Borisovka Rus. Fed.
116 C2 Borken Ger.
108 G2 Borkenes Norway

116 C1 Borkum Ger.
116 C1 Borkum i. Ger.
109 G3 Borlänge Sweden
117 F2 Borna Ger.
116 C1 Borne Neth.
77 C1 Borneo i. Asia
109 F4 Bornholm i. Denmark
127 C3 Bornova Turkey
106 B1 Borodyanka Ukr.
93 E2 Borohoro Shan mts China
130 B3 Boron Mali
105 D2 Borovichi Rus. Fed.
105 E2 Borovsk Rus. Fed.
92 C1 Borovskoy Kazakh.
67 C1 Borroloola Austr.
126 B1 Borşa Romania
92 B2 Borsakelmas sho'rxogi salt marsh Uzbek.
106 B2 Borshchiv Ukr.
85 D1 Borshchovochnyy Khrebet mts Rus. Fed.
117 E1 Börßum Ger.
Bortala China see Bole
97 C2 Borūjerd Iran
106 A2 Boryslav Ukr.
106 C1 Boryspil' Ukr.
107 C1 Borzna Ukr.
85 D1 Borzya Rus. Fed.
125 C1 Bosanska Dubica Bos.-Herz.
125 C1 Bosanska Gradiška Bos.-Herz.
125 C1 Bosanska Krupa Bos.-Herz.
125 C1 Bosanski Novi Bos.-Herz.
125 C1 Bosanski Grahovo Bos.-Herz.
87 A3 Bose China
139 C2 Boshof S. Africa
125 C2 Bosnia-Herzegovina country Europe
134 C2 Bosobolo Dem. Rep. Congo
127 C2 Bosporus str. Turkey
158 B2 Bosque U.S.A.
134 B2 Bossangoa C.A.R.
134 B2 Bossembélé C.A.R.
156 B2 Bossier City U.S.A.
138 A2 Bossiesvlei Namibia
84 B2 Bosten Hu l. China
115 C3 Boston U.K.
155 F2 Boston U.S.A.
156 B1 Boston Mountains U.S.A.
69 C2 Botany Bay Austr.
136 B3 Boteti r. Botswana
126 B2 Botev mt. Bulg.
96 A1 Botevgrad Bulg.
108 G3 Bothnia, Gulf of Fin./Sweden
126 C1 Botoşani Romania
86 B2 Botou China
139 C2 Botshabelo S. Africa
136 B3 Botswana country Africa
125 C2 Botte Donato, Monte mt. Italy
152 C1 Bottineau U.S.A.
116 C2 Bottrop Ger.
170 C2 Botucatu Brazil
130 B4 Bouaké Côte d'Ivoire
134 B2 Bouar C.A.R.
130 B1 Bouârfa Morocco
147 D3 Bouctouche Can.
123 E2 Bougaa Alg.
64 G4 Bougainville Island P.N.G.
Bougie Alg. see Bejaïa
130 B3 Bougouni Mali
116 B3 Bouillon Belgium
123 D2 Bouira Alg.
130 A2 Boujdour Western Sahara
66 B3 Boulder Austr.
152 B2 Boulder CO U.S.A.
150 D1 Boulder MT U.S.A.
151 D3 Boulder City U.S.A.
Boulhaut Morocco see Ben Slimane
67 C2 Boulia Austr.
120 C2 Boulogne-Billancourt France
120 C1 Boulogne-sur-Mer France
134 C2 Boulouba C.A.R.
134 B3 Boumango Dem. Rep. Congo
134 B2 Boumba r. Cameroon
123 D2 Boumerdes Alg.
130 B4 Bouna Côte d'Ivoire
130 B4 Boundiali Côte d'Ivoire
150 D2 Bountiful U.S.A.
65 I8 Bounty Islands N.Z.
130 B3 Bourem Mali
120 C2 Bourganeuf France
121 D2 Bourg-en-Bresse France
120 C2 Bourges France
Bourgogne reg. France see Burgundy
121 D2 Bourgoin-Jallieu France
69 C2 Bourke Austr.
115 C3 Bourne U.K.
115 C4 Bournemouth U.K.
134 C2 Bourtoutou Chad
131 C1 Bou Saâda Alg.
131 D3 Bousso Chad
130 A3 Boutilimit Maur.
62 Bouvetøya S. Atlantic Ocean
144 C2 Bow r. Can.
Bowa China see Muli
67 D2 Bowen Austr.
69 C3 Bowen, Mount Austr.
145 C3 Bow Island Can.
158 B3 Bowling Green KY U.S.A.
153 E3 Bowling Green MO U.S.A.
154 C2 Bowling Green OH U.S.A.
152 C1 Bowman U.S.A.
69 D2 Bowral Austr.
117 D3 Boxberg Ger.
116 B2 Boxtel Neth.
96 B1 Boyabat Turkey

Boyang China see Poyang
113 B2 Boyle Ireland
113 C2 Boyne r. Ireland
152 B2 Boysen Reservoir U.S.A.
168 B2 Boyuibe Bol.
127 C3 Bozburun Turkey
127 C3 Bozcaada i. Turkey
127 C3 Bozdağ mt. Turkey
127 C3 Boz Dağları mts Turkey
127 C3 Bozdoğan Turkey
150 D1 Bozeman U.S.A.
134 B2 Bozoum C.A.R.
127 C3 Bozüyük Turkey
125 C2 Brač i. Croatia
146 B2 Bracebridge Can.
109 G3 Bräcke Sweden
115 C4 Bracknell U.K.
125 C2 Bradano r. Italy
157 D3 Bradenton U.S.A.
163 B3 Brades Montserrat
114 C3 Bradford U.K.
155 D2 Bradford U.S.A.
159 D2 Brady U.S.A.
112 C2 Braemar U.K.
122 B1 Braga Port.
167 E3 Bragança Brazil
122 B1 Bragança Port.
171 C2 Bragança Paulista Brazil
105 D3 Brahin Belarus
91 D2 Brahmanbaria Bangl.
91 C3 Brahmapur India
78 A1 Brahmaputra r. China/India
69 C3 Braidwood Austr.
126 C1 Brăila Romania
153 E1 Brainerd U.S.A.
115 D4 Braintree U.K.
116 B2 Braives Belgium
117 D1 Brake (Unterweser) Ger.
138 A1 Brakwater Namibia
114 B2 Brampton U.K.
117 D1 Bramsche Ger.
166 C3 Branco r. Brazil
117 F1 Brandenburg Ger.
145 E3 Brandon Can.
156 C2 Brandon U.S.A.
113 A2 Brandon Mountain h. Ireland
138 B3 Brandvlei S. Africa
119 D1 Braniewo Pol.
146 B3 Brantford Can.
69 D2 Branxton Austr.
147 D3 Bras d'Or Lake Can.
171 D3 Brasil, Planalto do plat. Brazil
170 C1 Brasilândia Brazil
170 C1 Brasília Brazil
171 D1 Brasília de Minas Brazil
104 C2 Braslaw Belarus
126 C1 Braşov Romania
119 D2 Bratislava Slovakia
99 H3 Bratsk Rus. Fed.
118 C2 Braunau am Inn Austria
117 E1 Braunschweig Ger.
108 □A2 Brautarholt Iceland
Bravo del Norte, Rio r. Mex./U.S.A. see Rio Grande
151 C4 Brawley U.S.A.
113 C2 Bray Ireland
166 B2 Brazil country S. America
174 E6 Brazil Basin N. Atlantic Ocean
60 Brazilian Highlands S. America
159 D3 Brazos r. U.S.A.
134 B3 Brazzaville Congo
125 C2 Brčko Bos.-Herz.
112 C2 Brechin U.K.
116 B2 Brecht Belgium
159 D2 Breckenridge U.S.A.
119 D2 Břeclav Czech Rep.
115 B4 Brecon U.K.
115 B4 Brecon Beacons reg. U.K.
116 B2 Breda Neth.
138 B3 Bredasdorp S. Africa
118 B2 Bregenz Austria
108 H1 Breivikbotn Norway
108 E3 Brekstad Norway
117 D1 Bremen Ger.
117 D1 Bremerhaven Ger.
Bremersdorp Swaziland see Manzini
150 B1 Bremerton U.S.A.
117 D1 Bremervörde Ger.
159 D2 Brenham U.S.A.
121 E2 Brennero Italy
118 C2 Brenner Pass Austria/Italy
115 D4 Brentwood U.K.
124 B1 Brescia Italy
116 A2 Breskens Neth.
121 E2 Bressanone Italy
112 □ Bressay i. U.K.
120 B2 Bressuire France
104 C2 Brest Belarus
120 B2 Brest France
Brest-Litovsk Belarus see Brest
Bretagne reg. France see Brittany
156 C3 Breton Sound b. U.S.A.
167 D3 Breves Brazil
69 C1 Brewarrina Austr.
150 C1 Brewster U.S.A.
105 E2 Breytovo Rus. Fed.
Brezhnev Rus. Fed. see Naberezhnyye Chelny
125 C2 Brezovo Polje plain Croatia
134 C2 Bria C.A.R.
121 D3 Briançon France
106 B2 Briceni Moldova
Brichany Moldova see Briceni
115 B4 Bridgend U.K.

155 E2 Bridgeport CT U.S.A.
152 C2 Bridgeport NE U.S.A.
163 E3 Bridgetown Barbados
147 D3 Bridgewater Can.
115 B3 Bridgnorth U.K.
115 B4 Bridgwater U.K.
115 B4 Bridgwater Bay U.K.
114 C2 Bridlington U.K.
114 C2 Bridlington Bay U.K.
115 B4 Bridport U.K.
121 D2 Brig Switz.
150 D2 Brigham City U.S.A.
69 C3 Bright Austr.
70 B3 Brighton N.Z.
115 C4 Brighton U.K.
152 C3 Brighton CO U.S.A.
154 C2 Brighton MI U.S.A.
121 D3 Brignoles France
130 A3 Brikama Gambia
117 D2 Brilon Ger.
125 C2 Brindisi Italy
　Brinlack Ireland see
　Bun na Leaca
69 D1 Brisbane Austr.
115 B4 Bristol U.K.
155 E2 Bristol CT U.S.A.
157 D1 Bristol TN U.S.A.
115 A4 Bristol Channel est. U.K.
144 B2 British Columbia prov. Can.
　British Guiana country S. America
　see Guyana
　British Honduras country
　Central America see Belize
72 C6 British Indian Ocean Territory terr.
　Indian Ocean
　British Solomon Islands country
　S. Pacific Ocean see
　Solomon Islands
139 C2 Brits S. Africa
138 B3 Britstown S. Africa
120 B2 Brittany reg. France
120 C2 Brive-la-Gaillarde France
122 C1 Briviesca Spain
115 B4 Brixham U.K.
119 D2 Brno Czech Rep.
　Broach India see Bharuch
157 D2 Broad r. U.S.A.
146 C2 Broadback r. Can.
69 C3 Broadford Austr.
112 B2 Broadford U.K.
112 C3 Broad Law h. U.K.
152 B1 Broadus U.S.A.
145 D2 Brochet Can.
145 D2 Brochet, Lac l. Can.
147 D3 Brochet, Lac au l. Can.
117 E1 Bröckel Ger.
117 E2 Brocken mt. Ger.
142 E1 Brock Island Can.
146 C2 Brockville Can.
143 G2 Brodeur Peninsula Can.
112 B3 Brodick U.K.
119 D1 Brodnica Pol.
106 B1 Brody Ukr.
159 D1 Broken Arrow U.S.A.
153 D2 Broken Bow U.S.A.
68 B2 Broken Hill Austr.
　Broken Hill Zambia see Kabwe
175 F6 Broken Plateau Indian Ocean
167 D2 Brokopondo Suriname
115 B3 Bromsgrove U.K.
109 E4 Brønderslev Denmark
139 C2 Bronkhorstspruit S. Africa
108 F2 Brønnøysund Norway
80 A3 Brooke's Point Phil.
156 B2 Brookhaven U.S.A.
150 B2 Brookings OR U.S.A.
153 D2 Brookings SD U.S.A.
144 C2 Brooks Can.
142 C2 Brooks Range mts U.S.A.
157 D3 Brooksville U.S.A.
155 D2 Brookville U.S.A.
112 B2 Broom, Loch inlet U.K.
66 B1 Broome Austr.
150 B2 Brothers U.S.A.
　Broughton Island Can. see
　Qikiqtarjuaq
106 C1 Brovary Ukr.
159 C2 Brownfield U.S.A.
144 C3 Browning U.S.A.
156 C1 Brownsville TN U.S.A.
159 D3 Brownsville TX U.S.A.
159 D2 Brownwood U.S.A.
108 □A2 Brú Iceland
120 C1 Bruay-la-Bussière France
154 B1 Bruce Crossing U.S.A.
146 B2 Bruce Peninsula Can.
119 D2 Bruck an der Mur Austria
　Bruges Belgium see Brugge
116 A2 Brugge Belgium
78 A1 Bruint India
144 C2 Brûlé Can.
167 E4 Brumado Brazil
109 F3 Brumunddal Norway
77 C1 Brunei country Asia
　Brunei Brunei see
　Bandar Seri Begawan
118 B2 Brunico Italy
　Brünn Czech Rep. see Brno
117 D1 Brunsbüttel Ger.
157 D2 Brunswick GA U.S.A.
155 F2 Brunswick ME U.S.A.
69 D1 Brunswick Heads Austr.
139 D2 Bruntville S. Africa
152 C2 Brush U.S.A.

116 B2 Brussels Belgium
　Bruxelles Belgium see Brussels
159 D2 Bryan U.S.A.
105 D3 Bryansk Rus. Fed.
107 D2 Bryn'kovskaya Rus. Fed.
107 D2 Bryukhovetskaya Rus. Fed.
119 D1 Brzeg Pol.
　Brześć nad Bugiem Belarus see Brest
130 A3 Buba Guinea-Bissau
127 C3 Buca Turkey
96 B2 Bucak Turkey
166 B2 Bucaramanga Col.
106 B2 Buchach Ukr.
69 C3 Buchan U.K.
130 A4 Buchanan Liberia
126 C2 Bucharest Romania
117 D1 Bucholz in der Nordheide Ger.
126 C1 Bucin, Pasul pass Romania
117 D1 Bückeburg Ger.
158 A2 Buckeye U.S.A.
112 C2 Buckhaven U.K.
112 C2 Buckie U.K.
115 C3 Buckingham U.K.
67 C1 Buckingham Bay Austr.
67 D2 Buckland Tableland reg. Austr.
68 A2 Buckleboo Austr.
155 F2 Bucksport U.S.A.
119 D2 Bučovice Czech Rep.
　Bucureşti Romania see Bucharest
105 D3 Buda-Kashalyova Belarus
119 D2 Budapest Hungary
91 B2 Budaun India
124 A2 Buddusò Italy
115 A4 Bude U.K.
103 D4 Budennovsk Rus. Fed.
　Budennoye Rus. Fed. see
　Krasnogvardeyskoye
105 D2 Budogoshch' Rus. Fed.
124 A2 Budoni Italy
　Budweis Czech Rep. see
　České Budějovice
134 A2 Buea Cameroon
151 B4 Buellton U.S.A.
166 B2 Buenaventura Col.
160 B2 Buenaventura Mex.
　Buena Vista i. N. Mariana Is see
　Tinian
122 C1 Buendia, Embalse de resr Spain
171 D1 Buenópolis Brazil
169 C3 Buenos Aires Arg.
169 A4 Buenos Aires, Lago l. Arg./Chile
155 D2 Buffalo NY U.S.A.
152 C1 Buffalo SD U.S.A.
159 D2 Buffalo TX U.S.A.
152 B2 Buffalo WY U.S.A.
145 D2 Buffalo Narrows Can.
137 C3 Buffalo Range Zimbabwe
138 A2 Buffels watercourse S. Africa
139 C1 Buffels Drift S. Africa
126 C2 Buftea Romania
119 E1 Bug r. Pol.
77 C2 Bugel, Tanjung pt Indon.
125 C2 Bugojno Bos.-Herz.
102 D2 Bugrino Rus. Fed.
80 A3 Bugsuk i. Phil.
103 E3 Bugul'ma Rus. Fed.
103 E3 Buguruslan Rus. Fed.
137 C2 Buhera Zimbabwe
126 C1 Buhuşi Romania
115 B3 Builth Wells U.K.
85 D1 Buir Nur l. Mongolia
136 A3 Buitepos Namibia
125 D2 Bujanovac Serbia
135 C3 Bujumbura Burundi
85 D1 Bukachacha Rus. Fed.
136 B2 Bukalo Namibia
135 C3 Bukavu Dem. Rep. Congo
　Bukhara Uzbek. see Buxoro
76 B2 Bukittinggi Indon.
135 D3 Bukoba Tanz.
119 D1 Bukowiec h. Pol.
75 C3 Bula Indon.
69 D2 Bulahdelah Austr.
137 B3 Bulawayo Zimbabwe
127 C3 Buldan Turkey
139 D2 Bulembu Swaziland
84 C1 Bulgan Mongolia
126 C2 Bulgaria country Europe
70 B2 Buller r. N.Z.
158 A1 Bullhead City U.S.A.
68 B1 Bulloo watercourse Austr.
68 B1 Bulloo Downs Austr.
138 A1 Büllsport Namibia
77 D2 Bulukumba Indon.
134 B3 Bulungu Dem. Rep. Congo
134 B3 Bumba Dem. Rep. Congo
134 C2 Bumba Dem. Rep. Congo
78 A1 Bumhkang Myanmar
134 B3 Buna Dem. Rep. Congo
　Bun Beg Ireland see An Bun Beag
66 A3 Bunbury Austr.
113 C2 Bunclody Ireland
113 C1 Buncrana Ireland
135 D3 Bunda Tanz.
67 E2 Bundaberg Austr.
69 C1 Bundarra Austr.
69 D2 Bundarra Austr.
90 B2 Bundi India
113 B1 Bundoran Ireland
91 C2 Bundu India
69 C3 Bungendore Austr.
135 D2 Bungoma Kenya
83 B4 Bungo-suidō sea chan. Japan
135 D2 Bunia Dem. Rep. Congo

134 C3 Bunianga Dem. Rep. Congo
113 B1 Bun na Leaca Ireland
79 B2 Buôn Ma Thuôt Vietnam
135 D3 Bura Kenya
133 C3 Buraan Somalia
　Burang China see Jirang
94 B2 Buraydah Saudi Arabia
117 D2 Burbach Ger.
133 C4 Burco Somalia
116 B1 Burdaard Neth.
127 D3 Burdur Turkey
　Burdwan India see Barddhaman
133 B3 Burē Eth.
115 D3 Bure r. U.K.
85 E1 Bureinskiy Khrebet mts Rus. Fed.
117 D2 Büren Ger.
90 B1 Burewala Pak.
　Bureya Range mts Rus. Fed. see
　Bureinskiy Khrebet
126 C2 Burgas Bulg.
117 E1 Burg bei Magdeburg Ger.
117 E1 Burgdorf Niedersachsen Ger.
117 E1 Burgdorf Niedersachsen Ger.
147 E3 Burgeo Can.
139 C3 Burgersdorp S. Africa
139 D1 Burgersfort S. Africa
116 A2 Burgh-Haamstede Neth.
117 F3 Burglengenfeld Ger.
161 C2 Burgos Mex.
122 C1 Burgos Spain
121 C2 Burgundy reg. France
127 C3 Burhaniye Turkey
90 B2 Burhanpur India
91 C2 Burhar-Dhanpuri India
117 D1 Burhave (Butjadingen) Ger.
170 C2 Buri Brazil
76 B2 Burial Indon.
80 B2 Burias i. Phil.
147 E3 Burin Can.
79 B2 Buriram Thai.
170 C1 Buriti Alegre Brazil
167 E3 Buriti Bravo Brazil
171 C1 Buritis Brazil
123 C2 Burjassot Spain
159 D2 Burkburnett U.S.A.
67 C1 Burketown Austr.
130 B3 Burkina country Africa
150 D2 Burley U.S.A.
152 C3 Burlington CO U.S.A.
153 E2 Burlington IA U.S.A.
153 E1 Burlington NC U.S.A.
155 E2 Burlington VT U.S.A.
　Burma country Asia see Myanmar
150 B2 Burney U.S.A.
67 D4 Burnie Austr.
114 B3 Burnley U.K.
150 C2 Burns U.S.A.
150 C2 Burns Junction U.S.A.
144 B2 Burns Lake Can.
153 E2 Burnsville U.S.A.
117 F1 Burow Ger.
93 E2 Burqin China
68 A2 Burra Austr.
125 D2 Burrel Albania
113 B2 Burren reg. Ireland
69 C2 Burrendong, Lake Austr.
69 C2 Burren Junction Austr.
123 C2 Burriana Spain
69 C2 Burrinjuck Reservoir Austr.
160 B2 Burro, Serranías del mts Mex.
127 C2 Bursa Turkey
132 B2 Bür Safājah Egypt
　Būr Sa'īd Egypt see Port Said
　Būr Sa'īd Egypt see Port Said
　Būr Sūdān Sudan see Port Sudan
146 C2 Burton, Lac l. Can.
　Burtonport Ireland see Ailt an
　Chorráin
115 C3 Burton upon Trent U.K.
68 B2 Burtundy Austr.
75 C3 Buru i. Indon.
135 C3 Burundi country Africa
135 C3 Bururi Burundi
112 C1 Burwick U.K.
114 B3 Bury U.K.
107 C1 Buryn' Ukr.
92 B2 Burynshyk Kazakh.
115 D3 Bury St Edmunds U.K.
134 C3 Busanga Dem. Rep. Congo
97 D3 Büshehr Iran
135 D3 Bushenyi Uganda
　Bushire Iran see Büshehr
134 C2 Businga Dem. Rep. Congo
66 A3 Busselton Austr.
159 C3 Bustamante Mex.
124 A1 Busto Arsizio Italy
80 A2 Busuanga Phil.
134 C2 Buta Dem. Rep. Congo
135 C3 Butare Rwanda
112 B3 Bute i. U.K.
135 C2 Butembo Dem. Rep. Congo
139 C2 Butha-Buthe Lesotho
155 D2 Butler U.S.A.
77 D2 Buton i. Indon.
150 D1 Butte U.S.A.
76 B1 Butterworth Malaysia
112 A1 Butt of Lewis hd U.K.
145 E2 Button Bay Can.
147 D1 Button Islands Can.
80 B3 Butuan Phil.
105 F3 Buturlinovka Rus. Fed.
91 C2 Butwal Nepal
117 D2 Butzbach Ger.
133 C4 Buulobarde Somalia

133 C5 Buur Gaabo Somalia
133 C4 Buurhabaka Somalia
94 A2 Buwāṭah Saudi Arabia
92 C3 Buxoro Uzbek.
117 D1 Buxtehude Ger.
114 C3 Buxton U.K.
105 F2 Buy Rus. Fed.
103 D4 Buynaksk Rus. Fed.
127 C3 Büyükmenderes r. Turkey
81 A1 Buyun Shan mt. China
90 B1 Buzai Gumbad Afgh.
126 C2 Buzău Romania
126 C1 Buzău r. Romania
137 C2 Búzi Moz.
103 E3 Buzuluk Rus. Fed.
104 C3 Byahoml' Belarus
126 C2 Byala Sliven Bulg.
126 C2 Byala Varna Bulg.
104 C3 Byalynichy Belarus
104 D3 Byarezina r. Belarus
104 B3 Byaroza Belarus
104 C3 Byarozawka Belarus
119 D1 Bydgoszcz Pol.
　Byelorussia country Europe see
　Belarus
104 C3 Byerazino Belarus
104 C3 Byeshankovichy Belarus
105 D3 Bykhaw Belarus
143 G2 Bylot Island Can.
69 C2 Byrock Austr.
69 D1 Byron Bay Austr.
99 J2 Bytantay r. Rus. Fed.
119 D1 Bytom Pol.
119 D1 Bytów Pol.

C

136 A2 Caála Angola
170 B2 Caarapó Brazil
171 C1 Caatinga Brazil
160 B2 Caballos Mesteños, Llano de los plain Mex.
122 B1 Cabañaquinta Spain
80 B1 Cabanatuan Phil.
133 C3 Cabdul Qaadir Somalia
170 A1 Cabeceira Rio Manso Brazil
170 C1 Cabeceiras Brazil
122 B2 Cabeza del Buey Spain
168 B1 Cabezas Bol.
166 B1 Cabimas Venez.
136 A1 Cabinda Angola
134 B3 Cabinda prov. Angola
167 F3 Cabo de Santo Agostinho Brazil
171 D2 Cabo Frio Brazil
171 D2 Cabo Frio, Ilha do i. Brazil
146 C2 Cabonga, Réservoir resr Can.
69 D1 Caboolture Austr.
166 B3 Cabo Pantoja Peru
137 C2 Cabora Bassa, Lake resr Moz.
160 A1 Caborca Mex.
147 D2 Cabot Strait Can.
122 C2 Cabra Spain
171 D1 Cabral, Serra do mts Brazil
123 D2 Cabrera, Illa de i. Spain
122 B1 Cabrera, Sierra de la mts Spain
145 D2 Cabri Can.
123 C2 Cabriel r. Spain
170 B3 Caçador Brazil
125 D2 Čačak Serbia
124 A2 Caccia, Capo c. Italy
122 B2 Cacém Port.
167 E4 Cáceres Brazil
122 B2 Cáceres Spain
144 B2 Cache Creek Can.
130 A3 Cacheu Guinea-Bissau
167 D3 Cachimbo, Serra do hills Brazil
170 B1 Cachoeira Alta Brazil
171 D2 Cachoeiro de Itapemirim Brazil
130 A3 Cacine Guinea-Bissau
136 A2 Cacolo Angola
136 A2 Caconda Angola
170 B1 Caçu Brazil
119 D2 Čadca Slovakia
117 D1 Cadenberge Ger.
161 B2 Cadereyta Mex.
154 C2 Cadillac U.S.A.
80 B2 Cadiz Phil.
122 B2 Cádiz Spain
122 B2 Cádiz, Golfo de g. Spain
144 C2 Cadotte Lake Can.
120 B2 Caen France
　Caerdydd U.K. see Cardiff
　Caerfyrddin U.K. see Carmarthen
　Caergybi U.K. see Holyhead
114 A3 Caernarfon U.K.
115 A3 Caernarfon Bay U.K.
　Caernarvon U.K. see Caernarfon
168 B2 Cafayate Arg.
170 C2 Cafelândia Brazil
136 A1 Cahama Angola
113 B3 Caha Mountains hills Ireland
113 A3 Cahermore Ireland
113 C2 Cahir Ireland
113 A3 Cahirsiveen Ireland
　Cahora Bassa, Lago de resr Moz. see
　Cabora Bassa, Lake

Coëtivy

66 A2 Chichester Range mts Austr.
159 D1 Chickasha U.S.A.
122 B2 Chiclana de la Frontera Spain
166 B3 Chiclayo Peru
169 B4 Chico Chubut r. Arg.
169 B4 Chico Santa Cruz r. Arg.
151 B3 Chico U.S.A.
155 E2 Chicopee U.S.A.
80 B2 Chico Sapocoy, Mount Phil.
147 C3 Chicoutimi Can.
147 D1 Chidley, Cape Can.
79 A3 Chieo Lan, Ang Kep Nam Thai.
124 B2 Chieti Italy
161 C3 Chietla Mex.
86 B1 Chifeng China
171 D1 Chifre, Serra do mts Brazil
137 C2 Chifunde Moz.
93 D2 Chiganak Kazakh.
161 C3 Chignahuapán Mex.
137 C3 Chigubo Moz.
78 A1 Chigu Co l. China
160 B2 Chihuahua Mex.
93 C2 Chiili Kazakh.
104 C2 Chikhachevo Rus. Fed.
83 C3 Chikuma-gawa r. Japan
144 B2 Chilanko r. Can.
90 B1 Chilas Pak.
159 C2 Childress U.S.A.
169 A3 Chile country S. America
174 C6 Chile Basin S. Pacific Ocean
168 B2 Chilecito Arg.
173 G8 Chile Rise S. Pacific Ocean
93 D2 Chilik Kazakh.
91 C3 Chilika Lake India
137 B2 Chililabombwe Zambia
144 B2 Chilko r. Can.
144 B2 Chilko Lake Can.
169 A3 Chillán Chile
154 B2 Chillicothe IL U.S.A.
153 E3 Chillicothe MO U.S.A.
154 C3 Chillicothe OH U.S.A.
144 B3 Chilliwack Can.
169 A4 Chiloé, Isla de i. Chile
161 C3 Chilpancingo Mex.
69 C3 Chiltern Austr.
115 C4 Chiltern Hills U.K.
136 B1 Chiluage Angola
87 C3 Chilung Taiwan
135 D3 Chimala Tanz.
137 C2 Chimanimani Zimbabwe
168 B3 Chimbas Arg.
166 B3 Chimborazo mt. Ecuador
166 B3 Chimbote Peru
92 B2 Chimboy Uzbek.
Chimishliya Moldova see Cimişlia
Chimkent Kazakh. see Shymkent
137 C2 Chimoio Moz.
93 C3 Chimtargha, Qullai mt. Tajik.
84 C2 China country Asia
161 C2 China Mex.
166 B4 Chincha Alta Peru
144 C2 Chinchaga r. Can.
161 D3 Chinchorro, Banco Mex.
137 C2 Chinde Moz.
81 B3 Chindo S. Korea
81 B3 Chin-do i. S. Korea
84 C2 Chindu China
78 A1 Chindwin r. Myanmar
81 B2 Chinghwa N. Korea
137 B2 Chingola Zambia
136 A2 Chinguar Angola
81 B2 Chinhae S. Korea
137 C2 Chinhoyi Zimbabwe
Chini India see Kalpa
Chining China see Jining
90 B1 Chiniot Pak.
160 B2 Chinipas Mex.
81 B2 Chinju S. Korea
134 C2 Chinko r. C.A.R.
158 B1 Chinle U.S.A.
87 B3 Chinmen Taiwan
Chinnamp'o N. Korea see Namp'o
83 C3 Chino Japan
151 C4 Chino U.S.A.
120 C2 Chinon France
150 E1 Chinook U.S.A.
158 A2 Chino Valley U.S.A.
93 C2 Chinoz Uzbek.
137 C2 Chinsali Zambia
124 B1 Chioggia Italy
127 C3 Chios Greece
127 C3 Chios i. Greece
137 C2 Chipata Zambia
136 A2 Chipindo Angola
Chipinga Zimbabwe see Chipinge
137 C3 Chipinge Zimbabwe
89 B3 Chiplun India
115 B4 Chippenham U.K.
154 A2 Chippewa Falls U.S.A.
115 C4 Chipping Norton U.K.
Chipuriro Zimbabwe see Guruve
161 D3 Chiquimula Guat.
93 C2 Chirchiq Uzbek.
137 C3 Chiredzi Zimbabwe
158 B2 Chiricahua Peak U.S.A.
162 B4 Chiriquí, Golfo de b. Panama
81 B2 Chiri-san mt. S. Korea
162 B4 Chirripó mt. Costa Rica
137 B2 Chirundu Zimbabwe
146 C2 Chisasibi Can.
153 E1 Chisholm U.S.A.
Chisimaio Somalia see Kismaayo
106 B2 Chişinău Moldova
103 E3 Chistopol' Rus. Fed.
85 D1 Chita Rus. Fed.
136 A2 Chitado Angola
Chitaldrug India see Chitradurga
137 C2 Chitambo Zambia
136 B1 Chitato Angola
137 C1 Chitipa Malawi
137 C3 Chitobe Moz.
Chitor India see Chittaurgarh
82 D2 Chitose Japan
89 B3 Chitradurga India
90 B1 Chitral Pak.
162 B4 Chitré Panama
91 D2 Chittagong Bangl.
90 B2 Chittaurgarh India
89 B3 Chittoor India
Chittorgarh India see Chittaurgarh
137 C2 Chitungwiza Zimbabwe
136 B2 Chiume Angola
137 C2 Chivhu Zimbabwe
86 B2 Chizhou China
Chkalov Rus. Fed. see Orenburg
130 C1 Chlef Alg.
123 D2 Chlef, Oued r. Alg.
117 F2 Chodov Czech Rep.
169 B3 Choele Choel Arg.
Chogori Feng mt. China/Pakistan see K2
64 G4 Choiseul i. Solomon Is
160 B2 Choix Mex.
118 C1 Chojna Pol.
119 D1 Chojnice Pol.
133 B3 Ch'ok'ē Eth.
Chokue Moz. see Chókwé
99 K2 Chokurdakh Rus. Fed.
137 C3 Chókwé Moz.
120 B2 Cholet France
161 C3 Cholula Mex.
136 B2 Choma Zambia
Chomo China see Yadong
118 C1 Chomutov Czech Rep.
99 I2 Chona r. Rus. Fed.
81 B2 Ch'ŏnan S. Korea
74 A2 Chon Buri Thai.
166 A3 Chone Ecuador
Chong'an China see Wuyishan
81 B1 Ch'ŏngjin N. Korea
81 B2 Chŏngju N. Korea
81 B2 Ch'ŏngju S. Korea
81 B2 Chŏngp'yŏng N. Korea
86 A3 Chongqing China
86 A2 Chongqing mun. China
81 B2 Chŏngŭp S. Korea
137 B2 Chongwe Zambia
87 A3 Chongzuo China
81 B2 Chŏnju S. Korea
169 A4 Chonos, Archipiélago de los is Chile
170 B3 Chopimzinho Brazil
127 B3 Chora Sfakion Greece
114 B3 Chorley U.K.
107 C2 Chornobay Ukr.
106 C1 Chornobyl' Ukr.
107 C2 Chornomors'ke Ukr.
106 B2 Chortkiv Ukr.
81 B2 Ch'ŏrwŏn S. Korea
81 B1 Ch'osan N. Korea
83 D3 Chōshi Japan
169 A3 Chos Malal Arg.
119 D1 Choszczno Pol.
150 D1 Choteau U.S.A.
130 A2 Choûm Maur.
85 D1 Choybalsan Mongolia
85 D1 Choyr Mongolia
70 B2 Christchurch N.Z.
115 C4 Christchurch U.K.
143 H2 Christian, Cape Can.
139 C2 Christiana S. Africa
Christianshåb Greenland see Qasigiannguit
70 A2 Christina, Mount N.Z.
74 B3 Christmas Island terr. Indian Ocean
127 B2 Chrysoupoli Greece
Chu Kazakh. see Shu
Chubarovka Ukr. see Polohy
169 B4 Chubut r. Arg.
105 F3 Chuchkovo Rus. Fed.
106 B1 Chudniv Ukr.
105 D2 Chudovo Rus. Fed.
142 C2 Chugach Mountains U.S.A.
83 B4 Chūgoku-sanchi mts Japan
Chuguchak China see Tacheng
82 B2 Chuguyevka Rus. Fed.
107 D2 Chuhuyiv Ukr.
Chukchi Peninsula pen. Rus. Fed. see Chukotskiy Poluostrov
176 J3 Chukchi Sea sea Rus. Fed./U.S.A.
105 F2 Chukhloma Rus. Fed.
99 N2 Chukotskiy Poluostrov pen. Rus. Fed.
Chulaktau Kazakh. see Karatau
151 C4 Chula Vista U.S.A.
98 G3 Chulym Rus. Fed.
168 B2 Chumbicha Arg.
99 K3 Chumikan Rus. Fed.
79 A2 Chumphon Thai.
81 B2 Ch'unch'ŏn S. Korea
Chungking China see Chongqing
Ch'ungmu S. Korea see T'ongyŏng
87 C3 Chungyang Shanmo mts Taiwan
99 H2 Chunya r. Rus. Fed.
135 D3 Chunya Tanz.
166 B4 Chuquibamba Peru
168 B2 Chuquicamata Chile
121 D2 Chur Switz.
78 A1 Churachandpur India
99 J2 Churapcha Rus. Fed.
145 E2 Churchill Can.
145 E2 Churchill r. Man. Can.
147 D2 Churchill r. Nfld. and Lab. Can.
145 E2 Churchill, Cape Can.
147 D2 Churchill Falls Can.
145 D2 Churchill Lake Can.
90 B2 Churu India
79 B2 Chu Sê Vietnam
158 B1 Chuska Mountains U.S.A.
102 E3 Chusovoy Rus. Fed.
147 C3 Chute-des-Passes Can.
64 G3 Chuuk is Micronesia
78 B1 Chuxiong China
107 C2 Chyhyryn Ukr.
Chymyshliya Moldova see Cimişlia
Ciadâr-Lunga Moldova see Ciadîr-Lunga
106 B2 Ciadîr-Lunga Moldova
76 B2 Ciamis Indon.
76 B2 Cianjur Indon.
170 B2 Cianorte Brazil
158 A2 Cibuta, Sierra mt. Mex.
96 B1 Cide Turkey
119 E1 Ciechanów Pol.
162 C2 Ciego de Ávila Cuba
163 C3 Ciénaga Col.
162 B2 Cienfuegos Cuba
123 C2 Cieza Spain
122 C2 Cigüela r. Spain
96 B2 Cihanbeyli Turkey
160 B3 Cihuatlán Mex.
122 C2 Cijara, Embalse de resr Spain
125 C2 Çikës, Maja e mt. Albania
76 B2 Cilacap Indon.
Cill Airne Ireland see Killarney
Cill Chainnigh Ireland see Kilkenny
159 C1 Cimarron r. U.S.A.
106 B2 Cimişlia Moldova
124 B2 Cimone, Monte mt. Italy
Cîmpina Romania see Câmpina
Cîmpulung Romania see Câmpulung
76 B2 Cina, Tanjung c. Indon.
154 C3 Cincinnati U.S.A.
Cinco de Outubro Angola see Xá-Muteba
127 C3 Çine Turkey
116 B2 Ciney Belgium
150 C2 Cinnabar Mountain U.S.A.
161 C3 Cintalapa Mex.
87 B3 Ciping China
Ciping China see Ciping
169 B3 Cipolletti Arg.
142 C2 Circle AK U.S.A.
152 B1 Circle MT U.S.A.
76 B2 Cirebon Indon.
115 C4 Cirencester U.K.
124 A1 Ciriè Italy
125 C3 Cirò Marina Italy
126 B1 Cisnădie Romania
125 C2 Čitluk Bos.-Herz.
138 A3 Citrusdal S. Africa
151 B3 Citrus Heights U.S.A.
126 C1 Ciucaş, Vârful mt. Romania
161 B2 Ciudad Acuña Mex.
161 B3 Ciudad Altamirano Mex.
166 C2 Ciudad Bolívar Venez.
163 C4 Ciudad Bolivia Venez.
160 B2 Ciudad Camargo Mex.
160 A2 Ciudad Constitución Mex.
161 C3 Ciudad Cuauhtémoc Mex.
161 C3 Ciudad del Carmen Mex.
170 B3 Ciudad del Este Para.
160 B2 Ciudad Delicias Mex.
161 C2 Ciudad de Valles Mex.
166 C2 Ciudad Guayana Venez.
158 B3 Ciudad Guerrero Mex.
160 B3 Ciudad Guzmán Mex.
161 C3 Ciudad Hidalgo Mex.
161 C3 Ciudad Ixtepec Mex.
160 B1 Ciudad Juárez Mex.
161 C2 Ciudad Madero Mex.
161 C2 Ciudad Mante Mex.
161 C2 Ciudad Mier Mex.
160 B2 Ciudad Obregón Mex.
122 C2 Ciudad Real Spain
161 C2 Ciudad Río Bravo Mex.
122 B1 Ciudad Rodrigo Spain
Ciudad Trujillo Dom. Rep. see Santo Domingo
161 C2 Ciudad Victoria Mex.
123 D1 Ciutadella Spain
124 B1 Cividale del Friuli Italy
124 B2 Civitanova Marche Italy
124 B2 Civitavecchia Italy
120 C2 Civray France
127 C3 Çivril Turkey
86 C2 Cixi China
115 D4 Clacton-on-Sea U.K.
144 C2 Claire, Lake Can.
121 C2 Clamecy France
156 C2 Clanton U.S.A.
138 A3 Clanwilliam S. Africa
113 C2 Clara Ireland
68 A2 Clare Austr.
154 C2 Clare U.S.A.
113 A2 Clare Island Ireland
155 E2 Claremont U.S.A.
113 B2 Claremorris Ireland
70 B2 Clarence N.Z.
71 B3 Clarence Island Antarctica
147 E3 Clarenville Can.
144 C2 Claresholm Can.
153 D2 Clarinda U.S.A.
160 A3 Clarión, Isla i. Mex.
139 C3 Clarkebury S. Africa
150 C1 Clark Fork r. U.S.A.
157 D2 Clark Hill Reservoir U.S.A.
154 C3 Clarksburg U.S.A.
156 B2 Clarksdale U.S.A.
150 C1 Clarkston U.S.A.
156 B1 Clarksville AR U.S.A.
156 C1 Clarksville TN U.S.A.
170 B1 Claro r. Brazil
159 C1 Claude U.S.A.
159 C1 Clayton U.S.A.
113 B3 Clear, Cape Ireland
142 C3 Cleare, Cape U.S.A.
153 E2 Clear Lake U.S.A.
151 B3 Clear Lake l. U.S.A.
144 C2 Clearwater Can.
145 C2 Clearwater r. Can.
157 D3 Clearwater U.S.A.
150 C1 Clearwater r. U.S.A.
159 D2 Cleburne U.S.A.
117 E1 Clenze Ger.
67 D2 Clermont Austr.
121 C2 Clermont-Ferrand France
116 C2 Clervaux Lux.
68 A2 Cleve Austr.
156 B2 Cleveland MS U.S.A.
154 C2 Cleveland OH U.S.A.
157 D1 Cleveland TN U.S.A.
150 D1 Cleveland, Mount U.S.A.
170 B3 Clevelândia Brazil
113 B2 Clew Bay Ireland
157 D3 Clewiston U.S.A.
113 A2 Clifden Ireland
69 D1 Clifton Austr.
158 B2 Clifton U.S.A.
158 B1 Clines Corners U.S.A.
144 B2 Clinton Can.
153 E2 Clinton IA U.S.A.
153 E3 Clinton MO U.S.A.
159 D1 Clinton OK U.S.A.
141 H8 Clipperton, Île terr. N. Pacific Ocean
112 A2 Clisham h. U.K.
114 B3 Clitheroe U.K.
113 B3 Clonakilty Ireland
67 D2 Cloncurry Austr.
113 C1 Clones Ireland
113 C2 Clonmel Ireland
117 D1 Cloppenburg Ger.
153 E1 Cloquet U.S.A.
152 B2 Cloud Peak U.S.A.
151 C3 Clovis CA U.S.A.
159 C2 Clovis NM U.S.A.
Cluain Meala Ireland see Clonmel
145 D2 Cluff Lake Mine Can.
126 B1 Cluj-Napoca Romania
67 C2 Cluny Austr.
121 D2 Cluses France
70 A3 Clutha r. N.Z.
112 B3 Clyde r. U.K.
112 B3 Clyde, Firth of est. U.K.
112 B3 Clydebank U.K.
143 H2 Clyde River Can.
160 B3 Coalcomán Mex.
144 C3 Coaldale Can.
151 C3 Coaldale U.S.A.
144 B2 Coal River Can.
166 C3 Coari Brazil
166 C3 Coari r. Brazil
157 C2 Coastal Plain U.S.A.
144 B2 Coast Mountains Can.
150 B2 Coast Ranges mts U.S.A.
112 B3 Coatbridge U.K.
145 F1 Coats Island Can.
71 C2 Coats Land reg. Antarctica
161 C3 Coatzacoalcos Mex.
162 A3 Cobán Guat.
69 C2 Cobar Austr.
113 B3 Cobh Ireland
168 B1 Cobija Bol.
Coblenz Ger. see Koblenz
146 C3 Cobourg Can.
66 C1 Cobourg Peninsula Austr.
69 C3 Cobram Austr.
117 E2 Coburg Ger.
168 B1 Cochabamba Bol.
116 C2 Cochem Ger.
Cochin India see Kochi
144 C2 Cochrane Alta Can.
146 B3 Cochrane Ont. Can.
169 A4 Cochrane Chile
68 A2 Cockaleechie Austr.
68 B2 Cockburn Austr.
Cockburn Town Turks and Caicos Is see Grand Turk
114 B2 Cockermouth U.K.
66 B3 Cocklebiddy Austr.
138 B3 Cockscomb mt. S. Africa
162 B3 Coco r. Hond./Nic.
141 J9 Coco, Isla de i. N. Pacific Ocean
175 F4 Cocos Basin Indian Ocean
74 A3 Cocos Islands terr. Indian Ocean
160 B2 Cocula Mex.
166 B2 Cocuy, Sierra Nevada del mt. Col.
155 E2 Cod, Cape U.S.A.
166 C3 Codajás Brazil
124 B2 Codigoro Italy
147 D2 Cod Island Can.
167 E3 Codó Brazil
152 B2 Cody U.S.A.
67 D1 Coen Austr.
116 C2 Coesfeld Ger.
129 I6 Coëtivy i. Seychelles

Coeur d'Alene

150 C1 Coeur d'Alene U.S.A.
116 C1 Coevorden Neth.
139 C3 Coffee Bay S. Africa
153 D3 Coffeyville U.S.A.
68 A2 Coffin Bay Austr.
69 D2 Coffs Harbour Austr.
139 C3 Cofimvaba S. Africa
120 B2 Cognac France
134 A2 Cogo Equat. Guinea
68 B3 Cohuna Austr.
162 B4 Coiba, Isla de i. Panama
169 A4 Coihaique Chile
89 B3 Coimbatore India
122 B1 Coimbra Port.
168 B1 Coipasa, Salar de salt flat Bol.
68 B3 Colac Austr.
171 D1 Colatina Brazil
152 C3 Colby U.S.A.
115 D4 Colchester U.K.
145 C2 Cold Lake Can.
112 C3 Coldstream U.K.
69 C2 Coleambally Austr.
159 D2 Coleman U.S.A.
68 B3 Coleraine Austr.
113 C1 Coleraine U.K.
139 C3 Colesberg S. Africa
169 A3 Colico Chile
160 B3 Colima Mex.
160 B3 Colima, Nevado de vol. Mex.
112 A2 Coll i. U.K.
69 C1 Collarenebri Austr.
159 D2 College Station U.S.A.
69 C1 Collerina Austr.
66 A3 Collie Austr.
66 B1 Collier Bay Austr.
154 C2 Collingwood Can.
70 B2 Collingwood N.Z.
142 F2 Collinson Peninsula Can.
117 F2 Collmberg h. Ger.
124 A3 Collo Alg.
113 B1 Collooney Ireland
121 D2 Colmar France
114 B3 Colne U.K.
116 C2 Cologne Ger.
Colomb-Béchar Alg. see Béchar
170 C2 Colômbia Brazil
166 B2 Colombia country S. America
89 B4 Colombo Sri Lanka
120 C3 Colomiers France
168 C3 Colón Arg.
162 C4 Colón Panama
75 D2 Colonia Micronesia
169 B4 Colonia Las Heras Arg.
125 C3 Colonna, Capo c. Italy
112 A2 Colonsay i. U.K.
169 B3 Colorado r. Arg.
158 A2 Colorado r. Mex./U.S.A.
159 D2 Colorado r. Texas U.S.A.
152 B3 Colorado state U.S.A.
151 C4 Colorado Desert U.S.A.
151 E3 Colorado Plateau U.S.A.
152 C3 Colorado Springs U.S.A.
160 B2 Colotlán Mex.
168 B1 Colquiri Bol.
152 B1 Colstrip U.S.A.
154 B3 Columbia KY U.S.A.
155 D3 Columbia MD U.S.A.
153 E3 Columbia MO U.S.A.
157 D2 Columbia SC U.S.A.
156 C1 Columbia TN U.S.A.
150 B1 Columbia r. U.S.A.
144 C2 Columbia, Mount Can.
150 D1 Columbia Falls U.S.A.
144 B2 Columbia Mountains Can.
150 C1 Columbia Plateau U.S.A.
157 D2 Columbus GA U.S.A.
154 B3 Columbus IN U.S.A.
156 C2 Columbus MS U.S.A.
150 E1 Columbus MT U.S.A.
153 D2 Columbus NE U.S.A.
158 B2 Columbus NM U.S.A.
154 C3 Columbus OH U.S.A.
159 D3 Columbus TX U.S.A.
150 C1 Colville U.S.A.
142 B2 Colville r. U.S.A.
142 D2 Colville Lake Can.
114 B3 Colwyn Bay U.K.
124 B2 Comacchio Italy
161 C3 Comalcalco Mex.
126 C1 Comănești Romania
146 C2 Comencho, Lac l. Can.
113 C2 Comeragh Mountains hills Ireland
159 D2 Comfort U.S.A.
91 D2 Comilla Bangl.
124 A2 Comino, Capo c. Italy
161 C3 Comitán de Domínguez Mex.
121 C2 Commentry France
159 D2 Commerce U.S.A.
143 G2 Committee Bay Can.
124 A1 Como Italy
Como, Lago di l. Italy see Como, Lake
124 A1 Como, Lake l. Italy
169 B4 Comodoro Rivadavia Arg.
161 B2 Comonfort Mex.
137 D2 Comoros country Africa
144 B3 Comox Can.
121 C2 Compiègne France
160 B2 Compostela Mex.
106 B2 Comrat Moldova
130 A4 Conakry Guinea
120 B2 Concarneau France
171 E1 Conceição da Barra Brazil
167 E3 Conceição do Araguaia Brazil
171 D1 Conceição do Mato Dentro Brazil
168 B2 Concepción Arg.
169 A3 Concepción Chile
160 B2 Concepción Mex.
151 B4 Conception, Point U.S.A.
170 C2 Conchas Brazil
158 C1 Conchas Lake U.S.A.
160 B2 Conchos r. Mex.
161 C2 Conchos r. Mex.
151 B3 Concord CA U.S.A.
155 E2 Concord NH U.S.A.
168 C3 Concordia Arg.
138 A2 Concordia S. Africa
153 D3 Concordia U.S.A.
69 C2 Condobolin Austr.
120 C3 Condom France
150 B1 Condon U.S.A.
124 B1 Conegliano Italy
67 E1 Conflict Group is P.N.G.
120 C2 Confolens France
151 D3 Confusion Range mts U.S.A.
91 C2 Congdü China
114 B3 Congleton U.K.
134 B3 Congo country Africa
134 B3 Congo r. Congo/Dem. Rep. Congo
Congo (Brazzaville) country Africa see Congo
Congo (Kinshasa) country Africa see Congo, Democratic Republic of the
134 C3 Congo, Democratic Republic of the country Africa
134 C3 Congo Basin Dem. Rep. Congo
Congo Free State country Africa see Congo, Democratic Republic of the
145 C2 Conklin Can.
113 B1 Conn, Lough l. Ireland
113 B2 Connacht reg. Ireland
155 E2 Connecticut r. U.S.A.
155 E2 Connecticut state U.S.A.
112 B2 Connel U.K.
113 B2 Connemara reg. Ireland
150 D1 Conrad U.S.A.
175 D7 Conrad Rise Southern Ocean
159 D2 Conroe U.S.A.
171 D2 Conselheiro Lafaiete Brazil
171 D1 Conselheiro Pena Brazil
116 B3 Consenvoye France
114 C2 Consett U.K.
79 B3 Côn Sơn, Đao i. Vietnam
Constance Ger. see Konstanz
121 D2 Constance, Lake Ger./Switz.
126 C2 Constanța Romania
122 B2 Constantina Spain
131 C1 Constantine Alg.
150 D2 Contact U.S.A.
171 D2 Contagalo Brazil
166 B3 Contamana Peru
169 A5 Contreras, Isla i. Chile
142 E2 Contwoyto Lake Can.
156 B1 Conway AR U.S.A.
155 E2 Conway NH U.S.A.
67 C2 Coober Pedy Austr.
Cooch Behar India see Koch Bihar
Cook, Mount mt. N.Z. see Aoraki
157 C1 Cookeville U.S.A.
142 B2 Cook Inlet sea chan. U.S.A.
65 K5 Cook Islands terr. S. Pacific Ocean
147 E2 Cook's Harbour Can.
113 C1 Cookstown U.K.
70 B2 Cook Strait N.Z.
67 D1 Cooktown Austr.
69 C2 Coolabah Austr.
69 C2 Coolamon Austr.
69 D1 Coolangatta Austr.
66 B3 Coolgardie Austr.
69 C3 Cooma Austr.
68 B2 Coombah Austr.
69 C2 Coonabarabran Austr.
68 A3 Coonalpyn Austr.
69 C2 Coonamble Austr.
69 C1 Coongoola Austr.
153 E1 Coon Rapids U.S.A.
68 A1 Cooper Creek watercourse Austr.
157 E3 Cooper's Town Bahamas
150 B2 Coos Bay U.S.A.
69 C2 Cootamundra Austr.
113 C1 Cootehill Ireland
161 C3 Copainalá Mex.
161 C3 Copala Mex.
109 F4 Copenhagen Denmark
125 C2 Copertino Italy
69 D1 Copeton Reservoir Austr.
168 A2 Copiapó Chile
159 D2 Copperas Cove U.S.A.
154 B1 Copper Harbor U.S.A.
Coppermine Can. see Kugluktuk
142 E2 Coppermine r. Can.
138 B2 Copperton S. Africa
Coquilhatville Dem. Rep. Congo see Mbandaka
168 A2 Coquimbo Chile
168 A2 Coquimbo, Bahía de b. Chile
126 B2 Corabia Romania
171 D1 Coração de Jesus Brazil
166 B4 Coracora Peru
69 D1 Coraki Austr.
66 A2 Coral Bay Austr.
143 G2 Coral Harbour Can.
172 D7 Coral Sea S. Pacific Ocean
64 G5 Coral Sea Islands Territory terr. Austr.
153 E2 Coralville U.S.A.
68 B3 Corangamite, Lake Austr.
115 C3 Corby U.K.
Corcaigh Ireland see Cork
151 C3 Corcoran U.S.A.
169 A4 Corcovado, Golfo de sea chan. Chile
157 D2 Cordele U.S.A.
80 B2 Cordilleras Range mts Phil.
171 D1 Cordisburgo Brazil
168 B3 Córdoba Arg.
161 C3 Córdoba Mex.
122 C2 Córdoba Spain
169 B3 Córdoba, Sierras de mts Arg.
142 C2 Cordova U.S.A.
67 D2 Corfield Austr.
127 A3 Corfu i. Greece
170 B1 Corguinho Brazil
122 B2 Coria Spain
122 B2 Coria del Río Spain
69 D2 Coricudgy mt. Austr.
127 B3 Corinth Greece
156 C2 Corinth U.S.A.
Corinth, Gulf of sea chan. Greece see Gulf of Corinth
171 D1 Corinto Brazil
113 B3 Cork Ireland
127 C2 Çorlu Turkey
170 B2 Cornélio Procópio Brazil
147 E3 Corner Brook Can.
69 C3 Corner Inlet b. Austr.
151 B3 Corning CA U.S.A.
155 D2 Corning NY U.S.A.
Corn Islands is Nic. see Maíz, Islas del
124 B2 Corno, Monte mt. Italy
146 C3 Cornwall Can.
142 F1 Cornwallis Island Can.
166 C1 Coro Venez.
171 D1 Coroaci Brazil
170 C1 Coromandel Brazil
89 C3 Coromandel Coast India
70 C1 Coromandel Peninsula N.Z.
80 B2 Coron Phil.
145 C2 Coronation Can.
142 E2 Coronation Gulf Can.
71 B3 Coronation Island S. Atlantic Ocean
171 D1 Coronel Fabriciano Brazil
168 C2 Coronel Oviedo Para.
170 B1 Coronel Ponce Brazil
169 B3 Coronel Pringles Arg.
170 A2 Coronel Sapucaia Brazil
169 B3 Coronel Suárez Arg.
125 D2 Çorovodë Albania
161 D3 Corozal Belize
159 D3 Corpus Christi U.S.A.
168 B1 Corque Bol.
167 E4 Corrente Brazil
170 B1 Correntes Brazil
167 E4 Correntina Brazil
113 B2 Corrib, Lough l. Ireland
168 C2 Corrientes Arg.
169 C3 Corrientes, Cabo c. Arg.
160 B2 Corrientes, Cabo c. Mex.
159 E2 Corrigan U.S.A.
69 C3 Corryong Austr.
Corse i. France see Corsica
121 D3 Corse, Cap c. France
121 D3 Corsica i. France
159 D2 Corsicana U.S.A.
121 D3 Corte France
122 B2 Cortegana Spain
152 B3 Cortez U.S.A.
124 B1 Cortina d'Ampezzo Italy
155 D2 Cortland U.S.A.
124 B2 Cortona Italy
122 B2 Coruche Port.
Çoruh Turkey see Artvin
96 B1 Çorum Turkey
167 D4 Corumbá Brazil
170 C1 Corumbá r. Brazil
170 C1 Corumbá de Goiás Brazil
Corunna Spain see A Coruña
150 B2 Corvallis U.S.A.
115 B3 Corwen U.K.
Cos i. Greece see Kos
160 B2 Cosalá Mex.
161 C3 Cosamaloapan Mex.
125 C3 Cosenza Italy
121 C2 Cosne-Cours-sur-Loire France
168 B3 Cosquín Arg.
123 C2 Costa Blanca coastal area Spain
123 D1 Costa Brava coastal area Spain
122 B2 Costa de la Luz coastal area Spain
123 C2 Costa del Azahar coastal area Spain
122 B2 Costa del Sol coastal area Spain
162 B3 Costa de Mosquitos coastal area Nic.
123 D1 Costa Dorada coastal area Spain
166 C4 Costa Marques Brazil
170 B1 Costa Rica Brazil
162 B3 Costa Rica country Central America
160 B2 Costa Rica Mex.
Costermansville Dem. Rep. Congo see Bukavu
126 B2 Costești Romania
80 B3 Cotabato Phil.
153 D1 Coteau des Prairies reg. U.S.A.
152 C1 Coteau du Missouri reg. U.S.A.
163 C3 Coteaux Haiti
121 D3 Côte d'Azur coastal area France
130 B4 Côte d'Ivoire country Africa
Côte Française de Somalis country Africa see Djibouti
121 C2 Côtes de Meuse ridge France
166 B3 Cotopaxi, Volcán vol. Ecuador
115 B4 Cotswold Hills U.K.
150 B2 Cottage Grove U.S.A.
118 C1 Cottbus Ger.
121 D3 Cottian Alps mts France/Italy
120 B2 Coubre, Pointe de la pt France
68 A3 Couedic, Cape du Austr.
121 C2 Coulommiers France
153 D2 Council Bluffs U.S.A.
104 B2 Courland Lagoon b. Lith./Rus. Fed.
116 A3 Courmelles France
144 B3 Courtenay Can.
120 B2 Coutances France
120 B2 Coutras France
116 B2 Couvin Belgium
115 C3 Coventry U.K.
122 B1 Covilhã Port.
157 D2 Covington GA U.S.A.
154 C3 Covington KY U.S.A.
154 C3 Covington VA U.S.A.
66 B3 Cowan, Lake imp. l. Austr.
112 C2 Cowdenbeath U.K.
68 A2 Cowell Austr.
69 C3 Cowes Austr.
150 B1 Cowlitz r. U.S.A.
69 C2 Cowra Austr.
170 B1 Coxim Brazil
170 B1 Coxim r. Brazil
91 D2 Cox's Bazar Bangl.
161 B3 Coyuca de Benitez Mex.
91 C1 Cozhê China
161 D2 Cozumel Mex.
161 D2 Cozumel, Isla de i. Mex.
68 A2 Cradock Austr.
139 C3 Cradock S. Africa
152 B2 Craig U.S.A.
118 C2 Crailsheim Ger.
126 B2 Craiova Romania
145 D2 Cranberry Portage Can.
69 C3 Cranbourne Austr.
144 C3 Cranbrook Can.
167 E3 Crateús Brazil
167 F3 Crato Brazil
170 C2 Cravinhos Brazil
152 C2 Crawford U.S.A.
154 B2 Crawfordsville U.S.A.
115 C4 Crawley U.K.
150 D1 Crazy Mountains U.S.A.
145 D2 Cree r. Can.
160 B2 Creel Mex.
145 D2 Cree Lake Can.
145 D2 Creighton Can.
120 C2 Creil France
116 B1 Creil Neth.
124 A1 Crema Italy
124 B1 Cremona Italy
124 B2 Cres i. Croatia
150 B2 Crescent City U.S.A.
69 D2 Crescent Head Austr.
151 E3 Crescent Junction U.S.A.
144 C3 Creston Can.
153 E2 Creston U.S.A.
156 C2 Crestview U.S.A.
127 B3 Crete i. Greece
123 D1 Creus, Cap de c. Spain
123 C2 Crevillent Spain
114 B3 Crewe U.K.
112 B2 Crianlarich U.K.
168 D2 Criciúma Brazil
112 C2 Crieff U.K.
124 B1 Crikvenica Croatia
107 C2 Crimea pen. Ukr.
117 F2 Crimmitschau Ger.
112 B2 Crinan U.K.
134 B2 Cristal, Monts de mts Equat. Guinea/Gabon
170 C1 Cristalina Brazil
126 B1 Crișul Alb r. Romania
117 E1 Crivitz Ger.
Crna Gora country Europe see Montenegro
125 C1 Črnomelj Slovenia
113 B2 Croagh Patrick h. Ireland
125 C1 Croatia country Europe
77 C1 Crocker, Banjaran mts Malaysia
159 D2 Crockett U.S.A.
75 C3 Croker Island Austr.
112 B2 Cromarty U.K.
115 D3 Cromer U.K.
70 A3 Cromwell N.Z.
163 C2 Crooked Island Bahamas
153 D1 Crookston U.S.A.
69 C2 Crookwell Austr.
69 D1 Croppa Creek Austr.
152 C1 Crosby U.S.A.
157 D3 Cross City U.S.A.
156 B2 Crossett U.S.A.
114 B2 Cross Fell h. U.K.
145 E2 Cross Lake Can.
157 C1 Crossville U.S.A.
125 C3 Crotone Italy
150 E1 Crow Agency U.S.A.
115 D4 Crowborough U.K.
156 B2 Crowley U.S.A.
69 D1 Crows Nest Austr.
144 C3 Crowsnest Pass Can.
61 Crozet Basin Indian Ocean
175 D7 Crozet, Îles is Indian Ocean
162 C3 Cruz, Cabo c. Cuba
168 C2 Cruz Alta Brazil
168 B3 Cruz del Eje Arg.
171 D2 Cruzeiro Brazil
166 B3 Cruzeiro do Sul Brazil
68 A2 Crystal Brook Austr.
159 D3 Crystal City U.S.A.
154 B1 Crystal Falls U.S.A.
156 B2 Crystal Springs U.S.A.
119 E2 Csongrád Hungary
119 D2 Csorna Hungary

D

Frankenwald

117 E2 Frankenwald *mts* Ger.
154 C3 Frankfort *KY* U.S.A.
154 B2 Frankfort *MI* U.S.A.
Frankfurt Ger. *see* Frankfurt am Main
117 D2 Frankfurt am Main Ger.
118 C1 Frankfurt an der Oder Ger.
118 C2 Fränkische Alb *hills* Ger.
117 E3 Fränkische Schweiz *reg.* Ger.
155 E2 Franklin *NH* U.S.A.
155 D2 Franklin *PA* U.S.A.
156 C1 Franklin *TN* U.S.A.
142 D2 Franklin Bay Can.
150 C1 Franklin D. Roosevelt Lake U.S.A.
144 B1 Franklin Mountains Can.
142 F2 Franklin Strait Can.
69 C3 Frankston Austr.
98 E1 Frantsa-Iosifa, Zemlya *is* Rus. Fed.
70 B2 Franz Josef Glacier N.Z.
Franz Josef Land *is* Rus. Fed. *see* Frantsa-Iosifa, Zemlya
124 A3 Frasca, Capo della *c.* Italy
144 B3 Fraser *r.* B.C. Can.
147 D2 Fraser *r. Nfld. and Lab.* Can.
138 B3 Fraserburg S. Africa
112 C2 Fraserburgh U.K.
146 B3 Fraserdale Can.
67 E2 Fraser Island Austr.
144 B2 Fraser Lake Can.
144 B2 Fraser Plateau Can.
169 C3 Fray Bentos Uru.
109 E4 Fredericia Denmark
159 D2 Frederick U.S.A.
159 D2 Fredericksburg *TX* U.S.A.
155 D3 Fredericksburg *VA* U.S.A.
144 A2 Frederick Sound *sea chan.* U.S.A.
147 D3 Fredericton Can.
Frederikshåb Greenland *see* Paamiut
109 F4 Frederikshavn Denmark
Fredrikshamn Fin. *see* Hamina
109 F4 Fredrikstad Norway
154 B2 Freeport *IL* U.S.A.
159 D3 Freeport *TX* U.S.A.
162 C2 Freeport City Bahamas
159 D3 Freer U.S.A.
139 C2 Free State *prov.* S. Africa
130 A4 Freetown Sierra Leone
122 B2 Fregenal de la Sierra Spain
120 B2 Fréhel, Cap *c.* France
118 B2 Freiburg im Breisgau Ger.
118 C2 Freising Ger.
118 C2 Freistadt Austria
121 D3 Fréjus France
66 A3 Fremantle Austr.
151 B3 Fremont *CA* U.S.A.
153 D2 Fremont *NE* U.S.A.
154 C2 Fremont *OH* U.S.A.
French Congo *country* Africa *see* Congo
167 D2 French Guiana *terr.* S. America
French Guinea *country* Africa *see* Guinea
150 E1 Frenchman *r.* U.S.A.
65 M5 French Polynesia *terr.* S. Pacific Ocean
French Somaliland *country* Africa *see* Djibouti
63 French Southern and Antarctic Lands *terr.* Indian Ocean
French Sudan *country* Africa *see* Mali
French Territory of the Afars and Issas *country* Africa *see* Djibouti
167 D3 Fresco *r.* Brazil
160 B2 Fresnillo Mex.
151 C3 Fresno U.S.A.
123 D2 Freu, Cap des *c.* Spain
121 D2 Freyming-Merlebach France
130 A3 Fria Guinea
168 B2 Frias Arg.
117 D2 Friedberg (Hessen) Ger.
118 B2 Friedrichshafen Ger.
117 F1 Friesack Ger.
116 C1 Friesoythe Ger.
159 C2 Friona U.S.A.
152 B3 Frisco U.S.A.
Frobisher Bay Can. *see* Iqaluit
143 H2 Frobisher Bay *b.* Can.
117 F2 Frohburg Ger.
103 D4 Frolovo Rus. Fed.
119 D1 Frombork Pol.
115 B4 Frome U.K.
68 A2 Frome, Lake *imp. l.* Austr.
68 A2 Frome Downs Austr.
116 C2 Fröndenberg Ger.
159 C3 Frontera Mex.
161 C3 Frontera Mex.
160 B1 Fronteras Mex.
155 D3 Front Royal U.S.A.
124 B2 Frosinone Italy
108 E3 Frøya *i.* Norway
Frunze Kyrg. *see* Bishkek
170 C2 Frutal Brazil
121 D2 Frutigen Switz.
119 D2 Frýdek-Místek Czech Rep.
87 B3 Fu'an China
87 C3 Fuding China
122 C1 Fuenlabrada Spain
168 C2 Fuerte Olimpo Para.
130 A2 Fuerteventura *i.* Islas Canarias
80 B2 Fuga *i.* Phil.
95 C2 Fujairah U.A.E.
83 C3 Fuji Japan
87 B3 Fujian *prov.* China
83 C3 Fujinomiya Japan
83 C3 Fuji-san *vol.* Japan
Fukien *prov.* China *see* Fujian
83 C3 Fukui Japan
83 B4 Fukuoka Japan
83 D3 Fukushima Japan
117 D2 Fulda Ger.
117 D2 Fulda *r.* Ger.
86 A3 Fuling China
153 E3 Fulton U.S.A.
121 C2 Fumay France
65 I4 Funafuti *atoll* Tuvalu
130 A1 Funchal Arquipélago da Madeira
171 D1 Fundão Brazil
122 B1 Fundão Port.
147 D3 Fundy, Bay of *g.* Can.
137 C3 Funhalouro Moz.
86 B2 Funing *Jiangsu* China
87 A3 Funing *Yunnan* China
131 C3 Funtua Nigeria
95 C2 Fürgun, Küh-e *mt.* Iran
105 F2 Furmanov Rus. Fed.
Furmanovka Kazakh. *see* Moyynkum
Furmanovo Kazakh. *see* Zhalpaktal
171 C2 Furnas, Represa *resr* Brazil
67 D4 Furneaux Group *is* Austr.
Furong China *see* Wan'an
116 C1 Fürstenau Ger.
117 E3 Fürth Ger.
82 D3 Furukawa Japan
143 G2 Fury and Hecla Strait Can.
86 C1 Fushun China
81 B1 Fusong China
95 C2 Fuwayriṭ Qatar
Fuxian China *see* Wafangdian
86 A2 Fuxian China
86 C1 Fuxin China
86 B2 Fuyang China
85 E1 Fuyu China
Fuyu China *see* Songyuan
84 B1 Fuyun China
87 B3 Fuzhou *Fujian* China
87 B3 Fuzhou *Jiangxi* China
109 F4 Fyn *i.* Denmark
112 B3 Fyne, Loch *inlet* U.K.
F.Y.R.O.M. *country* Europe *see* Macedonia

G

133 C4 Gaalkacyo Somalia
136 A2 Gabela Angola
Gaberones Botswana *see* Gaborone
131 D1 Gabès Tunisia
131 D1 Gabès, Golfe de *g.* Tunisia
134 B3 Gabon *country* Africa
139 C1 Gaborone Botswana
95 C2 Gābrīk Iran
126 C2 Gabrovo Bulg.
130 A3 Gabú Guinea-Bissau
89 B3 Gadag India
91 C2 Gadchiroli India
117 E1 Gadebusch Ger.
156 C2 Gadsden U.S.A.
134 B2 Gadzi C.A.R.
126 C2 Găeşti Romania
124 B2 Gaeta Italy
124 B2 Gaeta, Golfo di *g.* Italy
157 D1 Gaffney U.S.A.
131 C1 Gafsa Tunisia
105 E2 Gagarin Rus. Fed.
125 C3 Gagliano del Capo Italy
130 B4 Gagnoa Côte d'Ivoire
147 D2 Gagnon Can.
Gago Coutinho Angola *see* Lumbala N'guimbo
97 C1 Gagra Georgia
138 A2 Gaiab *watercourse* Namibia
127 C3 Gaïdouronisi *i.* Greece
120 C3 Gaillac France
Gaillimh Ireland *see* Galway
157 D3 Gainesville *FL* U.S.A.
157 D2 Gainesville *GA* U.S.A.
159 D2 Gainesville *TX* U.S.A.
114 C3 Gainsborough U.K.
68 A2 Gairdner, Lake *imp. l.* Austr.
112 B2 Gairloch U.K.
138 B2 Gakarosa *mt.* S. Africa
135 E3 Galana *r.* Kenya
119 D2 Galanta Slovakia
Galápagos, Islas *is* Ecuador *see* Galapagos Islands
141 I10 Galapagos Islands *is* Ecuador
173 G6 Galapagos Rise Pacific Ocean
112 C3 Galashiels U.K.
126 C1 Galaţi Romania
109 E3 Galdhøpiggen *mt.* Norway
161 B2 Galeana Mex.
144 C2 Galena Bay Can.
154 A2 Galesburg U.S.A.
138 B2 Galeshewe S. Africa
105 F2 Galich Rus. Fed.
122 B1 Galicia *aut. comm.* Spain
96 B2 Galilee, Sea of *l.* Israel
94 A3 Gallabat Sudan
156 C1 Gallatin U.S.A.
89 C4 Galle Sri Lanka
173 G6 Gallego Rise Pacific Ocean
166 B1 Gallinas, Punta *pt* Col.
125 C2 Gallipoli Italy
127 C2 Gallipoli Turkey
108 H2 Gällivare Sweden
158 B1 Gallup U.S.A.
130 A2 Galtat Zemmour Western Sahara
113 B2 Galtymore *h.* Ireland
159 E3 Galveston U.S.A.
159 E3 Galveston Bay U.S.A.
159 E3 Galveston Island U.S.A.
113 B2 Galway Ireland
113 B2 Galway Bay Ireland
170 C1 Gamá Brazil
139 D3 Gamalakhe S. Africa
133 B4 Gambēla Eth.
130 A3 Gambia *r.* Gambia
130 A3 Gambia, The *country* Africa
65 N6 Gambier, Îles *is* Fr. Polynesia
68 A3 Gambier Islands Austr.
147 E3 Gambo Can.
134 B3 Gamboma Congo
144 C1 Gamêtî Can.
108 H2 Gammelstaden Sweden
158 B1 Ganado U.S.A.
97 C1 Gäncä Azer.
77 C2 Gandadiwata, Bukit *mt.* Indon.
134 C3 Gandajika Dem. Rep. Congo
147 E3 Gander Can.
147 E3 Gander *r.* Can.
117 D1 Ganderkesee Ger.
123 D1 Gandesa Spain
90 B2 Gandhidham India
90 B2 Gandhinagar India
90 B2 Gandhi Sagar *resr* India
123 C2 Gandia Spain
Ganga *r.* Bangl./India *see* Ganges
169 B4 Gangán Arg.
90 B2 Ganganagar India
78 A1 Gangaw Myanmar
84 C2 Gangca China
91 C1 Gangdisê Shan *mts* China
91 D2 Ganges *r.* Bangl./India
121 C3 Ganges France
91 C2 Ganges, Mouths of the Bangl./India
175 E2 Ganges Cone Indian Ocean
91 C2 Gangtok India
91 C3 Ganjam India
87 A3 Ganluo China
121 C2 Gannat France
152 B2 Gannett Peak U.S.A.
138 A3 Gansbaai S. Africa
86 A1 Gansu *prov.* China
131 D4 Ganye Nigeria
87 B3 Ganzhou China
130 B3 Gao Mali
Gaoleshan China *see* Xianfeng
113 B1 Gaoth Dobhair Ireland
130 B3 Gaoua Burkina
130 A3 Gaoual Guinea
86 B2 Gaoyou China
86 B2 Gaoyou Hu *l.* China
121 D3 Gap France
80 B2 Gapan Phil.
91 C1 Gar China
113 B2 Gara, Lough *l.* Ireland
92 C3 Garabil Belentligi *hills* Turkm.
92 B2 Garabogaz Turkm.
92 B2 Garabogazköl Turkm.
92 B2 Garabogazköl Aýlagy *b.* Turkm.
133 C4 Garacad Somalia
69 C1 Garah Austr.
167 F3 Garanhuns Brazil
139 C2 Ga-Rankuwa S. Africa
134 C1 Garar, Plaine de *plain* Chad
133 C4 Garbahaarrey Somalia
151 B2 Garberville U.S.A.
97 D2 Garbosh, Küh-e *mt.* Iran
117 D1 Garbsen Ger.
170 C2 Garça Brazil
170 B2 Garcias Brazil
124 B1 Garda, Lake *l.* Italy
124 A3 Garde, Cap de *c.* Alg.
117 E1 Gardelegen Ger.
152 C3 Garden City U.S.A.
145 E2 Garden Hill Can.
93 C3 Gardēz Afgh.
155 F2 Gardiner U.S.A.
Gardner *atoll* Micronesia *see* Faraulep
151 C3 Gardnerville U.S.A.
152 B3 Garfield U.S.A.
104 B2 Gargždai Lith.
139 C3 Gariep Dam *dam* S. Africa
138 A3 Garies S. Africa
135 D3 Garissa Kenya
104 B2 Garkalne Latvia
159 D2 Garland U.S.A.
118 C2 Garmisch-Partenkirchen Ger.
68 B2 Garnpung Lake *imp. l.* Austr.
120 B3 Garonne *r.* France
133 C4 Garoowe Somalia
90 B2 Garoth India
134 B2 Garoua Cameroon
134 B2 Garoua Boulai Cameroon
Garqêntang China *see* Sog
112 B2 Garry *r.* U.K.
142 F2 Garry Lake Can.
135 E3 Garsen Kenya
92 B2 Garşy Turkm.
138 A2 Garub Namibia
76 B2 Garut Indon.
154 B2 Gary U.S.A.
161 B2 Garza García Mex.
84 C2 Garzê China
Gascogne *reg.* France *see* Gascony
Gascogne, Golfe de *g.* France *see* Gascony, Gulf of
120 B3 Gascony *reg.* France
120 B3 Gascony, Gulf of France
66 A2 Gascoyne *r.* Austr.
134 B2 Gashaka Nigeria
131 D3 Gashua Nigeria
75 E3 Gasmata P.N.G.
147 D3 Gaspé Can.
147 D3 Gaspésie, Péninsule de la *pen.* Can.
157 E1 Gaston, Lake U.S.A.
157 D1 Gastonia U.S.A.
123 C2 Gata, Cabo de *c.* Spain
104 D2 Gatchina Rus. Fed.
114 C2 Gateshead U.K.
159 D2 Gatesville U.S.A.
155 D1 Gatineau Can.
146 C3 Gatineau *r.* Can.
Gatooma Zimbabwe *see* Kadoma
69 D1 Gatton Austr.
145 E2 Gauer Lake Can.
109 E4 Gausta *mt.* Norway
139 C2 Gauteng *prov.* S. Africa
95 C2 Gāvbandī Iran
127 B3 Gavdos *i.* Greece
109 G3 Gävle Sweden
109 G3 Gävlebukten *b.* Sweden
105 F2 Gavrilov Posad Rus. Fed.
105 E2 Gavrilov-Yam Rus. Fed.
138 A2 Gawachab Namibia
78 A1 Gawai Myanmar
68 A2 Gawler Austr.
68 A2 Gawler Ranges *hills* Austr.
91 C2 Gaya India
130 C3 Gaya Niger
130 C3 Gayéri Burkina
154 C1 Gaylord U.S.A.
102 E2 Gayny Rus. Fed.
132 B1 Gaza *terr.* Asia
96 B2 Gaza Gaza
96 B2 Gaziantep Turkey
92 C2 Gazojak Turkm.
130 B4 Gbarnga Liberia
134 A2 Gboko Nigeria
119 D1 Gdańsk Pol.
104 A3 Gdańsk, Gulf of Pol./Rus. Fed.
104 C2 Gdov Rus. Fed.
119 D1 Gdynia Pol.
132 B3 Gedaref Sudan
117 D2 Gedern Ger.
127 C3 Gediz Turkey
127 C3 Gediz *r.* Turkey
118 C1 Gedser Denmark
116 B2 Geel Belgium
68 B3 Geelong Austr.
117 E1 Geesthacht Ger.
91 C1 Gê'gyai China
145 D2 Geikie *r.* Can.
109 E3 Geilo Norway
135 D3 Geita Tanz.
87 A3 Gejiu China
124 B3 Gela Italy
124 B3 Gela, Golfo di *g.* Italy
107 D3 Gelendzhik Rus. Fed.
Gelibolu Turkey *see* Gallipoli
116 C2 Gelsenkirchen Ger.
134 B2 Gemena Dem. Rep. Congo
127 C2 Gemlik Turkey
124 B1 Gemona del Friuli Italy
133 C4 Genalē Wenz *r.* Eth.
97 D3 Genāveh Iran
169 B3 General Acha Arg.
169 B3 General Alvear Arg.
169 C3 General Belgrano Arg.
160 B2 General Cepeda Mex.
General Freire Angola *see* Muxaluando
General Machado Angola *see* Camacupa
169 B3 General Pico Arg.
169 B3 General Roca Arg.
170 B2 General Salgado Brazil
80 B3 General Santos Phil.
155 D2 Genesee *r.* U.S.A.
154 A2 Geneseo *IL* U.S.A.
155 D2 Geneseo *NY* U.S.A.
121 D2 Geneva Switz.
155 D2 Geneva U.S.A.
121 D2 Geneva, Lake *l.* France/Switz.
Genève Switz. *see* Geneva
122 B2 Genil *r.* Spain
116 B2 Genk Belgium
69 C3 Genoa Austr.
124 A2 Genoa Italy
124 A2 Genoa, Gulf of *g.* Italy
Genova Italy *see* Genoa
Gent Belgium *see* Ghent
77 C2 Genteng *i.* Indon.
117 F1 Genthin Ger.
66 A3 Geographe Bay Austr.
147 D2 George *r.* Can.
138 B3 George S. Africa
68 A3 George, Lake Austr.
157 D3 George, Lake *FL* U.S.A.
155 E2 George, Lake *NY* U.S.A.
162 C2 George Town Bahamas
130 A3 Georgetown Gambia
167 D2 Georgetown Guyana
76 B1 George Town Malaysia
154 C3 Georgetown *KY* U.S.A.
157 E2 Georgetown *SC* U.S.A.
159 D2 Georgetown *TX* U.S.A.
71 L2 George V Land *reg.* Antarctica
97 C1 Georgia *country* Asia
157 D2 Georgia *state* U.S.A.
146 B3 Georgian Bay Can.
67 C2 Georgina *watercourse* Austr.
Georgiu-Dezh Rus. Fed. *see* Liski
93 E2 Georgiyevka Kazakh.
103 D4 Georgiyevsk Rus. Fed.

H

Hermidale

81 B2 Haeju-man b. N. Korea
81 B3 Haenam S. Korea
94 B2 Ḥafar al Bāṭin Saudi Arabia
90 B1 Hafizabad Pak.
91 D2 Haflong India
108 □A3 Hafnarfjörður Iceland
94 A3 Hagar Nish Plateau Eritrea/Sudan
75 D2 Hagåtña Guam
117 F1 Hagelberg h. Ger.
116 C2 Hagen Ger.
117 E1 Hagenow Ger.
144 B2 Hagensborg Can.
155 D3 Hagerstown U.S.A.
109 F3 Hagfors Sweden
150 D1 Haggin, Mount U.S.A.
83 B4 Hagi Japan
78 B1 Ha Giang Vietnam
113 B2 Hag's Head hd Ireland
120 B2 Hague, Cap de la c. France
85 F3 Hahajima-rettō is Japan
135 D3 Hai Tanz.
Haicheng China see Haifeng
86 C1 Haicheng China
78 B1 Hai Dương Vietnam
96 B2 Haifa Israel
87 B3 Haifeng China
Haikang China see Leizhou
87 B3 Haikou China
94 B2 Ḥā'il Saudi Arabia
Hailar China see Hulun Buir
Hailong China see Meihekou
108 H2 Hailuoto i. Fin.
85 D3 Hainan i. China
87 A4 Hainan prov. China
144 A2 Haines U.S.A.
144 A1 Haines Junction Can.
117 E2 Hainich ridge Ger.
117 E2 Hainleite ridge Ger.
78 B1 Hai Phong Vietnam
Haiphong Vietnam see Hai Phong
163 C3 Haiti country West Indies
132 B3 Haiya Sudan
119 E2 Hajdúböszörmény Hungary
119 E2 Hajdúszoboszló Hungary
83 C3 Hajiki-zaki pt Japan
94 B3 Ḥajjah Yemen
97 D3 Ḥājjīābād Iran
119 E1 Hajnówka Pol.
78 A1 Haka Myanmar
97 C2 Hakkâri Turkey
82 D2 Hakodate Japan
138 B2 Hakseen Pan salt pan S. Africa
Ḥalab Syria see Aleppo
94 B2 Ḥalabān Saudi Arabia
97 C2 Ḥalabja Iraq
132 B2 Halaib Sudan
94 A2 Halaib Triangle terr. Egypt/Sudan
95 C3 Ḥalāniyāt, Juzur al is Oman
94 A2 Ḥālat 'Ammār Saudi Arabia
Halban Mongolia see Tsetserleg
117 E2 Halberstadt Ger.
80 B2 Halcon, Mount Phil.
109 F4 Halden Norway
117 E1 Haldensleben Ger.
91 B2 Haldwani India
95 C2 Hāleh Iran
70 A3 Halfmoon Bay N.Z.
155 D1 Haliburton Highlands hills Can.
147 D3 Halifax Can.
114 C3 Halifax U.K.
155 D3 Halifax U.S.A.
81 B3 Halla-san mt. S. Korea
143 G2 Hall Beach Can.
116 B2 Halle Belgium
117 E2 Halle (Saale) Ger.
118 C2 Hallein Austria
117 E2 Halle-Neustadt Ger.
64 G3 Hall Islands Micronesia
153 D1 Hallock U.S.A.
143 H2 Hall Peninsula Can.
66 B1 Halls Creek Austr.
75 C2 Halmahera i. Indon.
109 F4 Halmstad Sweden
78 B1 Ha Long Vietnam
Hälsingborg Sweden see Helsingborg
116 B2 Halsteren Neth.
114 B2 Haltwhistle U.K.
83 B4 Hamada Japan
97 C2 Hamadān Iran
96 B2 Ḥamāh Syria
83 C4 Hamamatsu Japan
109 F3 Hamar Norway
132 B2 Ḥamāṭah, Jabal mt. Egypt
89 C4 Hambantota Sri Lanka
117 D1 Hamburg Ger.
139 C3 Hamburg S. Africa
156 B2 Hamburg U.S.A.
94 A2 Ḥamḍ, Wādī al watercourse Saudi Arabia
94 B3 Ḥamḍah Saudi Arabia
155 E2 Hamden U.S.A.
109 H3 Hämeenlinna Fin.
117 D1 Hameln Ger.
66 A2 Hamersley Range mts Austr.
81 B1 Hamgyŏng-sanmaek mts N. Korea
81 B2 Hamhŭng N. Korea
84 C2 Hami China
132 B2 Hamid Sudan
68 B3 Hamilton Austr.
146 C3 Hamilton Can.
Hamilton r. Can. see Churchill
70 C1 Hamilton N.Z.
112 B3 Hamilton U.K.
156 C2 Hamilton AL U.S.A.
150 D1 Hamilton MT U.S.A.
154 C3 Hamilton OH U.S.A.
131 E1 Hamīm, Wādī al watercourse Libya
109 I3 Hamina Fin.
116 C2 Hamm Ger.
131 D1 Hammamet, Golfe de g. Tunisia
97 C2 Ḥammār, Hawr al imp. l. Iraq
117 D2 Hammelburg Ger.
108 G3 Hammerdal Sweden
108 H1 Hammerfest Norway
156 B2 Hammond U.S.A.
155 E3 Hammonton U.S.A.
155 D3 Hampton U.S.A.
155 E2 Hampton Bays U.S.A.
131 D2 Ḥamrā', Al Ḥamādah al plat. Libya
94 A2 Ḥanak Saudi Arabia
82 D3 Hanamaki Japan
117 D2 Hanau Ger.
85 D2 Hanbogd Mongolia
86 B2 Hancheng China
154 B1 Hancock U.S.A.
86 B2 Handan China
135 D3 Handeni Tanz.
151 C3 Hanford U.S.A.
84 C1 Hangayn Nuruu mts Mongolia
Hangchow China see Hangzhou
Hanggin Houqi China see Xamba
Hangö Fin. see Hanko
86 B2 Hangu China
86 C2 Hangzhou China
86 C2 Hangzhou Wan b. China
95 B2 Ḥanīdh Saudi Arabia
Hanjia China see Pengshui
Hanjiang China see Yangzhou
109 H4 Hanko Fin.
151 D3 Hanksville U.S.A.
70 B2 Hanmer Springs N.Z.
144 C2 Hanna Can.
152 B2 Hanna U.S.A.
153 E3 Hannibal U.S.A.
117 D1 Hannover Ger.
117 D2 Hannoversch Münden Ger.
109 F4 Hanöbukten b. Sweden
78 B1 Ha Nôi Vietnam
Hanoi Vietnam see Ha Nôi
146 B3 Hanover Can.
Hanover Ger. see Hannover
138 B3 Hanover S. Africa
155 E2 Hanover NH U.S.A.
155 D3 Hanover PA U.S.A.
108 G2 Hansnes Norway
109 E4 Hanstholm Denmark
104 C3 Hantsavichy Belarus
91 C2 Hanumana India
90 B2 Hanumangarh India
86 A2 Hanzhong China
65 M5 Hao atoll Fr. Polynesia
91 C2 Haora India
108 H2 Haparanda Sweden
116 B2 Hapert Neth.
147 D2 Happy Valley-Goose Bay Can.
94 A2 Ḥaql Saudi Arabia
95 B2 Ḥaraḍh Saudi Arabia
104 C2 Haradok Belarus
94 B3 Ḥarajā Saudi Arabia
137 C2 Harare Zimbabwe
95 C3 Ḥarāsīs, Jiddat al des. Oman
85 D1 Har-Ayrag Mongolia
131 E3 Haraze-Mangueigne Chad
130 A4 Harbel Liberia
85 E1 Harbin China
154 C2 Harbor Beach U.S.A.
147 E3 Harbour Breton Can.
90 B2 Harda India
108 E4 Hardangerfjorden sea chan. Norway
77 C1 Harden, Bukit mt. Indon.
116 C1 Hardenberg Neth.
116 B1 Harderwijk Neth.
138 A3 Hardeveld mts S. Africa
150 E1 Hardin U.S.A.
144 C1 Hardisty Lake Can.
109 E3 Hareid Norway
116 C1 Haren (Ems) Ger.
133 C4 Hārer Eth.
133 C4 Hargeysa Somalia
126 C1 Harghita-Mădăraş, Vârful mt. Romania
84 C2 Har Hu l. China
104 B2 Hari kurk sea chan. Estonia
90 B1 Haripur Pak.
90 A1 Hari Rūd r. Afgh./Iran
126 C1 Hârlău Romania
116 B1 Harlingen Neth.
159 D3 Harlingen U.S.A.
115 D4 Harlow U.K.
150 E1 Harlowton U.S.A.
150 C2 Harney Basin U.S.A.
150 C2 Harney Lake U.S.A.
109 G3 Härnösand Sweden
85 E1 Har Nur China
84 C1 Har Nuur l. Mongolia
112 □ Haroldswick U.K.
130 B4 Harper Liberia
117 D1 Harpstedt Ger.
146 C2 Harricana, Rivière d' r. Can.
69 D2 Harrington Austr.
147 E2 Harrington Harbour Can.
112 A2 Harris reg. U.K.
112 A2 Harris, Sound of sea chan. U.K.
154 B3 Harrisburg IL U.S.A.
150 B2 Harrisburg OR U.S.A.
155 D2 Harrisburg PA U.S.A.
139 C2 Harrismith S. Africa
156 B1 Harrison U.S.A.
147 E2 Harrison, Cape Can.
142 B2 Harrison Bay U.S.A.
155 D3 Harrisonburg U.S.A.
144 B3 Harrison Lake Can.
153 E3 Harrisonville U.S.A.
114 C3 Harrogate U.K.
126 C2 Hârşova Romania
108 G2 Harstad Norway
138 B2 Hartbees watercourse S. Africa
119 D2 Hartberg Austria
155 E2 Hartford CT U.S.A.
153 D2 Hartford SD U.S.A.
115 A4 Hartland Point U.K.
114 C2 Hartlepool U.K.
Hartley Zimbabwe see Chegutu
144 B2 Hartley Bay Can.
139 B2 Harts r. S. Africa
157 D2 Hartwell Reservoir U.S.A.
84 C1 Har Us Nuur l. Mongolia
152 C1 Harvey U.S.A.
115 D4 Harwich U.K.
90 B2 Haryana state India
117 E2 Harz hills Ger.
117 E2 Harzgerode Ger.
94 B2 Ḥasan, Jabal h. Saudi Arabia
96 B2 Hasan Dağı mts Turkey
115 C4 Haslemere U.K.
89 B3 Hassan India
116 B2 Hasselt Belgium
117 E2 Haßfurt Ger.
131 C2 Hassi Bel Guebbour Alg.
131 C1 Hassi Messaoud Alg.
109 F4 Hässleholm Sweden
116 B2 Hastière-Lavaux Belgium
69 C3 Hastings Austr.
70 C1 Hastings N.Z.
115 D4 Hastings U.K.
153 E2 Hastings MN U.S.A.
153 D2 Hastings NE U.S.A.
Hatay Turkey see Antakya
158 B2 Hatch U.S.A.
145 D2 Hatchet Lake Can.
126 B1 Haţeg Romania
68 B2 Hatfield Austr.
84 C1 Hatgal Mongolia
78 B2 Ha Tinh Vietnam
68 B2 Hattah Austr.
157 E1 Hatteras, Cape U.S.A.
173 H3 Hatteras Abyssal Plain S. Atlantic Ocean
156 C2 Hattiesburg U.S.A.
116 C2 Hattingen Ger.
79 B3 Hat Yai Thai.
133 C4 Haud reg. Eth.
109 E4 Haugesund Norway
109 E4 Haukeligrend Norway
108 I2 Haukipudas Fin.
70 C1 Hauraki Gulf N.Z.
70 A3 Hauroko, Lake N.Z.
130 B1 Haut Atlas mts Morocco
147 D3 Hauterive Can.
Haute-Volta country Africa see Burkina
130 B1 Hauts Plateaux Alg.
162 B2 Havana Cuba
115 C4 Havant U.K.
117 E1 Havel r. Ger.
117 F1 Havelberg Ger.
70 B2 Havelock N.Z.
Havelock Swaziland see Bulembu
70 C1 Havelock North N.Z.
115 A4 Haverfordwest U.K.
116 C2 Havixbeck Ger.
119 D2 Havlíčkův Brod Czech Rep.
108 H1 Havøysund Norway
127 C3 Havran Turkey
150 E1 Havre U.S.A.
147 D3 Havre-Aubert Can.
147 D2 Havre-St-Pierre Can.
65 L2 Hawai'i i. U.S.A.
172 E4 Hawai'ian Islands is N. Pacific Ocean
94 B2 Ḥawallī Kuwait
114 B3 Hawarden U.K.
70 A2 Hawea, Lake N.Z.
70 B1 Hawera N.Z.
114 B2 Hawes U.K.
112 C3 Hawick U.K.
70 C1 Hawke Bay N.Z.
68 A2 Hawker Austr.
68 B1 Hawkers Gate Austr.
138 A3 Hawston S. Africa
151 C3 Hawthorne U.S.A.
68 B2 Hay Austr.
144 C1 Hay r. Can.
116 C3 Hayange France
150 C1 Hayden U.S.A.
145 E2 Hayes r. Man. Can.
142 F2 Hayes r. Nunavut Can.
95 C3 Haymā' Oman
93 C2 Hayotboshi tog'i mt. Uzbek.
127 C2 Hayrabolu Turkey
144 C1 Hay River Can.
153 D3 Hays U.S.A.
94 B3 Ḥays Yemen
106 B2 Haysyn Ukr.
151 B3 Hayward U.S.A.
115 C4 Haywards Heath U.K.
97 D2 Hazar Turkm.
90 A1 Hazarajat reg. Afgh.
154 C3 Hazard U.S.A.
91 C2 Hazaribagh India
91 C2 Hazaribagh Range mts India
120 C1 Hazebrouck France
144 B2 Hazelton Can.
155 D2 Hazleton U.S.A.
151 B3 Healdsburg U.S.A.
69 C3 Healesville Austr.
175 E7 Heard Island Indian Ocean
159 D2 Hearne U.S.A.
146 B3 Hearst Can.
71 A3 Hearst Island Antarctica
86 B2 Hebei prov. China
69 C1 Hebel Austr.
156 B1 Heber Springs U.S.A.
86 B2 Hebi China
147 D2 Hebron Can.
144 A2 Hecate Strait Can.
87 A3 Hechi China
116 B2 Hechtel Belgium
70 C2 Hector, Mount N.Z.
109 F3 Hede Sweden
116 C1 Heerde Neth.
116 B1 Heerenveen Neth.
116 B1 Heerhugowaard Neth.
116 B2 Heerlen Neth.
Ḥefa Israel see Haifa
86 B2 Hefei China
86 B3 Hefeng China
85 E1 Hegang China
135 D1 Heiban Sudan
118 B1 Heide Ger.
138 A1 Heide Namibia
117 D3 Heidelberg Ger.
138 B3 Heidelberg S. Africa
85 E1 Heihe China
118 B2 Heilbronn Ger.
85 E1 Heilong Jiang r. China
109 I3 Heinola Fin.
Hejaz reg. Saudi Arabia see Hijaz
108 A3 Hekla vol. Iceland
108 F3 Helagsfjället mt. Sweden
86 A2 Helan Shan mts China
156 B2 Helena AR U.S.A.
150 D1 Helena MT U.S.A.
112 B2 Helensburgh U.K.
118 B1 Helgoland i. Ger.
118 B1 Helgoländer Bucht g. Ger.
Heligoland i. Ger. see Helgoland
Heligoland Bight g. Ger. see Helgoländer Bucht
Helixi China see Ningguo
108 □A3 Hella Iceland
116 B2 Hellevoetsluis Neth.
123 C2 Hellín Spain
Hell-Ville Madag. see Andoany
92 C3 Helmand r. Afgh.
117 E2 Helmbrechts Ger.
138 A2 Helmeringhausen Namibia
116 B2 Helmond Neth.
112 C1 Helmsdale U.K.
112 C1 Helmsdale r. U.K.
114 C2 Helmsley U.K.
117 E1 Helmstedt Ger.
81 B1 Helong China
159 D3 Helotes U.S.A.
109 F4 Helsingborg Sweden
Helsingfors Fin. see Helsinki
109 F4 Helsingør Denmark
109 H3 Helsinki Fin.
115 A4 Helston U.K.
113 C2 Helvick Head hd Ireland
115 C4 Hemel Hempstead U.K.
117 D1 Hemmoor Ger.
108 F2 Hemnesberget Norway
86 B2 Henan prov. China
127 D2 Hendek Turkey
154 B3 Henderson KY U.S.A.
157 E1 Henderson NC U.S.A.
151 D3 Henderson NV U.S.A.
159 E2 Henderson TX U.S.A.
65 O6 Henderson Island Pitcairn Is
157 D1 Hendersonville U.S.A.
115 C4 Hendon U.K.
78 A1 Hengduan Shan mts China
116 C1 Hengelo Neth.
Hengnan China see Hengyang
87 B3 Hengshan China
86 B2 Hengshui China
87 A3 Hengxian China
87 B3 Hengyang China
Hengzhou China see Hengxian
107 C2 Heniches'k Ukr.
155 D3 Henlopen, Cape U.S.A.
116 C2 Hennef (Sieg) Ger.
146 B2 Henrietta Maria, Cape Can.
Henrique de Carvalho Angola see Saurimo
155 D3 Henry, Cape U.S.A.
159 D1 Henryetta U.S.A.
143 H2 Henry Kater, Cape Can.
117 D1 Henstedt-Ulzburg Ger.
136 A3 Hentiesbaai Namibia
117 D3 Heppenheim (Bergstraße) Ger.
87 A3 Hepu China
92 C3 Herāt Afgh.
145 D2 Herbert Can.
70 C2 Herbertville N.Z.
117 D2 Herbstein Ger.
125 C2 Herceg-Novi Montenegro
115 B3 Hereford U.K.
159 C2 Hereford U.S.A.
117 D1 Herford Ger.
116 C2 Herkenbosch Neth.
112 □ Herma Ness hd U.K.
138 A3 Hermanus S. Africa
69 C2 Hermidale Austr.

J

Kara Sea

102 F1 **Kara Sea** Rus. Fed.
108 I2 **Karasjok** Norway
Kara Strait *str.* Rus. Fed. *see* **Karskiye Vorota, Proliv**
127 D2 **Karasu** Turkey
Karasubazar Ukr. *see* **Bilohirs'k**
93 D1 **Karasuk** Rus. Fed.
93 D2 **Karatau** Kazakh.
93 C2 **Karatau, Khrebet** *mts* Kazakh.
102 F2 **Karatayka** Rus. Fed.
83 A4 **Karatsu** Japan
127 B3 **Karavas** Greece
76 B2 **Karawang** Indon.
97 C2 **Karbalā'** Iraq
119 E2 **Karcag** Hungary
Kardeljevo Croatia *see* **Ploče**
127 B3 **Karditsa** Greece
104 B2 **Kärdla** Estonia
138 B3 **Kareeberge** *mts* S. Africa
91 B2 **Kareli** India
104 C3 **Karelichy** Belarus
108 H2 **Karesuando** Sweden
Karghalik China *see* **Yecheng**
90 B1 **Kargil** India
Kargilik China *see* **Yecheng**
102 C2 **Kargopol'** Rus. Fed.
134 B1 **Kari** Nigeria
137 B2 **Kariba** Zimbabwe
137 B2 **Kariba, Lake** *resr* Zambia/Zimbabwe
76 B2 **Karimata, Pulau-pulau** *is* Indon.
76 B2 **Karimata, Selat** *str.* Indon.
89 B3 **Karimnagar** India
77 C2 **Karimunjawa, Pulau-pulau** *is* Indon.
107 C2 **Karkinits'ka Zatoka** *g.* Ukr.
107 D2 **Karlivka** Ukr.
Karl-Marx-Stadt Ger. *see* **Chemnitz**
125 C1 **Karlovac** Croatia
118 C1 **Karlovy Vary** Czech Rep.
Karlsburg Romania *see* **Alba Iulia**
109 F4 **Karlshamn** Sweden
109 F4 **Karlskoga** Sweden
109 G4 **Karlskrona** Sweden
118 B2 **Karlsruhe** Ger.
109 F4 **Karlstad** Sweden
117 D3 **Karlstadt** Ger.
105 D3 **Karma** Belarus
109 E4 **Karmøy** *i.* Norway
91 D2 **Karnafuli Reservoir** Bangl.
90 B2 **Karnal** India
126 C2 **Karnobat** Bulg.
90 A2 **Karodi** Pak.
137 B2 **Karoi** Zimbabwe
137 C1 **Karonga** Malawi
132 B3 **Karora** Eritrea
127 C3 **Karpathos** Greece
127 C3 **Karpathos** *i.* Greece
127 B3 **Karpenisi** Greece
Karpilovka Belarus *see* **Aktsyabrski**
102 D2 **Karpogory** Rus. Fed.
66 A2 **Karratha** Austr.
97 C1 **Kars** Turkey
104 C2 **Kārsava** Latvia
Karshi Uzbek. *see* **Qarshi**
127 C3 **Karşıyaka** Turkey
102 E2 **Karskiye Vorota, Proliv** *str.* Rus. Fed.
Karskoye More *sea* Rus. Fed. *see* **Kara Sea**
117 E1 **Karstädt** Ger.
127 C2 **Kartal** Turkey
103 F3 **Kartaly** Rus. Fed.
97 C2 **Kārūn, Rūd-e** *r.* Iran
89 B3 **Karwar** India
99 I3 **Karymskoye** Rus. Fed.
127 B3 **Karystos** Greece
127 C3 **Kaş** Turkey
146 B2 **Kasabonika Lake** Can.
134 C3 **Kasaï, Plateau du** Dem. Rep. Congo
134 C4 **Kasaji** Dem. Rep. Congo
137 C2 **Kasama** Zambia
136 B2 **Kasane** Botswana
134 B3 **Kasangulu** Dem. Rep. Congo
89 B3 **Kasaragod** India
145 D1 **Kasba Lake** Can.
136 B2 **Kasempa** Zambia
135 C4 **Kasenga** Dem. Rep. Congo
135 C3 **Kasese** Dem. Rep. Congo
135 D2 **Kasese** Uganda
Kasevo Rus. Fed. *see* **Neftekamsk**
97 D2 **Kāshān** Iran
Kashgar China *see* **Kashi**
93 D3 **Kashi** China
83 D3 **Kashima-nada** *b.* Japan
105 E2 **Kashin** Rus. Fed.
105 E3 **Kashira** Rus. Fed.
105 E3 **Kashirskoye** Rus. Fed.
83 C3 **Kashiwazaki** Japan
92 B3 **Kāshmar** Iran
Kashmir *terr.* Asia *see* **Jammu and Kashmir**
90 A2 **Kashmore** Pak.
135 C3 **Kashyukulu** Dem. Rep. Congo
105 F3 **Kasimov** Rus. Fed.
154 B3 **Kaskaskia** *r.* U.S.A.
109 H3 **Kaskinen** Fin.
135 C3 **Kasongo** Dem. Rep. Congo
134 B3 **Kasongo-Lunda** Dem. Rep. Congo
127 C3 **Kasos** *i.* Greece
Kaspiyskiy Rus. Fed. *see* **Lagan'**
132 B3 **Kassala** Sudan
117 D2 **Kassel** Ger.
131 C1 **Kasserine** Tunisia
96 B1 **Kastamonu** Turkey
Kastellorizon *i.* Greece *see* **Megisti**
127 B2 **Kastoria** Greece
105 D3 **Kastsyukovichy** Belarus
135 D3 **Kasulu** Tanz.
137 C2 **Kasungu** Malawi
155 F1 **Katahdin, Mount** U.S.A.
134 C3 **Katako-Kombe** Dem. Rep. Congo
135 D2 **Katakwi** Uganda
66 A3 **Katanning** Austr.
79 A3 **Katchall** *i.* India
127 B2 **Katerini** Greece
135 D3 **Katesh** Tanz.
144 A2 **Kate's Needle** *mt.* Can./U.S.A.
137 C2 **Katete** Zambia
78 A1 **Katha** Myanmar
66 C1 **Katherine** Austr.
66 C1 **Katherine** *r.* Austr.
90 B2 **Kathiawar** *pen.* India
91 C2 **Kathmandu** Nepal
138 B2 **Kathu** S. Africa
90 B1 **Kathua** India
130 B3 **Kati** Mali
91 C2 **Katihar** India
70 C1 **Katikati** N.Z.
139 C3 **Katikati** S. Africa
136 B2 **Katima Mulilo** Namibia
130 B4 **Katiola** Côte d'Ivoire
139 C2 **Katlehong** S. Africa
Katmandu Nepal *see* **Kathmandu**
127 B3 **Kato Achaïa** Greece
135 C3 **Katompi** Dem. Rep. Congo
69 D2 **Katoomba** Austr.
119 D1 **Katowice** Pol.
96 B3 **Kātrīnā, Jabal** *mt.* Egypt
109 G4 **Katrineholm** Sweden
131 C3 **Katsina** Nigeria
131 C4 **Katsina-Ala** Nigeria
83 D3 **Katsuura** Japan
93 C3 **Kattaqo'rg'on** Uzbek.
109 F4 **Kattegat** *str.* Denmark/Sweden
116 B1 **Katwijk aan Zee** Neth.
117 D3 **Katzenbuckel** *h.* Ger.
65 L1 **Kaua'i** *i.* U.S.A.
109 H3 **Kauhajoki** Fin.
104 B3 **Kaunas** Lith.
131 C3 **Kaura-Namoda** Nigeria
Kaushany Moldova *see* **Căuşeni**
108 H2 **Kautokeino** Norway
125 D2 **Kavadarci** Macedonia
125 C2 **Kavajë** Albania
127 B2 **Kavala** Greece
82 C2 **Kavalerovo** Rus. Fed.
89 C3 **Kavali** India
89 B3 **Kavaratti** *atoll* India
126 C2 **Kavarna** Bulg.
75 E3 **Kavieng** P.N.G.
97 D2 **Kavīr, Dasht-e** *des.* Iran
83 C3 **Kawagoe** Japan
70 B1 **Kawakawa** N.Z.
137 B1 **Kawambwa** Zambia
83 C3 **Kawanishi** Japan
146 C3 **Kawartha Lakes** Can.
83 C3 **Kawasaki** Japan
70 C1 **Kawerau** N.Z.
79 A2 **Kawkareik** Myanmar
78 A1 **Kawlin** Myanmar
79 A2 **Kawmapyin** Myanmar
132 B2 **Kawm Umbū** Egypt
79 A2 **Kawthaung** Myanmar
Kaxgar China *see* **Kashi**
93 D3 **Kaxgar He** *r.* China
130 B3 **Kaya** Burkina
127 C3 **Kayacı Dağı** *h.* Turkey
137 C1 **Kayambi** Zambia
77 C1 **Kayan** *r.* Indon.
152 B2 **Kaycee** U.S.A.
Kaydanovo Belarus *see* **Dzyarzhynsk**
158 A1 **Kayenta** U.S.A.
130 A3 **Kayes** Mali
93 D2 **Kaynar** Kazakh.
96 B2 **Kayseri** Turkey
150 D2 **Kaysville** U.S.A.
76 B2 **Kayuagung** Indon.
Kazakhskaya S.S.R. *country* Asia *see* **Kazakhstan**
93 D1 **Kazakhskiy Melkosopochnik** *plain* Kazakh.
92 B2 **Kazakhskiy Zaliv** *b.* Kazakh.
92 C2 **Kazakhstan** *country* Asia
Kazakhstan Kazakh. *see* **Aksay**
103 D3 **Kazan'** Rus. Fed.
Kazandzhik Turkm. *see* **Bereket**
126 C2 **Kazanlŭk** Bulg.
Kazan-rettō *is* Japan *see* **Volcano Islands**
92 A2 **Kazbek** *mt.* Georgia/Rus. Fed.
97 D3 **Kāzerūn** Iran
119 E2 **Kazincbarcika** Hungary
134 C3 **Kazumba** Dem. Rep. Congo
82 D2 **Kazuno** Japan
102 F2 **Kazymskiy Mys** Rus. Fed.
127 B3 **Kea** *i.* Greece
113 C1 **Keady** U.K.
153 D2 **Kearney** U.S.A.
158 A2 **Kearny** U.S.A.
131 C1 **Kebili** Tunisia
132 A3 **Kebkabiya** Sudan
108 G2 **Kebnekaise** *mt.* Sweden
133 C4 **K'ebrī Dehar** Eth.
76 B2 **Kebumen** Indon.
144 B2 **Kechika** *r.* Can.
127 D3 **Keçiborlu** Turkey
119 D2 **Kecskemét** Hungary
104 B2 **Kėdainiai** Lith.
130 A3 **Kédougou** Senegal
119 D1 **Kędzierzyn-Koźle** Pol.
144 B1 **Keele** *r.* Can.
144 A1 **Keele Peak** Can.
Keelung Taiwan *see* **Chilung**
155 E2 **Keene** U.S.A.
138 A2 **Keetmanshoop** Namibia
145 E3 **Keewatin** Can.
Kefallonia *i.* Greece *see* **Cephalonia**
75 C3 **Kefamenanu** Indon.
108 □A3 **Keflavík** Iceland
93 D2 **Kegen** Kazakh.
144 C2 **Keg River** Can.
104 C2 **Kehra** Estonia
78 A1 **Kehsi Mansam** Myanmar
114 C3 **Keighley** U.K.
104 B2 **Keila** Estonia
138 B2 **Keimoes** S. Africa
108 I3 **Keitele** *l.* Fin.
68 B3 **Keith** Austr.
112 C2 **Keith** U.K.
144 B1 **Keith Arm** *b.* Can.
150 B2 **Keizer** U.S.A.
119 E2 **Kékes** *mt.* Hungary
133 C4 **K'elafo** Eth.
Kelang Malaysia *see* **Klang**
108 J2 **Keles-Uayv, Gora** *h.* Rus. Fed.
118 C2 **Kelheim** Ger.
92 C3 **Kelif Uzboýy** *marsh* Turkm.
96 B1 **Kelkit** *r.* Turkey
144 B1 **Keller Lake** Can.
150 C1 **Kellogg** U.S.A.
108 I2 **Kelloselkä** Fin.
113 C2 **Kells** Ireland
104 B2 **Kelmė** Lith.
131 D4 **Kélo** Chad
144 C3 **Kelowna** Can.
112 C3 **Kelso** U.K.
150 B1 **Kelso** U.S.A.
76 B1 **Keluang** Malaysia
145 D2 **Kelvington** Can.
102 C2 **Kem'** Rus. Fed.
Ke Macina Mali *see* **Macina**
144 B2 **Kemano (abandoned)** Can.
134 C2 **Kembé** C.A.R.
127 C3 **Kemer** Turkey
98 G3 **Kemerovo** Rus. Fed.
108 H2 **Kemi** Fin.
108 I2 **Kemijärvi** Fin.
108 I2 **Kemijärvi** *l.* Fin.
108 I2 **Kemijoki** *r.* Fin.
152 A2 **Kemmerer** U.S.A.
108 I3 **Kempele** Fin.
71 G2 **Kemp Land** *reg.* Antarctica
71 A2 **Kemp Peninsula** Antarctica
69 D2 **Kempsey** Austr.
146 C3 **Kempt, Lac** *l.* Can.
118 C2 **Kempten (Allgäu)** Ger.
139 C2 **Kempton Park** S. Africa
77 C2 **Kemujan** *i.* Indon.
142 B2 **Kenai** U.S.A.
145 D2 **Kenaston** Can.
114 B2 **Kendal** U.K.
157 D3 **Kendall** U.S.A.
77 D2 **Kendari** Indon.
76 C2 **Kendawangan** Indon.
131 D3 **Kendégué** Chad
130 A4 **Kenema** Sierra Leone
134 B3 **Kenge** Dem. Rep. Congo
78 A1 **Kengtung** Myanmar
138 B2 **Kenhardt** S. Africa
130 B1 **Kenitra** Morocco
113 B3 **Kenmare** Ireland
152 C1 **Kenmare** U.S.A.
113 A3 **Kenmare River** *inlet* Ireland
116 C3 **Kenn** Ger.
159 C2 **Kenna** U.S.A.
155 F2 **Kennebec** *r.* U.S.A.
Kennedy, Cape *c.* U.S.A. *see* **Canaveral, Cape**
156 B3 **Kenner** U.S.A.
115 C4 **Kennet** *r.* U.K.
153 E3 **Kennett** U.S.A.
150 C1 **Kennewick** U.S.A.
146 A3 **Kenora** Can.
154 B2 **Kenosha** U.S.A.
158 C2 **Kent** U.S.A.
93 C2 **Kentau** Kazakh.
154 B3 **Kentucky** *r.* U.S.A.
154 C3 **Kentucky** *state* U.S.A.
154 B3 **Kentucky Lake** U.S.A.
156 B2 **Kentwood** U.S.A.
135 D2 **Kenya** *country* Africa
135 D3 **Kenya, Mount** *mt.* Kenya
76 B1 **Kenyir, Tasik** *resr* Malaysia
153 E2 **Keokuk** U.S.A.
91 C2 **Keonjhar** India
127 C3 **Kepsut** Turkey
68 B3 **Kerang** Austr.
107 D2 **Kerch** Ukr.
75 D3 **Kerema** P.N.G.
144 C3 **Keremeos** Can.
132 B3 **Keren** Eritrea
97 C2 **Kerend** Iran
175 E7 **Kerguélen, Îles** *is* Indian Ocean
175 E7 **Kerguelen Plateau** Indian Ocean
135 D3 **Kericho** Kenya
70 B1 **Kerikeri** N.Z.
76 B2 **Kerinci, Gunung** *vol.* Indon.
Kerintji *vol.* Indon. *see* **Kerinci, Gunung**
116 C2 **Kerkrade** Neth.
127 A3 **Kerkyra** Greece
Kerkyra *i.* Greece *see* **Corfu**
132 B3 **Kerma** Sudan
65 J7 **Kermadec Islands** S. Pacific Ocean
95 C1 **Kermān** Iran
97 C2 **Kermānshāh** Iran
Kermine Uzbek. *see* **Navoiy**
159 C2 **Kermit** U.S.A.
151 C3 **Kern** *r.* U.S.A.
130 B4 **Kérouané** Guinea
116 C2 **Kerpen** Ger.
145 D2 **Kerrobert** Can.
159 D2 **Kerrville** U.S.A.
113 B2 **Kerry Head** *hd* Ireland
Keryneia Cyprus *see* **Kyrenia**
146 B2 **Kesagami Lake** Can.
127 C2 **Keşan** Turkey
82 D3 **Kesennuma** Japan
90 B2 **Keshod** India
116 C2 **Kessel** Neth.
114 B2 **Keswick** U.K.
119 D2 **Keszthely** Hungary
98 G3 **Ket'** *r.* Rus. Fed.
76 C2 **Ketapang** Indon.
144 A2 **Ketchikan** U.S.A.
150 D2 **Ketchum** U.S.A.
130 B4 **Kete Krachi** Ghana
134 B2 **Ketté** Cameroon
115 C3 **Kettering** U.K.
154 C3 **Kettering** U.S.A.
150 C1 **Kettle River Range** *mts* U.S.A.
109 H3 **Keuruu** Fin.
116 C2 **Kevelaer** Ger.
154 B2 **Kewanee** U.S.A.
154 B1 **Keweenaw Bay** U.S.A.
154 B1 **Keweenaw Peninsula** U.S.A.
157 D3 **Key Largo** U.S.A.
115 B4 **Keynsham** U.K.
155 D3 **Keyser** U.S.A.
157 D4 **Key West** U.S.A.
139 C2 **Kgotsong** S. Africa
85 F1 **Khabarovsk** Rus. Fed.
107 D3 **Khadyzhensk** Rus. Fed.
91 D2 **Khagrachari** Bangl.
90 A2 **Khairpur** Pak.
138 B1 **Khakhea** Botswana
92 B3 **Khalīlābād** Iran
102 F2 **Khal'mer"yu** Rus. Fed.
84 C1 **Khamar-Daban, Khrebet** *mts* Rus. Fed.
90 B2 **Khambhat** India
90 B3 **Khambhat, Gulf of** India
90 B2 **Khamgaon** India
95 C2 **Khamīr** Iran
94 B3 **Khamir** Yemen
94 B3 **Khamis Mushayţ** Saudi Arabia
93 C3 **Khānābād** Afgh.
90 B2 **Khandwa** India
99 K2 **Khandyga** Rus. Fed.
90 B1 **Khanewal** Pak.
Khan Hung Vietnam *see* **Soc Trăng**
99 J3 **Khani** Rus. Fed.
82 B2 **Khanka, Lake** China/Rus. Fed.
131 C2 **Khannfoussa** *h.* Alg.
90 B2 **Khanpur** Pak.
93 D2 **Khantau** Kazakh.
99 H2 **Khantayskoye, Ozero** *l.* Rus. Fed.
102 F2 **Khanty-Mansiysk** Rus. Fed.
79 A3 **Khao Chum Thong** Thai.
79 A2 **Khao Laem, Ang Kep Nam** Thai.
90 B1 **Khaplu** Pak.
103 D4 **Kharabali** Rus. Fed.
91 C2 **Kharagpur** India
95 C2 **Khārān** *r.* Iran
Kharga Oasis *oasis* Egypt *see* **Wāḩāt al Khārijah**
90 B2 **Khargon** India
107 D2 **Kharkiv** Ukr.
Khar'kov Ukr. *see* **Kharkiv**
127 C2 **Kharmanli** Bulg.
105 F2 **Kharovsk** Rus. Fed.
132 B3 **Khartoum** Sudan
103 D4 **Khasavyurt** Rus. Fed.
95 D2 **Khāsh** Iran
102 F2 **Khashgort** Rus. Fed.
94 A3 **Khashm el Girba** Sudan
94 A3 **Khashm el Girba Dam** Sudan
97 C1 **Khashuri** Georgia
91 D2 **Khasi Hills** India
127 C2 **Khaskovo** Bulg.
99 H2 **Khatanga** Rus. Fed.
139 C3 **Khayamnandi** S. Africa
94 A2 **Khaybar** Saudi Arabia
138 A3 **Khayelitsha** S. Africa
123 D2 **Khemis Miliana** Alg.
79 B2 **Khemmarat** Thai.
131 C1 **Khenchela** Alg.
97 D3 **Kherāmeh** Iran
107 C2 **Kherson** Ukr.
99 H2 **Kheta** *r.* Rus. Fed.
85 D1 **Khilok** Rus. Fed.
105 E2 **Khimki** Rus. Fed.
90 A2 **Khipro** Pak.
105 E3 **Khlevnoye** Rus. Fed.
79 B2 **Khlung** Thai.
106 B2 **Khmel'nyts'kyy** Ukr.
Khmer Republic *country* Asia *see* **Cambodia**
92 B1 **Khobda** Kazakh.
Khodzheyli Uzbek. *see* **Xo'jayli**
105 E3 **Khokhol'skiy** Rus. Fed.
90 B2 **Khokhropar** Pak.
90 A1 **Kholm** Afgh.
105 D2 **Kholm** Rus. Fed.
105 D2 **Kholm-Zhirkovskiy** Rus. Fed.
138 A1 **Khomas Highland** *hills* Namibia
105 E3 **Khomutovo** Rus. Fed.
95 C2 **Khonj** Iran

Komsomol'skiy

79 B2 **Khon Kaen** Thai.
78 A1 **Khonsa** India
99 K2 **Khonuu** Rus. Fed.
102 E2 **Khoreyver** Rus. Fed.
85 D1 **Khorinsk** Rus. Fed.
136 A3 **Khorixas** Namibia
82 B2 **Khorol** Rus. Fed.
107 C2 **Khorol** Ukr.
97 C2 **Khorramābād** Iran
97 C2 **Khorramshahr** Iran
93 D3 **Khorugh** Tajik.
93 C3 **Khōst** Afgh.
Khotan China *see* **Hotan**
106 B2 **Khotyn** Ukr.
130 B1 **Khouribga** Morocco
104 C3 **Khoyniki** Belarus
78 A1 **Khreum** Myanmar
92 B1 **Khromtau** Kazakh.
Khrushchev Ukr. *see* **Svitlovods'k**
106 B2 **Khrystynivka** Ukr.
139 B1 **Khudumelapye** Botswana
93 C2 **Khŭjand** Tajik.
79 B2 **Khu Khan** Thai.
94 A2 **Khulays** Saudi Arabia
91 C2 **Khulna** Bangl.
Khūnīnshahr Iran *see* **Khorramshahr**
97 D2 **Khunsar** Iran
95 B2 **Khurayş** Saudi Arabia
90 B1 **Khushab** Pak.
106 A2 **Khust** Ukr.
139 C2 **Khutsong** S. Africa
90 A2 **Khuzdar** Pak.
97 D3 **Khvormūj** Iran
97 C2 **Khvoy** Iran
105 D2 **Khvoynaya** Rus. Fed.
93 D3 **Khyber Pass** Afgh./Pak.
69 D2 **Kiama** Austr.
80 B3 **Kiamba** Phil.
135 C3 **Kiambi** Dem. Rep. Congo
Kiangsi *prov.* China *see* **Jiangxi**
Kiangsu *prov.* China *see* **Jiangsu**
135 D3 **Kibaha** Tanz.
135 D3 **Kibaya** Tanz.
135 D3 **Kibiti** Tanz.
135 C3 **Kibombo** Dem. Rep. Congo
135 D3 **Kibondo** Tanz.
135 D2 **Kibre Mengist** Eth.
135 D3 **Kibungo** Rwanda
127 B2 **Kičevo** Macedonia
130 C3 **Kidal** Mali
115 B3 **Kidderminster** U.K.
130 A3 **Kidira** Senegal
90 B1 **Kidmang** India
70 C1 **Kidnappers, Cape** N.Z.
118 C1 **Kiel** Ger.
119 E1 **Kielce** Pol.
114 B2 **Kielder Water** *resr* U.K.
135 C4 **Kienge** Dem. Rep. Congo
106 C1 **Kiev** Ukr.
130 A3 **Kiffa** Maur.
135 D3 **Kigali** Rwanda
135 C3 **Kigoma** Tanz.
104 B2 **Kihnu** *i.* Estonia
108 I2 **Kiiminki** Fin.
83 B4 **Kii-suidō** *sea chan.* Japan
125 D1 **Kikinda** Serbia
135 C3 **Kikondja** Dem. Rep. Congo
75 D3 **Kikori** P.N.G.
75 D3 **Kikori** *r.* P.N.G.
134 B3 **Kikwit** Dem. Rep. Congo
81 B1 **Kilchu** N. Korea
113 C2 **Kilcock** Ireland
113 C2 **Kildare** Ireland
134 B3 **Kilembe** Dem. Rep. Congo
159 E2 **Kilgore** U.S.A.
135 D3 **Kilifi** Kenya
135 D3 **Kilimanjaro** *vol.* Tanz.
135 D3 **Kilindoni** Tanz.
96 B2 **Kilis** Turkey
106 B2 **Kiliya** Ukr.
113 B2 **Kilkee** Ireland
113 D1 **Kilkeel** U.K.
113 C2 **Kilkenny** Ireland
127 B2 **Kilkis** Greece
113 B1 **Killala** Ireland
113 B1 **Killala Bay** Ireland
113 B2 **Killaloe** Ireland
144 C2 **Killam** Can.
113 B2 **Killarney** Ireland
159 D2 **Killeen** U.S.A.
112 B2 **Killin** U.K.
147 D1 **Killiniq** Can.
113 B2 **Killorglin** Ireland
113 B1 **Killybegs** Ireland
112 B3 **Kilmarnock** U.K.
69 B3 **Kilmore** Austr.
135 D3 **Kilosa** Tanz.
113 B2 **Kilrush** Ireland
135 C3 **Kilwa** Dem. Rep. Congo
135 D3 **Kilwa Masoko** Tanz.
135 D3 **Kimambi** Tanz.
68 A2 **Kimba** Austr.
152 C2 **Kimball** U.S.A.
75 E3 **Kimbe** P.N.G.
144 C3 **Kimberley** Can.
138 B2 **Kimberley** S. Africa
66 B1 **Kimberley Plateau** Austr.
81 B1 **Kimch'aek** N. Korea
81 B2 **Kimch'ŏn** S. Korea
81 B2 **Kimhae** S. Korea
143 H2 **Kimmirut** Can.
105 E3 **Kimovsk** Rus. Fed.
134 C3 **Kimpanga** Dem. Rep. Congo
134 B3 **Kimpese** Dem. Rep. Congo
105 E2 **Kimry** Rus. Fed.
77 C1 **Kinabalu, Gunung** *mt.* Malaysia
144 C2 **Kinbasket Lake** Can.
112 C1 **Kinbrace** U.K.
146 B3 **Kincardine** Can.
78 A1 **Kinchang** Myanmar
135 C3 **Kinda** Dem. Rep. Congo
114 C3 **Kinder Scout** *h.* U.K.
145 D2 **Kindersley** Can.
130 A3 **Kindia** Guinea
135 C3 **Kindu** Dem. Rep. Congo
105 F2 **Kineshma** Rus. Fed.
134 B3 **Kingandu** Dem. Rep. Congo
67 E2 **Kingaroy** Austr.
151 B3 **King City** U.S.A.
146 C2 **King George Islands** Can.
104 C2 **Kingisepp** Rus. Fed.
67 D3 **King Island** Austr.
Kingisseppa Estonia *see* **Kuressaare**
66 B1 **King Leopold Ranges** *hills* Austr.
158 A1 **Kingman** U.S.A.
151 B3 **Kings** *r.* U.S.A.
68 A3 **Kingscote** Austr.
113 C2 **Kingscourt** Ireland
115 D3 **King's Lynn** U.K.
66 B1 **King Sound** *b.* Austr.
150 D2 **Kings Peak** U.S.A.
157 D1 **Kingsport** U.S.A.
67 D4 **Kingston** Austr.
146 C3 **Kingston** Can.
162 C3 **Kingston** Jamaica
155 E2 **Kingston** U.S.A.
68 A3 **Kingston South East** Austr.
114 C3 **Kingston upon Hull** U.K.
163 D3 **Kingstown** St Vincent
159 D3 **Kingsville** U.S.A.
115 B4 **Kingswood** U.K.
112 B2 **Kingussie** U.K.
142 F2 **King William Island** Can.
139 C3 **King William's Town** S. Africa
83 D3 **Kinka-san** *i.* Japan
112 B2 **Kinlochleven** U.K.
109 F4 **Kinna** Sweden
113 B3 **Kinsale** Ireland
134 B3 **Kinshasa** Dem. Rep. Congo
157 E1 **Kinston** U.S.A.
104 B2 **Kintai** Lith.
130 B4 **Kintampo** Ghana
112 C2 **Kintore** U.K.
112 B3 **Kintyre** *pen.* U.K.
78 A1 **Kin-U** Myanmar
135 D3 **Kiomboi** Tanz.
146 C3 **Kipawa, Lac** *l.* Can.
135 D3 **Kipembawe** Tanz.
135 D3 **Kipengere Range** *mts* Tanz.
145 D2 **Kipling** Can.
Kipling Station Can. *see* **Kipling**
135 C4 **Kipushi** Dem. Rep. Congo
135 C4 **Kipushia** Dem. Rep. Congo
117 D2 **Kirchhain** Ger.
117 D3 **Kirchheim-Bolanden** Ger.
99 I3 **Kirenga** *r.* Rus. Fed.
99 I3 **Kirensk** Rus. Fed.
105 E3 **Kireyevsk** Rus. Fed.
Kirghizia *country* Asia *see* **Kyrgyzstan**
93 D2 **Kirghiz Range** *mts* Kazakh./Kyrg.
Kirgizskaya S.S.R. *country* Asia *see* **Kyrgyzstan**
65 J4 **Kiribati** *country* Pacific Ocean
96 B2 **Kırıkkale** Turkey
105 E2 **Kirillov** Rus. Fed.
Kirin China *see* **Jilin**
Kirin *prov.* China *see* **Jilin**
Kirinyaga *mt.* Kenya *see* **Kenya, Mount**
105 D2 **Kirishi** Rus. Fed.
64 L3 **Kiritimati** *atoll* Kiribati
127 C3 **Kırkağaç** Turkey
114 B3 **Kirkby** U.K.
114 B2 **Kirkby Stephen** U.K.
112 C2 **Kirkcaldy** U.K.
112 B3 **Kirkcudbright** U.K.
108 J2 **Kirkenes** Norway
104 B1 **Kirkkonummi** Fin.
146 B3 **Kirkland Lake** Can.
127 C2 **Kırklareli** Turkey
153 E2 **Kirksville** U.S.A.
97 C2 **Kirkūk** Iraq
112 C1 **Kirkwall** U.K.
Kīrov Kazakh. *see* **Balpyk Bi**
105 D3 **Kirov** *Kaluzhskaya Oblast'* Rus. Fed.
102 D3 **Kirov** *Kirovskaya Oblast'* Rus. Fed.
Kirovabad Azer. *see* **Gäncä**
Kirovakan Armenia *see* **Vanadzor**
Kirovo Ukr. *see* **Kirovohrad**
102 E3 **Kirovo-Chepetsk** Rus. Fed.
Kirovo-Chepetskiy Rus. Fed. *see* **Kirovo-Chepetsk**
107 C2 **Kirovohrad** Ukr.
102 C2 **Kirovsk** Rus. Fed.
107 D2 **Kirovs'ke** Ukr.
Kirovskiy Kazakh. *see* **Balpyk Bi**
82 B1 **Kirovskiy** Rus. Fed.
112 C2 **Kirriemuir** U.K.
102 E3 **Kirs** Rus. Fed.
103 D3 **Kirsanov** Rus. Fed.
96 B2 **Kırşehir** Turkey
90 A2 **Kirthar Range** *mts* Pak.
108 H2 **Kiruna** Sweden
83 C3 **Kiryū** Japan
105 E2 **Kirzhach** Rus. Fed.
135 D3 **Kisaki** Tanz.
135 C2 **Kisangani** Dem. Rep. Congo
134 B3 **Kisantu** Dem. Rep. Congo
76 A1 **Kisaran** Indon.
98 G3 **Kiselevsk** Rus. Fed.
91 C2 **Kishanganj** India
131 C4 **Kishi** Nigeria
Kishinev Moldova *see* **Chişinău**
83 C4 **Kishiwada** Japan
93 D1 **Kishkenekol'** Kazakh.
91 D2 **Kishoreganj** Bangl.
90 B1 **Kishtwar** India
135 D3 **Kisii** Kenya
119 D2 **Kiskunfélegyháza** Hungary
119 D2 **Kiskunhalas** Hungary
103 D4 **Kislovodsk** Rus. Fed.
133 C5 **Kismaayo** Somalia
Kismayu Somalia *see* **Kismaayo**
135 C3 **Kisoro** Uganda
127 B3 **Kissamos** Greece
130 A4 **Kissidougou** Guinea
157 D3 **Kissimmee** U.S.A.
157 D3 **Kissimmee, Lake** U.S.A.
145 D2 **Kississing Lake** Can.
Kistna *r.* India *see* **Krishna**
135 D3 **Kisumu** Kenya
119 E2 **Kisvárda** Hungary
Kisykkamys Kazakh. *see* **Dzhangala**
130 B3 **Kita** Mali
83 D3 **Kitaibaraki** Japan
82 D3 **Kitakami** Japan
82 D3 **Kitakami-gawa** *r.* Japan
83 B4 **Kita-Kyūshū** Japan
135 D2 **Kitale** Kenya
82 D2 **Kitami** Japan
146 B3 **Kitchener** Can.
109 J3 **Kitee** Fin.
135 D2 **Kitgum** Uganda
144 B2 **Kitimat** Can.
134 B3 **Kitona** Dem. Rep. Congo
108 H2 **Kittilä** Fin.
157 E1 **Kitty Hawk** U.S.A.
135 D3 **Kitunda** Tanz.
144 B2 **Kitwanga** Can.
137 B2 **Kitwe** Zambia
118 C2 **Kitzbühel** Austria
117 E3 **Kitzingen** Ger.
75 D3 **Kiunga** P.N.G.
108 I3 **Kiuruvesi** Fin.
108 I2 **Kivalo** *ridge* Fin.
106 B1 **Kivertsi** Ukr.
104 C2 **Kiviõli** Estonia
107 D2 **Kivsharivka** Ukr.
135 C3 **Kivu, Lake** Dem. Rep. Congo/Rwanda
127 C2 **Kıyıköy** Turkey
102 E3 **Kizel** Rus. Fed.
127 C3 **Kızılca Dağ** *mt.* Turkey
96 B1 **Kızılırmak** *r.* Turkey
103 D4 **Kizlyar** Rus. Fed.
Kizyl-Arbat Turkm. *see* **Serdar**
108 I1 **Kjøllefjord** Norway
108 G2 **Kjøpsvik** Norway
118 C1 **Kladno** Czech Rep.
118 C2 **Klagenfurt** Austria
104 B2 **Klaipėda** Lith.
110 B1 **Klaksvík** Faroe Is
150 B2 **Klamath** *r.* U.S.A.
150 B2 **Klamath Falls** U.S.A.
150 B2 **Klamath Mountains** U.S.A.
76 B1 **Klang** Malaysia
118 C2 **Klatovy** Czech Rep.
138 A3 **Klawer** S. Africa
144 A2 **Klawock** U.S.A.
144 B2 **Kleena Kleene** Can.
138 B2 **Kleinbegin** S. Africa
138 A2 **Klein Karas** Namibia
138 A2 **Kleinsee** S. Africa
139 C2 **Klerksdorp** S. Africa
106 B1 **Klesiv** Ukr.
105 D3 **Kletnya** Rus. Fed.
116 C2 **Kleve** Ger.
104 C3 **Klichaw** Belarus
105 D3 **Klimavichy** Belarus
105 D3 **Klimovo** Rus. Fed.
105 E2 **Klimovsk** Rus. Fed.
105 E2 **Klin** Rus. Fed.
117 F2 **Klingenthal** Ger.
117 F2 **Klínovec** *mt.* Czech Rep.
109 G4 **Klintehamn** Sweden
105 D3 **Klintsy** Rus. Fed.
125 C2 **Ključ** Bos.-Herz.
119 D1 **Kłodzko** Pol.
116 C1 **Kloosterhaar** Neth.
119 D2 **Klosterneuburg** Austria
117 E1 **Klötze (Altmark)** Ger.
144 A1 **Kluane Lake** Can.
Kluang Malaysia *see* **Keluang**
119 D1 **Kluczbork** Pol.
Klukhori Rus. Fed. *see* **Karachayevsk**
144 A2 **Klukwan** U.S.A.
105 F2 **Klyaz'ma** *r.* Rus. Fed.
104 C3 **Klyetsk** Belarus
99 L3 **Klyuchi** Rus. Fed.
114 C2 **Knaresborough** U.K.
109 F3 **Knästen** *h.* Sweden
145 E2 **Knee Lake** Can.
117 E1 **Knesebeck** Ger.
117 E3 **Knetzgau** Ger.
125 C2 **Knin** Croatia
119 C2 **Knittelfeld** Austria
125 D2 **Knjaževac** Serbia
Knob Lake Can. *see* **Schefferville**
113 B3 **Knockboy** *h.* Ireland
116 A2 **Knokke-Heist** Belgium
157 D1 **Knoxville** U.S.A.
143 H1 **Knud Rasmussen Land** *reg.* Greenland
138 B3 **Knysna** S. Africa
76 B2 **Koba** Indon.
83 C4 **Kōbe** Japan
København Denmark *see* **Copenhagen**
116 C2 **Koblenz** Ger.
75 C3 **Kobroör** *i.* Indon.
104 B3 **Kobryn** Belarus
Kocaeli Turkey *see* **İzmit**
127 B2 **Kočani** Macedonia
127 C2 **Kocasu** *r.* Turkey
125 B1 **Kočevje** Slovenia
91 C2 **Koch Bihar** India
105 F3 **Kochetovka** Rus. Fed.
89 B4 **Kochi** India
83 B4 **Kōchi** Japan
103 D4 **Kochubey** Rus. Fed.
91 C2 **Kodarma** India
142 B3 **Kodiak** U.S.A.
142 B3 **Kodiak Island** U.S.A.
139 C1 **Kodibeleng** Botswana
133 B4 **Kodok** Sudan
106 B2 **Kodyma** Ukr.
127 C2 **Kodzhaele** *mt.* Bulg./Greece
138 A2 **Koës** Namibia
138 C2 **Koffiefontein** S. Africa
130 B4 **Koforidua** Ghana
83 C3 **Kōfu** Japan
147 D2 **Kogaluk** *r.* Can.
130 B3 **Kogoni** Mali
90 B1 **Kohat** Pak.
88 D2 **Kohima** India
104 C2 **Kohtla-Järve** Estonia
144 A1 **Koidern** Can.
Kokand Uzbek. *see* **Qo'qon**
104 B2 **Kökar** Fin.
Kokchetav Kazakh. *see* **Kokshetau**
138 A2 **Kokerboom** Namibia
104 C3 **Kokhanava** Belarus
105 F2 **Kokhma** Rus. Fed.
108 H3 **Kokkola** Fin.
104 C2 **Koknese** Latvia
154 B2 **Kokomo** U.S.A.
138 B1 **Kokong** Botswana
139 C2 **Kokosi** S. Africa
93 E2 **Kokpekti** Kazakh.
93 C1 **Kokshetau** Kazakh.
147 D2 **Koksoak** *r.* Can.
139 C3 **Kokstad** S. Africa
Koktokay China *see* **Fuyun**
77 D2 **Kolaka** Indon.
102 C2 **Kola Peninsula** Rus. Fed.
108 H2 **Kolari** Fin.
Kolarovgrad Bulg. *see* **Shumen**
130 A3 **Kolda** Senegal
109 E4 **Kolding** Denmark
135 C2 **Kole** Dem. Rep. Congo
123 D2 **Koléa** Alg.
102 D2 **Kolguyev, Ostrov** *i.* Rus. Fed.
89 B3 **Kolhapur** India
104 B2 **Kolkasrags** *pt* Latvia
91 C2 **Kolkata** India
89 B4 **Kollam** India
116 C1 **Kollum** Neth.
Köln Ger. *see* **Cologne**
119 D1 **Koło** Pol.
119 D1 **Kołobrzeg** Pol.
130 B3 **Kolokani** Mali
105 E2 **Kolomna** Rus. Fed.
106 B2 **Kolomyya** Ukr.
130 B3 **Kolondiéba** Mali
77 D2 **Kolonedale** Indon.
138 B2 **Kolonkwaneng** Botswana
98 G3 **Kolpashevo** Rus. Fed.
105 E3 **Kolpny** Rus. Fed.
Kol'skiy Poluostrov *pen.* Rus. Fed. *see* **Kola Peninsula**
94 B3 **Koluli** Eritrea
108 F3 **Kolvereid** Norway
135 C4 **Kolwezi** Dem. Rep. Congo
99 L2 **Kolyma** *r.* Rus. Fed.
Kolyma Lowland *lowland* Rus. Fed. *see* **Kolymskaya Nizmennost'**
Kolyma Range *mts* Rus. Fed. *see* **Kolymskiy, Khrebet**
99 L2 **Kolymskaya Nizmennost'** *lowland* Rus. Fed.
99 M2 **Kolymskiy, Khrebet** *mts* Rus. Fed.
138 A2 **Komaggas** S. Africa
83 C3 **Komaki** Japan
99 M3 **Komandorskiye Ostrova** *is* Rus. Fed.
119 D2 **Komárno** Slovakia
139 D2 **Komati** *r.* S. Africa/Swaziland
139 D2 **Komatipoort** S. Africa
83 C3 **Komatsu** Japan
136 A2 **Kombat** Namibia
135 C3 **Kombe** Dem. Rep. Congo
Komintern Ukr. *see* **Marhanets'**
106 C2 **Kominternivs'ke** Ukr.
125 C2 **Komiža** Croatia
119 D2 **Komló** Hungary
Kommunarsk Ukr. *see* **Alchevs'k**
134 B3 **Komono** Congo
127 C2 **Komotini** Greece
Kompong Som Cambodia *see* **Sihanoukville**
Komrat Moldova *see* **Comrat**
138 B3 **Komsberg** *mts* S. Africa
99 H1 **Komsomolets, Ostrov** *i.* Rus. Fed.
105 F2 **Komsomol'sk** Rus. Fed.
107 C2 **Komsomol's'k** Ukr.
Komsomol'skiy Rus. Fed. *see* **Yugorsk**

Komsomol'skiy

99 M2 Komsomol'skiy Chukotskiy Avtonomnyy Okrug Rus. Fed.
103 D4 Komsomol'skiy Respublika Kalmykiya-Khalm'g-Tangch Rus. Fed.
99 K3 Komsomol'sk-na-Amure Rus. Fed.
105 E2 Konakovo Rus. Fed.
91 C3 Kondagaon India
102 F2 Kondinskoye Rus. Fed.
Kondinskoye Rus. Fed. see Oktyabr'skoye
135 D3 Kondoa Tanz.
102 C2 Kondopoga Rus. Fed.
105 E3 Kondrovo Rus. Fed.
143 J2 Kong Christian IX Land reg. Greenland
143 K2 Kong Christian X Land reg. Greenland
143 J2 Kong Frederik VI Kyst coastal area Greenland
140 P2 Kong Frederik VIII Land coastal area Greenland
81 B2 Kongju S. Korea
135 C3 Kongolo Dem. Rep. Congo
109 E4 Kongsberg Norway
109 F3 Kongsvinger Norway
93 D3 Kongur Shan mt. China
116 C2 Königswinter Ger.
119 D1 Konin Pol.
125 C2 Konjic Bos.-Herz.
138 A2 Konkiep watercourse Namibia
102 D2 Konosha Rus. Fed.
107 C1 Konotop Ukr.
119 E1 Końskie Pol.
Konstantinograd Ukr. see Krasnohrad
118 B2 Konstanz Ger.
131 C3 Kontagora Nigeria
79 B2 Kon Tum Vietnam
79 B2 Kon Tum, Cao Nguyên Vietnam
96 B2 Konya Turkey
93 D2 Konyrat Kazakh.
116 C3 Konz Ger.
102 E3 Konzhakovskiy Kamen', Gora mt. Rus. Fed.
150 C1 Kooskia U.S.A.
144 C3 Kootenay Lake Can.
69 D2 Kootingal Austr.
138 B3 Kootjieskolk S. Africa
108 □B2 Kópasker Iceland
124 B1 Koper Slovenia
109 G4 Köping Sweden
139 C1 Kopong Botswana
109 G4 Kopparberg Sweden
125 C1 Koprivnica Croatia
105 F3 Korablino Rus. Fed.
89 C3 Koraput India
91 C2 Korba India
117 D2 Korbach Ger.
125 D2 Korçë Albania
125 C2 Korčula Croatia
125 C2 Korčula i. Croatia
86 C2 Korea Bay g. China/N. Korea
81 B1 Korea, North country Asia
81 B2 Korea, South country Asia
81 B3 Korea Strait Japan/S. Korea
105 D3 Korenevo Rus. Fed.
107 D2 Korenovsk Rus. Fed.
Korenovskaya Rus. Fed. see Korenovsk
106 B1 Korets' Ukr.
127 C2 Körfez Turkey
130 B4 Korhogo Côte d'Ivoire
Korinthos Greece see Corinth
119 D2 Kőris-hegy h. Hungary
125 D2 Koritnik mt. Albania/Kosovo
Koritsa Albania see Korçë
83 D3 Kōriyama Japan
103 F3 Korkino Rus. Fed.
127 D3 Korkuteli Turkey
93 E2 Korla China
119 D2 Körmend Hungary
65 I5 Koro i. Fiji
130 B3 Koro Mali
147 D2 Koroc r. Can.
107 D1 Korocha Rus. Fed.
135 D3 Korogwe Tanz.
75 C2 Koror Palau
119 E2 Körös r. Hungary
106 B1 Korosten' Ukr.
106 B1 Korostyshiv Ukr.
131 D3 Koro Toro Chad
109 H3 Korpo Fin.
82 D1 Korsakov Rus. Fed.
107 C2 Korsun'-Shevchenkivs'kyy Ukr.
119 E1 Korsze Pol.
132 B3 Korti Sudan
116 A2 Kortrijk Belgium
99 L3 Koryakskaya, Sopka vol. Rus. Fed.
99 M2 Koryakskoye Nagor'ye mts Rus. Fed.
102 D2 Koryazhma Rus. Fed.
81 B2 Koryŏng S. Korea
107 C1 Koryukivka Ukr.
127 C3 Kos Greece
127 C3 Kos i. Greece
107 D2 Kosa Biryuchyy Ostriv i. Ukr.
81 B2 Kosan N. Korea
119 D1 Kościan Pol.
Kosciusko, Mount mt. Austr. see Kosciuszko, Mount
69 C3 Kosciuszko, Mount Austr.
93 E2 Kosh-Agach Rus. Fed.
83 A4 Koshikijima-rettō is Japan
119 E2 Košice Slovakia
108 H2 Koskullskulle Sweden
81 B2 Kosŏng N. Korea
125 D2 Kosovo country Europe
Kosovska Mitrovica Kosovo see Mitrovicë
64 H3 Kosrae atoll Micronesia
130 B4 Kossou, Lac de l. Côte d'Ivoire
92 C1 Kostanay Kazakh.
126 B2 Kostenets Bulg.
139 C2 Koster S. Africa
132 B3 Kosti Sudan
108 J3 Kostomuksha Rus. Fed.
106 B1 Kostopil' Ukr.
105 F2 Kostroma Rus. Fed.
105 F2 Kostroma r. Rus. Fed.
118 C1 Kostrzyn Pol.
107 D2 Kostyantynivka Ukr.
119 D1 Koszalin Pol.
119 D2 Kőszeg Hungary
90 B2 Kota India
76 B2 Kotaagung Indon.
77 C2 Kotabaru Indon.
77 C1 Kota Belud Malaysia
76 B1 Kota Bharu Malaysia
76 B2 Kotabumi Indon.
77 C1 Kota Kinabalu Malaysia
91 C3 Kotaparh India
77 C1 Kota Samarahan Malaysia
102 D3 Kotel'nich Rus. Fed.
103 D4 Kotel'nikovo Rus. Fed.
99 K1 Kotel'nyy, Ostrov i. Rus. Fed.
105 D1 Kotel'va Ukr.
117 E2 Köthen (Anhalt) Ger.
135 D2 Kotido Uganda
109 I3 Kotka Fin.
102 D2 Kotlas Rus. Fed.
142 B2 Kotlik U.S.A.
125 C2 Kotor Varoš Bos.-Herz.
105 D3 Kotovo Rus. Fed.
107 E1 Kotovsk Rus. Fed.
106 B2 Kotovs'k Ukr.
89 C3 Kottagudem India
134 C2 Kotto r. C.A.R.
99 H2 Kotuy r. Rus. Fed.
142 B2 Kotzebue U.S.A.
142 B2 Kotzebue Sound sea chan. U.S.A.
130 A3 Koubia Guinea
116 A2 Koudekerke Neth.
130 B3 Koudougou Burkina
138 B3 Kougaberge mts S. Africa
134 B3 Koulamoutou Gabon
130 B3 Koulikoro Mali
134 B2 Koum Cameroon
134 B2 Koumra Chad
130 A3 Koundâra Guinea
Kounradskiy Kazakh. see Konyrat
167 D2 Kourou Fr. Guiana
130 B3 Kouroussa Guinea
131 D3 Kousséri Cameroon
130 B3 Koutiala Mali
109 I3 Kouvola Fin.
125 D1 Kovačica Serbia
108 J2 Kovdor Rus. Fed.
106 A1 Kovel' Ukr.
Kovno Lith. see Kaunas
105 F2 Kovrov Rus. Fed.
67 D1 Kowanyama Austr.
70 B2 Kowhitirangi N.Z.
127 C3 Köyceğiz Turkey
102 D2 Koyda Rus. Fed.
142 B2 Koyukuk r. U.S.A.
127 B2 Kozani Greece
106 C1 Kozelets' Ukr.
105 E3 Kozel'sk Rus. Fed.
89 B3 Kozhikode India
106 B2 Kozyatyn Ukr.
130 C4 Kpalimé Togo
79 A2 Kra, Isthmus of Myanmar/Thai.
79 A3 Krabi Thai.
79 A2 Kra Buri Thai.
79 B2 Krâchéh Cambodia
109 E4 Kragerø Norway
116 B1 Kraggenburg Neth.
125 D2 Kragujevac Serbia
76 B2 Krakatau i. Indon.
119 D1 Kraków Pol.
125 D2 Kraljevo Serbia
107 D2 Kramators'k Ukr.
109 G3 Kramfors Sweden
127 B3 Kranidi Greece
118 C2 Kranj Slovenia
139 D2 Kranskop S. Africa
102 E1 Krasino Rus. Fed.
104 C2 Krāslava Latvia
117 F2 Kraslice Czech Rep.
105 D3 Krasnapollye Belarus
105 D3 Krasnaya Gora Rus. Fed.
105 F2 Krasnaya Gorbatka Rus. Fed.
Krasnoarmeysk Kazakh. see Taiynsha
103 D3 Krasnoarmeysk Rus. Fed.
Krasnoarmeyskaya Rus. Fed. see Poltavskaya
107 D2 Krasnoarmiys'k Ukr.
102 D2 Krasnoborsk Rus. Fed.
107 D2 Krasnodar Rus. Fed.
107 D2 Krasnodon Ukr.
104 C2 Krasnogorodskoye Rus. Fed.
107 D1 Krasnogvardeyskoye Rus. Fed.
107 D2 Krasnohrad Ukr.
107 C2 Krasnohvardiys'ke Ukr.
102 E3 Krasnokamsk Rus. Fed.
105 D2 Krasnomayskiy Rus. Fed.
107 C2 Krasnoperekops'k Ukr.
103 D3 Krasnoslobodsk Rus. Fed.
102 F3 Krasnotur'insk Rus. Fed.
102 E3 Krasnoufimsk Rus. Fed.
102 E2 Krasnovishersk Rus. Fed.
Krasnovodsk Turkm. see Türkmenbaşy
99 H3 Krasnoyarsk Rus. Fed.
105 E3 Krasnoye Rus. Fed.
99 M2 Krasnoye, Ozero l. Rus. Fed.
105 F2 Krasnoye-na-Volge Rus. Fed.
119 E1 Krasnystaw Pol.
105 D3 Krasnyy Rus. Fed.
Krasnyy Kamyshanik Rus. Fed. see Komsomol'skiy
105 E2 Krasnyy Kholm Rus. Fed.
107 D2 Krasnyy Luch Ukr.
107 E2 Krasnyy Sulin Rus. Fed.
106 B2 Krasyliv Ukr.
Kraulshavn Greenland see Nuussuaq
116 C2 Krefeld Ger.
107 C2 Kremenchuk Ukr.
107 C2 Kremenchuts'ke Vodoskhovyshche resr Ukr.
106 B1 Kremenets' Ukr.
119 D2 Křemešník h. Czech Rep.
Kremges Ukr. see Svitlovods'k
107 D2 Kreminna Ukr.
152 B2 Kremmling U.S.A.
119 D2 Krems an der Donau Austria
105 D2 Kresttsy Rus. Fed.
104 B2 Kretinga Lith.
116 C2 Kreuzau Ger.
117 C2 Kreuztal Ger.
134 A2 Kribi Cameroon
139 C2 Kriel S. Africa
127 B3 Krikellos Greece
82 D1 Kril'on, Mys c. Rus. Fed.
127 B3 Krios, Akrotirio pt Greece
89 C3 Krishna r. India
89 C3 Krishna, Mouths of the India
91 C2 Krishnanagar India
109 E4 Kristiansand Norway
109 F4 Kristianstad Sweden
108 E3 Kristiansund Norway
109 F4 Kristinehamn Sweden
Kristinopol' Ukr. see Chervonohrad
Kriti i. Greece see Crete
127 C3 Kritiko Pelagos sea Greece
126 B2 Kriva Palanka Macedonia
Krivoy Rog Ukr. see Kryvyy Rih
125 C1 Križevci Croatia
124 B1 Krk i. Croatia
108 F3 Krokom Sweden
107 C1 Krolevets' Ukr.
105 E3 Kromy Rus. Fed.
117 E2 Kronach Ger.
79 B2 Krŏng Kaôh Kŏng Cambodia
143 J2 Kronprins Frederik Bjerge nunataks Greenland
139 C2 Kroonstad S. Africa
107 E2 Kropotkin Rus. Fed.
119 E2 Krosno Pol.
119 D1 Krotoszyn Pol.
76 B2 Krui Indon.
138 B3 Kruisfontein S. Africa
125 C2 Krujë Albania
127 C2 Krumovgrad Bulg.
Krung Thep Thai. see Bangkok
104 C3 Krupki Belarus
125 D2 Kruševac Serbia
117 E2 Krušné hory mts Czech Rep.
144 A2 Kruzof Island U.S.A.
105 D3 Krychaw Belarus
107 D2 Krylovskaya Rus. Fed.
107 D3 Krymsk Rus. Fed.
Krymskaya Rus. Fed. see Krymsk
Kryms'kyy Pivostriv pen. Ukr. see Crimea
Krystynopol Ukr. see Chervonohrad
107 C2 Kryvyy Rih Ukr.
106 B2 Kryzhopil' Ukr.
130 B2 Ksabi Alg.
123 D2 Ksar el Boukhari Alg.
130 B1 Ksar el Kebir Morocco
Ksar-es-Souk Morocco see Er Rachidia
105 E3 Kshenskiy Rus. Fed.
94 B2 Kū', Jabal al h. Saudi Arabia
77 C1 Kuala Belait Brunei
Kuala Dungun Malaysia see Dungun
76 B1 Kuala Kangsar Malaysia
76 B1 Kuala Kerai Malaysia
76 B1 Kuala Lipis Malaysia
76 B1 Kuala Lumpur Malaysia
77 C2 Kualapembuang Indon.
76 B1 Kuala Terengganu Malaysia
76 B2 Kualatungal Indon.
77 C1 Kuamut Malaysia
81 A1 Kuandian China
76 B1 Kuantan Malaysia
107 D2 Kuban' r. Rus. Fed.
105 E2 Kubenskoye, Ozero l. Rus. Fed.
126 C2 Kubrat Bulg.
76 B2 Kubu Indon.
77 C1 Kubuang Indon.
76 C1 Kuching Malaysia
125 C2 Kuçovë Albania
77 C1 Kudat Malaysia
77 C2 Kudus Indon.
118 C2 Kufstein Austria
143 G2 Kugaaruk Can.
107 D2 Kugey Rus. Fed.
142 E2 Kugluktuk Can.
142 D2 Kugmallit Bay Can.
108 I3 Kuhmo Fin.
95 C2 Kūhrān, Kūh-e mt. Iran
138 A1 Kuis Namibia
Kuitin China see Kuytun
136 A2 Kuito Angola
108 I2 Kuivaniemi Fin.
81 B2 Kujang N. Korea
82 D2 Kuji Japan
83 B4 Kujū-san vol. Japan
125 D2 Kukës Albania
92 B3 Kükürtli Turkm.
127 C3 Kula Turkey
91 D2 Kula Kangri mt. Bhutan/China
92 B2 Kulandy Kazakh.
104 B2 Kuldīga Latvia
Kuldja China see Yining
138 B1 Kule Botswana
117 E2 Kulmbach Ger.
93 C3 Kŭlob Tajik.
92 B2 Kul'sary Kazakh.
127 D3 Kulübe Tepe mt. Turkey
93 D1 Kulunda Rus. Fed.
93 D1 Kulundinskoye, Ozero salt l. Rus. Fed.
143 J2 Kulusuk Greenland
83 C3 Kumagaya Japan
83 B4 Kumamoto Japan
83 C4 Kumano Japan
126 B2 Kumanovo Macedonia
130 B4 Kumasi Ghana
134 A2 Kumba Cameroon
Kum-Dag Turkm. see Gumdag
94 B2 Kumdah Saudi Arabia
103 E3 Kumertau Rus. Fed.
81 B2 Kumi S. Korea
135 D2 Kumi Uganda
127 C3 Kumkale Turkey
109 G4 Kumla Sweden
131 D3 Kumo Nigeria
78 A1 Kumon Range mts Myanmar
78 B2 Kumphawapi Thai.
Kumul China see Hami
136 A2 Kunene r. Angola/Namibia
93 D2 Kungei Alatau mts Kazakh./Kyrg.
109 F4 Kungsbacka Sweden
134 B2 Kungu Dem. Rep. Congo
102 E3 Kungur Rus. Fed.
78 A1 Kunhing Myanmar
78 A1 Kunlong Myanmar
91 B1 Kunlun Shan mts China
87 A3 Kunming China
81 B2 Kunsan S. Korea
66 B1 Kununurra Austr.
117 D3 Künzelsau Ger.
108 I3 Kuopio Fin.
125 C1 Kupa r. Croatia/Slovenia
75 C3 Kupang Indon.
104 B2 Kupiškis Lith.
127 C2 Küplü Turkey
144 A2 Kupreanof Island U.S.A.
107 D2 Kup"yans'k Ukr.
93 E2 Kuqa China
97 C2 Kür r. Azer.
83 B4 Kurashiki Japan
91 C2 Kurasia India
83 B3 Kurayoshi Japan
105 E3 Kurchatov Rus. Fed.
93 E2 Kurchum Kazakh.
127 C2 Kŭrdzhali Bulg.
83 B4 Kure Japan
73 T7 Kure Atoll U.S.A.
104 B2 Kuressaare Estonia
103 F3 Kurgan Rus. Fed.
Kuria Muria Islands is Oman see Ḩalāniyāt, Juzur al
109 H3 Kurikka Fin.
172 C2 Kuril Basin Sea of Okhotsk
85 F1 Kuril Islands is Rus. Fed.
85 F1 Kuril'sk Rus. Fed.
Kuril'skiye Ostrova is Rus. Fed. see Kuril Islands
172 C3 Kuril Trench N. Pacific Ocean
105 E3 Kurkino Rus. Fed.
Kurmashkino Kazakh. see Kurchum
133 B3 Kurmuk Sudan
89 B3 Kurnool India
83 D3 Kuroiso Japan
69 D2 Kurri Kurri Austr.
104 B2 Kuršėnai Lith.
94 B2 Kursh, Jabal mt. Saudi Arabia
105 E3 Kursk Rus. Fed.
125 D2 Kuršumlija Serbia
138 B2 Kuruman S. Africa
138 B2 Kuruman watercourse S. Africa
83 B4 Kurume Japan
99 I3 Kurumkan Rus. Fed.
89 C4 Kurunegala Sri Lanka
97 D1 Kuryk Kazakh.
127 C3 Kuşadası Turkey
127 C3 Kuşadası Körfezi b. Turkey
127 C2 Kuş Gölü l. Turkey
107 D2 Kushchevskaya Rus. Fed.
82 D2 Kushiro Japan
Kushka Turkm. see Serhetabat
92 C1 Kushmurun Kazakh.
91 C2 Kushtia Bangl.
142 B2 Kuskokwim r. U.S.A.
142 B2 Kuskokwim Mountains U.S.A.
82 D2 Kussharo-ko l. Japan
Kustanay Kazakh. see Kostanay
79 B2 Kut, Ko i. Thai.
127 C3 Kütahya Turkey
97 C1 K'ut'aisi Georgia
Kutaraja Indon. see Banda Aceh
Kutch, Gulf of g. India see Kachchh, Gulf of

Laughlin Peak

125 C1 Kutjevo Croatia
119 D1 Kutno Pol.
134 B3 Kutu Dem. Rep. Congo
132 A3 Kutum Sudan
142 E2 Kuujjua r. Can.
147 D2 Kuujjuaq Can.
146 C2 Kuujjuarapik Can.
108 I2 Kuusamo Fin.
136 A2 Kuvango Angola
105 D2 Kuvshinovo Rus. Fed.
94 B2 Kuwait country Asia
94 B2 Kuwait Kuwait
98 G3 Kuybyshev Rus. Fed.
Kuybyshev Rus. Fed. see Samara
107 D2 Kuybysheve Ukr.
Kuybyshevka-Vostochnaya Rus. Fed. see Belogorsk
103 D3 Kuybyshevskoye Vodokhranilishche resr Rus. Fed.
93 E2 Kuytun China
127 C3 Kuyucak Turkey
103 D3 Kuznetsk Rus. Fed.
106 B1 Kuznetsovs'k Ukr.
102 C2 Kuzomen' Rus. Fed.
108 H1 Kvalsund Norway
139 D2 KwaMashu S. Africa
77 D1 Kwandang Indon.
Kwangchow China see Guangzhou
81 B2 Kwangju S. Korea
Kwangtung prov. China see Guangdong
81 B1 Kwanmo-bong mt. N. Korea
139 C3 Kwanobuhle S. Africa
139 C3 KwaNojoli S. Africa
138 B3 KwaNonzame S. Africa
131 C3 Kwatarkwashi Nigeria
139 C3 Kwatinidubu S. Africa
139 C2 KwaZamokuhle S. Africa
138 B3 KwaZamukucinga S. Africa
139 C2 KwaZanele S. Africa
139 D2 KwaZulu-Natal prov. S. Africa
Kweichow prov. China see Guizhou
Kweiyang China see Guiyang
137 B2 Kwekwe Zimbabwe
134 B3 Kwenge r. Dem. Rep. Congo
139 C3 Kwezi-Naledi S. Africa
119 D1 Kwidzyn Pol.
75 D3 Kwikila P.N.G.
134 B3 Kwilu r. Angola/Dem. Rep. Congo
75 C3 Kwoka mt. Indon.
134 B2 Kyabé Chad
69 C3 Kyabram Austr.
78 A2 Kyaikto Myanmar
79 A2 Kya-in Seikkyi Myanmar
84 D1 Kyakhta Rus. Fed.
68 A2 Kyancutta Austr.
78 A1 Kyaukpadaung Myanmar
78 A2 Kyaukpyu Myanmar
104 B3 Kybartai Lith.
78 A2 Kyebogyi Myanmar
70 B3 Kyeburn N.Z.
78 A2 Kyeintali Myanmar
90 B1 Kyelang India
Kyiv Ukr. see Kiev
106 C1 Kyivs'ke Vodoskhovyshche resr Ukr.
Kyklades is Greece see Cyclades
145 D2 Kyle Can.
112 B2 Kyle of Lochalsh U.K.
116 C3 Kyll r. Ger.
127 B3 Kyllini mt. Greece
127 B3 Kymi Greece
68 B3 Kyneton Austr.
135 D2 Kyoga, Lake Uganda
69 D1 Kyogle Austr.
81 B2 Kyŏnggi-man b. S. Korea
81 B2 Kyŏngju S. Korea
83 C4 Kyōto Japan
127 B3 Kyparissia Greece
127 B3 Kyparissiakos Kolpos b. Greece
93 C1 Kypshak, Ozero salt l. Kazakh.
127 B3 Kyra Panagia i. Greece
96 B2 Kyrenia Cyprus
93 D2 Kyrgyzstan country Asia
117 F1 Kyritz Ger.
109 H3 Kyrönjoki r. Fin.
102 E2 Kyrta Rus. Fed.
102 D2 Kyssa Rus. Fed.
99 J2 Kytalyktakh Rus. Fed.
127 B3 Kythira i. Greece
127 B3 Kythnos i. Greece
144 B2 Kyuquot Can.
83 B4 Kyūshū i. Japan
126 B2 Kyustendil Bulg.
78 A2 Kywebwe Myanmar
108 H3 Kyyjärvi Fin.
84 C1 Kyzyl Rus. Fed.
92 C2 Kyzylkum Desert Kazakh./Uzbek.
93 C2 Kyzylorda Kazakh.
Kzyl-Orda Kazakh. see Kyzylorda
Kzyltu Kazakh. see Kishkenekol'

L

161 C3 La Angostura, Presa de resr Mex.
133 C4 Laascaanood Somalia
133 C3 Laasgoray Somalia
166 C1 La Asunción Venez.
130 A2 Laâyoune Western Sahara
103 D4 Laba r. Rus. Fed.
160 B2 La Babia Mex.
77 D2 Labala Indon.
168 B2 La Banda Arg.
77 C1 Labang Malaysia
120 B2 La Baule-Escoublac France
118 C1 Labe r. Czech Rep.
130 A3 Labé Guinea
144 A1 Laberge, Lake Can.
144 C2 La Biche, Lac l. Can.
124 B1 Labin Croatia
103 D4 Labinsk Rus. Fed.
80 B2 Labo Phil.
120 B3 Labouheyre France
169 B3 Laboulaye Arg.
147 D2 Labrador reg. Can.
147 D2 Labrador City Can.
143 I2 Labrador Sea Can./Greenland
166 C3 Lábrea Brazil
77 C1 Labuan Malaysia
77 C2 Labuhanbajo Indon.
76 B1 Labuhanbilik Indon.
75 C3 Labuna Indon.
79 A2 Labutta Myanmar
102 F2 Labytnangi Rus. Fed.
125 C2 Laç Albania
123 D2 La Cabaneta Spain
La Calle Alg. see El Kala
121 C2 La Capelle France
89 B3 Laccadive Islands India
145 E2 Lac du Bonnet Can.
162 B3 La Ceiba Hond.
68 A3 Lacepede Bay Austr.
150 B1 Lacey U.S.A.
121 D2 La Chaux-de-Fonds Switz.
69 B2 Lachlan r. Austr.
162 C4 La Chorrera Panama
155 E1 Lachute Can.
121 D3 La Ciotat France
144 C2 Lac La Biche Can.
Lac la Martre Can. see Whatî
155 E1 Lac-Mégantic Can.
144 C2 Lacombe Can.
162 B4 La Concepción Panama
161 C3 La Concordia Mex.
124 A3 Laconi Italy
155 E2 Laconia U.S.A.
144 C2 La Crete Can.
154 A2 La Crosse U.S.A.
160 B2 La Cruz Mex.
160 B2 La Cuesta Mex.
171 D1 Ladainha Brazil
90 B1 Ladakh Range mts India/Pak.
138 B3 Ladismith S. Africa
95 D2 Lādīz Iran
105 D1 Ladoga, Lake Rus. Fed.
Ladozhskoye Ozero l. Rus. Fed. see Ladoga, Lake
157 D2 Ladson U.S.A.
139 C3 Lady Grey S. Africa
144 B3 Ladysmith Can.
139 C2 Ladysmith S. Africa
75 D3 Lae P.N.G.
159 C3 La Encantada, Sierra mts Mex.
168 B2 La Esmeralda Bol.
109 F4 Læsø i. Denmark
Lafayette Alg. see Bougaa
157 C2 La Fayette U.S.A.
154 B2 Lafayette IN U.S.A.
156 B2 Lafayette LA U.S.A.
131 C4 Lafia Nigeria
120 B2 La Flèche France
157 D1 La Follette U.S.A.
146 C2 Laforge Can.
95 C2 Lāft Iran
124 A3 La Galite i. Tunisia
103 D4 Lagan' Rus. Fed.
167 F4 Lagarto Brazil
134 B2 Lagdo, Lac de l. Cameroon
131 C1 Laghouat Alg.
171 D1 Lagoa Santa Brazil
130 A2 La Gomera i. Islas Canarias
130 C4 Lagos Nigeria
122 B2 Lagos Port.
150 C1 La Grande U.S.A.
146 C2 La Grande 3, Réservoir resr Can.
146 C2 La Grande 4, Réservoir resr Can.
66 B1 La Grange Austr.
157 C2 La Grange U.S.A.
166 C2 La Gran Sabana plat. Venez.
168 D2 Laguna Brazil
160 A2 Laguna, Picacho de la mt. Mex.
166 B3 Lagunas Peru
163 C3 Lagunillas Venez.
La Habana Cuba see Havana
77 C1 Lahad Datu Malaysia
76 B2 Lahat Indon.
94 B3 Laḥij Yemen
97 C2 Lāhījān Iran
116 C2 Lahnstein Ger.
90 B1 Lahore Pak.
90 A2 Lahri Pak.
109 I3 Lahti Fin.
131 D4 Laï Chad
69 D1 Laidley Austr.
120 C2 L'Aigle France
127 B3 Laimos, Akrotirio pt Greece
138 B3 Laingsburg S. Africa
108 H2 Lainioälven r. Sweden
112 B1 Lairg U.K.
124 B1 Laives Italy
86 B2 Laiwu China
86 C2 Laiyang China
86 B2 Laiyuan China
86 B2 Laizhou China
86 B2 Laizhou Wan b. China
66 C1 Lajamanu Austr.
168 C2 Lajes Brazil
160 B2 La Junta Mex.
152 C3 La Junta U.S.A.
133 B4 Lake Abaya l. Eth.
119 D2 Lake Balaton l. Hungary
69 C2 Lake Cargelligo Austr.
69 D2 Lake Cathie Austr.
156 B2 Lake Charles U.S.A.
157 D2 Lake City FL U.S.A.
157 E2 Lake City SC U.S.A.
144 B3 Lake Cowichan Can.
Lake Harbour Can. see Kimmirut
158 A2 Lake Havasu City U.S.A.
159 D3 Lake Jackson U.S.A.
66 A3 Lake King Austr.
157 D3 Lakeland U.S.A.
144 C2 Lake Louise Can.
150 B1 Lake Oswego U.S.A.
70 A2 Lake Paringa N.Z.
156 B2 Lake Providence U.S.A.
69 C3 Lakes Entrance Austr.
133 B3 Lake Tana l. Eth.
150 B2 Lakeview U.S.A.
153 E2 Lakeville U.S.A.
152 B3 Lakewood CO U.S.A.
155 E2 Lakewood NJ U.S.A.
157 D3 Lake Worth U.S.A.
90 A2 Lakhpat India
90 B1 Lakki Marwat Pak.
127 B3 Lakonikos Kolpos b. Greece
130 B4 Lakota Côte d'Ivoire
108 H1 Lakselv Norway
123 C1 L'Alcora Spain
162 A3 La Libertad Guat.
122 B1 Lalín Spain
122 B2 La Línea de la Concepción Spain
90 B2 Lalitpur India
Lalitpur Nepal see Patan
145 D2 La Loche Can.
116 B2 La Louvière Belgium
124 A2 La Maddalena Italy
77 C1 Lamag Malaysia
La Manche str. France/U.K. see English Channel
152 C3 Lamar U.S.A.
95 C2 Lamard Iran
124 A3 La Marmora, Punta mt. Italy
144 C1 La Martre, Lac l. Can.
120 B2 Lamballe France
134 B3 Lambaréné Gabon
138 A3 Lambert's Bay S. Africa
108 □A2 Lambeyri Iceland
122 B1 Lamego Port.
147 D3 Lamèque, Île i. Can.
166 B4 La Merced Peru
68 B3 Lameroo Austr.
159 C2 Lamesa U.S.A.
127 B3 Lamia Greece
153 E2 Lamoni U.S.A.
78 A2 Lampang Thai.
159 D2 Lampasas U.S.A.
161 B2 Lampazos Mex.
115 A3 Lampeter U.K.
78 A2 Lamphun Thai.
135 E3 Lamu Kenya
121 D3 La Mure France
112 C3 Lanark U.K.
79 A2 Lanbi Kyun i. Myanmar
78 A1 Lancang China
Lancang Jiang r. China see Mekong
114 B2 Lancaster U.K.
151 C4 Lancaster CA U.S.A.
154 C3 Lancaster OH U.S.A.
155 D2 Lancaster PA U.S.A.
157 D2 Lancaster SC U.S.A.
143 G2 Lancaster Sound str. Can.
66 A3 Lancelin Austr.
Lanchow China see Lanzhou
118 C2 Landeck Austria
152 B2 Lander U.S.A.
115 A4 Land's End pt U.K.
118 C2 Landshut Ger.
109 F4 Landskrona Sweden
157 C2 Lanett U.S.A.
138 B2 Langberg mts S. Africa
153 D1 Langdon U.S.A.
109 F4 Langeland i. Denmark
117 D1 Langen Ger.
116 C1 Langeoog Ger.
116 C1 Langeoog i. Ger.
98 G2 Langepas Rus. Fed.
86 B2 Langfang China
117 D2 Langgöns Ger.
112 C3 Langholm U.K.
108 □A3 Langjökull Iceland
76 A1 Langkawi i. Malaysia
121 C3 Langogne France
120 B3 Langon France
122 B1 Langreo Spain
121 D2 Langres France
76 A1 Langsa Indon.
78 B1 Lang Sơn Vietnam
121 C3 Languedoc reg. France
117 D1 Langwedel Ger.
145 D2 Lanigan Can.
169 A3 Lanín, Volcán vol. Arg./Chile
97 C2 Länkäran Azer.
120 B2 Lannion France
154 B1 L'Anse U.S.A.
155 E1 L'Anse-St-Jean Can.
154 C2 Lansing U.S.A.
87 B3 Lanxi China
133 B4 Lanya Sudan
130 A2 Lanzarote i. Islas Canarias
86 A2 Lanzhou China
80 B2 Laoag Phil.
78 B1 Lao Cai Vietnam
86 B2 Laohekou China
84 C2 Laojunmiao China
81 B1 Laoling China
81 B1 Lao Ling mts China
121 C2 Laon France
78 B2 Laos country Asia
81 B1 Laotougou China
82 A2 Laoye Ling mts China
170 C3 Lapa Brazil
130 A2 La Palma i. Islas Canarias
162 C4 La Palma Panama
166 C2 La Paragua Venez.
168 B1 La Paz Bol.
161 D3 La Paz Hond.
160 A2 La Paz Mex.
166 C3 La Pedrera Col.
154 C2 Lapeer U.S.A.
82 D1 La Pérouse Strait Japan/Rus. Fed.
161 C2 La Pesca Mex.
160 B2 La Piedad Mex.
169 C3 La Plata Arg.
169 C3 La Plata, Río de sea chan. Arg./Uru.
108 H3 Lappajärvi l. Fin.
109 I3 Lappeenranta Fin.
108 G2 Lappland reg. Europe
127 C2 Lâpseki Turkey
Laptevo Rus. Fed. see Yasnogorsk
99 J1 Laptev Sea Rus. Fed.
Laptevykh, More sea Rus. Fed. see Laptev Sea
109 H3 Lapua Fin.
168 B2 La Quiaca Arg.
124 B2 L'Aquila Italy
151 C4 La Quinta U.S.A.
95 C2 Lār Iran
130 B1 Larache Morocco
152 B2 Laramie U.S.A.
152 B2 Laramie Mountains U.S.A.
170 B3 Laranjeiras do Sul Brazil
77 D2 Larantuka Indon.
75 C3 Larat i. Indon.
123 D2 Larba Alg.
L'Ardenne, Plateau de plat. Belgium see Ardennes
122 C1 Laredo Spain
159 D3 Laredo U.S.A.
157 D3 Largo U.S.A.
112 B3 Largs U.K.
131 D1 L'Ariana Tunisia
168 B2 La Rioja Arg.
127 B3 Larisa Greece
90 A2 Larkana Pak.
96 B2 Larnaca Cyprus
Larnaka Cyprus see Larnaca
113 D1 Larne U.K.
116 B2 La Roche-en-Ardenne Belgium
120 B2 La Rochelle France
120 B2 La Roche-sur-Yon France
123 C2 La Roda Spain
163 D3 La Romana Dom. Rep.
145 D2 La Ronge Can.
145 D2 La Ronge, Lac l. Can.
66 C1 Larrimah Austr.
71 A3 Larsen Ice Shelf Antarctica
109 F4 Larvik Norway
152 C3 Las Animas U.S.A.
Las Anod Somalia see Laascaanood
146 C3 La Sarre Can.
158 B2 Las Cruces U.S.A.
168 A2 La Serena Chile
169 C3 Las Flores Arg.
169 B3 Las Heras Arg.
78 A1 Lashio Myanmar
92 C3 Lashkar Gāh Afgh.
125 C3 La Sila reg. Italy
168 B2 Las Lomitas Arg.
122 B2 Las Marismas marsh Spain
160 B2 Las Nieves Mex.
130 A2 Las Palmas de Gran Canaria Islas Canarias
124 A2 La Spezia Italy
169 C3 Las Piedras Uru.
169 B4 Las Plumas Arg.
171 D1 Lassance Brazil
145 D2 Last Mountain Lake Can.
168 B2 Las Tórtolas, Cerro mt. Arg./Chile
134 B3 Lastoursville Gabon
125 C2 Lastovo i. Croatia
160 A2 Las Tres Vírgenes, Volcán vol. Mex.
162 C2 Las Tunas Cuba
160 B2 Las Varas Chihuahua Mex.
160 B2 Las Varas Nayarit Mex.
158 B1 Las Vegas NM U.S.A.
151 C3 Las Vegas NV U.S.A.
147 E2 La Tabatière Can.
96 B2 Latakia Syria
120 B3 La Teste-de-Buch France
124 B2 Latina Italy
163 D3 La Tortuga, Isla i. Venez.
80 B2 La Trinidad Phil.
105 E2 Latskoye Rus. Fed.
146 C3 La Tuque Can.
104 B2 Latvia country Europe
Latviyskaya S.S.R. country Europe see Latvia
75 E3 Lau P.N.G.
118 C1 Lauchhammer Ger.
117 E3 Lauf an der Pegnitz Ger.
121 D2 Laufen Switz.
108 □A3 Laugarás Iceland
143 H1 Lauge Koch Kyst reg. Greenland
158 C1 Laughlin Peak U.S.A.

Lumajangdong Co

91 C1 **Lumajangdong Co** *salt l.* China
Lumbala Angola *see* **Lumbala Kaquengue**
Lumbala Angola *see* **Lumbala N'guimbo**
136 B2 **Lumbala Kaquengue** Angola
136 B2 **Lumbala N'guimbo** Angola
156 C2 **Lumberton** *MS* U.S.A.
157 E2 **Lumberton** *NC* U.S.A.
77 C1 **Lumbis** Indon.
122 B1 **Lumbrales** Spain
79 B2 **Lumphăt** Cambodia
145 D2 **Lumsden** Can.
70 A3 **Lumsden** N.Z.
109 F4 **Lund** Sweden
137 C2 **Lundazi** Zambia
115 A4 **Lundy** U.K.
117 E1 **Lüneburg** Ger.
117 E1 **Lüneburger Heide** *reg.* Ger.
116 C2 **Lünen** Ger.
121 D2 **Lunéville** France
136 B2 **Lunga** *r.* Zambia
130 A4 **Lungi** Sierra Leone
Lungleh India *see* **Lunglei**
91 D2 **Lunglei** India
136 B2 **Lungwebungu** *r.* Zambia
90 B2 **Luni** *r.* India
104 C3 **Luninyets** Belarus
120 C3 **L'Union** France
130 A4 **Lunsar** Sierra Leone
93 E2 **Luntai** China
87 A3 **Luodian** China
87 B3 **Luoding** China
86 B2 **Luohe** China
86 B2 **Luoyang** China
134 B3 **Luozi** Dem. Rep. Congo
137 B2 **Lupane** Zimbabwe
87 A3 **Lupanshui** China
126 B1 **Lupeni** Romania
137 C2 **Lupilichi** Moz.
117 F2 **Luppa** Ger.
111 B3 **Lurgan** U.K.
Luring China *see* **Gêrzê**
137 D2 **Lúrio** Moz.
137 D2 **Lurio** *r.* Moz.
108 F2 **Lurøy** Norway
137 B2 **Lusaka** Zambia
134 C3 **Lusambo** Dem. Rep. Congo
125 C2 **Lushnjë** Albania
86 C2 **Lüshunkou** China
139 C3 **Lusikisiki** S. Africa
152 C2 **Lusk** U.S.A.
Luso Angola *see* **Luena**
92 B3 **Lut, Dasht-e** *des.* Iran
115 C4 **Luton** U.K.
77 C1 **Lutong** Malaysia
145 C1 **Łutselk'e** Can.
106 B1 **Luts'k** Ukr.
71 F3 **Lützow-Holm Bay** Antarctica
138 B2 **Lutzputs** S. Africa
138 A3 **Lutzville** S. Africa
133 C4 **Luuq** Somalia
153 D2 **Luverne** U.S.A.
135 C3 **Luvua** *r.* Dem. Rep. Congo
136 B2 **Luvuei** Angola
139 D1 **Luvuvhu** *r.* S. Africa
135 D3 **Luwegu** *r.* Tanz.
135 D2 **Luwero** Uganda
77 D2 **Luwuk** Indon.
116 C3 **Luxembourg** *country* Europe
116 C3 **Luxembourg** Lux.
121 D2 **Luxeuil-les-Bains** France
78 A1 **Luxi** China
139 C3 **Luxolweni** S. Africa
132 B2 **Luxor** Egypt
116 B2 **Luyksgestel** Neth.
102 D2 **Luza** Rus. Fed.
Luzern Switz. *see* **Lucerne**
78 B1 **Luzhai** China
87 A3 **Luzhi** China
87 A3 **Luzhou** China
170 C1 **Luziânia** Brazil
167 E3 **Luzilândia** Brazil
80 B2 **Luzon** *i.* Phil.
80 B1 **Luzon Strait** Phil./Taiwan
125 C3 **Luzzi** Italy
106 A2 **L'viv** Ukr.
L'vov Ukr. *see* **L'viv**
Lwów Ukr. *see* **L'viv**
104 C3 **Lyakhavichy** Belarus
Lyallpur Pak. *see* **Faisalabad**
105 D2 **Lychkovo** Rus. Fed.
108 G3 **Lycksele** Sweden
71 C2 **Lyddan Island** Antarctica
104 C3 **Lyel'chytsy** Belarus
104 C3 **Lyepyel'** Belarus
152 A2 **Lyman** U.S.A.
115 B4 **Lyme Bay** U.K.
115 B4 **Lyme Regis** U.K.
155 D3 **Lynchburg** U.S.A.
68 A2 **Lyndhurst** Austr.
145 D2 **Lynn Lake** Can.
150 B1 **Lynnwood** U.S.A.
145 D1 **Lynx Lake** Can.
121 C2 **Lyon** France
Lyons France *see* **Lyon**
105 D2 **Lyozna** Belarus
119 E1 **Łysica** *h.* Pol.
102 E3 **Lys'va** Rus. Fed.
107 D2 **Lysychans'k** Ukr.
103 D3 **Lysyye Gory** Rus. Fed.
114 B3 **Lytham St Anne's** U.K.
104 C3 **Lyuban'** Belarus
106 C2 **Lyubashivka** Ukr.
105 E2 **Lyubertsy** Rus. Fed.
106 B1 **Lyubeshiv** Ukr.
105 F2 **Lyubim** Rus. Fed.
106 A1 **Lyuboml'** Ukr.
107 D2 **Lyubotyn** Ukr.
105 D2 **Lyubytino** Rus. Fed.
105 D3 **Lyudinovo** Rus. Fed.

M

96 B2 **Ma'ān** Jordan
86 B2 **Ma'anshan** China
104 C2 **Maardu** Estonia
94 B3 **Ma'āriḍ, Banī** *des.* Saudi Arabia
96 B2 **Ma'arrat an Nu'mān** Syria
116 B1 **Maarssen** Neth.
116 B2 **Maas** *r.* Neth.
116 B2 **Maaseik** Belgium
80 B2 **Maasin** Phil.
116 B2 **Maastricht** Neth.
137 C3 **Mabalane** Moz.
94 B3 **Ma'bar** Yemen
166 D2 **Mabaruma** Guyana
114 D3 **Mablethorpe** U.K.
139 C2 **Mabopane** S. Africa
137 C3 **Mabote** Moz.
138 B2 **Mabule** Botswana
138 B1 **Mabutsane** Botswana
171 D2 **Macaé** Brazil
137 C2 **Macaloge** Moz.
142 F2 **MacAlpine Lake** Can.
87 B3 **Macao** *aut. reg.* China
167 D2 **Macapá** Brazil
166 B3 **Macará** Ecuador
171 D1 **Macarani** Brazil
Macassar Indon. *see* **Makassar**
Macassar Strait *str.* Indon. *see* **Makassar, Selat**
137 C2 **Macatanja** Moz.
167 F3 **Macau** Brazil
137 C3 **Maccaretane** Moz.
114 B3 **Macclesfield** U.K.
66 B2 **Macdonald, Lake** *imp. l.* Austr.
66 C2 **Macdonnell Ranges** *mts* Austr.
146 A2 **MacDowell Lake** Can.
112 C2 **Macduff** U.K.
122 B1 **Macedo de Cavaleiros** Port.
68 B3 **Macedon** *mt.* Austr.
127 B2 **Macedonia** *country* Europe
167 F3 **Maceió** Brazil
124 B2 **Macerata** Italy
68 A2 **Macfarlane, Lake** *imp. l.* Austr.
113 B3 **Macgillycuddy's Reeks** *mts* Ireland
90 A2 **Mach** Pak.
171 C2 **Machado** Brazil
137 C3 **Machaila** Moz.
135 D3 **Machakos** Kenya
166 B3 **Machala** Ecuador
137 C3 **Machanga** Moz.
Machaze Moz. *see* **Chitobe**
86 B2 **Macheng** China
154 B2 **Machesney Park** U.S.A.
155 F2 **Machias** U.S.A.
89 C3 **Machilipatnam** India
137 C2 **Machinga** Malawi
166 B1 **Machiques** Venez.
166 B4 **Machu Picchu** *tourist site* Peru
115 B3 **Machynlleth** U.K.
139 D2 **Macia** Moz.
Macias Nguema *i.* Equat. Guinea *see* **Bioko**
126 C1 **Măcin** Romania
130 B3 **Macina** Mali
69 D1 **Macintyre** *r.* Austr.
67 D2 **Mackay** Austr.
66 B2 **Mackay, Lake** *imp. l.* Austr.
144 C1 **MacKay Lake** Can.
144 B2 **Mackenzie** Can.
144 A1 **Mackenzie** *r.* Can.
Mackenzie Guyana *see* **Linden**
Mackenzie *atoll* Micronesia *see* **Ulithi**
71 H3 **Mackenzie Bay** Antarctica
142 C2 **Mackenzie Bay** Can.
142 E1 **Mackenzie King Island** Can.
144 A1 **Mackenzie Mountains** Can.
Mackillop, Lake *imp. l.* Austr. *see* **Yamma Yamma, Lake**
145 D2 **Macklin** Can.
69 D2 **Macksville** Austr.
69 D1 **Maclean** Austr.
139 C3 **Maclear** S. Africa
66 A2 **MacLeod, Lake** *dry lake* Austr.
154 A2 **Macomb** U.S.A.
124 A2 **Macomer** Italy
137 D2 **Macomia** Moz.
121 C2 **Mâcon** France
157 D2 **Macon** *GA* U.S.A.
153 E3 **Macon** *MO* U.S.A.
156 C2 **Macon** *MS* U.S.A.
69 C2 **Macquarie** *r.* Austr.
64 G9 **Macquarie Island** S. Pacific Ocean
69 C2 **Macquarie Marshes** Austr.
69 C2 **Macquarie Mountain** Austr.
172 D9 **Macquarie Ridge** S. Pacific Ocean
71 H2 **Mac. Robertson Land** *reg.* Antarctica
113 B3 **Macroom** Ireland
68 A1 **Macumba** *watercourse* Austr.
161 C3 **Macuspana** Mex.
160 B2 **Macuzari, Presa** *resr* Mex.
139 D2 **Madadeni** S. Africa
137 □D3 **Madagascar** *country* Africa
175 D5 **Madagascar Ridge** Indian Ocean
131 D2 **Madama** Niger
127 B2 **Madan** Bulg.
75 D3 **Madang** P.N.G.
155 D1 **Madawaska** *r.* Can.
78 A1 **Madaya** Myanmar
166 D3 **Madeira** *r.* Brazil
130 A1 **Madeira** *terr.* N. Atlantic Ocean
147 D3 **Madeleine, Îles de la** *is* Can.
115 B3 **Madeley** U.K.
160 B2 **Madera** Mex.
151 B3 **Madera** U.S.A.
89 B3 **Madgaon** India
90 B2 **Madhya Pradesh** *state* India
139 C2 **Madibogo** S. Africa
134 B3 **Madingou** Congo
137 □D2 **Madirovalo** Madag.
154 B3 **Madison** *IN* U.S.A.
153 D2 **Madison** *SD* U.S.A.
154 B2 **Madison** *WI* U.S.A.
154 C3 **Madison** *WV* U.S.A.
150 D1 **Madison** *r.* U.S.A.
154 B3 **Madisonville** U.S.A.
77 C2 **Madiun** Indon.
135 D2 **Mado Gashi** Kenya
84 C2 **Madoi** China
104 C2 **Madona** Latvia
94 A2 **Madrakah** Saudi Arabia
95 C3 **Madrakah, Ra's** *c.* Oman
Madras India *see* **Chennai**
150 B2 **Madras** U.S.A.
161 C2 **Madre, Laguna** *lag.* Mex.
159 D3 **Madre, Laguna** *lag.* U.S.A.
166 C4 **Madre de Dios** *r.* Peru
161 B3 **Madre del Sur, Sierra** *mts* Mex.
160 B2 **Madre Occidental, Sierra** *mts* Mex.
161 B2 **Madre Oriental, Sierra** *mts* Mex.
122 C1 **Madrid** Spain
122 C2 **Madridejos** Spain
77 C2 **Madura** *i.* Indon.
77 C2 **Madura, Selat** *sea chan.* Indon.
89 B4 **Madurai** India
137 B2 **Madziwadzido** Zimbabwe
83 C3 **Maebashi** Japan
78 A2 **Mae Hong Son** Thai.
78 A1 **Mae Sai** Thai.
78 A2 **Mae Sariang** Thai.
115 B4 **Maesteg** U.K.
78 A2 **Mae Suai** Thai.
137 □D2 **Maevatanana** Madag.
Mafeking S. Africa *see* **Mafikeng**
139 C2 **Mafeteng** Lesotho
69 C3 **Maffra** Austr.
135 D3 **Mafia Island** Tanz.
139 C2 **Mafikeng** S. Africa
135 D3 **Mafinga** Tanz.
170 C3 **Mafra** Brazil
99 L3 **Magadan** Rus. Fed.
Magallanes Chile *see* **Punta Arenas**
Magallanes, Estrecho de *sea chan.* Chile *see* **Magellan, Strait of**
166 B2 **Magangue** Col.
156 B1 **Magazine Mountain** *h.* U.S.A.
130 A4 **Magburaka** Sierra Leone
85 E1 **Magdagachi** Rus. Fed.
160 A1 **Magdalena** Mex.
158 B2 **Magdalena** U.S.A.
160 A2 **Magdalena, Bahía** *b.* Mex.
117 E1 **Magdeburg** Ger.
169 A5 **Magellan, Strait of** *sea chan.* Chile
Maggiore, Lago *l.* Italy *see* **Maggiore, Lake**
124 A1 **Maggiore, Lake** *l.* Italy
132 B2 **Maghāghah** Egypt
113 C1 **Magherafelt** U.K.
103 E3 **Magnitogorsk** Rus. Fed.
156 B2 **Magnolia** U.S.A.
137 C2 **Màgoé** Moz.
146 C3 **Magog** Can.
147 D2 **Magpie, Lac** *l.* Can.
130 A3 **Magṭa' Laḥjar** Maur.
97 D2 **Magtymguly** Turkm.
135 D3 **Magu** Tanz.
167 E3 **Maguarinho, Cabo** *c.* Brazil
139 D2 **Magude** Moz.
106 B2 **Măgura, Dealul** *h.* Moldova
78 A1 **Magwe** Myanmar
97 C2 **Mahābād** Iran
90 B2 **Mahajan** India
137 □D2 **Mahajanga** Madag.
77 C2 **Mahakam** *r.* Indon.
139 C1 **Mahalapye** Botswana
137 □D2 **Mahalevona** Madag.
91 C2 **Mahanadi** *r.* India
137 □D2 **Mahanoro** Madag.
90 B3 **Maharashtra** *state* India
79 B2 **Maha Sarakham** Thai.
137 □D2 **Mahavavy** *r.* Madag.
84 B3 **Mahbubnagar** India
94 B2 **Mahd adh Dhahab** Saudi Arabia
123 D2 **Mahdia** Alg.
166 D2 **Mahdia** Guyana
129 I6 **Mahé** *i.* Seychelles
91 C3 **Mahendragiri** *mt.* India
135 D3 **Mahenge** Tanz.
70 B3 **Maheno** N.Z.
90 B2 **Mahesana** India
90 B2 **Mahi** *r.* India
70 C1 **Mahia Peninsula** N.Z.
105 D3 **Mahilyow** Belarus
123 D2 **Mahón** Spain
130 B3 **Mahou** Mali
Mahsana India *see* **Mahesana**
90 B2 **Mahuva** India
127 C2 **Mahya Dağı** *mt.* Turkey
122 B1 **Maia** Port.
Maiaia Moz. *see* **Nacala**
163 C3 **Maicao** Col.
90 A1 **Maīdān Shahr** Afgh.
145 D2 **Maidstone** Can.
115 D4 **Maidstone** U.K.
131 D3 **Maiduguri** Nigeria
91 D2 **Maijdi** Bangl.
91 C2 **Mailani** India
117 D2 **Main** *r.* Ger.
134 B3 **Mai-Ndombe, Lac** *l.* Dem. Rep. Congo
117 E3 **Main-Donau-Kanal** *canal* Ger.
155 F1 **Maine** *state* U.S.A.
147 D3 **Maine, Gulf of** Can./U.S.A.
78 A1 **Maingkwan** Myanmar
112 C1 **Mainland** *i. Scotland* U.K.
112 □ **Mainland** *i. Scotland* U.K.
137 □D2 **Maintirano** Madag.
117 D2 **Mainz** Ger.
166 C1 **Maiquetía** Venez.
136 B3 **Maitengwe** Botswana
69 D2 **Maitland** *N.S.W.* Austr.
68 A2 **Maitland** *S.A.* Austr.
162 B3 **Maíz, Islas del** *is* Nic.
83 C3 **Maizuru** Japan
125 C2 **Maja Jezercë** *mt.* Albania
77 C2 **Majene** Indon.
135 D2 **Majī** Eth.
123 D2 **Majorca** *i.* Spain
Majunga Madag. *see* **Mahajanga**
139 C2 **Majwemasweu** S. Africa
134 B3 **Makabana** Congo
77 C2 **Makale** Indon.
135 C3 **Makamba** Burundi
93 E2 **Makanchi** Kazakh.
134 B2 **Makanza** Dem. Rep. Congo
106 B1 **Makariv** Ukr.
85 F1 **Makarov** Rus. Fed.
176 B1 **Makarov Basin** Arctic Ocean
125 C2 **Makarska** Croatia
77 C2 **Makassar** Indon.
77 C2 **Makassar, Selat** Indon.
92 B2 **Makat** Kazakh.
135 D3 **Makatapora** Tanz.
139 D2 **Makatini Flats** *lowland* S. Africa
130 A4 **Makeni** Sierra Leone
136 B3 **Makgadikgadi** *depr.* Botswana
103 D4 **Makhachkala** Rus. Fed.
92 B2 **Makhambet** Kazakh.
135 D3 **Makindu** Kenya
93 D1 **Makinsk** Kazakh.
107 D2 **Makiyivka** Ukr.
Makkah Saudi Arabia *see* **Mecca**
147 E2 **Makkovik** Can.
119 E2 **Makó** Hungary
134 B2 **Makokou** Gabon
135 D3 **Makongolosi** Tanz.
138 B2 **Makopong** Botswana
135 C2 **Makoro** Dem. Rep. Congo
134 B3 **Makoua** Congo
127 B3 **Makrakomi** Greece
95 D2 **Makran** *reg.* Iran/Pak.
90 A2 **Makran Coast Range** *mts* Pak.
105 E2 **Maksatikha** Rus. Fed.
97 C2 **Mākū** Iran
78 A1 **Makum** India
83 B4 **Makurazaki** Japan
131 C4 **Makurdi** Nigeria
108 G2 **Malå** Sweden
162 B4 **Mala, Punta** *pt* Panama
89 B3 **Malabar Coast** India
134 A2 **Malabo** Equat. Guinea
171 D1 **Malacacheta** Brazil
Malacca Malaysia *see* **Melaka**
76 A1 **Malacca, Strait of** Indon./Malaysia
150 D2 **Malad City** U.S.A.
104 C3 **Maladzyechna** Belarus
122 C2 **Málaga** Spain
Malagasy Republic *country* Africa *see* **Madagascar**
137 □D3 **Malaimbandy** Madag.
113 B1 **Málainn Mhóir** Ireland
64 H4 **Malaita** *i.* Solomon Is
133 B4 **Malakal** Sudan
64 H5 **Malakula** *i.* Vanuatu
77 D2 **Malamala** Indon.
77 C2 **Malang** Indon.
Malange Angola *see* **Malanje**
136 A1 **Malanje** Angola
109 G4 **Mälaren** *l.* Sweden
169 B3 **Malargüe** Arg.
146 C3 **Malartic** Can.
104 B3 **Malaryta** Belarus
96 B2 **Malatya** Turkey
137 C2 **Malawi** *country* Africa
Malawi, Lake *l.* Africa *see* **Nyasa, Lake**
105 D2 **Malaya Vishera** Rus. Fed.
80 B3 **Malaybalay** Phil.
97 C2 **Malāyer** Iran
76 B1 **Malaysia** *country* Asia
97 C2 **Malazgirt** Turkey
119 D1 **Malbork** Pol.
117 F1 **Malchin** Ger.
116 A2 **Maldegem** Belgium
64 L4 **Malden Island** Kiribati
72 C5 **Maldives** *country* Indian Ocean
115 D4 **Maldon** U.K.
72 I9 **Male** Maldives
127 B3 **Maleas, Akrotirio** *pt* Greece
119 D2 **Malé Karpaty** *hills* Slovakia
135 C3 **Malela** Dem. Rep. Congo

Maryborough

132 A3 Malha Sudan
150 C2 Malheur Lake U.S.A.
130 B3 Mali *country* Africa
130 A3 Mali Guinea
75 C3 Maliana East Timor
74 C3 Malili Indon.
113 C1 Malin Ireland
135 E3 Malindi Kenya
113 C1 Malin Head *hd* Ireland
Malin More Ireland *see* Málainn Mhór
127 C2 Malkara Turkey
104 C3 Mal'kavichy Belarus
126 C2 Malko Tŭrnovo Bulg.
69 C3 Mallacoota Austr.
69 C3 Mallacoota Inlet *b.* Austr.
112 B2 Mallaig U.K.
132 B2 Mallawī Egypt
145 E1 Mallery Lake Can.
Mallorca *i.* Spain *see* Majorca
113 B2 Mallow Ireland
108 F3 Malm Norway
108 H2 Malmberget Sweden
116 C2 Malmédy Belgium
138 A3 Malmesbury S. Africa
109 F4 Malmö Sweden
87 A3 Malong China
134 C4 Malonga Dem. Rep. Congo
102 C2 Maloshuyka Rus. Fed.
109 E3 Måløy Norway
105 E2 Maloyaroslavets Rus. Fed.
105 E2 Maloye Borisovo Rus. Fed.
102 D2 Malozemel'skaya Tundra *lowland* Rus. Fed.
141 J9 Malpelo, Isla de *i.* N. Pacific Ocean
100 F5 Malta *country* Europe
104 C2 Malta Latvia
150 E1 Malta U.S.A.
138 A1 Maltahöhe Namibia
114 C2 Malton U.K.
Maluku *is* Indon. *see* Moluccas
109 F3 Malung Sweden
139 C2 Maluti Mountains Lesotho
89 B3 Malvan India
156 B2 Malvern U.S.A.
133 B4 Malwal Sudan
106 B1 Malyn Ukr.
99 L2 Malyy Anyuy *r.* Rus. Fed.
Malyy Kavkaz *mts* Asia *see* Lesser Caucasus
99 K2 Malyy Lyakhovskiy, Ostrov *i.* Rus. Fed.
139 C2 Mamafubedu S. Africa
167 F3 Mamanguape Brazil
80 B3 Mambajao Phil.
135 C2 Mambasa Dem. Rep. Congo
134 B2 Mambéré *r.* C.A.R.
80 B2 Mamburao Phil.
139 C2 Mamelodi S. Africa
134 A2 Mamfe Cameroon
151 C3 Mammoth Lakes U.S.A.
104 A3 Mamonovo Rus. Fed.
166 C4 Mamoré *r.* Bol./Brazil
130 A3 Mamou Guinea
130 B4 Mampong Ghana
77 C2 Mamuju Indon.
130 B4 Man Côte d'Ivoire
166 C3 Manacapuru Brazil
123 D2 Manacor Spain
75 C2 Manado Indon.
162 B3 Managua Nic.
137 □D3 Manakara Madag.
94 B3 Manākhah Yemen
95 C2 Manama Bahrain
75 D3 Manam Island P.N.G.
137 □D3 Mananara *r.* Madag.
137 □D2 Mananara Avaratra Madag.
137 □D3 Mananjary Madag.
130 A3 Manantali, Lac de *l.* Mali
70 A3 Manapouri, Lake N.Z.
93 E2 Manas Hu *l.* China
91 C2 Manaslu *mt.* Nepal
Manastir Macedonia *see* Bitola
75 C3 Manatuto East Timor
78 A2 Man-aung Kyun Myanmar
166 C3 Manaus Brazil
96 B2 Manavgat Turkey
132 A3 Manawashei Sudan
114 B3 Manchester U.K.
155 E2 Manchester *CT* U.S.A.
155 E2 Manchester *NH* U.S.A.
156 C1 Manchester *TN* U.S.A.
61 Manchurian Plain China
97 D3 Mand, Rūd-e *r.* Iran
133 A4 Manda, Jebel *mt.* Sudan
137 □D3 Mandabe Madag.
109 E4 Mandal Norway
75 D3 Mandala, Puncak *mt.* Indon.
78 A1 Mandalay Myanmar
84 D1 Mandalgovĭ Mongolia
152 C1 Mandan U.S.A.
134 B1 Mandara Mountains Cameroon/Nigeria
124 A3 Mandas Italy
135 E2 Mandera Kenya
116 C2 Manderscheid Ger.
90 B1 Mandi India
130 B3 Mandiana Guinea
Mandidzuzure Zimbabwe *see* Chimanimani
91 C2 Mandla India
137 □D2 Mandritsara Madag.
90 B2 Mandsaur India
66 A3 Mandurah Austr.
89 B3 Mandya India
124 B1 Manerbio Italy
106 B1 Manevychi Ukr.
125 C2 Manfredonia Italy
125 C2 Manfredonia, Golfo di *g.* Italy
130 B3 Manga Burkina
134 B3 Mangai Dem. Rep. Congo
65 L6 Mangaia *i.* Cook Is
70 C1 Mangakino N.Z.
126 C2 Mangalia Romania
89 B3 Mangalore India
139 C2 Mangaung S. Africa
76 B2 Manggar Indon.
Mangghyshlaq Kazakh. *see* Mangistau
92 B2 Mangistau Kazakh.
77 C1 Mangkalihat, Tanjung *pt* Indon.
84 C2 Mangnai China
137 C2 Mangochi Malawi
137 □D3 Mangoky *r.* Madag.
75 C3 Mangole *i.* Indon.
70 B1 Mangonui N.Z.
Mangshi China *see* Luxi
122 B1 Mangualde Port.
170 B3 Mangueirinha Brazil
85 E1 Mangui China
Mangyshlak Kazakh. *see* Mangistau
153 D3 Manhattan U.S.A.
137 C3 Manhica Moz.
171 D2 Manhuaçu Brazil
137 □D2 Mania *r.* Madag.
124 B1 Maniago Italy
137 C2 Maniamba Moz.
166 C3 Manicoré Brazil
147 D3 Manicouagan *r.* Can.
147 D2 Manicouagan, Petit Lac *l.* Can.
147 D2 Manicouagan, Réservoir *resr* Can.
95 B2 Manīfah Saudi Arabia
65 K5 Manihiki *atoll* Cook Is
80 B2 Manila Phil.
69 D2 Manilla Austr.
Manipur India *see* Imphal
127 C3 Manisa Turkey
123 C2 Manises Spain
114 A2 Man, Isle of *i.* Irish Sea
154 B2 Manistee U.S.A.
154 B1 Manistique U.S.A.
145 E2 Manitoba *prov.* Can.
145 E2 Manitoba, Lake Can.
154 B1 Manitou Islands U.S.A.
146 B3 Manitoulin Island Can.
152 C3 Manitou Springs U.S.A.
146 B3 Manitouwadge Can.
154 B2 Manitowoc U.S.A.
146 C3 Maniwaki Can.
166 B2 Manizales Col.
137 □D3 Manja Madag.
137 C3 Manjacaze Moz.
153 E2 Mankato U.S.A.
130 B4 Mankono Côte d'Ivoire
145 D3 Mankota Can.
89 C4 Mankulam Sri Lanka
90 B2 Manmad India
68 A2 Mannahill Austr.
89 B4 Mannar Sri Lanka
89 B4 Mannar, Gulf of India/Sri Lanka
117 D3 Mannheim Ger.
144 C2 Manning Can.
68 A2 Mannum Austr.
145 C2 Mannville Can.
75 C3 Manokwari Indon.
135 C3 Manono Dem. Rep. Congo
79 A2 Manoron Myanmar
121 D3 Manosque France
147 C2 Manouane, Lac *l.* Can.
81 B1 Manp'o N. Korea
123 D1 Manresa Spain
137 B2 Mansa Zambia
143 G2 Mansel Island Can.
108 I2 Mansel'kya *ridge* Fin./Rus. Fed.
69 C3 Mansfield Austr.
114 C3 Mansfield U.K.
156 B1 Mansfield *AR* U.S.A.
156 B2 Mansfield *LA* U.S.A.
154 C2 Mansfield *OH* U.S.A.
155 D2 Mansfield *PA* U.S.A.
166 A3 Manta Ecuador
80 A3 Mantalingajan, Mount Phil.
171 D1 Mantena Brazil
157 E1 Manteo U.S.A.
120 C2 Mantes-la-Jolie France
171 C2 Mantiqueira, Serra da *mts* Brazil
Mantova Italy *see* Mantua
104 C1 Mäntsälä Fin.
124 B1 Mantua Italy
102 D3 Manturovo Rus. Fed.
167 D3 Manuelzinho Brazil
77 D2 Manui *i.* Indon.
70 B1 Manukau N.Z.
75 D3 Manus Island P.N.G.
156 B2 Many U.S.A.
137 C2 Manyame *r.* Moz./Zimbabwe
135 D3 Manyara, Lake *salt l.* Tanz.
Manyas Gölü *l.* Turkey *see* Kuş Gölü
103 D4 Manych-Gudilo, Ozero *l.* Rus. Fed.
158 B1 Many Farms U.S.A.
135 D3 Manyoni Tanz.
122 C2 Manzanares Spain
162 C2 Manzanillo Cuba
160 B3 Manzanillo Mex.
135 C3 Manzanza Dem. Rep. Congo
85 D1 Manzhouli China
139 D2 Manzini Swaziland
131 D3 Mao Chad
Maó Spain *see* Mahón
75 D3 Maoke, Pegunungan *mts* Indon.
139 C2 Maokeng S. Africa
81 A1 Maokui Shan *mt.* China
86 A2 Maomao Shan *mt.* China
87 B3 Maoming China
137 C3 Mapai Moz.
91 C1 Mapam Yumco *l.* China
77 D2 Mapane Indon.
161 C3 Mapastepec Mex.
160 B2 Mapimí Mex.
137 C3 Mapinhane Moz.
145 D3 Maple Creek Can.
172 D4 Mapmakers Seamounts N. Pacific Ocean
75 D3 Maprik P.N.G.
139 D1 Mapulanguene Moz.
137 C3 Maputo Moz.
139 D2 Maputo *r.* Moz./S. Africa
139 C2 Maputsoe Lesotho
130 A2 Maqṭeïr *reg.* Maur.
91 C2 Maquan He *r.* China
136 A1 Maquela do Zombo Angola
169 B4 Maquinchao Arg.
153 E2 Maquoketa U.S.A.
139 C1 Mara S. Africa
166 C3 Maraã Brazil
167 E3 Marabá Brazil
167 D2 Maracá, Ilha de *i.* Brazil
166 B1 Maracaibo Venez.
Maracaibo, Lago de *inlet* Venez. *see* Maracaibo, Lake
166 B2 Maracaibo, Lake *inlet* Venez.
170 A2 Maracaju Brazil
170 A2 Maracaju, Serra de *hills* Brazil
166 C1 Maracay Venez.
131 D2 Marādah Libya
131 C3 Maradi Niger
97 C2 Marāgheh Iran
166 C2 Marahuaca, Cerro *mt.* Venez.
167 E3 Marajó, Baía de *est.* Brazil
167 D3 Marajó, Ilha de *i.* Brazil
95 C2 Marākī Iran
135 D2 Maralal Kenya
Maralbashi China *see* Bachu
66 C3 Maralinga Austr.
Maralwexi China *see* Bachu
158 A2 Marana U.S.A.
97 C2 Marand Iran
Marandellas Zimbabwe *see* Marondera
166 B3 Marañón *r.* Peru
Maraş Turkey *see* Kahramanmaraş
126 C1 Mărăşeşti Romania
146 B3 Marathon Can.
157 D4 Marathon U.S.A.
122 C2 Marbella Spain
66 A2 Marble Bar Austr.
139 C1 Marble Hall S. Africa
139 D3 Marburg S. Africa
117 D2 Marburg an der Lahn Ger.
119 D2 Marcali Hungary
153 E3 Marceline U.S.A.
115 D3 March U.K.
116 B2 Marche-en-Famenne Belgium
122 B2 Marchena Spain
168 B3 Mar Chiquita, Laguna *l.* Arg.
166 B4 Marcona Peru
155 E2 Marcy, Mount U.S.A.
90 B1 Mardan Pak.
169 C3 Mar del Plata Arg.
97 C2 Mardın Turkey
112 B2 Maree, Loch *l.* U.K.
67 D1 Mareeba Austr.
124 B3 Marettimo, Isola *i.* Italy
105 D2 Marevo Rus. Fed.
158 C2 Marfa U.S.A.
Margao India *see* Madgaon
66 A3 Margaret River Austr.
166 C1 Margarita, Isla de *i.* Venez.
139 D3 Margate S. Africa
115 D4 Margate U.K.
78 A1 Margherita India
Margherita, Lake *l.* Eth. *see* Lake Abaya
135 C2 Margherita Peak Dem. Rep. Congo/Uganda
92 C3 Mārgow, Dasht-e *des.* Afgh.
107 C2 Marhanets' Ukr.
78 A1 Mari Myanmar
168 B2 María Elena Chile
172 C5 Mariana Trench N. Pacific Ocean
Mariánica, Cordillera *mts* Spain *see* Morena, Sierra
156 B2 Marianna *AR* U.S.A.
157 C2 Marianna *FL* U.S.A.
118 C2 Mariánské Lázně Czech Rep.
160 B2 Marías, Islas *is* Mex.
94 B3 Ma'rib Yemen
125 C1 Maribor Slovenia
Maricourt Can. *see* Kangiqsujuaq
135 C2 Maridi Sudan
133 A4 Maridi *watercourse* Sudan
71 P2 Marie Byrd Land *reg.* Antarctica
163 D3 Marie-Galante *i.* Guadeloupe
109 G3 Mariehamn Fin.
138 A1 Mariental Namibia
109 F4 Mariestad Sweden
157 D2 Marietta *GA* U.S.A.
154 C3 Marietta *OH* U.S.A.
121 D3 Marignane France
99 K3 Marii, Mys *pt* Rus. Fed.
104 B3 Marijampolė Lith.
170 C2 Marília Brazil
122 B1 Marín Spain
151 B3 Marina U.S.A.
125 C3 Marina di Gioiosa Ionica Italy
104 C3 Mar"ina Horka Belarus
154 B1 Marinette U.S.A.
170 B2 Maringá Brazil
122 B2 Marinha Grande Port.
154 B2 Marion *IN* U.S.A.
154 C2 Marion *OH* U.S.A.
157 E2 Marion *SC* U.S.A.
154 C3 Marion *VA* U.S.A.
157 D2 Marion, Lake U.S.A.
68 A3 Marion Bay Austr.
168 B2 Mariscal José Félix Estigarribia Para.
121 D3 Maritime Alps *mts* France/Italy
126 C2 Maritsa *r.* Bulg.
107 D2 Mariupol' Ukr.
133 C4 Marka Somalia
84 C3 Markam China
139 C1 Marken S. Africa
116 B1 Markermeer *l.* Neth.
114 C3 Market Rasen U.K.
114 C3 Market Weighton U.K.
99 I2 Markha *r.* Rus. Fed.
155 D2 Markham Can.
107 D2 Markivka Ukr.
134 B2 Markounda C.A.R.
156 B2 Marksville U.S.A.
117 D3 Marktheidenfeld Ger.
117 F2 Marktredwitz Ger.
116 C2 Marl Ger.
67 C2 Marla Austr.
116 A3 Marle France
159 D2 Marlin U.S.A.
69 C3 Marlo Austr.
120 C3 Marmande France
127 C2 Marmara, Sea of *g.* Turkey
Marmara Denizi *g.* Turkey *see* Marmara, Sea of
127 C3 Marmaris Turkey
121 C2 Marne *r.* France
121 C2 Marne-la-Vallée France
134 B2 Maro Chad
137 □D2 Maroantsetra Madag.
70 B1 Marokopa N.Z.
117 E2 Maroldsweisach Ger.
137 □D2 Maromokotro *mt.* Madag.
137 C2 Marondera Zimbabwe
167 D2 Maroni *r.* Fr. Guiana
67 E2 Maroochydore Austr.
77 C2 Maros Indon.
65 M6 Marotiri *is* Fr. Polynesia
134 B1 Maroua Cameroon
137 □D2 Marovoay Madag.
65 N4 Marquesas Islands Fr. Polynesia
157 D4 Marquesas Keys *is* U.S.A.
171 D2 Marquês de Valença Brazil
154 B1 Marquette U.S.A.
132 A3 Marra, Jebel *mt.* Sudan
132 A3 Marra, Jebel Sudan
139 D2 Marracuene Moz.
130 B1 Marrakech Morocco
Marrakesh Morocco *see* Marrakech
68 A1 Marree Austr.
102 F2 Marresale Rus. Fed.
137 C2 Marromeu Moz.
137 C2 Marrupa Moz.
132 B2 Marsá al 'Alam Egypt
131 D1 Marsa al Burayqah Libya
135 D2 Marsabit Kenya
94 A2 Marsa Delwein Sudan
124 B3 Marsala Italy
132 A1 Marsá Maṭrūḥ Egypt
117 D2 Marsberg Ger.
124 B2 Marsciano Italy
69 C2 Marsden Austr.
116 B1 Marsdiep *sea chan.* Neth.
121 D3 Marseille France
Marseilles France *see* Marseille
156 B1 Marshall *AR* U.S.A.
153 D2 Marshall *MN* U.S.A.
153 E3 Marshall *MO* U.S.A.
159 E2 Marshall *TX* U.S.A.
64 H2 Marshall Islands *country* N. Pacific Ocean
153 E2 Marshalltown U.S.A.
154 A2 Marshfield U.S.A.
162 C2 Marsh Harbour Bahamas
156 B3 Marsh Island U.S.A.
109 G4 Märsta Sweden
Martaban, Gulf of *g.* Myanmar *see* Mottama, Gulf of
77 C2 Martapura Indon.
76 B2 Martapura Indon.
155 E2 Martha's Vineyard *i.* U.S.A.
121 D2 Martigny Switz.
119 D2 Martin Slovakia
152 C2 Martin U.S.A.
161 C2 Martínez Mex.
157 D2 Martinez U.S.A.
171 C1 Martinho Campos Brazil
163 D3 Martinique *terr.* West Indies
163 D3 Martinique Passage Dominica/Martinique
155 D3 Martinsburg U.S.A.
154 D3 Martinsville U.S.A.
70 C2 Marton N.Z.
123 D1 Martorell Spain
122 C2 Martos Spain
92 B1 Martuk Kazakh.
97 D3 Marv Dasht Iran
121 C3 Marvejols France
92 C3 Mary Turkm.
67 E2 Maryborough Austr.

138 B2 Marydale S. Africa
155 D3 Maryland state U.S.A.
114 B2 Maryport U.K.
153 D3 Marysville U.S.A.
153 E2 Maryville MO U.S.A.
157 D1 Maryville TN U.S.A.
135 D3 Masai Steppe plain Tanz.
135 D3 Masaka Uganda
77 C2 Masalembu Besar i. Indon.
77 D2 Masamba Indon.
81 B2 Masan S. Korea
135 D4 Masasi Tanz.
80 B2 Masbate Phil.
80 B2 Masbate i. Phil.
123 D2 Mascara Alg.
171 E1 Mascote Brazil
139 C2 Maseru Lesotho
          Mashaba Zimbabwe see Mashava
137 C3 Mashava Zimbabwe
92 B3 Mashhad Iran
139 D2 Mashishing S. Africa
90 A2 Mashkel, Hamun-i- salt flat Pak.
139 C3 Masibambane S. Africa
95 C3 Masīlah, Wādī al watercourse Yemen
139 C2 Masilo S. Africa
134 B3 Masi-Manimba Dem. Rep. Congo
135 D2 Masindi Uganda
138 B3 Masinyusane S. Africa
          Masira, Gulf of b. Oman see
          Maşīrah, Khalīj
95 C3 Maşīrah, Khalīj Oman
97 C2 Masjed Soleymān Iran
113 B2 Mask, Lough l. Ireland
137 □E2 Masoala, Tanjona c. Madag.
153 E2 Mason City U.S.A.
          Masqaṭ Oman see Muscat
124 A2 Massa Italy
155 E2 Massachusetts state U.S.A.
155 E2 Massachusetts Bay U.S.A.
131 D3 Massaguet Chad
131 D3 Massakory Chad
137 C3 Massangena Moz.
136 A1 Massango Angola
132 B3 Massawa Eritrea
155 E2 Massena U.S.A.
131 D3 Massenya Chad
144 A2 Masset Can.
121 C2 Massif Central mts France
154 C2 Massillon U.S.A.
137 C3 Massinga Moz.
139 D1 Massingir Moz.
94 A2 Mastābah Saudi Arabia
70 C2 Masterton N.Z.
90 B1 Mastuj Pak.
90 A2 Mastung Pak.
94 A2 Mastūrah Saudi Arabia
104 B3 Masty Belarus
83 B4 Masuda Japan
          Masuku Gabon see Franceville
137 C3 Masvingo Zimbabwe
135 D3 Maswa Tanz.
85 D1 Matad Mongolia
134 B3 Matadi Dem. Rep. Congo
162 B3 Matagalpa Nic.
146 C3 Matagami Can.
146 C3 Matagami, Lac l. Can.
159 D3 Matagorda Island U.S.A.
159 D3 Matagorda Peninsula U.S.A.
136 A2 Matala Angola
130 A3 Matam Senegal
70 C1 Matamata N.Z.
160 B2 Matamoros Chihuahua Mex.
161 C2 Matamoros Tamaulipas Mex.
135 D3 Matandu r. Tanz.
147 D3 Matane Can.
162 B2 Matanzas Cuba
          Matapan, Cape c. Greece see
          Taínaro, Akra
89 C4 Matara Sri Lanka
77 C2 Mataram Indon.
66 C1 Mataranka Austr.
123 D1 Mataró Spain
139 C3 Matatiele S. Africa
70 A3 Mataura N.Z.
70 A3 Mataura r. N.Z.
70 C1 Matawai N.Z.
168 B3 Mategua Bol.
161 B2 Matehuala Mex.
125 C2 Matera Italy
124 A3 Mateur Tunisia
145 E2 Matheson Island Can.
159 D3 Mathis U.S.A.
90 B2 Mathura India
80 B3 Mati Phil.
161 C3 Matías Romero Mex.
114 C3 Matlock U.K.
166 D4 Mato Grosso Brazil
170 B1 Mato Grosso state Brazil
170 B1 Mato Grosso, Planalto do plat. Brazil
170 B1 Mato Grosso do Sul state Brazil
139 D2 Matola Moz.
122 B1 Matosinhos Port.
          Matou China see Pingguo
95 C2 Maṭraḥ Oman
83 B3 Matsue Japan
82 D2 Matsumae Japan
83 C3 Matsumoto Japan
83 C4 Matsusaka Japan
87 D3 Matsu Tao i. Taiwan
83 B4 Matsuyama Japan
146 B2 Mattagami r. Can.
146 C3 Mattawa Can.
121 D2 Matterhorn mt. Italy/Switz.
150 C2 Matterhorn mt. U.S.A.

157 D1 Matthews U.S.A.
95 C2 Maṭṭī, Sabkhat salt pan Saudi Arabia
154 B3 Mattoon U.S.A.
166 C2 Maturín Venez.
107 D2 Matveyev Kurgan Rus. Fed.
139 C2 Matwabeng S. Africa
121 C1 Maubeuge France
120 C3 Maubourguet France
71 E3 Maud Seamount sea feature
          S. Atlantic Ocean
65 L1 Maui i. U.S.A.
157 D2 Mauldin U.S.A.
154 C2 Maumee r. U.S.A.
77 D2 Maumere Indon.
136 B2 Maun Botswana
91 C2 Maunath Bhanjan India
78 A1 Maungdaw Myanmar
91 B2 Mau Ranipur India
66 C2 Maurice, Lake imp. l. Austr.
130 A3 Mauritania country Africa
129 I8 Mauritius country Indian Ocean
136 B2 Mavinga Angola
139 C3 Mavuya S. Africa
94 B2 Māwān, Khashm mt. Saudi Arabia
134 B3 Mawanga Dem. Rep. Congo
87 B3 Mawei China
78 A1 Mawkmai Myanmar
78 A1 Mawlaik Myanmar
79 A2 Mawlamyaing Myanmar
94 B2 Mawqaq Saudi Arabia
71 L1 Mawson Peninsula Antarctica
94 B3 Mawza Yemen
124 A3 Maxia, Punta mt. Italy
137 C3 Maxixe Moz.
70 B1 Maxwell N.Z.
99 J2 Maya r. Rus. Fed.
163 C2 Mayaguana i. Bahamas
163 D3 Mayagüez Puerto Rico
97 D2 Mayamey Iran
112 B3 Maybole U.K.
132 B3 Maych'ew Eth.
133 C3 Maydh Somalia
116 C2 Mayen Ger.
120 B2 Mayenne France
120 B2 Mayenne r. France
144 C2 Mayerthorpe Can.
154 B3 Mayfield U.S.A.
107 E3 Maykop Rus. Fed.
92 C3 Maymanah Afgh.
144 A1 Mayo Can.
134 B3 Mayoko Congo
          Mayo Landing Can. see Mayo
80 B2 Mayon vol. Phil.
137 D2 Mayotte terr. Africa
99 J3 Mayskiy Rus. Fed.
154 C3 Maysville U.S.A.
134 B3 Mayumba Gabon
153 D1 Mayville U.S.A.
136 B2 Mazabuka Zambia
          Mazagan Morocco see El Jadida
167 D3 Mazagão Brazil
120 C3 Mazamet France
90 B1 Mazar China
124 B3 Mazara del Vallo Italy
93 C3 Mazār-e Sharīf Afgh.
123 C2 Mazarrón Spain
123 C2 Mazarrón, Golfo de b. Spain
160 A2 Mazatán Mex.
162 A3 Mazatenango Guat.
160 B2 Mazatlán Mex.
104 B2 Mažeikiai Lith.
104 B2 Mazirbe Latvia
119 E1 Mazowiecka, Nizina lowland Pol.
137 B3 Mazunga Zimbabwe
119 E1 Mazurskie, Pojezierze reg. Pol.
104 C3 Mazyr Belarus
139 D2 Mbabane Swaziland
134 B2 Mbaïki C.A.R.
134 B2 Mbakaou, Lac de l. Cameroon
137 C1 Mbala Zambia
137 B3 Mbalabala Zimbabwe
135 D2 Mbale Uganda
134 B2 Mbalmayo Cameroon
134 B2 Mbandaka Dem. Rep. Congo
134 B2 Mbandjok Cameroon
134 A2 Mbanga Cameroon
136 A1 M'banza Congo Angola
134 B3 Mbanza-Ngungu Dem. Rep. Congo
135 D3 Mbarara Uganda
134 B2 Mbé Cameroon
135 D3 Mbeya Tanz.
135 D4 Mbinga Tanz.
135 D3 Mbizi Mountains Tanz.
135 C2 Mboki C.A.R.
134 B2 Mbomo Congo
134 B2 Mbouda Cameroon
130 A3 Mbour Senegal
130 A3 Mbout Maur.
134 C3 Mbuji-Mayi Dem. Rep. Congo
135 D3 Mbuyuni Tanz.
155 F1 McAdam Can.
159 D3 McAlester U.S.A.
159 D3 McAllen U.S.A.
144 B2 McBride Can.
150 C2 McCall U.S.A.
159 C2 McCamey U.S.A.
144 B2 McClintock Channel Can.
142 F2 McClure Strait Can.
156 B2 McComb U.S.A.
152 C2 McConaughy, Lake U.S.A.
152 C2 McCook U.S.A.
157 D2 McDermitt U.S.A.
175 E7 McDonald Islands Indian Ocean

150 D1 McDonald Peak U.S.A.
151 D3 McGill U.S.A.
142 B2 McGrath U.S.A.
150 D2 McGuire, Mount U.S.A.
137 C2 Mchinji Malawi
156 C1 McKenzie U.S.A.
67 D2 McKinlay Austr.
142 B2 McKinley, Mount U.S.A.
150 B2 McKinleyville U.S.A.
144 C2 McLennan Can.
144 B2 McLeod Lake Can.
150 B1 McMinnville OR U.S.A.
156 C1 McMinnville TN U.S.A.
153 D3 McPherson U.S.A.
144 C1 McTavish Arm b. Can.
139 C3 Mdantsane S. Africa
123 E2 M'Doukal Alg.
151 D3 Mead, Lake resr U.S.A.
152 C3 Meade U.S.A.
145 D2 Meadow Lake Can.
154 C2 Meadville U.S.A.
82 D2 Meaken-dake vol. Japan
122 B1 Mealhada Port.
147 E1 Mealy Mountains Can.
144 C2 Meander River r. Can.
94 A2 Mecca Saudi Arabia
155 D3 Mechanicsville U.S.A.
116 B2 Mechelen Belgium
116 B2 Mechelen Neth.
116 C2 Mechernich Ger.
116 C2 Meckenheim Ger.
117 E1 Mecklenburgische Seenplatte reg.
          Ger.
122 B1 Meda Port.
76 A1 Medan Indon.
169 B4 Medanosa, Punta pt Arg.
89 C4 Medawachchiya Sri Lanka
123 D2 Médéa Alg.
166 B2 Medellín Col.
131 D1 Medenine Tunisia
150 B2 Medford U.S.A.
126 C2 Medgidia Romania
126 B1 Mediaș Romania
152 B2 Medicine Bow Mountains U.S.A.
152 B2 Medicine Bow Peak U.S.A.
145 C2 Medicine Hat Can.
153 D3 Medicine Lodge U.S.A.
171 D1 Medina Brazil
94 A2 Medina Saudi Arabia
122 C1 Medinaceli Spain
122 C1 Medina del Campo Spain
122 B1 Medina de Rioseco Spain
91 C2 Medinipur India
100 E5 Mediterranean Sea
145 C2 Medley Can.
103 E3 Mednogorsk Rus. Fed.
78 A1 Mêdog China
104 B2 Medvėgalio kalnas h. Lith.
99 L2 Medvezh'i, Ostrova is Rus. Fed.
102 C2 Medvezh'yegorsk Rus. Fed.
66 A2 Meekatharra Austr.
152 B2 Meeker U.S.A.
90 B2 Meerut India
116 A2 Meetkerke Belgium
135 C3 Mêga Eth.
76 B2 Mega i. Indon.
135 D2 Mega Escarpment Eth./Kenya
127 B3 Megalopoli Greece
91 D2 Meghalaya state India
91 C2 Meghasani mt. India
127 C3 Megisti i. Greece
108 I1 Mehamn Norway
66 A2 Meharry, Mount Austr.
153 E3 Mehlville U.S.A.
95 C2 Mehrān watercourse Iran
90 B1 Mehtar Lām Afgh.
135 D3 Meia Meia Tanz.
170 C1 Meia Ponte r. Brazil
134 B2 Meiganga Cameroon
65 B1 Meihekou China
          Meijiang China see Ningdu
78 A1 Meiktila Myanmar
117 E2 Meiningen Ger.
118 C1 Meißen Ger.
          Meixian China see Meizhou
87 B3 Meizhou China
168 A2 Mejicana mt. Arg.
168 A2 Mejillones Chile
132 B3 Mek'elē Eth.
130 C2 Mekerrhane, Sebkha salt pan Alg.
130 B1 Meknès Morocco
79 B2 Mekong r. Asia
79 B3 Mekong, Mouths of the Vietnam
76 B1 Melaka Malaysia
172 D4 Melanesia is Pacific Ocean
172 D5 Melanesian Basin Pacific Ocean
69 B3 Melbourne Austr.
157 D3 Melbourne U.S.A.
124 A2 Mele, Capo c. Italy
          Melekess Rus. Fed. see Dimitrovgrad
105 F2 Melenki Rus. Fed.
147 C2 Mélèzes, Rivière aux r. Can.
131 D3 Melfi Chad
125 C2 Melfi Italy
145 D2 Melfort Can.
108 F3 Melhus Norway
122 B1 Melide Spain
130 B1 Melilla N. Africa
145 D3 Melita Can.
107 D2 Melitopol' Ukr.
135 C2 Melka Guba Eth.
117 D1 Melle Ger.
109 F4 Mellerud Sweden

117 E2 Mellrichstadt Ger.
117 D1 Mellum i. Ger.
139 D2 Melmoth S. Africa
168 C3 Melo Uru.
131 C1 Melrhir, Chott salt l. Alg.
112 C3 Melrose U.K.
          Melsetter Zimbabwe see Chimanimani
68 B3 Melton Austr.
115 C3 Melton Mowbray U.K.
121 C2 Melun France
145 D2 Melville Can.
67 C1 Melville, Cape Austr.
147 E2 Melville, Lake Can.
66 C1 Melville Island Austr.
142 E1 Melville Island Can.
143 G2 Melville Peninsula Can.
77 C2 Memboro Indon.
118 C2 Memmingen Ger.
76 B1 Mempawah Indon.
96 B3 Memphis tourist site Egypt
156 B1 Memphis TN U.S.A.
159 C1 Memphis TX U.S.A.
107 C1 Mena Ukr.
156 B2 Mena U.S.A.
137 □D3 Menabe mts Madag.
130 C3 Ménaka Mali
          Mènam Khong r. Laos/Thai. see
          Mekong
121 C3 Mende France
133 B4 Mendebo Eth.
132 B3 Mendefera Eritrea
176 B1 Mendeleyev Ridge Arctic Ocean
161 C2 Méndez Mex.
133 B4 Mendi Eth.
75 D3 Mendi P.N.G.
115 B4 Mendip Hills U.K.
154 B2 Mendota U.S.A.
169 B3 Mendoza Arg.
127 C3 Menemen Turkey
116 A2 Menen Belgium
86 B2 Mengcheng China
76 B2 Menggala Indon.
87 A3 Mengzi China
147 D2 Menihek Can.
68 B2 Menindee Austr.
68 B2 Menindee Lake Austr.
68 A3 Meningie Austr.
120 C2 Mennecy France
154 B1 Menominee U.S.A.
136 A2 Menongue Angola
          Menorca i. Spain see Minorca
77 C1 Mensalong Indon.
76 A1 Mentawai, Kepulauan is Indon.
76 B2 Mentok Indon.
77 C1 Menyapa, Gunung mt. Indon.
124 A3 Menzel Bourguiba Tunisia
66 B2 Menzies Austr.
160 B2 Meoqui Mex.
116 C1 Meppel Neth.
116 C1 Meppen Ger.
137 C3 Mepuze Moz.
139 C2 Meqheleng S. Africa
124 B1 Merano Italy
75 D3 Merauke Indon.
68 B2 Merbein Austr.
          Merca Somalia see Marka
151 B3 Merced U.S.A.
168 C2 Mercedes Arg.
159 D3 Mercedes U.S.A.
143 H2 Mercy, Cape Can.
159 C1 Meredith, Lake U.S.A.
107 D2 Merefa Ukr.
132 A3 Merga Oasis Sudan
79 A2 Mergui Archipelago is Myanmar
126 C2 Meriç r. Greece/Turkey
127 C2 Meriç Turkey
161 D2 Mérida Mex.
122 B2 Mérida Spain
166 B2 Mérida Venez.
163 C2 Mérida, Cordillera de mts Venez.
150 C2 Meridian ID U.S.A.
156 C2 Meridian MS U.S.A.
159 D2 Meridian TX U.S.A.
120 B3 Mérignac France
109 H3 Merikarvia Fin.
104 B3 Merimbula Austr.
104 B3 Merkinė Lith.
132 A3 Merowe Sudan
66 A3 Merredin Austr.
112 B3 Merrick h. U.K.
154 B1 Merrill U.S.A.
152 C2 Merrillville U.S.A.
152 C2 Merriman U.S.A.
144 B2 Merritt Can.
69 C2 Merrygoen Austr.
132 C3 Mersa Fatma Eritrea
116 C3 Mersch Lux.
117 E2 Merseburg (Saale) Ger.
114 B2 Mersey r. U.K.
127 B2 Mersin Turkey
76 B1 Mersing Malaysia
115 D4 Mers-les-Bains France
90 B2 Merta India
115 B4 Merthyr Tydfil U.K.
132 C3 Merti Plateau Kenya
122 B2 Mértola Port.
92 B2 Mertvyy Kultuk, Sor dry lake Kazakh.
135 D3 Meru vol. Tanz.
138 B3 Merweville S. Africa
96 B1 Merzifon Turkey
116 C2 Merzig Ger.
158 A2 Mesa AZ U.S.A.
158 C2 Mesa NM U.S.A.

O

R

Salton Sea

151 C4 **Salton Sea** *salt l.* U.S.A.
170 B3 **Salto Osório, Represa** *resr* Brazil
170 B3 **Salto Santiago, Represa de** *resr* Brazil
157 D2 **Saluda** U.S.A.
92 B3 **Saluq, Kūh-e** *mt.* Iran
124 A2 **Saluzzo** Italy
167 F4 **Salvador** Brazil
95 C2 **Salwah** Saudi Arabia
78 A2 **Salween** *r.* China/Myanmar
97 C2 **Salyan** Azer.
154 C3 **Salyersville** U.S.A.
138 A1 **Salzbrunn** Namibia
118 C2 **Salzburg** Austria
117 E1 **Salzgitter** Ger.
117 D2 **Salzkotten** Ger.
117 E1 **Salzwedel** Ger.
160 B1 **Samalayuca** Mex.
82 D2 **Samani** Japan
80 B2 **Samar** *i.* Phil.
103 E3 **Samara** Rus. Fed.
Samarahan Malaysia *see* **Sri Aman**
75 E3 **Samarai** P.N.G.
77 C2 **Samarinda** Indon.
93 C3 **Samarqand** Uzbek.
97 C2 **Sāmarrā'** Iraq
97 C1 **Şamaxı** Azer.
135 C3 **Samba** Dem. Rep. Congo
77 C1 **Sambaliung** *mts* Indon.
91 C2 **Sambalpur** India
76 C2 **Sambar, Tanjung** *pt* Indon.
76 B1 **Sambas** Indon.
137 □E2 **Sambava** Madag.
90 B2 **Sambhar** India
106 A2 **Sambir** Ukr.
77 C2 **Sambo** Indon.
77 C2 **Samboja** Indon.
169 C3 **Samborombón, Bahía** *b.* Arg.
81 B2 **Samch'ŏk** S. Korea
Samch'ŏnp'o S. Korea *see* **Sach'on**
97 C2 **Samdi Dag** *mt.* Turkey
135 D3 **Same** Tanz.
137 B2 **Samfya** Zambia
94 B2 **Samīrah** Saudi Arabia
81 B1 **Samjiyŏn** N. Korea
Sam Neua Laos *see* **Xam Nua**
64 J5 **Samoa** *country* S. Pacific Ocean
172 E6 **Samoa Basin** S. Pacific Ocean
Samoa i Sisifo *country* S. Pacific Ocean *see* **Samoa**
125 C1 **Samobor** Croatia
126 B2 **Samokov** Bulg.
127 C3 **Samos** *i.* Greece
Samothrace *i.* Greece *see* **Samothraki**
127 C2 **Samothraki** Greece
127 C2 **Samothraki** *i.* Greece
77 C2 **Sampit** Indon.
135 C3 **Sampwe** Dem. Rep. Congo
159 E2 **Sam Rayburn Reservoir** U.S.A.
78 B2 **Sâm Sơn** Vietnam
96 B1 **Samsun** Turkey
97 C1 **Samtredia** Georgia
79 B3 **Samui, Ko** *i.* Thai.
79 B2 **Samut Songkhram** Thai.
130 B3 **San** Mali
94 B3 **Şan'ā'** Yemen
134 A2 **Sanaga** *r.* Cameroon
97 C2 **Sanandaj** Iran
162 B3 **San Andrés, Isla de** *i.* Caribbean Sea
122 B1 **San Andrés del Rabanedo** Spain
158 B2 **San Andres Mountains** U.S.A.
161 C3 **San Andrés Tuxtla** Mex.
159 C2 **San Angelo** U.S.A.
159 D3 **San Antonio** U.S.A.
151 C4 **San Antonio, Mount** U.S.A.
168 B2 **San Antonio de los Cobres** Arg.
169 B4 **San Antonio Oeste** Arg.
124 B2 **San Benedetto del Tronto** Italy
160 A3 **San Benedicto, Isla** *i.* Mex.
151 C4 **San Bernardino** U.S.A.
151 C4 **San Bernardino Mountains** U.S.A.
158 B3 **San Blas** Mex.
157 C3 **San Blas, Cape** U.S.A.
162 C4 **San Blas, Punta** *pt* Panama
168 B1 **San Borja** Bol.
160 B2 **San Buenaventura** Mex.
80 B2 **San Carlos** Phil.
163 D4 **San Carlos** Venez.
169 A4 **San Carlos de Bariloche** Arg.
163 C4 **San Carlos del Zulia** Venez.
120 C2 **Sancerrois, Collines du** *hills* France
151 C4 **San Clemente** U.S.A.
151 C4 **San Clemente Island** U.S.A.
121 C2 **Sancoins** France
64 H5 **San Cristobal** *i.* Solomon Is
166 B2 **San Cristóbal** Venez.
161 C3 **San Cristóbal de las Casas** Mex.
162 C2 **Sancti Spíritus** Cuba
139 D1 **Sand** *r.* S. Africa
77 C1 **Sandakan** Malaysia
109 E3 **Sandane** Norway
127 B2 **Sandanski** Bulg.
130 A3 **Sandaré** Mali
112 C1 **Sanday** *i.* U.K.
159 C2 **Sanderson** U.S.A.
166 C4 **Sandia** Peru
151 C4 **San Diego** U.S.A.
127 D3 **Sandıklı** Turkey
109 E4 **Sandnes** Norway
108 F2 **Sandnessjøen** Norway
134 C3 **Sandoa** Dem. Rep. Congo
119 E1 **Sandomierz** Pol.
105 E2 **Sandovo** Rus. Fed.
110 B1 **Sandoy** *i.* Faroe Is
150 C1 **Sandpoint** U.S.A.
87 B3 **Sandu** China
110 B1 **Sandur** Faroe Is
154 C2 **Sandusky** U.S.A.
138 A3 **Sandveld** *mts* S. Africa
138 A2 **Sandverhaar** Namibia
109 F4 **Sandvika** Norway
109 G3 **Sandviken** Sweden
147 E2 **Sandwich Bay** Can.
151 D2 **Sandy** U.S.A.
145 D2 **Sandy Bay** Can.
67 E2 **Sandy Cape** Austr.
146 A2 **Sandy Lake** Can.
146 A2 **Sandy Lake** *l.* Can.
157 D2 **Sandy Springs** U.S.A.
160 A1 **San Felipe** Mex.
161 B2 **San Felipe** Mex.
166 C1 **San Felipe** Venez.
160 A2 **San Fernando** Mex.
161 C2 **San Fernando** Mex.
80 B2 **San Fernando** *Luzon* Phil.
80 B2 **San Fernando** *Luzon* Phil.
122 B2 **San Fernando** Spain
163 D3 **San Fernando** Trin. and Tob.
166 C2 **San Fernando de Apure** Venez.
157 D3 **Sanford** *FL* U.S.A.
155 E2 **Sanford** *ME* U.S.A.
157 E1 **Sanford** *NC* U.S.A.
168 B3 **San Francisco** Arg.
151 B3 **San Francisco** U.S.A.
123 D2 **San Francisco Javier** Spain
90 B3 **Sangamner** India
99 J2 **Sangar** Rus. Fed.
124 A3 **San Gavino Monreale** Italy
117 E2 **Sangerhausen** Ger.
77 C1 **Sanggau** Indon.
134 B3 **Sangha** *r.* Congo
125 C3 **San Giovanni in Fiore** Italy
75 C2 **Sangir** *i.* Indon.
75 C2 **Sangir, Kepulauan** *is* Indon.
81 B2 **Sangju** S. Korea
79 A2 **Sangkhla Buri** Thai.
77 C1 **Sangkulirang** Indon.
89 B3 **Sangli** India
134 B2 **Sangmélima** Cameroon
137 C3 **Sango** Zimbabwe
San Gottardo, Passo del *pass* Switz. *see* **St Gotthard Pass**
152 B3 **Sangre de Cristo Range** *mts* U.S.A.
91 C2 **Sangsang** China
160 A2 **San Hipólito, Punta** *pt* Mex.
161 D3 **San Ignacio** Belize
168 B1 **San Ignacio** Bol.
160 A2 **San Ignacio** Mex.
146 C2 **Sanikiluaq** Can.
87 A3 **Sanjiang** China
Sanjiang China *see* **Jinping**
83 C3 **Sanjō** Japan
151 B3 **San Joaquin** *r.* U.S.A.
169 B4 **San Jorge, Golfo de** *g.* Arg.
162 B4 **San José** Costa Rica
80 B2 **San Jose** Phil.
80 B2 **San Jose** Phil.
151 B3 **San Jose** U.S.A.
160 A2 **San José, Isla** *i.* Mex.
160 B2 **San José de Bavicora** Mex.
80 B2 **San Jose de Buenavista** Phil.
160 A2 **San José de Comondú** Mex.
160 B2 **San José del Cabo** Mex.
166 B2 **San José del Guaviare** Col.
168 B3 **San Juan** Arg.
162 B3 **San Juan** *r.* Costa Rica/Nic.
163 C3 **San Juan** Dom. Rep.
163 D3 **San Juan** Puerto Rico
151 D3 **San Juan** *r.* U.S.A.
168 C2 **San Juan Bautista** Para.
161 C3 **San Juan Bautista Tuxtepec** Mex.
163 D4 **San Juan de los Morros** Venez.
161 C2 **San Juan del Río** Mex.
150 B1 **San Juan Islands** U.S.A.
160 B2 **San Juanito** Mex.
152 B3 **San Juan Mountains** U.S.A.
169 B4 **San Julián** Arg.
91 C2 **Sankh** *r.* India
79 B2 **San Khao Phang Hoei** *mts* Thai.
116 C2 **Sankt Augustin** Ger.
121 D2 **Sankt Gallen** Switz.
121 D2 **Sankt Moritz** Switz.
Sankt-Peterburg Rus. Fed. *see* **St Petersburg**
118 C2 **Sankt Veit an der Glan** Austria
116 C3 **Sankt Wendel** Ger.
96 B2 **Şanlıurfa** Turkey
158 B3 **San Lorenzo** Mex.
122 B2 **Sanlúcar de Barrameda** Spain
160 B2 **San Lucas** Mex.
169 B3 **San Luis** Arg.
161 B2 **San Luis de la Paz** Mex.
158 A2 **San Luisito** Mex.
151 B3 **San Luis Obispo** U.S.A.
151 B3 **San Luis Obispo Bay** U.S.A.
161 B2 **San Luis Potosí** Mex.
160 A1 **San Luis Río Colorado** Mex.
159 D3 **San Marcos** U.S.A.
124 B2 **San Marino** *country* Europe
124 B2 **San Marino** San Marino
160 B2 **San Martín de Bolaños** Mex.
169 A4 **San Martín de los Andes** Arg.
151 B3 **San Mateo** U.S.A.
169 B4 **San Matías, Golfo** *g.* Arg.
86 B2 **Sanmenxia** China
162 B3 **San Miguel** El Salvador
168 B2 **San Miguel de Tucumán** Arg.
151 B4 **San Miguel Island** U.S.A.
161 C3 **San Miguel Sola de Vega** Mex.
87 B3 **Sanming** China
169 B3 **San Nicolás de los Arroyos** Arg.
151 C4 **San Nicolas Island** U.S.A.
126 B1 **Sânnicolau Mare** Romania
139 C2 **Sannieshof** S. Africa
130 B4 **Sanniquellie** Liberia
119 E2 **Sanok** Pol.
80 B2 **San Pablo** Phil.
160 B2 **San Pablo Balleza** Mex.
168 B2 **San Pedro** Arg.
168 B1 **San Pedro** Bol.
130 B4 **San-Pédro** Côte d'Ivoire
160 A2 **San Pedro** Mex.
158 A2 **San Pedro** *watercourse* U.S.A.
122 B2 **San Pedro, Sierra de** *mts* Spain
160 B2 **San Pedro de las Colonias** Mex.
168 C2 **San Pedro de Ycuamandyyú** Para.
158 A3 **San Pedro el Saucito** Mex.
162 B3 **San Pedro Sula** Hond.
124 A3 **San Pietro, Isola di** *i.* Italy
112 C3 **Sanquhar** U.K.
160 A1 **San Quintín, Cabo** *c.* Mex.
169 B3 **San Rafael** Arg.
124 A2 **San Remo** Italy
159 D2 **San Saba** U.S.A.
163 C2 **San Salvador** *i.* Bahamas
162 B3 **San Salvador** El Salvador
168 B2 **San Salvador de Jujuy** Arg.
124 B2 **Sansepolcro** Italy
125 C2 **San Severo** Italy
125 C2 **Sanski Most** Bos.-Herz.
168 B1 **Santa Ana** Bol.
162 B3 **Santa Ana** El Salvador
160 A1 **Santa Ana** Mex.
151 C4 **Santa Ana** U.S.A.
168 B1 **Santa Ana de Yacuma** Bol.
160 B2 **Santa Bárbara** Mex.
151 C4 **Santa Barbara** U.S.A.
170 B2 **Santa Bárbara, Serra de** *hills* Brazil
168 B2 **Santa Catalina** Chile
151 C4 **Santa Catalina Island** U.S.A.
170 B3 **Santa Catarina** *state* Brazil
166 C3 **Santa Clara** Col.
162 C2 **Santa Clara** Cuba
151 B3 **Santa Clara** U.S.A.
151 C4 **Santa Clarita** U.S.A.
123 D1 **Santa Coloma de Gramanet** Spain
Santa Comba Angola *see* **Waku-Kungo**
125 C3 **Santa Croce, Capo** *c.* Italy
169 B5 **Santa Cruz** *r.* Arg.
168 B1 **Santa Cruz** Bol.
80 B2 **Santa Cruz** Phil.
151 B3 **Santa Cruz** U.S.A.
161 C3 **Santa Cruz Barillas** Guat.
171 E1 **Santa Cruz Cabrália** Brazil
123 C2 **Santa Cruz de Moya** Spain
130 A2 **Santa Cruz de Tenerife** Islas Canarias
168 C2 **Santa Cruz do Sul** Brazil
151 C4 **Santa Cruz Island** U.S.A.
64 H5 **Santa Cruz Islands** Solomon Is
123 D2 **Santa Eulalia del Río** Spain
168 B3 **Santa Fé** Arg.
158 B1 **Santa Fe** U.S.A.
170 B2 **Santa Fé do Sul** Brazil
170 B1 **Santa Helena de Goiás** Brazil
169 B3 **Santa Isabel** Arg.
Santa Isabel Equat. Guinea *see* **Malabo**
64 G4 **Santa Isabel** *i.* Solomon Is
170 B1 **Santa Luisa, Serra de** *hills* Brazil
167 E3 **Santa Luzia** Brazil
160 A2 **Santa Margarita, Isla** *i.* Mex.
168 C2 **Santa Maria** Brazil
160 B1 **Santa María** *r.* Mex.
151 B4 **Santa Maria** U.S.A.
139 D2 **Santa Maria, Cabo de** *c.* Moz.
122 B2 **Santa Maria, Cabo de** *c.* Port.
171 C1 **Santa Maria, Chapadão de** *hills* Brazil
167 E3 **Santa Maria das Barreiras** Brazil
125 C3 **Santa Maria di Leuca, Capo** *c.* Italy
171 D1 **Santa Maria do Suaçuí** Brazil
166 B1 **Santa Marta** Col.
151 C4 **Santa Monica** U.S.A.
167 E4 **Santana** Brazil
126 B1 **Sântana** Romania
122 C1 **Santander** Spain
124 A3 **Sant'Antioco** Italy
124 A3 **Sant'Antioco, Isola di** *i.* Italy
123 D2 **Sant Antoni de Portmany** Spain
167 D3 **Santarém** Brazil
122 B2 **Santarém** Port.
170 B1 **Santa Rita do Araguaia** Brazil
169 B3 **Santa Rosa** Arg.
168 C2 **Santa Rosa** Brazil
151 B3 **Santa Rosa** *CA* U.S.A.
158 C2 **Santa Rosa** *NM* U.S.A.
162 B3 **Santa Rosa de Copán** Hond.
151 B4 **Santa Rosa Island** *CA* U.S.A.
156 C2 **Santa Rosa Island** *FL* U.S.A.
160 A2 **Santa Rosalía** Mex.
150 C2 **Santa Rosa Range** *mts* U.S.A.
122 B1 **Santa Uxía de Ribeira** Spain
170 B1 **Santa Vitória** Brazil
123 D1 **Sant Carles de la Ràpita** Spain
151 C4 **Santee** U.S.A.
168 C2 **Santiago** Brazil
169 A3 **Santiago** Chile
163 C3 **Santiago** Dom. Rep.
160 B2 **Santiago** Mex.
162 B4 **Santiago** Panama
80 B2 **Santiago** Phil.
122 B1 **Santiago de Compostela** Spain
162 C2 **Santiago de Cuba** Cuba
160 B2 **Santiago Ixcuintla** Mex.
160 B2 **Santiago Papasquiaro** Mex.
122 C1 **Santillana** Spain
123 D2 **Sant Joan de Labritja** Spain
123 D1 **Sant Jordi, Golf de** *g.* Spain
171 D2 **Santo Amaro de Campos** Brazil
170 B2 **Santo Anastácio** Brazil
171 C2 **Santo André** Brazil
168 C2 **Santo Angelo** Brazil
170 B2 **Santo Antônio da Platina** Brazil
167 F4 **Santo Antônio de Jesus** Brazil
166 C3 **Santo Antônio do Içá** Brazil
171 C2 **Santo Antônio do Monte** Brazil
163 D3 **Santo Domingo** Dom. Rep.
160 A2 **Santo Domingo** Mex.
158 B1 **Santo Domingo Pueblo** U.S.A.
127 C3 **Santorini** *i.* Greece
171 C2 **Santos** Brazil
171 D2 **Santos Dumont** Brazil
173 I7 **Santos Plateau** S. Atlantic Ocean
168 C2 **Santo Tomé** Arg.
169 A4 **San Valentín, Cerro** *mt.* Chile
162 B3 **San Vicente** El Salvador
160 A1 **San Vicente** Mex.
80 B2 **San Vicente** Phil.
166 B4 **San Vicente de Cañete** Peru
124 B2 **San Vincenzo** Italy
124 B3 **San Vito, Capo** *c.* Italy
87 A4 **Sanya** China
171 C2 **São Bernardo do Campo** Brazil
168 C2 **São Borja** Brazil
170 C2 **São Carlos** Brazil
171 D1 **São Felipe, Serra de** *hills* Brazil
167 D4 **São Félix** Brazil
167 D3 **São Félix** Brazil
171 D2 **São Fidélis** Brazil
171 D1 **São Francisco** Brazil
167 F4 **São Francisco** *r.* Brazil
170 C3 **São Francisco, Ilha de** *i.* Brazil
170 C3 **São Francisco do Sul** Brazil
168 C3 **São Gabriel** Brazil
171 D2 **São Gonçalo** Brazil
171 C1 **São Gonçalo do Abaeté** Brazil
171 C1 **São Gotardo** Brazil
170 B1 **São Jerônimo, Serra de** *hills* Brazil
171 D2 **São João da Barra** Brazil
171 C2 **São João da Boa Vista** Brazil
122 B1 **São João da Madeira** Port.
171 D1 **São João da Ponte** Brazil
171 D2 **São João del Rei** Brazil
171 D1 **São João do Paraíso** Brazil
171 D1 **São João Evangelista** Brazil
171 D2 **São João Nepomuceno** Brazil
170 C2 **São Joaquim da Barra** Brazil
168 D2 **São José** Brazil
170 C2 **São José do Rio Preto** Brazil
171 C2 **São José dos Campos** Brazil
170 C3 **São José dos Pinhais** Brazil
170 A1 **São Lourenço** Brazil
171 C2 **São Lourenço** Brazil
167 E3 **São Luís** Brazil
170 C2 **São Manuel** Brazil
170 C1 **São Marcos** *r.* Brazil
167 E3 **São Marcos, Baía de** *b.* Brazil
171 E1 **São Mateus** Brazil
170 B3 **São Mateus do Sul** Brazil
121 C2 **Saône** *r.* France
170 C2 **São Paulo** Brazil
170 C1 **São Paulo** *state* Brazil
171 D2 **São Pedro da Aldeia** Brazil
167 E3 **São Raimundo Nonato** Brazil
171 C1 **São Romão** Brazil
São Salvador Angola *see* **M'banza Congo**
São Salvador do Congo Angola *see* **M'banza Congo**
171 C2 **São Sebastião, Ilha do** *i.* Brazil
170 C2 **São Sebastião do Paraíso** Brazil
170 B1 **São Simão** Brazil
170 B1 **São Simão, Barragem de** *resr* Brazil
75 C2 **Sao-Siu** Indon.
129 D5 **São Tomé** São Tomé and Príncipe
129 D5 **São Tomé** *i.* São Tomé and Príncipe
171 D2 **São Tomé, Cabo de** *c.* Brazil
129 D5 **São Tomé and Príncipe** *country* Africa
171 C2 **São Vicente** Brazil
122 B2 **São Vicente, Cabo de** *c.* Port.
75 C3 **Saparua** Indon.
123 D2 **Sa Pobla** Spain
105 F3 **Sapozhok** Rus. Fed.
82 D2 **Sapporo** Japan
125 C2 **Sapri** Italy
159 D1 **Sapulpa** U.S.A.
97 C2 **Saqqez** Iran
97 C2 **Sarāb** Iran
79 B2 **Sara Buri** Thai.
Saragossa Spain *see* **Zaragoza**
105 F3 **Sarai** Rus. Fed.
125 C2 **Sarajevo** Bos.-Herz.
103 E3 **Saraktash** Rus. Fed.
78 A1 **Saramati** *mt.* India/Myanmar
155 E2 **Saranac Lake** U.S.A.
125 D3 **Sarandë** Albania
80 B3 **Sarangani Islands** Phil.
103 D3 **Saransk** Rus. Fed.
103 E3 **Sarapul** Rus. Fed.
157 D3 **Sarasota** U.S.A.
106 B2 **Sarata** Ukr.
152 B2 **Saratoga** U.S.A.

155 E2 Saratoga Springs U.S.A.
77 C1 Saratok Malaysia
103 D3 Saratov Rus. Fed.
95 D2 Saravan Iran
77 C1 Sarawak *state* Malaysia
127 C2 Saray Turkey
127 C3 Sarayköy Turkey
95 D2 Sarbāz Iran
92 B3 Sarbīsheh Iran
90 B2 Sardarshahr India
Sardegna *i.* Italy *see* Sardinia
124 A2 Sardinia *i.* Italy
108 G2 Sarektjåkkå *mt.* Sweden
93 C3 Sar-e Pol Afgh.
174 C3 Sargasso Sea *sea* N. Atlantic Ocean
90 B1 Sargodha Pak.
131 D4 Sarh Chad
95 D2 Sarhad *reg.* Iran
97 D2 Sārī Iran
127 C3 Sarıgöl Turkey
97 C1 Sarıkamış Turkey
77 C1 Sarikei Malaysia
67 D2 Sarina Austr.
131 D2 Sarīr Tibesti *des.* Libya
81 B2 Sariwŏn N. Korea
127 C2 Sarıyer Turkey
93 D2 Sarkand Kazakh.
127 C2 Şarköy Turkey
120 C3 Sarlat-la-Canéda France
75 D3 Sarmi Indon.
169 B4 Sarmiento Arg.
154 C2 Sarnia Can.
106 B1 Sarny Ukr.
76 B2 Sarolangun Indon.
127 B3 Saronikos Kolpos *g.* Greece
127 C2 Saros Körfezi *b.* Turkey
119 E2 Sárospatak Hungary
103 D3 Sarova Rus. Fed.
Sarpan *i.* N. Mariana Is *see* Rota
121 D2 Sarrebourg France
122 B1 Sarria Spain
123 C1 Sarrión Spain
121 D3 Sartène France
Sartu China *see* Daqing
127 C3 Saruhanlı Turkey
119 D2 Sárvár Hungary
97 D3 Sarvestān Iran
92 B2 Sarykamyshskoye Ozero *salt l.* Turkm./Uzbek.
93 D2 Saryozek Kazakh.
93 D2 Saryshagan Kazakh.
93 C2 Sarysu *watercourse* Kazakh.
93 D3 Sary-Tash Kyrg.
91 C2 Sasaram India
83 A4 Sasebo Japan
145 D2 Saskatchewan *prov.* Can.
145 D2 Saskatchewan *r.* Can.
145 D2 Saskatoon Can.
99 I2 Saskylakh Rus. Fed.
139 C2 Sasolburg S. Africa
103 D3 Sasovo Rus. Fed.
130 B4 Sassandra Côte d'Ivoire
124 A2 Sassari Italy
118 C1 Sassnitz Ger.
130 A3 Satadougou Mali
152 C3 Satanta U.S.A.
89 B3 Satara India
139 D1 Satara S. Africa
103 E3 Satka Rus. Fed.
91 C2 Satna India
93 C2 Satpayev Kazakh.
90 B2 Satpura Range *mts* India
79 B2 Sattahip Thai.
126 B1 Satu Mare Romania
79 B3 Satun Thai.
160 B2 Saucillo Mex.
109 E4 Sauda Norway
108 □B2 Sauðárkrókur Iceland
94 B2 Saudi Arabia *country* Asia
121 C3 Saugues France
153 E1 Sauk Center U.S.A.
121 C2 Saulieu France
104 B2 Saulkrasti Latvia
146 B3 Sault Sainte Marie Can.
154 C1 Sault Sainte Marie U.S.A.
93 C1 Saumalkol' Kazakh.
75 C3 Saumlakki Indon.
120 B2 Saumur France
136 B1 Saurimo Angola
125 D2 Sava *r.* Europe
65 J5 Savai'i *i.* Samoa
107 E1 Savala *r.* Rus. Fed.
130 C4 Savalou Benin
157 D2 Savannah *GA* U.S.A.
156 C1 Savannah *TN* U.S.A.
157 D2 Savannah *r.* U.S.A.
79 B2 Savannakhét Laos
146 A2 Savant Lake Can.
127 C3 Savaştepe Turkey
130 C4 Savè Benin
121 D2 Saverne France
105 F2 Savino Rus. Fed.
102 D2 Savinskiy Rus. Fed.
Savoie *reg.* France *see* Savoy
124 A2 Savona Italy
109 I3 Savonlinna Fin.
121 D2 Savoy *reg.* France
109 F4 Sävsjö Sweden
75 C3 Savu *i.* Indon.
108 I2 Savukoski Fin.
Savu Sea *sea* Indon. *see* Laut Sawu
90 B2 Sawai Madhopur India
78 A1 Sawan Myanmar
78 A2 Sawankhalok Thai.
152 B3 Sawatch Range *mts* U.S.A.
Sawhāj Egypt *see* Sūhāj
137 B2 Sawmills Zimbabwe
95 C3 Şawqirah, Dawḩat *b.* Oman
Şawqirah Bay *b.* Oman *see* Şawqirah, Dawḩat
69 D2 Sawtell Austr.
150 C2 Sawtooth Range *mts* U.S.A.
84 C1 Sayano-Shushenskoye Vodokhranilishche *resr* Rus. Fed.
92 C3 Saýat Turkm.
95 C3 Sayḩūt Yemen
109 I3 Säynätsalo Fin.
85 D2 Saynshand Mongolia
155 D2 Sayre U.S.A.
160 B3 Sayula Mex.
161 C3 Sayula Mex.
144 B2 Sayward Can.
Sayyod Turkm. *see* Saýat
105 E2 Sazonovo Rus. Fed.
130 B1 Sbaa Alg.
114 B2 Scafell Pike *h.* U.K.
125 C3 Scalea Italy
112 □ Scalloway U.K.
124 B2 Scandicci Italy
112 C1 Scapa Flow *inlet* U.K.
112 B2 Scarba *i.* U.K.
146 C3 Scarborough Can.
163 D3 Scarborough Trin. and Tob.
114 C2 Scarborough U.K.
80 A2 Scarborough Shoal *sea feature* S. China Sea
112 A2 Scarinish U.K.
Scarpanto *i.* Greece *see* Karpathos
116 B2 Schaerbeek Belgium
121 D2 Schaffhausen Switz.
116 B1 Schagen Neth.
118 C2 Schärding Austria
116 A2 Scharendijke Neth.
117 D1 Scharhörn *i.* Ger.
117 D1 Scheeßel Ger.
147 D2 Schefferville Can.
151 D3 Schell Creek Range *mts* U.S.A.
155 E2 Schenectady U.S.A.
159 D3 Schertz U.S.A.
117 E3 Scheßlitz Ger.
116 C1 Schiermonnikoog *i.* Neth.
116 B2 Schilde Belgium
124 B1 Schio Italy
117 F2 Schkeuditz Ger.
117 E1 Schladen Ger.
118 C2 Schladming Austria
117 E2 Schleiz Ger.
118 B1 Schleswig Ger.
117 D2 Schloss Holte-Stukenbrock Ger.
117 D2 Schlüchtern Ger.
117 E3 Schlüsselfeld Ger.
117 E2 Schmalkalden, Kurort Ger.
117 D2 Schmallenberg Ger.
Schmidt Island *i.* Rus. Fed. *see* Shmidta, Ostrov
117 F2 Schmölln Ger.
117 D1 Schneverdingen Ger.
117 E1 Schönebeck (Elbe) Ger.
117 E1 Schöningen Ger.
116 B2 Schoonhoven Neth.
75 D3 Schouten Islands P.N.G.
113 B3 Schull Ireland
117 E3 Schwabach Ger.
118 B2 Schwäbische Alb *mts* Ger.
117 F3 Schwandorf Ger.
77 C2 Schwaner, Pegunungan *mts* Indon.
117 E1 Schwarzenbek Ger.
117 F2 Schwarzenberg Ger.
138 A2 Schwarzrand *mts* Namibia
Schwarzwald *mts* Ger. *see* Black Forest
118 C2 Schwaz Austria
118 C1 Schwedt an der Oder Ger.
117 E2 Schweinfurt Ger.
117 E1 Schwerin Ger.
117 E1 Schweriner See *l.* Ger.
121 D2 Schwyz Switz.
124 B3 Sciacca Italy
111 B4 Scilly, Isles of U.K.
154 C3 Scioto *r.* U.S.A.
152 B1 Scobey U.S.A.
69 D2 Scone Austr.
126 B2 Scorniceşti Romania
71 C3 Scotia Ridge S. Atlantic Ocean
165 F8 Scotia Sea S. Atlantic Ocean
112 C2 Scotland *admin. div.* U.K.
144 B2 Scott, Cape Can.
139 D3 Scottburgh S. Africa
152 C3 Scott City U.S.A.
152 C2 Scottsbluff U.S.A.
156 C2 Scottsboro U.S.A.
112 B1 Scourie U.K.
155 D2 Scranton U.S.A.
114 C3 Scunthorpe U.K.
121 E2 Scuol Switz.
Scutari Albania *see* Shkodër
115 D4 Seaford U.K.
114 C2 Seaham U.K.
145 E2 Seal *r.* Can.
138 B3 Seal, Cape S. Africa
68 B3 Sea Lake Austr.
159 D3 Sealy U.S.A.
156 B1 Searcy U.S.A.
114 B2 Seascale U.K.
150 B1 Seattle U.S.A.
155 E2 Sebago Lake U.S.A.
160 A2 Sebastián Vizcaíno, Bahía *b.* Mex.
Sebastopol Ukr. *see* Sevastopol'
Sebenico Croatia *see* Šibenik
126 B1 Sebeş Romania
76 B2 Sebesi *i.* Indon.
104 C2 Sebezh Rus. Fed.
96 B1 Şebinkarahisar Turkey
157 D3 Sebring U.S.A.
77 C2 Sebuku *i.* Indon.
144 B3 Sechelt Can.
166 A3 Sechura Peru
89 B3 Secunderabad India
153 E3 Sedalia U.S.A.
121 C2 Sedan France
70 B2 Seddon N.Z.
130 A3 Sédhiou Senegal
158 A2 Sedona U.S.A.
117 E2 Seeburg Ger.
117 E1 Seehausen (Altmark) Ger.
138 A2 Seeheim Namibia
120 C2 Sées France
117 E2 Seesen Ger.
117 E1 Seevetal Ger.
130 A4 Sefadu Sierra Leone
139 C1 Sefare Botswana
109 F3 Segalstad Norway
76 B1 Segamat Malaysia
102 C2 Segezha Rus. Fed.
130 B3 Ségou Mali
122 C1 Segovia Spain
102 C2 Segozerskoye, Ozero *resr* Rus. Fed.
131 D2 Séguédine Niger
130 B4 Séguéla Côte d'Ivoire
159 D3 Seguin U.S.A.
123 C2 Segura *r.* Spain
122 C2 Segura, Sierra de *mts* Spain
136 B3 Sehithwa Botswana
109 H3 Seinäjoki Fin.
120 C2 Seine *r.* France
120 B2 Seine, Baie de *b.* France
121 C2 Seine, Val de *val.* France
119 E1 Sejny Pol.
76 B2 Sekayu Indon.
130 B4 Sekondi Ghana
150 B1 Selah U.S.A.
75 C3 Selaru *i.* Indon.
77 C2 Selatan, Tanjung *pt* Indon.
142 B2 Selawik U.S.A.
114 C3 Selby U.K.
152 C1 Selby U.S.A.
127 C3 Selçuk Turkey
136 B3 Selebi-Phikwe Botswana
Selebi-Pikwe Botswana *see* Selebi-Phikwe
121 D2 Sélestat France
Seletyteniz, Oz. *salt l.* Kazakh. *see* Siletiteniz, Ozero
108 □A3 Selfoss Iceland
130 A3 Sélibabi Maur.
158 A1 Seligman U.S.A.
132 A2 Selîma Oasis Sudan
127 C3 Selimiye Turkey
130 B3 Sélingué, Lac de *l.* Mali
105 D2 Selizharovo Rus. Fed.
109 E4 Seljord Norway
145 E2 Selkirk Can.
112 C3 Selkirk U.K.
144 C2 Selkirk Mountains Can.
158 A2 Sells U.S.A.
156 C2 Selma *AL* U.S.A.
151 C3 Selma *CA* U.S.A.
121 D2 Selongey France
115 C4 Selsey Bill *hd* U.K.
105 D3 Sel'tso Rus. Fed.
Selukwe Zimbabwe *see* Shurugwi
166 B3 Selvas *reg.* Brazil
150 C1 Selway *r.* U.S.A.
145 D1 Selwyn Lake Can.
144 A1 Selwyn Mountains Can.
67 C2 Selwyn Range *hills* Austr.
76 B2 Semangka, Teluk *b.* Indon.
77 C2 Semarang Indon.
76 B1 Sematan Malaysia
134 B2 Sembé Congo
97 C2 Şemdinli Turkey
107 C1 Semenivka Ukr.
103 D3 Semenov Rus. Fed.
77 C2 Semeru, Gunung *vol.* Indon.
107 E2 Semikarakorsk Rus. Fed.
105 E3 Semiluki Rus. Fed.
152 B2 Seminoe Reservoir U.S.A.
159 C2 Seminole U.S.A.
157 D2 Seminole, Lake U.S.A.
93 E1 Semipalatinsk Kazakh.
77 C1 Semitau Indon.
Sem Kolodezey Ukr. *see* Lenine
97 D2 Semnān Iran
77 C1 Semporna Malaysia
121 C2 Semur-en-Auxois France
Semyonovskoye Rus. Fed. *see* Bereznik
Semyonovskoye Rus. Fed. *see* Ostrovskoye
166 C3 Sena Madureira Brazil
136 B2 Senanga Zambia
83 B4 Sendai Japan
83 D3 Sendai Japan
157 D2 Seneca U.S.A.
130 A3 Senegal *country* Africa
130 A3 Sénégal *r.* Maur./Senegal
118 C1 Senftenberg Ger.
135 D3 Sengerema Tanz.
167 E3 Senhor do Bonfim Brazil
119 D2 Senica Slovakia
124 B2 Senigallia Italy
125 B2 Senj Croatia
108 G2 Senja *i.* Norway
138 B2 Senlac S. Africa
121 C2 Senlis France
79 B2 Senmonorom Cambodia
132 B3 Sennar Sudan
146 C3 Senneterre Can.
139 C3 Senqu *r.* Lesotho
121 C2 Sens France
125 D1 Senta Serbia
144 B2 Sentinel Peak Can.
139 C1 Senwabarwana S. Africa
91 B2 Seoni India
81 B2 Seoul S. Korea
171 D2 Sepetiba, Baía de *b.* Brazil
75 D3 Sepik *r.* P.N.G.
77 C1 Sepinang Indon.
147 D2 Sept-Îles Can.
103 D4 Serafimovich Rus. Fed.
116 B2 Seraing Belgium
75 C3 Seram *i.* Indon.
76 B2 Serang Indon.
76 B1 Serasan, Selat *sea chan.* Indon.
125 D2 Serbia *country* Europe
92 B3 Serdar Turkm.
133 C3 Serdo Eth.
105 E3 Serebryanyye Prudy Rus. Fed.
76 B1 Seremban Malaysia
135 D3 Serengeti Plain Tanz.
137 C2 Serenje Zambia
106 B2 Seret *r.* Ukr.
103 D3 Sergach Rus. Fed.
102 F2 Sergino Rus. Fed.
105 E2 Sergiyev Posad Rus. Fed.
Sergo Ukr. *see* Stakhanov
90 A1 Serhetabat Turkm.
77 C1 Seria Brunei
77 C1 Serian Malaysia
127 B3 Serifos *i.* Greece
96 B2 Serik Turkey
75 C3 Sermata, Kepulauan *is* Indon.
Sernyy Zavod Turkm. *see* Kükürtli
102 F3 Serov Rus. Fed.
136 B3 Serowe Botswana
122 B2 Serpa Port.
Serpa Pinto Angola *see* Menongue
105 E3 Serpukhov Rus. Fed.
171 D2 Serra Brazil
171 C1 Serra das Araras Brazil
124 A3 Serramanna Italy
170 B1 Serranópolis Brazil
116 A3 Serre *r.* France
127 B2 Serres Greece
167 F4 Serrinha Brazil
171 D1 Sêrro Brazil
170 C2 Sertãozinho Brazil
75 D3 Serui Indon.
136 B3 Serule Botswana
77 C2 Seruyan *r.* Indon.
84 C2 Sêrxü China
136 A2 Sesfontein Namibia
124 B2 Sessa Aurunca Italy
124 A2 Sestri Levante Italy
121 C3 Sète France
171 D1 Sete Lagoas Brazil
108 G2 Setermoen Norway
109 E4 Setesdal *val.* Norway
131 C1 Sétif Alg.
83 B4 Seto-naikai *sea* Japan
130 B1 Settat Morocco
114 B2 Settle U.K.
122 B2 Setúbal Port.
122 B2 Setúbal, Baía de *b.* Port.
146 A2 Seul, Lac *l.* Can.
97 C1 Sevan Armenia
92 A2 Sevan, Lake Armenia
Sevana Lich *l.* Armenia *see* Sevan, Lake
107 C3 Sevastopol' Ukr.
Seven Islands Can. *see* Sept-Îles
147 D2 Seven Islands Bay Can.
115 D4 Sevenoaks U.K.
121 C3 Sévérac-le-Château France
146 B2 Severn *r.* Can.
138 B2 Severn S. Africa
115 B4 Severn *r.* U.K.
102 D2 Severnaya Dvina *r.* Rus. Fed.
99 H1 Severnaya Zemlya *is* Rus. Fed.
102 D2 Severnyy Rus. Fed.
102 F2 Severnyy Rus. Fed.
99 I3 Severobaykal'sk Rus. Fed.
102 C2 Severodvinsk Rus. Fed.
99 L3 Severo-Kuril'sk Rus. Fed.
108 J2 Severomorsk Rus. Fed.
102 C2 Severoonezhsk Rus. Fed.
99 H2 Severo-Yeniseyskiy Rus. Fed.
107 D3 Severskaya Rus. Fed.
151 D3 Sevier *r.* U.S.A.
151 D3 Sevier Lake U.S.A.
Sevilla Spain *see* Seville
122 B2 Seville Spain
Sevlyush Ukr. *see* Vynohradiv
105 D3 Sevsk Rus. Fed.
142 C2 Seward U.S.A.
142 B2 Seward Peninsula U.S.A.
144 A2 Sewell Inlet Can.
144 C2 Sexsmith Can.
160 B2 Sextín *r.* Mex.
102 G1 Seyakha Rus. Fed.
129 I6 Seychelles *country* Indian Ocean
108 □C2 Seyðisfjörður Iceland
Seyhan Turkey *see* Adana
96 B2 Seyhan *r.* Turkey
107 C1 Seym *r.* Rus. Fed./Ukr.

116 A2 Sint-Laureins Belgium
163 D3 Sint Maarten i. Neth. Antilles
116 B2 Sint-Niklaas Belgium
159 D3 Sinton U.S.A.
81 A1 Sinŭiju N. Korea
80 B3 Siocon Phil.
119 D2 Siófok Hungary
121 D2 Sion Switz.
153 D2 Sioux Center U.S.A.
153 D2 Sioux City U.S.A.
153 D2 Sioux Falls U.S.A.
146 A2 Sioux Lookout Can.
81 A1 Siping China
145 E2 Sipiwesk Lake Can.
71 P2 Siple, Mount Antarctica
71 P2 Siple Island Antarctica
Sipolilo Zimbabwe see Guruve
76 A2 Sipura i. Indon.
80 B3 Siquijor Phil.
109 E4 Sira r. Norway
Siracusa Italy see Syracuse
67 C1 Sir Edward Pellew Group is Austr.
126 C1 Siret Romania
126 C1 Siret r. Romania
94 A1 Sirhān, Wādī an watercourse Saudi Arabia
95 C2 Sīrīk Iran
77 C1 Sirik, Tanjung pt Malaysia
78 B2 Siri Kit, Khuan Thai.
144 B1 Sir James MacBrien, Mount Can.
95 C2 Sīrjān Iran
97 C2 Şırnak Turkey
90 B2 Sirohi India
76 A1 Sirombu Indon.
90 B2 Sirsa India
131 D1 Sirte Libya
131 D1 Sirte, Gulf of Libya
104 B2 Širvintos Lith.
125 C1 Sisak Croatia
79 B2 Sisaket Thai.
161 C2 Sisal Mex.
138 B2 Sishen S. Africa
97 C2 Sisian Armenia
143 I2 Sisimiut Greenland
145 D2 Sisipuk Lake Can.
79 B2 Sisŏphŏn Cambodia
121 D3 Sisteron France
Sitang China see Sinan
91 C2 Sitapur India
127 C3 Siteia Greece
139 D2 Siteki Swaziland
144 A2 Sitka U.S.A.
116 B2 Sittard Neth.
78 A1 Sittaung Myanmar
78 A2 Sittaung r. Myanmar
78 A1 Sittwe Myanmar
77 C2 Situbondo Indon.
96 B2 Sivas Turkey
127 C3 Sivaslı Turkey
96 B2 Siverek Turkey
104 D2 Siverskiy Rus. Fed.
96 B2 Sivrihisar Turkey
132 A2 Sīwah Egypt
91 B1 Siwalik Range mts India/Nepal
Siwa Oasis oasis Egypt see Wāḩāt Sīwah
121 D3 Six-Fours-les-Plages France
86 B2 Sixian China
139 C2 Siyabuswa S. Africa
Sjælland i. Denmark see Zealand
125 D2 Sjenica Serbia
108 G2 Sjøvegan Norway
107 C2 Skadovs'k Ukr.
109 F4 Skagen Denmark
109 E4 Skagerrak str. Denmark/Norway
150 B1 Skagit r. U.S.A.
144 A2 Skagway U.S.A.
108 G2 Skaland Norway
109 F4 Skara Sweden
90 B1 Skardu Pak.
119 E1 Skarżysko-Kamienna Pol.
119 D2 Skawina Pol.
130 A2 Skaymat Western Sahara
144 B2 Skeena r. Can.
144 B2 Skeena Mountains Can.
114 D3 Skegness U.K.
108 H3 Skellefteå Sweden
108 H3 Skellefteälven r. Sweden
113 C2 Skerries Ireland
109 F4 Ski Norway
127 B3 Skiathos i. Greece
113 B3 Skibbereen Ireland
108 □B2 Skíðadals-jökull glacier Iceland
114 B2 Skiddaw h. U.K.
109 E4 Skien Norway
119 E1 Skierniewice Pol.
131 C1 Skikda Alg.
68 B3 Skipton Austr.
114 B3 Skipton U.K.
109 E4 Skive Denmark
108 H1 Skjervøy Norway
Skobelev Uzbek. see Farg'ona
127 B3 Skopelos i. Greece
105 E3 Skopin Rus. Fed.
127 B2 Skopje Macedonia
127 B3 Skoutaros Greece
109 F4 Skövde Sweden
99 J3 Skovorodino Rus. Fed.
155 F2 Skowhegan U.S.A.
108 H2 Skröven Sweden
104 B2 Skrunda Latvia
144 A1 Skukum, Mount Can.
138 B1 Skukuza S. Africa
104 B2 Skuodas Lith.

106 B2 Skvyra Ukr.
112 A2 Skye i. U.K.
127 B3 Skyros Greece
127 B3 Skyros i. Greece
109 F4 Slagelse Denmark
76 B2 Slamet, Gunung vol. Indon.
113 C2 Slaney r. Ireland
104 C2 Slantsy Rus. Fed.
125 C1 Slatina Croatia
126 B2 Slatina Romania
159 C2 Slaton U.S.A.
145 C1 Slave r. Can.
130 C4 Slave Coast Africa
144 C2 Slave Lake Can.
93 D1 Slavgorod Rus. Fed.
104 C2 Slavkovichi Rus. Fed.
Slavonska Požega Croatia see Požega
125 C1 Slavonski Brod Croatia
106 B1 Slavuta Ukr.
106 C1 Slavutych Ukr.
82 B2 Slavyanka Rus. Fed.
Slavyanskaya Rus. Fed. see Slavyansk-na-Kubani
107 D2 Slavyansk-na-Kubani Rus. Fed.
105 D3 Slawharad Belarus
119 D1 Sławno Pol.
115 C3 Sleaford U.K.
113 A2 Slea Head hd Ireland
146 C2 Sleeper Islands Can.
113 D1 Slieve Donard h. U.K.
112 A2 Sligachan U.K.
Slieve Gamph hills Ireland see Ox Mountains
Sligeach Ireland see Sligo
113 B1 Sligo Ireland
113 B1 Sligo Bay Ireland
109 G4 Slite Sweden
126 C2 Sliven Bulg.
Sloboda Rus. Fed. see Ezhva
126 C2 Slobozia Romania
144 B3 Slocan Can.
104 C3 Slonim Belarus
116 B1 Sloten Neth.
115 C4 Slough U.K.
119 D2 Slovakia country Europe
124 B1 Slovenia country Europe
107 D2 Slov''yans'k Ukr.
118 C1 Słubice Pol.
106 B1 Sluch r. Ukr.
116 A2 Sluis Neth.
119 D1 Słupsk Pol.
104 C3 Slutsk Belarus
113 A2 Slyne Head hd Ireland
84 E1 Slyudyanka Rus. Fed.
147 D2 Smallwood Reservoir Can.
104 C3 Smalyavichy Belarus
104 C3 Smarhon' Belarus
145 D2 Smeaton Can.
125 D2 Smederevo Serbia
125 D2 Smederevska Palanka Serbia
107 C2 Smila Ukr.
104 C3 Smilavichy Belarus
104 C2 Smiltene Latvia
153 D3 Smith Center U.S.A.
144 B2 Smithers Can.
157 E1 Smithfield NC U.S.A.
150 D2 Smithfield UT U.S.A.
155 D3 Smith Mountain Lake U.S.A.
146 C3 Smiths Falls Can.
69 D2 Smithton Austr.
69 D2 Smoky Cape Austr.
153 D3 Smoky Hills U.S.A.
108 E3 Smøla i. Norway
105 D3 Smolensk Rus. Fed.
105 D3 Smolensko-Moskovskaya Vozvyshennost' hills Belarus/Rus. Fed.
127 B2 Smolyan Bulg.
82 B2 Smolyoninovo Rus. Fed.
146 B3 Smooth Rock Falls Can.
Smyrna Turkey see İzmir
107 D2 Smyrnove Ukr.
108 □B3 Snæfell mt. Iceland
114 A2 Snaefell h. Isle of Man
144 A1 Snag (abandoned) Can.
150 C1 Snake r. U.S.A.
150 D2 Snake River Plain U.S.A.
Snare Lakes Can. see Wekweètì
108 F3 Snåsvatn l. Norway
116 B1 Sneek Neth.
113 B3 Sneem Ireland
138 B3 Sneeuberge mts S. Africa
Snegurovka Ukr. see Tetiyiv
119 D1 Sněžka mt. Czech Rep.
124 B1 Snežnik mt. Slovenia
119 E1 Śniardwy, Jezioro l. Pol.
Sniečkus Lith. see Visaginas
107 C2 Snihurivka Ukr.
109 E3 Snøhetta mt. Norway
Snovsk Ukr. see Shchors
145 D1 Snowbird Lake Can.
115 A3 Snowdon mt. U.K.
Snowdrift Can. see Łutselk'e
145 C1 Snowdrift r. Can.
158 A2 Snowflake U.S.A.
145 D2 Snow Lake Can.
150 C1 Snowshoe Peak U.S.A.
68 A2 Snowtown Austr.
69 C3 Snowy r. Austr.
69 C3 Snowy Mountains Austr.
159 C2 Snyder U.S.A.
137 □D2 Soalala Madag.
137 □D2 Soanierana-Ivongo Madag.
106 B2 Sob r. Ukr.

81 B2 Sobaek-sanmaek mts S. Korea
133 B4 Sobat r. Sudan
105 F2 Sobinka Rus. Fed.
167 E4 Sobradinho, Barragem de resr Brazil
167 E3 Sobral Brazil
107 D3 Sochi Rus. Fed.
81 B2 Sŏch'ŏn S. Korea
65 L5 Society Islands Fr. Polynesia
166 B2 Socorro Col.
158 B2 Socorro NM U.S.A.
158 B2 Socorro TX U.S.A.
160 A3 Socorro, Isla i. Mex.
72 B4 Socotra i. Yemen
79 B3 Soc Trăng Vietnam
122 C2 Socuéllamos Spain
108 I2 Sodankylä Fin.
150 D2 Soda Springs U.S.A.
109 G3 Söderhamn Sweden
109 G4 Södertälje Sweden
132 A3 Sodiri Sudan
133 B4 Sodo Eth.
109 G3 Södra Kvarken str. Fin./Sweden
139 C1 Soekmekaar S. Africa
Soerabaia Indon. see Surabaya
117 D2 Soest Ger.
69 C2 Sofala Austr.
126 B2 Sofia Bulg.
137 □D2 Sofia r. Madag.
Sofiya Bulg. see Sofia
Sofiyevka Ukr. see Vil'nyans'k
91 B1 Sog China
109 E3 Sognefjorden inlet Norway
127 D2 Söğüt Turkey
Sohâg Egypt see Sūhāj
Sohar Oman see Şuḩār
116 B3 Soignies Belgium
121 C2 Soissons France
106 A1 Sokal' Ukr.
81 B2 Sokch'o S. Korea
127 C3 Söke Turkey
97 C1 Sokhumi Georgia
130 C4 Sokodé Togo
105 F2 Sokol Rus. Fed.
117 F2 Sokolov Czech Rep.
131 C3 Sokoto Nigeria
131 C3 Sokoto r. Nigeria
106 B2 Sokyryany Ukr.
89 B3 Solapur India
151 B3 Soledad U.S.A.
105 F2 Soligalich Rus. Fed.
115 C3 Solihull U.K.
102 E3 Solikamsk Rus. Fed.
103 E3 Sol'-Iletsk Rus. Fed.
116 C2 Solingen Ger.
138 A1 Solitaire Namibia
108 G3 Sollefteå Sweden
109 G4 Sollentuna Sweden
123 D2 Sóller Spain
117 D2 Solling hills Ger.
105 E2 Solnechnogorsk Rus. Fed.
76 B2 Solok Indon.
64 H4 Solomon Islands country S. Pacific Ocean
64 G4 Solomon Sea S. Pacific Ocean
77 D2 Solor, Kepulauan is Indon.
121 D2 Solothurn Switz.
97 D2 Solţānābād Iran
117 D1 Soltau Ger.
105 D2 Sol'tsy Rus. Fed.
112 C3 Solway Firth est. U.K.
136 B2 Solwezi Zambia
127 C3 Soma Turkey
133 C4 Somalia country Africa
61 Somali Basin Indian Ocean
136 B1 Sombo Angola
125 C1 Sombor Serbia
160 B2 Sombrerete Mex.
154 C3 Somerset U.S.A.
139 C3 Somerset East S. Africa
142 F2 Somerset Island Can.
138 A3 Somerset West S. Africa
126 B1 Someş r. Romania
117 E2 Sömmerda Ger.
162 B3 Somoto Nic.
91 C2 Son r. India
81 C1 Sŏnbong N. Korea
109 E5 Sønderborg Denmark
117 E2 Sondershausen Ger.
Søndre Strømfjord Greenland see Kangerlussuaq
124 B1 Sondrio Italy
79 B2 Sông Câu Vietnam
78 B1 Sông Đa, Hô resr Vietnam
135 D4 Songea Tanz.
81 B1 Sŏnggan N. Korea
81 B1 Songhua Hu resr China
81 B1 Songjianghe China
Sŏngjin N. Korea see Kimch'aek
79 B3 Songkhla Thai.
81 B2 Songnam S. Korea
81 B2 Songnim N. Korea
136 A1 Songo Angola
137 D2 Songo Moz.
Songololo Dem. Rep. Congo see Mbanza-Ngungu
85 E1 Songyuan China
Sonid Youqi China see Saihan Tal
90 B2 Sonipat India
105 E2 Sonkovo Rus. Fed.
78 B1 Sơn La Vietnam
90 A2 Sonmiani Pak.
90 A2 Sonmiani Bay Pak.
117 E2 Sonneberg Ger.
158 A2 Sonoita Mex.

160 A2 Sonora r. Mex.
151 B3 Sonora CA U.S.A.
159 C2 Sonora TX U.S.A.
162 B3 Sonsonate El Salvador
Soochow China see Suzhou
133 A4 Sopo watercourse Sudan
119 D2 Sopron Hungary
90 B1 Sopur India
124 B2 Sora Italy
146 C3 Sorel Can.
67 D4 Sorell Austr.
122 C1 Soria Spain
106 B2 Soroca Moldova
154 C2 Sorocaba Brazil
103 E3 Sorochinsk Rus. Fed.
Soroki Moldova see Soroca
75 D2 Sorol atoll Micronesia
75 C3 Sorong Indon.
135 D2 Soroti Uganda
108 H1 Sørøya i. Norway
124 B2 Sorrento Italy
108 G2 Sorsele Sweden
80 B2 Sorsogon Phil.
102 C2 Sortavala Rus. Fed.
108 G2 Sortland Norway
81 B2 Sŏsan S. Korea
139 C2 Soshanguve S. Africa
105 E3 Sosna r. Rus. Fed.
169 B3 Sosneado mt. Arg.
102 E2 Sosnogorsk Rus. Fed.
102 D2 Sosnovka Rus. Fed.
104 C2 Sosnovyy Bor Rus. Fed.
119 D1 Sosnowiec Pol.
107 C1 Sosnytsya Ukr.
102 F3 Sos'va Rus. Fed.
107 D2 Sosyka r. Rus. Fed.
161 C2 Soto la Marina Mex.
134 B2 Souanké Congo
127 B3 Souda Greece
120 C3 Souillac France
Soûl S. Korea see Seoul
120 B2 Soulac-sur-Mer France
120 B3 Soulom France
Soûr Lebanon see Tyre
123 D2 Sour el Ghozlane Alg.
145 D3 Souris Man. Can.
147 D3 Souris P.E.I. Can.
145 E3 Souris r. Can.
167 F3 Sousa Brazil
131 D1 Sousse Tunisia
120 B3 Soustons France
138 B3 South Africa, Republic of country Africa
115 C4 Southampton U.K.
145 F1 Southampton, Cape Can.
145 F1 Southampton Island Can.
89 D3 South Andaman i. India
68 A1 South Australia state Austr.
156 B3 Southaven U.S.A.
158 B2 South Baldy mt. U.S.A.
146 B3 South Baymouth Can.
154 B3 South Bend U.S.A.
157 D2 South Carolina state U.S.A.
74 B2 South China Sea N. Pacific Ocean
South Coast Town Austr. see Gold Coast
152 C2 South Dakota state U.S.A.
115 C4 South Downs hills U.K.
175 E6 Southeast Indian Ridge Indian Ocean
71 O2 Southeast Pacific Basin S. Pacific Ocean
145 D2 Southend Can.
115 D4 Southend-on-Sea U.K.
70 B2 Southern Alps mts N.Z.
66 A3 Southern Cross Austr.
145 E2 Southern Indian Lake Can.
175 D7 Southern Ocean
157 E1 Southern Pines U.S.A.
Southern Rhodesia country Africa see Zimbabwe
112 B3 Southern Uplands hills U.K.
71 J2 South Geomagnetic Pole (2008) Antarctica
165 G8 South Georgia terr. S. Atlantic Ocean
165 G8 South Georgia and the South Sandwich Islands terr. S. Atlantic Ocean
154 B2 South Haven U.S.A.
145 E1 South Henik Lake Can.
135 D2 South Horr Kenya
70 B2 South Island N.Z.
81 B2 South Korea country Asia
151 B3 South Lake Tahoe U.S.A.
71 L3 South Magnetic Pole (2008) Antarctica
165 F9 South Orkney Islands S. Atlantic Ocean
152 C2 South Platte r. U.S.A.
114 B3 Southport U.K.
157 E2 Southport U.S.A.
145 C3 South River Can.
112 C1 South Ronaldsay i. U.K.
139 D3 South Sand Bluff pt S. Africa
165 H8 South Sandwich Islands S. Atlantic Ocean
71 C4 South Sandwich Trench S. Atlantic Ocean
145 D2 South Saskatchewan r. Can.
145 E2 South Seal r. Can.
165 H9 South Shetland Islands Antarctica
114 C2 South Shields U.K.
70 B1 South Taranaki Bight b. N.Z.
172 C8 South Tasman Rise Southern Ocean

T

Varzino

102 C2 Varzino Rus. Fed.
Vasa Fin. see Vaasa
104 C3 Vasilyevichy Belarus
104 C2 Vasknarva Estonia
126 C1 Vaslui Romania
109 G4 Västerås Sweden
109 G3 Västerdalälven r. Sweden
104 A2 Västerhaninge Sweden
109 G4 Västervik Sweden
124 B2 Vasto Italy
107 D2 Vasylivka Ukr.
106 C1 Vasyl'kiv Ukr.
107 D2 Vasyl'kivka Ukr.
120 C2 Vatan France
127 B3 Vatheia Greece
124 B2 Vatican City Europe
108 □B3 Vatnajökull Iceland
126 C1 Vatra Dornei Romania
Vätter, Lake l. Sweden see Vättern
109 F4 Vättern l. Sweden
158 B2 Vaughn U.S.A.
121 C3 Vauvert France
137 □D2 Vavatenina Madag.
65 J5 Vava'u Group is Tonga
104 B3 Vawkavysk Belarus
109 F4 Växjö Sweden
Vayenga Rus. Fed. see Severomorsk
102 E1 Vaygach, Ostrov i. Rus. Fed.
170 C1 Vazante Brazil
117 D1 Vechta Ger.
126 C2 Vedea r. Romania
116 C1 Veendam Neth.
116 B1 Veenendaal Neth.
108 F2 Vega i. Norway
144 C2 Vegreville Can.
122 B2 Vejer de la Frontera Spain
109 E4 Vejle Denmark
126 B2 Velbŭzhdki Prokhod pass Bulg./Macedonia
138 A3 Velddrif S. Africa
116 B2 Veldhoven Neth.
125 B2 Velebit mts Croatia
116 C2 Velen Ger.
125 C1 Velenje Slovenia
125 D2 Veles Macedonia
122 C2 Vélez-Málaga Spain
171 D1 Velhas r. Brazil
125 D2 Velika Plana Serbia
104 C2 Velikaya r. Rus. Fed.
105 D2 Velikiye Luki Rus. Fed.
105 D2 Velikiy Novgorod Rus. Fed.
102 D2 Velikiy Ustyug Rus. Fed.
126 C2 Veliko Tŭrnovo Bulg.
124 B2 Veli Lošinj Croatia
105 D2 Velizh Rus. Fed.
124 B2 Velletri Italy
89 B3 Vellore India
102 D2 Vel'sk Rus. Fed.
117 F1 Velten Ger.
107 D1 Velykyy Burluk Ukr.
Velykyy Tokmak Ukr. see Tokmak
175 E4 Vema Trench Indian Ocean
124 B2 Venafro Italy
170 C2 Venceslau Bráz Brazil
120 C2 Vendôme France
124 B1 Veneta, Laguna lag. Italy
105 E3 Venev Rus. Fed.
Venezia Italy see Venice
166 C2 Venezuela country S. America
166 B1 Venezuela, Golfo de g. Venez.
124 B1 Venice Italy
157 D3 Venice U.S.A.
124 B1 Venice, Gulf of Europe
116 C2 Venlo Neth.
109 E4 Vennesla Norway
116 B2 Venray Neth.
104 B2 Venta r. Latvia/Lith.
104 B2 Venta Lith.
139 C2 Ventersburg S. Africa
139 C3 Venterstad S. Africa
124 A2 Ventimiglia Italy
115 C4 Ventnor U.K.
104 B2 Ventspils Latvia
151 C4 Ventura U.S.A.
159 C3 Venustiano Carranza, Presa resr Mex.
123 C2 Vera Spain
170 C2 Vera Cruz Brazil
161 C3 Veracruz Mex.
90 B2 Veraval India
124 A1 Verbania Italy
124 A1 Vercelli Italy
121 D3 Vercors reg. France
108 F3 Verdalsøra Norway
170 B1 Verde r. Brazil
170 B2 Verde r. Brazil
160 B2 Verde r. Mex.
158 A2 Verde r. U.S.A.
171 D1 Verde Grande r. Brazil
117 D1 Verden (Aller) Ger.
170 B1 Verdinho, Serra do mts Brazil
121 D3 Verdon r. France
121 D2 Verdun France
139 C2 Vereeniging S. Africa
122 B1 Verín Spain
107 D3 Verkhnebakanskiy Rus. Fed.
105 D3 Verkhnedneprovskiy Rus. Fed.
108 J2 Verkhnetulomskiy Rus. Fed.
108 J2 Verkhnetulomskoye Vodokhranilishche resr Rus. Fed.
103 D4 Verkhniy Baskunchak Rus. Fed.
107 E1 Verkhniy Mamon Rus. Fed.
102 D2 Verkhnyaya Toyma Rus. Fed.
105 E3 Verkhov'ye Rus. Fed.
106 A2 Verkhovyna Ukr.
99 J2 Verkhoyanskiy Khrebet mts Rus. Fed.
145 C2 Vermilion Can.
153 D2 Vermillion U.S.A.
146 A3 Vermillion Bay Can.
155 E2 Vermont state U.S.A.
151 E2 Vernal U.S.A.
138 B2 Verneuk Pan salt pan S. Africa
144 C2 Vernon Can.
159 D2 Vernon U.S.A.
157 D3 Vero Beach U.S.A.
127 B2 Veroia Greece
124 B1 Verona Italy
154 B2 Verona U.S.A.
120 C2 Versailles France
120 B2 Vertou France
139 D2 Verulam S. Africa
116 B2 Verviers Belgium
121 C2 Vervins France
121 D3 Vescovato France
103 E3 Veselaya, Gora mt. Rus. Fed.
107 C2 Vesele Ukr.
107 E2 Veselyy Rus. Fed.
121 D2 Vesoul France
156 C2 Vestavia Hills U.S.A.
108 F2 Vesterålen is Norway
108 F2 Vestfjorden sea chan. Norway
110 B1 Vestmanna Faroe Is
108 □A3 Vestmannaeyjar Iceland
108 □A3 Vestmannaeyjar is Iceland
109 E3 Vestnes Norway
Vesuvio vol. Italy see Vesuvius
124 B2 Vesuvius vol. Italy
105 E2 Ves'yegonsk Rus. Fed.
119 D2 Veszprém Hungary
109 G4 Vetlanda Sweden
102 D3 Vetluga Rus. Fed.
102 D3 Vetluzhskiy Rus. Fed.
116 A2 Veurne Belgium
135 D2 Veveno r. Sudan
121 D2 Vevey Switz.
107 D1 Veydelevka Rus. Fed.
96 B1 Vezirköprü Turkey
Vialar Alg. see Tissemsilt
168 C3 Viamao Brazil
167 E3 Viana Brazil
122 B1 Viana do Castelo Port.
Viangchan Laos see Vientiane
78 B1 Viangphoukha Laos
127 C3 Viannos Greece
170 C1 Vianópolis Brazil
124 B2 Viareggio Italy
109 E4 Viborg Denmark
Viborg Rus. Fed. see Vyborg
125 C3 Vibo Valentia Italy
123 D1 Vic Spain
160 A1 Vicente Guerrero Mex.
124 B1 Vicenza Italy
105 F2 Vichuga Rus. Fed.
121 C2 Vichy France
156 B2 Vicksburg U.S.A.
171 D2 Viçosa Brazil
68 A3 Victor Harbor Austr.
66 C1 Victoria r. Austr.
68 B3 Victoria state Austr.
Victoria Cameroon see Limbe
144 B3 Victoria Can.
169 A3 Victoria Chile
Victoria Malaysia see Labuan
129 I6 Victoria Seychelles
159 D3 Victoria U.S.A.
135 D3 Victoria, Lake Africa
68 B2 Victoria, Lake Austr.
78 A1 Victoria, Mount Myanmar
75 D3 Victoria, Mount P.N.G.
170 B3 Victoria, Sierra de la hills Arg.
136 B2 Victoria Falls waterfall Zambia/Zimbabwe
136 B2 Victoria Falls Zimbabwe
142 E2 Victoria Island Can.
71 M2 Victoria Land coastal area Antarctica
66 C1 Victoria River Downs Austr.
155 E1 Victoriaville Can.
138 B3 Victoria West S. Africa
151 C4 Victorville U.S.A.
157 D2 Vidalia U.S.A.
126 C2 Videle Romania
108 □A2 Víðidalsá Iceland
126 B2 Vidin Bulg.
90 B2 Vidisha India
156 B2 Vidor U.S.A.
169 B4 Viedma Arg.
169 A4 Viedma, Lago l. Arg.
118 C2 Viehberg mt. Austria
123 D1 Vielha Spain
116 B2 Vielsalm Belgium
117 E2 Vienenburg Ger.
119 D2 Vienna Austria
154 C3 Vienna U.S.A.
121 C2 Vienne France
120 C2 Vienne r. France
78 B2 Vientiane Laos
116 C2 Viersen Ger.
120 C2 Vierzon France
160 B2 Viesca Mex.
125 C2 Vieste Italy
78 B2 Vietnam country Asia
78 B1 Viêt Tri Vietnam
80 B2 Vigan Phil.
124 A1 Vigevano Italy
122 B1 Vigo Spain
Viipuri Rus. Fed. see Vyborg
89 C3 Vijayawada India
108 □B3 Vík Iceland
127 B2 Vikhren mt. Bulg.
144 C2 Viking Can.
108 F3 Vikna i. Norway
Vila Alferes Chamusca Moz. see Guija
Vila Arriaga Angola see Bibala
Vila Bugaço Angola see Camanongue
Vila Cabral Moz. see Lichinga
Vila da Ponte Angola see Kuvango
Vila de Aljustrel Angola see Cangamba
Vila de Almoster Angola see Chiange
Vila de João Belo Moz. see Xai-Xai
Vila de Trego Morais Moz. see Chókwé
Vila Fontes Moz. see Caia
122 B2 Vila Franca de Xira Port.
122 B1 Vilagarcía de Arousa Spain
139 D1 Vila Gomes da Costa Moz.
122 B1 Vilalba Spain
Vila Luísa Moz. see Marracuene
Vila Marechal Carmona Angola see Uíge
Vila Miranda Moz. see Macaloge
137 □D2 Vilanandro, Tanjona c. Madag.
104 C2 Viļāni Latvia
122 B1 Vila Nova de Gaia Port.
123 D1 Vilanova i la Geltrú Spain
Vila Paiva de Andrada Moz. see Gorongosa
Vila Pery Moz. see Chimoio
122 B1 Vila Real Port.
122 B1 Vilar Formoso Port.
Vila Salazar Angola see N'dalatando
Vila Salazar Zimbabwe see Sango
Vila Teixeira de Sousa Angola see Luau
171 D2 Vila Velha Brazil
166 B4 Vilcabamba, Cordillera mts Peru
98 F1 Vil'cheka, Zemlya i. Rus. Fed.
108 G3 Vilhelmina Sweden
166 C4 Vilhena Brazil
104 C2 Viljandi Estonia
139 C2 Viljoenskroon S. Africa
104 B3 Vilkaviškis Lith.
99 H1 Vil'kitskogo, Proliv str. Rus. Fed.
160 B1 Villa Ahumada Mex.
122 B1 Villablino Spain
118 C2 Villach Austria
Villa Cisneros Western Sahara see Ad Dakhla
160 B2 Villa de Cos Mex.
168 B3 Villa Dolores Arg.
161 C3 Villa Flores Mex.
169 C3 Villa Gesell Arg.
161 C2 Villagrán Mex.
161 C3 Villahermosa Mex.
160 A2 Villa Insurgentes Mex.
123 C2 Villajoyosa-La Vila Joíosa Spain
168 B3 Villa María Arg.
169 B3 Villa Mercedes Arg.
168 B2 Villa Montes Bol.
160 B2 Villanueva Mex.
122 B2 Villanueva de la Serena Spain
122 C2 Villanueva de los Infantes Spain
168 C2 Villa Ocampo Arg.
158 B3 Villa Ocampo Mex.
124 A3 Villaputzu Italy
168 C2 Villarrica Para.
122 C2 Villarrobledo Spain
Villasalazar Zimbabwe see Sango
168 B2 Villa Unión Arg.
160 B2 Villa Unión Mex.
160 B2 Villa Unión Mex.
166 B2 Villavicencio Col.
168 B2 Villazon Bol.
120 C3 Villefranche-de-Rouergue France
121 C2 Villefranche-sur-Saône France
123 C2 Villena Spain
116 A2 Villeneuve-d'Ascq France
120 C3 Villeneuve-sur-Lot France
156 B2 Ville Platte U.S.A.
116 A3 Villers-Cotterêts France
121 C2 Villeurbanne France
139 C2 Villiers S. Africa
118 B2 Villingen Ger.
153 E2 Villisca U.S.A.
104 C3 Vilnius Lith.
107 C2 Vil'nohirs'k Ukr.
107 D2 Vil'nyans'k Ukr.
116 B2 Vilvoorde Belgium
104 C3 Vilyeyka Belarus
99 J2 Vilyuy r. Rus. Fed.
109 G4 Vimmerby Sweden
169 A3 Viña del Mar Chile
123 D1 Vinaròs Spain
154 B3 Vincennes U.S.A.
71 J3 Vincennes Bay Antarctica
155 D3 Vineland U.S.A.
78 B2 Vinh Vietnam
79 B2 Vinh Long Vietnam
159 D1 Vinita U.S.A.
106 B2 Vinnytsya Ukr.
71 R2 Vinson Massif mt. Antarctica
109 E3 Vinstra Norway
121 E2 Vipiteno Italy
80 B2 Virac Phil.
90 B2 Viramgam India
96 B2 Viranşehir Turkey
145 D3 Virden Can.
120 B2 Vire France
136 A2 Virei Angola
171 D1 Virgem da Lapa Brazil
158 A1 Virgin r. U.S.A.
139 C2 Virginia S. Africa
153 E1 Virginia U.S.A.
155 D3 Virginia state U.S.A.
155 D3 Virginia Beach U.S.A.
151 C3 Virginia City U.S.A.
163 D3 Virgin Islands (U.K.) terr. West Indies
163 D3 Virgin Islands (U.S.A.) terr. West Indies
79 B2 Virôchey Cambodia
125 C1 Virovitica Croatia
116 B3 Virton Belgium
104 B2 Virtsu Estonia
89 B4 Virudhunagar India
125 C2 Vis i. Croatia
104 C2 Visaginas Lith.
151 C3 Visalia U.S.A.
90 B2 Visavadar India
80 B2 Visayan Sea Phil.
109 G4 Visby Sweden
142 E2 Viscount Melville Sound sea chan. Can.
167 E3 Viseu Brazil
122 B1 Viseu Port.
126 B1 Vişeu de Sus Romania
89 C3 Vishakhapatnam India
104 C2 Višķi Latvia
125 C2 Visoko Bos.-Herz.
119 D1 Vistula r. Pol.
Vitebsk Belarus see Vitsyebsk
124 B2 Viterbo Italy
65 I5 Viti Levu i. Fiji
99 I3 Vitim r. Rus. Fed.
171 D2 Vitória Brazil
167 E4 Vitória da Conquista Brazil
122 C1 Vitoria-Gasteiz Spain
120 B2 Vitré France
121 C2 Vitry-le-François France
105 D2 Vitsyebsk Belarus
121 D2 Vittel France
124 B3 Vittoria Italy
124 B1 Vittorio Veneto Italy
122 B1 Viveiro Spain
152 C2 Vivian U.S.A.
Vizagapatam India see Vishakhapatnam
158 A3 Vizcaíno, Desierto de des. Mex.
160 A2 Vizcaíno, Sierra mts Mex.
127 C2 Vize Turkey
89 C3 Vizianagaram India
116 B2 Vlaardingen Neth.
103 D4 Vladikavkaz Rus. Fed.
105 F2 Vladimir Rus. Fed.
82 B2 Vladivostok Rus. Fed.
125 D2 Vlasotince Serbia
116 B1 Vlieland i. Neth.
116 A2 Vlissingen Neth.
125 C2 Vlorë Albania
118 C1 Vltava r. Czech Rep.
118 C2 Vöcklabruck Austria
125 C2 Vodice Croatia
Vogelkop Peninsula pen. Indon. see Doberai, Jazirah
117 D2 Vogelsberg hills Ger.
Vohémar Madag. see Iharaña
Vohibinany Madag. see Ampasimanolotra
Vohimarina Madag. see Iharaña
137 □D3 Vohimena, Tanjona c. Madag.
137 □D3 Vohipeno Madag.
135 D3 Voi Kenya
121 D2 Voiron France
147 D2 Voisey's Bay Can.
125 C1 Vojvodina prov. Serbia
108 J3 Voknavolok Rus. Fed.
Volcano Bay b. Japan see Uchiura-wan
85 F3 Volcano Islands is Japan
Volchansk Ukr. see Vovchans'k
105 E2 Volga Rus. Fed.
105 F2 Volga r. Rus. Fed.
103 D4 Volgodonsk Rus. Fed.
103 D4 Volgograd Rus. Fed.
103 D4 Volgogradskoye Vodokhranilishche resr Rus. Fed.
105 D2 Volkhov Rus. Fed.
105 D1 Volkhov r. Rus. Fed.
117 E2 Volkstedt Ger.
107 D2 Volnovakha Ukr.
106 B2 Volochys'k Ukr.
107 D2 Volodars'ke Ukr.
Volodarskoye Kazakh. see Saumalkol'
106 B1 Volodars'k-Volyns'kyy Ukr.
106 B1 Volodymyrets' Ukr.
106 A1 Volodymyr-Volyns'kyy Ukr.
105 E2 Vologda Rus. Fed.
105 E2 Volokolamsk Rus. Fed.
107 D1 Volokonovka Rus. Fed.
127 B3 Volos Greece
104 C2 Volosovo Rus. Fed.
105 D2 Volot Rus. Fed.
105 E3 Volovo Rus. Fed.
103 D3 Vol'sk Rus. Fed.
130 C4 Volta r. Ghana
130 C4 Volta, Lake resr Ghana
171 D2 Volta Redonda Brazil
126 C2 Voluntari Romania
103 D4 Volzhskiy Rus. Fed.
108 □C2 Vopnafjörður Iceland
104 C3 Voranava Belarus

W

Westmalle

Xuefeng China *see* **Mingxi**
Xujiang China *see* **Guangchang**
87 B3 Xun Jiang *r.* China
87 B3 Xunwu China
123 C2 Xúquer, Riu *r.* Spain
87 B3 Xuwen China
87 A3 Xuyong China
86 B2 Xuzhou China
Xuzhou China *see* **Xuzhou**
127 B3 Xylokastro Greece

Y

86 A2 Ya'an China
133 B4 Yabēlo Eth.
85 D1 Yablonovyy Khrebet *mts* Rus. Fed.
157 D1 Yadkin *r.* U.S.A.
91 C2 Yadong China
86 A1 Yagan China
71 A4 Yaghan Basin S. Atlantic Ocean
105 E2 Yagnitsa Rus. Fed.
99 K2 Yagodnoye Rus. Fed.
134 B1 Yagoua Cameroon
144 C3 Yahk Can.
107 C1 Yahotyn Ukr.
160 B2 Yahualica Mex.
96 B2 Yahyalı Turkey
83 C4 Yaizu Japan
150 B1 Yakima U.S.A.
150 C1 Yakima *r.* U.S.A.
90 A2 Yakmach Pak.
130 B3 Yako Burkina
82 D2 Yakumo Japan
83 B4 Yaku-shima *i.* Japan
142 C3 Yakutat U.S.A.
144 A2 Yakutat Bay U.S.A.
99 J2 Yakutsk Rus. Fed.
107 D2 Yakymivka Ukr.
79 B3 Yala Thai.
134 C2 Yalinga C.A.R.
69 C3 Yallourn Austr.
127 C2 Yalova Turkey
106 B2 Yalpuh, Ozero *l.* Ukr.
107 C3 Yalta Ukr.
81 A1 Yalu Jiang *r.* China/N. Korea
102 F3 Yalutorovsk Rus. Fed.
83 D3 Yamagata Japan
83 B4 Yamaguchi Japan
Yamal, Poluostrov *pen.* Rus. Fed. *see* **Yamal Peninsula**
102 F1 Yamal Peninsula *pen.* Rus. Fed.
Yamankhalinka Kazakh. *see* **Makhambet**
69 D1 Yamba Austr.
166 B2 Yambi, Mesa de *hills* Col.
133 A4 Yambio Sudan
126 C2 Yambol Bulg.
102 G2 Yamburg Rus. Fed.
78 A1 Yamethin Myanmar
104 C2 Yamm Rus. Fed.
67 D2 Yamma Yamma, Lake *imp. l.* Austr.
130 B4 Yamoussoukro Côte d'Ivoire
107 C1 Yampil' Ukr.
106 B2 Yampil' Ukr.
91 C2 Yamuna *r.* India
78 A1 Yamzho Yumco *l.* China
99 K2 Yana *r.* Rus. Fed.
86 A2 Yan'an China
166 B4 Yanaoca Peru
94 A2 Yanbu' al Baḩr Saudi Arabia
86 C2 Yancheng China
66 A3 Yanchep Austr.
130 B3 Yanfolila Mali
134 C2 Yangambi Dem. Rep. Congo
86 B2 Yangcheng China
87 B3 Yangchun China
81 B2 Yangdok N. Korea
87 B3 Yangjiang China
Yangôn Myanmar *see* **Rangoon**
86 B2 Yangquan China
87 B3 Yangshuo China
79 B3 Yang Sin, Chư *mt.* Vietnam
78 B1 Yangtouyan China
86 C2 Yangtze *r.* China
86 C2 Yangtze, Mouth of the China
Yangtze Kiang *r.* China *see* **Yangtze**
86 A2 Yangxian China
86 B2 Yangzhou China
81 B1 Yanji China
153 D2 Yankton U.S.A.
99 K2 Yano-Indigirskaya Nizmennost' *lowland* Rus. Fed.
86 B1 Yanqing China
87 A3 Yanshan China
99 K2 Yanskiy Zaliv *g.* Rus. Fed.
69 C1 Yantabulla Austr.
86 C2 Yantai China
134 B2 Yaoundé Cameroon
75 D2 Yap *i.* Micronesia
75 D3 Yapen *i.* Indon.
75 D3 Yapen, Selat *sea chan.* Indon.
160 A2 Yaqui *r.* Mex.
67 D2 Yaraka Austr.
102 F3 Yaransk Rus. Fed.
64 H4 Yaren Nauru
94 B3 Yarim Yemen
Yarkand China *see* **Shache**
Yarkant China *see* **Shache**
93 C2 Yarkant He *r.* China
Yarlung Zangbo *r.* China *see* **Brahmaputra**

147 D3 Yarmouth Can.
158 A2 Yarnell U.S.A.
102 F2 Yarongo Rus. Fed.
105 E2 Yaroslavl' Rus. Fed.
82 B2 Yaroslavskiy Rus. Fed.
69 C3 Yarra Junction Austr.
69 C3 Yarram Austr.
105 D2 Yartsevo Rus. Fed.
105 E3 Yasnogorsk Rus. Fed.
79 B2 Yasothon Thai.
69 C2 Yass Austr.
97 D2 Yāsūj Iran
127 C3 Yataǧan Turkey
135 D3 Yata Plateau Kenya
145 E1 Yathkyed Lake Can.
83 B4 Yatsushiro Japan
166 C3 Yavari *r.* Brazil/Peru
89 B2 Yavatmal India
106 A2 Yavoriv Ukr.
83 B4 Yawatahama Japan
78 A1 Yawng-hwe Myanmar
Yaxian China *see* **Sanya**
97 D2 Yazd Iran
156 B2 Yazoo *r.* U.S.A.
156 B2 Yazoo City U.S.A.
127 B3 Ydra Greece
127 B3 Ydra *i.* Greece
79 A2 Ye Myanmar
93 D3 Yecheng China
123 C2 Yecla Spain
160 B2 Yécora Mex.
105 E3 Yefremov Rus. Fed.
107 E2 Yegorlykskaya Rus. Fed.
105 E2 Yegor'yevsk Rus. Fed.
133 B4 Yei Sudan
102 F3 Yekaterinburg Rus. Fed.
Yekaterinodar Rus. Fed. *see* **Krasnodar**
Yekaterinoslav Ukr. *see* **Dnipropetrovs'k**
Yekaterinovskaya Rus. Fed. *see* **Krylovskaya**
Yelenovskiye Kar'yery Ukr. *see* **Dokuchayevs'k**
105 E3 Yelets Rus. Fed.
105 D2 Yeligovo Rus. Fed.
130 A3 Yélimané Mali
Yelizavetgrad Ukr. *see* **Kirovohrad**
112 □ Yell *i.* U.K.
144 C1 Yellowknife Can.
69 C2 Yellow Mountain *h.* Austr.
86 B2 Yellow River *r.* China
85 E2 Yellow Sea N. Pacific Ocean
152 C1 Yellowstone *r.* U.S.A.
152 A2 Yellowstone Lake U.S.A.
104 C3 Yel'sk Belarus
94 B3 Yemen *country* Asia
106 B1 Yemil'chyne Ukr.
102 E2 Yemva Rus. Fed.
107 D2 Yenakiyeve Ukr.
78 A1 Yenangyaung Myanmar
78 B1 Yên Bai Vietnam
130 B4 Yendi Ghana
127 C3 Yenice Turkey
127 C3 Yenifoça Turkey
84 C1 Yenisey *r.* Rus. Fed.
Yeotmal India *see* **Yavatmal**
69 C2 Yeoval Austr.
115 B4 Yeovil U.K.
67 E2 Yeppoon Austr.
Yeraliyev Kazakh. *see* **Kuryk**
99 I2 Yerbogachen Rus. Fed.
97 C1 Yerevan Armenia
93 D1 Yereymentau Kazakh.
Yermentau Kazakh. *see* **Yereymentau**
159 C3 Yermo Mex.
151 C4 Yermo U.S.A.
105 D3 Yershichi Rus. Fed.
103 D3 Yershov Rus. Fed.
166 B4 Yerupaja *mt.* Peru
Yerushalayim Israel/West Bank *see* **Jerusalem**
81 B2 Yesan S. Korea
93 C1 Yesil' Kazakh.
127 C3 Yeşilova Turkey
99 H2 Yessey Rus. Fed.
115 A4 Yes Tor *h.* U.K.
69 D1 Yetman Austr.
78 A1 Ye-U Myanmar
120 B2 Yeu, Île d' *i.* France
103 D4 Yevlax Azer.
107 C2 Yevpatoriya Ukr.
Yexian China *see* **Laizhou**
107 D2 Yeya *r.* Rus. Fed.
107 D2 Yeysk Rus. Fed.
104 C2 Yezyaryshcha Belarus
Y Fenni U.K. *see* **Abergavenny**
170 A2 Ygatimí Para.
87 A3 Yibin China
86 B2 Yichang China
85 E1 Yichun *Heilong.* China
87 B3 Yichun *Jiangxi* China
Yidu China *see* **Qingzhou**
82 A3 Yilan China
126 C2 Yıldız Dağları *mts* Turkey
96 B2 Yıldızeli Turkey
Yilong China *see* **Shiping**
86 A2 Yinchuan China
81 B1 Yingchengzi China
87 B3 Yingde China
86 C1 Yingkou China
87 B3 Yingshan *Hubei* China
86 A2 Yingshan *Sichuan* China

87 B3 Yingtan China
Yining China *see* **Xiushui**
93 E2 Yining China
78 A1 Yinmabin Myanmar
86 A1 Yin Shan *mts* China
133 B4 Yirga Alem Eth.
135 D2 Yirga Ch'efē Eth.
135 D2 Yirol Sudan
Yishan China *see* **Yizhou**
86 B2 Yishui China
78 A1 Yi Tu, Nam *r.* Myanmar
84 C2 Yiwu China
86 C1 Yixian China
86 B2 Yixing China
87 B3 Yiyang China
87 B3 Yizhang China
87 A3 Yizhou China
Yizhou China *see* **Yixian**
108 I2 Yli-Kitka *l.* Fin.
108 H2 Ylitornio Fin.
108 H3 Ylivieska Fin.
109 H3 Ylöjärvi Fin.
99 K2 Ynykchanskiy Rus. Fed.
Ynys Môn *i.* U.K. *see* **Anglesey**
77 C2 Yogyakarta Indon.
134 B2 Yokadouma Cameroon
134 B2 Yoko Cameroon
83 C3 Yokohama Japan
82 D3 Yokote Japan
131 D4 Yola Nigeria
83 D3 Yonezawa Japan
87 B3 Yong'an China
Yongbei China *see* **Yongsheng**
87 B3 Yongchun China
86 A2 Yongdeng China
81 B2 Yŏngdŏk S. Korea
81 B2 Yŏnghŭng N. Korea
Yongjing China *see* **Xifeng**
81 B2 Yŏngju S. Korea
87 C3 Yongkang China
Yongle China *see* **Zhen'an**
78 B1 Yongren China
78 B1 Yongsheng China
87 B3 Yongzhou China
155 E2 Yonkers U.S.A.
121 C2 Yonne *r.* France
166 B2 Yopal Col.
66 A3 York Austr.
114 C3 York U.K.
156 C2 York AL U.S.A.
153 D2 York NE U.S.A.
155 D3 York PA U.S.A.
67 D1 York, Cape Austr.
68 A3 Yorke Peninsula Austr.
68 A3 Yorketown Austr.
114 C3 Yorkshire Wolds *hills* U.K.
145 D2 Yorkton Can.
103 D3 Yoshkar-Ola Rus. Fed.
113 C3 Youghal Ireland
69 C2 Young Austr.
68 A3 Younghusband Peninsula Austr.
154 C2 Youngstown U.S.A.
130 B3 Youvarou Mali
87 A3 Youyang China
93 E2 Youyi Feng *mt.* China/Rus. Fed.
96 B2 Yozgat Turkey
170 A2 Ypé-Jhú Para.
150 B2 Yreka U.S.A.
Yr Wyddfa *mt.* U.K. *see* **Snowdon**
75 D3 Ysabel Channel P.N.G.
121 C2 Yssingeaux France
109 F4 Ystad Sweden
Ysyk-Köl Kyrg. *see* **Balykchy**
93 D2 Ysyk-Köl *salt l.* Kyrg.
Y Trallwng U.K. *see* **Welshpool**
108 □A3 Ytri-Rangá *r.* Iceland
99 J2 Ytyk-Kyuyel' Rus. Fed.
87 A3 Yuanbao Shan *mt.* China
87 A3 Yuanjiang China
78 B1 Yuan Jiang *r.* China
87 B3 Yuanling China
87 A3 Yuanmou China
86 B2 Yuanping China
151 B3 Yuba City U.S.A.
82 D2 Yūbari Japan
161 C3 Yucatán *pen.* Mex.
162 B2 Yucatan Channel Cuba/Mex.
Yuci China *see* **Jinzhong**
66 C2 Yuendumu Austr.
87 C3 Yueqing China
87 B3 Yueyang China
102 F2 Yugorsk Rus. Fed.
87 B3 Yujiang China
99 L2 Yukagirskoye Ploskogor'ye *plat.* Rus. Fed.
105 D2 Yukhnov Rus. Fed.
142 B2 Yukon *r.* Can./U.S.A.
159 D1 Yukon U.S.A.
144 A1 Yukon Territory *admin. div.* Can.
66 C2 Yulara Austr.
87 B3 Yulin *Guangxi* China
86 A2 Yulin *Shaanxi* China
78 B1 Yulong Xueshan *mt.* China
158 A2 Yuma AZ U.S.A.
152 C2 Yuma CO U.S.A.
151 D4 Yuma Desert U.S.A.
Yumen China *see* **Laojunmiao**
96 B2 Yunak Turkey
86 B2 Yuncheng China
87 B3 Yunfu China
87 A3 Yungui Gaoyuan *plat.* China
Yunjinghong China *see* **Jinghong**
Yunling China *see* **Yunxiao**
87 A3 Yunnan *prov.* China

68 A2 Yunta Austr.
87 B3 Yunxiao China
86 B2 Yunyang China
87 A3 Yuping China
Yuping China *see* **Libo**
98 G3 Yurga Rus. Fed.
166 B2 Yurimaguas Peru
91 C1 Yurungkax He *r.* China
Yuryev Estonia *see* **Tartu**
87 C3 Yü Shan *mt.* Taiwan
86 B2 Yushe China
84 C2 Yushu China
Yushuwan China *see* **Huaihua**
97 C1 Yusufeli Turkey
91 C1 Yutian China
87 A3 Yuxi China
105 F2 Yuzha Rus. Fed.
99 K3 Yuzhno-Sakhalinsk Rus. Fed.
107 C2 Yuzhnoukrayins'k Ukr.
86 B2 Yuzhou China
Yuzovka Ukr. *see* **Donets'k**
121 D2 Yverdon Switz.
120 C2 Yvetot France

Z

116 B1 Zaandam Neth.
85 D1 Zabaykal'sk Rus. Fed.
135 C2 Zabia Dem. Rep. Congo
94 B3 Zabīd Yemen
95 D1 Zābol Iran
95 D2 Zābolī Iran
161 D3 Zacapa Guat.
160 B3 Zacapu Mex.
160 B2 Zacatecas Mex.
161 C3 Zacatepec Mex.
161 C3 Zacatlán Mex.
127 B3 Zacharo Greece
107 C2 Zachepylivka Ukr.
160 B2 Zacoalco Mex.
161 C2 Zacualtipán Mex.
125 C2 Zadar Croatia
79 A3 Zadetkyi Kyun *i.* Myanmar
105 E3 Zadonsk Rus. Fed.
96 B3 Za'farânah Egypt
122 B2 Zafra Spain
Zagazig Egypt *see* **Az Zaqāzīq**
130 B1 Zagora Morocco
Zagorsk Rus. Fed. *see* **Sergiyev Posad**
125 C1 Zagreb Croatia
Zagros, Kūhhā-ye *mts* Iran *see* **Zagros Mountains**
97 C2 Zagros Mountains *mts* Iran
95 D2 Zāhedān Iran
96 B2 Zahlé Lebanon
94 B3 Ẓahrān Saudi Arabia
Zaire *country* Africa *see* **Congo, Democratic Republic of the**
125 D2 Zaječar Serbia
137 C3 Zaka Zimbabwe
105 E3 Zakharovo Rus. Fed.
97 C2 Zākhō Iraq
102 C2 Zakhrebetnoye Rus. Fed.
127 B3 Zakynthos Greece
127 B3 Zakynthos *i.* Greece
119 D2 Zalaegerszeg Hungary
126 B1 Zalău Romania
94 B2 Zalim Saudi Arabia
132 A3 Zalingei Sudan
106 B2 Zalishchyky Ukr.
94 A2 Ẓalmā, Jabal az *mt.* Saudi Arabia
144 C2 Zama City Can.
Zambeze *r.* Moz. *see* **Zambezi**
136 C2 Zambezi *r.* Africa
136 B2 Zambezi Zambia
136 B2 Zambezi Escarpment Zambia/Zimbabwe
136 B2 Zambia *country* Africa
80 B3 Zamboanga Phil.
80 B3 Zamboanga Peninsula Phil.
119 E1 Zambrów Pol.
122 B1 Zamora Spain
160 B3 Zamora de Hidalgo Mex.
119 E1 Zamość Pol.
Zamost'ye Pol. *see* **Zamość**
91 B1 Zanda China
116 B2 Zandvliet Belgium
116 B1 Zandvoort Neth.
154 C3 Zanesville U.S.A.
93 D3 Zangguy China
91 C1 Zangsêr Kangri *mt.* China
97 C2 Zanjān Iran
90 B1 Zanskar Mountains India
Zante *i.* Greece *see* **Zakynthos**
135 D3 Zanzibar Tanz.
135 D3 Zanzibar Island Tanz.
105 E3 Zaokskiy Rus. Fed.
131 C2 Zaouatallaz Alg.
Zaouet el Kahla Alg. *see* **Bordj Omer Driss**
86 B2 Zaoyang China
99 H3 Zaozernyy Rus. Fed.
86 B2 Zaozhuang China
105 D2 Zapadnaya Dvina *r.* Europe
105 D2 Zapadnaya Dvina Rus. Fed.
Zapadno-Sibirskaya Ravnina *plain* Rus. Fed. *see* **West Siberian Plain**
84 B1 Zapadnyy Sayan *reg.* Rus. Fed.
159 D3 Zapata U.S.A.
108 J2 Zapolyarnyy Rus. Fed.
107 D2 Zaporizhzhya Ukr.

117	E2	**Zappendorf** Ger.
97	C1	**Zaqatala** Azer.
		Zara Croatia *see* **Zadar**
96	B2	**Zara** Turkey
161	B2	**Zaragoza** Mex.
123	C1	**Zaragoza** Spain
95	C1	**Zarand** Iran
92	C3	**Zaranj** Afgh.
104	C2	**Zarasai** Lith.
105	E3	**Zaraysk** Rus. Fed.
166	C2	**Zaraza** Venez.
131	C3	**Zaria** Nigeria
106	B1	**Zarichne** Ukr.
97	D3	**Zarqān** Iran
82	B2	**Zarubino** Rus. Fed.
119	D1	**Żary** Pol.
131	C1	**Zarzis** Tunisia
104	C3	**Zaslawye** Belarus
139	C3	**Zastron** S. Africa
		Zavitaya Rus. Fed. *see* **Zavitinsk**
85	E1	**Zavitinsk** Rus. Fed.
105	F2	**Zavolzhsk** Rus. Fed.
		Zavolzh'ye Rus. Fed. *see* **Zavolzhsk**
119	D1	**Zawiercie** Pol.
131	E1	**Zāwiyat Masūs** Libya
93	E2	**Zaysan** Kazakh.
93	E2	**Zaysan, Lake** *l.* Kazakh.
		Zaysan, Ozero *l.* Kazakh. *see* **Zaysan, Lake**
106	B2	**Zbarazh** Ukr.
106	B1	**Zdolbuniv** Ukr.
109	F4	**Zealand** *i.* Denmark
116	A2	**Zedelgem** Belgium
116	A2	**Zeebrugge** Belgium
139	C2	**Zeerust** S. Africa
117	F1	**Zehdenick** Ger.
66	C2	**Zeil, Mount** Austr.
117	F2	**Zeitz** Ger.
125	C2	**Zelena Gora** *mt.* Bos.-Herz.
103	D3	**Zelenodol'sk** Rus. Fed.
104	C1	**Zelenogorsk** Rus. Fed.
105	E2	**Zelenograd** Rus. Fed.
104	B3	**Zelenogradsk** Rus. Fed.
104	B3	**Zel'va** Belarus
135	C2	**Zémio** C.A.R.
123	D2	**Zemmora** Alg.
161	C3	**Zempoaltépetl, Nudo de** *mt.* Mex.
125	D2	**Zemun** Serbia
81	B1	**Zengfeng Shan** *mt.* China
125	C2	**Zenica** Bos.-Herz.
123	D2	**Zenzach** Alg.
117	F2	**Zerbst** Ger.
92	C4	**Zereh, Gowd-e** *depr.* Afgh.
121	D2	**Zermatt** Switz.
107	E2	**Zernograd** Rus. Fed.
		Zernovoy Rus. Fed. *see* **Zernograd**
117	E2	**Zeulenroda** Ger.
117	D1	**Zeven** Ger.
116	C2	**Zevenaar** Neth.
116	B2	**Zevenbergen** Neth.

99	J3	**Zeya** Rus. Fed.
95	C2	**Zeydābād** Iran
95	C2	**Zeynālābād** Iran
99	J3	**Zeyskoye Vodokhranilishche** *resr* Rus. Fed.
119	D1	**Zgierz** Pol.
104	B3	**Zhabinka** Belarus
		Zhabye Ukr. *see* **Verkhovyna**
		Zhaksy Sarysu *watercourse* Kazakh. *see* **Sarysu**
92	A2	**Zhalpaktal** Kazakh.
93	C1	**Zhaltyr** Kazakh.
		Zhambyl Kazakh. *see* **Taraz**
92	B2	**Zhanaozen** Kazakh.
		Zhangaqazaly Kazakh. *see* **Ayteke Bi**
		Zhangde China *see* **Anyang**
		Zhangdian China *see* **Zibo**
82	A1	**Zhangguangcai Ling** *mts* China
87	B3	**Zhangjiajie** China
86	B1	**Zhangjiakou** China
87	B3	**Zhangping** China
87	B3	**Zhangshu** China
81	A1	**Zhangwu** China
86	A2	**Zhangxian** China
84	C2	**Zhangye** China
87	B3	**Zhangzhou** China
92	A2	**Zhanibek** Kazakh.
87	B3	**Zhanjiang** China
87	B3	**Zhao'an** China
85	E1	**Zhaodong** China
		Zhaoge China *see* **Qixian**
87	B3	**Zhaoqing** China
87	A3	**Zhaotong** China
91	C1	**Zhari Namco** *salt l.* China
93	E2	**Zharkent** Kazakh.
105	D2	**Zharkovskiy** Rus. Fed.
93	E2	**Zharma** Kazakh.
106	C2	**Zhashkiv** Ukr.
		Zhaxi China *see* **Weixin**
93	D2	**Zhayrem** Kazakh.
		Zhdanov Ukr. *see* **Mariupol'**
87	C3	**Zhejiang** *prov.* China
98	F1	**Zhelaniya, Mys** *c.* Rus. Fed.
		Zheleznodorozhnyy Rus. Fed. *see* **Yemva**
		Zheleznodorozhnyy Uzbek. *see* **Qo'ng'irot**
105	E3	**Zheleznogorsk** Rus. Fed.
		Zheltyye Vody Ukr. *see* **Zhovti Vody**
86	A2	**Zhen'an** China
86	A2	**Zhenba** China
87	A3	**Zheng'an** China
87	B3	**Zhenghe** China
86	B2	**Zhengzhou** China
86	B2	**Zhenjiang** China
		Zhenjiang China *see* **Zhenjiang**
87	A3	**Zhenyuan** China
107	E1	**Zherdevka** Rus. Fed.
102	D2	**Zheshart** Rus. Fed.
93	C2	**Zhezkazgan** Kazakh.

93	C2	**Zhezkazgan** Kazakh.
99	J2	**Zhigansk** Rus. Fed.
86	B2	**Zhijiang** China
92	C1	**Zhitikara** Kazakh.
105	D3	**Zhizdra** Rus. Fed.
104	D3	**Zhlobin** Belarus
106	B2	**Zhmerynka** Ukr.
90	A1	**Zhob** Pak.
104	C3	**Zhodzina** Belarus
99	L1	**Zhokhova, Ostrov** *i.* Rus. Fed.
		Zholkva Ukr. *see* **Zhovkva**
		Zhongba China *see* **Jiangyou**
91	C2	**Zhongba** China
		Zhongduo China *see* **Youyang**
		Zhongning China *see* **Xiushan**
86	A2	**Zhongning** China
		Zhongping China *see* **Huize**
87	B3	**Zhongshan** China
		Zhongshan China *see* **Lupanshui**
86	A2	**Zhongwei** China
		Zhongxin China *see* **Xangyi'nyilha**
86	B2	**Zhoukou** China
86	C2	**Zhoushan** China
106	A1	**Zhovkva** Ukr.
107	C2	**Zhovti Vody** Ukr.
81	A2	**Zhuanghe** China
86	B2	**Zhucheng** China
105	D3	**Zhukovka** Rus. Fed.
105	E2	**Zhukovskiy** Rus. Fed.
86	B2	**Zhumadian** China
		Zhuoyang China *see* **Suiping**
87	B3	**Zhuzhou** *Hunan* China
87	B3	**Zhuzhou** *Hunan* China
106	A2	**Zhydachiv** Ukr.
104	C3	**Zhytkavichy** Belarus
106	B1	**Zhytomyr** Ukr.
119	D2	**Žiar nad Hronom** Slovakia
86	B2	**Zibo** China
119	D1	**Zielona Góra** Pol.
116	A2	**Zierikzee** Neth.
78	A1	**Zigaing** Myanmar
131	E2	**Zīghan** Libya
87	A3	**Zigong** China
		Zigui China *see* **Guojiaba**
130	A3	**Ziguinchor** Senegal
160	B3	**Zihuatanejo** Mex.
119	D2	**Žilina** Slovakia
131	D2	**Zillah** Libya
99	H3	**Zima** Rus. Fed.
161	C2	**Zimapán** Mex.
137	B2	**Zimbabwe** *country* Africa
130	A4	**Zimmi** Sierra Leone
126	C2	**Zimnicea** Romania
102	C2	**Zimniy Bereg** *coastal area* Rus. Fed.
131	C3	**Zinder** Niger
94	B3	**Zinjibār** Yemen
107	C1	**Zin'kiv** Ukr.
		Zinoyevsk Ukr. *see* **Kirovohrad**
166	B2	**Zipaquirá** Col.
119	D2	**Zirc** Hungary

91	D2	**Ziro** India
95	C2	**Zīr Rūd** Iran
119	D2	**Zistersdorf** Austria
161	B3	**Zitácuaro** Mex.
119	C1	**Zittau** Ger.
103	E3	**Zlatoust** Rus. Fed.
119	D2	**Zlín** Czech Rep.
131	D1	**Zlīṭan** Libya
119	D1	**Złotów** Pol.
105	D3	**Zlynka** Rus. Fed.
105	E3	**Zmiyevka** Rus. Fed.
107	D2	**Zmiyiv** Ukr.
105	E3	**Znamenka** Rus. Fed.
107	E1	**Znamenka** Rus. Fed.
107	C2	**Znam"yanka** Ukr.
119	D2	**Znojmo** Czech Rep.
138	B3	**Zoar** S. Africa
86	A2	**Zoigê** China
107	D1	**Zolochiv** Ukr.
106	A2	**Zolochiv** Ukr.
107	C2	**Zolotonosha** Ukr.
105	E3	**Zolotukhino** Rus. Fed.
137	C2	**Zomba** Malawi
134	B2	**Zongo** Dem. Rep. Congo
128	B1	**Zonguldak** Turkey
121	D3	**Zonza** France
130	B3	**Zorgho** Burkina
130	B4	**Zorzor** Liberia
131	D2	**Zouar** Chad
130	A2	**Zouérat** Maur.
125	D1	**Zrenjanin** Serbia
105	D2	**Zubtsov** Rus. Fed.
121	D2	**Zug** Switz.
97	C1	**Zugdidi** Georgia
		Zuider Zee *l.* Neth. *see* **IJsselmeer**
122	B2	**Zújar** *r.* Spain
116	C2	**Zülpich** Ger.
116	A2	**Zulte** Belgium
137	C2	**Zumbo** Moz.
161	C3	**Zumpango** Mex.
158	B1	**Zuni Mountains** U.S.A.
87	A3	**Zunyi** China
125	C1	**Županja** Croatia
121	D2	**Zürich** Switz.
121	D2	**Zürichsee** *l.* Switz.
116	C1	**Zutphen** Neth.
131	D1	**Zuwārah** Libya
106	D1	**Zvenyhorodka** Ukr.
137	C3	**Zvishavane** Zimbabwe
119	D2	**Zvolen** Slovakia
125	C2	**Zvornik** Bos.-Herz.
130	B4	**Zwedru** Liberia
139	C3	**Zwelitsha** S. Africa
119	D2	**Zwettl** Austria
117	F2	**Zwickau** Ger.
116	C1	**Zwolle** Neth.
99	L2	**Zyryanka** Rus. Fed.
93	E2	**Zyryanovsk** Kazakh.

Acknowledgements

pages 52–53
Land Cover map data courtesy of
Center for Remote Sensing, Boston University, USA

pages 54–55
Population map data:
Gridded Population of the World (GPW), Version 3.
Palisades, NY: CIESN, Columbia University. Available at
http://sedac.ciesin.columbia.edu/plue/gpw

pages 56–57n
Telecommunications traffic data:
TeleGeography Research, Washington D.C. USA
www.telegeography.com

Cover
Image courtesy of
NASA / SCIENCE PHOTO LIBRARY

KEY TO MAP PAGES AFRICA, NORTH AMERICA, SOUTH AMERICA

(see front endpapers for Oceania, Asia and Europe)

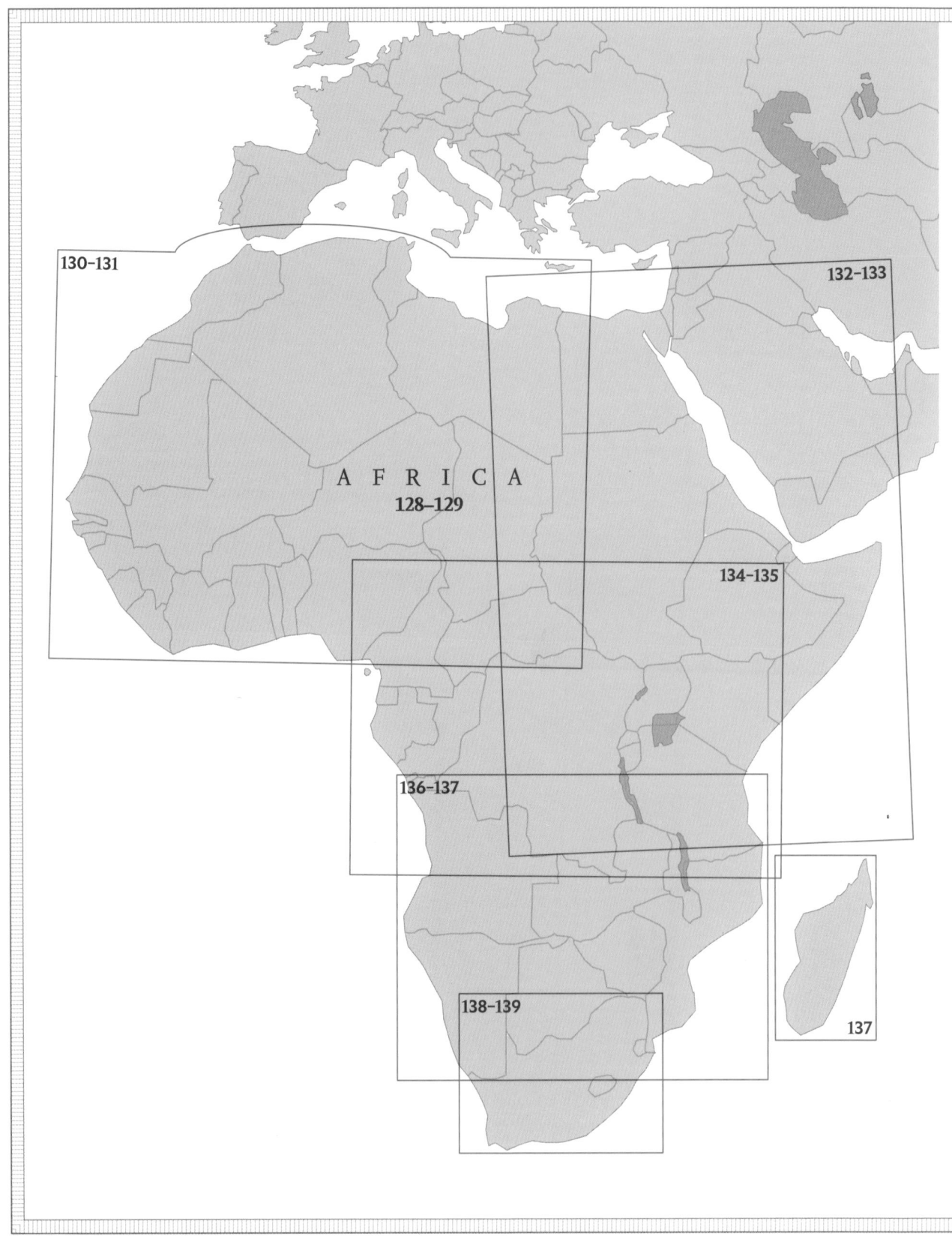

130–131

132–133

A F R I C A
128–129

134–135

136–137

138–139

137